Henry Thomas Riley

The Pharsalia

Literally translated into English Prose

Henry Thomas Riley

The Pharsalia
Literally translated into English Prose

ISBN/EAN: 9783337372934

Printed in Europe, USA, Canada, Australia, Japan

Cover: Foto ©Thomas Meinert / pixelio.de

More available books at **www.hansebooks.com**

THE

PHARSALIA

OF

L U C A N

LITERALLY TRANSLATED INTO ENGLISH PROSE,
WITH COPIOUS NOTES.

BY

H. T. RILEY, B.A.,

LATE SCHOLAR OF CLARE HALL, CAMBRIDGE.

LONDON: GEORGE BELL & SONS, YORK STREET,
COVENT GARDEN.
1889.

PREFACE.

In the following Translation, the text of Weise has been adopted, except in a few instances, where the readings of Cortius, Weber, or the older Commentators, appeared preferable. It is much to be regretted that, notwithstanding their labours, the text still remains in a corrupt state.

The Pharsalia has not been previously translated into English prose; but there have been two poetical versions, one by Thomas May, in 1627, the other by Nicholas Rowe. The latter is too well known to require comment; the former, though replete with the quaint expressions peculiar to the early part of the seventeenth century, has the merit of adhering closely to the original, and is remarkable for its accuracy.

The present translation has been made on the same principle as those of Ovid and Plautus in the CLASSICAL LIBRARY; it is strictly literal, and is intended to be a faithful reflex, not only of the author's meaning, but, as nearly as possible, of his actual modes of expression.

To enhance the value of the work in an historical point of view, the narrative has been illustrated by a comparison with parallel passages in the Commentaries of Cæsar, and the works of other ancient historians who have treated of the wars between Pompey and Cæsar.

H. T. R.

CONTENTS.

b

CONTENTS.

BOOK VIII.

LUCAN'S
PHARSALIA.

BOOK THE FIRST.

CONTENTS.

WARS more than civil[1] upon the Emathian plains[2], and license conceded to lawlessness, I sing; and a powerful people turning with victorious right-hand against its own vitals, and kindred armies *engaged;* and, the compact of rule rent

---

[1] *Wars more than civil*) ver. 1. There is some doubt as to the meaning of this expression. It has been suggested that the Poet refers to the circumstance of foreign nations taking part in a warfare which had originated between the citizens of Rome ; while another opinion is, that he alludes to the fact of Cæsar and Pompey being not only fellow citizens but connected by marriage.

[2] *The Emathian plains*) ver. 1. Emathia was properly that part of Macedonia which lay between the rivers Haliacmon and Axius. The poets, however, frequently give the name of Emathia to Thessaly, which adjoined Macedonia, and in which Pharsalia was situate,

ß

asunder[1], a contest waged with all the might of the shaken
earth for the universal woe, and standards meeting with hostile standards, the eagles alike[2], and darts threatening darts[3].
    What madness, this, O citizens! what lawlessness so great
of the sword, while nations are your hate, for you to shed the
Latian blood?   And, while proud Babylon was to be spoiled[4]
of the Ausonian trophies, and the shade of Crassus was wandering unavenged, has it pleased you that wars, doomed to
produce no triumphs, should be waged?   Alas! how much
of land and of sea might have been won with that self-same
blood which the right-hands of fellow-citizens have shed.
Whence Titan makes his approach, and where the night conceals the stars, and where the mid-day intensely burns with
its scorching moments; where too, the winter, frozen and unused to be relaxed by the spring, binds fast the icy ocean with
Scythian cold!   By this beneath the yoke should the Seres[5],
by this the barbarian Araxes[6], have come, and the race, if
any there be, that lies situate contiguous to the rising Nile[7].

[1] *The compact of rule rent asunder*) ver. 4.   By the use of the word
"regnum," he probably refers to the compact which had been originally made
between the Triumvirs Pompey, Cæsar, and Crassus, to divide the sovereign
power among themselves.
[2] *The eagles alike*) ver. 7.   "Pares aquilas."   More literally "matched."
The figure is derived from the "comparatio" or "matching" of the gladiators
at the gladiatorial games.
[3] *And darts threatening darts*) ver. 7.   "Pila."   Rowe, who translates
it "pile," has the following Note here :—"I have chosen to translate the Latin
word 'pilum' thus nearly, or indeed rather to keep it and make it English;
because it was a weapon, as eagles were the ensigns, peculiar to the Romans, and
made use of here by Lucan purposely to denote the war made among themselves."
It was a javelin or dart about five feet in length, which the Roman infantry
discharged against the enemy at the commencement of the engagement.
[4] *Babylon was to be spoiled*) ver. 10.   He speaks of Babylon as then
belonging to the Parthians, who had recently conquered the Crassi with immense slaughter, a disaster which had not been avenged.
[5] *Beneath the yoke should the Seres*) ver. 19.   Seres was the name given
to the inhabitants of Serica, an indefinite region situate in the north-western
parts of Asia ; but it is generally supposed that a part of China was so called.
The great wall of China is called by Ammianus Marcellinus "Aggeres Se-
rium," "The bulwarks of the Seres."
[6] *The barbarian Araxes*) ver. 19.   There were rivers of this name in
Armenia, Mesopotamia, Persia, and Thessaly.   Probably the first is the one
here alluded to.
[7] *Contiguous to the rising Nile*) ver. 20.   The subject of the rise of the
Nile is fully treated of in the speech of Achoreus, in the Tenth Book.

Then, Rome, if so great thy love for an accursed warfare,
when thou hast subjected the whole earth to Latian laws,
turn thy hands against thyself; not as yet has a foe been
wanting to thee. But now that the walls are tottering with
the dwellings half overthrown throughout the cities of Italy,
and, the fortifications falling away, vast stones are lying
there, and the houses are occupied by no protector, and but
few inhabitants are wandering amid the ancient cities, that
Hesperia has remained unsightly with brambles and un-
ploughed for many a year, and that hands are wanting
for the fields requiring them—not thou, fierce Pyrrhus,
nor yet the Carthaginian[1], will prove the cause of ruin
so great; to no sword has it been allowed to penetrate
the vitals; deep-seated are the wounds of the fellow-citizen's right hand.

But if the Fates have decreed no other way[2] for Nero to
succeed, and at a costly price eternal realms are provided
for the Gods, and heaven could only obey its own Thunderer
after the wars of the raging Giants[3]; then in no degree, O
Gods above, do we complain; crimes themselves, and law
lessness, on these conditions, are approved; let Pharsalia
fill her ruthless plains, and let the shades of the Carthaginians be sated with blood; let the hosts meet for the last
time at tearful Munda[4]. To these destined *wars*, Cæsar,

[1] *Pyrrhus, nor yet the Carthaginian*) ver. 30. He alludes to Pyrrhus,
king of Epirus, and Hannibal the Carthaginian, two of the most terrible enemies of Rome.

[2] *Have decreed no other way*) ver. 33. One of the Scholiasts thinks that
this is said in bitter irony against the Emperor Nero. It is, however, more
probable that it is intended in a spirit of adulation; as the First Book was
evidently written under very different political feelings from the latter ones;
in which he takes every opportunity of indirectly censuring the tyrant.

[3] *Wars of the raging Giants*) ver. 36. He alludes to the Giganto
machia, or war between the Gods and the Giants. By this expression he
either intends a compliment to the fame of Cæsar and Pompey individually,
or to the prowess of the Roman people.

[4] *At tearful Munda*) ver. 40. Munda was a village of Spain near
Malaga, or, according to some, in the neighbourhood of Cordova, where Cæsar,
in the year B.C. 45, defeated the sons of Pompey with the loss of 30,000
men. Cneius, the eldest, was slain there. The Poet alludes in the preceding
line to the war carried on in the north of Africa, where Juba sided with the
partisans of Pompey.

let the famine of Perusia[1] and the struggles of Mutina[2] be
added, the fleets, too, which rugged Leucadia overwhelmed[3],
and the servile wars beneath the burning Ætna[4]; still, much
does Rome owe to the arms of her citizens, since for thy
sake these events have come to pass.

When, thy allotted duties fulfilled, thou shalt late repair
to the stars, the palace of heaven, preferred *by thee*, shall
receive thee[5], the skies rejoicing; whether it please thee to
wield the sceptre, or whether to ascend the flaming chariot
of Phœbus, and with thy wandering fire to survey the earth,
in no way alarmed at the change of the sun[6]; by every
Divinity will it be yielded unto thee, and to thy free choice
will nature leave it what God thou shalt wish to be, where
to establish the sovereignty of the world. But do thou
neither choose thy abode in the Arctic circle, nor where the
sultry sky of the south behind us declines; whence with
thy star obliquely thou mayst look upon Rome[7]. If thou

---

[1] *The famine of Perusia*) ver. 41.   Perusia was an ancient city of Etruria.   L. Antonius, the brother of the Triumvir, took refuge here, and was
besieged by Augustus for several months, till he was compelled by famine to
surrender. This lengthened siege gave occasion to that campaign being called
" Bellum Perusinum."

[2] *And the struggles of Mutina*) ver. 41.   He alludes to the siege of
Mutina, now Modena, in the years B.C. 44, 43.   Decimus Brutus being besieged there by Marc Antony, the Consuls Hirtius and Pansa hastened to
relieve him, and perished in battle under its walls.

[3] *Which rugged Leucadia overwhelmed*) ver. 43.   Reference is made to
the sea fight at Actium near the isle of Leucas or Leucadia, off the coast of
Acarnania, in which Augustus defeated Antony and Cleopatra.

[4] *Servile wars beneath the burning Ætna*) ver. 44.   He alludes to the
defeat of Sextus, the son of Pompey, in the Sicilian seas; where a vast number
of slaves had ranged under his banners.   He was first defeated by Agrippa,
the son-in-law of Augustus, off Mylæ, and again off Naulochus, a seaport between Mylæ and Pelorum in Sicily, B.C. 36.

[5] *The palace of heaven shall receive thee*) ver. 46.   This is more abject
flattery than we could expect from a Poet whose works breathe the intense
spirit of liberty to be found in the latter books of this Poem.

[6] *Alarmed at the change of the sun*) ver. 49.   He probably alludes to
the disastrous result of Phaeton guiding the chariot of the Sun, when the
world was set in flames.   Nero prided himself upon his skill as a charioteer,
and not improbably the Poet intends here to flatter him on his weak point.
As to the disaster of Phaeton, see the Metamorphoses of Ovid, at the commencement of the Second Book.

[7] *Obliquely thou mayst look upon Rome*) ver. 55.   Some of the Scho-

shouldst press upon one side of the boundless æther, the sky will be sensible of the burden[1]. Keep thy weight in the mid sphere of the balanced heavens; may all that part of the æther with sky serene be free *from mist*, and may no clouds interpose before Cæsar.

Then, arms laid aside, may the human race consult its own good, and may all nations love one another; may Peace, sent throughout the world, keep close the iron thresholds[2] of the warlike Janus. But to myself already *art thou* a Divinity; and, if I, a bard, receive thee in my breast, I could not wish to invoke the God who moves the mystic shrines of Cirrha[3], and to withdraw Bacchus from Nysa[4]. Sufficient art thou to supply inspiration for Roman song.

My design leads me[5] to recount the causes of events so great, and a boundless task is commenced upon; what it was that impelled a frantic people to arms — what that drove away Peace from the world. The envious course of the Fates, and the denial to what is supreme to be of long duration; the heavy fall, too, beneath a weight too great; and Rome that could not support herself. So when, its structure dissolved, the last hour shall have closed so many ages of the universe, all things shall return once more to former chaos; constellations shall rush on against mingled constellations; fiery stars shall fall into the deep; earth shall refuse to extend her shores, and shall cast away the ocean; Phœbe shall come into collision with her bro-

liasts, fancying that all this is said in irony, would have this word 'obliquum,' 'sidelong,' or 'oblique,' to refer to the squint or cast observable in Nero's eye. There seems, however, no ground for this notion.

[1] *Will be sensible of the burden*) ver. 57. The same Scholiasts think that satirical allusion is here made to the fatness of Nero.

[2] *Keep close the iron thresholds*) ver. 62. He alludes to the Temple of Janus, which was shut in time of peace.

[3] *The mystic shrines of Cirrha*) ver. 64. Cirrha was a town of Phocis, situate on Mount Parnassus, near Delphi, sacred to Apollo, who is here referred to.

[4] *Withdraw Bacchus from Nysa*) ver. 65. Nysa was the name of several cities sacred to Bacchus. One was in India, which is also supposed to have been called Dionysopolis. Another was in Æthiopia. The others were in Caria, Cappadocia, Thrace, and Bœotia. As the latter was, like Cyrrha, situate on Mount Parnassus, it is not improbable that it is the one here referred to.

[5] *My design leads me*) ver. 67. The Metamorphoses of Ovid begin with the same expression, "fert animus."

ther, and, disdaining to guide her two-horsed chariot in its sidelong course, will demand the day for herself; and the whole mechanism, discordant, will confuse the ties of the universe rent asunder.

Mighty things fall of themselves; this limit to increase have the Deities assigned to a prosperous state. Nor yet to the advantage of any *other* nations does Fortune turn her hate against a people all-powerful by land and by sea. Thou, Rome, *wast* the cause of *thy own* woes, becoming the common property of three masters[1]; the fatal compact[2], too, for sway never *successfully* entrusted to a number. O ye, disastrously concordant, and blinded by desires too great, why does it please you to unite your strength and to share the world in common? While the earth shall support the sea, and the air the earth[3], and his long courses shall whirl on Titan *in his career*, and night shall succeed the day through signs as many, no faith is there in partners in rule, and all power will be impatient of a sharer.

And believe not any nations, nor let the examples of *this* fatality be sought from afar; the rising walls *of Rome* were steeped with a brother's blood[4]. Nor was the earth and the ocean then the reward of frenzy so great; an humble retreat[5] brought into collision its lords.

---

[1] *The common property of three masters*) ver. 85. He alludes to the first Triumvirate or compact secretly made between Pompey, Cæsar, and Crassus to share the Roman power between them. By this arrangement Pompey had Spain and Africa, Crassus Syria, while Cæsar's government over Gaul was prolonged for five years.

[2] *The fatal compact, too*) ver. 85, 6. "Nec umquam In turbam missi feralia fœdera regni!" The meaning is, "The sovereign sway divided among several, fatal in its consequences, and a thing never successfully done before;" the Romans having hitherto, except in the disastrous times of Sulla and Marius, been governed by the laws of the Republic, from the period when the kings ceased to reign.

[3] *And the air the earth*) ver. 90, 1. Ovid has a very similar passage in the Metamorphoses, B. i. l. 11. "The earth did not as yet hang in the surrounding air, balanced by its own weight."

[4] *Steeped with a brother's blood*) ver. 95. He alludes to the death of Remus, who, according to some, was slain by the hand of his brother Romulus; Ovid, however, in the Fasti, B. iv. l. 839, says, that he was slain by Celer, one of the followers of Romulus. His offence was the contempt which he displayed in leaping over the walls of infant Rome.

[5] *An humble retreat*) ver. 97. "Asylum."—Under the name "asylum," he probably alludes to the whole of the spot on which Rome then stood. Romu-

The discordant concord lasted for a short time; and peace there was, through no inclination of the chieftains. For Crassus, interposing, was the sole impediment to the destined war. Just as the narrow Isthmus[1] which cleaves and barely divides the two seas, nor yet allows them to meet together; if the earth were to withdraw, the Ionian would dash itself against the Ægean main : so, when Crassus, who kept asunder the ruthless arms of the chieftains, by a fate much to be deplored stained Assyrian Carrhæ[2] with Latian blood, the Parthian misfortunes let loose the frenzy of Rome. More, ye descendants of Arsaces[3], was effected by you in that battle than you suppose ; civil warfare you conferred upon the conquered.

The sway is cut asunder by the sword ; and the fortunes of a powerful people, which embrace the sea, the land, the whole earth, brook not two *leaders*. For Julia, cut off by the ruthless hand[4] of the Destinies[5], bore away to the shades below the ties of allied blood, and the marriage

lus constituted a grove near the Tiber a place of refuge for the slaves and criminals of neighbouring states, that he might thereby augment the number of his own-citizens. In later times the Asylum was walled in. From a passage in the Fasti of Ovid, B. ii. l. 67, it seems that, running down to the banks of the Tiber, it skirted the Capitolium.

[1] *Just as the narrow Isthmus*) ver. 101. He alludes to the Isthmus of Corinth, which connects the Peloponnesus with the main land, and has the Ionian Sea on the west, and the Ægean on the east.

[2] *Stained Assyrian Carrhæ*) ver. 105. Carrhæ or Carræ, the Haran of Scripture, was a city of Osroëne in Mesopotamia, not far from Edessa. Crassus was slain in battle there with the Parthians, B.C. 53.

[3] *Ye descendants of Arsaces*) v. 108. The kings of Parthia were called Arsacidæ from Arsaces, the founder of the Parthian empire. He was a person of obscure origin, and said to have been a mountain robber. About 250 B.C. he headed a revolt of the Parthians against Antiochus II., which being successful, he became their first monarch.

[4] *Julia, cut off by the ruthless hand*) ver. 113. Julia was the daughter of Julius Cæsar by his wife Cornelia, and his only child in marriage. She was betrothed to Servilius Cæpio, but was married to Pompey, B.C. 59. She died B.C. 54, and her only child, which some writers state to have been a son, some a daughter, died a few days after. Seneca says that Cæsar was in Britain at the time of Julia's death. Though she was twenty-three years younger than Pompey, she was devotedly attached to him, and received a shock which proved fatal to her on believing him to have been slain in a popular tumult.

[5] *Of the Destinies*) ver. 113. "Parcarum." Literally, "of the Parcæ." This was a name of the Fates or Destinies, Clotho, Lachesis, and Atropos.

torches[1], with direful omen, portentous of woe. But if the
Fates had allowed thee a longer sojourn in life, thou alone
hadst been able to restrain on the one side the husband and
on the other the parent, and, the sword dashed down, to join
the armed hands, just as the Sabine women, interposing[2],
united the sons-in-law with the fathers-in-law. By thy death
is friendship rent asunder, and license granted to the chieftains to commence the warfare. The ambition of rivalry adds
its spur.

Thou, Magnus, art afraid lest recent exploits should eclipse
former triumphs, and the laurels gained from the pirates should
be eclipsed by[3] the conquest of the Gauls; thee, *Cæsar*, does
the continuance of thy labours and thy experience *gained by
them* now elevate, and Fortune[4] that cannot brook a second
place. Neither can Cæsar now endure any one his superior,
nor Pompey *any one* his equal. Who with the more justice took
up arms it is not permitted us to know[5]; each one defends
himself with a mighty abettor; the conquering cause was
pleasing to the Gods, but the conquered one to Cato[6].

[1] *And the marriage torches*) ver. 112. "Tædæ" were the marriage torches
borne before the bride when being led to her husband's house. By the
use of the word "feralia," he means that her marriage torch was ominously
soon supplanted by the torch which lighted her funeral pile.

[2] *As the Sabine women interposing*) ver. 118. He alludes to the reconciliation effected by the Sabine women, who had been carried off by Romulus
and his Romans, between their relatives and their husbands, when about to
engage in mortal combat. The story is prettily told by Ovid in the Fasti,
B. iii. l. 201, et seq.—See the Translation in *Bohn's Classical Library*, p. 97.

[3] *Laurels gained from the pirates should be eclipsed by*) ver. 122. He
alludes to the victories of Cæsar in Gaul, and those gained by Pompey over
the Cilician pirates, who had swarmed in vast numbers in the Mediterranean, and whom Pompey had defeated with a fleet of 500 ships. The Poet
alludes to the laurel crown with which Pompey would be graced when proceeding in triumph to the Capitol. It may be here remarked that the Poet
throughout the work calls Pompey by his surname of "Magnus."

[4] *And Fortune*) ver. 124. "Fortuna." Cæsar was in the habit of paying especial veneration to the Goddess "Fortune."

[5] *It is not permitted us to know*) ver. 126. This passage does not at all
correspond with the spirit in which the latter books are written; where every
possible invective as a tyrant and murderer is unsparingly lavished upon
Cæsar. It is not improbable that this book was written several years before the latter ones, and while the Poet was still enjoying the favour of Nero.

[6] *But the conquered one to Cato*) ver. 128. This is a great compliment to
Cato, who is made the hero of the Ninth Book. He was the great-grandson
of Cato the Censor, and was doubtless the most virtuous of all the illustrious
Romans of his day.

Nor did they meet on equal terms; the one, with his years tending downward to old age, and grown tranquil amid a long practice of the arts of peace[1], had now in tranquillity[2] forgotten the general; and, an aspirant for fame, *had been wont to confer* upon the public many a largess[3]; solely to be wafted on by the popular gales, and to exult in the applause of a theatre his own[4]; not to recruit his strength afresh, and principally to rely upon his former successes. *There* stood the shadow of a glorious name[5]: just as the lofty oak, in a fertile field, which bears the spoils[6] of an ancient people and the consecrated gifts of chieftains, now no longer standing fast by its firm roots, is fixed by its own weight; and sending forth its bared branches into the air, with its trunk, and not its leaves, forms a shade; and although it threatens to fall at the first eastern blast, *and* trees so many around it lift themselves with firmly-rooted strength, still it alone is venerated.

But in Cæsar not only was there a name as great, and the fame of the general; but a valour that knew not how to rest in *one* place, and a shame only *felt* at not conquering in

[1] *Of the arts of peace*) ver. 130. "Togæ." Literally " of the toga." This was the robe or gown worn by the Roman citizens in domestic life.

[2] *In tranquillity forgotten the general*) ver. 131. Pompey triumphed over Mithridates B.C. 62, since which time, for a period of fourteen years, he had been unused to active warfare. He was only six years older than Cæsar.

[3] *To confer many a largess*) ver. 133. "Dare multa." By the word "dare" he alludes to the largesses of corn which Pompey plentifully bestowed on the Roman populace, and the gladiatorial shows which he exhibited.

[4] *Applause of a theatre his own*) ver. 133. He alludes to the theatre which Pompey built at Rome. It was the first one of stone there erected, and was large enough to accommodate 40,000 spectators. It was built in the Campus Martius, on the model of one at Mytilene, in the isle of Lesbos. It was opened with scenic representations, gladiatorial combats, and fights of wild beasts. Five hundred lions were killed, and eighteen elephants were hunted, and a rhinoceros exhibited for the first time.

[5] *Stood the shadow of a glorious name*) ver. 135. The Poet probably alludes here to Pompey's title or surname of " Magnus," or " Great," which was given to him by the Roman people after he had conquered Domitius Ahenobarbus and Hiarbas in Sicily. Plutarch informs us that Pompey did not use that name himself till he was appointed to the command against Sertorius in Spain.

[6] *That bears the spoils*) ver. 137. He compares Pompey, enriched with the spoil of nations and the rewards of his fellow-citizens, to an oak, upon which a trophy has been erected composed of spoils and gifts.

war. Fierce and unrestrained; *ready* to lead his troops whither hope and whither vengeance should summon, and never to spare fleshing his sword; to press on his own advantages, to rely on the favour of the Deity; bearing down whatever opposed himself as he sought the summit, and rejoicing amid ruin to have made his way.

Just as the lightning forced by the winds through the clouds flashes forth with the echoes of the riven æther and with a crash throughout the universe, and overwhelms the light of day, and terrifies the alarmed nations, dazzling the eyes with its sidelong flame. It rages against temples its own[1]; and, no matter impeding its going forth, both falling, it sends vast, and returning, vast devastation far and wide, and collects again its scattered fires.

These were the motives secretly existing with the chieftains; but *there were* public grounds for the warfare, which have ever overwhelmed mighty nations. For when, the world subdued, Fortune introduced wealth too great, and the manners gave way before prosperity, and booty and the spoils of the enemy induced luxurious habits; no moderation *was there* in gold or in houses; hunger, too, disdained the tables of former times; dresses hardly suitable for the matrons to wear, the males seized hold upon[2]; poverty fruitful in men[3] was shunned; and that was fetched from the entire earth by means of which each nation falls. Then did they join the lengthened boundaries of the fields, and the extended lands once turned up by the hard ploughshare of Camillus[4], and which had submitted to the ancient mattocks of the Curii[5], lay far and wide beneath the charge of husbandmen unknown *to their employers.*

[1] *Against temples its own*) ver. 155. He means that as the lightnings rage amid the clouds and the air, their own realms, so Cæsar displayed his warlike fury among his own fellow-citizens.

[2] *The males seized hold upon*) ver. 164. He probably alludes to the use of "multitia," certain thin garments and silken textures which had been recently introduced into Rome.

[3] *Fruitful in men*) ver. 165. "Virorum." In the sense of "manly spirits."

[4] *Ploughshare of Camillus*) ver. 168. He alludes to M. Furius Camillus, the Roman Dictator, who was said to have been taken from the plough to lead his fellow-citizens against the enemy. He died of the plague, B.C. 365.

[5] *Mattocks of the Curii*) ver. 169. He alludes to Marius Curius Dentatus, who held the Consulship with P. Cornelius Rufinus, and enabled the Romans to withstand Pyrrhus, and triumphed over the Samnites. When their

This was not the people whom tranquil peace might avail, whom its own liberty might satisfy with arms unmoved. Thence *arose* ready broils, and the contemptible wickedness which poverty could prompt; and the great honor, and one worthy to be sought with the sword, to have been able to do more than one's own country; might, too, was the measure of right; hence laws and decrees of the people[1] constrained, and Tribunes confounding their rights with Consuls. / Hence the Fasces [2] snatched up at a price, and the populace itself the vendor of its own applause, and canvassing fatal to the city, bringing round the annual contests on the venal Plain *of Mars*[3]; hence devouring usury, and interest greedy for each moment, and credit shaken, and warfare profitable to the many[4].

Now had Cæsar in his course[5] passed the icy Alps, and revolved in his mind the vast commotions and the future war. When he had arrived at the waves of the little Rubicon[6], the mighty image of his trembling country distinctly appeared to the chieftain in the darkness of the night, bear-

ambassadors came with the intention of bribing him, they found him at work in his field, and in answer to their solicitations, he told them that he would rather be the ruler of the rich than be rich himself, and that, invincible in the field, he could not be conquered by money. He died B.C. 270.

[1] *Laws and decrees of the people*) ver. 176. At Rome the " leges," or " laws " were approved by the Senate ; while the " plebiscita," or " decrees of the people," were passed at the " Comitia Tributa," or meetings of the tribes, on the rogation of a Tribune.

[2] *Hence the Fasces*) ver. 178. " Fasces." These, which were formed of a bundle of rods inclosing an axe, were the insignia of the Consular dignity ; and the word is frequently used to denote the office itself. Lucan here alludes to the corrupt and venal manners of the Roman people at this period.

[3] *The venal Plain of Mars*) ver. 180. He alludes to the elections of the Roman magistrates in the Campus Martius at Rome, and the system of bribery by which the suffrages of the people were purchased.

[4] *Profitable to the many*) ver. 182. Those, namely, who had nothing to lose.

[5] *Cæsar in his course*) ver. 185. On his march from Gaul to Italy.

[6] *The waves of the little Rubicon*) ver. 185. This was a small river between Cæsenum and Ariminum, in the north of Italy, falling into the Adriatic. It was the ancient boundary of Gaul, which was Cæsar's province. It is said to have received its name from the red (rubri) stones with which it abounded. It is uncertain whether it was the stream called Lusa, or that named Pisatello at the present day. It is said that on the bank of this river a pillar was placed by a decree of the Senate, with an inscription importing that whoever should pass in arms into the Roman territory would be deemed an enemy to the state.

ing marks of extreme sadness on her features, letting loose
the white hair from her tower-bearing head, with her long
locks dishevelled, standing with her arms *all* bare, and
uttering *these words*, mingled with sighs :
  " Whither beyond this do you proceed ?   Whither, *ye* men,
do you bear my standards?   If rightfully you come, if as
citizens, thus far you may."   Then did horror smite the limbs
of the chieftain, his hair stood on end, and a languor that
checked his course withheld his steps on the verge of the
bank.   Soon he exclaims, " O Thunderer, who dost look
down[1] upon the walls of the mighty city from the Tarpeian
rock, and ye Phrygian Penates of the Julian race[2], ye secret mysteries, too, of Quirinus borne away[3], and Jove
of Latium, who dost reside in lofty Alba[4], and ye Vestal
hearths[5], and thou, O Rome, equal to a supreme Deity, favour
my designs!   With no fatal arms am I pursuing thee ; lo !

---

  [1] *Thunderer, who dost look down*) ver. 196.   He alludes to Jupiter Capitolinus, whose temple was on the Capitoline hill, a part of which was called
the Tarpeian rock, from the virgin Tarpeia, who was killed and buried there.
  [2] *Phrygian Penates of the Julian race*) ver. 197.   Æneas rescued his
Penates or household gods from the flames of Troy, the capital of Phrygia.
Ascanius or Iulus, his son, was said to have been the ancestor of the Julian
family, of which Julius Cæsar was a member.   Jupiter had a temple, which
was built on the mountain of Alba by Ascanius, and was there worshipped
under the name of Jupiter Latialis.   The holy fire sacred to Vesta was
first preserved there, until it was removed from Alba to Rome by Numa.
  [3] *Mysteries of Quirinus borne away*) ver. 197.   Quirinus was a name of
Romulus, derived, according to Dionysius of Halicarnassus, from the Sabine
language.   Some suppose it to have originated in the Sabine word " curis," a
spear.   Lucan here alludes to the mysterious manner in which Romulus disappeared.   It is not improbable that he was slain by his nobles, and that
through their agent Julius Proculus they spread the report that he had been
taken up to heaven.   In the Fasti of Ovid, B. ii. l. 505, he is represented
as saying, " Forbid the Quirites to lament, and let them not offend my
Godhead with their tears.   Let them offer me frankincense, and let the
multitude pay adoration to Quirinus, their new God, and let them practise
my father's arts and warfare."
  [4] *Who dost reside in lofty Alba*) ver. 198.   Alba Longa was said to be
the most ancient town in Latium, and to have been founded by Ascanius,
the son of Æneas.   It derived its name of Longa from its extending in a
long line down the Alban mount toward the Alban lake.   It was totally destroyed by Tullus Hostilius, and its inhabitants were removed to Rome.
  [5] *And ye Vestal hearths*) ver. 199.   He alludes to the sacred fire which
was tended by the Vestal virgins in the Temple of Vesta, said to have
been brought from Troy by Æneas.

here am I, Cæsar, the conqueror by land and by sea, every-where (if only it is permitted me) thine own soldier even still. He will it be, he the guilty one, who shall make me thy foe!"

Then did he end the respite from the warfare, and swiftly bore the standards through the swollen stream. Just as when in the parched plains of sultry Libya a lion, his enemy perceived at hand, crouches undecided until he collects all his fury; soon as he has aroused himself by the lashings of his infuriate tail, and has raised his mane erect, and from his vast throat the loud roar re-echoes; then, if the light lance of the Moor, hurled, pierces him, or the hunt-ing spears enter his broad chest, amid the weapons, careless of wounds so great, he rushes on.

From a small spring rises the ruddy Rubicon, and, when fervid summer glows, is impelled with humble waves, and through the lowly vales it creeps along, and, a fixed boundary, separates from the Ausonian husbandmen the Gallic fields. At that time winter[1] gave it strength, and now the showery Cynthia with her blunted horn for the third time[2] had swollen the waves, and the Alps were thawed by the watery blasts of the eastern breeze. First of all the charger[3] is opposed obliquely to the stream, to bear the brunt of the floods; then the rest of the throng bursts through the pliant waves of the river, now broken in *its course*, across the easy ford. When Cæsar, the stream surmounted, reached the opposite banks, and stood upon the forbidden fields of Hesperia; "Here," said he, "here do I leave peace, and the violated laws behind; thee, Fortune, do I follow; henceforth, far hence be treaties! The Desti-nies have we trusted; War as our umpire we must adopt."

Thus having said, the active leader in the shades of night hurries on his troops, and swifter than the hurled

---

[1] *At that time winter*) ver. 217. Cæsar passed the Rubicon at the end of the month of January.

[2] *With her blunted horn for the third time*) ver. 218. "Tertia Cynthia" is probably the third night after the change of the moon. The passage seems to mean that it had rained three nights (and probably days) successively.

[3] *The charger*) ver. 220. "Sonipes," "sounding hoof," is the name gene-rally used by Lucan when he speaks of the charger or war-horse.

charge of the Balearic sling[1]. and the arrow[2] shot behind the back of the Parthian; and threatening he surprises Ariminum[3]. Lucifer left behind, the stars fled from the fires of the sun, and now arose the day doomed to behold the first outbreak of the war. Whether by the will of the Gods, or whether the murky south wind impelled them, clouds obscured the saddened light. When in the captured Forum the soldier halted, commanded to pitch his standard, the clash of clarions and the clang of trumpets sounded the ill-omened signals[4] together with the hoarse-sounding horn. The rest of the people was broken, and, aroused from their beds, the youth snatched down the arms fixed up near the hallowed Penates, which a prolonged peace *still* afforded; they laid hold of shields decaying with the frames now bare, and darts with blunted points, and swords rough with the cankering of swarthy rust.

When the well-known eagles glittered, and the Roman standards, and Cæsar mounted aloft was beheld in the midst of the ranks, they grew chilled with alarm, icy dread bound fast their limbs, and they revolved *these* silent complaints within their speechless breasts:—" O walls ill founded, these, with the Gauls for their neighbours[5]! O *walls*

[1] *Of the Balearic sling*) ver. 229. The Baleares were islands in the Mediterranean, off the coast of Spain, and were called " Major" and " Minor;" whence their present names Majorca and Minorca. Their inhabitants were noted for their great skill in the use of the sling, and were much employed in the Roman and Carthaginian armies.

[2] *The arrow*) ver. 230. The Parthians were famed for the dexterity with which they used the bow when retreating on horseback at the swiftest speed.

[3] *He surprises Ariminum*) ver. 231. Ariminum, now called Rimini, was a city of Umbria, on the coast of the Adriatic; about nine miles south of the Rubicon. The Via Flaminia and the Via Æmilia led to it from Rome. Cæsar took possession of it immediately after passing the Rubicon, as being a spot from which he could conveniently direct his operations against Etruria and Picenum. Cæsar informs us in his account of the Civil War, B. i., c. 8, that he took possession of this place with the 13th legion, and that here he met the Tribunes who had fled to him from Rome for protection.

[4] *The ill-omened signals*) ver. 238. Because sounding the note of civil war.

[5] *The Gauls for their neighbours*) ver. 248. Ariminum was originally inhabited by the Umbrians, then by the Senonian Gauls, who were expelled by the Romans in the year B.C. 268, when it was colonized from Roma.

condemned to a hapless site! Profound peace and tranquil
repose is there throughout all nations, we are the prey and the
first encampment for *these thus* frenzied. Far better, Fortune, wouldst thou have afforded an abode in an eastern
clime, and under the icy north, and wandering abodes[1],
rather than to have to protect the threshold of Latium. We
were the first to behold the commotions of the Senones[2],
the Cimbrian[3], too, rushing on, and the hosts of Libya[4],
and the career of the Teutonic rage. As oft as Fortune
aims a blow at Rome, this is the passage for the warfare."

Thus with a secret sigh *spoke* each, not venturing to express his alarm aloud; no voice was entrusted to anguish;
but in the same degree in which, when the winter keeps in
the birds, the fields are silent, and the mid ocean without a
murmur is still, thus profound was the silence. / Light has
now dispelled the cold shades of night; lo! the Fates supply to his wavering mind the torches of war and induce-
ments provoking to battle, and rend asunder all the pauses
of moderation; Fortune struggles that the movements of
the chieftain shall be justified, and discovers pretexts for
his arms.

[1] *And wandering abodes*) ver. 253. He alludes either to the wandering life of the Numidian tribes or of the Scythians, who were said to move
from place to place, and to live in waggons.

[2] *The commotions of the Senones*) ver. 254. The Senonian Gauls were
originally from Gallia Lugdunensis, dwelling near the Sequana or Seine. A
part of their people passed into Italy by way of the Alps about B.C. 400,
and penetrating to the south, they took up their abode on the borders of the
Adriatic, after expelling the Umbrians. Marching against Rome they took
all the City except the Capitol, B.C. 390. They were finally subdued by the
Romans, and the greater part of them destroyed by the Consul Dolabella, B.C.
283. Of course Ariminum, being at the very verge of Italy, would be exposed to their first attacks.

[3] *The Cimbrian, too*) ver. 254. The Cimbri are supposed to have originally
inhabited the Chersonesus Cimbrica, or Jutland. Migrating south with the
Teutoni and Ambrones, they overran Gaul, which they ravaged in all directions. They repulsed several Roman armies with great slaughter, but were ultimately defeated by Caius Marius near Aquæ Sextiæ (now Aix) in Gaul, and
by Marius and Catulus at the battle of Campi Raudii, near Verona, B.C. 101.

[4] *And the hosts of Libya*) ver. 255. Under the name of "Mars Libyes"
he alludes to the Punic wars; in the second of which Ariminum played a
distinguished part. In the year B.C. 218 Sempronius directed his legions
thither in order to oppose Hannibal in Cisalpine Gaul; and throughout that
war it was one of the points to which the greatest importance was attached
from its commanding position.

The threatening Senate, the law violated, expelled from the divided city the differing Tribunes [1], the Gracchi being thrown in their teeth [2]. These now repairing to the standards of the chieftain moving *onward* and in their vicinity, the daring Curio, with his venal tongue [3], accompanies ; a voice that once was the people's, and that had dared to defend liberty, and to place armed potentates on a level with the lower classes [4].

And when he beheld the chieftain revolving his various cares in his breast, he said, "While, Cæsar, thy party could be aided by my voice, although against the will of the Senate, then did we prolong thy rule [5], so long as I had

[1] *Expelled the differing Tribunes*) ver. 266. Cæsar offered to lay down his command if Pompey would do the same ; but the party of the latter would listen to no proposals for an accommodation. Quintus Cassius Longinus, and Marc Antony, the Tribunes of the people, ventured to speak boldly in behalf of Cæsar, but were violently censured by the Consuls Marcellus and Lentulus, who reminded them very significantly of the conduct and fate of the Gracchi, and threatened them with a similar end; on which they escaped from the city by night, disguised like slaves, and fled to Cæsar at Ariminum. This the Poet considers to be unfortunate, inasmuch as it would consequently appear that Cæsar marched towards Rome for no other reason than to preserve the privileges of the Tribunes, and to support the laws of his country.

[2] *The Gracchi being thrown in their teeth*) ver. 267. Tiberius and Caius Gracchus devoted their public career to asserting the rights of the Plebeians against the Patricians of Rome, for which reason their names became bywords for sedition and violence. They both met with violent deaths at different periods.

[3] *The daring Curio, with his venal tongue*) ver. 269. C. Scribonius Curio was an orator of great natural talents. He first belonged to the party of Pompey; but having run deeply into debt, he abandoned him and joined Cæsar, on the understanding that he would pay off all his liabilities. When the Senate demanded that Cæsar should lay down his command before coming into the city, Curio proposed that Pompey should do the same. While he was opposing the party of Pompey in the Senate, the year of his Tribuneship came to a close, and, fearing for his own safety, he fled from the city and joined Cæsar at Ariminum ; or, according to some, at Ravenna.

[4] *On a level with the lower classes*) ver. 271. By his eloquence he was able to counteract the ambition of great men, and to reduce them to a private station. It is supposed by some that Curio is the person referred to by Virgil in the sixth Book of the Æneid, in the famous words, " Vendidit hic auro patriam." " This man sold his country for gold."

[5] *Then did we prolong thy rule*) ver. 275. He takes to himself the credit of having obtained for Cæsar a prolongation of his government of Gaul for another five years.

the liberty to occupy the Rostra[1], and to bring over to thee
the wavering Quirites. But after the laws, coerced by warfare, were dumb, we were driven from our paternal homes,
and of our own accord we endured exile ; 't is thy victory will
make us citizens *again*. While, strengthened with no
support, the factions are *still* in doubt, away with delay ! it
always injures *men* prepared to procrastinate. Equal labours
and anxieties are being sought for a greater reward[2]. Gaul
has kept thee engaged in war for twice five years[3], a portion
of the earth how trifling ! If with a happy result thou hast
fought a few battles, Rome for thee will subdue the world[4]!

  " Now neither does the procession of the lengthened
triumph[5] receive thee returning, nor does the Capitol
demand the consecrated laurels. Cankering envy denies
thee everything; and hardly wilt thou escape with impunity having subdued the foe; it is the determination of
the son-in-law to deprive the father-in-law[6] of the sway.
Thou canst not share the earth ; alone thou mayst possess it."

[1] *To occupy the Rostra*) ver. 275. " Rostra," or " The Beaks," was the
name given to the stage in the Forum at Rome, from which the Orators
addressed the populace. It was so called from having been adorned with
the "rostra," or " beaks " of the ships of war taken from the Antiates. The
Rostra were transferred by Julius Cæsar to another part of the Forum, from
which time the spot where the ancient Rostra had stood was called " Rostra
Vetera," while the other was styled the " Rostra Nova," or " Rostra Julia."

[2] *Are sought for a greater reward*) ver. 282. Meaning, " The risk and
labour are equal to those you encountered in the Gallic war, but the reward
will be far greater."

[3] *For twice five years*) ver. 283. " Geminis lustris." The original meaning of the word " lustrum " (which was derived from " luo," " to cleanse,"
or " atone for,") was, " a purifying sacrifice," offered in behalf of the whole
people by one of the Censors, after finishing the census or review of the
Roman people, at the end of every five years, or four years according to
the Julian Calendar. The Gallic campaigns of Cæsar extended over a
period of ten years.

[4] *Rome for thee will subdue the world*) ver. 285. That is to say, " in
conquering Rome you will have conquered the world."

[5] *Procession of the lengthened triumph*) ver. 286. He alludes to the unjust refusal which Cæsar had met with when he demanded a triumph for his
conquests in Gaul.

[6] *The son-in-law to deprive the father-in-law*) ver. 289. Throughout his
poem, Lucan generally styles Cæsar " socer," " the father-in-law," and
Pompey " gener," " the son-in-law," relatively to each other. The marriage
of Pompey to Julia, the daughter of Cæsar, has been previously referred to.

After he had thus spoken, and had aroused in him, though eager already for the war, much anger *still*, and had inflamed the chieftain, in the same degree as the Elean courser is urged on by the shouts [1], although, the starting place now closed [2], he struggles against the door, and headlong loosens the bolts. Forthwith he summons the armed maniples [3] to the standards, and when, the multitudes collecting, he has well calmed their hurrying tumultuousness, with his countenance and his right hand he enjoins silence :—

" O companions in war!" he exclaims, " who together with me have experienced the thousand hazards of battle, now in the tenth year that you have conquered, has your blood, shed in the regions of the north, deserved this, and wounds and death, and winters passed at the foot of the Alps? Not otherwise is Rome convulsed by the vast tumultuous preparations for war, than if the Punic Hannibal were descending from the Alps. With stout recruits the cohorts are being filled; for the fleet every forest is falling; and both by sea and by land is Cæsar ordered to be expelled. What, if my standards had lain prostrate in adverse warfare, and if the fierce nations of the Gauls had been rushing close on our backs? Now, when Fortune acts with me in prospering circumstances, and the Gods *are* summoning us to the mastery, we are challenged. Let him come to the war, the chieftain, enfeebled by prolonged peace [4], with his soldiery *so* hastily levied, his toga-clad partisans, too, and

---

[1] *Elean courser is urged on by the shouts*) ver. 294. He alludes to the coursers in the chariot races at the Olympic games, which were celebrated in the territory of Elis, in the Peloponnesus.

[2] *The starting place closed*) ver. 295. The "carceres" were vaults at the end of the race-course, closed by gates of open woodwork, which, on the signal being given, were simultaneously opened by the aid of men and ropes, and the chariots came forth, ready for starting. The "carceres" were fastened with "repagula," "bars " or " bolts."

[3] *Summons the armed maniples*) ver. 296. In the early times of the Roman state a bundle of hay on the end of a pole served the Roman army for the purposes of a standard. To each troop of a hundred men, a " manipulus," or " wisp " of hay (so called from " manum implere," " to fill the hand," as forming a handful), was assigned as a standard, and hence in time the company itself obtained the name of " manipulus," and the soldier, as a member of it, was called " manipularis."

[4] *The chieftain, enfeebled by prolonged peace*) ver. 311. He alludes to Pompey, in recent years grown unused to warfare.

the loquacious Marcellus[1], the Catos as well, *mere* idle names[2]. Will, forsooth, men from afar[3] and purchased dependants still associate Pompey with the sway for years so many? Is he to be guiding the *triumphal* chariot, his years not yet permitting it[4]? Is he never to resign the honors which he has once usurped? Why need I now complain of the fields placed under restraint[5] throughout the whole earth, and how that starvation at his command has become his slave? Who does not know how the camp has been intermingled with the trembling Forum? When the swords ominously threatening surrounded the terrified judgment seat[6] with an unwonted array, and, the soldiery presuming to burst in upon the midst of the legal proceedings,

[1] *The loquacious Marcellus*) ver. 313. C. Claudius Marcellus is referred to, who, when Consul, together with his colleague, Cornelius Lentulus, distinguished himself by his fierce animosity against Cæsar. He appears to have been a person of slender abilities, and a tool in the hands of the partisans of Pompey. Judging from the present passage, he was probably noted for his garrulity. It is supposed that he perished in the Civil War.

[2] *The Catos, as well, mere idle names*) ver. 313. The plural number is used here as a contemptuous mode of expression. M. Porcius Cato was the only one of the family who was distinguished at this period.

[3] *Men from afar*) ver. 314. Cortius thinks that the word " extremi " refers to the " lowest," or " dregs " of the people. It is more probable that it alludes to persons or nations from a distance, as Pompey had gained victories and subdued nations in Spain, Africa, Asia Minor, and other parts of the world.

[4] *His years not yet permitting it*) ver. 316. According to the laws of Rome, a general was not allowed to enjoy a triumph till he had arrived at his thirtieth year. Pompey having conquered Hiarbas, King of Numidia, who had espoused the cause of Cn. Domitius Ahenobarbus, the Marian leader, obtained a triümph before he had attained his twenty-fifth year.

[5] *Fields placed under restraint*) ver. 318. We are informed by Cicero, in his Epistles to Atticus, and by Plutarch, in the Life of Pompey, that by a law passed for the purpose, the whole power of importing corn was entrusted to Pompey for five years; and Plutarch states that it was asserted by Clodius that the law was not made by reason of the scarcity of corn, but that the scarcity of corn was made that it might give rise to a law to invest Pompey with a power almost supreme. Pompey was accused of having, by his agents, used under-hand means to create this scarcity.

[6] *Surrounded the terrified judgment seat*) ver. 321. He alludes to the conduct of Pompey, on the occasion when T. Annius Papianus Milo was accused of the murder of Clodius, and defended by Cicero, who then pronounced his oration pro Milone, or rather a part of it, as, being intimidated, he forgot a large portion of what he had intended to say in favour of his client. Pompey was then the sole Consul, and to prevent the tumults

the standards of Pompey closed around the accused Milo.
Now, too, lest an old age spent in privacy should await him
in his feebleness, he is preparing for contests accursed,
accustomed to civil warfare, and, trained by crimes, to
surpass his master Sulla[1]. And as the fierce tigers never
lay aside their fury, which, in the Hyrcanian forest[2], while
they haunted the lairs of their dams, the blood deep-drawn
of the slain herds has nurtured; so too, Magnus, does thy
thirst survive to thee accustomed to lick the sword of Sulla.
Once received within the lips, no blood allows the polluted
jaws to become satiated. Still, what end will power meet
with, th῾   ῾ⁿᵍed? What limit is there to crimes? At
least, diᵛ   ᴎ, let this Sulla of thine teach thee[3]
now to d᷄.   this supreme sway. Shall then, after
the wandₑ   nsᵗ, and the Pontic battles of the exhausted m   th difficulty ended through barbarian

---

that were threatened by ᵥₑ friends of Clodius, he lined the Forum and the
surrounding hills with soldiers. This was contrary to law, and though
Pompey aided the prosecution of Milo, Cæsar is made to insinuate, in the
present speech, that it was done to protect him; whereas, in all probability,
Pompey acted thus solely with the view of maintaining the public peace.
Milo was condemned, and retired in exile to Massilia or Marseilles.

[1] *To surpass his master Sulla*) ver. 326. Pompey was one of the most
successful legates of the Dictator Sulla, in the latter part of the civil wars
against the Marian faction. He married Æmilia, the step-daughter of Sulla,
having put away his wife, Antistia, for that purpose.

[2] *In the Hyrcanian forest*) ver. 328. The Hyrcanian forest was situate
on the shores of the Caspian Sea. It was said to be the haunt of numerous
panthers, leopards, and tigers, to which reference is here made. The country
of Hyrcania flourished most under the Parthian kings, who often resided
there during the summer.

[3] *Let this Sulla of thine teach thee*) ver. 335. He alludes to the retirement of Sulla from public life, who, at the age of sixty, resigned the Dictatorship, and retired to the town of Puteoli.

[4] *After the wandering Cilicians*) ver. 336. The pirates are alluded to,
who were conquered by Pompey, and whose strongholds were on the coast
of Cilicia, in Asia Minor.

[5] *The Pontic battles of the exhausted monarch*) ver. 336. He alludes to
the death of Mithridates, king of Pontus, who waged war with the Romans
for a period of forty years. Having received many overthrows from Sulla
and Lucullus, he was ultimately conquered by Pompey. Being closely besieged in a fortress by his son Pharnaces, he attempted to poison himself,
but from his previous continued use of antidotes, he was unable to do so;
on which he fell on his sword and perished. In the next line Cæsar refers
to the protracted length of this war.

poison, Cæsar be granted to Pompey as a last province, because, commanded to lay down my conquering eagles, I did not obey? If from myself the reward of my labours is torn away, to these, at least, let the rewards of their prolonged service be granted, *though* not with their general; under some leader, whoever he is, let these troops enjoy their triumph. Whither, after the wars, shall pallid old age betake itself? What settlement is there to be for those who have served their time? What lands shall be granted[1] for our veterans to plough[2]? What walls for the invalided? Or, Magnus, shall pirates, in preference, become the settlers[3]? Victorious already, raise, raise your standards; the might we must employ, which we have acquired; to him who wields arms does he surrender everything who refuses what is his due. The Deities, too, will not forsake us; for neither is plunder nor sovereignty sought by my arms; we are tearing away its tyrants[4] from a City ready to be enslaved."

Thus he speaks; but the hesitating ranks mutter among themselves words of indecision in whispers far from distinct; duty and their paternal Penates check their feelings although rendered fierce with carnage, and their swelling spirits; but through ruthless love of the sword and dread of their general, they are brought back. Then Lælius, who held the rank[5] of first centurion, and wore the

---

[1] *What lands shall be granted*) ver. 344. The "emeriti" in the Roman armies were those who had served for the stipulated time, and were entitled to immunity for the future.

[2] *For our veterans to plough*) ver. 345. When an "emeritus" was induced to continue in the service, either from attachment to his general, or from hopes of promotion, he was called "veteranus." When the "emeriti" retired from the service, it was usual to bestow on them grants of the public land.

[3] *Pirates, in preference, become the settlers*) ver. 346. He refers to the manner in which Pompey disposed of the Cilician pirates after he had conquered them; some of whom he distributed among the cities of Cilicia, and many were settled at Soli, on the Cicilian coast, which had lately been depopulated by Tigranes, king of Armenia, and which was thenceforth called Pompeiopolis. Others received grants of land at Dymæ, in Achaia, others in Calabria.

[4] *We are tearing away its tyrants*) ver. 351. He probably alludes here to the sons of Pompey, as well as their father.

[5] *Lælius, who held the rank*) ver. 357. Lælius was the "primipilus," or "first centurion" of the thirteenth legion. The "primipilus" commanded the first maniple of the "Triarii," and was next in rank to the military Tribunes. In his charge was the eagle of the legion, which, perhaps, is here

insignia of the decoration won in service[1], the oak that bespoke the reward for saving a citizen[2], exclaimed:

" If it is lawful, O greatest guardian of the Roman fame, and if it is allowed to utter the accents of truth—that a patience so long enduring has withheld thy might, do we complain. Was it that confidence in us was wanting to thee? So long as the warm blood imparts motion to these breathing bodies, and so long as stalwart arms have might to hurl the javelin, wilt thou be submitting to the degenerate arts of peace[3], and the sovereign sway of the Senate?\ Is it so very dreadful to prove the conqueror in civil war? Come, lead us amid the tribes of Scythia, amid the inhospitable shores of Syrtis[4], amid the sultry sands of thirsting Libya. This army, when it left the conquered world behind its back, stilled the swelling waves of Ocean[5] with its oars, and subdued the foaming Rhine at its northern mouth[6]. To me, in following thy commands, it is as much a matter of course to do, as

referred to under the title of "insignia." The vine sapling with which they had the power of inflicting punishment on refractory soldiers was another of the insignia of the centurions.

[1] *Won in service*) ver. 357. "Emeriti." On the meaning of this word, see the Note to l. 344.

[2] *The reward for saving a citizen*) ver. 358. The "corona civica," or "civic crown," was the second in honor and importance in the Roman armies, and was presented to the soldier who had saved the life of a fellow-citizen in battle. It was originally made from the "ilex," afterwards from the "æsculus," and, finally, from the "quercus," three different kinds of oak. The elder Pliny informs us that before the claim was allowed it was necessary to satisfy the following requisitions—to have saved the life of a fellow-citizen in battle, slain his opponent, and maintained his ground.

[3] *Degenerate arts of peace*) ver. 365. "Togam." Literally, the "toga," or "gown," which was worn by the citizens in time of peace.

[4] *Inhospitable shores of Syrtis*) ver. 367. There were two quicksands off the coast of Africa, known by the name of "Syrtis" or "Syrtes." The greater Syrtis was a wide gulf on the shores of Tripolita and Cyrenaica, opposite the mouth of the Adriatic. It was especially dangerous for its sandbanks and quicksands, and its exposure to the northern winds; while on the shore it was skirted by loose burning sands. The lesser Syrtis lay considerably to the west of the other one, and was dangerous from its rocky shores and the variableness of its tides.

[5] *Stilled the swelling waves of Ocean*) ver. 370. He alludes to the passage of Cæsar from the coast of Gaul to that of Britain.

[6] *At its northern mouth*) ver. 371. "Vertice;" literally, "heights." There is considerable doubt among the Commentators as to the exact meaning of this word in the present passage.

it is to will. And no fellow-citizen of mine, Cæsar, is he against whom I shall hear thy trumpet-signal. By the prospering standards of thy ten campaigns I swear, and by thy triumphs *gained* over every foe; if thou shouldst bid me bury my sword in the breast of my brother, in the throat too of my parent, and in the entrails of my wife teeming with her burden, still, though with unwilling right hand, I will do all this; if to despoil the Gods, and to set fire to the Temples, the flames of thy camp[1] shall envelope the Divinity of *Juno* Moneta; if to pitch the camp above the waves of Etrurian Tiber[2], a bold marker-out of the encampment will I enter upon the Hesperian fields. Whatever walls thou shalt desire to level with the plain, impelled by these arms the battering-ram shall scatter the stones far and wide; even though that city which thou shouldst order to be utterly razed should be Rome *herself.*"

To these words the cohorts at once shout assent, and pledge themselves with hands lifted on high, for whatever wars he shall summon them to. An uproar ascends to the skies as vast, as, when the Thracian Boreas beats against the crags of pine-bearing Ossa[3], the trunks bending of the woods bowed down, or returning again *upright* into the air, the roar *of the forests* arises.

Cæsar, when he perceives that the war is embraced by the soldiers thus heartily, and that the Fates are favouring, that by no indecision he may impede his fortune, summons forth the cohorts scattered throughout the Gallic fields, and with standards moved from every direction marches upon Rome.

---

[1] *The flames of thy camp*) ver. 380. "Numina miscebit castrensis flamma Monetæ." The exact meaning of this passage has caused much discussion among the Commentators, but it seems most probable that the veteran is expressing his readiness, at the command of his general, to melt the statues of the Gods in the flames for his master's purposes. Under the name Moneta, as the protectress of money, Juno had a Temple on the Capitoline Hill, in which was the mint of Rome. The speaker probably means to hint his readiness, if necessary, to march into the very heart of Rome to seize the statues of the Divinities.

[2] *Waves of Etrurian Tiber*) ver. 381. The Tiber takes its rise in the ancient country of Etruria.

[3] *The crags of pine-bearing Ossa*) ver. 389. Ossa was a mountain much celebrated by the poets. It was in the north of Magnesia, in Thessaly, and was in the vicinity of Pelion and Olympus, but was much less lofty than the latter.

They deserted the tents pitched by the cavity of Lemanus[1], and the camp which soaring aloft above the curving rock of Vogesus[2] used to overawe the pugnacious Lingones[3] with their painted arms. Those left the shallows of Isara[4], which running with its own flood through such an extent, falling into a stream of greater fame, bears not *its own* name down to the ocean waves. The yellow-haired Ruteni[5] are relieved from the prolonged garrison; the placid Atax[6] rejoices at no longer bearing the Latian keels; the Varus, too[7], the limit of Hesperia, her boundaries *now* extended[8]; where, too, beneath the divine authority of Hercules, the consecrated harbour adjoins the sea[9] with its hollowed

[1] *Lemanus*) ver. 396. Now the Lake of Geneva.

[2] *Curving rock of Vogesus*) ver. 397. Vogesus, or Vosgesus, now the Vosges, was the name of a range of mountains in Gaul, running parallel to the river Rhine. The rivers Seine, Saône, and Moselle rise in these mountains.

[3] *The pugnacious Lingones*) ver. 398. The Lingones were a powerfu. people of Transalpine Gaul, separated from the Sequani by the river Arar, or Saône. Their chief town was Andematurinum, afterwards Lingones, now called Langres. Tacitus informs us that the Germans were also accustomed to paint their arms.

[4] *The shallows of Isara*) ver. 399. Isara, now the Isère, a river of Gaul, flows into the Rhone, north of Valentia.

[5] *The yellow-haired Ruteni*) ver. 402. The Ruteni, or Rutheni, were a people of Gallia Aquitanica. Their chief town was Segodunum, afterwards Civitas Rutenorum, now called Rodez.

[6] *The placid Atax*) ver. 403. The Atax, or Narbo, was a river of Gallia Narbonensis, rising in the Pyrenees: it is now called Aude.

[7] *The Varus, too*) ver. 404. The Varus, now called Var, or Varo, was a river of Gallia Narbonensis, rising in Mount Cema, in the Alps, and falling into the Mediterranean.

[8] *Her boundaries now extended*) ver. 404. " Promoto limite." This passage has presented difficulties to some of the Commentators; but it is pretty clear that he alludes to the period when, the Roman state having extended beyond its former limits, the Rubicon was no longer considered the boundary which separated Italy from Gaul, and the Varus, which lay far to the north-west of it, was substituted as such in its place. Hesperia, or the " country of the West," was one of the ancient names of Italy. Spain also was sometimes called by that name.

[9] *The consecrated harbour adjoins the sea*) ver. 405. This was the "Portus Monœci," a seaport on the coast of Liguria, founded by the Massilians. The town was situate on a promontory, and possessed a temple of Hercules Monœcus, from whom the place derived its name. The harbour was of importance, as being the only one on this part of the coast of Liguria. Hercules was said to have touched here when on his expedition against Geryon, king of Spain.

rocks; no Corus[1] holds sway over it, nor yet the Zephyr; alone does Circius[2] disturb the shores his own, and withholds *the ships* from the safe harbour of Monœcus. Where, too, the doubtful coast extends[3], which land and sea claim at alternate periods, when the vast ocean is poured forth *upon it*, or when with ebbing waves it retreats. *Whether it is that* the wind thus rolls[4] on the sea from distant climes, and bearing it on *there* leaves it; or whether the waves of wandering Tethys[5], influenced by the second of the heavenly bodies[6], flow at the lunar hours; or whether the flaming Titan, that he may quaff the refreshing waves, uplifts the ocean, and raises the billows to the stars—do you enquire, whom the economy of the universe engages; but to me, thou Cause, whatever thou art, that dost govern movements thus regular, as the Gods of heaven have willed it *so*, for ever lie concealed!

Then does he, who occupies the fields of Nemetis[7] and the banks of the Aturus[8], where on the curving shore, flowing by Tarbela[9], it encloses the sea gently flowing in, move his

[1] *No Corus holds sway*) ver. 406. Corus, or Caurus, the Argestes of the Greeks, is considered a stormy wind in Italy. It blows from the north-west.

[2] *Alone does Circius*) ver. 407. Circius was a violent wind which was said to blow in the ancient Gallia Narbonensis. According to some it blew from the north-north-west, while others call it a south wind. The latter seems most probably the case, as if, as is sometimes represented, the harbour of Monœcus opened to the south-west, it could not well be exposed to any wind blowing from the north.

[3] *Where the doubtful coast extends*) ver. 409. He probably alludes to the flat coast off Belgium and the present kingdom of Holland.

[4] *It is that the wind thus rolls*) ver. 412. Pomponius Mela, in his Third Book, mentions the same three theories. The second is the right one.

[5] *Waves of wandering Tethys*) ver. 414. Tethys is a name very generally given by the poets to the ocean. She was one of the most ancient of the Deities, and was the wife of Oceanus, daughter of Cœlus and Vesta, and the foster-mother of Juno.

[6] *The second of the heavenly bodies*) ver. 413. "Sidere secundo." Under this name he refers to the moon, as being the next in apparent magnitude to the sun.

[7] *Who occupies the fields of Nemetis*) ver. 419. The Nemetes, or Nemetæ. were a people of Gallia Belgica, on the Rhine. Their chief town was Noviomagus, afterwards Nemetæ, on the site of the present Spires.

[8] *The banks of the Aturus*) ver. 420. The Aturus, or Atur, now called the Adour, was a river of Gallia Aquitanica, rising in the Pyrenees, and flowing through the territory of the Tarbelli into the ocean.

[9] *Flowing by Tarbela*) ver. 421. The city of the Tarbelli, who were a

standards, and the Santonian exults[1], the enemy removed;
the Biturigian[2], too, and the active Suessones[3] with their
long arms; the Leucan[4] and the Rheman[5], most adroit in
extending the arm *with the poised javelin;* the Sequanian
race most adroit with the reins guided in the circle; the
Belgian, too[6], the skilful guide of the scythed chariot[7]; the

powerful people of Gallia Aquitanica, lying between the ocean and the
Pyrenees. Their chief town was ' Aquæ Tarbellicæ,' or ' Augustæ,' on
the Atur or Adour. It is now called Dacqs.

[1] *The Santonian exults*) ver. 422. The Santoni, or Santones, were
a nation of Gallia Aquitanica, dwelling near the ocean, to the north of the
Garumna, or Garonne. Their chief town was called Mediolanum, afterwards Santones, now Saintes.

[2] *The Biturigian, too,* ver. 423. The Bituriges were a powerful people
of Gallia Aquitanica. They were divided into the Bituriges Cubi, who inhabited the district now called Bourges, having Avaricum for their capital;
and the Bituriges Vivisci, or Ubisci, on the Garonne, whose capital was
Burdigala, now Bordeaux.

[3] *And the active Suessones*) ver. 423. The Suessones, or Suessiones, were
a warlike nation of Gallia Belgica. Their king, Divitiacus, in the time of
Cæsar, was reckoned the most powerful chief in Gaul. They inhabited a
fertile country to the west of the Rhine, and possessed twelve towns, of
which the capital was Noviodunum, afterwards Augusta Suessonum, or
Suessones, now Soissons. They were noted for the height of their stature,
and the length of their spears and shields.

[4] *The Leucan*) ver. 424. The Leuci were a people in the south-east of
Gallia Belgica, between the rivers Matrona and Mosella. Their chief town
was Tullum, now Toul.

[5] *And the Rheman*) ver. 424. The Remi, or Rhemi, were a very powerful people of Gallia Belgica, lying to the east of the Suessones and the
Bellovaci. They formed an alliance with Cæsar, when the rest of the
Belgæ made war against him, B.C. 57. Their chief town was Durocortorum,
afterwards called Remi, now Rheims. From the expression "optimus
excusso lacerto," it appears that the Rhemi were especially famed for their
skill in the use of the javelin.

[6] *The Belgian, too*) ver. 426. The Belgæ formed one of the three great
peoples into which Cæsar divides the population of Gaul. They were
bounded on the north by the Rhine, on the west by the ocean, on the south
by the Sequana or Seine and the Matrona or Marne, and on the east by
the territory of the Treviri. They were of German origin, and had settled
in the country, on dispossessing the former inhabitants. Though mentioned
here separately from the Nervii, Remi, and Suessones, all the latter were
really tribes of the Belgæ.

[7] *Skilful guide of the scythed chariot*) ver. 426. "Rostrati—covini."
The "covinus" was a kind of chariot much in use among the Belgæ and
the ancient Britons. Its spokes were armed with long scythes, which are here
referred to in the epithet "rostrati," literally "beaked." From the Romans
having designated a covered travelling carriage by the same name, it is

Arverni, likewise[1], who have presumed to pretend them-selves[2] of Latian brotherhood, descended from the race of the people of Ilium ; the Nervian, also[3], too fatally re-bellious[4], and defiled by the *broken* treaty with the slaugh-tered Cotta ; the Vangiones, too[5], who imitate thee, Sarma-tian, with the loosely-flowing trowsers[6]; the fierce Batavians,

---

supposed that the "covinus" was covered on all sides except the front, and that it was occupied by one person only, the "covinarius," or driver of the chariot. We learn from Tacitus, that the "covinarii" constituted a regular part of the British army.

[1] *The Arverni, likewise*) ver. 427. The Arverni were a powerful nation of Celtica, and, in the time of Cæsar, the rivals of the Ædui for the supre-macy. They are supposed to have possessed a large portion of the high lands of central France, in the valley of the Allier. Their territory gave its name to the modern Auvergne.

[2] *Who have presumed to pretend themselves*) ver. 427. It has been suggested that either this remark is a mistake of the Poet, or that he simply alludes to the pride of the Arverni before they were conquered by the Romans, whose equals they considered themselves to be. It has been, how-ever, supposed by some that the Arverni really did claim descent from Antenor, the Trojan. One of the Scholiasts says that a Trojan named Alvernus founded the colony, and that Cicero makes mention of them in the words—"In-venti sunt qui etiam fratres populi Romani vocarentur." "There have been found some who were even called the brothers of the Roman people." This passage, however, is to be found in none of the fragments of Cicero's works which have come down to us.

[3] *The Nervian, also*) ver. 429. The Nervii were a warlike people of Gallia Belgica, whose territory extended from the river Sabis (now Sambre) to the ocean, and part of which was covered by the forest of Arduenna or Ardennes. They were divided into several smaller tribes, the Centrones, Grudii, Levaci, Pleumoxii, and Geiduni.

[4] *Too fatally rebellious*) ver. 429. He alludes to the fate of Q. Aurun-culeius Cotta, an officer in the army of Julius Cæsar. He and Q. Titurius Sabinus had the command of one legion and four cohorts, with which they took up their position in the territory of the Eburones. Listening to the advice of Sabinus, he was drawn into an ambuscade by Ambiorix and Cati-volcus, on which they, with the greater part of their soldiers, were cut to pieces.

[5] *The Vangiones, too*) ver. 431. The Vangiones were a people of Ger-many, in the neighbourhood of the modern Worms.

[6] *With the loosely-flowing trowsers*) ver. 430. Ovid, speaking of the people of Tomi, in Thrace, bordering on Sarmatia, refers to this peculiarity in their dress. In the Tristia, B. iii. El. 10, l. 19, he says—"The in-habitants barely defend themselves from the cold by skins and sewn trow-sers." And again, in B. v. El. 10, l. 34, he says—"Even those who are supposed to derive their origin from the Grecian city, the Persian trowsers cover instead of the dress of their country;" and in B. iv. El. 6, l. 47—"Here there is a Scythian multitude, and crowds of the Getæ, wearing

too[1], whom the harsh-sounding trumpets of crooked brass[2] inflame to war; where Cinga flows around[3] with its tide; where the Rhone bears to the sea the Arar[4], swept along with its impetuous waves; where the race dwells upon the heights on the mountain summits, the Gebennæ precipitous[5] with their snow-white crags. [The Pictones, left at liberty[6], cultivate their fields[7]: and no more does the camp pitched around keep in check the fickle Turones[8]. The Andian disdaining, Meduana[9], to pine amid thy fogs, is

trowsers." The following nations are read of in ancient times as wearing "braccæ," or "trowsers:"—the Medes and Persians, the Parthians, the Phrygians, the Sacæ, the Sarmatians, the Dacians, the Getæ, the Gauls, the Britons, the Belgæ, and the Teutones.

[1] *The fierce Batavians, too*) ver. 431. The Batavi were a people who inhabited the country between the Maas and the Waal, at the mouth of the Rhine, now Holland. Their country was first styled "Insula Batavorum," and at a later period Batavia. Their chief towns were Batavodurum and Lugdunum, now Leyden. These people were long the allies of the Romans in their wars against the Germans, and were of great service by means of their excellent cavalry.

[2] *Harsh-sounding trumpets of crooked brass*) ver. 432. The "tuba" or trumpet of the Roman armies was straight, while the "cornu" and the "lituus" were curved. Probably the peculiarity of the "tubæ" of the Batavi was, that while they preserved the sound of the "tuba," they had the form of the "cornu."

[3] *Where Cinga flows around*) ver. 432. Cinga, now Cinca, a river of Hispania Tarraconensis, rising in the Pyrenees, falling with the Sicoris into the Iberus, or Ebro.

[4] *Bears to the sea the Arar*) ver. 433. The Arar, now the Saône, is a river of Gaul, which, rising in the Vosges, flows into the Rhodanus or Rhone, at Lugdunum or Lyons.

[5] *The Gebennæ precipitous*) ver. 435. Gebennæ, or Cebenna Mons, was the range of mountains now called the Cevennes, situate in the middle of Gaul, extending northwards to Lugdunum or Lyons, and separating the Arverni from the Helvii.

[6] *The Pictones, left at liberty*) ver. 436. This and the next five lines are generally looked upon as spurious. According to some, they were first found by Cujacius; but Cortius says, that the report was, that Marbodus Andinus, the Bishop of Rennes, inserted these verses in the Poem to gratify his countrymen.

[7] *Cultivate their fields*) ver. 436. The Pictones, who were afterwards called the Pictavi, were a powerful people on the coast of Gallia Aquitanica. Their chief town was Limonum, subsequently called Pictavi, now Poitiers.

[8] *Keep the fickle Turones*) ver. 437. The Turones, Turoni, or Turonii, were a people in the interior of Gallia Lugdunensis. Their chief town was Cæsarodunum, subsequently Turoni, now Tours.

[9] *Meduana*) ver. 438. A river of Gaul, flowing into the L'geris, now called the Mayne.

now refreshed by the placid stream of Liger[1]; from the squadrons of Cæsar renowned Genabos[2] is set free.]

Thou, too, Trevirian[3], overjoyed that the course of warfare is turned back; and *thou*, Ligurian[4], now shorn, in former times with thy locks hanging adown thy graceful neck, preferred to the whole of long-haired Gaul[5]; *those*, too, by whom the relentless Teutates[6] is appeased by direful bloodshed, and Hesus, dreadful[7] with his merciless altars; and the shrine of Taranis[8], not more humane than *that* of Scythian Diana[9]. You, too, *ye* Bards[10], who, *as* poets, hand down in your praises to remote ages spirits valiant,

---

[1] *Stream of Liger*) ver. 439. Liger, or Ligeris, now the Loire, is one of the largest rivers of France, and rises in the Cevennes.

[2] *Renowned Genabos*) ver. 440. Genabum, or Cenabum, was a town of Gallia Lugdunensis, on the north bank of the Ligeris, and the chief town of the Carnutes; it was plundered and burnt by Cæsar, but was afterwards rebuilt. The present city of Orleans stands on its site.

[3] *Thou, too, Trevirian*) ver. 441. The Treviri were a powerful nation of Gallia Belgica, and were faithful allies of the Romans. They were famous for the excellence of their cavalry. Their territory lay to the eastward of that of the Rhemi, and the Mosella flowed through it. Their chief town was made a Roman colony by Augustus, and was called Augusta Trevirorum, now Trier, or Treves.

[4] *And thou, Ligurian*) ver. 442. The Ligurian tribes were divided by the Romans into the Ligures Transalpini and Cisalpini. Those who inhabited the Maritime Alps were called "Capillati," or "Comati," from the custom of wearing their hair long.

[5] *The long-haired Gaul*) ver. 443. "Gallia Comata" was the name given to that part of Gaul which was the last conquered by the Romans, and received its name from the inhabitants continuing to wear their hair long and flowing, while the other nations of Gallia Cisalpina had adopted the Roman manners.

[6] *The relentless Teutates*) ver. 445. Teutas, or Teutates, is supposed to have been the name of a Gallic Divinity corresponding to the Roman Mercury. Human victims were offered to him.

[7] *And Hesus, dreadful*) ver. 445. Hesus was the Mars of the Gauls, and to him the prisoners taken in battle were sacrificed.

[8] *The shrine of Taranis*) ver. 446. Taranis is supposed to have been the Jupiter of the Celtic nations.

[9] *That of Scythian Diana*) ver. 446. He alludes to the worship of Diana at Tauris in Scythia, where, by order of Thoas, the king, all strangers were slain and sacrificed to the Gods. Iphigenia was her priestess, and narrowly escaped sacrificing her own brother Orestes. See the story related in the Tristia of Ovid, B. ii. El. 2, p. 425 of the Translation in *Bohn's Classical Library*.

[10] *You too, Bards*) ver. 449. The "Bardi" were the Poets of Gaul and Germany, whose province it was to sing the praises of their chieftains and of the heroes who had died in combat.

and cut off in war, freed from alarm, did *then* pour forth full
many a strain; and you, Druids[1], after arms were laid aside,
sought once again your barbarous ceremonials and the ruthless usages of your sacred rites. To you alone[2] has it been
granted to know the Gods and the Divinities of heaven, or
alone to know that they do not exist. In remote forests do
you inhabit the deep glades. On your authority[3] the shades
seek not the silent abodes of Erebus, and the pallid realms
of Pluto[4] in the depths below; the same spirit controls other
limbs in another world[5]; death is the mid space in a prolonged existence, if you sing what is ascertained *as truth.*
Assuredly the nations whom the Northern Bear looks down
upon *are* happy in their error, whom this, the very greatest
of terrors, does not move, the fear of death. Thence have
the people spirits *ever* ready to rush to arms, and souls
that welcome death; and *they deem it* cowardice to be sparing
of a life destined to return. You, too, stationed to prevent
the Cauci[6], with their curling locks, from warfare, repair to

[1] *And you, Druids*) ver. 451. The "Druidæ," or Druids, were the high-
priests of the Gauls, and performed many mysterious rites. By "positis
armis," the Poet does not mean that they wielded arms, but that after arms
were laid aside in Gaul by reason of the civil wars, they resumed their superstitious practices, which had been checked by Cæsar. Cæsar says, in his
Gallic War, B. vi. ch. 14—"The Druids do not go to war, nor do they pay
tribute together with the rest."

[2] *To you alone*) ver. 453. The meaning seems to be, "To you alone is
it granted to know the mysteries of the Gods, or the fact that there are
no Gods."

[3] *On your authority*) ver. 454. The meaning is, that the Druids taught
the doctrine of the immortality of the soul.

[4] *The pallid realms of Pluto*) ver. 455. Dis was an epithet of Pluto,
the king of Erebus, or the infernal regions.

[5] *In another world*) ver. 457. "Orbe alio" may mean simply "in
another region" of the earth; but it most probably refers to the idea prevalent with those who taught the doctrine of the transmigration of the soul, that
it animated various bodies in the stars in a certain cycle or routine. The
doctrine of the Druids differed from that of Pythagoras, who is said, but
upon very slender authority, to have derived his notions on this subject
from them. The Druids believed that the soul passed from man into man
alone; while Pythagoras thought that on leaving the human body it passed
into the bodies of various animals in succession.

[6] *To prevent the Cauci*) ver. 464. The Cauci, Caÿci, or Chauci, were a
powerful people in the north-east of Germany, whose country was divided
by the Visurgis or Weser. Tacitus describes them as the noblest and most
courageous of the German tribes. In the use of the word "cirrigeros," he

Rome, and desert the savage banks of the Rhine, and the
world *now* laid open to the nations.

Cæsar, when his immense resources, with their collected
strength, had created confidence for daring still greater
things, spread throughout all Italy, and filled the neighbouring fortified towns[1]. Idle rumours, too, were added
to well-founded fears, and burst upon the feelings of the
public, and presented to them the destined slaughter, and,
a swift forerunner of the hastening warfare, let loose tongues
innumerable to false alarms. Some there are who, where
Mevania displays itself[2] in the plains that rear the bulls,
aver that the audacious squadrons are pushing onward to
the combat, and that, where Nar flows[3] on to the stream of
Tiber, the barbarian troops of the ruthless Cæsar are spreading far and wide; that he himself, leading all his eagles
and his collected standards, is advancing with no single
column, and with a camp densely thronged. And not such
as they remember him do they *now* behold him; both more
terrible and relentless does he seem to their imaginations,
and more inhuman than the conquered foe[4]. That after
him the nations lying between the Rhine and the Alps,
torn from the Arctic regions and from their paternal homes,
are following close, and that the City has been ordered, a
Roman looking on, to be sacked by barbarous tribes.

Thus, by his fears, does each one give strength to
rumour; and no one the author of their woes, what they
have invented they dread. And not alone is the lower
class alarmed, smitten by a groundless terror; but the Senate

alludes to the custom of the German nations of wearing the hair long and
curling.

[1] *Filled the neighbouring fortified towns*) ver. 468. We learn from
Cæsar's Civil War, B. i. c. 11, 12, that the next places which he took
after Ariminum, were Arretium, Pisaurus, Fanum, Iguvium, and Auximum.

[2] *Mevania displays itself*) ver. 473. This was an ancient city in the
interior of Umbria, on the river Tinea. It was situate on the road from
Rome to Ancona, and was very strongly fortified. The Clitumnus was a
river in the neighbourhood, famous for a breed of white oxen fed on its
banks.

[3] *And where Nar flows*) ver. 475. This was a river of Central Italy, on
the frontiers of Umbria and Picenum. Passing by Interamna and Narnia, it
fell into the Tiber, not far from Ocriculum.

[4] *More inhuman than the conquered foe*) ver. 480. Namely, the Gauls
and the Britons.

house, and the Fathers themselves rush forth from their
seats, and the Senate taking to flight gives its hateful decrees[1] for the warfare into the charge of the Consuls. Then
uncertain what to seek as safe, and what to leave as worthy
to be feared, whither the anxiety for flight directs each one,
it urges the populace headlong, and the throng, connected in
one long line, bursts forth.

You would suppose either that accursed torches had set
fire to the abodes, or that now, the ruins shaking, the
nodding houses were tottering to their fall ; thus does the
panic-stricken multitude at random rush throughout the City
with precipitate steps, as though there had been but one
hope in their ruined fortunes, to desert their paternal
walls.   Just as, when the stormy south wind has repulsed
from the Libyan Syrtes the boundless ocean, and the
broken mass of the sail-bearing mast has sent forth its
crash, and the pilot, the ship deserted, leaps into the waves,
the seaman, too, and *thus*, the structure of the vessel not yet
torn asunder, each one makes a shipwreck for himself ; so
the City forsaken, do they fly unto the warfare.   The parent,
now weakened with old age, was able to call no one back[2] :
nor yet the wife her husband with her tears ; nor did the
household Lares detain them, while they were breathing
prayers for their safety *thus* doubtful ; nor did any one
pause at the threshold, and then, filled with perhaps his
last glimpse of the beloved City, take his departure ; not
to be called back, the crowd rushes on.

O Deities, ready to grant supreme prosperity, and loth
to preserve the same !   The cowardly throngs left the City a

---

[1] *Gives its hateful decrees*) ver. 489.   Speaking of this crisis, Cæsar
says, in the Civil War, B. i. ch. 5—" Recourse was had to that extreme
and formal decree of the Senate " (which was never resorted to even by daring
proposers except when the City was in danger of being set on fire, or when
the public safety was despaired of), " that the Consuls, Prætors, Tribunes of
the people, and Proconsuls in the City, should take care that the State received no detriment."   Of course these decrees would be odious to the partizans of Cæsar.

[2] *Was able to call no one back*) ver. 505.   There is a similar passage in
the Tristia of Ovid, B. i. El. 3, l. 54, where, describing the night of his
leaving Rome in banishment, he says :—" Thrice did I touch the threshold ;
thrice was I called back, and my lingering foot itself paused indulgent to
my feelings ; often, having bade him farewell, did I again give utterance to
many a word and, as if now departing, I gave the last kiss."

prey on Cæsar's approach, filled with the people and with
conquered nations, and able to hold the human race, if the
multitude were collected together. When, in foreign regions, the Roman soldier, pressed by the foe, is hemmed in
he escapes the dangers of the night by a simple trench,
and the rampart suddenly formed with the protection of
some clods torn up affords secure slumbers within the
tents. Thou Rome, on the name only of war being heard
art being deserted; a single night has not been trusted to
thy walls.

Still, pardon must be granted, *yes*, must be granted for
alarms thus great. Pompey flying, they were in dread[1].
Besides, that even no hope in the future might cheer
their failing spirits, there was added the disclosed assurance
of a still worse future, and the threatening Gods of heaven
filled with prodigies the earth, the seas, the skies. The
gloomy nights beheld stars unknown, and the sky burning with flames, and torches flying obliquely through the
expanse along the heavens, and the train of a fear-inspiring
meteor, and a comet threatening tyranny to the earth[2].
Incessant lightnings flashed in the deceptive clear sky, and
the fire described various forms in the dense atmosphere;
now a javelin, with a prolonged *flame, and* now a torch,
with a scattered light, flashed in the heavens. Lightning in
silence without any clouds, and bringing its fires from the
Arctic regions[3], smote the Capital of Latium[4]; the lesser
stars, too, that were wont to speed onwards in the still
hours of the night, came in the middle of the day; and,
her horns closed, when Phœbe was now reflecting her

---

[1] *Pompey flying, they were in dread*) ver. 522. According to Cæsar,
Civil War, B. i. ch. 14, Pompey left the City on his road to the legions
which he had placed in winter quarters in Apulia.

[2] *Threatening tyranny to the earth*) ver. 529. By its appearance threatening tyranny to the earth; such as it had suffered under Marius and Sulla.

[3] *From the Arctic regions*) ver. 534. This was considered portentous
of ill, inasmuch as lightning was supposed generally to proceed from the
south.

[4] *The Capital of Latium*) ver. 535. By "Latiale caput" some understand Rome, as being the chief city of Latium. It is not improbable that
the Temple of Jupiter on the Capitoline Hill is meant. Jupiter Latialis is
mentioned in l. 198.

brother on her whole orb, struck by the sudden shadow of
the earth she turned pale. Titan himself, when he was
raising his head in mid Olympus, concealed his glowing
chariot in dense darkness, and enwrapped the earth in
shade, and forced the nations to despair of day; just as,
the Sun retreating by the east, Mycenæ of Thyestes brought
on the night[1].

Grim Mulciber opened the mouths of Sicilian Etna[2];
nor did it raise its flames to the heavens, but with its crest
bending low the flame fell downwards on the Hesperian
side. The black Charybdis stirred up from her depths sea
of the colour of blood; the savage dogs barked in dismal
tones. The fire was torn from the Vestal altars; and the
flame that showed that the Latin rites[3] were completed was
divided into *two* parts, and rose with a twofold point, resembling the funeral piles of Thebes[4]. Then did the Earth
withdraw from her axis, and, their ridges quaking, the Alps
shook off their ancient snows. With billows more mighty

---

[1] *Mycenæ of Thyestes brought on the night*) ver. 544. Atreus and
Thyestes, the sons of Pelops and Hippodamia, slew their half-brother
Chrysippus. Thyestes having seduced Ærope, the wife of Atreus, sent
Pleisthenes, the son of Atreus, whom he had brought up, to murder his
father, on which Atreus, supposing him to be the son of Thyestes, slew him.
According to another version of the story, which is the one here referred to,
Atreus, feigning a reconciliation, invited Thyestes to his kingdom, and
killed and dressed the bodies of Tantalus and Pleisthenes, the sons of Thyestes, and, while his brother was enjoying the meal, had their hands and
heads brought in and shown to him, on which Thyestes fled to the court of
Thesprotus. The Sun is said to have hid his face in horror, and turned back
in his course, on seeing this transaction.

[2] *Opened the mouths of Sicilian Etna*) ver. 545. This is a poetical
method of stating that there was an eruption of Etna at this period.
Mulciber was a name of Vulcan, derived from "mulceo" "to soften," from
his being the inventor of working iron.

[3] *Showed that the Latin rites*) ver. 550. The festival called "Latinæ
feriæ," or simply "Latinæ," was performed in honour of Jupiter Latialis
on the Alban Mount, when an ox was sacrificed there by night: multitudes flocked thither, and the season was one of great rejoicings and
feasting.

[4] *Resembling the funeral piles of Thebes*) ver. 552. Eteocles and Polynices, the Theban brothers, sons of Œdipus, having slain each other in
combat, their bodies were burnt on the same funeral pile, but their animosity
was said to have survived in death, and the flames refused to unite.

Tethys did overwhelm Hesperian Calpe[1] and the heights of Atlas[2]. We have heard how that the native Deities[3] wept, and how with sweat the Lares attested the woes of the City, how, too, that the presented gifts fell down in their Temples, and birds of ill omen[4] polluted the day; and how that the wild beasts, emboldened, the woods at nightfall deserted, made their lairs in the midst of Rome. Then were the tongues of cattle adapted[5] to human accents; monstrous births, too, *there were* of human beings, both as to the number and the formation of the limbs, and her own infant struck the mother with horror; the fatal lines[6], too, of the Pro-

---

[1] *Hesperian Calpe*) ver. 555. The rock of Gibraltar in Hesperia, or Spain, which was also called the Columns of Hercules.

[2] *The heights of Atlas*) ver. 555. Atlas was the name of a mountain range in the north-west of Africa, situate between the Mediterranean and the Great Desert, now called the Desert of Sahara.

[3] *The native Deities*) ver. 556. The " Dii Indigetes " were those Gods of the Romans who were supposed to have once lived on earth as mortals, and were after their death raised to the rank of Gods, such as Janus, Faunus, Picus, Æneas, Evander, Hercules, Latinus, and Romulus. Some take them to have been only such Deities as took part in the foundation of Rome, as Mars, Venus, Vesta, and others; while others think that they were those whose worship was introduced into Latium from Troy.

[4] *And birds of ill omen*) ver. 558. He probably means screech-owls and bats, which were considered birds of ill omen.

[5] *Tongues of cattle adapted*) ver. 561. Livy and Valerius Maximus tell us that an ox spoke and warned Rome of the disasters which would ensue on Hannibal's arrival in Italy. We learn from one of the Scholiasts that in these Civil Wars an ass spoke. Another informs us that an ox spoke when ploughing, in reproof of his driver, and told him that it was useless to urge him on, for soon there would be no people left in Italy to consume the produce of the fields.

[6] *The fatal lines*) ver. 564. He alludes to the Prophecies of the Sibyl ; a name given to several mysterious personages of antiquity, of whom ten are mentioned by Varro. The one here alluded to, resided at Cumæ, on the sea-coast of Italy. Erythrea was her usual name, but she is sometimes called Herophile, Daphne, Deiphobe, Manto, &c. Apollo granted her a life to equal in the years of its duration the grains contained in a handful of sand. Forgetting to add to her request the enjoyment of health and strength, decrepitude and infirmity became her lot as her years advanced. There was another Sibyl of Cumæ in Ætolia, who is represented as a different personage from the former. According to the Scholiasts, Lucan here alludes to a prophecy of the Sibyl couched under the following letters: R.R.R. P.P.P.P. F.F.F., which was said to mean " Romanum ruit regnum, Pompeius, pater patriæ, pellitur ferro, flammâ, fame." " The Roman state comes to ruin, Pompey, the father of his country, is expelled

phetess of Cumæ were repeated among the populace. Then did those, whom with their hacked arms the savage Bellona inspires[1], sing of the Gods enraged; and tossing their blood-stained hair, the Galli howled forth[2] sad accents to the throng. Urns filled with bones laid at rest sent forth groans.

Then arose the crash of arms, and loud voices were heard amid the remote parts of the groves, and ghosts came nigh to *men*[3]. Those, too, who till the fields adjacent to the extremities of the walls, fled in all directions; the mighty Erinnys was encompassing the City about, shaking her pitch-tree torch down-turned with flaming top, and her hissing locks; such as when the Fury impelled the Theban Agave[4], or whirled *in air* the weapons of the savage Lycurgus[5]; or such

by sword, flames, and hunger." According to one account a frantic woman ran through the streets of Rome calling out these initial letters. For a full account of the Sibyls see the Translation of Ovid's Metamorphoses, in *Bohn's Classical Library*, p. 484 *et seq.*

[1] *The savage Bellona inspires*) ver. 565. Bellona, the Goddess of war, was probably a Sabine divinity, and is represented as the companion of Mars, sometimes as his sister or his wife. Her priests at Rome, to whom reference is here made, were called "Bellonarii," and when they offered sacrifice to her they wounded their own arms and legs, and offered up the blood, and sometimes even drank thereof, that they might become inspired with a warlike enthusiasm. This sacrifice was performed on the 24th of March, which was thence called "Dies sanguinis," "the Day of blood."

[2] *The Galli howled forth*) ver. 567. The Galli were eunuch priests of Cybele, whose worship was introduced into Rome from Phrygia, B.C. 204. Their wild and boisterous rites are here referred to, and, like the priests of Bellona, they were in the habit of mutilating their own bodies. The origin of their name is uncertain, but it was most probably derived from the river Gallus in Phrygia, which flowed near the temple of Cybele. One of the Scholiasts says, that to insult the Galli, after the conquest of Gaul, Cæsar had some persons castrated and shut up in the temple of Cybele. Papias relates the same story.

[3] *Ghosts came nigh to men*) ver. 570. "Venientes cominus umbræ." It has been suggested that this passage means that the shadows of the body ominously fell in front at a time when they ought to have fallen behind. The translation given in the text is, however, the preferable one.

[4] *Impelled the Theban Agave*) ver. 574. Pentheus having forbidden the people to worship Bacchus, and, having ordered him to be captured, his mother Agave and the other Bacchantes became inspired by the Furies and tore him to pieces. See the Metamorphoses of Ovid, Book vii. l. 510, *et seq.*

[5] *The weapons of the savage Lycurgus*) ver. 575. Lycurgus, king of Thrace, having denied the Divinity of Bacchus, was punished with insanity, on which he slew his own wife and child, and cut off his own legs, mistaking them for vine branches. According to one account he was murdered by his

as, when, by the command of the unjust Juno, Pluto now
visited, Alcides shuddered at Megæra[1]. Trumpets re
sounded, and black night, amid the silent shades, sent forth
an uproar as loud as that with which the cohorts are min
gled *in combat*. The shade of Sulla, too, seeming to arise in
the middle of the Plain *of Mars*[2], uttered ill-boding prophecies; and the husbandmen fled from Marius raising his head
at the cold waves of Anio[3], his sepulchre burst asunder.

By reason of these things it seemed good that, according
to the ancient usage, the Etrurian prophets[4] should be

subjects, who were forbidden by an oracle to taste wine till he had been
dispatched, while another version states that he was slain by the panthers
sacred to Bacchus. The fates of Pentheus and Lycurgus are mentioned in
conjunction, in the Fasti of Ovid, B. iii. l. 721-2. "Thou also, unhappy
prey of thy Theban mother, shalt remain unmentioned; thou too, Lycurgus,
impelled by madness to assail thy own knee."

[1] *Alcides shuddered at Megæra*) ver. 577. He alludes to a tradition
relative to Hercules, which stated that when he had returned from the Infernal Regions, he was seized with madness, which Megæra, the chief of the
Furies, had, by the command of Juno, his relentless persecutor, sent upon
him; on which he slew Megara, the daughter of Creon (who had been his
wife, and whom he had given to Iolaüs), and her children by Iolaüs. This
madness was inflicted upon him for having slain Lycus, king of Thebes.
Hercules was called Alcides, probably from the Greek word, ἀλκὸς, strength.

[2] *In the middle of the Plain of Mars*) ver 581. After the death of
Sulla the Senate paid him the honor of a public funeral, and, with the
Priests, Vestal Virgins, and Equites, accompanied the funeral procession to
the Campus Martius, where, according to the express desire of the deceased,
his body was burnt, as he feared that his enemies might insult his remains,
as he had done those of Marius, which had been taken out of the grave and
thrown into the Anio at his command. This circumstance was the more
striking, as it had been previously the custom of the Cornelian family, of
which he was a member; to bury and not burn their dead. A monument
was erected to him in the Campus Martius, the inscription on which he is
said to have composed himself. It stated that none of his friends ever did
him a service, and none of his enemies a wrong, without being fully repaid.

[3] *The cold waves of Anio*) ver. 582. The Anio was a small stream
which ran into the Tiber. In using the word "fracto," "burst asunder,"
the Poet probably alludes to the circumstance above-mentioned, of the violation of his tomb by the orders of the vengeful Sulla.

[4] *The Etrurian prophets*) ver. 584. The Romans received their superstitions relative to augury and soothsaying from Etruria, which was always famous for the skill of its natives in those branches, and was for many centuries
the nursery of the Roman priesthood. Ovid says, in the Metamorphoses,
B. xv. l. 559, that Tages, who was fabled to have sprung out of the earth, was
the first to teach the Etrurian nation how to foretell future events.—See l. 637
of this Book, and the Translation in *Bohn's Classical Library*, p. 543.

summoned. Of whom, Aruns, the one most stricken in
years, inhabited the walls of deserted Luca[1], well-skilled
in the movements of the lightnings, and the throbbing
veins of the entrails, and the warnings of the wing[2] hovering in the air. In the first place he orders the monsters,
which revolting nature has produced from no seed, to be
seized, and *then bids them* burn the accursed progeny of the
barren womb in ill-omened flames[3]. Then next he orders
the whole City to be perambulated by the trembling citizens, and the priests, who purify the walls at the festive lustrum, to whom is granted the power to perform the rite, to
go round about the lengthened spaces without the walls[4],
at the extreme boundaries. The inferior throng follows,
tightly girt in the Gabinian fashion[5], and the filleted priestess
leads the Vestal choir, to whom alone it is permitted to
behold the Trojan Minerva[6]. Next, those who have charge

[1] *Deserted Luca*) ver. 586. Luca, now Lucca, was a Ligurian city in
upper Italy, at the foot of the Apennines. Luna is another reading here ;
it was a town of Etruria, situate on the left bank of the Macra, about four
miles from the sea-shore. It was famed for its white marble, which now
takes its name from the neighbouring town of Carrara. The character of
Aruns here mentioned is probably a fabulous one, invented by the Poet.

[2] *Warnings of the wing*) ver. 588. Auspices were derived from the
flight and from the voice of birds. Those which afforded the former were
called " Præpetes," those which gave the latter were called " Oscines."

[3] *In ill-omened flames*) ver. 591. Infaustis—flammis. One of the Scholiasts tells us that those flames were called "infaustæ" which were kindled
from wood which had been struck by lightning, or which had been used in
burning the dead.

[4] *Spaces without the walls*) ver. 594. Pomœria. This word is probably
compounded of "post" and "mœrium," the old name for "a wall," and sig-
nified a space of ground adjoining the city walls. The limits of the
Pomœrium were marked out by stone pillars at certain distances. The
Pomœrium was probably described to denote the space within which the
City auspices were to be taken.

[5] *In the Gabinian fashion*) ver. 596. According to Servius, the "Cinctus
Gabinius" was formed by girding the toga tight round the body by one of its
"laciniæ," or loose ends. This was done by forming a part of the toga into
a girdle, drawing its outer edge round the body, and tying it in a knot in
the front, at the same time that the head was covered with another portion of
the garment. The Lares were generally represented in the Gabinian habit.

[6] *To behold the Trojan Minerva*) ver. 598. He alludes to the Palladium
or image of Minerva which had been brought by Æneas from Troy, and was
deposited in the Temple of Vesta under the care of the Vestal Virgins, who
alone were permitted to look upon it.

of the decrees of the Gods and the mystic prophecies,
and who reconduct Cybele, when bathed, from the little
Almo[1]: the Augur, too, skilled in observing the birds on the
left hand; and the Septemvir[2], joyous at the festivals, and
the fellowship of the Titii[3],—the Salian, likewise[4], carrying

[1] *When bathed from the little Almo*) ver. 600. It was a yearly custom
with the Romans to wash the statue of the Goddess Cybele and her chariot
in the waters of the Almo, a small river near Rome. Ovid mentions this
practice in the Fasti, B. iv. l. 338, *et seq.* "There is a spot where the rapid
Almo flows into the Tiber, and the lesser stream loses its name in that of
the greater. There does the hoary priest, in his purple vestments, lave the
lady Goddess and her sacred utensils in the waters of the Almo." One
of the Scholiasts says that there was a river of the same name in Phrygia,
whence the worship of Cybele was brought. This line is by some thought to
be spurious. In the previous line the Poet alludes to the "Quindecimviri,"
or "Fifteen," whose duty it was to preserve the Sibylline books, which
were supposed to reveal the destinies of Rome. Their number was originally
two, next ten, and by Sulla they were increased to fifteen.

[2] *And the Septemvir*) ver. 602. "Septemvir." He alludes to the "Septemviri Epulones," who were originally three in number, and whose office
was first instituted in the year B.C. 196. Their duty was, to attend to the
"Epulum Jovis," or "Feast of Jove," and the banquets, or "lectisternia,"
given in honor of the other Gods; a duty which had originally belonged to
the Pontifices. Julius Cæsar added three to their number, but they were
afterwards reduced to seven. They formed a Collegium, and were one of
the four religious corporations of Rome, the other three being those of the
Pontifices, Augures, and Quindecimviri.

[3] *Fellowship of the Titii*) ver. 602. The "Titii Sodales" formed a Colleg¿
of priests at Rome, who represented the Titii or second tribe of the Romans,
which was descended from the Sabines, and continued to perform their
ancient rites. This body is said to have been instituted by Titus Tatius, the
king of the Sabines, who reigned jointly with Romulus. According to
Tacitus, it would seem that Romulus made the worship of Tatius after his
death a part of the Sabine sacred rites. Varro derives the name from
"Titiæ aves," the "Titian birds," which were observed by these priests in
certain auguries, and it is not improbable that they kept the auguries peculiar
to the Sabines distinct from those used by the other tribes. It is very
doubtful whether the office of the "Titii Sodales," as the preservers of the
Sabine ritual, was in existence in the time of Lucan.

[4] *The Salian, likewise*) ver. 603. The Salii were priests of Mars, who
were instituted by Numa to keep the sacred shields or "ancilia;" they received their name from "salio," to "leap" or "dance," because in the procession round the City they danced with the shields suspended from their
necks. Some writers say that they received their name from Salius, an Arcadian, a companion of Æneas, who taught the Italian youths to dance in
armour. After the processions had lasted some days, the shields were
replaced in the Temple of Mars. The dress of the Salii was an embroidered
tunic, with a brazen belt, the "trabea," and the "apex," or tufted conical cap;

the ancilia[1] on his exulting neck; and the Flamen[2], who wears the tuft[3] upon his noble head.

And while in prolonged circuit they go round about the emptied City, Arruns collects the dispersed *objects struck by* flames of lightning, and with a lamenting murmur buries them in the earth, and bestows a name upon the consecrated spots[4]. Then does he urge onward to the altar a male, with selected neck. Now had he begun to pour the

each having a sword by his side, and a spear or staff in his hand, with which, while dancing, he struck the ancile, kept time with the voice and the movements of the dance.

[1] *Carrying the ancilia*) ver. 603. The "ancile" was a sacred shield, which was said to have fallen from heaven in the time of King Numa. To prevent its being stolen, as the destiny of the Roman state was supposed to depend on its preservation, Numa ordered a number of shields to be made by Mamurius exactly resembling it, in order that those having criminal designs might not be able to steal it. The "ancilia" were under the especial charge of the Salii. See the Fasti of Ovid, B. iii. l. 363, *et seq.*

[2] *And the Flamen*) ver. 604. The Flamens were priests who dedicated their services to one particular Deity, while the Pontifices offered sacrifice to all. The "Flamen Dialis," or "Flamen of Jupiter," held the highest office of the Roman priesthood, though his political influence was less than that or the "Pontifex Maximus." Among other privileges, that of having a lictor was one.

[3] *Who wears the tuft*) ver. 604. "Apicem." Under the name of "apex" he refers to a peculiar cap worn by the Flamens and Salii at Rome. That name, however, properly belonged to a pointed piece of olive wood, the base of which was surrounded with wool. This was held on the head by fillets or by a cap, which was fastened by two bands called "apicula," or "offendices." The cap was of a conical form, and was generally made of sheep-skin with the wool on; and from the "apex" on its summit it at length acquired that name. The Flamens were chosen from the higher classes; hence the present epithet "generoso."

[4] *A name upon the consecrated spots*) ver. 608. He alludes to the consecration of the "bidental." This was a name given to a place struck by lightning, which was held sacred ever afterwards. Similar veneration was also paid to a place where a person who had been killed by lightning was buried. Priests collected the earth that had been torn up, the branches broken off by the lightning, and everything that had been scorched, and buried them in the ground with lamentations. The spot was then consecrated by sacrificing a two-year old sheep, which being called "bidens," gave its name to the place. An altar was also erected there, and it was not allowable to tread on the spot, or to touch it, or even to look at it. When the altar had fallen to decay, it might be repaired, but to enlarge its boundaries was deemed sacrilege, and madness was supposed to ensue on committing such an offence; Seneca mentions a belief that wine which had been struck by lightning would produce death or madness in those who drank it.

wine, and to place on it the salted corn[1], with knife pointed
downwards; and long *was* the victim impatient of the rites[2]
not grateful to him; when the aproned attendants pressed
upon the threatening horns, sinking on his knees he presented his subdued neck. And no blood as usual spurted
forth; but from the gaping wound there was black venom
poured forth instead of ruddy gore.´ Astounded at the ill-
omened rites Aruns turned pale, and sought the wrath
of the Gods of heaven in the torn-out entrails. The very
colour alarmed the prophet; for a pervading lividness
streaked with spots of blood the pallid vitals, tinted with
foul spots and gorged with congealed blood. He perceives
the liver reeking with corruption, and beholds the veins
threatening on the enemy's side[3]. The fibres of the panting lungs lie concealed, and a narrow line separates the
vital parts. The heart lies still; and through gaping clefts
the vitals emit corrupt matter; the cauls, too, disclose
their retreats; and, shocking sign! that which has appeared
with impunity in no entrails, lo! he sees growing upon
the head of the entrails the mass of another head[4]—a part
hangs weak and flabby, a part throbs and with a rapid
pulsation incessantly moves the veins.

When, by these means, he understood the fated allotment
of vast woes, he exclaimed, "Hardly is it righteous, Gods of
heaven, for me to disclose to the people what you warn
me of! nor indeed, supreme Jupiter, have I propitiously
offered unto thee[5] this sacrifice; and into the breast of the

[1] *The salted corn*) ver. 610. The "mola," used in sacrifice, was a mixture of salt and spelt, which, together with wine, was poured between the
horns of the victim before it was offered in sacrifice. "Obliquo cultro"
seems to mean "with the knife pointed downwards," vertically, and not
obliquely, which latter, however, is the more usual meaning of "obliquus."

[2] *Impatient of the rites*) ver. 611. For the victim to struggle when about
to be sacrificed was considered an ill omen.

[3] *On the enemy's side*) ver. 622. In divining by the entrails, it was the
custom for the priests to divide them into two portions; one being assigned
to those whom they favoured, the other to the enemy. In this instance the
enemy's part, which was assigned to Cæsar, was replete with appearances of
the most fatal ominousness.

[4] *Mass of another head*) ver. 628. He finds a twofold portion of what they
called the head of the liver. This, which was a portentous omen, was supposed to denote the increase of Cæsar's prosperity at the expense of Pompey.

[5] *Offered unto thee*) ver. 633. He means that from the appearance of the
victim it would seem as though he had not been sacrificing to Jupiter, but to

slaughtered bull have the infernal Deities entered! Things
not to be uttered do we dread; but things still greater than
our apprehensions will come to pass. May the Gods grant
a prosperous result to what has been seen, and may there
be no truth in the entrails; but *rather* may Tages, the founder of the art[1], have *fondly* invented *all* these things!"
Thus did the Etrurian, obscuring the omens and concealing them in much perplexing doubt, utter his prophecies.

But Figulus[2], to whom it was a care to know the Gods
and the secrets of the heavens, whom not Egyptian Memphis[3] could equal in the science of the stars and in the
principles which regulate the heavenly bodies, exclaimed :—
"Either this world wanders without any laws throughout all
ages, and the Constellations run to and fro with uncertain
movements; or else, if the Fates hold sway, a speedy destruction is preparing for the City and the human race. Will
the earth yawn, and cities be swallowed up? Or will the
glowing atmosphere deprive us of all moderate temperature?
Will the faithless earth refuse her crops of corn? Will all

the Furies and the other Deities of the Infernal Regions, who have answered
him with direful omens.

[1] *Tages, the founder of the art*) ver. 637. See the note to l. 584. Cicero
mentions Tages as having sprung from the earth, in his book On Divination,
B. ii. c. 23.

[2] *But Figulus*) ver. 639. He probably alludes to P. Nigidius Figulus, a
Roman Philosopher, who had a great reputation for learning. Aulus Gellius
pronounces him as, next to Varro, the most learned among the Romans. He
was noted for his mathematical and physical investigations, and followed the
tenets of the Pythagorean school of Philosophy. He was also famed as an
astrologer, and, in the Eusebian Chronicle, he is called a magician. He was
an intimate friend of Cicero, and was one of the Senators selected by him to
take down the examinations of the witnesses who gave evidence with regard
to Catiline's conspiracy, B.C. 63. He was Prætor four years afterwards, and
took an active part in the Civil War on the side of Pompey. He was, consequently, compelled by Cæsar to live in banishment, and died B.C. 44. A
letter of Cicero to him is still extant, in his Epistles Ad Familiares, B. iv.
Ep. 13. He is said to have received the name of Figulus, which means
"a potter," from the circumstance of having promulgated on his return from
Greece that the globe whirled round with the rapidity of the potter's wheel.

[3] *Not Egyptian Memphis*) ver. 640. This was the second city in importance in ancient Egypt, but sank into insignificance after the foundation of
Alexandria. It was of unknown antiquity, its foundation being ascribed
to Menes. It stood on the banks of the Nile, and was connected by canals
with the lakes Mœris and Marcotis. It was the seat of the worship of the
Egyptian Ptha, or the Hephæstus of the Greeks. The Egyptian priesthood
were especially famed for their skill in astrology and divination.

the water be mingled with poison infused *therein?* What kind of ruin, O Gods of heaven, with what plagues do you furnish your vengeance? At the same instant the closing days of many have met. If the cold star of Saturn, with its evil influence in the lofty heaven, had lighted up its dusky fires, Aquarius would have poured forth showers worthy of Deucalion [1], and the whole earth would have been concealed in the ocean spread over it. If, Phœbus, thou wast now urging the fierce Nemean lion [2] with thy rays, flames would be making their way over the whole world, and, set on fire by thy chariot, the sky would be in a blaze. Those fires pause: thou, Gradivus, who dost inflame the threatening Scorpion with his burning tail, and dost scorch his claws, why dost thou make preparations thus mighty? For with his remote setting propitious Jupiter [3] is going down, and the healthful star of Venus is dim, and the Cyllenian *Deity* [4], rapid in his movements, is retarded, and Mars occupies the heavens alone.

"Why have the Constellations forsaken their courses, and *why* in obscurity are they borne along throughout the universe? Why *thus* intensely shines the side of the sword-girt Orion [5]? The frenzy of arms is threatening; and the might of the sword shall confound all right by force; and for many a year shall this madness prevail. And what avails it to ask an end from the Gods of heaven? That peace comes with a tyrant *alone.* Prolong, Rome, the continuous series of thy woes; protract for a length of time thy calamities, only now free during civil war."

[1] *Showers worthy of Deucalion*) ver. 653. For an account of the flood of Deucalion, see the First Book of Ovid's Metamorphoses.

[2] *The fierce Nemean lion*) ver. 655. The Constellation Leo in the Zodiac was fabled to have been formed by the Lion of the Nemean forest, which was conquered by Hercules.

[3] *Propitious Jupiter*) ver. 661. He means the star so called.

[4] *And the Cyllenian Deity*) ver. 662. Mercury was called "Cyllenius," from Mount Cyllene in Arcadia, on which he was said to have been born.

[5] *Side of the sword-girt Orion*) ver. 665. "The unguarded words of Orion excited the anger of the Gods. 'There is no wild beast,' said he, 'that I am unable to conquer.' The Earth sent a scorpion; it attempted to fasten its crooked claws on the Goddess, the mother of the twins; Orion opposed it. Latona added him to the number of the radiant stars, and said, 'Enjoy the reward of thy deserts.'" Such is the account which Ovid gives in the Fasti, B. v. l. 540, of the origin of the Constellation of Orion. See also the curious story of his birth related in the same Book, l. 493, *et seq.* Hesiod, however, says that he was the son of Neptune by Euryale, the daughter of Minos. Pindar makes the isle of Chios to have been his birth-place, and not Bœotia.

These presages g eatly alarm the trembling multitude, but greater ones confound them. For just as on the heights of Pindus[1] the Edonian female[2], filled with the Ogygian Lyæus[3], hurries along, so likewise is a matron[4], borne along through the astounded City, disclosing by these words how Phœbus is exciting her breast: " Whither, O Pæan[5], am I being borne? In what land art thou placing me, hurried along amid the skies? I see Pangæum[6], white with its snowy ridges, and extended Philippi beneath the crags of Hæmus[7]. What frenzy this is, O Phœbus, tell

---

[1] *On the heights of Pindus*) ver. 674.   Pindus was the name of that part of the mountain range running through Greece which separated Thessaly from Epirus.

[2] *The Edonian female*) ver. 675.   The Edoni or Edones were a Thracian people, situate between the Nestus and the Strymon.   They were celebrated by their devotion to the orgies of Bacchus; whence "Edonis" in the Latin Poets, as in the present instance, signifies a female worshipper of Bacchus.

[3] *The Ogygian Lyæus*) ver. 675.   Bacchus was called Lyæus, from the Greek word λύειν, to "loosen" or "relax," because wine dispels care.   He was probably styled "Ogygian" from the circumstance of his having been born at Thebes, which was called Ogygia, from Ogyges, one of its early kings.

[4] *Is a matron*) ver. 676.   Sulpitius says that her name was Oritia.

[5] *Whither, O Pæan*) ver. 678.   Pæan was originally a name given to a Deity who was the physician of the Gods.   In that sense it came from the Greek παιών, " healing." Similarly it afterwards became a surname of Æsculapius, a God who had the power of healing.   It was also given to Apollo and Thanatos, or Death, perhaps as being liberators of mankind from suffering and sorrow.   It may, however, have been applied to the two last as coming from παίειν, " to strike," Death being supposed to strike with his dart, and Apollo, as the Deity of the Sun, striking with his rays. Apollo was frequently appealed to under this name, as all-powerful to avert evil.

[6] *I see Pangæum*) ver. 679.   Pangæum, or Pangæus, was a range of mountains in Macedonia, between the Strymon and the Nestus, in the vicinity of Philippi.

[7] *The crags of Hæmus*) ver. 680.   The Hæmus formed a lofty range of mountains (now called the Balkan chain) separating Thrace from Mœsia. Though famed among the Poets for their immense height, they do not exceed 4000 feet above the level of the sea.   Lucan here falls into the error of confounding Pharsalia with Philippi, the place where Brutus and Cassius were afterwards defeated by Antony and Augustus Cæsar.   Rowe has the following Note here:—"It is pretty strange that so many great names of antiquity, as Virgil, Ovid, Petronius, and Lucan should be guilty of such a blunder in geography, as to confound the field of battle between Julius Cæsar and Pompey with that between Octavius Cæsar and Brutus, when it was very plain one was in the middle of Thessaly and the other in Thrace, a great part of Macedonia lying between them.   Sulpitius, indeed, one of the commentators on Lucan, says, there was a town called Philippi,

me; why do Roman armies mingle their weapons and their bands? Without an enemy[1] is there war? Torn away, whither am I being borne? Thou art conducting me to the distant east, where the sea is changed by the stream of the Nile of Lagus[2]. Him who is lying a hideous trunk[3] on the river's sand, do I recognize. Over the seas am I borne to the shifting Syrtes[4] and the parched Libya, whither the direful Erinnys has transferred the ranks of Emathia[5]. Now above the heights of the cloud-capt Alps and the aërial Pyrenees[6] am I torn away. To the abodes of my native City I return, and in the midst of the Senate impious warfare[7] is being waged. Factions again[8] arise, and once more throughout all the earth do I proceed. Permit me to behold fresh shores of the sea[9], and fresh lands; now, Phœbus, have I beheld Philippi!"

Thus she said; and exhausted by her wearied frenzy she laid her down.

in whose neighbourhood the battle between Cæsar and Pompey was fought, but upon what authority I know not; but supposing that, it is undeniable that these two battles were fought in two different countries. I must own it seems to me the fault originally of Virgil (upon what occasion so correct a writer could commit so great an error is not easy to imagine), and that the rest took it very easily from him, without making any further enquiry."

[1] *Without an enemy*) ver. 6S2. That is, " without a foreign foe."

[2] *The Nile of Lagus*) ver. 6S4. The Nile is so called, as being under the sway of Ptolemy, the descendant of the Macedonian Lagus; it was said to change the waters of the sea at its mouth in colour and taste.

[3] *A hideous trunk*) ver. 6S5. In allusion to the death of Pompey, which is related in the Eighth Book.

[4] *To the shifting Syrtes*) ver. 6S6. He alludes to the march of the Roman army along the desert sands of Libya under the command of Cato, related at length in the Ninth Book.

[5] *The ranks of Emathia*) ver. 6S8. They are called Emathian from the circumstance of their then recent defeat in Emathia or Thessaly.

[6] *The aërial Pyrenees*) ver. 6S9. She alludes to the war in Spain waged by Cæsar against the sons of Pompey, whom he defeated at the battle of Munda.

[7] *Impious warfare*) ver. 691. Allusion is made to the death of Cæsar by the hands of Brutus and Cassius and the other assassins in the Senate-house.

[8] *Factions again arise*) ver. 692. The Civil Wars waged between Augustus and Antony on one side against Brutus and Cassius on the other, and afterwards between Augustus and Antony.

[9] *Fresh shores of the sea*) ver. 693. By the use of the word " Pontus" he seems vaguely to refer to the Euxine Sea lying off the coast of Thrace, in which Philippi was situate.

46

BOOK THE SECOND.

CONTENTS.

Reflections on the Prodigies, 1-15. The alarm at Rome described. The complaints of the matrons, 16-42. The complaints of the men, 43-66. A long speech is spoken by an aged man in reference to the Civil Wars carried on between Sulla and Marius, 67-233. Brutus repairs to Cato at night, and asks his advice, 234-285. Cato answers that he shall follow Pompey, and advises Brutus to do the same, 286-325. While they are conversing, Marcia appears, whom, formerly his own wife, Cato had given to his friend Hortensius, since whose death she has sought him again as her husband, 326 -349. In the presence of Brutus they renew the nuptial vow, 350- 391. Pompey has in the meantime retired to Campania. The Apennines, with their streams, are described, 392-438. Cæsar takes possession of the whole of Italy. The flight of Libo, Thermus, Sulla, Varus, Lentulus, and Scipio, from the cities which they hold, 439-477. Domitius Ahenobarbus, by breaking down the bridge, endeavours to impede the course of Cæsar at Corfinium. Cæsar crosses the river, and while he is preparing to lay siege to Corfinium, the citizens deliver Domitius to him. Cæsar gives him his liberty against his wish, 478-525. Pompey addresses his troops, and promises to lead them to battle, 526-595. He retreats to Brundisium, 596-609. The situation of that place is described, 610-627. Pompey sends his son to Asia to request the assistance of the eastern Kings. He himself prepares to cross over to Epirus, 628-649. Cæsar follows Pompey, and endeavours to cut him off from the sea. 650-679. Pompey leaves Italy, 680-703. Cæsar enters Brundisium, 704-736.

AND now was the wrath of the Deities displayed, and the universe gave manifest signs of war; foreknowing nature by her monster-bearing confusion overthrew the laws and the compacts of things, and proclaimed the fatality. Why, ruler of Olympus, has it seemed good to thee to add this care to anxious mortals, that by means of direful omens they should know of misfortunes about to come? Whether it is that, when first the parent of the world, the flame receding, set apart the shapeless realms and unformed matter, he established causes to endless time, by which he rules all things, binding himself as well by a law, and, with the immovable boundaries of fate, allotted the world to endure its destined ages; or whether it is that nothing is preordained, but Chance wanders in uncertainty, and brings and brings round again events, and accident rules the affairs of mortals: may that be instantaneous, whatever thou dost intend;

may the mind of man be blind to his future fate ; to him who dreads may it be allowed to hope.

Therefore when they perceived at the price of how vast calamity to the world the truthfulness of the Gods of heaven was about to be realized, *there* was a general mourning[1] in token of woe throughout the City; clad in the plebeian garb [2] all honors lay concealed ; the purple accompanied no fasces. Then did they withhold expression of their griefs, and great anguish without a voice pervaded all. Thus at the moment of death the astounded house is silent while the body is lying not yet called upon by name [3], nor *as yet* does the mother with her dishevelled locks prompt the arms of the female domestics to the cruel beatings on their breasts ; but when, life fled, she presses the stiffened limbs and the lifeless features, and the eyes swimming in death, no longer is it anguish, but now it is dread ; distractedly she throws herself down, and is astounded at her woes. The matron has laid aside her former habit, and sorrowing throngs occupy the shrines. These sprinkle the Gods with tears ; these dash their breasts against the hard ground, and, awe-stricken, throw their torn-out hair upon the sacred threshold, and with repeated howlings strike upon the ears accustomed to be addressed in prayer.

And not all lay in the Temple of the Supreme Thunderer ;

[1] *There was a general mourning*) ver. 18. "Justitium." This term doubtless originally signified a cessation of judicial business, but came afterwards to denote a time when public business of every kind was suspended. At this period the courts of law and the treasury were closed, and no ambassadors were received by the Senate. The justitium was formally proclaimed by the Senate and the magistrates in times of public alarm and danger. In the lapse of time, a justitium was usually ordered as a mark of public mourning, and under the Empire it was only employed under such circumstances.

[2] *Clad in the plebeian garb*) ver. 19. By this expression he means that the Consuls forbore to wear the purple, which was one of the insignia of their office. Their being attended by lictors, with the fasces, was another of their badges of office.

[3] *Called upon by name*) ver. 23. "Conclamata." After a person was dead, those who were present lamented aloud, and called on the party by name, to ascertain if he was only in a trance. According to some authorities this was repeated daily for seven days, and was done for the last time when the body was placed on the funeral pile, on which occasion it was finally said "conclamatum est," signifying that no hope of life now remained.

:they made division of the Deities, and at no altar was there wanting a parent to create discontent[1]; one of whom, tearing her bedewed cheeks, *and* blackened with blows, upon her livid arms, exclaimed, "Now, O wretched matrons, beat your breasts, now tear your locks, nor defer this grief and preserve it for our crowning woes. Now have you the power to weep, while the fortune of the chieftains is undecided; when one shall have proved the conqueror, you must rejoice." With these incentives did grief encourage itself.

The men likewise, repairing to the hostile camps, are pouring forth well-grounded complaints against the relentless Divinities. "Oh luckless lot, that we were not born for the Punic days of Cannæ[2] and of Trebia[3], a youthful race! Gods of heaven, we do not ask for peace; inspire with anger *foreign* nations; at once arouse the enraged cities; let the world conspire in arms; let the Median ranks descend from Achæmenian[4] Susa[5]; let the Scythian Ister[6] not confine

[1] *To create discontent*) ver. 36. "Invidiam factura." By addressing prayers to the Gods which were not likely to be fulfilled, and thus causing the Deities to be censured for their inattention to the wishes of their worshippers.

[2] *Punic days of Cannæ*) ver. 46. Cannæ was a village of Apulia, situate in a plain near the rivers Aufidus and Vergellus. It was famed for the memorable defeat there of the Romans under L. Æmilius Paulus and C. Terentius Varro, the Consuls, by Hannibal, the Carthaginian general, B.C. 216. From forty to fifty thousand Romans are said to have perished in this battle.

[3] *And of Trebia*) ver. 46. Trebia was a small river in Gallia Cisalpina, falling into the Padus, or Po, near Placentia. Hannibal gained a victory there over the Romans, B.C. 218.

[4] *Achæmenian*) ver. 49. This epithet refers to Achæmenes, the founder of the race of the Achæmenidæ, and the ancestor of the Persian kings. He was said to have been nurtured by an eagle. The epithet in the present instance, and, in general, as used by the Latin Poets, has the signification of "Persian."

[5] *Susa*) ver. 49. Susa (which is called Shushan in the Old Testament) was the winter residence of the Persian kings, and was situate in the province of Susiana, on the banks of the river Choaspes. The climate was very hot here, and hence the choice of it for a winter palace. Its site is now marked by huge mounds, in which are found fragments of bricks and pottery.

[6] *The Scythian Ister*) ver. 50. The river, the whole whereof is now called the Danube, was, from its source as far as Vienna, called "Danubius" by the Romans; from there to the Black Sea it received the name of "Ister."

the Massagetan[1]; let the Albis[2] pour forth the yellow
haired Suevi[3] from the extreme north and the unsubdued
sources of the Rhine[4]; make us the foes of all nations;
but avert civil warfare. On the one side let the Dacian
press-*upon us*[5], the Getan on the other[6]; let the one meet
the Iberians[7], the other turn his standards against the
eastern quivers.   Let no hand, Rome, of thine[8], enjoy

---

[1] *The Massagetan*) ver. 50.   The Massagetæ were a warlike race of
Scythia, to the north of the Araxes, and the present Sea of Aral.   Their
country corresponds to that of the Kirghiz Tartars at the present day, in
the north of Independent Tartary.   Herodotus appears to include under this
name all the Nomadic tribes of Asia east of the Caspian.   It was said that
it was their custom to kill and eat their aged people.

[2] *Let the Albis*) ver. 52.   The Albis, now the Elbe, was the most easterly
river of Germany with which the Romans became acquainted.   According
to Tacitus it rose in the country of the Hermunduri.   The Romans first
reached this river B.C. 9, and crossed it for the first time B.C. 3, under
Domitius Ahenobarbus.

[3] *The yellow-haired Suevi*) ver. 51.   The term "Suevi" is supposed to
have been the collective name of a large number of German tribes, who
were remarkable for a migratory mode of life.   Their locality has not been
with any exactness ascertained.   In the third century a race of people
called "Suevi" settled in and gave the name to the present Suabia.

[4] *Sources of the Rhine*) ver. 52.   The Rhæti lived about the sources of
the Rhine.   Suetonius says that Augustus crippled, but did not subdue,
them.

[5] *Let the Dacian press upon us*) ver. 54.   The Daci inhabited Dacia,
which lay to the north of the Danube, and comprehended the present countries of Transylvania, Moldavia, Wallachia, and part of Hungary.   They
were of similar race with the Getæ, and spoke the same language.   In
the reign of Augustus, this warlike people crossed the Danube, and, after
plundering the allies of Rome, were repulsed by the generals of Augustus.
In the reign of Domitian they obliged the Romans to purchase peace by
the payment of a tribute.   They were finally conquered by Trajan.

[6] *The Getan on the other*) ver. 54.   The Getæ are said to have been the
same people as the Daci.   In the later periods of the Roman Empire their
country was occupied by the Goths, who had migrated from the southern
shores of the Baltic, from which circumstance the Getæ and the Goths have
often been erroneously looked upon as the same people.   The Getæ furnished slaves to Greece and Italy; and Geta figures as a crafty servant in
the Plays of Terence.   Davus similarly means a Dacian slave; he, too, is
introduced in the Latin Comedy.

[7] *Meet the Iberians*) ver. 54.   The Iberi were the nations of Spain, who
dwelt in the vicinity of the Iberus, now called the Ebro, in the north-east
of that country.

[8] *Let no hand, Rome, of thine*) ver. 56.   That is, "Let every hand be
engaged in war against a foreign enemy."

E

leisure. Or if, ye Gods of heaven, it is your pleasure to blot out the Hesperian name, gathered into fires let the entire æther [1] descend in lightnings upon the earth. Enraged Parent, at the same instant smite both partisans and leaders, while not as yet they have deserved it. Do they with an extent so great of unheard of crimes, seek *to know* which of the two is to rule the City? Hardly would it have been worth the while to levy civil war, that neither *might*."

Such complaints did piety, doomed to be bootless, pour forth; but a care their own afflicted wretched parents, and they detested the long-lived destiny of a sorrowing old age, and years reserved for civil warfare a second time. And one, seeking precedents for their great alarm, exclaimed, "Not other commotions did the Fates intend at the time when, victorious after the Teutonic [2] and the Libyan triumphs [3], the exiled Marius concealed his head amid the slimy sedge [4]. The pools of the plashy soil and the fenny marshes concealed, Fortune, thy deposit; next did the chains of iron [5]

[1] *Let the entire æther*) ver. 58. Probably by the term "æther," he means the fiery element which was supposed to range in the firmament, above the regions of the air.

[2] *After the Teutonic*) ver. 69. The speaker probably alludes to the victory which Marius, the Consul, gained at Aquæ Sextiæ (now Aix) against the combined forces of the Teutones and Ambrones. According to some accounts there were 200,000 slain and 80,000 taken prisoners at this battle.

[3] *And the Libyan triumphs*) ver. 69. He alludes to the conquest of Jugurtha, king of Numidia, by Marius; which, however, was effected by the treachery of Bocchus, king of Mauritania, as much as by the generalship of either Marius or his predecessor Metellus.

[4] *Amid the slimy sedge*) ver. 70. Allusion is made to the circumstance of Marius hiding in the sedge and mud of the marshes of Minturnæ, in Latium. when pursued by the vengeance of Sulla. He was, however, discovered, dragged from his retreat, and, with a rope round his neck, delivered up to the authorities of Minturnæ.

[5] *The chains of iron*) ver. 72. Marius, when taken captive, was not, as the present passage would seem to imply, thrown into a dungeon, but placed in the charge of a woman named Fannia, who was supposed to be his personal enemy, but was secretly his friend. It was while he was here that a Gallic or a Cimbrian soldier was sent into his apartment to put him to death. The part of the room where the aged Marius lay was in the shade, and with a terrible voice he exclaimed—"Man, dost thou dare to murder C. Marius?" The barbarian, imagining that fire flashed from his eyes, dropped his sword, and rushed out of the house, exclaiming "I cannot murder C. Marius!"

eat into the aged man, and prolonged squalor in prison. A Consul, and fated to die successful[1] in the subdued City, beforehand did he pay the penalty of his crimes. Death herself fled full oft from the hero, and in vain *was* power granted to his enemy[2] over the hated blood; who, at the very stroke of death stood riveted and from his faltering hand let fall the sword. He had beheld an intense light in the darkened cell, and the dread Goddesses of crime, and the Marius of a future day, and in alarm he had heard. 'It is not right for thee to touch this neck; to the laws of fate does he owe many deaths before his own; lay aside thy vain fury. If it is your wish to avenge the destruction of your extinct race, Cimbrians, do you preserve this aged man!' Not by the favour of the Deity, *but* by the mighty anger of the Gods of heaven was this cruel man protected, and he sufficed for Fate when desiring to ruin Rome.

" He, too, borne over the stormy main[3] to a hostile land. and driven among the deserted cottages[4], lay amid the spoiled realms of the conquered Jugurtha[5], and trod upon the Punic ashes[6]. Carthage and Marius exchanged consolation for their fates, and equally prostrate, patiently

---

[1] *Fated to die successful*) ver. 74. Being afterwards restored to power at Rome, he died in the 71st year of his age, and on the 18th day of his seventh Consulship.

[2] *Power granted to his enemy*) ver. 76. The Cimbrian or Gallic soldier referred to in the Note to l. 72.

[3] *Borne over the stormy main*) ver. 88. He alludes to the departure of Marius from Minturnæ, where he was furnished with a small ship, and, after touching at the isle of Ænaria (now Ischia) and Eryx, in Sicily, he landed in Africa, the country of his former enemy, Jugurtha.

[4] *Among the deserted cottages*) ver. 89. "Mapalia" were moveable huts or cottages, which the Numidians carried on waggons when they moved from place to place, seeking new pastures for their flocks.

[5] *Of the conquered Jugurtha*) ver. 90. Jugurtha, the king of Numidia, an illegitimate son of Mastanabal, despite of numerous defeats, long made head against Metellus, the Roman general, but was finally conquered by Marius, who enjoyed the honour of a triumph on the occasion, and Jugurtha was finally thrown into a dungeon and starved to death.

[6] *Trod upon the Punic ashes*) ver. 91. Landing near Carthage, Marius was forbidden, by the lictor of Sextilius, the Prætor, to set foot on the African shore; on which he exclaimed, "Go tell thy master that thou hast seen Caius Marius sitting amid the ruins of Carthage;" not inaptly comparing the downfall of that great city to his own ruined fortunes.

submitted to the Gods. There did he collect together the resentfulness of Libya[1]. When first, his fortune returning, he set free troops of slaves[2], the iron wrought up[3] *into swords*, the slaves' dungeons[4] sent forth the ruthless bands. To no one were entrusted the ensigns of their leader to be carried, except to him who had now gained experience in wickedness, and had brought crime into the camp. Oh ye Fates! what *a day*, what a day was that, on which the victorious Marius seized the walls! and with strides how vast did cruel Death hurry on! With the commonalty the nobles fall; and far and wide stalks the sword, and the weapon is withdrawn from the breast of none. Gore stands in the temples, and red with plenteous slaughter the slippery stones are wet. To no one was his age[5] a protection.

---

[1] *The resentfulness of Libya*) ver. 93. By " Libycas iras," he perhaps means such a thirst for vengeance as Libyans or Africans alone usually display. It has been suggested that there is an intended reference here to the giant Antæus, who (as Lucan says in the Fourth Book, l. 597) was born in the caves of Libya and of whom it was fabled that every time he touched the earth he received additional strength, and that similarly Marius always rose from the most depressed state superior to his misfortunes. The serpents of Africa were said to gain fresh fury and venom from their contact with the earth.

[2] *He set free troops of slaves*) ver. 94. He alludes to the circumstance of Marius landing in Etruria from Africa, and, by proclaiming freedom to the slaves, collecting a large army, with which he joined L. Cornelius Cinna, the Consul, who had been driven from Rome by his colleague, Cn. Octavius. Marius, with Cinna and Carbo, shortly afterwards entered Rome, and, in their thirst for vengeance, were guilty of the most dreadful atrocities.

[3] *The iron wrought up*) ver. 95. " Conflato ferro," probably means, as one of the Scholiasts suggests, that the iron chains and fetters with which the slaves were bound, were used to make swords and other weapons. Another suggestion is, that " ferro " means the spades and mattocks which were used in cultivating the fields.

[4] *The slaves' dungeons*) ver. 95. The " ergastula " were private prisons attached to most of the country residences of the more wealthy Romans, for the confinement and punishment of their refractory slaves. They were probably underground, as appears from passages in Columella, and in the Aulularia of Plautus, ll. 301. 319, where the dungeon is called by the name of " puteus." Columella also says, that the " ergastulum " was lighted by narrow windows, too high to be touched by the hand. Plutarch says that these prisons became necessary throughout Italy by reason of the numerous conquests of the Romans, and the great number of foreign slaves introduced to cultivate the lands.

[5] *To no one was his age*) ver. 104. He alludes to the dreadful butcheries perpetrated by the body-guard of Marius, which he had formed out of the

There was no shame at having hurried on the closing day
of the aged man in his declining years; nor in the very
threshold of life at cutting short the rising destiny of the
wretched infant. By what criminality could little children be deserving of slaughter? But now enough is it
to be able to die. The very impetuosity of frenzy hurries
them on, and it seems like sluggishness to be in search
of the guilty. To swell the number a large portion falls:
and the blood-stained victor seizes the head cut off from
an unknown neck, as he is ashamed to go with an empty
hand. The only hope of safety is to imprint trembling
kisses[1] on the polluted right hand. Although a thousand
swords attended the unheard-of signals for death, O degenerate people, hardly would it be becoming for men
thus to earn lengthened ages *of existence,* much less
the short-lived disgrace of surviving, and life until Sulla
returns[2].

"Who has the leisure to bewail the deaths of the multitude?
Hardly thee, Bæbius[3], rent asunder by thine entrails, and
how that the countless hands of the dismembering throng
tore thy limbs to pieces; or thee, Antonius, foreteller of
woes, whose features, hanging by the torn white hair[4],

slaves attending him, who slew indiscriminately all of the aristocratic party
they could lay hands upon.

[1] *To imprint trembling kisses*) ver. 114. Marius had given instructions to his guards that all in the streets whom he did not salute, or to
whom he did not extend his hands to be kissed, were to be put to death
indiscriminately. Under these circumstances Q. Ancharius was killed; and
one of the Scholiasts mentions Euanthius, a former friend of Marius, who
was thus slain.

[2] *Until Sulla returns*) ver. 118. Who dealt equal vengeance on the
Marian party.

[3] *Hardly thee, Bæbius*) ver. 120. He alludes to the death of M.
Bæbius, who was torn to pieces by the hands of the Marian faction. Connected with his fate one of the Scholiasts relates a story not to the credit of
Terence, the Comic Poet. He says that Terence, being surrounded by the
partisans of Marius, promised, probably as the price of his own safety, that
he would discover to them an enemy of Marius, who had used his influence
in the Senate to his prejudice, and thereupon informed them where they
would find Bæbius.

[4] *Hanging by the torn white hair*) ver. 122. M. Antonius, who is spoken
of by Cicero as one of the greatest of the Roman Orators, having belonged
to the party of Sulla, was marked out for destruction by Marius, on his
return to the City. Touched by his eloquence, the soldiers who were sent

dripping *with blood*, the soldier carrying placed upon the festive table. Fimbia mangled [1] the beheaded Crassi [2]. The relentless prison was steeped with Tribunitial gore. Thee also, Scævola [3], neglected by the unscrupulous right hand, before the very shrine of the Goddess and her ever-burning hearths they slew; but exhausted old age poured forth little blood from thy throat, and spared the flames. These things his seventh *Consular* year followed [4], the fasces regained. That was the closing period of the life of Marius, who had endured all things which evil fortune is able *to effect*, and who had enjoyed all things which a better *fortune can bring*, and had experienced what fortune can destine for man.

refused to execute their commands, on which P. Annius, the Tribune, their commander, cut off his head, and carried it to Marius, while he was at table. After he had handled it with scorn and derision, he ordered it to be placed on the Rostra.

[1] *Fimbria mangled*) ver. 124. C. Flavius Fimbria was one of the most violent partisans of the Marian faction. Cicero styles him—" homo audacissimus et insanissimus," "a most audacious and most insane man." Being finally defeated by Sulla, he fell by the hands of one of his own slaves, whom he commanded to slay him. His career seems to have been that of a madman.

[2] *The beheaded Crassi*) ver. 124. According to some accounts P. Licinius Crassus, the father, and his son of the same name, were slain in each other's sight by Fimbria. It is, however, more generally stated that the son was put to death before his father's eyes, who afterwards stabbed himself to escape a more ignominious death at the hands of the Marian faction. Appian relates the story in a different manner. He says that the father, after slaying the son, was himself slain by the partisans of Marius. Crassus, the Triumvir, was a younger son of the elder of these Crassi.

[3] *Thee also, Scævola*) ver. 126. Mucius Scævola, the Pontifex Maximus, notwithstanding his virtuous character, was proscribed by the Marian faction, on which he fled for refuge to the temple of Vesta. He was, however, slain by the younger Marius, and the altars were drenched with his blood. " Neglectum violatæ dextræ " has been supposed by some to refer to the story of his ancestor, Mucius Scævola, having thrust his hand into the flames to show his firmness when taken prisoner by Porsenna. Weisse, however, thinks that it refers to the right hand of Marius, which was extended to be kissed by those whom he intended to sa re, and that (certainly by a forced construction) it means " unregarded by the unscrupulous right hand." " Neglectu violatæ Vestæ," " with heedlessness of the outraged Vesta," is another reading, and perhaps a preferable one, as Scævola was not put to death till some years after the death of the elder Marius.

[4] *Seventh Consular year followed*) ver. 130. Thirteen years intervened between the sixth and seventh Consulship of Marius. He died at the commencement of his seventh Consulship.

" Now at Sacriportus [1] how many dead bodies fell prostrate, or how many slaughtered troops did the Collinian
Gate [2] endure, at the time when the sovereignty of
the world and the sway of power, transferred, had almost
changed its site [3], and the Samnite hoped for Roman
wounds exceeding the Caudine Forks [4]! Sulla, too, added
as an avenger to the boundless slaughter. He shed the
little blood that was remaining to the City, and while he
amputated the limbs now too corrupt, the healing art exceeded its limits, and the hand followed too far where the
malady led it. The guilty perished; but when now the
guilty alone could possibly be surviving. Then was scope
given to hatred, and, let loose from the rein of the laws,
anger rushed on. Not for one *crime* were all sacrificed, but
each one framed a criminality of his own. Once for all had
the victor given his commands. Through the entrails of his
master [5] did the servant plunge the accursed sword; sons

[1] *Now at Sacriportus*) ver. 134. Marius having died, and Cinna being
slain, Sulla returned from Asia, where he had been carrying on the war
against Mithridates, and after landing at Brundisium, defeated the younger
Marius with great slaughter at Sacriportus, in Latium, B.C. 82.

[2] *Did the Collinian Gate*) ver. 135. The Samnites and Lucanians, who
favoured the cause of the younger Marius, under Pontius Telesinus and L.
Lamponius, marched towards Rome, which, on Marius being shut up in
Præneste, was left by Sulla without any protection. Sulla, however,
came up with them at the Colline Gate, and a battle was fought, which was
most obstinately contested, as Telesinus had vowed that he would level
Rome to the ground, and transfer the dominion to his own native place.
The victory was gained by Sulla, but 50,000 men are said to have fallen
on each side. Telesinus was among the slain. The Porta Collina was the
most northernly of the gates of Rome; it was situate near the Quirinal
Esquinal and Viminal Hills (Colles), from which it took its name.

[3] *Had almost changed its site*) ver. 136. He alludes to the resolution
abovementioned, which had been formed by Pontius Telesinus and the
younger Marius, to remove the seat of government from Rome to Samnium.

[4] *Exceeding the Caudine Forks*) ver. 138. The " Furcæ Caudinæ," or
"Caudine Forks," were narrow passes in the mountains near Caudium, a
town of Samnium. Here the Roman army had been defeated by the Samnites, and were sent under the yoke, B.C. 321.

[5] *Through the entrails of his master*) ver. 149. One of the Scholiasts
suggests that this is said particularly in allusion to the fate of the younger
Marius, who, being shut up in Præneste, and, despairing of holding out any
longer, endeavoured, with the brother of Telesinus, to make his escape by a
subterranean passage, but was betrayed by a slave; on which, finding their

were steeped in a father's blood. The contention was, to
whom the severed head of the parent belonged ; brothers fell
as a reward to brothers. The tombs were filled by flight,
and living bodies were intermingled with the buried, and
the dens of wild beasts received the throng. This one
broke his neck and his compressed throat with the halter ;
another hurling himself. with weight falling headlong,
dashed against the hard ground, burst asunder ; and from
the blood-stained victor they snatched away their own
slaughter ; this one himself heaped up the oaken fabric of
his own funeral pile, and, all his blood not yet poured forth,
leaped down into the flames, and, while *yet* he might, took
possession of the fires. The heads of chieftains *are* carried
on javelins throughout the trembling City, and heaped up
in the midst of the Forum. Whatever crime there is anywhere existing is then known. Not Thrace beheld so many
hanging in the stables [1] of the Bistonian tyrant, nor Libya
upon the posts of Antæus ; nor did lamenting Greece weep
for torn limbs so many in the halls of Pisa [2]. When now
they had mouldered away in corruption, and confused, in
length of time lost their marks, the right hand of the
wretched parents collected them, and, recognized, stealthily
removed them with timid theft. I remember, too, that I
myself, anxious to place the disfigured features of my slain
brother upon the pile and the forbidden flames, searched
about among all the carcases of *this* Sullanian peace, and
amid all the trunks sought for one with which the head
lopped from the neck would correspond.

flight discovered, they slew each other. According to other accounts Marius
killed himself, or, at his own request, was stabbed by his own slave.

[1] *Hanging in the stables*) ver. 163. Diomedes, king of Thrace (which
was also called Bistonia), was said to have fed his mares upon the flesh of
strangers, and to have fixed their heads on his doors. Antæus, the Libyan
giant, who was slain by Hercules, was also said to have perpetrated similar
cruelties.

[2] *In the halls of Pisa*) ver. 165. He alludes to the practice of Œnomaüs,
king of Pisa in Elis, who made it a condition that those who came forward
as suitors for the hand of his daughter, Hippodamia, should contend with
himself in a chariot race ; and that those who were conquered should be
put to death. After many had been sacrificed in the attempt, Pelops,
through bribing Myrtilus, the charioteer of Œnomaüs, won the hand of
Hippodamia.

" Why shall I make mention of the shades of Catulus appeased[1]? When Marius the victim[2] made, a sad sacrifice to perhaps an unwilling shade, an unutterable atonement to an insatiate tomb[3]; when we beheld the mangled limbs, and the wounds equal in number with the members, and no one given fatal to life, although upon a body mangled all over, and the ruthless usage of an accursed cruelty to forego the death of him who was *thus* perishing. Hands torn off fell down, and the tongue cut out *still* quivered, and with noiseless movement beat the vacant air. This one cuts off the ears, another the nostrils of the aquiline nose; that one gouges out the eye-balls from their hollow sockets, and, his *mangled* limbs viewed *by himself*, put out his eyes the last. Hardly will there be any believing that one person could have endured the punishments thus numerous of a crime so dreadful. Thus under the mass of ruins limbs are broken beneath the vast weight; nor more disfigured do the headless carcases come to shore which have perished in the midst of the ocean.

" Why has it pleased you to lose your pains, and to disfigure the features of Marius, as though an ignoble person? That this criminality and slaughter on being made known might please Sulla, he ought to have been able to be recognized. Prænestine Fortune beheld[4] all her citizens cut off

---

[1] *The shades of Catulus appeased*) ver. 174. Q. Lutatius Catulus, who had formerly been the colleague of Marius in the Consulship, :'n his expedition against the Cimbri, having espoused the cause of Sulla, his name was included among the rest of victims in the Marian proscription of B.C. 87. Finding escape impossible, he shut himself in a room, and, kindling a charcoal fire, died of suffocation.

[2] *When Marius the victim*) ver. 175. He alludes to the cruel death of M. Marius Gratidianus, the friend and fellow-townsman of Cicero. He was the son of M. Gratidius, but was adopted by one of the Marii, probably a brother of the elder Marius. In revenge for the death of Catulus, his brother, or, according to some, his son, obtained of Sulla the proscription of Gratidianus, on account of his connexion with the family of the Marii. He was butchered by the infamous Catiline, according to some accounts, at the tomb of Catulus. His tongue, nose, and ears were cut off, and his eyes dug out, and his head was then carried in triumph through the City.

[3] *To an insatiate tomb*) ver. 176. " Inexpleto busto." " A tomb that would be content with no propitiatory sacrifice."

[4] *Prænestine Fortune beheld*) ver. 194. By the direction of Sulla, Lutretius Ofella laid siege to the town of Præneste, and, after it was taken, 5000 of the inhabitants were put to the sword, although they had thrown

together by the sword—a people perishing at a moment by a single death. Then fell the flower of Italy, now the sole youth of Latium, and stained the sheepfolds of wretched Rome.* So many youths at the same instant to fall by a hostile death, full oft has famine, the rage too of the ocean, and sudden earthquake *caused*, or pestilence of climate and locality, or slaughter in warfare, vengeance it never was *that did so*. Hardly, amid the masses of the dense multitude, and the pallid throngs, could the victors, death inflicted, move their hands. Hardly, the slaughter completed, do they fall, and with neck still dubious² they totter; but the vast carnage bears them down, and the carcases perform the part of slaughter; the trunks falling heavily smother the living³. Unconcerned he sat above, a careless spectator of wickedness so great; he repented not that he had ordered so many thousands of the hapless multitude to die.

"The Etrurian stream received⁴ all the Sullanian corpses heaped together. Into the river the first ones fell, upon the bodies the last. Ships sailing with the tide stuck fast, and, choked up in its waters by the bloody carnage, the

themselves upon the mercy of the conquerors. The Goddess Fortuna had a temple at Præneste, where her prophecies were highly esteemed, under the name of "Prænestinæ Sortes." The town was situate about twenty miles to the south-east of Rome, and, from its cool situation, was much frequented by the Romans in the summer season. It is now called Palestrina.

¹ *The sheepfolds of wretched Rome*) ver. 197. "Ovilia." By this name, which properly signifies "the sheepfolds," the enclosures on the Campus Martius were called, in which the centuries were enclosed on the occasion of giving their votes for the magistrates of Rome. On the third day after the battle at the Colline Gate, in which he had conquered Pontius Telesinus, Sulla directed all the Samnite and Lucanian prisoners to be collected in the ovilia of the Campus Martius, and ordered his soldiers to slaughter them. Their shrieks alarming the Senators, who had been convened by Sulla in the Temple of Bellona, he requested them to take no notice of what was going on, as he was only inflicting due chastisement on some rebels.

² *With neck still dubious*) ver. 204. It is doubtful what "dubiâ cervice" exactly means. Cortius thinks that it signifies that the head is still remaining attached to the body, not being cut clean off. It seems more likely, however, to mean those who have received wounds in the throat, and have not fallen but are only staggering, and who are borne down by the weight of others who are slain outright.

³ *Smother the living*) ver. 206. By suffocating the others, who are not as yet dead or mortally wounded.

⁴ *The Etrurian stream received*) ver. 210. The bodies were generally thrown into the Tiber and thus carried down to the sea.

mouth of the river flowed out into the sea. The following waves stood still at the mass, until the stream of deep blood made a passage for itself, and, pouring forth over all the plain and rushing with headlong stream down to the floods of Tiber, aided the impeded waters; and now no longer does its bed nor yet its banks, contain the river, and it throws back the corpses on the plain. At length having struggled with difficulty down to the Etrurian waves, with the flowing blood it divided the azure sea. For this did Sulla merit to be styled the saviour of the state; for this to be called the Fortunate[1]; for this to raise for himself a tomb in the middle of the Plain *of Mars?*

" These wrongs await us to be again endured; in this order of warfare will they proceed; this conclusion will await the civil strife. Although still greater *calamities* do our alarms anticipate, and they rush to battle with much greater detriment to the human race. Rome recovered was the greatest reward of war to the exiled Marii, nor more did victory afford to Sulla than utterly to destroy the hated faction. These, Fortune[2], on other grounds thou dost invite, and, raised to power already, they meet in combat. Neither would be commencing civil war, if content with that with which Sulla was." Thus did old age lament, sorrowing and mindful of the past, and fearful of the future.

But terror did not strike the breast of the noble Brutus[3], nor was he a portion of the trembling populace weeping in alarm so great at the commotion; but in the drowsy

---

[1] *To be called the Fortunate*) ver. 221. After the death of the younger Marius, on the occasion of his triumph over Mithridates, B.C. 81, Sulla claimed for himself the title of Felix, or " Fortunate," as being the especial favourite of the Gods. He believed himself to be especially under the protection of Venus and Hercules. His son and daughter were also named Faustus and Fausta, on account of the good fortune of their father.

[2] *These Fortune*) ver. 230. Namely, Cæsar and Pompey.

[3] *Of the noble Brutus*) ver. 234. M. Junius Brutus, professing to follow M. Porcius Cato as his political model, sided with Pompey. After the battle of Pharsalia he fled to Larissa, whence he wrote a letter to Cæsar, soliciting pardon, which was not only granted, but the conqueror even requested Brutus to come to him. According to Plutarch, it was Brutus who informed Cæsar of Pompey's flight into Egypt. Notwithstanding the favours which he had received from Cæsar, he joined Cassius and the band of conspirators who murdered Cæsar in the Senate-house. Being defeated at Philippi by Antony and Augustus, he fell upon his own sword.

night, when the Parrhasian Helice[1] was turning her cha
riot obliquely, he knocked at the not extensive halls of his
kinsman Cato[2]. He found him with sleepless anxiety reflecting on the public affairs, the fates of men, and the
fortunes of the City, both fearful for all and regardless for
himself; and in these words he began to address him :—

"Do thou, now the sole refuge for virtue expelled and long
since banished from all lands, whom by no tempestuous
shock Fortune shall tear away from thee, direct me wavering in mind, do thou confirm me in doubt with assured
strength; for let others follow Magnus or the arms of
Cæsar, Cato shall be the sole leader of Brutus. Dost thou
adhere to peace, keeping thy footsteps unshaken while the
world is in doubt? Or has it been thy pleasure, mingling
in slaughter with the leaders of crime and of the maddened
populace, to forgive the civic strife? Each one do his own
reasons hurry away to the accursed combat: these a polluted house[3], and laws to be dreaded in peace; these hunger
to be driven away by means of the sword, and plighted faith
to be lost sight of[4] amid the ruins of the world. Fury has
impelled no one to arms; overcome by a vast reward,
they are repairing to the camps: for its own sake is the
warfare pleasing to thee alone? What has it availed *thee*
so many years to have remained untouched by the man-

---

[1] *Parrhasian Helice*) ver. 237. The constellation of the Greater Bear
was called Helice, from the Greek word ἱλίσσω, to revolve, because it revolves round the Pole. It was fabled that Calisto, of whom Jupiter was
enamoured, was changed by the vengeful Juno into the Greater Bear. See
her story related in the Second Book of Ovid's Fasti, l. 153, *et seq.* She
was a daughter of Lycaon, king of Arcadia, in which country there was a
town and a mountain called by the name of Parrhasia, which was said to
have been derived from Parrhasus, a son of Lycaon.

[2] *Of his kinsman Cato*) ver. 238. Servilia, the mother of Brutus, was
the half-sister of Cato, they being the children of Livia, by different mar-
riages. Brutus also married Porcia, the daughter of Cato.

[3] *A polluted house*) ver. 252. Sulpitius supposes "polluta domus" to
refer to acts of violation committed against the females of the families of
those who consequently thirsted for vengeance. It may also mean, as suggested by one of the Scholiasts, that members of a family, having murdered
the others, had become desperate, and resorted to civil war to screen their
own offences.

[4] *To be lost sight of*) ver. 253. "Permiscenda." Literally, to be "mingled," or "involved in;" he here alludes to the debts of the extravagant
and unprincipled.

ners of a corrupt age? This sole reward of thy long-prac-
tised virtues shalt thou receive; others the wars shall find
thyself they shall make, guilty. O Gods of heaven, let
not so much be allowed to the fatal arms as even to have
moved these hands; and let no javelins hurled by thy arms
be borne in the dense cloud of weapons; nor let valour
so great be thrown away on chance[1]. All the fortune of
the war will rest itself on thee. Who shall be unwilling,
although falling by the wound from another, to die by this
sword, and for the crime to be thine own? Better alone
without arms wilt thou live in tranquil inactivity, just as the
stars of heaven ever unmoved roll onward in their course.
The air nearer to the earth is inflamed with the lightnings,
and the lowermost regions of earth receive the winds and
the flashing streaks of flame; Olympus, by the will of the
Gods, stands above the clouds. The least of things does
discord disturb; the highest enjoy peace.

" How joyously will the ears of Cæsar learn that a citizen
so great has come forth to battle! For that the rival camp
of the chieftain Magnus has been preferred to his own he
will never grieve. Too much does he please himself[2], if
civil war is pleasing to Cato. A large portion of the Senate
and a Consul, about to wage war under a general a private
person[3], and other nobles as well, cause me anguish; to
whom add Cato under the yoke of Pompey, then throughout the whole world Cæsar alone will be free[4]. But if for

[1] *Be thrown away on chance*) ver. 263. " Nec tanta in casum virtus eat."
There have been some doubts about the readings and meaning of this passage. It probably means that Cato is not to throw away his wisdom and
valour in a cause where the successful result will be sure to be solely attributed to the chances of war.

[2] *Too much does he please himself*) ver. 276. " Nimium placet ipse." It
is a matter of doubt to whom " ipse " refers, whether to Cato or to Cæsar.
It most probably relates to Cæsar, and if so, the meaning may be that
Cæsar will be extremely pleased with himself, if the Civil War which he has
caused shall be pleasing to Cato; if it refers to Cato, it may mean that
Cæsar will be receiving too high a compliment at the hands of Cato, if the
latter takes part in the Civil War.

[3] *Under a general a private person*) ver. 279. The meaning is, " It
grieves me to see the Senate and the Consul under the command of a general,
merely a private person;" it being the duty of the Consuls to wage war, and
lead the armies of the state.

[4] *Cæsar alone will be free*) ver. 281. Because Pompey, though general,
would, in some degree, be under the control of the Senate.

the laws of thy country it pleases thee to take up arms, and
to defend liberty, already thou dost have Brutus the
enemy neither of Pompey nor of Cæsar, *but* after the war,
of the conqueror."

Thus he speaks. But Cato utters to him from his
secret breast *these* hallowed words:—" Brutus, I confess that
civil warfare is wickedness in the extreme; but·whither
the fates lead, virtue with clear conscience shall follow. It
shall be the crime of the Gods of heaven to have made even
me guilty. Who is able to look upon the stars and the
world falling to ruin, void of fear himself? Who, when
the lofty sky is rushing downwards, the earth is quaking,
the weight of the confused universe mingling together,
can keep his hands folded *in inactivity?* Shall stranger
nations follow the frenzy of Hesperia and the Roman
wars, and Kings be led over the seas beneath other
climes, *and* shall I alone live in inactivity? Far hence
avert, O Gods of heaven, the frantic notion that Rome
may fall, in its ruin to affect the Dahans[1] and the Getans,
while I am free from care. As grief itself bids the parent
bereaved by the death of his sons, to head the long funereal procession to the tomb; it gives him satisfaction to
have thrust his hands amidst the blackening flames, and
himself to have held the swarthy torches[2] in the heaped-up
structure of the pile; I will not be torn away, before, Rome,
I shall have embraced thee lifeless, and Liberty, thy name,
and shall have followed thy unsubstantial shade. So let it
be; let the unappeased Gods receive a full expiatory sacrifice, of no blood let us defraud the warfare. And would that
it were possible for the Gods of heaven and of Erebus to expose this head *of mine* condemned to every punishment!

" The hostile troops bore down the devoted Decius[3]; me

---

[1] *To affect the Dahans*) ver. 296. The Dahæ were a great nation of
Scythia, who roamed at large in the country to the east of the Caspian (which
from them still bears the name of Daghesan), on the banks of the Axus and
the Jaxartes. They were famed for their skill as archers on horseback.

[2] *To have held the swarthy torches*) ver. 301. He alludes to the custom
of the nearest relative of the deceased setting fire to the pile.

[3] *Bore down the devoted Decius*) ver. 308. It is impossible to say to
which of the Decii he here refers, as two individuals of the name of P. Decius Mus, father and son, devoted themselves to death for the Roman cause.
The elder was commander jointly with T. Manlius Torquatus in the Latin

let two armies assail, me let the barbarian multitude from
the Rhine aim at with their darts ; may I, accessible, in the
midst, receive from all the lances the wounds of the entire
warfare. May this blood redeem the people; by my fate
may it be atoned for, whatever the Roman manners have
deserved to pay the penalty for. Why should the people
ready for the yoke—why should those desirous to endure a
harsh sway, perish? Myself alone attack with the sword—
myself who in vain maintain our laws and empty rights; this
throat, this, will provide peace, and an end of their hardships for the nations of Hesperia; after I am gone there is
no need of war for him who wishes to reign. Why do we
not then follow the standards of the state and Pompey as
our leader? And yet, if Fortune shall favour, it has been
well ascertained that he as well promises himself the sway
over the whole world. Let him conquer therefore, myself
his soldier, that he may not suppose that for himself he
has conquered." Thus he spoke, and he applied sharp
incentives to his indignation and aroused the warm blood
of the youth to too great fondness for civil war.

In the meantime, Phœbus dispelling the chilly shades *of
night*, the door, being knocked at, sent forth a sound; and
the hallowed Marcia[1] entered in grief, having left the tomb

War. Learning from a vision that the general of the one side and the army
of the other, were devoted to the Gods of the dead, he rushed into the
thickest of the enemy, wearing the sacrificial dress, and was slain. Zonaras,
however, says that he was slain, as a devoted victim, by a Roman soldier.
His son, who commanded the left wing of the Roman army at the battle of
Sentinum against the Gauls, resolved to imitate the example of his father,
and dedicating himself and the army of the enemy to the Gods of the dead,
he fell a sacrifice for his country.

[1] *The hallowed Marcia*) ver. 328. Marcia was the daughter of L. Mar-
cius Philippus, and was the second wife of Cato. After she had borne him
three children, he ceded her to his friend Hortensius, with the sanction of
her father. After the death of Hortensius she returned to Cato, and it was
sneeringly remarked that Cato was not a loser, in a pecuniary way, by the
transaction. In Dr. Smith's Dictionary of Greek and Roman Biography, we
find the following remarks on this transaction. "Heineccius infers, from
the words of Plutarch, that Cato did not, according to the common belief,
lend his wife, but that she was divorced from him by the ceremony of sale,
and married to Hortensius. Heineccius quotes the case as an instance of a
marriage contracted by ' *coemptio*,' and dissolved by ' *remancipatio*.' But
it does not seem that Cato formally married her again after the death of Hortensius, though it appears that she returned to her former relation of wife."

of Hortensius[1] : once, a virgin, joined in wedlock to a better
husband; afterwards when, the price and the reward of wedlock, her third progeny was born, she in her pregnancy was
given to fill another home *with her offspring*, destined to
unite two houses by a mother's blood. But after she had
enclosed in the urn the last ashes, hurrying with tearful
countenance, tearing her dishevelled hair, and beating her
breast with repeated blows, and bearing the ashes of the
tomb, not destined to please her husband in other guise,
thus in sadness did she speak :—

" While I had in me the *strengthening* blood, while strength
to endure a mother's pains, Cato, I performed thy commands, and pregnant, two husbands did I receive[2]. My
vitals wearied and exhausted by child-bearing I now return,
to no other husband to be handed over. Grant the unenjoyed
ties of our former union; grant only the empty name of
wedlock; let it be allowed to inscribe on my tomb, 'Marcia,
the wife of Cato;' nor let it be enquired as doubtful in
remote posterity whether I abandoned my first marriage
torch, repudiated or *only* transferred. Thou dost not receive
me as a partner in joyous circumstances; amid thy
cares and to share thy griefs, do I come. Allow me to
attend the camp. Why shall I be left in the safety of
peace, and Cornelia be near to the civic strife?"

These words influenced the hero, and though the times
were unsuited for wedlock, Fate now summoning him to
the war, still a solitary union pleased him, and nuptials
devoid of empty pomp, and the admission of the Gods
alone[3] as witnesses of the solemnities. No festive garlands
hang from the wreath-bound threshold, and no white fillet[4]

[1] *The tomb of Hortensius*) ver. 328. Q. Hortensius was one of the most
famous of the Roman Orators, and, for many years, the rival of Cicero. He
had the adroitness to escape being enrolled on the lists of either the Marian
or the Sullane faction, and died a natural death, B.C. 50, in his sixty-fourth
year. He was noted for his luxurious habits, and at his death left 10,000
casks of Chian wine to his heir. At the time when he took Marcia as his
wife she was pregnant by Cato, her first husband.

[2] *Pregnant, two husbands did I receive*) ver. 339. In allusion to her
pregnancy when married to Hortensius.

[3] *Admission of the Gods alone*) ver. 353. The Deities thus adjured as
witnesses would probably be Jupiter, Juno, Venus, Suada, and Diana.

[4] *No white fillet*) ver. 355. " Infulae," or "fillets" of wool, were hung by
the bride on the doorposts of the house of the bridegroom.

runs along the two doorposts, nor *are there* the usual torches[1], nor does the couch stand on high[2] with its ivory steps[3], or variegate its coverings with embroidered gold: and no matron, pressing her forehead with the turreted crown[4], forbids her, with foot lifted over[5], to touch the threshold. No saffron-coloured veil[6] lightly to hide the timid blushes of the bride, concealed her downcast features; the girdle with its gems did not encircle her flowing robes[7], no necklace her graceful neck[8]; and no scanty under-tunic[9],

[1] *The usual torches*) ver. 356. He alludes to the torches which were carried before the bride by boys dressed in the prætexta, when she was conducted to her husband's house.

[2] *Couch stand on high*) ver. 357. He alludes to the "torus genialis," or marriage bed, which was generally placed in the "atrium," or great room on the ground floor of the Roman houses.

[3] *With its ivory steps*) ver. 357. The bedsteads used by the Romans were, in general, rather high, so that persons were in the habit of entering the bed by means of steps placed beside it, which Varro calls by the name of "scamnum." The bedsteads were sometimes made of metal or of costly wood, or else veneered with tortoise-shell or ivory. We find, from the present passage, that the "scamnum" was similarly ornamented.

[4] *With the turreted crown*) ver. 358. One of the Scholiasts states that a turreted crown was generally worn by the bride during the nuptial cere-monies.

[5] *With foot lifted over*) ver. 359. When the procession arrived at the house of the bridegroom, the door of which was adorned with garlands and flowers, the bride was carried across the threshold by "pronubi," or men who had been married to but one woman, that she might not strike against it with her foot, which would be an evil omen. See the Casina of Plautus, Act iv. Sc. iv. l. 1, 2.

[6] *No saffron-coloured veil*) ver. 361. The bridal veil which the bride wore was called "flammeum," and was of a bright yellow colour, which was also the colour of her shoes.

[7] *Her flowing robes*) ver. 362. The bride was dressed in a long white robe with a purple fringe, or adorned with ribands. This dress was called "tunica recta," and was bound round the waist with a girdle or zone.

[8] *No necklace her graceful neck*) ver. 363. Necklaces were much worn in an-cient times by the Indians, Persians, and Egyptians. They were especially used (as mentioned in the present instance) by the Greek and Roman females as bridal ornaments. The "monile baccatum," or "bead necklace," was the most common, being made of berries, glass, or other materials strung toge-ther, with thread, silk, wire, or hooks of gold. Emeralds were used for a similar purpose, and amber was much employed. Thus Ovid says in the second Book of the Metamorphoses, l. 366, that the amber distilled from the trees, into which the sisters of Phaëton were changed, was sent to be worn by the Latian matrons.

[9] *No scanty under-tunic*) ver. 364. The "supparus," or "supparum," is

clinging to the lower part of the shoulders, enveloped her bared arms. Even so, just as she was, she preserved the mournful *ensigns* of the garb of woe, and in the way in which her sons, in the same her husband, did she embrace. Covered by the funereal wool the purple was concealed. None of the wonted jests[1] acted their . '.y part, nor after the Sabine usage[2] did the sorrowing husband receive the festive taunts. No pledges of the house[3], no relations met together. They were united in silence, and contented with the auspices of Brutus. Nor did *Cato* remove the grim long hair from his hallowed face, or admit of joyousness on his rigid features.

Since first he had beheld the deadly arms upraised, he had allowed the unshorn white hair to descend upon his rugged brow and the woeful beard to grow upon his cheeks. Because, forsooth, he had leisure for one thing alone—free from factions and from hate—to weep for mankind. Nor were the ties of their former connexion renewed; his continence[4] withheld from even lawful love. These *were* the manners, this was the unswerving rule of the rigid Cato; to observe moderation, and to adhere to his end; to follow *the guidance of* nature, and to lay down his life for his country; and not to believe himself born for himself, but for the

said by Festus to have been made of linen, and to have been the same as the "subucula," or under tunic; but Varro says that it was an outer garment, and contrasts it with the "subucula," which he derives from "subter," "under,' while "supparus" he derives from "supra," "over." Judging from the present passage, it appears to have been an outer garment, which left the arms and shoulders bare. It was, perhaps, peculiar to the nuptial ceremony.

[1] *None of the wonted jests*) ver. 368. He alludes to the Fescennine verses which, full of broad jests and railleries, were sung at the door of the bridal apartment, by girls, when the other persons had left. These verses were also called epithalamia. Ovid relates a curious story, by way of accounting for the origin of this custom. See the Fasti, B. iii. l. 675, *et seq.*

[2] *Nor after the Sabine usage*) ver. 369. The custom of singing these songs, and of joking the bridegroom on this occasion, was said to have been derived from the Sabines.

[3] *No pledges of the house*) ver. 370. "Pignora," "pledges," or "ties," meaning relations or children.

[4] *His continence withheld*) ver. 378. Shortly after his reunion with Marcia Cato fled from Rome, but left her there to protect his property and interests.

whole world. To subdue hunger *was* a banquet to him, and to keep away by a *mere* roof the winter's cold, an opulent abode; to wrap a shaggy toga around his limbs, after the manner of the Roman follower of Quirinus[1], *was* a costly robe; to him, too, the especial object of sexual desire was offspring; he was the City's husband[2], and the City's sire: a worshipper of justice, an observer of strict honor; *he was* a good man for the common weal: and upon none of Cato's deeds did pleasure, born but for herself, make inroad and exact her share.

In the mean time, Magnus departing with the hastening throng, took possession of the Campanian walls of the Dardanian colonist[3]. This seat of war was to his mind, for him, exerting all his might, thence to spread abroad his scattered party to meet the foe, where with its shady hills Apennine raises on high the mid part of Italy, than which no land swells with its peaks to a loftier height, or approaches more nigh to Olympus. The mountain in the midst extends itself between the two waters of the Lower and the Upper sea[4]; and on the one side does Pisa, that, with its shallows, breaks the Etrurian waves, on the other, Ancona, opposed to the Dalmatian billows, bound the mountain ridges.

From vast sources does it produce boundless streams, and extend its rivers along the space that separates the two seas. On the left side descend both the swift Metaurus[5],

[1] *Follower of Quirinus*) ver. 386. " Quiritis " here means one of the lower classes of the people in the city which had been founded by Quirinus or Romulus, and not, as some have supposed, one of the ancient Romans in contradistinction to those of the more modern Rome.

[2] *He was the City's husband*) ver. 388. The whole state received from him the affections of a father and a husband.

[3] *Campanian walls of the Dardanian colonist*) ver. 393. Capua, the capital of Campania, was said to have been founded by Capys, one of the Trojans who accompanied Æneas from Troy. See Virgil's Æneid, B. x. l. 145.

[4] *The Lower and the Upper sea*) ver. 400. The Adriatic, or the Lower, and the Etrurian, or the Higher, Sea. He is speaking of that part of Italy where Pisa is on the coast on the Etrurian side, and Ancona, which is somewhat more southerly, on the Adriatic. Ancona is opposite the coast of Dalmatia, whence the expression " obnoxia fluctibus Dalmaticis."

[5] *The swift Metaurus*) ver. 405. This was the name of two rivers of Italy, one of which was a small river of Umbria, now called the Metauro, flowing into the Adriatic Sea, and rendered memorable by the defeat and

and the rapid Crustumium[1], and the Sapis[2] uniting with
the Isaurus[3], and the Sena[4], the Aufidus[5], too, that beats
the Adriatic waves; and, (into a river more vast than which
no region dissolves itself,) the Eridanus rolls down [6] dismantled forests into the main, and by its waters empties Hesperia
of streams. The story *is,* that this river[7] was the first to
shade its banks with a poplar crown; and that, when
Phaëton, his bounds overstepped, bringing headlong downwards the light of day, set the skies on fire with his blazing
reins, the streams throughout the scorched earth being
swept away, this one had waves equal to *quenching* the fires
of Phœbus. Not less is it than the Nile, if the Nile did
not lie stagnant *far and wide* over the flat surface of level
Egypt, the Libyan sands. Nor less *is* it than the Ister, except
that while the Ister flows through the globe, it receives
streams that might have fallen *as rivers* into any seas whatever, and not by itself is discharged into the Scythian waves.

The waters that seek the right-hand declivities of the
mountain range form the Tiber, and the Rutuba[8] in its

death of Hasdrubal, the brother of Hannibal, on its banks, B.C. 207. The
second, now called the Marro, was a stream on the east coast of Bruttium.
The "lævum latus," or "left side," here mentioned, is the Adriatic.

[1] *Rapid Crustumium*) ver. 406. The Crustumium was a river falling
into the Adriatic, near the town of Ariminum.

[2] *And the Sapis*) ver. 406. The Sapis, now called the Savio, was a small
river of Gallia Cisalpina, rising in the Apennines, and flowing into the
Adriatic, south of Ravenna.

[3] *With the Isaurus*) ver. 406. This river was also called the Pisaurus,
and, flowing through Umbria, falls into the Adriatic. It is now called La
Foglia.

[4] *And the Sena*) ver. 407. The Sena was a small river of Umbria, which
flowed past the town of Senogallia, founded by the Galli Senones. It is now
called La Nevola.

[5] *The Aufidus*) ver. 407. The Aufidus, now called the Ofanto, was the
principal river of Apulia. It rose in the territory of the Hirpini in Samnium,
flowing at first with a rapid current, and then more slowly into the Adriatic.

[6] *The Eridanus rolls down*) ver. 409. Eridanus, also called the Padus,
now the Po, flows into the Adriatic near the city of Ravenna.

[7] *The story is, that this river*) ver. 410. He refers to the tradition which
stated that, when Phaëton was smitten by the thunderbolts of Jupiter, he
fell into the river Eridanus or Padus, and his sisters Phaëthusa, Lampetie,
and Phœbe, the Naiads of Italy, were changed into poplars on its banks.
See the story in the Metamorphoses of Ovid, B. ii. l. 325, *et seq.*

[8] *And the Rutuba*) ver. 422. The Rutuba, now the Roya, is a small
river on the coast of Liguria, which flows between very high banks.

cavities. Thence downward glide both the swift Vulturnus [1], and the Sarnus [2], the producer of night-like mists, and the Liris [3] impelled by the Vestine waters [4] through the realms of shady Marica [5], and the Siler [6], skimming along the cultivated fields of Salernum [7]; the Macra [8], too, which in its shallows admits of no barks, runs into the sea of neighbouring Luna. Where, extending still beyond, it rises with its ridges elevated in the air, it beholds the Gallic fields, and looks down upon the declining Alps. Then, fertile for the Umbrians [9] and the Marsians [10], and subdued by

[1] *The swift Vulturnus*) ver. 423. The Vulturnus, now called Volturno, was the chief river of Campania, rising in the Apennines in Samnium, and falling into the Etrurian sea.

[2] *And the Sarnus*) ver. 424. The Sarnus, now called Sarno, is a river of Campania, flowing by Nuceria, and falling into the sea at Puteoli near Pompeii. Being in the vicinity of Mount Vesuvius, its mephitic vapours here alluded to were probably owing to the action of that volcano.

[3] *And the Liris*) ver. 424. The Liris, more anciently called the Clanis, and now the Garigliano, is one of the principal rivers of Central Italy, rising in the Apennines and flowing into the bay of Caieta near Minturnæ, at the boundary between Latium and Campania. Horace speaks of the "quieta aqua," "the placid waters" of the Liris.

[4] *Impelled by the Vestine waters*) ver. 425. The Vestini were a Sabellian race of Central Italy, lying between the Apennines, and the Adriatic Sea.

[5] *Of shady Marica*) ver. 424. Marica was a nymph of Latium, who was worshipped at Minturnæ, and had a sacred grove on the banks of the river Liris. Virgil mentions her as being the mother of Latinus by Faunus. Servius remarks, that some considered her identical with Aphrodite, and others with Circe.

[6] *And the Siler*) ver. 426. The Siler, now called the Silaro, was a river of lower Italy, forming the boundary between Lucania and Campania. Rising in the Apennines it falls into the Etrurian Sea, north of Pæstum.

[7] *Fields of Salernum*) ver. 425. Salernum, now called Salerno, was an ancient town of Campania, on the bay of Pæstum. It was made a Roman colony B.C. 194, but attained a greater prosperity in the middle ages, when a College of Health was established there.

[8] *The Macra*) ver. 426. The Macra, now called the Magra, was a small river rising in the Apennines, and discharging itself into the Ligurian Sea, near Luna. As here stated by the Poet, it was unnavigable for ships.

[9] *Fertile for the Umbrians*) ver. 430. He speaks of a former time, when, before the rise of Rome, Italy was inhabited by the Umbri, the Marsi, and the Sabines. The Umbri were one of the most ancient nations of Italy, and at the same time very powerful; their country, which was afterwards that called Etruria, extending across the peninsula from the Adriatic to the Etrurian Sea. The Umbrians were subdued by the Romans B.C. 307.

[10] *And the Marsians*) ver. 430. The Marsi were a brave and warlike people of Central Italy, in the high lands surrounded by the Apennines, near

the Sabine ploughshare[1], embracing with its pine-clad rocks
all the native races of Latium, it deserts not Hesperia
before it is cut short by the waves of Scylla[2], and extends
its rocks to the Lacinian temples[3]; longer than Italy, until[4]
the sea pressing on cut short its boundaries, and the ocean
forced back the land. But after the earth was separated by
the two seas, the extremity of the range ended in Sicilian
Pelorus[5].

Cæsar, furious for war, is not pleased at[6] having a way

Lake Fucinus. Marruvium was their chief town. Being probably acquainted
with the medicinal qualities of many plants, they acquired the reputation
among their Italian neighbours of being magicians, and were said to have
descended from Circe, the enchantress.

[1] *By the Sabine ploughshare*) ver. 430.   The Sabini were an ancient and
powerful race in Central Italy, situate at the foot of the Apennines, and
extending to the confines of Lucania and Apulia.   The term "Sabellus," as
in the present instance, is often applied to the Sabines, though properly this
race was divided into three classes, the Sabini, the Sabelli, and the Samnites.   The Marsi were, properly speaking, a tribe of the Sabelli.

[2] *Waves of Scylla*) ver. 433.   Scylla was a dangerous whirlpool lying
between the coasts of Italy and Sicily.

[3] *To the Lacinian temples*) ver. 434.   Lacinium, or Lacinia, was a Promontory on the eastern coast of Bruttium, a few miles south of Croton, and
forming the western boundary of the Tarentine Gulf.   It had a celebrated
Temple of Juno, who was worshipped here under the surname of Lacinia.
The Temple was situate on the Promontory, and the remains of it are still
extant.   The spot is said, by one of the Scholiasts, to have taken its name
from Lacinius, a robber, who was slain there by Hercules.

[4] *Longer than Italy, until*) ver. 435.   He means that the Apennines were
once longer in extent than the present Italy, at the time when Sicily was
not broken off from Italy by the intervening sea, and these mountains ran
through it as far as Pelorus.

[5] *Sicilian Pelorus*) ver. 438.   Pelorus was a Promontory, or mountain,
forming the north-east angle of Sicily.   The common story was, that it
received its name from the pilot of Hannibal, who was slain and buried
there; but, unfortunately for the truth of the story, it is called by this name
by Thucydides long before the time of Hannibal.

[6] *Is not pleased at*) ver. 439.   Owing to the peculiar manner in which
Lucan makes use of the conjunctions copulative and negative, this passage
may be translated in two different ways, of exactly opposite meaning:
"Cæsar, most anxious for civil war, is not pleased at making his way without effusion of blood, and is not pleased at marching through the Italian
territories free from an enemy, and at not being able to sally forth against
the fields in hostile form."   This is the translation suggested by Sulpitius,
Ascensius, and Farnabius, and approved of by Weise, Grotius, &c.   Cortius,
however, would render it,—"Cæsar, most anxious for civil war, is pleased at
not making his way, except with effusion of blood, and at not marching

otherwise than by the shedding of blood, *and* that he cannot lay waste the limits of Hesperia *now* free from an enemy. and rush down upon the deserted fields. and he would not lose the advantage of his march[1], and would be leading on force hand to hand with force. It delights him not so much to enter the opening gates, as to have broken them down; nor so much for the fields to be ploughed by the submitting husbandman, as if *the land* were laid waste with fire and sword. By paths permitted he is reluctant to proceed, and to appear to be a fellow-citizen. Then the cities of Latium, in doubt, and wavering with varying party feelings, although about to yield at the first alarm of the approaching warfare, still with stout ramparts strengthen their walls, and surround them on every side with the deep trench. Round masses of stone, too, and darts which may be hurled from above against the foe, they provide upon the lofty towers of the walls.

The multitude *is* more favourable to Magnus, and attachment struggles with threatening terror; just as when the south wind, with his dread-sounding blasts, possesses the sea, him do all the billows follow: if again the earth[2], loosened by the stroke of the Æolian trident, sends forth the eastern gales over the swelling waves, although swept by *this* fresh one, the billows *still* retain *the effects of* the former wind, and while the heavens give way to the eastern

through the Italian territories free from an enemy, and at being able to sally forth against the fields in hostile form." The first is probably the correct translation, for Weise very justly asks, where were the persons to defend the fields? It is notorious, on the other hand, that the only partizans of Pompey and the Senate were shut up in the fortified towns of Italy. Besides, the first mode of translation would tend to blacken the character of Cæsar, as making him (though contrary to the real fact), gratuitously a lover of bloodshed, which is quite consistent with the design of Lucan throughout the work. This is the more clear, as we find that the march of Cæsar through the boundaries of Italy was unimpeded, for Pompey had withdrawn his forces to the south, and awaited him in Campania.

[1] *Would not lose the advantage of his march*) ver. 442. "Non perdat iter." " Would not wish to lose the benefit of a march, as though through an enemy's country, and thereupon gaining the opportunity of gathering spoil as he proceeds."

[2] *If again the earth*) ver. 456. He probably means the land of Strongyle, now Stromboli, one of the Liparian or Æolian Islands, of the coast of Italy, where Æolus, the God of the Winds was said to have his abode. See the Æneid of Virgil, B. i. l. 51, *et seq.*

winds sweeping along the clouds, the waves *still* obey the
southern gales. But terror was able readily to change their
feelings, and fortune swayed their wavering attachment.

The Etrurian race was left defenceless by the flight of
frightened Libo [1], and now, Thermus repulsed [2], Umbria
lost the disposal of itself. Nor with his father's auspices
did Sulla wage the civic warfare [3], turning his back, on
hearing the name of Cæsar. Varus, when [4] the approaching troops attacked Auximum [5], rushing through the

[1] *Flight of frightened Libo*) ver. 462. Scribonius Libo was the father-in-
law of Sextus Pompeius, the son of Pompey the Great. He was entrusted
with the command of Etruria, but on the rapid approach of Cæsar, forsook
his charge and hastened to join the Consuls in Campania. Augustus afterwards married his sister, Scribonia, and he was Consul with M. Antony in
the year B.C. 34. It is not known at what time he died.

[2] *Now, Thermus repulsed*) ver. 463. Cæsar says, in his History of the
Civil War, B. i. ch. 12:—" In the meantime, being informed that Thermus,
the Prætor, was in possession of Iguvium [an important city of Umbria], with
five cohorts, and was fortifying the town, but that the feelings of all the inhabitants were very well inclined towards himself, he detached Curio, with
three cohorts, which he had at Ariminum and Pisaurus. Upon notice of
his approach, Thermus, distrusting the affections of the townsmen, drew his
cohorts out of it, and made his escape; his soldiers deserted him on the
road, and returned home.' This was Q. Minutius Thermus, formerly Proprætor in Asia. After the death of Pompey, he followed the fortunes of
his son Sextus, but finally deserted him, B.C. 35, and went over to M.
Antony.

[3] *Did Sulla wage the civic warfare*) ver. 465. This was Faustus Cornelius
Sulla, a son of the Dictator, by his fourth wife, Cæcilia Metella. He was
the son-in-law of Pompey, and, joining his party, crossed over into Greece,
on the approach of Cæsar. Being taken prisoner by Cæsar after the battle
of Thapsus, he was murdered in a tumult of the soldiers, in the victor's camp.

[4] *Varus, when*) ver. 466. This was P. Attius Varus, a zealous partizan of
Pompey in the Civil War. When Pompey left Italy, he crossed over to
Africa, which, with the assistance of Juba, he subdued for the Pompeian
party. He afterwards burnt several of Cæsar's ships at Adrumetum. Joining Cneius Pompeius in Spain, he was defeated in a naval battle by C. Didius.
He fell at the battle of Munda, and his head, with that of Labienus, was
carried to Cæsar.

[5] *Attacked Auximum*) ver. 466. Auximum was a large town of Picenum,
and a Roman colony. Cæsar thus relates the present circumstance in his
Civil War, B. i. c. 13:—"On news of Cæsar's approach, the senate of Auximum went in a body to Attius Varus, and told him that it was not a subject
for them to determine upon, yet neither they nor the rest of the freemen
were willing that Caius Cæsar, a general who had merited so well of the
state, after performing such great achievements, should be excluded from their
town and walls; wherefore he ought to pay some regard to the opinion of

walls[1] on the opposite side, his rear neglected, flies where are the woods, where *are* the rocks. Lentulus is driven[2] from the citadel of Asculum[3]. The victor presses upon them retreating, and draws over the troops; and alone out of a force so great the commander escapes, and standards that escort no cohorts[4]. Thou, too, Scipio, dost forsake the deserted citadel of Nuceria[5], entrusted to thy charge; although a most hardy youthful band is posted in this camp, some time before withdrawn from Cæsar's arms by reason of the Parthian panic; with which Magnus reinstated the Gallic losses, and, whilst he himself summoned them to the warfare, gave to his father-in-law the loan of Roman blood.

posterity, and his own danger. Alarmed at this declaration, Attius Varus drew out of the town the garrison he had placed there, and fled. A few of Cæsar's front rank having pursued him, obliged him to halt, and when the battle began, Varus was deserted by his troops, some of whom dispersed to their homes, and the rest came over to Cæsar."

[1] *Rushing through the walls*) ver. 467. By the mention of his mode of escape, it is not improbable that Lucan has confounded Attius Varus with C. Attius the Pelignian, who, on the approach of Cæsar, leaped from the walls of Sulmo with the intention of escaping.

[2] *Lentulus is driven*) ver. 469. This was P. Cornelius Lentulus Spinther, the Consul, who afterwards joined Pompey in Greece, and fled with him to the isle of Rhodes. His subsequent fate is not known.

[3] *Citadel of Asculum*) ver. 469. This was Asculum, a town of Picenum; it was a Roman municipium. There was another town in Apulia of the same name. Cæsar thus mentions this circumstance in his Civil War, B. i. c. 15:—" In the meantime, the twelfth legion came to join Cæsar; with these two he marched to Asculum, the chief town of Picenum. Lentulus Spinther occupied that town with ten cohorts; but on being informed of Cæsar's approach, he fled from the town, and in attempting to bring off his cohorts with him, was deserted by a great part of his men."

[4] *That escort no cohorts*) ver. 471. This was not the case, as some of his men still remained with him, whom he added shortly afterwards to the forces of Vibullius Rufus, the Pompeian partizan.

[5] *The citadel of Nuceria*) ver. 473. Nuceria, sometimes called " Luceria," was a town of Apulia, on the borders of Samnium. It was situate on a steep hill, and had a Temple of Minerva. This was now held by L. Scipio, the father-in-law of Pompey. In reference to the preceding passage, Marcellus, for the purpose probably of weakening Cæsar, had prevailed on the Senate to make a decree that Cæsar should give up one legion and Pompey another, which they pretended to be about to send to the Parthian war. In obedience to this decree, Cæsar delivered to Bibulus one legion as his own, and another which had formerly been raised and lent to him by Pompey, to supply the great loss which he had sustained by the defeat of his legates, Titurius and Cotta. These legions were now with Scipio in the town of Nuceria.

But thee, valiant Domitius [1], the abodes of Corfinium [2],
surrounded by strong walls, receive; those recruits, which
once were placed around the polluted Milo, obey thy
trumpet's call. When he beheld afar an immense cloud
arising on the plain, and the ranks shining with weapons
glittering in the glistening sun, "Run down, my comrades,"
said he, "to the banks of the river, and sink the bridge
under water; and thou, stream, now come forth, in all thy
strength, from thy mountain sources, and collect together
all the waters, that with thy foaming tide, thou mayst, the
structure broken, bear off the alder timbers. At this line
let the war come to a stand; upon these banks let the foe at
his leisure take his ease. Put a check upon the headlong
leader; Cæsar first coming to a stop at this spot shall be
to us a victory."

No more having said, he leads down from the walls his
active band, in vain. For when first, from the plains, the
river set at liberty [3], Cæsar beheld his passage being cut off,
excited by boiling indignation, *he said*, "Is it not enough
to have sought a lurking-place for your cowardice within
walls? Do you close up the plains, ye cowards, and attempt
to keep me in check with streams? Not, if Ganges with
his swelling tide were to separate me, should Cæsar now
come to a stand at any river, after the waters of Rubicon.
Hasten on, ye squadrons of horse; onward, too, ye foot;

[1] *Thee, valiant Domitius*) ver. 479. L. Domitius Ahenobarbus was one of
the most active opponents of Pompey and Cæsar on their coalition, and followed the opinions of Cato, whose sister Porcia he had married. He afterwards became more closely allied with Pompey. Being abandoned by Pompey,
he was obliged by his soldiers to surrender Corfinium; on which, offended at
the remissness of his leader, he retired to Massilia, which he defended
against Cæsar. He afterwards joined Pompey in Thessaly, and was slain at
the battle of Pharsalia, where he commanded the left wing. Cicero asserts
in his Second Philippic, that he fell by the hand of M. Antony.

[2] *The abodes of Corfinium*) ver. 478. Corfinium was the chief town of
the Peligni in Samnium: it is now called Popolo. Ahenobarbus had gar-
risoned it with twenty cohorts, among which were those soldiers who had
enclosed the Forum when Milo was arraigned for the death of Clodius. He
sent five cohorts to break down the bridge of the river, which was three
miles from the town, but these, meeting the advance-guard of Cæsar's army,
were repulsed. See the Civil War of Cæsar, B. i. c. 16.

[3] *The river set at liberty*) ver. 492. "Amne soluto." "The river being
about to be let loose," or "set free," as it were, by reason of the bridge
being in the act of being broken down.

ascend the bridge about to fall!" When this had been said, the light horsemen gave full rein along the plain, and their stalwart arms hurled the darts to the opposite bank, much like a shower thickly falling. Cæsar enters upon [1] the stream left vacant, its guard being put to flight, and is brought safe to the citadel of the enemy.

And now he was erecting towers to discharge vast masses, and the mantelet [2] had moved on beneath the midst of the walls; when lo! a crime in warfare [3], the gates being opened, the troops dragged forth their captive chief, and before the feet of his haughty fellow-citizen he stood. Still, his features contemptuously scowling, with undaunted neck did his high-born courage demand the sword. Cæsar was aware both that punishment was wished for and that pardon was dreaded [4]. "Live on," said he [5], "although thou art unwill-

---

[1] *Cæsar enters upon*) ver. 503. It is hard to say whether "ingreditur" here means that he crossed the river by the bridge, or that, disdaining the bridge, he forded it with his troops. Cæsar, however, in the Civil War, B. i. c. 16, speaks of marching his legions "over," so that a passage by the bridge is probably meant.

[2] *And the mantelet*) ver. 506. The "vineæ," which were similar to what are called "mantelets" in modern warfare, were roofs or sheds, under which the besiegers protected themselves from the darts, stones, and fires hurled from the walls of the besieged town on the assailants. The roof and sides were formed of wicker-work, while planks, covered with wet cloth or raw hides, also supported the sides. They were on light frames, and were either carried or wheeled by the soldiers to the walls. They received their name from their resemblance to a leafy bower, formed by the branches of vines.

[3] *A crime in warfare*) ver. 507. According to Cæsar (Civil War, B. i. c. 19, 20), the facts were these :—Domitius, having sent to Pompey for aid, received an answer that Pompey would not encounter the risk of relieving him, as he had retreated to Corfinium without his own advice or consent, and that if any opportunity should offer, he, Domitius, was to come to Pompey with his whole force. On this, Domitius determined on escaping from the town, imparting his design to a few of his friends. His intentions becoming suspected, his troops mutinied, and, seizing him, sent dispatches to Cæsar, to say that they were ready to deliver the town and Domitius into his hands.

[4] *That pardon was dreaded*) ver. 511. According to some accounts, Domitius had endeavoured to poison himself on being about to fall in the hands of Cæsar, but his physician only gave him a sleeping potion.

[5] *Live on, said he*) ver. 512. Cæsar says that Lentulus Spinther interceded with him for the lives of Domitius and the other nobles taken at Corfinium, on which the conqueror replied that he had not left his Province to injure any one, but to protect himself against the malice of his enemies, and to restore the Tribunes of the people, who had been expelled from the City He not only dismissed Domitius, but even returned him sixty sestertia,

ing; and by my bounty behold the light of day. To the conquered faction now let there be bright hopes, and the example of myself; even if it pleases thee try arms once more; and nothing for this pardon do I stipulate, if thou shalt be overcome."

He *thus* speaks, and orders the chains to be loosened on his tightened hands. Alas! even his murder perpetrated, how much more becomingly might Fortune have spared a Roman's shame; to whom it is the very greatest of punishments, to be pardoned because he has followed the camp of his country and Magnus for his leader, and the whole of the Senate. He, undismayed, checks his heavy wrath, and to himself *he says*, "And wilt thou repair, degenerate man, to Rome, and the retreats of peace? Dost thou not prepare to go into the midst of the frenzy of war, destined soon to die? Rush on assured, and burst asunder all delay to *losing* thy life, and *thus* be rid of Cæsar's gift."

In the meantime, not aware of the chieftain being taken, Magnus was preparing arms, that, with strength intermingled, he might recruit his party. And now, on the ensuing day, about to order the trumpet *to sound*, and thinking that the resentment of the soldiers about to move might be ascertained, with a voice moving veneration he addressed the silent cohorts: "O avengers of crimes, and who have followed the preferable standards, O truly Roman band, to whom the Senate has given arms in no private cause [1], in your aspirations demand the fight. With ruthless ravages the fields of Hesperia glow; along the icy Alps is poured forth the Gallic rage [2]; already has blood touched the polluted swords of Cæsar. Well *have* the Gods *provided*, that we were the first to endure the casualties of war On their side let the criminality commence.

"Now, e'en now, myself the umpire, let Rome seek punishment and vengeance. Nor indeed is it right for these to be called real battles, but *rather* the wrath of an

though he knew that it was a sum originally provided to pay the adherents of Pompey. See the Civil War, B. i. c. 22, 23.

. [1] *In no private cause*) ver. 533. "Non privata," " in no private cause," he having been enjoined to undertake the war against Cæsar on behalf of the state.

[2] *The Gallic rage*) ver. 535. In allusion to the Gallic forces who accompanied Cæsar.

avenging country. No more is this a war than when Catiline prepared[1] the torches to blaze amid the houses, and Lentulus the partner in his fury, and the frantic band of Cethegus, with his naked shoulders[2]. O frenzy of the leader *greatly* to be pitied! When, Cæsar, the Fates could wish to enrol thee among the Camilli[3] and the great Metelli[4], among the Cinnæ[5] and the Marii dost thou come. Assuredly thou shalt be laid prostrate, as by Catulus Lepidus fell[6], and Carbo, who, submitting[7] to my axe, is buried

[1] *When Catiline prepared*) ver. 541. He alludes to the intended rebellion of L. Sergius Catilina, when, in conjunction with P. Cornelius Lentulus Sura, who had lost his seat in the Senate, and other conspirators, he had destined the City of Rome to the flames. Information of the conspiracy was given to Cicero, who took instant measures to quell it; on which, Catiline and others left the City, and, raising an army, waged open war against the state. He was defeated by M. Petreius, and was slain in battle fighting with desperate courage.

[2] *Cethegus, with his naked shoulders*) ver. 543. He alludes to an ancient fashion which seems to have prevailed among the Cethegi, of wearing the arms bare. Horace, in his Art of Poetry, l. 50, refers to the same custom. The person here mentioned was C. Cornelius Cethegus, one of the most abandoned of the associates of Catiline. It was to have been his part to murder the leading Senators. He was, however, arrested, and put to death, the evidence against him being the swords and daggers which he had collected in his house.

[3] *Among the Camilli*) ver. 544. He, no doubt, though using the plural number, refers more especially to M. Furius Camillus, the patriotic Dictator, and the deliverer of Rome from Gallic bondage.

[4] *And the great Metelli*) ver. 545. He probably alludes in particular to L. Cæcilius Metellus, who, when Consul, successfully opposed the Carthaginians in the first Punic war. When high priest, he rescued the Palladium from the Temple of Vesta when on fire, but lost his sight in consequence; he was therefore allowed the privilege, previously granted to no one, of riding to the Senate-house in a chariot, and was rewarded with a statue in the Capitol.

[5] *Among the Cinna*) ver. 546. He alludes to L. Cornelius Cinna, the partizan of Marius, who endeavoured to recall Marius to Rome when in banishment in Africa. He at length succeeded in regaining power, and became Consul jointly with Marius, when he distinguished himself by his cruelty. He was finally slain by his own troops when marching against Sulla.

[6] *By Catulus Lepidus fell*) ver. 547. M. Æmilius Lepidus, the father of the Triumvir, being declared by the Senate an enemy to the state, collected an army in Etruria, and marched against Rome. Here he was defeated in the Campus Martius by Pompey and Catulus, and fled with the remainder of his troops to Sardinia, where he was again repulsed, and is supposed to have died of grief.

[7] *Carbo, who, submitting*) ver. 548. Cn. Papirius Carbo was one of the leaders

in a Sicilian sepulchre, Sertorius, too[1], who, an exile, aroused the fierce Iberians. And yet, if there is any belief *in me*, I grudge, Cæsar, to add thee as well to these, and that Rome has opposed my hands to thee in thy madness.

" Would that Crassus had returned safe after the battles of the Parthians, and victorious from the regions of Scythia, that thou mightst fall by a like cause to that by which the foeman Spartacus *fell*[2]. If the Gods of heaven have ordained that thou as well shalt be added to my titles *of triumph*, mighty is my right arm at hurling the javelin; this glowing blood has again waxed warm around my heart; thou shalt learn, that not all who could submit to peace are cowards in war. Although he styles me enfeebled and worn out, let not my age alarm you. In this camp let the chief be more aged[3], so long as the soldier *is more aged* in that.

of the Marian faction. He conducted the war in Cisalpine Gaul and Spain against the generals of Sulla, and with Norbanus was finally defeated near Faventia, in Italy, by Metellus. He fled first to Africa and thence to Sicily. Going thence to the isle of Cossyra, near Malta, he was taken prisoner by the emissaries of Pompey. He was brought in chains to Pompey at Lilybæum, in Sicily, who, after rebuking him, had his head struck off, which he sent to Sulla.

[1] *Sertorius, too*) ver. 549.   Q. Sertorius, one of the most gallant of the Romans, though fully sensible of the faults of Marius, his old commander, espoused his cause against the aristocratic party.   Though he commanded one of the four armies which besieged Rome under Marius and Cinna, he was entirely averse to the bloodshed which ensued.   Long after the death of Marius he asserted his own independence in Spain, and for many years kept the forces of Pompey and Metellus at bay, and destroyed a great portion of their troops. He was assassinated, B.C. 72, by Perperna and some others of his officers, who had long been jealous of him. Regardless of his merits, Lucan unjustly quotes him as an instance of the prowess of Pompey having dealt retribution against rebellion.

[2] *The foeman Spartacus fell*) ver. 554. Spartacus was a Thracian by birth, and originally a shepherd, then a soldier, and afterwards a leader of banditti. Being taken prisoner, he was sold to a trainer of gladiators. Regaining his freedom, he headed his fellow slaves, and defeated several of the Roman armies. After a successful career, M. Licinius Crassus, the Roman Prætor, was appointed to the command of the war against him, and, after gaining several advantages, defeated him at the river Silarus in a decisive battle, in which Spartacus was slain.

[3] *Let the chief be more aged*) ver. 561.   Alluding to his being the senior of Cæsar, while Cæsar had the veterans in his camp, and he himself a larger number of young recruits.

To whatever height a free people could elevate a citizen, *thither* have I ascended, and nothing have I left above *me* but the sovereignty. No private station does he desire, whoever in the Roman City attempts to be higher than Pompey. Here on our side either Consul is, here on our side are the ranks of our nobles to take their stand. Shall Cæsar be the conqueror of the Senate? Not to that degree, O Fortune! dost thou drag onward all things in thy blind career and feel ashamed at nothing.

"Does Gaul, rebellious now for many a year[1], and an age spent in labours, impart courage? Is it, because he fled from the cold waves[2] of the Rhine, and, calling the shallows[3] of a fluctuating sea the ocean, he showed his frightened back to the Britons he had sought out? Or do vain menaces swell, because the rumour of his frenzy has driven the City in arms from its paternal abodes? Alas! madman, they fly not from thee; all are following me! who, when I raised my standards gleaming over the whole ocean, before Cynthia had twice filled her completed orb, the pirate abandoned every ford of the sea, and asked for a home[4] in a narrow allotment of land. I too, more fortunate than Sulla[5], pursued to the death, the monarch *hitherto* unsubdued[6] and who stayed the destinies of Rome, flying in exile through the retreats of Scythian Pontus.

"No portion of the world is unconnected with me, but the whole earth is occupied by my trophies, under whatever sun it lies. Hence do the Arctic regions own me as a victor at the cold waves of Phasis[7]; a meridian clime is known to

---

[1] *For many a year*) ver. 568, 69. "Multis lustris," literally "for many 'lustra,'" or periods of four or five years.

[2] *Fled from the cold waves*) ver. 570. He alludes to the return of Cæsar from Germany into Gaul, and for the sake of a rhetorical artifice, pretends to call it a flight.

[3] *Calling the shallows*) ver. 571. See B. i. l. 410.

[4] *And asked for a home*) ver. 579. Alluding to his conquest of the Cilician pirates and their subsequent settlements.

[5] *More fortunate than Sulla*) ver. 512. This is said antithetically, and the words "although he was called fortunate (felix)," must be supposed to be supplied. Sulla had previously gained some victories over Mithridates.

[6] *The monarch hitherto unsubdued*) ver. 581. In allusion to his victories over Mithridates.

[7] *The cold waves of Phasis*) ver. 585. Phasis, now the Faz or Rioni, was a famous river of Colchis. In ancient times it was crossed by 120

me in hot Egypt[1], and in Syene[2], which on no side diverts
its shades.   The west obeys my laws, and the Hesperian
Bætis[3], that beyond all rivers dashes into the retreating
Tethys.   The subdued Arab[4] has known me; me the Heniochi, fierce in war[5], and the Colchians, famed for the fleece
borne away.   My standards do the Cappadocians dread, and
Judæa, devoted to the rites of an unknown God[6], and the
luxurious Sophene[7].   The Armenians, and the fierce Cilicians, and the Taurians[8] have I subdued.   What war but a
civil one to my father-in-law have I left?"

His partizans followed the words of the chieftain with no

bridges, and had many towns on its banks.   When conquered by Pompey,
Mithridates took refuge in the wild and inaccessible regions beyond the
Phasis, whither Pompey found himself unable to pursue him.

[1] *Known to me in hot Egypt*) ver. 587.   He had been sent by the Roman
Senate to Egypt to be the guardian of Ptolemy, the youthful king of that
country.

[2] *And in Syene*) ver. 587.   Syene was a city of Upper Egypt, on the
eastern bank of the Nile, just below the first Cataract, and was considered
the southern frontier city of Egypt against Æthiopia.   It was an important
point in the geography and astronomy of the ancients, as appears from the
expression used in the present instance.   It lay just under the tropic of
Cancer, and was therefore chosen as the place through which they drew their
chief parallel of latitude.   The sun was vertical to Syene at the time of the
summer solstice, and a well was shown there where the face of the sun was
seen at noon at that time.

[3] *The Hesperian Bætis*) ver. 589.   The Bætis, now the Guadalquivir, a
river in the south of Spain, was also called Tartessus and Certis.   It falls
into the Atlantic to the north of Gades, now Cadiz.   Pompey refers most
probably to his campaigns against Sertorius, which, however, certainly did not
redound to his credit as a general.

[4] *The subdued Arab*) ver. 590.   In his campaign in Syria and Palestine,
where he replaced Hyrcanus in possession of the government in opposition to
his brother Aristobulus.

[5] *The Heniochi, fierce in war*) ver. 591.   The Heniochi were a people of
Colchis famed for their piratical habits.

[6] *Rites of an unknown God*) ver. 593.   "Incerti Dei," a God unknown
to other nations.   It was at this period that Pompey restored Ariobarzanes,
king of Cappadocia, to his kingdom.

[7] *The luxurious Sophene*) ver. 593.   Sophene was a district of Greater
Armenia, lying between the ranges of Antitaurus and Masius, near the banks
of the Euphrates.   According to one of the Scholiasts it is here called
"mollis" from the heat of the sun in those regions, but more probably it is
so termed by reason of the effeminacy of its inhabitants.

[8] *And the Taurians*) ver. 594.   "Tauros."   By this term he probably
means the inhabitants of the country adjoining the great mountain range of
Taurus in Central Asia.

applause, nor did they demand the speedy trumpet signal
for the promised fight. Magnus too himself perceived
their fears, and it pleased him that his standards should be
borne back, and not to expose to the risks of a combat so
decisive troops already vanquished by the fame of Cæsar
not yet seen *by them*. Just as among the herds a bull,
worsted in the first combat, seeks the recesses of the
woods, and, exiled amid the vacant fields, tries his horns
upon the opposing trunks; and returns not to the pastures,
but when, his neck reinvigorated, *his* muscles exercised
give him confidence; then, soon victorious, the bulls accompanying, he leads the recovered herds, maugre the shepherd,
to any pastures he lists; so, unequal in strength, Magnus
surrendered Hesperia, and taking to flight over the Apulian fields ascended the secure towers of Brundisium[1].

This is a city once possessed by Dictæan colonists[2],
whom, flying from Crete, the Cecropian ships bore along
the seas, with sails that falsely told[3] that Theseus was conquered. In this *region*, the coast of Hesperia, which now
contracts itself into a narrow *arch*, extends into the sea
a small tongue, which, with its curving horns, shuts in the
waves of the Adriatic. Nor yet would this water inclosed
in the narrowed inlet form a harbour, if an island did not
receive upon its rocks the violent north-west gales, and
turn back the dashing waves. On the one side and on the
other nature has opposed mountains with craggy cliffs to
the open main, and has warded off the blasts, so that, held
fast by the shaking cables, ships can stand *there*. Hence
far and wide extends all the ocean, whether the sails are

[1] *Secure towers of Brundisium*) ver. 609. Cæsar says, in his "Civil War,"
B. i. c. 84, "Pompey, being informed of what had passed at Corfinium,
marched from Luceria to Canusium, and thence to Brundisium." This was
a town of Calabria, on a small bay of the Adriatic, forming an excellent
harbour, to which the place owed its importance.

[2] *Dictaan colonists*) ver. 610. Or Cretan colonists, so called from
Dicte, a mountain in the eastern part of Crete, where Jupiter is said to have
been reared.

[3] *With sails that falsely told*) ver. 612. He alludes to the story of
Theseus having returned from Crete, by inadvertence, with black sails, when
they ought, according to the arrangement previously made, to have been
white; on which Ægeus, his father, threw himself into the sea. He
means that Brundisium was colonized by the Cretans who had escaped
from Crete with Theseus in the Cecropian or Athenian ships.

C

borne, Corcyra, to thy harbours [1], or whether on the left
Illyrian Epidamnus [2] is sought, bordering upon the Ionian
waves. Hither is the flight of mariners, when the Adriatic
has put forth all its strength, and the Ceraunia [3] have disappeared in clouds, and when the Calabrian Sason [4] is
washed by the foaming main.

Therefore, when there is no hope in the affairs that have
been left behind, and there is no means of turning the
warfare to the hardy Iberians, since the Alps, with their
immense tracts, lie extended between, then that son [5], *one
of a progeny so great, whose age is more advanced,* he
thus addresses :—

"I bid you try the distant regions of the world.
Arouse the Euphrates and the Nile [6], even as far as the fame
of my name has reached, cities through which the fame of
Rome has been spread abroad after myself as her general.
Bring back to the seas the Cilician colonists scattered amid
the fields. On the one side arouse the Pharian kings [7] and
my *friend* Tigranes. And neglect not, I advise thee, the
arms of Pharnaces [8], nor yet do thou the tribes that wander

---

[1] *Corcyra, to thy harbours*) ver. 623. Corcyra, now Corfu, was an island
in the Ionian Sea, off the coast of Epirus, long famed for the naval enterprise of its inhabitants.

[2] *Illyrian Epidamnus*) ver. 624. Epidamnus was a town in Greek Illyria, on the Adriatic Sea. It was founded by the Corcyreans, and received
from them the name of Epidamnus; but when the Romans became masters
of the country, they changed the name to Dyrrhachium, as it reminded them
of their word " damnum," signifying " loss," or " misfortune." It was the
usual place of landing for those who crossed over from Brundisium.

[3] *And the Ceraunia*) ver. 626. The Ceraunia, or Acroceraunia, were
immense rocks on the coast of Epirus.

[4] *When the Calabrian Sason*) ver. 627. Sason, or Saso, was a small
rocky island off the coast of Illyria, to the north of the promontory of
Acroceraunia, much frequented by pirates. It is now called Sasseno, or
Sassa.

[5] *Then that son*) ver. 631. His son Cneius Pompeius.

[6] *Arouse the Euphrates and the Nile*) ver. 633. He is to repair to the
Euphrates and the Nile to invoke the aid of the kings of Parthia and Egypt.

[7] *Arouse the Pharian kings*) ver. 636. Lucan frequently calls the Egyptians " Pharii," " Pharians," from the island of Pharos, situate at the mouth
of the Nile. Tigranes was king of Armenia, and was indebted to Pompey
for his kingdom.

[8] *The arms of Pharnaces*) ver. 637. Pharnaces, king of Pontus or, more
properly, of the Bosporus, was a son of Mithridates the Great. He com-

in either Armenia, and the fierce nations along the shores of Pontus, and the Rhipæan bands[1], and those whom on its frozen waves the sluggish swamp of Mæotis[2], enduring the Scythian waggon, bears. But why do I any further delay? Throughout the entire East, my son, thou wilt carry the warfare, and awaken all the cities that have been subdued throughout the entire world; let all my triumphs repair once again to my camp. You too, who mark the Latian annals with your names, let the first northern breeze bear you to Epirus; thence, throughout the fields of the Greeks and the Macedonians acquire new strength, while winter affords time for peace." Thus he speaks, and all obey his commands, and unmoor their hollow ships from the shore.

But, never enduring peace and a long cessation from arms, lest it may be in the power of the Fates to work any change, Cæsar follows, and presses hard on the footsteps of his son-in-law. To others would have sufficed so many fortified towns[3] captured at the first assault, so many towers overwhelmed, the enemy expelled; thou thyself, Rome, the Capital of the world, the greatest reward of the warfare, so easy to be taken. But Cæsar, precipitate in everything, thinking nothing done while anything remains to be done, fiercely pursues; and still, although he is in possession of the whole of Italy, because Magnus is located on its extreme shores, does he grieve that as yet it is common to them; nor on the other hand is he willing

pelled his father to put an end to his own life; and, to secure himself on the throne, sent offers of submission with hostages to Pompey in Syria, and the body of his father to Sinope to be at the disposal of the Roman general. Pompey accepted his submission, and gave him the kingdom of the Bosporus, with the title of friend and ally of the Roman people. Pharnaces afterwards took advantage of the Civil Wars, and reconquered nearly the whole of his father's dominions, but was defeated by Cæsar at the battle of Zela, and shortly afterwards perished.

[1] *And the Rhipæan bands*) ver. 640. Rhipæan was a general and indefinite name for the northern nations of Scythia; but the Rhipæan mountains are supposed to have been a western branch of the Uralian chain.

[2] *Swamp of Mæotis*) ver. 641. He alludes to the Palus Mæotis, or Sea of Azof, which, when frozen, was said to be crossed by the Nomad tribes of Scythia with their waggons.

[3] *So many fortified towns*) ver. 653. Of which number the Poet has already specified Ariminum, Auximum, Asculum, Luceria, and Corfinium.

that the foe should wander on the open main, but with
moles he dams out the waves[1], and the expansive ocean
with rocks hurled down.

To no purpose is *this* labour bestowed on the immense
undertaking; the voracious sea sucks in all the rocks, and
mingles the mountains with its sands; just as, if the lofty
Eryx[2] were thrown down into the midst of the waves of
the Ægean Sea, still no rocky heights would tower above
the main; or if Gaurus[3], his pinnacles rooted up, were to
fall down to the very depths of stagnant Avernus. Therefore, when in the shoals no mass retained its weight, then
it pleased him, the woods cut down, to connect rafts, and
to fasten together with wide extent the trunks of trees by
immense chains.

Fame relates that exulting Xerxes constructed[4] such a

---

[1] *Dams out the waves*) ver. 662. This passage is best explained by a portion of what Cæsar himself has written on the subject. He states that he
was afraid that if Pompey remained at Brundisium he might command
the whole Adriatic Sea, with the extremity of Italy and the coast of Greece,
and be able to conduct the war on either side of it, and, fearing that he would
not relinquish Italy, he determined to deprive him of his means of communication. For that purpose (Civil War, B. i. c. 25), "where the mouth of
the port was narrowest, he threw up a mole of earth on either side, because
in these places the sea was shallow. Having gone out so far that the mole
could not be continued into deep water, he fixed double floats, thirty feet on
either side, before the mole. These he fastened with four anchors at the four
corners, that they might not be carried away by the waves. Having completed and secured them, he then joined to them other floats of equal size.
These he covered over with earth and mould, that he might not be prevented
from access to them to defend them, and on the front and both sides he protected them with a parapet of wicker-work: and on every fourth one he
raised a turret two stories high, to secure them the better from being attacked
by shipping and set on fire."

[2] *As, if the lofty Eryx*) ver. 666. Eryx was a lofty mountain of Sicily,
on the summit of which there was a Temple sacred to Venus.

[3] *Or if Gaurus*) ver. 667. Gaurus was the name of a volcanic range of
mountains in Campania. Avernus was a small lake seated near their foot,
filling the crater of an extinct volcano. It was supposed to be connected
with the Infernal Regions. The mephitic vapours were so powerful as to be
said to kill the birds that attempted to fly over it.

[4] *Exulting Xerxes constructed*) ver. 672. Xerxes, king of Persia, the
son of Darius and Atossa, when invading Europe, had a bridge of boats
thrown across the Hellespont from the vicinity of Abydos on the Asiatic
side, to the coast between Sestos and Abydos on the European, where the
straits are about a mile in width. The first bridge having been destroyed by

passage over the seas, when, daring great things, with his
bridges he joined both Europe to Asia, and Sestos to Abydos[1], and walked over the straits of the rapid Hellespont,
not fearing Eurus and Zephyrus; *at the time* when he would
have borne his sails and ships through the midst of Athos[2].
In such manner are the inlets of the deep narrowed by the
fall of the woods; then with many a mound the work
rises apace, and the tall towers vibrate over the seas.

Pompey, seeing the inlets of the deep choked up with land
newly-formed, vexed his mind with carking cares how to open
the sea, and to spread the warfare over the main. Full oft,
filled by the southern gales, and dragged by extended cables[3]
through the obstructions of the sea themselves, ships dashed
down into the salt tide the summits of the mass, and
made room for the barks[4] *to enter;* the balista, too, hurled
by stalwart arms amid the shades *of night,* hurled torches
cleft into many parts. When at length the occasion
suited for a stolen flight, he first ordered his followers that
no sailors' clamour should arouse, or clarion divide[5] the

a storm, the despot caused the heads of the chief engineers to be cut off, and
commanded the Straits to be scourged, and a set of fetters to be cast therein.
A new bridge was then formed consisting of a double line of ships. (See
Herodotus, B. viii. c. 36.)

[1] *And Sestos to Abydos*) ver. 674. Sestos and Abydos have been famed
in story for the loves of Hero and Leander. See their Epistles in the
Heroïdes of Ovid.

[2] *Through the midst of Athos*) ver. 677. Athos is a mountain which was
also called Acte, projecting from Chalcidice in Macedonia. Lucan here
alludes to the canal which Xerxes ordered to be cut through the Isthmus of
Mount Athos, from the Strymonic to the Toronaic Gulf, that his ships
might pass through; the remains of which work are to be seen at the
present day.

[3] *Dragged by extended cables*) ver. 683. They were not only impelled by
sails, but were also dragged on by means of ropes from the shore, on account
of their unwieldy size.

[4] *Made room for the barks*) ver. 685. Cæsar, in the Civil War, B. i.
c. 26, gives the following account of these operations :—" To counteract this,
Pompey fitted out large merchant ships, which he found in the harbour of
Brundisium ; on them he erected turrets three stories high, and, having furnished them with several engines and all sorts of weapons, drove them
amongst Cæsar's works, to break through the floats and interrupt the works;
thus there occurred skirmishes every day with slings, arrows, and other
weapons."

[5] *Or clarion divide*) ver. 689. The " buccina " was properly a trumpet
made from the conch-shell, and as such, in the hands of Triton, is described

hours, or trumpet lead the sailors, instructed beforehand, out to sea.

Now had the Virgin, towards her close[1], begun to precede the claws *of the Scorpion* that were to bring on Phœbus, when in silence the ships were unmoored. No anchor arouses their voices[2] while from the dense sands its hook is being dragged. While the sailyards are being set *to the wind*, and while the lofty pine-tree mast is being raised, the anxious masters of the fleet are silent; and the sailors, hanging *by the ropes*, unfurl the tightened sails, nor shake the stout shrouds, lest the air should breathe a whisper. The chieftain, too, in his aspirations, Fortune, entreats thee, that Italy, which thou dost forbid him to retain, it may be at least allowed him to quit. Hardly do the Fates permit it; for with a loud noise, impelled by beaks *of ships*, the sea re-echoes, the waters dash, and the billows with the tracks of so many ships *there* intermingled[3].

by Ovid in the Metamorphoses, B. i. l. 335, *et seq.* In after times it was made of metal to resemble the shell. It was probably distinct in form from the "cornu;" but is often confounded with it. As mentioned in the present instance, it was used chiefly to proclaim the watches of the night and day, which were hence called "buccina prima," "secunda," &c. The present orders were given that Cæsar's troops might not be put on the alert.

[1] *The Virgin, towards her close*) ver. 691. Weise has the following Note here:—"The time after midnight is meant, before the dawn and the rising of the sun, which the Poet describes as then being in Sagittarius. For the 'Chelæ' are [the claws] of the Scorpion. By 'Virgo ultima' he means that part of the constellation Virgo in the Zodiac which is nearest before the Scorpion. At this hour Pompey sets sail from the harbour, being aided by the darkness. The meaning of the Poet seems to be that this took place in autumn, although others write to a contrary effect."

[2] *No anchor arouses their voices*) ver. 694. He alludes to the "celeusma," or call, with which sailors keep time in heaving the anchor.

[3] *Ships there intermingled*) ver. 703. Cæsar gives the following interesting account of this escape of Pompey, in his Civil War, B. i. c. 27, 28 :—"Pompey now began to prepare for his departure on the arrival of the ships; and the more effectually to retard Cæsar's attack, lest his soldiers should force their way into the town at the moment of his departure, he stopped up the gates, built walls across the streets and avenues, sunk trenches across the ways, and fixed on them palisadoes and sharp stakes which he made level with the ground by means of hurdles and clay. But he barricaded with large beams, fastened in the ground and sharpened at the ends, two passages and roads without the walls, which led to the port. After making these arrangements, he ordered his soldiers to go on board without noise, and dis

Therefore, the enemy being received by the gates, all of which throughout the city attachment changing with fortune has opened, and within the walls, winding along the piers, with precipitate course seek the entrance to the harbour, and are vexed that the fleet has reached the sea. O shame! a slight victory is the flight of Pompey!

A narrow pass let the ships out to sea, more limited than the Euboean tide where it beats upon Chalcis[1]. Here stuck fast two ships, and received the grappling-irons prepared for the fleet; and the warfare being *thus* dragged to the shore[2], here, for the first time, did Nereus grow red with the blood of citizens. The rest of the fleet departs, despoiled of the *two* last ships; just as, when the bark from Pagasæ[3] sought the waves of Phasis, the earth shot forth the Cyanean rocks[4] into the deep; less by its stern torn off

posed here and there, on the walls and turrets, some light-armed veterans, archers, and slingers. These he designed to call off by a certain signal, when all the soldiers were embarked, and left galleys for them in a secure place. The people of Brundisium, irritated by the insolence of Pompey's soldiers, and the insults received from Pompey himself, were in favour of Cæsar's party. Therefore, as soon as they were aware of Pompey's departure, whilst his men were running up and down, and busied about their voyage, they made signs from the tops of the houses; Cæsar, being apprised of the design by them, ordered scaling-ladders to be got ready and his men to take arms, that he might not lose any opportunity of coming to an action. Pompey weighed anchor at nightfall. The soldiers who had been posted on the wall to guard it, were called off by the signal which had been agreed on, and, knowing the road, ran down to the ships."

[1] *Where it beats upon Chalcis*) ver. 710. He compares the narrow passage leading out of the harbour to the Euripus or Straits of Euboea, now the straits of Negropont, which separated it from the main land. Chalcis was a city of Euboea.

[2] *To the shore*) ver. 712. Cæsar, in his Civil War, B. i. c. 28, gives this account of their capture :—" Cæsar's soldiers fixed their ladders and scaled the walls; but, being cautioned by the people to beware of the hidden stakes and covered trenches, they halted, and being conducted by the inhabitants by a long circuit, they reached the port and captured with their boats and small craft two of Pompey's ships, full of soldiers, which had struck against Cæsar's moles." The " manus," or " hands," mentioned by Lucan, were probably " harpagones," or " grappling irons."

[3] *The bark from Pagasæ*) ver. 715. He speaks of the expedition of Jason to Colchis, to recover the Golden Fleece, in the ship Argo, which was built at Pagasæ in Thessaly.

[4] *The Cyanean rocks*) ver. 716. The story was, that when Jason's ship passed between the Symplegades, or Cyanean Islands, which floated at the

did the Argo escape from the mountains, and in vain
did the Symplegas strike at the vacant sea, and, destined
to stand, it bounded back[1].

Now, the complexion of the eastern sky no longer the same
warns that Phœbus is pressing on, and the pale light is not
yet ruddy, and is withdrawing their flames from the nearer
stars; and now the Pleiades[2] are dim, now the Wain of the
declining Boötes[3], growing faint, returns to the appearance of
the serene heavens, and the larger stars lie hid, and Lucifer
himself flies from the warm day. Now, Magnus, thou hadst
gained the open sea, not bearing *with thee* those destinies
which *thou wast wont*, when over the waves throughout all
seas thou didst give chase to the pirate. Exhausted by thy
triumphs, Fortune has forsaken *thee*. Banished with wife
and children, and dragging all thy household Gods to the
warfare, still, a mighty exile thou dost go, nations accompanying thee.

A distant spot is sought for thy unworthy downfall[4]. Not
because the Gods of heaven prefer to deprive thee of a
sepulchre in thy native land are the Pharian sands condemned to be thy tomb. It is Hesperia that is spared; in
order that, afar off, in a remote region, Fortune may hide
the horrid deed, and the Roman land be preserved un-
spotted by the blood of her own Magnus.

mouth of the Euxine Sea, the isles closed and struck off the stern of the
Argo.

[1] *Destined to stand, it bounded back*) ver. 719. It was ordained by the
Fates that if any ship should pass in safety between the Symplegades, they
should ever after remain fixed to one spot.

[2] *And now the Pleiades*) ver. 722. The Pleiades were the daughters of
Atlas and Pleione. They were changed into stars, of which six were visible
and the seventh invisible, because, as the story was, when on earth she was
united to a mortal; whereas her sisters had intercourse only with Divinities.
The Romans called them " Vergiliæ."

[3] *The Wain of the declining Boötes*) ver. 722. The Constellation before
the Great Bear was called Boötes, Arcturus, or Arctophylax. The name
Boötes was derived from the position of the star before the wain, resembling
that of the driver of a team.

[4] *For thy unworthy downfall*) ver. 731. The meaning is, that Egypt is
appointed by the Fates as the scene of the death of Pompey.

BOOK THE THIRD.

CONTENTS.

WHEN the south wind pressing upon the yielding sails urged on the fleet, and the ships set in motion the middle of the deep, each sailor looked upon the Ionian waves; Magnus alone did not turn his eyes from the Hesperian land, while he beheld his country's harbours, and the shores destined never to return to his gaze, and the peaks hidden in clouds, and the dim mountains, vanish. Then did the wearied limbs of the chieftain yield to soporiferous slumber. Then, a ghost, full of dread horror, Julia[1] seemed to raise her sorrowing head through the yawning earth, and to stand like a Fury[2] above the lighted pyre.

"Exiled," said she[3], "from the Elysian abodes and the

---

[1] *Julia*) ver. 10. His former wife, the daughter of Cæsar.

[2] *To stand like a Fury*) ver. 11. The term "furialis" is used because it was her errand, as she states to him, to follow him with vengeance throughout the Civil Warfare.

[3] *Exiled, said she*) ver. 12. "Expulsa." This term does not mean that she is expelled from the abodes of the Blessed by force, but that she is aroused by the portentousness of the Civil War, and is unable, from the interest she feels in it, to remain there any longer.

fields of the Blessed, unto the Stygian shades and the guilty
ghosts, since the civil warfare have I been dragged. I myself have beheld the Eumenides holding torches, the which
to brandish against your arms. The ferryman of scorched
Acheron[1] is preparing boats innumerable, *and* Tartarus is
expanding for manifold punishments. Hardly with plying
right hand do all the Sisters suffice for the work ; those
who are breaking their threads *quite* weary the Destinies.
While I was thy wife, Magnus, thou didst head the joyous
triumphal processions ; with thy marriage Fortune has
changed ;   and   ever   condemned   by   fate   to   drag   her
mighty husbands to ruin, lo ! my funereal pile *still* warm,
the supplanter Cornelia[2] has married *thee.*

  " Let her, in war and upon the deep, adhere to thy
standards, so long as it is allowed me to break thy slumbers
not secure from care, and let no time be left at leisure for
your love, but both let Cæsar occupy thy days and Julia thy
nights[3]. Me, husband, not the obliviousness of the Lethæan
shore has made forgetful of thyself, and the princes of
the dead have allowed me to follow *thee.*   Thou waging
the warfare, I will come into the midst of the ranks.
Never, Magnus, by the Shades and by my ghost shall
it be allowed thee not to have been his son-in-law. In
vain dost thou sever thy ties with the sword, the civic
warfare shall make thee mine." Thus having said, the
ghost, gliding away through the embrace of her trembling husband, fled.

---

  [1] *The ferryman of scorched Acheron*) ver. 17. Charon, the ferryman of hell.
  [2] *The supplanter Cornelia*) ver 23. Cornelia was the daughter of P. Cornelius Scipio, sometimes called Q. Cæcilius Metellus Scipio on account of his
adoption by Q. Metellus. She was first married to Crassus, the son of the
Triumvir, who perished with his father in the Parthian expedition. In the
next year she was married to Pompey, shortly after the death of his wife
Julia. After the death of Pompey she was pardoned by Cæsar, and returning to Rome, received from him the ashes of her husband, which she preserved on his Alban estate. The usual period of mourning among the Romans for a husband or wife was ten months (see the Fasti of Ovid, B. i.
!. 36), within which space of time it was deemed infamous to marry ; Cornelia, having been married to Pompey very shortly after Julia's death, is consequently here called by the opprobious name of " pellex," " supplanter," or
" paramour."
  [3] *And Julia thy nights*) ver. 27. By haunting his thoughts and his
dreams.

He, although the Deities and the Shades threaten de
struction, rushes the more boldly to arms, with a mind
assured of ill. And, "Why," says he, "are we alarmed
at the phantom of an unsubstantial dream? Either there
is no sense left in the mind after death, or else death itself
is nothing." Now the setting Titan was sinking in the
waves, and had plunged into the deep as much of his fiery
orb as is wont to be wanting to the moon, whether she is
about to be at full, or whether she has just been full;
then did the hospitable land present an easy access to
the ships; they coiled up the ropes, and, the masts laid
down, with oars they made for the shore.

Cæsar, when the winds bore off the ships *thus* escaping,
and the seas had hidden the fleet, and he stood the sole
ruler on the Hesperian shore, no glory in the expulsion of
Magnus caused joy to him; but he complained that the
enemy had turned their backs in safety upon the deep.
Nor, indeed, did any fortune now suffice for the eager
hero; nor was conquest of such value that he should delay
the warfare. Then did he expel from his breast the care
for arms and become intent upon peace, and in what
manner he might conciliate the fickle attachment of the
populace, fully aware that both the causes of anger and the
highest grounds of favour originate in supplies of corn. For
it is famine alone that makes cities free, and respect is
purchased when the powerful are feeding a sluggish multitude. A starving commonalty knows not how to fear[1].

Curio *is* ordered to pass over[2] into the Sicilian cities, where
the sea has either overwhelmed the land with sudden waves or
has cut it asunder and made the mid-land[3] a shore for itself.

[1] *Knows not how to fear*) ver. 58. Being always ready for insurrection.
[2] *Ordered to pass over*) ver. 59. The movements of Cæsar at this con-
juncture are thus related by himself in the Civil War, B. i. c. 30:—"Therefore, for the present, he relinquished all intention of pursuing Pompey, and
resolved to march to Spain, and commanded the magistrates of the free
towns to procure him ships, and to have them conveyed to Brundisium. He
detached Valerius, his lieutenant, with one legion to Sardinia; Curio, the
Proprætor, to Sicily with three legions; and ordered him, when he had
recovered Sicily, immediately to transport his army to Africa." The object of
Cæsar was, as Lucan states, to procure supplies of corn from Sardinia and
Sicily, two of the great granaries of Rome.
[3] *Made the mid-land*) ver. 61. Has made that which was the middle of a

There, is a vast conflict of the main, and the waves are
ever struggling, that the mountains, burst asunder, may
not reunite their utmost verges.   The war, too[1], is extended
even to the Sardinian coasts.   Each island is famous for its
corn-bearing fields ; nor more do any lands fill Hesperia with
harvests brought from afar, nor to a greater extent *supply*
the Roman granaries.   Hardly in fertility of soil does it
excel them, when, the south winds pausing[2], Boreas sweeping the clouds downwards to a southern clime, Libya
bears a plenteous year from the falling showers.

When these things had been provided for by the chieftain, then, victorious, he repaired to the abodes of his
country, not bringing *with him* bands of armed men,
but having the aspect of peace.   Oh! if he had returned to the City, the nations of the Gauls and the
North only subdued, what a long line of exploits might
he have paraded before him in the lengthened procession
of triumph[3], what representations of the warfare!   How
might he have placed chains upon the Rhine and upon
the ocean!   How high-spirited Gaul would have followed
his lofty chariot, and mingled with the yellow-haired
Britons!   Alas! by conquering still more what a triumph
was it[4] that he lost!   Not with joyous crowds did the
cities see him as he went along, but silent they beheld
him with alarm.   Nowhere was there the multitude coming
forth to meet the chieftain.   Still, he rejoiced that he was
held in such dread by the people, and he would prefer
himself not to be loved.

And now, too, he has passed over the steep heights of

continent into sea-shore.   He has mentioned in the Second Book the
belief that Sicily once joined the continent of Italy.

[1] *The war, too*) ver. 64.   Weise thinks that " bella" does not here literally
mean war, but " ships of war," sent for the purpose of collecting corn in the
isle of Sardinia.   See the Note to l. 59.

[2] *The south winds pausing*) ver. 68.   The " Austri," or south winds of
Africa, brought dry weather and kept away the fertilizing showers.

[3] *In the lengthened procession of triumph*) ver. 75.   Lucan, in his zeal,
overlooks the fact that a refusal to allow Cæsar to do this, or, in other
words, to have a triumph for his Gallic wars, was one of the main causes
which led him to engage in the Civil War.

[4] *What a triumph was it*) ver. 79.   No triumphs were permitted for conquests in civil warfare.

Anxur[1], and where the watery way divides the Pontine marshes. Where, *too*, is the lofty grove, where the realms of Scythian Diana[2]; and where there is the road for the Latian fasces[3] to lofty Alba. Afar from a lofty rock he now views the City, not beheld *by him* during the whole period of his northern wars; and, thus speaking, he admires the walls of his Rome:—

" And have there been men, forced by no warfare, to desert thee, the abode of the Gods! For what city will they fight? The Gods have proved more favouring in that it is no Eastern fury that now presses upon the Latian shores, nor yet the swift Sarmatian in common with the Pannonian, and the Getans mingled with the Dacians. Fortune, Rome, has spared thee, having a chief so cowardly[4], in that the warfare was a civil one."

Thus he speaks, and he enters Rome stupefied with terror; for he is supposed to be about to overthrow the walls of Rome as though captured, with dusky fires, and to scatter abroad the Gods. This is the extent of their fear; they think that he is ready *to do* whatever he is able. No festive omens *are there.* no pretending feigned applause with joyous uproar; hardly is there time to hate. The throng

---

[1] *Steep heights of Anxur*) ver. 84. Anxur, which was the former name of Terracina, was an ancient town of Latium, situate 58 miles to the south-east of Rome, on the Appian Way, and upon the coast; it had a citadel on a high hill, on which stood the Temple of Jupiter Anxurus.

[2] *Realms of Scythian Diana*) ver. 86. He alludes to the town of Aricia at the foot of the Alban Mount, on the Appian Way, about 16 miles from Rome. In its vicinity was a celebrated grove and temple of Diana Aricina, on the borders of the Lacus Nemorensis. Diana was worshipped here in a barbarous manner. Her priest, who was called " Rex nemorensis," was always a runaway slave, who obtained his office by slaying his predecessor, and he was obliged to fight with any slave who succeeded in breaking off a branch of a certain tree in the sacred grove. The worship of Diana was said to have been introduced here from the Tauric Chersonesus by Orestes and his sister Iphigenia, when flying from the cruelty of king Thoas. See the story related in the Pontic Epistles of Ovid, B. iii. Ep. 2.

[3] *Road for the Latian fasces*) ver. 87. He alludes to the " Latinæ Feriæ," which were celebrated by the Roman Consuls on the Alban Mount. See the First Book, l. 550, and the Note to the passage.

[4] *Having a chief so cowardly*) ver. 96. A chief so timid as Pompey has proved himself by his flight.

of Senators fills the Palatine halls of Phœbus[1] drawn forth
from their concealment, by no right of convoking the Senate.
The sacred seats are not graced with the Consul, no Prætor is there, the next power according to law; and the
empty curule seats[2] have been removed from their places.
Cæsar is everything. The Senate is present, witness to
the words of a private person. The Fathers sit, prepared to
give their sanction, whether he shall demand a kingdom,
whether a Temple for himself. the throats, too, of the
Senate, and their exile.

Fortunate *was it* that he blushed at commanding, more
than Rome *did* at obeying. Still, liberty, making the ex-
periment in one man whether the laws can possibly withstand force, gives rise to anger; and the resisting Metellus[3],

[1] *Palatine halls of Phœbus*) ver. 103. On arriving at Rome Cæsar convoked the Senate—not in the Senate-house, but in the Temple of Apollo, on
the Palatine hill.

[2] *The empty curule seats*) ver. 107. The curule seats were graced
by neither the Consuls nor the Prætors, as they were in arms with Pompey. In the account of the Civil War, B. i. c. 32, Cæsar relates what he
said on this occasion. He excused the war which he had undertaken as
he was compelled in his own defence to protect himself against the malice
and envy of a few, and at the same time requested that they would send
messengers to Pompey and the Consuls to propose a treaty for adjusting
the present differences. This proposition of Cæsar is suppressed by Lucan,
who throughout endeavours to place Cæsar's conduct in the most invidious
light. Cæsar tells us, c. 33, "The Senate approved of sending deputies, but
none could be found fit to execute the commission; for every person by reason
of his own private fears declined the office. For Pompey, on leaving the
city, had declared in the open Senate, that he would hold in the same degree
of estimation those who stayed in Rome and those in Cæsar's camp. Thus
three days were wasted in disputes and excuses. Besides, Lucius Metellus,
one of the Tribunes, was suborned by Cæsar's enemies, to prevent this, and
to embarrass everything else which Cæsar should propose."

[3] *The resisting Metellus*) ver. 114. This was L. Cæcilius Metellus Creticus, the Tribune of the people, and one of the adherents of Pompey. Remaining behind in the City on the approach of Cæsar, he did not fly with
Pompey and the rest of his party. The public treasury of Rome was in the
Temple of Saturn, in which Appian states that there was a large sum of
money especially deposited as a tund to defray the expenses of any war that
might arise from the Gauls invading the Roman territory. Cæsar laid hands
on this, alleging that as he had conquered the Gauls there was no longer any
use for it. Metellus attempted to prevent him, but he drew his sword in an
attitude of menace, saying, "Young man, it is as easy to do this as to say
it." It is supposed that this was the same Metellus who fought on the side

when he beholds the Temple of Saturn being forced open
by vast efforts, hurries his steps, and bursting through the
troops of Cæsar, takes his stand before the doors of the
Temple not yet opened. (To such a degree does the love
of gold alone know not how to fear the sword and death.
Swept away, the laws perish with no contest; but thou,
pelf, the most worthless portion of things, dost excite the
contest;) and, forbidding the conqueror the plunder, the
Tribune with loud voice addresses *him* :

" Only through my sides shall the Temple struck by thee
be opened, and, plunderer, thou shalt carry off no scattered
wealth except by *shedding* sacred blood. Surely this violated
power will find the Gods *its avengers.* The Tribune's curse,
too[1], following Crassus to the warfare, prayed for the direful
battles. Now unsheathe the sword; for the multitude is
not to be regarded by thee, the spectator of thy crimes: in
a deserted City do we stand. No soldier accursed shall
bear off his reward from our *Treasury;* nations there are for
thee to overthrow, walls for thee to grant. Want does not
drive thee to the spoils of exhausted peace; Cæsar, thou
hast a war of thy own."[2]

The victor, aroused by these words to extreme anger,
exclaims, " Thou dost conceive vain hopes of a glorious
death: my hand, Metellus, shall not pollute itself with that
throat *of thine.* No honor shall make thee deserving of the
resentment of Cæsar. Has liberty been left safe, thee its
assertor? Not to that degree has length of time confounded the highest with the lowest, that the laws, if
they are to be preserved by the voice of Metellus, would
not prefer by Cæsar to be uprooted."

of Antony against Augustus, and on being taken prisoner was pardoned at
the intercession of his son, who had sided with Augustus.

[1] *The Tribune's curse, too*) ver. 127. C. Ateius Capito and Aquillius Gallus,
the Tribunes of the people, were the opponents of Pompey and Crassus when
Consuls. They endeavoured to stop the levy of troops and to render the campaigns which they wished to undertake impossible; Crassus, however, continuing to make preparation for an expedition against the Parthians. Capito
uttered curses against him, and announced the appearance of dreadful prodigies, which were disregarded by Crassus. The overthrow and death of
Crassus were by many looked upon as the result of his disregard of the
warnings of Capito.

[2] *A war of thy own*) ver. 133. You have the war in Gaul, in which you
may gain sufficient spoil.

He spoke, and, the Tribune not yet retreating from the
door, his anger became more intense; he looked around
upon the ruthless swords, forgetful to pretend that there was
peace [1]. Then did Cotta [2] persuade Metellus to desist from
his too audacious purpose. "The liberty of a people," said
he, "which a tyrant's sway is ruling, perishes through
excess of liberty; of it thou mayst preserve the shadow, if
thou art ready *to do* whatever thou art commanded. To
so many unjust things have we, conquered, submitted; this
is the sole excuse for our shame and our degenerate fears,
that nothing can possibly now be dared. Quickly let him
carry off the evil incentives to direful warfare. Injuries
move the people, if any there are, whom their laws protect. Not to ourselves, but to our tyrant, is the poverty
dangerous that acts the slave."

Forthwith, Metellus led away, the Temple was opened
wide. Then did the Tarpeian rock re-echo, and with a loud
peal attest that the doors were opened; then, stowed away
in the lower part of the Temple, was dragged up, untouched for many a year, the wealth of the Roman people,
which the Punic wars [3], which Perseus [4], which the booty of
the conquered Philip [5], had supplied; that which, Rome,
Pyrrhus left to thee in his hurrying flight, the gold for

[1] *That there was peace*) ver. 143. "Togam;" literally, the "toga" or
gown, worn by citizens in the time of peace, and consequently employed as
the emblem of peace.

[2] *Then did Cotta*) ver. 143. This was L. Aurelius Cotta, a relative of
Aurelia, the mother of Cæsar, to whose party he belonged in the Civil War.
He had been Consul, Prætor, and Censor, and was an intimate friend of Cicero,
by whom he is much praised as a man of great talent and extreme prudence.
Lucan is probably in error in representing him as unwillingly submitting to
Cæsar.

[3] *Which the Punic wars*) ver. 157. At the end of the first Punic war the
Carthaginians were obliged to pay 1200 talents, and of the second 10,000.

[4] *Which Perseus*) ver. 158. Perses, or Perseus, the last king of Macedon, was conquered by Paulus Æmilius, B.C. 168. The booty was of immense value, and was paid into the Roman treasury, much to the chagrin of
the soldiers, who were so indignant at their small share of the plunder, that
it was not without much opposition that Æmilius obtained his triumph.

[5] *Of the conquered Philip*) ver. 158. Philip the Fifth, king of Macedon,
was conquered by Quintus Flamininus, who acquired a large amount of
booty, and celebrated a magnificent triumph which lasted three days. Philip
was the father of Perseus.

which Fabricius did not sell himself[1] to the king, whatever you saved, manners of our thrifty forefathers; that which, as tribute, the wealthy nations of Asia[2] had sent, and Minoïan Crete[3] had paid to the conqueror Metellus; that, too, which Cato brought from Cyprus[4] over distant seas. Besides, the wealth of the East, and the remote treasures of captive kings, which were borne before *him* in the triumphal processions of Pompey[5], were carried forth; the Temple was spoiled with direful rapine; and then for the first time was Rome poorer than Cæsar[6].

In the meantime the fortune of Magnus throughout the whole earth has aroused to battle the cities destined to fall with him. Greece near at hand affords forces for the neighbouring war. Amphissa sends[7] Phocian bands, the rocky Cirrha[8] too, and Parnassus deserted on either mountain ridge. The Bœotian leaders assemble, whom the swift Cephisus[9] surrounds with its fate-foretelling

[1] *Fabricius did not sell himself*) ver. 160. He alludes to the vain attempt made by Pyrrhus, king of Epirus, when he invaded Italy, to bribe C. Fabricius Luscinus. The money, according to Lucan, being left behind, was put in the public treasury.

[2] *The wealthy nations of Asia*) ver. 162. He probably alludes to treasures acquired from Antiochus, king of Syria, and Attalus, king of Pergamus, the latter of whom made the Roman people his heirs.

[3] *And Minoïan Crete*) ver. 163. Crete, formerly the kingdom of Minos, was subdued by Q. Metellus Creticus.

[4] *Cato brought from Cyprus*) ver. 164. The island of Cyprus was made a Roman province in the year B.C. 58, and M. Porcius Cato was sent to reduce it to submission. The money which he had collected there was put in the public treasury, and afterwards fell into Cæsar's hands. It was said to have amounted to 7000 talents.

[5] *Triumphal processions of Pompey*) ver. 166. Those which he had gained from Mithridates, king of Pontus, Tigranes, king of Armenia, and Aristobulus, king of Judæa.

[6] *Poorer than Cæsar*) ver. 168. Cæsar, in consequence of the large sums which he had expended in promoting his interests, was now greatly in debt.

[7] *Amphissa sends*) ver. 172. Amphissa, now Salona, was one of the chief towns of the Ozolian Locrians, on the borders of Phocis, seven miles from Delphi.

[8] *The rocky Cirrha*) ver. 172. Cirrha was a town of Phocis, a country of Greece between Ætolia and Bœotia, in which was the mountain of Parnassus, the fountain of Hippocrene and Helicon, and the city of Delphi.

[9] *The swift Cephisus*) ver. 175. The Cephisus here alluded to was the chief river of Bœotia and Phocis, rising near Lilæa in the latter country.

F

waters.   Cadmean Dirce, too[1], and the bands of Pisæ[2].
and the Alpheus[3] that sends beneath the main its waters to
the peoples of Sicily.   Then does the Arcadian leave
Mænalus[4], and the Trachynian soldier Herculean Œta[5]
The Thesprotians[6] and the Dryopians[7] rush on, and the
ancient Sellæ[8] forsake the silent oaks on the Chaonian
heights.   Although the levy has exhausted[9] the whole of
Athens, three little barks keep possession of the Phœbean

and falling into the lake Copais. Its waters are called "fatidica" from its
rising in Phocis, in which was situate Delphi, the oracle of Apollo.

[1] *Cadmean Dirce, too*) ver. 175.   Dirce was a fountain near Thebes, which
city was founded by Cadmus, the son of Agenor, king of Phœnicia.

[2] *The bands of Pisæ*) ver. 176.   Pisa was a city of Elis, near which the
Olympic games were celebrated.

[3] *And the Alpheus*) ver. 177.   The Alpheus was a river of Arcadia, famed
in story for his love for Arethusa, a water nymph of Sicily, and fabled to
have passed under the earth from Greece to Sicily.   See the story related in
the Metamorphoses of Ovid, B. v. l. 487 and 576, *et seq.*

[4] *Leave Mænalus*) ver. 177.   Mænalus was the name of a mountain
and a wood in Arcadia, in the Peloponnesus, sacred to Pan.

[5] *Herculean Œta*) ver. 178.   Œta was the name given to a pile of mountains in the south of Thessaly.   It was on one of these, that, according to
ancient mythology, Hercules put himself to death, by burning on his funeral
pile.   See the Metamorphoses of Ovid, Book x.   Trachyn was also called
Heraclea, and was celebrated as having been for a time the residence of
Hercules.   It was a town of Thessaly, situate in the district Malis.   There
was another of the same name in Phocis.

[6] *The Thesprotians*) ver. 179.   The Thesproti were a people on the coast
of Epirus.   They were said to have been the most ancient race, and to have
derived their name from Thesprotus, the son of Lycaon.

[7] *And the Dryopians*) ver. 179.   The Dryopes dwelt first in Thessaly,
and afterwards in Doris.   Being driven thence by the Dorians, they migrated
to other countries, and settled in Peloponnesus, Eubœa, and Asia Minor.

[8] *And the ancient Sella*) ver. 180.   The Sellæ were probably a people of
Chaonia, in the neighbourhood of Dodona.   The priests of the Temple of
Jupiter there were called Selli or Helli.   The will of the Divinity was said
to be declared by the wind rustling through the oaks; and in order to render
the sounds more distinct, brazen vessels were suspended on the branches of
the trees, which, being set in motion by the wind, came in contact with one
another.   The oracle, as mentioned by Lucan, had now been long extinct,
for in the year B.C. 219 the Temple was destroyed by the Ætolians, and the
sacred oaks cut down.

[9] *The levy has exhausted*) ver. 181.   This passage has greatly puzzled
the commentators, but the sense is pretty evidently that suggested by Cortius: "Although it was but a levy, still it exhausted the resources of
Athens, which was now weak, and but thinly inhabited."

dockyards[1], and demand Salamis to be believed as true[2].
Now, beloved by Jove[3], ancient Crete with its hundred
peoples resorts to arms, both Gnossus skilled[4] at wielding
the quiver, and Gortyna not inferior to the arrows of the
East[5].

Then, too, he who possesses Dardanian Oricum[6], and
the wandering Athamanians[7] dispersed amid the towering
woods, and the Enchelians[8] with their ancient name, who
witnessed the end of the transformed Cadmus, the Colchian

[1] *Phœbean dockyards*) ver. 182. The dockyards of Athens are probably
called "Phœbea" from the circumstance of Minerva, the tutelar Divinity of
Athens, having dedicated the Piræus to Apollo, as she did the Areopagus or
Hill of Justice to Mars.

[2] *Salamis to be believed as true*) ver. 183. The levy has so weakened
Athens, that there are only three ships of war left in the harbour, to ask
you to believe that this is the maritime state which once vanquished the Persians at the battle of Salamis. These three ships of war may probably have
been those which were used for sacred or state purposes, namely, the Theoris,
which performed a yearly voyage to Delos ; the Paralos, which, according to
the Scholiast on Aristophanes, was sent to Delphi or other places on sacred
missions ; and the Salaminia, which, according to Plutarch, was used for the
conveyance of those summoned from abroad for trial.

[3] *Now, beloved by Jove*) ver. 184. Crete was said to have been the birth-
place of Jupiter, and, according to some accounts, he was *buried* there.
Minos, its first king and lawgiver, was the son of Jupiter by Europa.

[4] *Both Gnossus skilled*) ver. 185. Gnossus and Gortyna were two of the
famed hundred cities of Crete. Its inhabitants were noted for their skill in
archery.

[5] *To the arrows of the East*) ver. 186. By the word "Eoïs" he refers to
the Parthians, who were remarkable for their expertness in the use of the
bow, even on horseback.

[6] *Dardanian Oricum*) ver. 187. Oricum or Oricus was a Greek town on
the coast of Illyria, near the Ceraunian Mountains and the frontiers of Epirus.
According to the tradition here followed in the use of the word "Darda-
nium," it was founded by Helenus, the son of Priam, who had then become
the husband of Andromache. Another account was that it was founded by
the Eubœans, who were cast here by a storm on their return from Troy ; while
a third legend stated that it was a Colchian colony.

[7] *The wandering Athamanians*) ver. 188. By the use of the word
"Athamas," he means the "Athamanes," a race living on the mountains of
Epirus.

[8] *And the Enchelians*) ver. 189. The Encheliæ were a people of Illyria,
into whose country Cadmus and his wife Harmonia retiring, were changed
into snakes or dragons. Lucan says that they received their name from this
circumstance : ἐγχέλυς being the Greek name for a kind of serpent. See
Ovid's Metamorphoses, B. iv. l. 563, *et seq.*

Absyrtis, too[1], that foams down to the Adriatic tide, and
those who cultivate the fields of Peneus[2], and by whose
labours the Thessalian ploughshare cleaves Hæmonian
Iolcos. From that spot for the first time was the sea attempted when the untaught Argo[3] mingled unknown races
upon a polluted sea-shore[4], and first committed the mortal
race to the winds and the raging waves of the ocean,
and through that bark one *more* death was added to the
destinies *of man.* Then Thracian Hæmus is deserted, and
Pholoë that feigned[5] the two-formed race. Strymon is
abandoned[6], accustomed to send the Bistonian birds to the
warm Nile, and the barbarian Cone[7], where one mouth of
the Ister, divided into many parts, loses the Sarmatian
waves, and washes Peuce sprinkled by the main; Mysia,
too[8], and the Idalian land bedewed by the cold Caïcus[9], and

[1] *The Colchian Absyrtis, too)* ver. 190. He alludes to the two islands off
the coast of Illyria called Absyrtides, where the Colchian Medea was said
to have slain her brother Absyrtus. It was, however, more generally believed
that this took place at Tomi, whither Ovid was banished, on the shores of
the Pontus Euxinus. The Absyrtis was probably a river at the mouth of
which these islands were situate.

[2] *The fields of Peneus)* ver. 191. The Peneus was a river of Thessaly,
of which Iolcos was a seaport, from which the Argonauts set sail for Colchis
in the ship Argo.

[3] *The untaught Argo)* ver. 193. The Argo was said to have been the
first ship launched on the sea by mankind.

[4] *A polluted sea-shore)* ver. 194. The shore might be considered polluted
or guilty, by reason of Medea's undutiful conduct to her father and her other
iniquities. In navigating the Argo, mankind for the first time incurred the
peril of shipwreck.

[5] *And Pholoë that feigned)* ver. 198. This was a mountain forming the
boundary between Arcadia and Elis. It was famed as having been one
of the abodes of the Centaurs.

[6] *Strymon is abandoned)* ver. 199. The Strymon was a river of Thrace,
whose banks were frequented by large flocks of cranes, which were said to
migrate to Egypt in the winter season.

[7] *And the barbarian Cone)* ver. 200. Cone was an island at the mouth
of the Ister or Danube. Peuce was also an island of Mœsia, formed by
the two southern mouths of the Danube. It was inhabited by the Peucini,
a tribe of the Bastarnæ. Lucan speaks here of its being washed by only
one mouth of the Danube.

[8] *Mysia, too)* ver. 203. Mysia was an extensive district of Asia Minor,
in which Troy was situate.

[9] *By the cold Caïcus)* ver. 203. The Caïcus was a river of Mysia
that flowed past Troy and the foot of Mount Ida.

Arisbe[1] very barren in its soil. Those, too, who inhabit
Pitane[2], and Celænæ[3], which, Pallas, condemned when
Phœbus was victor, laments thy gifts. Where, too, the swift
Marsyas[4] descending with his straight banks approaches the
wandering Mæander, and, mingling, is borne back again;
the land, too, that permits the Pactolus[5] to flow forth from
its gold-bearing mines, not less invaluable than which the
Hermus divides[6] the fields. The bands of Ilium, too, with
omens their own[7], seek the standards and the camp doomed
to fall; nor does the story of Troy restrain them, and Cæsar
declaring himself[8] the descendant of Phrygian Iulus.

The nations of Syria came; the deserted Orontes[9], and
Ninos *so* wealthy[10] (as the story is), and windy Damascus[11],

[1] *And Arisbe*) ver. 204. Arisbe was a small town situate in the Troad.

[2] *Who inhabit Pitane*) ver. 205. Pitane was a seaport town of Mysia,
on the shores of the Elaitic gulf, at the mouth of the Evenus, or, according
to some, of the Caïcus. It was the birth-place of the Academic philosopher
Arcesilaüs.

[3] *And Celænæ*) ver. 206. Celænæ was a great city of southern Phrygia, which lay at the sources of the rivers Mæander and Marsyas. Near the
source of the latter river there was a grotto which was said to have been
the scene of the punishment of Marsyas by Apollo. After he had been
flayed alive, his skin was hung up in the town of Celænæ. The story of the
musical contest between Apollo and Marsyas is told in Ovid's Metamorphoses,
B. vi. l. 383.

[4] *The swift Marsyas*) ver. 207. This river was said to have been formed
by the tears which were shed by the rural Deities in sympathy for the
tragical death of Marsyas.

[5] *Permits the Pactolus*) ver. 209. The Pactolus was a river of Lydia in
Asia Minor, said to have golden sands. The word "passa," "allowing" or
"permitting," is used, inasmuch as flowing forth from the mines it would tend
to waste the precious metal.

[6] *The Hermus divides*) ver. 210. The Hermus was another river of
Lydia, which was also said to have golden sands.

[7] *With omens their own*) ver. 212. "Ominibus suis;" meaning "with their
usual ill-luck," that of being conquered, whenever they had recourse to arms.

[8] *Cæsar declaring himself*) ver. 213. Julius Cæsar boasted of being
descended from Iulus or Ascanius, the son of Æneas, through the kings of
Alba Longa.

[9] *The deserted Orontes*) ver. 214. He means the country about the river
Orontes, which flowed past Antioch in Syria.

[10] *And Ninos so wealthy*) ver. 215. Ninus or Nineveh, according to
Scripture, was founded by Nimrod. According to profane historians, it was
founded by Ninus, the husband of Semiramis.

[11] *The windy Damascus*) ver. 215. Damascus in Cœle-Syria is probably

and Gaza[1], and Idumæa[2] rich in its groves of palms. Unstable Tyre as well[3], and Sidon precious with its purple dye. These ships did the Cynosure conduct[4] to the warfare by no winding track along the sea, more certain for no other barks. The Phœnicians first, if belief is given to report, ventured to represent in rude characters the voice destined to endure. Not yet had Memphis learned to unite[5] the rushes of the stream; and only animals engraved upon stones, both birds and wild beasts, kept in existence the magic tongues[6]. The forest, too, of Taurus is

called "ventosa" from the circumstance of its being situate on a plain and exposed to the winds. Notwithstanding this epithet, its situation is considered one of the finest in the globe.

[1] *And Gaza*) ver. 216. There were two cities of the name of Gaza. One was the strongly-fortified city of the Philistines, so called, on the sea-coast, while the other was a city in the Persian province of Sogdiana.

[2] *And Idumæa*) ver. 216. Idumæa in the later Jewish history and the Roman annals means the southern part of Judea and a small part of the northern part of Arabia Petræa, extending beyond the ancient Edom of Scripture.

[3] *Unstable Tyre as well*) ver. 217. The famous city of Tyre was on the sea-coast of Syria: at this period it had considerably fallen from its opulence. According to some, it is called "instabilis" from its liability to earthquakes, while others would have the word to mean "fickle" or "deceitful." Virgil speaks in the First Book of the Æneid of the "Tyrii bilingues," "the double-tongued Tyrians." Sidon was the neighbour of Tyre, and the rival of its commercial enterprise and opulence. These cities were famed for the production of the "murex" or purple dye extracted from the shell-fish so called, which was extremely valuable.

[4] *Did the Cynosure conduct*) ver. 219. The Constellation of the Lesser Bear was called Cynosura from Κυνὸς οὐρὰ "the Dog's tail," the stars in their sequence being fancifully thought to resemble that object. According, however, to another account, Cynosura was the name of a nymph who nursed Jupiter on Mount Ida, and for that service was raised to the stars. The Phœnicians of Tyre and Sidon, in navigating the ocean, took their observations from this Constellation, while the Greeks for that purpose used Helice or the Greater Bear. See the Fasti of Ovid, B. iii. l. 107, *et seq.*

[5] *Memphis learned to unite*) ver. 222. He means that the Phœnicians were the inventors of the art of writing, before it was known to the Egyptians, who had not then discovered the art of making paper from the byblus or papyrus, and only knew the use of hieroglyphics, which they carved on stone.

[6] *Kept in existence the magic tongues*) ver. 224. By "magicas linguas" he probably means the secrets known to the priesthood of Egypt, who professed to be skilled in the magic art.

deserted, and Persean Tarsus[1], and the Corycian cave[2] opening with its rocks worn away. Mallus[3] and remote Ægæ[4] resound with their dockyards, and the Cilician ship[5] goes forth obedient to the law, no longer a pirate now.

The rumour, too, of the warfare has moved the corners of the East, where Ganges is worshipped, who alone through out all the world dares to discharge himself by a mouth opposite[6] to the rising sun, and impels his waves towards the opposing eastern winds; here *it was* that the chieftain from Pella[7], *arriving* beyond the seas of Tethys, stopped short, and confessed that he was conquered by the vast earth. Where, too, Indus carrying along his rapid stream with di vided flood is not sensible of the Hydaspes mingling[8] with his waters. Those also, who drink the sweet juices[9] from the

[1] *And Persean Tarsus*) ver. 225. Tarsus was a very ancient city of Syria. According to the tradition here alluded to, it was founded by Perseus, the son of Jupiter and Danaë, and was said to have been so called from the Greek ταρσός, "a hoof," which the winged horse Pegasus was said to have lost there. Other accounts ascribe its foundation to the Assyrian king Sardanapalus. It was the birth-place of St. Paul.

[2] *And the Corycian cave*) ver. 226. Corycus was a city of Cilicia. About two miles from it there was a cave or glen in the mountains, called the "Corycian cave," celebrated by the Poets, and famous for its saffron. There was another Corycian cave in Mount Parnassus, also famed as a retreat of the Muses.

[3] *Mallus*) ver. 227. Mallus was an ancient city of Cilicia, said to have been founded at the time of the Trojan war by Mopsus and Amphilochus.

[4] *And remote Ægæ*) ver. 227. Ægæ was a seaport town of Cilicia. There were also towns of the same name in Achaia, Macedonia, Eubœa, and Æolia.

[5] *And the Cilician ship*) ver. 228. The Cilician pirates, in return for the clemency they had experienced from Pompey when conquered by him, espoused his cause against Cæsar.

[6] *By a mouth opposite*) ver. 230. He probably means that the Ganges was the only river that discharged itself into the Eastern Ocean, whence the sun was supposed to rise. This river is still an object of worship by those who live upon its banks.

[7] *The chieftain from Pella*) ver. 233. He alludes to Alexander the Great, who was born at Pella in Macedonia, and who paused in his conquests at the Eastern Ocean. The remark is intended as a reproach against his inordinate ambition in wishing that there was another world for him to conquer.

[8] *The Hydaspes mingling*) ver. 236. The Hydaspes, now called the Jelum, was the most northerly of the five great tributaries of the Indus. This river formed the limit of Alexander's progress in Asia.

[9] *Drink the sweet juices*) ver. 237. Salmasius, rather perversely, thinks

tender cane, and those, who, tinting their hair[1] with the
yellow drug, bind their flowing linen garments[2] with coloured
gems. Those also, who build up their own funereal pyres,
and, alive, ascend the heated piles[3]. Oh! how great a glory
is it to this race to hasten their fate by their own hands,
and, full of life, to present to the Deities what still remains!
The fierce Cappadocians come; the people, now inhabitants of the hardy Amanus[4], and the Armenian who
possesses the Niphates[5] that rolls down rocks; the Coatræ[6]
have quitted the woods that touch the skies. You, Arabians,
have come into a world to you unknown, wondering how
the shadows of the groves do not fall on the left hand[7].

that reference is here made to the manna or aerial honey of the Arabians;
whereas Vossius and most others agree that it refers to the extraction of
sugar from the sugar-cane by the natives of India. Arrian, in his Periplus
of the Erythræan Sea, speaks of the Indians as drinking honey from canes,
called 'sacchari,' clearly alluding to sugar.

[1] Tinting their hair) ver. 238. He speaks of the tribes of India as not
only using dyes for staining their hair of a golden hue, but using girdles or
zones decked with precious stones of various colours.

[2] Flowing linen garments) ver. 239. Under the name "carbasa" he
probably alludes to fine textures of cotton or linen, or perhaps silk, used
by the natives of India.

[3] Alive, ascend the heated piles) ver. 240. He alludes to the Brahmins
and their ceremony of Suttee or burning alive. Calanus, who is called by
the Greek writers one of the Gymnosophists of India, was one of this class,
and burnt himself on a pyre in the presence of the whole Macedonian army.

[4] Of the hardy Amanus) ver. 244. Amanus was a mountain of Cilicia.
He probably speaks of the natives of Cilicia, being now the "cultores," "inhabitants" or "tillers" of the land, in contradistinction to their former roving
and piratical habits.

[5] Possesses the Niphates) ver. 245. Niphates was a mountain chain of
Armenia, forming a prolongation of the Taurus from where it is crossed by
the Euphrates.

[6] The Coatræ) ver. 246. The Coatræ were a nation living in the mountains, probably between Assyria and Media. Virgil, in the Georgics, B. ii.
l. 124, speaks of the height of their trees as such that no arrow could
pass over them.

[7] Do not fall on the left hand) ver. 248. That is to say, on the left
hand or southward, if they stood facing the west. Under the name
"Arabes" he intends to include the Æthiopians and other nations living on
or near to the Equator. He probably alludes to the story told by Pliny in
his Natural History, B. vi. l. 22, relative to the inhabitants of Taprobana or Ceylon. Their ambassadors, who came to Rome to pay homage to
Claudius, were especially surprised to see their shadows fall northward, and
not towards the south, as in their own country.

Then did the Roman frenzy influence the extreme Oretæ [1], and the Caramanian chieftains [2], whose sky declining towards the south [3], beholds Arctus set, but not the whole of it; and there the swiftly-moving Boötes shines but a small part of the night. The region, too, of the Æthiopians, which would not be overhung by any portion of the sky that bears the Constellations [4], did not, his knee inclining downward, the extremity of the hoof of the bending Bull extend beyond *the Zodiac*. And where with the rapid Tigris [5] the vast Euphrates takes his rise, *streams* which Persia sends forth from no different sources; and it is uncertain, if the earth were to mix the rivers, which name in preference there would be for the waters. But, spreading over the fields the fertile Euphrates performs the part of [6] the Pharian waves; while the earth with a sudden chasm sucks up the Tigris [7], and

[1] *The extreme Oretæ*) ver. 249. The Oritæ, Oretæ, or Oræ, were a people of Gedrosia who inhabited the coast of a part of India now called Urboo in Beloochistan.

[2] *Caramanian chieftains*) ver. 250. The Caramanians inhabited the modern Kirman, a province of the ancient Persian empire, bounded on the south by the Indian Ocean.

[3] *Declining towards the south*) ver. 250. He means that the elevation of the North Pole is so very small in those regions that those Constellations which never set with us, appear there but very little above the horizon.

[4] *Sky that bears the Constellations*) ver. 254. By "signiferi poli" he means the Zodiac, and intends to say that Æthiopia lies beyond that part of the earth which is beneath the Zodiac, except that the hoof of the Constellation Taurus projects over it.

[5] *With the rapid Tigris*) ver. 256. Though they do not rise in the same spot, both the Euphrates and the Tigris rise in the mountains of Armenia; and opposite the city of Seleucia they come within 200 stadia, or about 20 miles, of each other. They then recede from each other, and unite about 60 miles above the mouth of the Persian Gulf. The Poet means to say that they are both such mighty streams, and so nearly equal in size, that if they were united it would be difficult to say which, as the smaller, would lose its name in the larger. We may here remark that Lucan is frequently very incorrect in his geographical descriptions.

[6] *Performs the part of*) ver. 260. He means that the Euphrates, by overflowing, like the Nile, fertilizes the country through which it passes.

[7] *Sucks up the Tigris*) ver. 261. Seneca and some others of the ancient writers mention that the Tigris disappears in its course, and then reappears in all its magnitude. It sinks under one of the mountains of the Taurus chain, and, having traversed underground 25 miles, reappears. One of the Scholiasts has in his commentary on this line preserved three lines composed by the Emperor Nero on the Tigris. As they are nowhere else to be found, they deserve to be quoted :—

conceals] is hidden course, and does not exclude the river born again from a new source from the waters of the sea.

Between the ranks of Cæsar and the opposing standards the warlike Parthians held a neutral ground, content that they had made them *but* two[1]. The wandering tribes of Scythia dipped their arrows, whom Bactros[2] encircles with its icy stream, and Hyrcania[3] with its vast forests. On this side the Lacedæmonian Heniochi[4], a nation fierce in wielding the rein, and the Sarmatian, the neighbour of the savage Moschi[5]. Where the Phasis cleaves the most wealthy fields of the Colchians; where *runs* the Halys[6] fatal to Crœsus; where falling from the Rhipæan heights the Tanais has given[7] the names of different parts of the world to its

> " Quique pererratam subductus Persida Tigris
> Deserit, et longo terrarum tractus hiatu,
> Reddit quæsitas jam non quærentibus undas."

" And the Tigris, which, traversing beneath Persia passed through, forsakes it, and, travelling in prolonged chasms of the earth, restores its waters that were sought for to those now seeking them no longer."

[1] *Made them but two*) ver. 266.   Content to have reduced their number to two and thus embroiled the Roman world, by slaying Crassus at Carrhæ; who, while he lived, was the mediator between Cæsar and Pompey.

[2] *Whom Bactros*) ver. 267.   Bactros was the name of the river that flowed by Bactra (now Balkh), the capital of the ancient Bactria, which occupied the locality of the modern Bokhara.   It was conquered by Alexander the Great.   Lucan is hardly correct in representing these tribes as preparing for the war, as they had been conquered by the Parthians, whom he has just described as being neutral.   The Bactrians were a wild and war-like race, and probably used poisoned arrows, as here represented.

[3] *And Hyrcania*) ver. 268.   Hyrcania was a fertile province of the ancient Persian empire.   Like Bactria it was at this time under the Parthian rule, whose kings often resided in it during the summer.

[4] *The Lacedæmonian Heniochi*) ver. 269.   He calls the Heniochi, a people of Colchis, Lacedæmonii, because the colony was said to have been founded by Amphitus and Telchius, Lacedæmonians, the charioteers of Castor and Pollux.   The story probably arose from the fact of the word Heniochi in Greek signifying "charioteers."

[5] *Of the savage Moschi*) ver. 270.   The Moschi were a people of Asia, whose territory was originally in Colchis, but in later times extended into Iberia and Armenia.

[6] *Where runs the Halys*) ver. 272.   The Halys was a river which served as the boundary between Lydia and Media.   It was rendered famous from the oracle given to Crœsus, the wealthy king of Lydia, that, " passing over the Halys, he should overthrow a mighty empire."   This he took to be the kingdom of Media, but the event proved that it was his own, which was conquered by Cyrus.

[7] *The Tanais has given*) ver. 273.   Or the river Don, which was usually

banks, and, the same boundary both of Europe and of Asia, cutting through the confines of the mid part of the earth, now in this direction, now in that, whichever way it turns, enlarges the world[1].

Where, too, the flowing strait pours forth the waves of Mæotis, and the Euxine sea is borne away, a vaunt *wrested* from[2] the limits of Hercules, and denies that Gades alone[3] admits the ocean. In this part the Essedonian nations[4], and thou, Arimaspian[5], tying thy locks bound up with gold; in this the bold Arian, and the Massagetan[6] satisfying the long fast of Sarmatian warfare with the horse on which he flies, and the rapid Geloni[7].

Not, when Cyrus leading forth his forces from the Memnonian realms[8], and with his troops counted by the throwing of their darts, the Persian came down[9], and, when the avenger

considered to be the boundary between Europe and Asia. This river rises in the centre of Russia.

[1] *Enlarges the world*) ver. 276. Where it extends within the Asiatic line it widens Europe as it were, and the same with regard to Asia.

[2] *A vaunt wrested from*) ver. 278. The meaning is that the Pontus Euxinus (now the Black Sea) by its magnitude detracts from the glories of the pillars of Hercules (now Gibraltar) by pouring into the Mediterranean a body of water almost as large.

[3] *That Gades alone*) ver. 279. Gades was founded by the Phœnicians. It occupied the site of the present Cadiz.

[4] *The Essedonian nations*) ver. 280. According to Pliny, the Essedonians were a people of Scythia, near the Palus Mæotis or sea of Azof.

[5] *And thou, Arimaspian*) ver. 281. The Arimaspi were a people of Scythia, who were fabled to have but one eye. They were said to live on the banks of a river of the same name, whose sands produced gold. They had also gold-mines, said to be watched by griffins.

[6] *And the Massagetan*) ver. 283. The Massagetæ were said to be in the habit, when overtaken by hunger, of opening veins in the bodies of their horses and sucking the blood.

[7] *And the rapid Geloni*) ver. 283. The Geloni were a people of Scythia who dwelt in Asiatic Sarmatia, east of the Tanais. They were said to have been of Grecian origin. The Arii were the inhabitants of a part of the ancient Persian empire, which is now the eastern part of Khorasan and to the west of Afghanistan.

[8] *From the Memnonian realms*) ver. 284. He calls the realms of Cyrus the Great, king of Persia, "Memnonian," from Memnon, who was the son of Aurora, and was fabled to have come from Ethiopia, which was considered as a part of the east, to the Trojan war.

[9] *The Persian came down*) ver. 286. Under the name "Perses" he alludes to Xerxes, the king of Persia, and his memorable expedition against Greece. Herodotus tells us that in order to count the numbers of his army,

of his brother's love[1] beat the waves with so many fleets, did sovereigns so numerous have one leader. Nor ever did races unite so varied in their dress, languages of people so different. Nations thus numerous did Fortune arouse to send as companions in his mighty downfall, and as obsequies worthy of the end of Magnus. Horn-bearing Ammon[2] did not delay to send the Marmarian troops[3] to the warfare; however far parched Libya extends from the western Moors, even to the Parætonian Syrtes[4] on the eastern shores. Lest fortunate Cæsar might not meet with all at once, Pharsalia gave the whole world to be subdued at the same moment.

He, when he quitted the walls of trembling Rome, swept across the cloud-capt Alps with his hastening troops; and while other nations were alarmed with terror at his fame, the Phocæan youth[5] amid doubtful fortunes dared to preserve their fidelity[6] with no Grecian fickleness, and their plighted faith, and to adhere to the cause *and* not the fortune. Yet first they attempted with peaceful words to modify the

he commanded each soldier as he passed by in review to discharge an arrow, by counting which he might have an exact account of their numbers.

[1] *Avenger of his brother's love*) ver. 286. This was Agamemnon, who led the Greek forces to Troy to avenge the injury done by Paris to the affections of his brother Menelaüs in carrying off his wife.

[2] *Horn-bearing Ammon*) ver. 292. The country situate near the Temple of Jupiter Ammon in Libya, where Jupiter was worshipped under the form of a ram.

[3] *The Marmarian troops*) ver. 293. The Marmaridæ were the inhabitants of Marmarica, a district between Cyrenaica and Egypt, and extending inland as far as the Oasis of Ammon.

[4] *The Parætonian Syrtes*) ver. 295. Parætonium was a city of Egypt, situate at one of the mouths of the Nile. The meaning of this circumlocution is, that all the nations extending from Mauritania to Egypt sided with Pompey.

[5] *The Phocæan youth*) ver. 301. We may here remark that Lucan repeatedly uses the word "juventus" to signify "an army," or the fighting men of a place; as, among the Romans, from the age of seventeen to forty-six, men were considered to be "juvenes," and were, as such, liable to military service.

[6] *Dared to preserve their fidelity*) ver. 301. He alludes to the inhabitants of Massilia, on the same site as the present city of Marseilles, in the south of France. It was founded by a colony of Phocæans from Asia Minor about B.C. 600. Lucan falls into the error of confounding these with the inhabitants of Phocis in Greece; and in the present instance he compliments them on not showing the usual " Graia levitas," the fickleness or want of good faith for which the Greeks were proverbially notorious.

impetuous wrath and stubborn feelings of the hero, and. a branch of the Cecropian Minerva[1] being borne before, they entreated the approaching enemy *in these terms :—*

" That always in foreign wars Massilia took part in common with your people, whatever age is comprehended in the Latian annals, *that same* bears witness. And now, if in an unknown world thou art seeking any triumphs, receive the right hands that are pledged to foreign warfare. But if, discordant, you are preparing a deadly strife, if direful battles, to civil arms we give our tears and our dissent. By our hands let no accursed wounds be meddled with. If to the inhabitants of heaven fury had given arms, or if the earth-born Giants were aiming at the stars, still not either by arms or by prayers would human piety presume to give aid to Jove ; and the mortal race, ignorant of the fortunes of the Gods, only by his lightnings would be sensible that still the Thunderer reigns in heaven. Besides, nations innumerable are meeting together on every side, nor does the slothful world so shudder at the contact of wickedness that the civil war stands in need of coerced swords.

" Would, indeed, that there were the same feelings in all, that they would refuse to *hurry on* your destiny, and that no strange soldier would wage these battles. On beholding his parent, whose right hand will not grow weak ? Brothers, too, on opposite sides, will forbear to hurl the darts. An end is there to your state, if you do not wage war with those[2] with whom it is lawful. This is the sum of our prayer ; leave the threatening eagles and the hostile standards afar from the city, and be willing to entrust thyself to our walls, and permit, Cæsar being admitted, the warfare to be shut out. Let *this* place, exempt from crime, be safe to Magnus and to thee. that, if fate wishes well to the unconquered City, if a treaty pleases, there may be *a place* to which you may repair unarmed.

" Or else, when the dangers so great of the Iberian warfare

---

[1] *A branch of the Cecropian Minerva*) ver. 306. A branch of olive, the symbol of peace, sacred to Minerva.

[2] *Wage war with those*) ver. 328. " Arma committere " here most probably means " to engage " or " fight;" and " illis " is the ablative plural. Most of the commentators take the phrase to mean " to entrust arms to," or " put arms in the hands of," and make " illis " the dative plural.

invite you, why do you turn aside *to us* in your rapid march?
We are of no weight in affairs, we are not of moment, a
multitude that never has enjoyed prospering arms, exiled
from the original abodes of our country, and, after the towers
of burnt Phocis[1] were transferred safe on foreign shores,
within humble walls, whom fidelity alone makes renowned
If by siege thou dost prepare to block up our walls, and by
force to break through our gates, *we are* prepared to receive
on our roofs the torches and the darts, to seek, the streams
being turned aside, draughts of water rescued[2] from *your
force*, and, thirsting, to suck at the dug up earth; and, if
bounteous Ceres should fail, then with stained jaws to eat
things horrid to be looked upon and foul to be touched.
Nor does this people fear to suffer for liberty that which
Saguntum, besieged[3] in the Punic warfare, underwent.
Torn from the bosoms of their mothers, and vainly drawing
at the breasts dried up with thirst, *the children* shall be
hurled into the midst of the flames. The wife, too, from
her dear husband shall demand her death. Brothers shall
exchange wounds, and by compulsion this civil war in preference will they wage."[4]

[1] *Towers of burnt Phocis*) ver. 340. By the word "Phocis" here, they
properly mean Phocæa in Asia Minor, from which their ancestors had been
expelled by Harpagus, the general of Cyrus the Great, on which they colonized Massilia. See the note to l. 301.

[2] *Draughts of water rescued*) ver. 345. "Haustus raptos," water withdrawn from them by turning the streams out of their course.

[3] *Saguntum, besieged*) ver. 350. Saguntum was a city of Spain, on the
site of the present Murviedro. It was faithful to the Romans, and was besieged by Hannibal for eight months in the second Punic war. When
taken, the inhabitants set fire to the city and threw themselves and their
wives and children into the flames.

[4] *In preference will they wage*) ver. 355. Cæsar gives the following
account of this interview in his Civil War, B. i. l. 35. Having heard that
Domitius Ahenobarbus, whom he had lately released, had been ordered to
seize Massilia, he hastened thither from Rome. "Cæsar sent for fifteen of
the principal persons of Massilia to attend him. To prevent the war commencing there, he remonstrated to the effect that they ought to follow the
precedent set by all Italy, rather than submit to the will of any one man;
and made use of such other arguments as he thought would tend to bring
them back to reason. The deputies reported this speech to their countrymen,
and by the authority of the state brought back this answer:—'That they
understood that the Roman people were divided into two factions; that they

Thus does the Grecian youth make an end; when, now betrayed by his agitated features, the anger of the chieftain at length in a loud voice testifies his sorrow:—

"Vainly does assurance of my haste encourage *you* Greeks. Even though we should be speeding onward to the furthest regions of the west, *still* there is time to raze Massilia. Rejoice, *ye* cohorts; by the favour of the Fates a war is presented before you. As the wind loses its strength unless the dense woods meet it with their oaks, being dissipated in empty space; so it is harmful to me that foes should be wanting; and we think it an injury to our arms, unless those who could be conquered rebel. But if I go alone, degenerate, with arms laid aside, then are their dwellings open to me. Now, not so much to shut me out, *but* to inclose me, do they wish. But yet they would keep afar the direful contagion of war *forsooth*. You shall suffer retribution[1] for suing for peace; and you shall learn that, during my life, there is nothing more safe than warfare, myself the leader."

After he has thus spoken, he turns his march towards[2] the fearless city; then he beholds the walls shut, and for-

themselves had neither judgment nor ability to decide which had the juster cause; that the heads of these factions were Cneius Pompey and Caius Cæsar, the two patrons of the state; the former of whom had granted to their state the lands of the Volcæ Arecomici and Helvii; the latter had assigned them a part of his conquests in Gaul, and had augmented their revenue. Wherefore, having received equal favours from both, they ought to show equal regard for both, and assist neither against the other, nor admit either into their city or harbours.'"

[1] *You shall suffer retribution*) ver. 370. If his own account is true, Cæsar had some grounds for being offended at the duplicity of the Massilians. He says, in the Civil War, B. i. c. 36, "While this treaty was going forward, Domitius arrived at Massilia with his fleet, and was received into the city, and made governor of it. The chief management of the war was entrusted to him. At his command they sent the fleet to all parts; they seized all the merchantmen they could meet with, and carried them into the harbour. They applied the sails, timber, and rigging with which they were furnished to rig and refit their other vessels."

[2] *Turns his march towards*) ver. 373. Cæsar says, in the Civil War, B. i. c. 37, "Provoked at such ill treatment, Cæsar led three legions against Massilia, and resolved to provide turrets and mantelets to assault the town, and to build twelve ships at Arelas, which, being completed and rigged in thirty days from the time the timber was cut down, and being brought to Massilia, he put under the command of Decimus Brutus, and left Caius Trebonius, his lieutenant, to invest the city."

tified by a dense band of youths. Not far from the walls a mound of earth rising aloft, its top widening, spreads out a little plain; this rock seems to the chieftain fitted to be surrounded with a long fortification, and very well suited for a safe encampment. The nearest part of the city rises with a high citadel, equal *in height* to the mound, and fields are situate in the valley between. Then did a thing please him, to be brought about with immense labour, to join the separated elevations by a vast mound. But first, that he might inclose the entire city, where it is surrounded by the earth, Cæsar drew a long work from the camp to the sea, and, encircling the springs and the pastures of the plain with a fosse, with turf and unmixed earth he raised out works that elevated their numerous towers.

Well worthy now to be remembered did this befall the Grecian city, and an eternal honor, that, not provoked *at first*[1], nor yet prostrated by very fear, it stayed the headlong course of a war that raged on every side, and all *others* being seized *instantaneously* by Cæsar, it alone was conquered with delay. How much is it that his destinies are stayed, and that Fortune, hastening to set *her* hero over the whole world, loses these days!

Then far and wide do all the forests fall, and the woods are spoiled of their oaks, that, as crumbling earth and twigs keep up the middle of the mass, *the wood* may keep close the earth knit together by the framed construction of its sides, that the mound being pressed down[2] may not give way beneath the towers.

There was a grove, never violated during long ages, which with its knitted branches shut in the darkened air and the cold shade, the rays of the sun being far removed. This no rustic Pans, and Fauns and Nymphs all-powerful in the groves, possessed, but sacred rites of the Gods barbarous in their ceremonial, and elevations crowned with ruthless

[1] *Not provoked at first*) ver. 389. "Non impulsa, nec ipso strata metu." Cortius suggests this translation of the passage:—"Not smitten down or laid prostrate with fear." "Non impulsa" seems, however, to mean, "not acting precipitately through provocation," and not to depend upon "metu."

[2] *The mound being pressed down*) ver. 398. According to Cæsar, these operations were carried on while he was fighting against Afranius and Petreius, the generals of Pompey, in Spain.

altars, and every tree was stained[1] with human gore. If at
all, antiquity, struck with awe at the Gods of heaven, has
been deserving of belief, upon these branches, too, the birds
of the air dread to perch, and the wild beasts to lie in the
caves; nor does any wind blow upon those groves, and
lightnings hurled from the dense clouds; a shuddering in
themselves[2] prevails among the trees that spread forth their
branches to no breezes. Besides, from black springs plenteous water falls, and the saddened images of the Gods[3] are
devoid of art, and stand unsightly *formed* from hewn trunks
The very mouldiness and paleness of the rotting wood now
renders *people* stricken with awe: not thus do they dread
the Deities consecrated with ordinary forms; so much does
it add to the terror not to know what Gods they are in
dread of. Fame, too, reported that full oft the hollow caverns roared amid the earthquake, and that yews that had
fallen rose again, and that flames shone from a grove that
did not burn, and that serpents embracing the oaks entwined around them.

The people throng that place with no approaching worship, but have left it to the Gods. When Phœbus is in
the mid sky, or dark night possesses the heavens, the priest
himself dreads the approach, and is afraid to meet with the
guardian of the grove[4].

This forest he commanded to fall beneath the aimed
iron; for close by the works and untouched in former war
it stood most dense in growth amid the bared mountains.
But the valiant bands trembled, and, moved by the venerable
sanctity of the place, they believed that if they should touch
the sacred oaks, the axes would rebound back[5] against their
own limbs. Cæsar, when he beheld his cohorts involved in

---

[1] *Every tree was stained*) ver. 405. By this he would seem to imply that
Druidical rites were performed in the wood.

[2] *A shuddering in themselves*) ver. 411. By the use of "suus" he means
that the leaves are left entirely undisturbed by the winds.

[3] *Images of the Gods*) ver. 412. These figures of the Deities were rough
unhewn logs of wood, of the kind called by the Greeks αὐτόξυλα.

[4] *The guardian of the grove*) ver. 425. It was a prevalent belief that
the Divinities walked on the earth at midday, and that they were especially
enraged against mortals who presented themselves in their path.

[5] *Would rebound back*) ver. 431. They believed that the axe would
rebound as a punishment for their profaneness.

I

great alarm, first daring to poise a hatchet snatched up, and with the iron to cut down the towering oak, the iron being buried in the violated wood, *thus* says : " Now then, that no one of you may hesitate to hew down the wood, believe that I have incurred the guilt."

Then did all the throng obey, not, *all* fear removed, free from care, but the wrath of the Gods and of Cæsar being weighed. Down fall the ashes, the knotty holm-oak is hurled down ; the wood of Dodona, too, and the alder more suited to the waves, the cypress, too, that bears witness to no ple-beian[1] *funeral* mourning, then first lay aside their foliage, and, spoiled of leaves, admit the day, and thrown down with its trunks thickly set the falling wood supports itself. Looking on, the nations of the Gauls lament, but the youth shut up within the walls exult. For who can suppose that the Gods are insulted with impunity? Fortune spares many that are guilty; and only with the wretched can the Deities be angered. And when enough of the grove is cut down. they bring waggons, sought amid the fields; and the hus-bandmen bewail, the oxen being carried off, the yearly pro-duce of the soil relaxed from the curving plough.

The general, however, impatient with a contest destined to linger on before the walls, turning towards the Spanish forces and the extremities of the world, orders the warfare to be carried on[2]. A mound is erected with props studded with iron[3], and receives two towers equalling the walls *in height;*

---

[1] *Witness to no plebeian*) ver. 442. The cypress was planted near the tombs of the rich, and was sometimes used for the purposes of the funeral pile. It was a tree of comparative rarity and great value. A branch of it was also placed at the door of the house in which a person of station was lying dead. This tree is said to have been considered an emblem of death from the fact that when once an incision has been made in it, it dies.

[2] *Orders the warfare to be carried on*) ver. 455. Leaving the conduct of the war to Caius Trebonius, his legate.

[3] *With props studded with iron*) ver. 455. "Stellatis axibus." This expression has caused great perplexity among the commentators, and Cortius has come to the conclusion that it alludes to the axle-trees of the wheels upon which the "agger" or mound was placed and then wheeled to the city. It is much more likely that it signifies cross beams studded with iron, which were used in constructing the agger which they were building round the city. This operation is described by Cæsar in the Civil War, B. ii. c. 15, and in the following passage the cross beams are referred to :—" They began, there-fore, to make a mound of a new construction, never heard of before, of two

these are fastened with no wood to the earth, but moved along a lengthened space, the cause lying concealed. When so great a mass was tottering, the youth supposed that the wind seeking to burst forth had shaken the empty recesses of the earth, and wondered that their walls were standing. Thence did the darts fall upon the lofty citadel of the city. But a greater power was there in the Grecian weapons against the Roman bodies. For the lance, not hurled by arms alone, but discharged by the tightened whirlwind force of the balista, did not, content to pass through but one side, cease *in its course ;* but, opening a way through both arms and through bones, death left behind, it flies on : after the wound a career still remains for the weapon.

But as often as a stone is hurled by the vast impulse of the blow, just as a rock, which old age, aided by the power of the winds, has separated from the height of the mountain, rushing onwards it bears down everything; and not only deprives of life the bodies it has dashed against, *but* scatters in every direction whole limbs together with the bl**o**od. But when, sheltered beneath the stout tortoise[1], valour approaches the hostile walls, and the foremost bear arms connected with the arms *of those behind,* and the uplifted shield protects the helmet, those which, before hurled from the distant retreats, proved destructive, now fall behind their backs ; nor is it now an easy task to the Greeks to direct their charges, or to change the level of their engines of war adapted for *hurling* weapons to a distance ; but, content with heavy masses alone, they hurl down stones with *their* bared arms. While the

---

walls of brick, each six feet thick, and to lay floors over them of almost the same breadth with the mound, made of timber. But wherever the space between the walls or the weakness of the timber seemed to require it, pillars were placed underneath and traversed beams laid on to strengthen the work, and the space which was floored was covered over with hurdles, and the hurdles plastered over with mortar."

[1] *Sheltered beneath the stout tortoise)* ver. 474. The "testudo" was a mode of attacking a besieged city, by the soldiers uniting their shields over their heads, locking one in the other, and thus making a compact covering for their bodies. The "testudo" also meant a kind of penthouse moving on wheels, under cover of which the besiegers worked the battering ram. The name in this case was suggested by the resemblance which the ram presented to a tortoise thrusting its head forwards from its shell and drawing it back again.

connected chain of arms[1] exists, just as roofs rattle, struck by
the harmless hailstones, so does it ward off all the missiles;
but after the excited valour of the men, the soldiers being
wearied, breaks down the lengthened fence, single arms give
way beneath the continuous blows.

Then, covered with light earth[2], the mantelet moves on,
concealed under the sheds and screened front of which they
now attempt to undermine the lower part of the walls, and
with iron implements to overthrow them; now the battering ram, more mighty with its suspended blows, impelled
endeavours to loosen the texture of the solid wall, and to
strike away one from the stones placed above. But struck
by flames from above and fragments of vast masses, and
many a stake, and the blows of oaks hardened by fire, the
hurdle roof, smitten, gives way; and, his labour spent in
vain, the wearied soldier seeks again the tents.

It was at first[3] the greatest wish of the Greeks that their
walls might stand. Now, still further, they prepare to make
a charge with their troops; and, attacking by night, they
conceal under their arms blazing torches, and the bold
youth sally forth[4]; no spear, no death-dealing bow, but fire,
is the weapon of the men, and the wind sweeping onward
the flames bears them throughout the Roman fortifications
with a swift course. Nor, although it struggles with green
timber, does the fire display slight strength; but borne
away from every torch it follows after extended volumes of
black smoke; it consumes not only the wood but huge
stones, and the solid rocks dissolve into dust. The mound
falls prostrate, and as it lies still longer does it appear.

Hope by land now departed from the conquered, and it

---

[1] *While the connected chain of arms*) ver. 482. "Dum fuit armorum
series." "So long as the shields kept firmly locked, the one in the other."

[2] *Covered with light earth*) ver. 487. The "vineæ," or mantelets, were
covered with earth to prevent them from being set on fire from above by the
enemy.

[3] *It was at first*) ver. 497. He means that it had been the limit of their
wishes that their walls might stand and the city remain uncaptured, but now
they prepare to sally forth and attack the enemy.

[4] *The bold youth sally forth*) ver. 500. The Poet conceals the fact related by Cæsar that this sally took place under circumstances of considerable
treachery, when, at their own request, a truce had been granted them, and
they were awaiting the arrival of Cæsar from Spain. See the Civil War,
B. ii. c. 12, 13, 14.

pleased them to try their fortune on the deep sea. Not with painted oak did the resplendent tutelary Deity[1] grace the ornamented barks, but rough, and just as the tree falls on the mountains, is a firm surface put together for the naval warfare. And now, attending the towered ship of Brutus[2], the fleet had come into the waves of the Rhone with the tide, making for the land of Stœchas[3]. The Grecian youth[4] as well was wishful to entrust all its strength to the Fates, and armed the aged men with the lads[5] intermingled. Not only did the fleet, which was *then* standing on the waves, receive the men; they sought again, too, the ships worn out in the dock-yards.

When Phœbus, spreading his morning rays upon the seas, has refracted them on the waters, and the sky is free from clouds, and, Boreas being banished and the south winds holding their peace, prepared for the warfare the sea lies calm, each one moves his ship from each station, and by equal arms on the one side the ships of Cæsar, on the other by Grecian rowers the fleet is impelled; urged on

[1] *The resplendent tutelary Deity*) ver. 510. The statue of the "tutela" or "tutelar Divinity" of the ship was placed at the stern. This was distinct from the "insigne," which was placed at the figure-head. See the Tristia of Ovid, where he says that the "insigne" of the vessel in which he sailed for Pontus was a helmet, while Minerva was the "tutela" of it.

[2] *The towered ship of Brutus*) ver. 514. His bark was thus distinguished as being the Prætorian or admiral's ship, he having been left in command of the fleet by Cæsar. This was D. Junius Brutus Albinus, who had served under Cæsar in Gaul. After the siege of Massilia, during the Civil War, Cæsar gave him the command of Further Gaul, and took every opportunity of showing him marks of favour. Notwithstanding this, he joined the murderers of Cæsar, and enjoying his full confidence, was sent to conduct him to the Senate-house for the purpose of assassination. He was afterwards deservedly put to death by Capenus, a Sequanian, by order of Antony.

[3] *The land of Stœchas*) ver. 516. The Stœchades were a cluster of islands, five in number, in the Mediterranean, to the east of Massilia, where the Massilians kept an armed force to protect their trade against pirates. They are now called the Isles d'Hières.

[4] *The Grecian youth*) ver. 516. He means the Massilians, as descendants of the Phocæans, whom Lucan supposes to have been Greeks. According to Cæsar, this naval engagement between Brutus and the Massilians took place before the attack by land; and the Massilians were aided by Lucius Nasidius, who had been sent by Pompey with sixteen ships. See the Civil War, B. ii. c. 3, 7.

[5] *With the lads*) ver. 518. "Ephebis." "Ephebi" was the name given to those between the ages of 16 and 20.

by oars the ships shake again, and the repeated strokes
move on the lofty barks. Both strong three-oared galleys,
and those which the rising ranks of rowers built up fourfold,
move on, and those which dip in the seas still more pine-
wood oars, ships in numbers, surround the wings of the
Roman fleet. This force breasts the open sea. In the
centre, in form of a crescent, the Liburnian barks[1], content
to increase with two ranks of oars, fall back. But the Prætorian ship of Brutus more lofty than all is impelled by six
tiers of oars, and carries a tower along the deep, and seeks
the seas from afar with its highest oars.

Where there is just so much sea intervening that either
fleet could cross over to the other with the oars once pulled,
innumerable voices are mingled in the vast expanse; and
the sound of the oars is drowned in the clamour, nor can
any trumpets be heard. Then they skim along the azure
main, and stretch along the benches, and strike their
breasts with the oars. When first beaks meeting beaks
send forth a sound, the ships run astern, and the hurled
darts as they fall fill the air and the vacant deep. And
now, the prows separated, the wings extend, and, the fleet
sundered, the opposing ships are received. Just as, so oft
as the tide struggles against the Zephyrs and the eastern
gales, in this direction run the waves, in that the sea; so,
when the ships in the ploughed-up tide describe their varying tracks, the sea which the one fleet impels onwards with
its oars, the other beats back.

But the pine-tree ships of the Greeks were skilful both to
challenge to the battle and to resort to flight, and to change
their course with no wide sweep, and with no tardiness to obey
the turning helm. But the Roman ship was more sure in
affording a keel firmly laid, and convenience to the warriors
equal to the dry land. Then said Brutus to the pilot sitting
at the ensign-bearing stern : " Dost thou suffer the battle to

[1] *The Liburnian barks*) ver. 534. " Liburna," or " Liburnica," was a
name given to every ship of war, from a " bireme" up to chose with six
ranks of oars. Pliny tells us that they were formed with sharp bows to
offer the least possible resistance to the water. They were originally constructed by the Liburnians, a people of Dalmatia, and were then probably
limited in size to two ranks of oars. They are said to have been first used
by the Romans at the battle of Actium. The " Liburnæ" here mentioned,
from the words " ordine gemino," appear to have had but two ranks of oars.

be shifting about upon the deep, and dost thou contend with
the vagaries of the ocean? Now close the warfare; oppose
the mid part of the vessels to the Phocæan beaks."

He obeyed, and sidelong he laid the alder barks before
the foe. Then, whatever ship tried the oaken sides of
that of Brutus, conquered by her own blow, captured, she
stuck fast[1] to the one she had struck. But others both
grappling-irons united and smooth chains, and they held
themselves on by the oars[2]; on the covered sea the warfare
stood *fixed to the same spot.*

Now no longer are the darts hurled from the shaken arms,
nor do the wounds fall from afar by means of the hurled
weapons; and hand meets hand. In a naval fight the sword
effects the most. Each one stands upon the bulwark of
his own ship, facing full the blows of the enemy; and none
fall slain in their own vessels. The deep blood foams in
the waves, and the tide *is* thickened with clotted gore. The
ships, too, which the chains of iron thrown on board are
dragging, the same do the dead bodies clogged together
hinder from being united. Some, half-dead, fall into the
vast deep, and drink of the sea mingled with their own
blood. Some, adhering to life struggling with slowly-coming
death, perish in the sudden wreck of the dismantled ships.
Javelins, missing their aim, accomplish their slaughter in
the sea, and whatever weapon falls, with its weight used to
no purpose, finds a wound on being received in the midst of
the waves.

A Roman ship hemmed in by Phocæan barks, its crew divided, with equal warfare defends the right side and the left;
from the high stern of which, while Tagus maintains the fight,
and boldly seizes hold of the Grecian flag[3], he is pierced both
in back and breast at the same moment by hurled darts; in

---

[1] *Captured, she stuck fast*) ver. 564. The shock was so great that she
was impaled, as it were, on the beak of the large ship of Brutus.

[2] *Held themselves on by the oars*) ver. 566. Oars being inserted between
oars, the ships lying broadside to broadside.

[3] *Hold of the Grecian flag*) ver. 586. "Aplustre." In the ancient ships
the upper part of the stern often had an ornament called "aplustre," which
formed the highest part of the poop. It is most probable that the form of it
was borrowed from the tail of the fish. The "aplustre" rising behind the
helmsman served in some measure to shelter him from wind and rain; and a
lantern was sometimes suspended from it.

the midst of his breast the iron meets, and the blood stands,
uncertain from which wound to flow, until the plenteous
gore at the same time expels both the spears, and rends
asunder his life, and scatters death in the wounds.

Hither also the right hand of hapless Telon directed his
ship, than which no hand more aptly, when the sea was
boisterous, did the barks obey; nor was the morrow's
weather better known to any one, whether he looks at Phœbus or whether at the horns of the moon, in order always to
trim the sails to the coming winds. He with the beak had
broken the ribs of a Latian bark; but quivering javelins
entered the middle of his breast, and the right hand of the
dying pilot turned away the ship. While Gyareus attempted
to leap on board the friendly bark, he received the iron
driven through his suspended entrails, and pinned to the
ship, the dart holding him back, *there* he hung.

Two twin brothers are standing, the glory of their fruitful
mother, whom the same womb bore to differing fates. Cruel
death separates the heroes : and the wretched parents recognize the one left behind, *all* mistake being *now* removed, a
cause for everlasting tears. He always renews their grief,
and presents his lost brother to them as they mourn. Of
these, the one, the oars *of two ships* being mingled sideways,
comb-like indented, dares from a Grecian stern to lay hands
upon[1] a Roman bark, but from above a heavy blow lops it
off; still, however, with the effort with which it has grasped
it keeps hold, and as it dies, holding fast with tightened
nerve, it stiffens. By his mischance his valour waxes
stronger: mutilated, more high-spirited wrath has he, and

---

[1] *To lay hands upon*) ver. 610. A similar story to this is told of Cynægyrus, the brother of the poet Æschylus, who, when the Persians were endeavouring to escape by sea, seized one of their ships with his right hand,
which was cut off. Justin magnifies the story, and states that he held with
both hands, which were successively cut off, and then held on with his teeth.
Lucan, with his usual distortion of facts at all favourable to Cæsar, here
attributes to the Massilians a valorous exploit which was, in reality, performed by a soldier of Cæsar's army. Suetonius says that, " Acilius, a soldier
of Cæsar, in the naval battle at Massilia, having seized with his right hand
the ship of the enemy, and it being cut off, imitating the memorable example
of Cynægyrus among the Greeks, leaped on board the ship and drove all before him with his shield." Plutarch and Valerius Maximus mention the same
circumstance.

he renews the combat with valorous left hand, and about to tear away his right hand he stretches out over the waves. This hand, too, is cut off with the entire arm. Now deprived of shield and weapons, he is not stowed away in the bottom of the ship, but, exposed and covering his brother's arms with his naked breast, pierced by many a spear, he *still* persists ; and weapons that were to have fallen to the destruction of many of his own friends he receives with a death that he has now earned. Then he summons his life, fleeting with many a wound, into his wearied limbs, and nerves his members with all the blood that is remaining, and, his members failing in strength, he leaps on board the hostile bark, destined to injure it by his weight alone.

The ship, heaped up with the slaughter of the men, and filled with much blood, received numerous blows on its slanting sides. But after, its ribs broken, it let in the sea being filled to the top of the hatches, it descended into the waves, sucking in the neighbouring waters with a whirling eddy. Cleft asunder by the sunk ship, the waves divided, and in the place of the bark the sea closed up. Many wondrous instances of various fates besides did that day afford upon the main.

While a grappling-iron was fastening its grasping hooks upon a ship, it fixed on Lycidas. He would have been sunk in the deep; but his friends hindered it and held fast his suspended thighs. Torn away he is rent in two : nor, as though from a wound, does his blood slowly flow ; the veins torn asunder[1], on every side it falls ; and the downward flow of his life's blood passing into his rent limbs is intercepted by the waters. The life of no one slain is parted with by a passage so great; the lower part of him mutilated gives to death the limbs deprived of their vitals ; but where the swelling lungs are situate, where the entrails are warm, there does death delay for a long time ; and having

---

[1] *The veins torn asunder*) ver. 639. This and the next four lines are said to have been repeated by Lucan when dying by a similar death ; his veins having been opened, at his own request, when commanded by Nero to slay himself. Many of the learned, however, do not believe this story, while others state that the lines beginning at l. 811 in the Ninth Book were the ones so repeated.

struggled much with this portion of the man, hardly does it take possession of all the limbs.

While, too eager for fight, the company of one ship is pressing straight against the side, and leaves the deck empty where it is free from the enemy, the vessel, overturned by the accumulated weight, within its hollow hull incloses both sea and sailors; nor is it allowed them to throw out their arms in the vast deep, but they perish in the inclosed waves.

Then was a remarkable kind of dreadful death beheld, when by chance ships of opposite sides transfixed with their beaks a youth as he swam. His breast divided in the middle at such mighty blows; nor with the ground bones were the limbs able to prevent the brazen beaks from re-echoing. His middle burst asunder, through his mouth the blood, mingled with the entrails, spouted forth corrupt matter. After they backed the ships with the oars, and the beaks withdrew, the body, with the pierced breast, being cast into the sea admitted the water into the wounds.

The greatest part of a crew being shipwrecked, struggling against death with expanded arms, rushed to receive the aid of a friendly ship; but when they caught hold of the woodwork on high with forbidden arms, and the bark, likely to perish, swayed to and fro from the multitude received, the impious crew from above struck at the middle of their arms with the sword: leaving their arms hanging from the Grecian ship, they were slain by the hands of their own side; no longer did the waves support on the surface of the sea the heavy trunks.

And now, all the soldiers stripped bare, the weapons being expended, fury finds arms; one hurls an oar at the foe; but others whirl round with stout arms the wrenched-up flagstaff [1], and the benches torn away, the rowers being driven off. For the purposes of fighting they break up the ships. The bodies slain they catch as they are falling overboard, and spoil the carcases of the weapons. Many, wanting darts, draw the deadly javelin wrenched out from their own entrails, and with the left hand clench fast their wounds, so that the blood may allow a firm blow, and may start forth after having hurled the hostile spear.

---

[1] *Wrenched-up flag-staff*) ver. 672. " Aplustre." See the Note to l. 586

Yet upon this ocean nothing causes more destruction than the antagonist opposed to the sea. For fire fixed to unctuous torches[1], and alive, beneath a covering of sulphur, is spread about; but the ships ready to afford a nutriment, now with pitch, now with melted wax, spread the confla gration. Nor do the waves conquer the flames; and, the barks now scattered over the sea, the fierce fire claims the fragments for itself. This one takes to the waves, that in the sea he may extinguish the flames; these, that they may not be drowned, cling to the burning spars. Amid a thousand forms of death, that single end is an object of dread, by which they have begun to perish. Nor is their valour idle in shipwreck. They collect darts thrown up by the sea, and supply them to the ships, and with failing efforts ply their erring hands through the waves. Now if but small the supply of weapons that is afforded, they make use of the sea. Fierce enemy clutches hold of enemy, and they delight to sink with arms entwined, and to die drowning *the foe.*

In that mode of fighting there was one Phocæan skilled at keeping his breath beneath the waves, and examining in the sea if anything had been sunk in the sands, and at wrenching up the tooth of the fluke too firmly fixed, as often as the anchor had proved insensible to the tightened rope. He took the enemy quite down when grappled with, and *then,* victorious, returned to the surface of the water; but, while he believed that he was rising amid the vacant waves, he met with the ships, and at last remained *for good* beneath the sea. Some threw their arms around the hostile oars, and withheld the flight of the ships. Not to throw away their deaths was the greatest care; many a one, dying, applied his wounds to the stern, and warded off the blows from the beaks.

Lygdamus, a slinger with the Balearic sling[2], aiming with

---

[1] *Fire fixed to unctuous torches*) ver. 681. This was probably a compo- sition which was sometimes called " Greek fire," and similar to our wildfire. Darts were used which they called "phalaricæ," and which being dipped into this combustible matter were then hurled against ships or wooden towers. This weapon was said to have been particularly used by the people of Saguntum. See the Sixth Book, l. 198.

[2] *The Balearic sling*) ver. 710. See the First Book, l. 229.

the hurled bullet at Tyrrhenus as he stood on the lofty elevation of the prow, shattered his hollow temples with the
solid lead. Expelled from their sockets, after the blood had
burst all the ligaments, the eyes started forth; his sight
destroyed, he stood amazed, and thought that this was the
darkness of death; but after he found that strength existed
in his limbs, he said: "You, O companions, just as you are
wont *to direct* the missiles, place me also straight in a direction for hurling darts. Employ, Tyrrhenus, what remains
of life in all the chances of war. This carcase, when dead,
in a great degree is of considerable use to the warriors;
in the place of one living shalt thou be struck *by the blow.*"
Thus having said, with aimless hand he hurled the dart
against the foe, but still not without effect.

This Argus, a youth of noble blood, received, not quite
where the midriff slopes down to the loins, and falling down
he aided the weapon with his own weight. Now stood the
unhappy sire of Argus in the opposite part of the conquered
ship; in the days of his youth he would not have yielded to
any one in Phocæan arms: conquered by age his strength
had decayed, and, worn out with old age, he was a model *of
valour*, not a soldier. He, seeing the death, often stumbling,
being an aged man, came between the benches of the long
ship to the stern, and found the panting limbs. No tears fell
from his cheeks, he did not beat his breast, but grew stiff
all over his body with distended hands. Night came on, and
dense shades spread over his eyes, and as he looked upon him
he ceased to recognize the wretched Argus. He sinking, on
seeing his father, raised his head and his now languid neck;
no voice issued from his loosened jaws; only with his silent
features did he ask a kiss and invite his father's right hand
to close his eyes. When the old man was relieved from his
torpor, and his grief, caused by the bloodshed, began to gain
strength, "I will not," he exclaimed, "lose the time granted
by the cruel Gods, and I will pierce my aged throat. Argus,
grant pardon to thy wretched parent, that I have fled from
thy embrace, thy last kisses. The warm blood has not yet
quitted thy wounds, and *but* half-dead thou dost lie, and
mayst still be the survivor."

Thus having said, although he had stained the hilt of the
sword driven through his entrails, still, with a headlong leap,

he descended beneath the deep waves.   His life hastening
to precede the end of his son he did not entrust to but one
form of death.

Now do the fates of the chieftains take a turn, nor is the
event of the warfare any longer doubtful: of the Grecian
fleet the greatest part is sunk; but other ships, changing
their rowers[1], carry their own conquerors; a few with precipitate flight reach *their* haven.   What wailing of parents
was there in the city!   What lamentations of matrons
along the shore!   Often did the wife, the features being
disfigured by the waves, embracing the dead body of a
Roman, believe *them to be* the features of her husband; and,
the funeral pile being lighted, wretched parents contended
for the mutilated body.

But Brutus, victorious on the deep, added to the arms of
Cæsar the first honor gained on the waves.

[1] *Changing their rowers*) ver. 754.   On being taken.   Cæsar says, in the
Civil War, B. ii. c. 7, that five of the Massilian ships were sunk, and four
taken.

BOOK THE FOURTH.

CONTENTS.

But afar in the remotest regions of the world stern Cæsar wages a warfare, not injurious with much slaughter[1], but destined to give the greatest impulse to the fate of the chieftains. With equal rights, Afranius[2] and Petreius[3]

---

[1] *Not injurious with much slaughter*) ver. 2. In consequence, as is seen in the sequel, of his having intercepted the supply of water of the enemy.

[2] *Afranius*) ver. 4. L. Afranius was a person of obscure origin, and was throughout the Civil War a warm friend and partisan of Pompey, under whom he had served against Sertorius in Spain and in the Mithridatic war. He was afterwards Consul, and obtained a triumph in B.C. 59, probably for some advantage gained over the Gauls. He was present at the battle of Pharsalia, where he had charge of the camp. He fled to Africa and was taken prisoner and put to death shortly after the battle of Thapsus. He now had the command of Hither Hispania, which, with three legions, had been given to him by Pompey.

[3] *And Petreius*) ver. 5. M. Petreius first served under Antony against

were rulers in that camp; an agreement divided the common command into equal shares; and the ever-watchful guard, protector of the trenches, obeyed alternate standards. With these, besides the Latian bands, there was the active Asturian[1] and the light-armed Vettones[2], and the Celts[3], who migrated from the ancient race of the Gauls, mingling their name with the Iberians.

The rich soil swells with a slight elevation, and with a hill of gentle slope increases on high; upon this rises Ilerda[4], founded by ancient hands; the Sicoris, not the last among the Hesperian rivers, flows by with its placid waves, which a stone bridge spans with its large arch, destined to endure the wintry waters[5]. But an adjoining rock bears the standard of Magnus; nor on a smaller hill does Cæsar rear his camp; a river in the middle divides the tents. The earth, expanding from here, unfolds extended fields, the eye scarcely catching the limits; and thou dost bound the plains, impetuous Cinga[6], being forbidden to repel the

Catiline. He was a person of considerable military experience, and a staunch partisan of Pompey. He was one of the legates of Pompey in Spain, and after his defeat by Cæsar, joined him in Greece. After the battle of Pharsalia he fled to Achaia and thence to Africa, where, after the fatal issue of the battle of Thapsus, he and king Juba fell by each other's hand, to avoid falling into the power of the enemy.

[1] *The active Asturian*) ver. 8. "Astur," though used in the singular, means the Asturians, or natives of the region now called "the Asturias," in Spain.

[2] *The light-armed Vettones*) ver. 9. The Vettones, or Vectones, were a people of Lusitania (now Portugal), separated from Asturia by the river Durius, now the Douro.

[3] *And the Celts*) ver. 10. He means the Ceitiberians, who were descended from the Celts who had originally crossed the Pyrenees, and, becoming mixed with the Iberians, the original inhabitants of the country, occupied the country now called Arragon. With reference to these levies of Pompey, Cæsar says, in his Civil War, B. i. c. 39, "Afranius had three legions, Petreius two. There were besides about eighty cohorts raised in Hispania (of which the troops belonging to Hither Hispania had shields, those belonging to Further Hispania leather targets), and about five thousand horse, raised in both provinces."

[4] *Upon this rises Ilerda*) ver. 13. Ilerda, now called Lerida, was a town of the Itergetes, in Hispania Tarraconensis, situate on an eminence over the river Sicoris (now the Segre), which was crossed here by a bridge of stone.

[5] *To endure the wintry waters*) ver. 16. Sufficiently strong and high to admit of the passage of the mountain floods of winter.

[6] *Impetuous Cinga*) ver. 21. Now called the Cinca, which, with the

waves and the shores of ocean in thy course; for, the streams
being mingled, the Iberus, that gives it to the region, takes
away *thy* name from thee.

The first day of the warfare refrained from blood-stained
battle, and drew out both the strength of the chieftains
and the numerous standards to be reviewed. They were
ashamed of their wickedness; fear restrained the arms of
them *thus* frenzied, and one day did they devote to country
and the broken laws. Then, the light of day declining[1],
Cæsar by night surrounded his troops with a trench suddenly formed, while the front ranks kept their post[2], and
ne deceived the foe, and, his maniples being drawn up near
each other in close ranks, enveloped the camp.

At early dawn he commanded[3] them with a sudden move-

Sicoris, falls into the river Iberus, or Ebro. The Cinga is supposed to have
lain to the east of the hostile camps, and the Sicoris to the west.

[1] *The light of day declining*) ver. 28. " Prono Olympo," literally
" Olympus falling;" " Olympus " being here used to signify the light of
the day.

[2] *The front ranks kept their post*) ver. 30. This passage is rendered
more intelligible by a reference to the narrative of Cæsar, in his Civil War,
B. i. c. 41, 2: " When Cæsar perceived that Afranius declined coming to an
engagement, he resolved to encamp at somewhat less than half a mile's distance from the very foot of the mountain; and that his soldiers, whilst engaged in their works, might not be terrified by any sudden attack of the
enemy, or disturbed in their work, he ordered them not to fortify it with a
wall, which must rise high and be seen at a distance, but to draw on the front
opposite the enemy a trench fifteen feet broad. The first and second lines
continued under arms, as was at first appointed. Behind them the third
line was carrying on the work without being seen; so that the whole was
completed before Afranius discovered that the camp was being fortified.
In the evening Cæsar drew his legions within this trench, and rested them
under arms the next night. The day following he kept his whole army
within it, and as it was necessary to bring materials from a considerable
distance, he for the present pursued the same plan in his work; and to
each legion, one after the other, he assigned one side of the camp to fortify,
and ordered trenches of the same magnitude to be cut. He kept the rest
of the legions under arms to oppose the enemy."

[3] *At early dawn he commanded*) ver. 32. This attack is thus described in
the Civil War, B. i. c. 43:—" Between the town of Ilerda and the next
hill, on which Afranius and Petreius were encamped, there was a plain
about three hundred paces broad, and near the middle of it an eminence
somewhat raised above the level. Cæsar hoped that if he could gain possession of this and fortify it he should be able to cut off the enemy from
the town, the bridge, and all the stores which they had laid up in the town.
In expectation of this, he led three legions out of the camp, and drawing

ment to ascend a hill, which in the middle separated Ilerda
in safety from the camp. Hither did both shame and terror
drive the foe, and, his troops hurried on, he first took possession of the hill; to these valour and the sword promised
the spot, but to those *possession of* the place itself. The
loaded soldiers struggled up the steep rocks; and with faces
upturned the ranks clung to the opposing mountain, and,
likely to fall upon their backs, were elevated by the shields
of those that followed. There was opportunity for no one to
poise his dart, while he was tottering and strengthening
his footsteps with his javelin fixed *in the ground*, while they
were clinging to crags and stumps of trees, and, the enemy
neglected, cut their way with the sword.

The chieftain beheld the troops likely to fail with disaster,
and ordered the cavalry to take part in the warfare, and by a
circuit to the left[1] to place before them its protected side.
Thus was the foot, readily, and with no one pressing upon
it, relieved, and the disappointed conqueror, the battle
being cut short, stood aloft.

Thus far were the vicissitudes of arms; the rest of its
fortunes did the weather give to the warfare, uncertain with
its varying fluctuations. The winter, clogged with the sluggish ice, and the dry north winds, kept the showers in the
clouds, the sky being frozen up. Snows pinched the mountain districts, and hoar-frosts destined not to last on
seeing the sun; and the whole earth nearer to the sky that
sinks the Constellations was parched, hardened beneath the
winter's clear sky.

up his army in an advantageous position, he ordered the advanced men of
one legion to hasten forward and take possession of the eminence. Upon
intelligence of this, the cohorts which were on guard before the camp of
Afranius were instantly sent a nearer way to occupy the same post. The
two parties engaged, and as the men of Afranius had reached the eminence
first, our men were repulsed, and on a reinforcement being sent, they were
obliged to turn their backs, and retreat to the standards of the legions."

[1] *By a circuit to the left*) ver. 41. Lucan seems here to confound the
attempt to take the rising ground with an attack on the town made by his
ninth legion, and described by Cæsar in the Civil War, B. i. c. 45, 6. The
aid given by the cavalry is thus described in the latter Chapter:—" Our
cavalry also, on either flank, though stationed on sloping or low ground,
yet bravely struggled up to the top of the hill, and riding between the
two armies, made our retreat more easy and secure."

K

But after the vernal carrier of Helle[1] who fell off, that
looks back upon the Constellations, brought back the warm
Titan, and once again, the hours having been made equal
according to the weights of the true Balance, the days
exceeded *in duration*[2]; then, the sun left behind, at the
time when Cynthia first shone dubious with her horn[3], she
excluded Boreas, and received flames from Eurus[4]. He,
whatever clouds he finds in his own region, hurls on
towards the western world with Nabathæan blasts[5]; both
those which the Arabian feels, and the mists which the Gan-
getic land exhales, *and* whatever the orient sun allows to
collect, whatever Corus, the darkener of the eastern sky,
has carried along, whatever has defended the Indians *from
the heat;* the clouds removed afar from the east rendered
tempestuous the day; nor could they with their heaviness
burst upon the mid region of the world, but hurried along
the showers in their flight.

Arctus and Notus are free from rains; towards Calpe
alone floats the humid air. Here, where now the lofty sky
of heaven[6] meets with the limits of Zephyrus and the
ocean, forbidden to pass beyond they roll in their dense
masses, and hardly does the space that separates the earth
from the heavens contain the mass of darkened air. And now,
pressed by the sky, they are thickened into dense showers.

[1] *The vernal carrier of Helle*) ver. 57. Aries, the Ram, who carried
Helle and Phryxus on his back over the Hellespont, when the former fell
off, and gave her name to that sea. He alludes to the entrance of the sun
into Aries in the Spring.

[2] *The days exceeded in duration*) ver. 59. When the days became
longer than the nights after the vernal Equinox.

[3] *Shone dubious with her horn*) ver. 60. Because her horns are then but
indistinctly seen.

[4] *Received flames from Eurus*) ver. 61. Virgil, in the First Book of
the Georgics, remarks that the approach of wind causes the moon to be
red; " vento semper rubet aurea Phœbe."

[5] *With Nabathæan blasts*) ver. 63. The Nabatæi, or Nabathæ, were a
people situate in the north-western parts of the Arabian peninsula, and were
said to be descended from Nabath, the eldest son of Ishmael. They afterwards extended into the original territory of the Edomites, or ancient Idumea.
The term " Nabatæis" here probably signifies " Eastern" generally.

[6] *The lofty sky of heaven*) ver. 73. " Summus cardo" here seems to
mean the horizon. Lucan uses the word " cardo " very indefinitely and
apparently with numerous significations.

and, united together, they flow downward ; nor do the lightnings preserve their flames, although they flash incessantly :
the bolts are quenched by the rains.　On this side, with
arch incomplete, the rainbow with its curve spans the air,
varying in colour with hardly any light, and drinks of the
ocean[1], and carries the waves, borne away, up to the clouds,
and restores to the heavens the ocean spread beneath.

And now, the Pyrenean snows[2], which Titan never was
able to melt, flow down, and the rocks are wet with broken
ice.　Then, the waters which spring forth from wonted
channels have no passage, such an extended stream does
all the bed of the river receive away beyond the banks.　Now
the shipwrecked arms of Cæsar are floating in the plain,
and, carried along with a vast torrent, the camp is swept
away; in the deep trench rivers overflow.　No capture of
cattle is easy, no fodder do the furrows under water bear ;
through mistake of the covered ways, the foragers, scattered abroad, are deceived amid the fields hidden *from
their sight*.

And now, ever the first attendant on great calamities,
ravening famine comes, and, besieged by no enemy, the
soldier is in want.　For a whole fortune[3], one, not a prodigal,
buys a little corn.　O the pallid thirst for gain !　The gold
proffered, a starving seller is not found wanting.　Now hills
and elevations lie concealed ; now one *continued* marsh hides
all the rivers, and sinks them in its vast gulf; entirely it
absorbs the rocks, and bears away the shelters of wild
beasts, and carries off themselves ; and, stronger *than they*,
it whirls in sudden vortices the roaring waters and repulses
the tides of ocean.　Nor is the night, spread over the
sky, sensible that Phœbus rises ; the disfigured face of

[1] *And drinks of the ocean*) ver. 81.　Virgil and Plautus also allude to
the popular belief that the rainbow drinks of the waters of the ocean.

[2] *The Pyrenean snows*) ver. 83.　The Pyrenees, which divide France
from Spain, were called " Pyrene," or " Pyrenæi Montes."　They are called
by both names by Lucan.

[3] *For a whole fortune*) ver. 95.　Livy, in his 28th Book, mentions an extraordinary instance of this species of avarice.　He says that during the
siege of Præneste, a soldier who was dying with hunger sold a mouse,
which he had caught, 'or 200 Roman denarii, but that he did not long survive the bargain.

K 2

heaven and the united shades mingle the varying traces of objects.

Thus lies the remotest part of the world, which the snowy zone and perpetual winters oppress; in the heavens no stars does it behold, not anything does it produce with its barren cold. but with ice it moderates the fires of the Con- stellations[1] in the middle *of the system.* Thus, O supreme Parent of the world, thus, Neptune, ruler in the second rank[2] of the ocean trident, mayst thou do, and mayst thou render dense the air with perpetual showers; do thou, *Neptune,* forbid to return, whatever streams thou hast sent forth. Let not the rivers find a downward course to the sea-shore, but be beaten back by the waters of the main; and let the shaken earth crumble into channels for the streams. These plains let the Rhine inundate, these the Rhone; *hither* let the rivers direct their vast resources. Hither send the Rhipæan snows to thaw; hither pour forth the pools and lakes, and, wherever they extend, the sluggish marshes, and rescue from civil wars[3] the wretched lands.

---

[1] *The fires of the Constellations*) ver. 109. By "ignes medios signorum," he means the supposed heat of the Constellations in the torrid zone, and that the northern regions counteract it, so as to render the countries habit- able which lie beneath them.

[2] *In the second rank*) ver. 110. "Sorte secundâ," "in the second rank." Neptune, as the king of the ocean, ranked next to his brother Jupiter, the king of the heavens.

[3] *Rescue from civil wars*) ver. 120. Cæsar, in the Civil War, B. i. c. 48, thus describes this tempest and its effects:—"In two days after this transaction, there happened an unexpected misfortune. For so great a storm arose, that it was agreed that there were never seen higher floods in those countries. It swept down the snow from all the mountains, and broke over the banks of the river, and in one day carried away both the bridges which Fabius had built—a circumstance which caused great dif- ficulties to Cæsar's army; for as one camp was pitched between two rivers, the Sicoris and the Cinga, and as neither of these could be forded for the space of thirty miles, they were all of necessity confined within these nar- row limits. Neither could the states which had espoused Cæsar's cause furnish him with corn, nor the troops which had gone far to forage return, as they were stopped by the floods; nor could the convoys coming from Italy and Gaul make their way to the camp. The states, too, were ex- hausted, because Afranius had conveyed almost all the corn, before Cæsar's arrival, into Ilerda, and whatever he had left had been already consumed by Cæsar. The cattle which might have served as a secondary resource against

But the Fortune of the hero, contented with *this* slight
alarm, returns in full career, and more than usual do the
propitious Deities favour him and merit his forgiveness.
Now the air *is* more serene, and Phœbus, equal to the waters,
has scattered the dense clouds into fleecy forms, and the
nights are reddening with the approaching light; and, the
due order of things observed, moisture departs from the
stars[1], and whatever of the water is poised aloft seeks
the lower regions.

The woods begin to raise their foliage, the hills to
emerge from the standing waters, and the valleys to become
hard, the light of day beheld. And when the Sicoris re-
gains its banks and leaves the plains, in the first place the
white willow, its twigs steeped in water, is woven into
small boats, and covered over, the bullock being slaughtered, adapted for passengers it floats along the swelling
stream. Thus does the Venetian on the flowing Padus,
and on the expanded ocean the Briton sail[2]; thus, when
the Nile covers everything, is the Memphitic boat framed
of the swampy papyrus[3].

want, had been removed by the states to a great distance on account of the
war."

[1] *Moisture departs from the stars*) ver. 126. He means that the
moisture now departed, which before, filling the clouds, had obscured the
light of the stars.

[2] *The Briton sail*) ver. 134. These were like the coracles, or light
boats, which Cæsar had seen used by the people of Britain. In the Civil
War, B. i. c. 54, he thus describes these operations :—"When Cæsar's
affairs were in this unfavourable position, and all the passes were guarded
by the soldiers and horse of Afranius, and the hedges could not be repaired, Cæsar ordered the soldiers to make ships of the kind that his knowledge of Britain a few years before had taught him. First, the keels and
ribs were made of light timber, then the rest of the hull of the ships was
wrought with wicker-work, and covered over with hides. When these were
finished, he drew them down to the river in waggons in one night, a distance of twenty-two miles from his camp, and transported in them some soldiers across the river, and on a sudden took possession of a hill adjoining
the bank. This he immediately fortified, before he was perceived by the
enemy. To this he afterwards transported a legion ; and having begun a
bridge on both sides, he finished it in two days. By this means he brought
safe to his camp the convoys and those who had gone out to forage, and
began to prepare a conveyance for the provisions."

[3] *Of the swampy papyrus*) ver. 136. Sulpitius, the Scholiast, says, that
he calls the papyrus "bibula," from its growing in the sand, which sucks
up the water.

Thrown across on these vessels the army hastens on
either side to curve the cut-down wood[1]; and dreading the
swelling of the threatening river, it does not place the wooden
foundations on the edges of the banks, *but* extends the
bridge into the midst of the fields.　And lest the Sicoris
may dare anything with its waters rising once again, it is
drawn away into channels, and, the stream being divided by
canals, it pays the penalty for the more swollen waters.
When Petreius sees that all things proceed with fortune to
Cæsar, he abandons the lofty Ilerda, and, distrusting the
might of the known world, seeks nations unsubdued[2], and
always fierce in arms by courting death, and he directs his
course to the limits of the world.

Cæsar, beholding the hills forsaken and the camp abandoned, bids them take up arms, and not look for bridge
or fords[3], but surmount the stream with hardy arms.
Obedience is given, and the soldier, rushing to the battle,
eagerly hastens on a path which in flight he would have
dreaded.　Afterwards, their arms regained, they warm their
soaking limbs, and, by running, reinvigorate their joints
chilled by the stream, until the shadows decrease, the day
speeding onwards to the noon.　And now the cavalry over
takes the hindmost ranks, and, undecided for flight and
for fight, they are detained.

[1] *To curve the cut-down wood*) ver. 137.　"Succisum curvare nemus;"
an elliptical method of expressing "to cut down wood and bend it into
arches for a bridge."

[2] *Seeks nations unsubdued*) ver. 146.　The object of Petreius and
Afranius, we learn from Cæsar, was to repair to Celtiberia.

[3] *Not look for bridge or fords*) ver. 149.　Because the route by the
bridge, as Cæsar informs us, required too large a circuit.　His cavalry
swam across the river.　He says, that "The foot being left behind, and
seeing that the cavalry had overtaken the enemy (Civil War, B. i. c. 54)
through the whole camp, the soldiers gathered in parties and declared their
regret that the enemy had been suffered to escape from their hands.　They
applied to their tribunes and centurions, and entreated them to inform
Cæsar that he need not be sparing of their labour: that they were ready
and able, and would venture to ford the river where the horse had crossed.
On this, Cæsar ordered all the weaker soldiers to be selected from each century, and left them with one legion besides to guard the camp.　The rest
of the legions he drew out without any baggage, and having disposed a
great number of horse in the river, above and below the ford, he led his
army over.　A few of his soldiers being carried away by the force of the
current were stopped by the horse and taken up, and not a man perished."

Two rocks raise[1] their craggy ridges from the plain, a hollow vale being in the midst. On the one side the elevated earth forms a chain of lofty hills, between which with darkened route safe paths lie concealed. These straits an enemy gaining possession of, Cæsar perceives that the warfare may be carried *thence* into the remote regions of the earth and into savage nations. " Go," says he, " without keeping your ranks[2], and in your speedy course turn back your hastening force, and present your faces and your threatening countenances to the battle; and let not the cowards fall by an ignoble death; as they fly let them receive the weapon straight in the breast."

He spoke, and he came in front of the foe speeding onward to the mountains. There they pitched their camps a little distant from each other, with a narrow trench *between*. After their eyes, straining by reason of no distance, had mutually caught sight[3] of each other's countenances in full view, and they beheld their own brothers, and children, and fathers, the wickedness of civil warfare was revealed.

For a little time they held their peace through fear; only with signs and the waving of the sword did they salute their friends. Soon, when, with more powerful impulses, ardent affection overpowered the rules *of war,* the soldiers ventured to pass the trench, *and* to stretch

---

[1] *Two rocks raise*) ver. 157. Cæsar finds that there is a passage through these defiles to remote regions and barbarous nations. It appears from his account that from his scouts he learnt " that there was a level road for the next five miles, and that there then succeeded a rough and mountainous country; and that whichever should first obtain possession of the defiles would have no trouble in preventing the other's progress."

[2] *Without keeping your ranks*) ver. 162. The meaning is, that Cæsar instructed his men to make all haste, leaving their ranks, to go by a circuitous path, and reaching the pass before the enemy, there to face about and charge him. Cæsar says, in the Civil War, B. i. c. 69, that, when his troops began to do this,—" At first the soldiers of Afranius ran in high spirits from their camp to look at us, and in contumelious language upbraided us, that we were forced for want of necessary subsistence to run away, and return to Ilerda. For our route was different from what we purposed, and we seemed to be going a contrary way."

[3] *Had mutually caught sight*) ver. 170. He means, that when they had encamped they were so close that they could easily recognize the countenances of each other.

the extended hands[1] for an embrace. One calls out the name of his host; another shouts to a neighbour; a youth spent together reminds another of their boyish pursuits; nor is there a Roman that does not recognize an enemy *as an acquaintance*. The arms are wet with tears, with sighs they interrupt their kisses; and, although stained with no blood, the soldier dreads to have done what he might *have done*.

Why dost thou beat thy breast? Why, madman, dost thou groan? Why dost thou pour forth empty laments, and not own that of thine own accord thou hast been obedient to criminality? Dost thou so greatly dread him, whom thou thyself dost make to be dreaded? Let the trumpet-call sound to battle, do thou neglect the ruthless signal; let them bear on the standards, stay behind; soon will the civic strife come to an end, and Cæsar, a private person, will love his son-in-law. Now, Concord, do thou approach, encircling all things in thine everlasting embrace, O thou salvation of things and of the harmonizing world, and hallowed love of the universe! now does our age hold a vast influence on what is to come. The skulking places of crimes so many have come to an end; pardon is torn away from an erring people; they have recognized their own friends.

---

[1] *To stretch the extended hands*) ver. 176. These circumstances are thus related in the Civil War, B. i. c. 283 :—" The soldiers having obtained a free opportunity of conversing with each other, came out in great numbers, and enquired each for whatever acquaintance or fellow-citizen he had in our camp, and invited him to him. First they returned them general thanks for sparing them the day before, and acknowledged that they were alive through their kindness. Then they enquired about the honor of our general, and whether they could with safety entrust themselves to him; and declared their sorrow that they had not done so in the beginning, and that they had taken up arms against their relations and kinsmen. Encouraged by these conferences, they desired the general's parole for the lives of Petreius and Afranius, that they might not appear guilty of a crime in having betrayed their generals. When they were assured of obtaining their demands, they promised that they would immediately remove their standards, and sent centurions of the first rank as deputies to treat with Cæsar about a peace. In the meantime some of them invite their acquaintances, and bring them to their camp, others are brought away by their friends, so that the two camps seemed to be united into one, and several of the tribunes and centurions came to Cæsar, and paid their respects to him."

O Fates, the Deity *thus* unpropitious, that by reason of a little respite increase calamities so great!

There was a truce, and the soldiers, mingled in either camp, wandered at large; in friendship on the hard turf they prepared the banquets; and with the mingled wine the libations flowed[1] on the grassy hearths, and, their couches united, the tale of the wars prolonged the sleepless night: on what plain they first came to a stand, from what right hand sped the lance. While they are boasting of the valiant things which they have done, and while they are disagreeing on many a point, what alone the Fates are seeking, confidence is renewed in them, wretched *beings*, and all the future criminality waxes the stronger by reason of their affection.

For after the treaty for a truce[2] is known to Petreius, and he sees himself and his own camp being betrayed, he arouses the right hands of his household troops to the accursed warfare, and, surrounded with a multitude, headlong drives the unarmed enemy from the camp, and separates them, joined in embraces, with the sword, and with plenteous bloodshed[3] disturbs the peace. Fierce anger adds words to provoke the battle:—

" O soldiers, unmindful of your country, forgetful of your standards, *if* you cannot bestow this on the cause of the Senate, to return, its champions, Cæsar being overcome; at least you can, to be overcome[4]. While *there is*

[1] *The libations flowed*) ver. 198. Libations of wine in honour of Bacchus were poured forth on the hearths that were temporarily made on the grass.

[2] *The treaty for a truce*) ver. 205. In allusion to the overtures made by his troops to Cæsar. See the Note to l. 176.

[3] *With plenteous bloodshed*) ver. 209. Cæsar, in the Civil War, B. i. c. 75, 76, mentions the conduct of Petreius in the following terms:—"Petreius did not neglect himself; he armed his domestics; with them and the Prætorian cohort of Spaniards and a few foreign horse, his dependents, whom he commonly kept near him to guard his person, he suddenly flew on the rampart, interrupted the conferences of the soldiers, drove our men from the camp, and put to death as many as he caught. Orders were given that whoever had any of Cæsar's soldiers should produce them; as soon as they were produced, they put them to death publicly in the Prætorium; but most of them concealed those whom they had entertained, and let them out at night over the rampart."

[4] *You can, to be overcome*) ver. 214. He means, that if they cannot be the champions of the Senate by the conquest of Cæsar, still they may fight, and though conquered, thus prove their fidelity.

the sword, and the Fates *are yet* uncertain, and blood shall not be wanting to flow from many a wound, will you be going over to a tyrant, and will you raise standards condemned *for treason?* And will Cæsar have to be entreated that he will make no distinction between his slaves? Is life also to be begged for[1] for your generals? Never shall my safety be the price and the reward of abominable treason; civil wars tend not to this, that we should live on.

" Under the name of peace we are betrayed. Nations would not be digging iron out of the mine that retreats far within *the earth*, no walls would be fortifying cities, no spirited steed would be going to the wars, no fleet upon the ocean to spread its tower-bearing ships upon the deep, if liberty were ever righteously bartered in return for peace. Oaths sworn in accursed criminality[2] are to bind my enemies, forsooth! but by you is your fidelity less esteemed, because it is allowed you fighting for a just cause to hope for pardon as well. O shocking compact of disgrace! Now, Magnus, ignorant of thy lot throughout the whole world thou art levying armies, and art arousing the monarchs who possess the extremities of the world, when perhaps by our treaty safety is already *basely* promised thee."

Thus he spoke, and he aroused all their feelings, and brought back the fondness for criminality. Thus, when, unused to the woods, wild beasts have grown tame in an inclosed prison, and have laid aside their threatening countenances, and have learned to submit to man; if a little blood comes to their burning mouths, their rage and fury return, and, reminded by the tasted gore, their jaws swell; their anger waxes hot, and hardly does it withhold from the trembling keeper. They rush on to all wickedness, and *broken* faith commits excesses, which, amid the dark night of battle, Fortune, to the disgrace of the Deities, might have been guilty of; amid the

[1] *Is life also to be begged for*) ver. 219. In allusion to the terms which they had proposed to Cæsar for the safety of their generals, he reproaches them with the readiness with which they were about to make themselves and their generals indiscriminately his slaves.

[2] *Sworn in accursed criminality*) ver. 228. In allusion to the promise of safety for their generals which Cæsar had given, contrary to his own wishes.

tables[1] and the couches[2], they stab the breasts which just before they have enfolded in their embraces. And, although at first lamenting they unsheathe their weapons, when the sword, the dissuader from right, adheres to the right hand, soon as they strike, they hate their own friends and strengthen their wavering spirits with the blow. Now the camp waxes hot with the tumult, and with the riot of criminality; the necks of parents are wrenched. And as though hidden criminality might be valueless, they expose all their monstrous deeds before the faces of their chieftains; they take delight in being guilty.

Thou, Cæsar, although despoiled of many a soldier, dost recognize[3] the Gods of heaven *as favouring thee*. Nor indeed in the Emathian plains[4] was thy fortune greater, nor in the waves of Phocæan Massilia; nor were exploits so great performed in the Pharian seas; since through this crime alone in the civil warfare thou shalt be the leader of the better cause. Polluted by an accursed slaughter, the generals dare not entrust their troops to an adjoining camp, and again they take flight towards the walls of lofty Ilerda. The cavalry, meeting them, cuts off all the plain, and encloses the enemy on the parched hills. Then Cæsar strives to surround them[5] destitute of water with a deep entrenchment, and not to permit the camp to reach the banks *of the river*, or the outworks to wind around plenteous springs.

[1] *Amid the tables*) ver. 245. This is contrary to the account of the conduct of the soldiers given by Cæsar himself. See the Note to l. 209.

[2] *And the couches*) ver. 245. The "tori" are the couches on which they reclined while taking the repast.

[3] *Dost recognize*) ver. 255. It is a matter of doubt with the Commentators what is the true meaning of "agnoscis" here. Some think that it means that Cæsar recognizes the Gods as propitious to him in this transaction; while others, perhaps with some reason, consider it to mean that Cæsar shows reverence for the Gods, in not violating the rites of hospitality and good faith by slaying the troops of Petreius which were in his camp.

[4] *Nor indeed in the Emathian plains*) ver. 255. He means to say that the cause of Cæsar was not more profited by his successes at Pharsalia, Massilia, and in Egypt, than by the favour which he found with the Gods on this occasion. It may be observed that this is one of the very few occasions on which the Poet speaks favourably of Cæsar. Indeed, as Rowe justly observes, the baseness and cruelty of Petreius were inexcusable.

[5] *Cæsar strives to surround them*) ver. 264. These events are related at length in the Civil War, B. i. c. 80-84.

When they beheld the road to death. their terror was
turned into headlong rage. The soldiers slew the
horses, no useful aid to people blockaded; and at length,
hope laid aside. being compelled to condemn *all* flight,
doomed to fall they are borne upon the foe. When Cæsar
saw them running down with extended front, and, devoted,
making their way to certain death, he said:—

"Soldiers, now keep back your darts, and withhold your
swords from them as they rush on; with no blood shall the
victory be gained for me; he is not conquered at no cost,
who with his throat *exposed* challenges the foe. See how
life being hated *by them*, valueless to themselves, the youths
rush on, now threatening to perish with loss to myself. They
will feel no wounds, they will fall on the swords, *and* rejoice in
shedding their blood. Let this zeal forsake their minds, let
this mad fit subside. Let them be rid of their wish to die."

Thus did he suffer them to be inflamed to no purpose
as they threatened, and, the war forbidden, to wax faint, until,
Phœbus having sunk, night substituted her lights. Then,
when no opportunity was given of mingling in the fight,
by degrees their fierce anger moderated, and their spirits
cooled; just as wounded breasts manifest the greatest courage
while the pain and the wound is recent, and the warm blood
gives an active impulse to the nerves, and the bones have
not as yet cleaved to the skin; if the victor stands conscious of the sword being driven home, and withholds his
hands, then a cold numbness fastens on the limbs and
spirit, the strength being withdrawn, after the congealed
blood has contracted the dried-up wounds.

And now deprived of water, the earth first dug up,
they seek hidden springs and concealed streams; and not
alone with mattocks and sturdy spades do they dig up the
fields, but with their own swords: and a well upon the
hollowed mountain is sunk as far as the surface of the
watery plain. Not so deeply down, not daylight left
so far behind, does the pale searcher [1] for the Asturian gold

---

[1] *Does the pale searcher*) ver. 298. Claudian also speaks of the gold-
mines in the country of the Asturians in Spain. Lemaire thinks, apparently with good reason, that " pallidus " is to be read in a literal or physical sense. Silius Italicus speaks of the avaricious Asturian as being "con-
color," " of the same colour," as the gold which he seeks, B. i. l. 231.

bury himself; still, neither do any rivers resoun1 in their
hidden course, nor *any* new streams gush forth, on the
pumice-stone being struck; nor do the sweating caverns
distil with small drops, nor is the gravel disturbed, moved
upwards by the little spring.   Then, exhausted with much
perspiration, the youths are drawn up above, wearied with
the hard incisions in the flinty rocks.   And you, waters,
in the search for you cause them to be the less able to
endure [1] the parching atmosphere.   Nor do they, wearied,
refresh their bodies with feasting, and, loathing food, they
make hunger their resource *against thirst.*   If a softer soil
betrays moisture, both hands squeeze the unctuous clods
over their mouths.   If turbid filth is lying unmoved upon
the black mud, all the soldiers vying with each other fall
down for the polluted draughts, and dying, quaff the waters,
which, likely to live, they would have been unwilling : after
the manner, too, of wild beasts, they dry the distended
cattle, and, milk denied, the loathsome blood is sucked
from the exhausted udder.   Then they wring the grass
and leaves, and strip off the branches dripping with dew,
and if at all *they can*, they squeeze juices from the crude
shoots or the tender sap.

   O happy *they*, whom the barbarian enemy, flying, has
slain amid the fields with poison mingled with the
springs[2]!   Though, Cæsar, thou shouldst openly pour
into these streams poison, and the gore of wild beasts,
and the pallid aconite that grows upon the Dictæan rocks,
the Roman youth, not deceived, would drink.   Their
entrails are scorchéd by the flame, and their parched mouths
are clammy, rough with scaly tongues.   Now do their
veins shrink up, and, refreshed with no moisture, their
lungs contract the alternating passages for the air; and hard-
drawn sighs hurt their ulcerated palates.   Still, however,
they open their mouths, and catch at the night air.   They
long for the showers, by whose onward force but just now

---

[1] *The less able to endure*) ver. 305.   The more they vainly searched for
water, the more thirsty they became.
[2] *With poison mingled with the springs*) ver. 320.   Several opponents
of the Romans are said to have poisoned the rivers and springs; Pyrrhus
king of Epirus, Jugurtha, king of Mauritania, Mithridates, and Juba, as
mentioned in history as having so done.

all things were inundated, and their looks are fixed upon the dry clouds. And that the more the want of water may afflict them in their wretchedness, they are not encamped upon the scorching Meroë[1] beneath the sky of the Crab. where the naked Garamantes[2] plough; but, the army, entrapped between the flowing Sicoris and the rapid Iberus, looks upon the adjacent streams.

Now subdued, the generals yielded, and, arms being laid down, Afranius, the adviser to sue for peace, dragging *after him* his half-dead squadrons into the enemy's camp, stood suppliantly before the feet of the conqueror. His dignity is preserved as he entreats, not beaten down by calamities, and he performs between his former *good* fortune and his recent misfortunes all the parts of one conquered, but *that one* a general, and with a breast void of care he sues for pardon[3] :—

" If the Fates had laid me prostrate under a degenerate enemy, there was not wanting the bold right hand for hurrying on *my own* death; but now the sole cause of my entreating for safety is, Cæsar, that I deem thee worthy to grant life. By no zeal for party are we influenced; nor have we taken up arms as foes to thy designs. Us in fact did the civil warfare find generals; and to our former cause was fidelity preserved so long as it could be. The Fates we

---

[1] *The scorching Meroë)* ver. 333. Meroë was a spot in Æthiopia called an island by the ancients, though not really so. It was the chief emporium for trade between Egypt, Æthiopia, Arabia, and India. Of course, from its southerly situation, the heat there would be intense.

[2] *The naked Garamantes)* ver. 334. The Garamantes were the most southerly people known to the ancients in North Africa. Herodotus places them nineteen days' journey from Æthiopia and the shores of the Indian Ocean, fifteen days' journey from Ammonium, and thirty days' journey from Egypt.

[3] *He sues for pardon)* ver. 343. The following is the speech of Afranius, on this occasion, given by Cæsar in the Civil War, B. i. c. 84 :—" That Cæsar ought not to be displeased either with him or his soldiers, for wishing to preserve their fidelity to their general, Cneius Pompeius. That they had now sufficiently discharged their duty to him, and had suffered punishment enough, in having endured the want of every necessary; but now, pent up almost like wild beasts, they were prevented from procuring water, and from walking abroad, and were unable to bear either the bodily pain or the mental anguish, but confessed themselves conquered, and begged and entreated, if there was any room left for mercy, that they might not be necessitated to suffer the most severe penalties."

do not withstand; the western nations we yield, the eastern ones we open *unto thee*, and we permit thee to feel assured of the world left behind thy back.

" Nor has blood, shed upon the plains, concluded the war for thee nor sword and wearied troops. This alone forgive thy foes, that thou dost conquer. And no great things are asked. Grant repose to the wearied; suffer us unarmed to pass the life which thou dost bestow; consider that our troops are lying prostrate along the plains; nor does it indeed befit *thee* to mingle with fortunate arms those condemned, and the captured to take part in thy triumphs; this multitude has fulfilled its destiny. This do we ask, that thou wilt not compel us, conquered, to conquer along with thyself."

He spoke; but *Cæsar*, readily prevailed upon, and serene in countenance, was appeased, and remitted continuance in the warfare [1] and *all* punishment. As soon as ever the compact for the desired peace had pleased them, the soldiers ran down to the *now* unguarded rivers; they fell down along the banks, and troubled the conceded streams. In many the long-continued draughts of water suddenly *gulped* not permitting the air to have a passage along the empty veins, compresses and shuts in the breath; nor even yet does the parching plague give way; but the craving malady, their entrails now filled with the stream, demands water for itself.

Afterwards strength returned to the nerves, and power to the men. O Luxury, prodigal of resources [2], never content with moderate provision, and gluttony, craving for food sought for over land and sea, and *thou*, pride of a sumptuous table, learn *from this* with how little we have the power to prolong life, and how much it is that nature de-

---

[1] *Continuance in the warfare*) ver. 364. " Usum belli " probably means " any further employment in the war," by being forced to serve on his side; so in the Civil War, B. i. c. 86: " Cæsar gave security that they should receive no damage, and that no person should be obliged, against his inclination, to take the military oath under him."

[2] *Prodigal of resources*) ver. 373. The Poet thus exclaims in a vein of Stoicism in which he sometimes indulges. See the Second Book, L 351, *et seq.*

mands. No wine, poured forth under a Consul gone out of memory[1], refreshes them fainting; from no gold and porcelain[2] do they drink; but from the pure water does life return. Enough for the people is the stream and bread. Ah, wretched they who engage in wars!

Then, leaving their arms to the victor, the soldiers, un-harmed with spoiled breast and free from cares, are dis-persed among their own cities. Oh! how much do they regret, on having obtained the granted peace, that they have ever with vibrated shoulders poised the weapon, *and* have endured thirst, and have in vain asked the Gods for pros-perous battles. To those, forsooth, who have experienced successful warfare, there *still* remain so many doubtful battles, so many toils throughout the world; should waver-ing Fortune never make a slip in success, so often must victory be gained, blood be poured forth upon all lands, and through his fortunes so numerous Cæsar be followed. Happy he, who was able then to know, the ruin of the world impending, in what place he was to lie[3]. No battles summoned them forth in their weariness; no trumpet-call broke their sound slumbers.

[1] *A Consul gone out of memory*) ver. 379. On the outside of the " am-phoræ," or " cadi," the titles of the wine were painted, the date of the vintage being denoted by the names of the Consuls then in office; and when the vessels were of glass, small tickets, called " pittacia," were suspended from them, stating to a similar effect. Ovid has a somewhat similar passage to the present, in his Art of Love, B. ii. l. 83 :—" For me, let the cask, stored up in the times of ancient Consuls, pour forth the wine of my an-cestors."

[2] *And porcelain*) ver. 380. The " murrhina," or " murrea vasa," " myrrhine vessels," were first introduced into Rome by Pompey. Their value was very great. Nero is said to have given three hundred talents for a drinking cup of this description. Pliny says that these vessels came from the east, principally from places within the Parthian empire, and chiefly from Caramania. He describes them as made of a substance formed by a moisture thickened in the earth by heat, and says that they were chiefly valued for their variety of colours. It has been suggested that they were made of a kind of glass, but it is, perhaps, more probable that they were made of Chinese porcelain.

[3] *He was to lie*) ver. 394. " Quo jaceat jam scire loco." There is some doubt about the exact meaning of " jaceat;" it may signify simply, " where in the ruin of the world he is to lie," without any stronger signification, or it may have the meaning of " where he is to die."

Now do the wives, and the innocent children, and the humble dwellings, and the land their own, receive no husbandmen draughted off[1]. This burden as well does Fortune remove from them at ease, that tormenting party spirit is removed from their minds. The one is the giver of *their* safety, the other was *their* leader. Thus do they alone, in happiness, look on upon the cruel warfare with no *favouring* wishes.

Not the same fortune of war lasted throughout the whole earth ; but against the side of Cæsar something did it dare, where the waves of the Adriatic sea beat against the extended Salonæ[2], and the warm Jader[3] flows forth towards the gentle Zephyrs. There, trusting in the warlike race of the Curictans[4], whom the land rears, flowed around by the Adriatic sea, Antony, taking up his position in *that* distant region, is shut up, safe from the onset[5] of war. if only famine, that besieges with certainty, would withdraw. The earth affords no forage for feeding the horses. the yellow-haired Ceres produces no crops of corn ; the soldiers strip the plains of grass, and, the fields now shorn close, with their wretched teeth they tear the dry grass from off the turf of their encampment. As soon as

---

[1] *No husbandmen draughted off*) ver. 397. Happy in not having to await the conclusion of the war, in order to be planted (deduci) in the enemy's country as military colonists, inasmuch as, being disbanded, they immediately retired to their own homes.

[2] *The extended Salona*) ver. 404. Salona, or Salonæ, was an important city of Illyria, and the capital of Dalmatia, situate on a small bay of the sea. It was the seat of a Roman colony. Here the Emperor Diocletian was born, and ended his days in retirement.

[3] *The warm Jader*) ver. 405. He alludes to a river so called near Salona ; there was also a town called Jader, or Jadera, on the Illyrian coast, with an excellent harbour.

[4] *Race of the Curictans*) ver. 406. Curicta was the name of an island in the Adriatic, off the coast of Illyria, where Dolabella commanded for Cæsar, while Caius Antonius encamped on the island, and was besieged by Libo. He must not be confounded with his brother, Marc Antony, who at this time was at Brundisium, in command of Cæsar's forces there. C. Antonius was Proconsul of Macedonia at the time of Cæsar's death, and being defeated by Brutus, was slain by him in revenge for the murder of Cicero by Marc Antony.

[5] *Safe from the onset*) ver. 409. "Cautus" has here the unusual meaning of "safe," or "secure."

L

they behold their friends[1] on the shore of the opposite mainland and Basilus their leader[2], a new stratagem for flight across the sea *is* discovered.

For, not according to wont do they extend the keels and build aloft the sterns, but with an unusual shape they fasten firm planks together for supporting a massive tower. For, on every side, empty caissons support the raft[3], a series of which, fastened together, with extended chains receives alder planks laid obliquely in double rows. Nor does it carry its oars exposed to the weapons in the open front: but that sea which it has surrounded with the beams *the oars* strike, and it shows the miracle of a silent course, because it neither carries sails nor beats the discovered waves. Then the straits are watched, while the ebbing tide is retreating with lessening waves, and the sands are laid bare by the sea flowing out. And now, the waters retiring, the shores increase; the raft, being launched, is borne gliding along on the receding tide, and its two companions. Upon them all a lofty tower is threatening above and the decks *are* formidable with nodding pinnacles.

Octavius, the guardian[4] of the Illyrian waves, was un

[1] *Behold their friends*) ver. 415. The "socii" here mentioned are Dolabella, who was commanding for Cæsar on the mainland, with his troops, and whom Basilus had joined with his fleet, while waiting to relieve Antonius.

[2] *Basilus their leader*) ver. 416. This was L. Minucius Basilus, whose original name was M. Satrius, before he assumed that of his uncle, by whom he was adopted. He served under Cæsar in Gaul, and in the Civil War commanded part of his fleet. Like Brutus and others, though a personal friend of Cæsar, he took part in his murder. He himself was slain by his own slaves about a year after. The fifteenth Epistle in the sixth book Ad Familiares, was written by Cicero to Basilus, congratulating him on the death of Cæsar.

[3] *Support the raft*) ver. 420. The whole of this account is very confused, and Lemaire suggests that it is one description formed from a mixture of several. The floats or rafts seem to have been of oblong form, and formed each of two tiers of caissons, or "cuppæ" (more literally "wine vats"), the space between which tiers was not covered over, for the purpose of rowing, while the outer sides of the raft were protected by hurdles. Being thus rowed from within, their motion would naturally astonish the enemy when at a distance. Lucan speaks of the floats being made by the forces of Antonius, whereas Florus mentions them as being sent by Basilus to the relief of the troops on the island.

[4] *Octavius, the guardian*) ver. 433. This was M. Octavius, a friend of

willing immediately to assault the raft, and withheld his swift ships, until his prey should be increased on a second passage[1], and invited them, rashly going on board, to try the deep once more through the pacific appearance of the sea. Thus, while the hunter encloses the scared deer in the feather-foil[2], as they dread the scent of the strong smelling feathers, or while he is lifting the nets on the forked sticks duly arranged, he holds the noisy mouth of the light Molossian *hound*[3], and restrains the Spartan and the Cretan *dogs;* neither is the wood permitted to any dog, except the one which, with nose pressed *to the ground,* scents the footsteps, and, the prey found, knows how not to bark, contented by shaking the leash[4] to point out the lair.

And no delay *is there;* the masses are filled again, and, the rafts greedily sought, the island is abandoned, at the time when at nightfall the waning light now opposes the first

Cicero and Curule Ædile B.C. 50. He espoused the cause of Pompey, and was appointed, with Q. Scribonius Libo, to the command of the Liburnian and Achæan fleets, serving as legate to M. Bibulus, the commander of Pompey's fleet. He and Libo defeated Dolabella on the Illyrian coast. After the battle of Pharsalia, he retreated first to Illyricum, and thence to Africa. The last time that he is mentioned in history is on the occasion of the battle of Actium, when, with M. Justeius, he commanded the middle of Antony's fleet.

[1] *On a second passage*) ver. 435. The meaning of this is obscure, but it seems to be that Octavius would not attack the floats till the first successful attempt had led them to return and fetch away more troops from the island.

[2] *In the feather-foil*) ver. 437. The " formido," or " feather-foil," was a toil or net used for catching deer, and covered with feathers of a red colour, for the purpose of scaring them away from breaking through the nets when inclosed. The " odorata penna " here mentioned is supposed by some to refer to the smell of the red dye in which the feathers were steeped; others, however, think that it refers to the smell of the feathers themselves, and cite the Cynægeticon of Gratius Faliscus, where he says that the feathers of vultures were used for foils, the strong smell of them driving away the wild beasts. As the feathers seem to have been used for scaring the deer, both by the sight and the smell, the line may mean, " the deer fearing the strong-smelling feathers as they move about in the breeze," or, " fearing the scent of the strong-smelling feathers."

[3] *The light Molossian hound*) ver. 440. The dogs of Molossus, in Epirus, were famed for their courage in the chase, while those of Sparta and Crete were prized for their swiftness.

[4] *By shaking the leash*) ver. 444. It appears from this passage, that when sent into dense thickets to find, the dogs were held by a long leash or cord, and, when successful, notice was given to the hunter by the shaking of it.

shades *of night*. But the Cilicians of Pompey with their
ancient skill¹ prepare to lay stratagems beneath the sea,
and suffering the surface of the main to be free, suspend
chains in the midst of the deep, and permit the connected
links to hang loose, and fasten them to the rocks² of the
Illyrian cliffs. Neither the first raft³ nor the one that
follows is retarded; but the third mass sticks fast, and by
a rope drawn⁴ follows on to the rocks. The hollow cliffs
hang over the sea, and, strange! the mass stands, always
about to fall, and with the woods overshadows the deep.
Hither did the ocean often bear ships, wrecked by the
north wind, and drowned bodies, and hide them in the
darkened caverns. The sea enclosed restores the spoil:
and when the caverns have vomited forth the water, the
waves of the eddying whirlpool surpass in rage the Tauromenian Charybdis⁵.

Here *one* mass, laden with colonists of Opitergium⁶,
stopped short; this the ships, unmoored from all their
stations, surrounded; others swarmed upon the rocks and
the sea-shore. Vulteius perceived⁷ the silent stratagems
beneath the waves (he was the captain of the raft),
who having in vain endeavoured to cut the chains with
the sword, without any hope⁸ demanded the fight, uncertain which way to turn his back, which way his breast,

¹ *With their ancient skill*) ver. 449. He alludes to the skill which, from
of old, the Cilicians had possessed in naval matters in consequence of their
former piratical mode of life.

² *Fasten them to the rocks*) ver. 452. One end of the chain or boom
was fastened to the rocks on the shore, while the other was probably fastened
down with anchors, thus extending nearly from the shore to the point of
embarkation in the island.

³ *Neither the first raft*) ver. 452. We learn from Florus that two were
carried over by the high tide.

⁴ *By a rope drawn*) ver. 454. Getting entangled by the chain or boom,
the float appears to have been dragged by the enemy upon the rocks off the
mainland, among which was the whirlpool here described.

⁵ *Tauromenian Charybdis*) ver. 461. The whirlpool of Charybdis, in
Sicily, was near the town of Tauromenus, or Tauromenium.

⁶ *Colonists of Opitergium*) ver. 462. This was a Roman colony of
Venetia, in the north of Italy. The present name is Oderzo.

⁷ *Vulteius perceived*) ver. 465. We learn from Florus that this brave
man was a tribune of Cæsar's army, but nothing more is known of him.

⁸ *Without any hope*) ver. 467. Wishes to fight, though with no hope of
being victorious.

to the warfare. Valour, however, in this calamity effected as much as, ensnared, it was able. The fight was between so many thousands pouring in upon the captured raft and scarcely on the other side a complete cohort; not long indeed, for black night concealed the dubious light, and darkness caused a truce.

Then thus with magnanimous voice did Vulteius encourage the cohort dismayed and dreading their approaching fate: "Youths, free no longer than one short night, consult in *this* limited time for your fortunes in *this* extremity. A short life remains for no one who in it has time to seek death for himself; nor, youths, is the glory of death inferior, in running to meet approaching fate. The period of their life to come being uncertain to all, equal is the praise of courage, both in sacrificing the years which you have hoped for, and in cutting short the moments of your closing existence, while by your own hand you hasten your fate. No one is compelled to wish to die. No way for flight is open; *our* fellow-citizens stand on every side bent against our throats. Determine on death, and all fear is gone; whatever is necessary, *that same* desire.

" Still, we have not to fall amid the dark haze of warfare, or when armies envelope their own darts with the shades intermingling, when heaped up bodies are lying on the plain, *and* every death goes to the common account, *and* valour perishes overwhelmed. In a ship have the Gods placed us conspicuous to our allies and to the foe. The seas will find us witnesses, the land will find them, the island from the summit of its cliffs will present them; the two sides from opposite shores[1] will be spectators. Fortune! an example in our deaths how great and memorable thou art contemplating I know not. Whatever memorials in ages *past* fidelity has afforded and a soldier's duty preserved by the sword, *the same* our youths will transcend.

---

[1] *From opposite shores*) ver. 495. " Diverso a littore." This description is very confused, and it is difficult to say what were the localities of the different parties. It would seem that the island was probably at the mouth of a river, and that the mainland on one side of the river was occupied by Antonius and his troops, while the Pompeians had possession of the mainland on the other side, on which they now dragged the raft of Vulteius.

" For, Cæsar, to fall upon our own swords for thee we
deem to be but little : but to us, hemmed in, no greater
ones are existing, for us to give as pledges of affection so
great.   An envious lot has cut off much from our praises,
in that we are not environed, captured together with our old
men and children[1].   Let the enemy know that we are men
unsubdued, and dread our courage, glowing and eager for
death, and be glad that[2] no more rafts have stuck fast.
They will be trying to corrupt us with treaties and with a
disgraced life.   O would that, in order that our distinguished death might gain the greater fame, they would prof-
fer pardon, *and* bid us hope for safety ; that they might
not, when we pierce our vitals with the warm weapon, think
that we are desperate.   By great valour must we deserve,
that Cæsar, a few among so many thousands being lost,
may call this a loss and a calamity.

" Though the Fates should afford an egress and let us
escape, I would not wish to avoid what is pressing on.
I have parted with life, companions, and am wholly impelled by the longing for approaching death. It is a frenzy.
To those alone is it granted to feel it whom now the
approach of doom is influencing : and the Gods conceal
from those destined to live, in order that they may endure
to live, that it is sweet to die."

Thus did courage arouse all the spirits of the magnanimous youths : whereas, before the words of their leader,
they all beheld with moistened eyes the stars of heaven,
and were in dread at the turning of the Wain of the Bear,
those same, when his precepts had influenced their brave
minds, *now* longed for day.   Nor was the sky then slow to
sink the stars in the main ; for the sun was occupying the
Ledæan Constellations[3] when his light is most elevated in

---

[1] *With our old men and children*) ver. 504.   Probably in allusion to the
Saguntines, who slew their aged people and children rather than allow them
to fall into the possession of the enemy.

[2] *And be glad that*) ver. 506. ' Because he must envy our glory in dying
thus valiantly.

[3] *The Ledæan Constellations*) ver. 526.   He means the Constellation
Gemini, supposed to have been formed by Castor and Pollux, the twin sons
of Jupiter and Leda.   The meaning of this circumlocution is, that the sun
was passing from Gemini into Cancer, and that it was about the beginning
of June.

the Crab. A short night was then urging the Thessalian arrows[1]. The rising day disclosed the Istrians[2] standing on the rocks, and the warlike Liburnians[3] on the sea with the Grecian fleet. The fight suspended, they first tried to conquer by a treaty, if *perchance* life might become more desirable to those entrapped, through the very delay of death.

Life now forsworn, the devoted youths stood resolved, and, secure in fight, their deaths assured to themselves by their own hands; and in no one *of them* did the outcry *of the enemy* shake the minds of the heroes prepared for the worst; and at the same time, both by sea and land, few in number, they bore up against innumerable forces, so great was their confidence in death. And when it seemed that in the warfare blood enough had flowed, their fury was turned from the enemy. First, Vulteius himself, the commander of the float, his throat bared, now demanding death, exclaims :—

" Is there any one of the youths whose right hand is worthy of my blood, and who, with certain assurance, can testify that with wounds from me he is ready to die?" Having said no more, already has not one sword alone pierced his entrails. He commends all, but him to whom he owes the first wounds, dying, he slays with a grateful stroke. The others rush to meet *each other*, and the whole horrors of warfare on one side do they perpetrate. Thus did the Dircæan band spring up from the seed *sown* by Cadmus[4],

---

[1] *The Thessalian arrows*) ver. 528. He alludes to the Constellation Sagittarius, or the Archer, which was supposed to be formed by Chiron, the Centaur, who dwelt in Thessaly. Being opposite to Gemini, it then rises at night.

[2] *Disclosed the Istrians*) ver. 529. The Histri, or Istri, here mentioned, were the inhabitants of Histria, a peninsula at the northern extremity of the Adriatic. They were a warlike Illyrian race, and were the partisans of Pompey, as here seen. Their chief towns were Tergeste and Pola.

[3] *The warlike Liburnians*) ver. 530. The Liburni were the inhabitants of Liburnia, a district of Illyricum ; they were very skilful sailors, and, on this occasion, were adherents to the cause of Pompey. Their light-sailing vessels were the original models of the " Liburnicæ " or " Liburnæ naves " of the Romans.

[4] *Seed sown by Cadmus*) ver. 550. He alludes to the occasion when Cadmus slew the dragon near the fountain of Dirce, and sowed its teeth in the ground, from which soldiers sprang up who slew each other. See the Metamorphoses of Ovid, B. iii. L. 100, *et seq.* This was ominous of the

and fall by the wounds of its own side, a dire presage to
the Theban brothers; the earth-born ones, too, sprung on
the plains of Phasis[1] from the wakeful teeth *of the dragon,*
the anger being enflamed by magic charms, filled the furrows so vast with kindred blood; and Medea herself shuddered at the crime[2] which she had wrought with herbs
before untried.

Thus engaged to mutual destruction do the youths fall,
and in the deaths of the heroes death has too great a
share in the valour; equally do they slay and fall with
deadly wounds; nor does his right hand deceive any one.
Nor are the wounds owing to the swords driven home;
the blade is run against by the breast, and with their
throats they press against the hand *of him who gives the
wound.* When with a blood-stained fate brothers rush upon
brothers, and the son upon the parent, still, with no trembling right hand, with all their might they drive home the
swords. There is but one mark of duty in those who
strike, not to repeat *the blow.* Now, half-dead, they drag
their entrails, gushing out, to the hatches, and they pour
into the sea plenteous blood. It gives them pleasure to behold the scorned light of day, and with proud looks to gaze
upon their conquerors, and to feel the approach of death.

Now is the raft beheld heaped up with the bloody
slaughter, and the victors give the bodies to the funeral
piles, the generals wondering[3] that to any one his leader
can be of value so great. Fame, spreading abroad over
the whole world, has spoken with greater praises of no ship
Still, after these precedents of the heroes, cowardly nations will not come to a sense how far from difficult it is

deaths of Eteocles and Polynices, the brothers, descendants of Cadmus, by
each other's hands.

[1] *On the plains of Phasis*) ver. 552. Jason also at Colchis, or "the
plains of Phasis," slew the dragon that guarded the Golden Fleece, and, sowing
its teeth in the ground, a race of men sprang up, on which, through the arts
of Medea, they turned their weapons against each other. See Ovid's Metamorphoses, B. vii. l. 122, *et seq.*

[2] *Shuddered at the crime*) ver. 556. The crime of fratricide which those
sprung from the teeth were committing, after Jason had thrown the stone
among them, as related by Ovid.

[3] *The generals wondering*) ver. 572. Octavius and Libo, the leaders of
Pompey's forces.

to escape slavery by *one's own* hand.   But tyrants' rule is
feared by reason of the sword, and liberty is galled by
cruel arms, and is ignorant that swords were given that
no one might be a slave.   Death, I wish that thou wouldst
refuse to withdraw the fearful from life, but that valour
alone could bestow thee!

Not more inactive than this warfare was the one which at
that time was raging in the Libyan fields.   For the bold
Curio unmoors his ships from the shore of Lilybæum [1],
and, no boisterous north wind being caught in his sails,
makes for the shores between the half-buried towers of
great Carthage and Clupea [2] with its well-known encampment [3]; and his first camp he pitches at a distance from
the surging sea, where the sluggish Bagrada [4] betakes itself, the plougher-up of the parched sand.

Thence he repairs to the hills and the rocks eaten away
on every side, which antiquity, not without reason, names
the realms of Antæus [5].   A rude countryman informed
him, desiring to know the reasons for the ancient name,
what was known *to him* through many ancestors.

[1] *The shore of Lilybæum*) ver. 583.   Lilybæum was a town on the
western coast of Sicily, on the site of the present Marsala, situate on a promontory of the same name, opposite to the coast of Africa.   Cæsar, in the
Civil War, B. ii. l. 23, thus mentions the departure of Curio for Africa:—
"About the same time Caius Curio, having sailed from Sicily to Africa, and,
from the first, despising the forces of Publius Attius Varus, transported only
two of the four legions which he had received from Cæsar, and five hundred
horse, and having spent two days and three nights on the voyage, arrived at
a place called Aquilaria, which is about twenty-two miles distant from
Clupea, and, in the summer season, has a convenient harbour."

[2] *And Clupea*) ver. 586.   Clupea, or Clypea, was originally called Aspis.
It was a city on a promontory so called, in the north-east of the Carthaginian territory.   It was founded by Agathocles, king of Sicily, and was
taken in the first Punic war by the Romans, who called it Clypea, the
translation of Aspis, meaning "a shield."   Its present name is Klibiah.

[3] *With its well-known encampment*) ver. 586.   Probably from the circumstance of Hercules having been said to have landed there, in his expedition
against Antæus.   Cornelius Scipio, as mentioned by Lucan, had formerly encamped in that neighbourhood, whence the spot was called "Castra Corneliana."

[4] *The sluggish Bagrada*) ver. 588.   This river, which is now called the
"Mejerdah," falls into the sea near the ancient Utica.

[5] *Realms of Antæus*) ver. 590.   Strabo mentions this mountain chain as
"the tomb of Antæus," and describes it as extending many hundreds of
miles, from Tingitana, in Mauritania, to the hills in the vicinity of Utica.

" Earth, not as yet barren. after the Giants being born,
conceived a dreadful offspring in the Libyan caves. Nor
to the Earth was Typhon so just a ground of pride, or
Tityus and the fierce Briareus; and she spared the heavens, in that she did not bring forth Antæus in the Phlegræan fields[1]. By this privilege as well did the Earth
redouble the strength so vast of her offspring, in that,
when they touched their parent, the limbs now exhausted
were vigorous again with renewed strength. This cavern
was his abode; they report that under the lofty rock he
lay concealed, *and* had caught lions for his food. For
his sleep no skins of wild beasts were wont to afford a
bed, no wood a couch. and lying on the bare earth he reco
vered his strength. The Libyans, tillers of the fields, perish; they perish whom the sea has brought; and his
strength, for a long time not using the aid of falling
slights the gift of the Earth; unconquered was he in
strength by all, although he kept standing.

" At length the report of the blood-stained pest *was*
spread abroad, and invited to the Libyan shores the magnanimous Alcides, who was relieving the land and sea from
monsters. He threw off the skin of the lion of Cleonæ[2],
Antæus *that* of a Libyan *lion.* The stranger besprinkled
his limbs with oil, the custom of the Olympic exercises[3]
observed; the other, not entirely trusting to touching his
mother with his feet, sprinkled warm sand[4] as an aid to his

---

[1] *The Phlegræan fields*) ver. 597. The Phlegræan plains were said to be
situate in Thessaly or Macedonia, and there the Earth gave birth to Typhon,
Tityus, and Briareus, who waged war against the Gods. The volcanic tract
extending from Capua to Cumæ in Campania was called by the same name,
and the tradition was, that there, too, the Giants warred with the Gods.

[2] *The lion of Cleonæ*) ver. 612. The Nemean lion, whose skin Hercules
wore, is so called from the town of Cleonæ, which was near the spot where
it was slain.

[3] *The Olympic exercises*) ver. 614. At the Olympic games, and at the
" palæstræ" in general, it was the custom of the wrestlers to anoint their
bodies with " ceroma," a mixture of oil and wax.

[4] *Sprinkled warm sand*) ver. 616. This must have been necessarily laid
upon the ceroma with which he anointed himself. Lucan says that it was
done in order to have some portion of the earth, from which he derived his
strength, always in contact with him; but dust or fine sand was universally used by wrestlers for sprinkling on their bodies after they had anointed
themselves.

limbs. With many a twist they linked their hands and
arms. For long, in vain were their throats tried at by their
ponderous arms, and with fixed features the head was held
unmoved; and they wondered at having found their match

" Nor in the beginning of the contest was Alcides willing
to employ his strength, and he wearied out the hero; which
his continued panting betrayed, and the cold sweat from
his fatigued body. Then his wearied neck *began* to shake :
then breast to be pressed upon by breast; then the thighs
to totter, struck sideways by the hand. Now does the victor
grasp the back of the hero as it is giving way, and, his
flanks squeezed up, he encircles him around the middle :
and his feet inserted, he spreads asunder his thighs, and
stretches the hero with *all* his limbs upon the ground.
The scorching earth carries off his sweat; with warm
blood his veins are filled. The muscles swell out, and in
all the limbs he grows hard, and, his body refreshed, he
loosens the Herculean grasp. Alcides stands astounded at
strength so vast; and not so much, although he was *then*
inexperienced, did he dread the Hydra cut asunder in the
Inachian waves[1], her snakes renewed.

" Equally matched they struggle. the one with strength
from the earth, the other with it his own. Never has it
been allowed his unrelenting stepdame[2] to be more in
hopes. She sees the limbs of the hero exhausted by sweat.
and his neck parched. upon which he bore Olympus. And
when again he lays hands upon his wearied limbs, Antæus, not waiting for the might of the foe, falls of his
own accord, and, strength received, rises more mighty.
Whatever vigour there is in the ground it is infused into
his weary limbs, and with the struggling hero the earth
labours.

" When at last Alcides perceived the aid of the contact of
his parent availing him, he said, ' Thou must stand, and no

---

[1] *In the Inachian waves*) ver. 634. Inachus was one of the ancient kings
of Argos, near which was situate the marsh or swamp of Lerna, where Hercules slew the Hydra with many heads, each of which, when cut off, was
replaced by two new ones.

[2] *His unrelenting stepdame*) ver. 637. " He never was in greater danger
of being destroyed, which would have gratified the vengeance of his im
placable step-mother, Juno."

further shalt thou be entrusted to the ground, and thou shalt be forbidden to be laid upon the earth. With thy compressed limbs thou shalt cling fast to my breast; thus far, Antæus, shalt thou fall.' Thus having said he raised aloft the youth, struggling to gain the ground. Earth was not able to infuse strength into the limbs of her dying son. Alcides held him by the middle; now was his breast numbed by a torpid chill; for long he did not entrust his foe to the earth. Hence, recording antiquity, the guardian of ancient times and the admirer of herself, has marked the land with his name. But a more noble name[1] has Scipio given to these hills, who called back the Punic foe from the Latian towers; for this was the encampment on the Libyan land being *first* reached. Look! you perceive the vestiges of the ancient entrenchment. Roman victory first took possession of these plains."

Curio, overjoyed, as though the fortune of the spot would wage the war, and preserve for himself the destinies of former commanders, pitching his unlucky tents upon the fortunate spot, indulged his camp *with hopes*, and took their omen away from the hills, and with unequal strength provoked the warlike foes. All Africa, which had submitted to the Roman standards, was then under the command of Varus[2]; who, though trusting in the Latian strength, still summoned from every side the forces of the king of the Libyan nation, and standards that attended their Juba[3] from the extremities of the world. Not a more extended

---

[1] *But a more noble name*) ver. 656. He alludes to the " Corneliana Castra," or " Cornelian Camp." It was so called from P. Cornelius Africanus Scipio the elder, who landed in that vicinity B.C. 204, and having vanquished Hasdrubal and Syphax, alarmed the Carthaginians to such a degree, that they were obliged to recall Hannibal and Mago from Italy.

[2] *Command of Varus*) ver. 667. This was Publius Attius Varus, whom we have already met with in B. ii. l. 466, as running away from Auximum in Italy. Cæsar, in the Civil War, B. i. c. 31, thus mentions his arrival in Africa:—" When Tubero arrived in Africa, he found Attius Varus in command of the province, who, having lost his cohorts, as already related, at Auximum, had straightway fled to Africa, and finding it without a governor, had seized it of his own accord, and, making levies, had raised two legions."

[3] *Attended their Juba*) ver. 670. He was the son of Hiempsal, who had been re-established on the Numidian throne by Pompey, whose cause Juba now espoused. He was also probably influenced by personal enmity against Curio, who, when Tribune of the people, had proposed a law for reducing the

region was there under any master. Where the realms are the longest, on the western extremity, Atlas, in the vicinity of Gades, terminates them; on the south[1], Ammon, adjacent to the Syrtes; but where in its breadth extends the scorching track of his vast realms, it divides the Ocean[2], and the burnt-up regions of the scorched zone suffice for the space *that intervenes.*

Races so numerous follow the camp; the Autoloples[3] and the wandering Numidians, and the Gætulian, ever ready with his uncaparisoned horse[4]; then the Moor, of the same colour as the Indian; the needy Nasamonian[5], the swift Marmaridæ, mingled with the scorched Garamantes, and the Mazagian[7],

kingdom of Juba to the condition of a Roman province. On the ultimate success of the arms of Cæsar, he fell at Utica, and, according to one account, he and Petreius were slain by each other's hand.

[1] *On the south*) ver. 673. It would appear curious that Lucan mentions the extent of Numidia from east to *south*, were it not the fact that the desert of Ammon and the adjacent coast lie in a considerably more southern latitude than the eastern extremity of the kingdom near Gades and Mount Atlas. Besides, Cyrene, the Libyan desert, and Egypt were universally considered as essentially *southern* climes by the Roman Poets.

[2] *It divides the Ocean*) ver. 675. He seems to mean that the whole region which lay between the Mediterranean and the southern ocean of Africa, bounded, as before mentioned, east and west, belonged to Juba. This seems a better explanation than that given by some who would have the Poet to mean that the whole track of country from north to south which lay between the Eastern (or Atlantic) Ocean and the Western Ocean (or Red Sea), belonged to Juba, as that would contradict what he has just said as to the breadth of the kingdom, and would include Egypt in his dominions, a mistake which Lucan certainly would not be guilty of.

[3] *The Autololes*) ver. 677. According to Pliny, the Autololes were a people of Mauritania Tingitana; but Ptolemy places them on the western coast of Africa, and south of the range of Atlas.

[4] *With his uncaparisoned horse*) ver. 678. He alludes to the custom of the Gætulians riding on horseback without saddles. In its widest sense, the region of Gætulia included the inhabitants of the regions between Mauritania, Numidia, Cyrene, and the Great Desert.

[5] *The needy Nasamonian*) ver. 679. The Nasamones were a people of Libya who originally dwelt on the shores of the Great Syrtis, but were driven inland by the Greek settlers of Cyrene, and afterwards by the Romans.

[6] *The swift Marmarida*) ver. 680. As to the Marmaridæ, see the Note to B iii. l. 293.

[7] *And the Mazagian*) ver. 681. The Mazagians were probably the same as the Maxyes, a people of the north of Africa, near the coast of the Lesser Syrtis, on the banks of the river Triton. They were said to claim descent from the Trojans.

that will rival the arrows of the Medes, when he hurls the
quivering spear; the Massylian nation[1], too, that sitting on
the bare back *of the horse*, with a slight wand guides the
mouth unacquainted with the bit; the African huntsman,
too, who is wont to wander with his empty cot, and at the
same time, *since* he has no confidence in his weapons, *accustomed* to cover the infuriate lions[2] with flowing garments.

Nor alone did Juba prepare arms in the cause of civil
strife, but aroused, he granted war to his private resentment. Him too, in the year in which[3] he had defiled the
Gods above and things human, by a tribunitial law Curio
had attempted to expel from the throne of his forefathers,
and to wrest Libya from its king, while, Rome, he was
making a kingdom[4] of thee. He, remembering his sorrows, fancies that this war is the fruit of *himself* retaining
the sceptre. At this report, therefore, of the king *approaching* Curio now trembles. And because those youths have
never been entirely devoted to the cause of Cæsar, nor as
soldiers had been tried in the waves of the Rhine, having
been taken in the citadel of Corfinium[5], both unfaithful to

[1] *The Massylian nation*) ver. 682. The Massyli were a people of Mauritania, who, like the Gætulians, rode without saddles.

[2] *To cover the infuriate lions*) ver. 685. Pliny the Elder, in his Eighth Book, informs us that the Gætulians were in the habit of catching lions by throwing a cloak or garment over their heads. The strength of the lion was commonly supposed to be centred in the eye.

[3] *In the year in which*) ver. 689. He means the year in which he was Tribune, and in which, according to report, he had been bribed by Cæsar to desert the aristocratic party.

[4] *He was making a kingdom*) ver. 692. While he was covertly trying to bring Rome under the despotic sway of Cæsar.

[5] *In the citadel of Corfinium*) ver. 697. His soldiers, to his sorrow, were not the veterans who had fought under Cæsar at the Rhine, but were those who, captured at Corfinium (see B. ii. l. 507), had gone over to the party of Cæsar. This circumstance is thus referred to in the Civil War, B. ii. c. 28:—
" In the army there was one Sextus Quintilius Varus, who, as we have mentioned before, was at Corfinium. When Cæsar gave him his liberty he went over to Africa. Now Curio had transported to Africa those legions which Cæsar had received under his command a short time before at Corfinium; so that the officers and companies were still the same, excepting the change of a few centurions. Quintilius, making this a pretext for addressing them, began to go round Curio's lines, and to entreat the soldiers not to lose all recollection of the oath which they first took to Domitius and to himself, their Quæstor, nor bear arms against those who had shared the same fortune, and endured the same hardships in siege, nor fight for those by whom they had opprobriously been called deserters."

their new leaders, and wavering to their former one, they deem either side *equally* right. But after he perceives all faint with inactive dread, and the nightly guards of the trenches forsaken by desertion, thus in his agitated mind does he speak :—

" By daring great fears are concealed; to arms will I resort the first. Let the soldiers descend to the level plains while they are *yet* my own ; rest ever produces a wavering disposition ; remove *all* consideration by fight. When the dire intent waxes strong with the sword grasped *in hand*, and helmets conceal their shame, who thinks of comparing the leaders, who of weighing the causes? The side he has taken to that does he wish well ; just as in the shows of the fatal sand[1] no ancient grudge compels those brought forward to combat together, *but* they hate those pitted against them.''

Thus having said[2], in the open plains he drew up his ranks, whom the fortune of war, about to deceive him with future woes, blandly received. For he drove Varus[3] from the field, and smote their backs exposed in disgraceful flight, until *their* camp prevented it. But after the sad battle of the worsted Varus was heard of by Juba; joyous that the glory of the warfare might be recovered by his own aid, by stealth he hurried on his troops, and by enjoined silence retarded the report of himself *approaching*, fearing this alone, through want of caution to be dreaded by the enemy. Sabura[4], next after the king among the Numidians, was sent *before* to provoke the commencing battle with a small troop and to draw them on, as though pretending[5] that the warfare was entrusted to himself.

[1] *In the shows of the fatal sand*) ver. 708, 9. "Fatalis arenæ Muneribus." He alludes to the " munera gladiatoria," or " gladiatorial shows," where the gladiators fought upon the "arena," or area covered with sand, of the Amphitheatre.

[2] *Thus having said*) ver. 710. The speeches of Curio to his council of war and his soldiers are set forth at length in Cæsar's Civil War, B. ii. c. 31, 32.

[3] *For he drove Varus*) ver. 714. The particulars of this defeat are related in the Civil War, B. ii. c. 34, 35. Cæsar says that of the enemy there were about six hundred killed and a thousand wounded.

[4] *Sabura*) ver. 722. This Sabura, or Saburra, was, with his forces, utterly defeated, B.C. 46, by P. Sittius. See the African War of Hirtius, c. 93.

[5] *As though pretending*) ver. 722. Sabura is to advance with a small force to lead Curio to believe that he alone is marching against him, and that Juba

He himself in a hollow valley keeps back the strength of the realm; just as the more crafty enemy [1] with his tail de· ceives the Pharian asps, and provokes them, enraged by a deceiving shadow; and obliquely seizes with safe grip the head of the serpent, stretching out in vain into the air, without its deadly matter; then the venom, baulked of its purpose, is squeezed out, and its jaws overflow with the wasted poison.

To the stratagems Fortune gives success; and fierce, the strength of the concealed foe not surveyed, Curio commands his cavalry to sally forth from the camp by night, and to spread far and wide over the unknown plains. He himself, about the first break of dawn, commands the signal *to sound* in the camp, often and vainly having begged them to apprehend Libyan stratagem and the Punic warfare, always fraught with treachery.

The destiny of approaching death had delivered up the youth to the Fates, and the civil warfare urged on its author *to his doom.* Over steep rocks, over crags, along an abrupt path he led *his* standards; when, espied afar from the tops of the hills, the enemy, in their stratagem, gave way a little, until, the hill being left, he entrusted his extended ranks to the wide plains. He, believing this a flight, *and* unacquainted with the concealed design, as though victorious, led forward his forces into the midst of the fields. Then first was the stratagem disclosed, and the flying Numidians, the mountains filled on every side, hemmed in the troops. At the same moment the leader himself was astounded, and the multitude, doomed to perish.

is not near at hand. So in the Civil War, B. ii. c. 38, Cæsar says, " Curio is informed by some deserters from the town that Juba has stayed behind in his own kingdom, being called home by a neighbouring war, and a dispute with the people of Leptis; and that Sabura, who has been sent with a small force, is drawing near to Utica. Curio, rashly believing this information, alters his design, and resolves to hazard a battle." It appears, however, by Cæsar's account, that there was no stratagem at first on the part of Juba, whose advanced guard was attacked unexpectedly by the cavalry of Curio, with great slaughter: shortly after which, Curio neglecting to make proper enquiries, again attacked Sabura, who, falling back, gradually surrounded him with his army, and destroyed him and his forces. See the Civil War, B. ii. c. 39-43.

[1] *The more crafty enemy*) ver. 724. He alludes to the ichneumon, or rat of Egypt, which was said to be a deadly enemy to the asp of that country, and, provoking it with the shadow of its own tail, to cause it to raise its head, on which it would seize it by the throat and kill it.

The fearful sought not flight, the valiant not battle ; since not there did the charger, moved by the clangor of trumpets, shake the rocks with the beating *of his hoof*, working at his mouth that champs the stiffened reins, and spread his mane, and prick up his ears, and not with the varying movement of the feet did he struggle not to be at rest. His wearied neck hangs down. His limbs reek with sweat, and his parched mouth is clammy, his tongue hanging out; his hoarse breast, which an incessant panting excites, groans *aloud;* and the breath, hardly drawn, contracts the spent flanks; the foam, too, grows hard upon the blood-stained bits. And now, compelled neither by whips nor goads, nor though prompted by frequent spurring, do they increase their speed. By wounds are the horses urged on. Nor avails it any one to have cut short the delay of his horny-hoofed *steed*, for they have neither space nor force for the onset; he is only carried on against the foe, and affords room for the javelins, the wound being offered.

But when first the skirmishing African sent forth his steeds in a troop, then did the plains re-echo with the sound; and, the earth loosened, the dust enveloped the air in its clouds, and brought on the shades, as vast as it is when hurled by the Bistonian whirlwind[1]. But when the miserable fate of war befell the foot, no fortune stood in suspense upon the decision of a doubtful conflict, but death occupied the duration of the battle. Nor yet had they the power to run straight against them, and to mingle their troops. Thus, the youths, hemmed in on every side, by those who fight hand to hand[2] and by those who send them from above, are overwhelmed with lances obliquely slanting and held horizontally; doomed to perish not by wounds or bloodshed, solely through the cloud of darts and the weight of the weapons.

[1] *The Bistonian whirlwind*) ver. 767. Thrace is called " Bistonia," from the Bistones, a people of that country between Mount Rhodope and the Ægean Sea, near Lake Bistonis.
[2] *Who fight hand to hand*) ver. 774. It seems not improbable that in this line " eminus" and " comminus" have changed places ; for the darts or spears that were thrown from a distance, " eminus," would fall obliquely, while the spears presented by those close at hand, " comminus," would be " rectæ," or " horizontally" pointed.

M

Therefore, ranks so numerous are crowded into a small compass, and if any one, fearing, creeps into the middle of the troop, hardly with impunity does he turn amid the swords of his own friends; and the mass is made more dense, inasmuch as the first rank, their feet bearing backwards, contract the circles. For them compressed there is now no room for wielding their arms, and their crowded limbs are trodden on; armed breast is broken by breast beaten against it. The victorious Moor did not enjoy a spectacle so joyous as Fortune *really* presented; he did not behold the streams of blood, and the fainting of the limbs, and the bodies as they struck the earth; squeezed up in the crowd every carcase stood upright.

Let Fortune arouse the hated ghosts of dire Carthage by *these* new funeral sacrifices[1]; let blood-stained Hannibal and the Punic shades receive this expiation so dire. 'Twere profane, ye Gods of heaven, for a Roman's fall on Libyan ground to benefit Pompey and the wishes of the Senate; rather for herself may Africa conquer us!

Curio, when he beheld his troops routed on the plain, and the dust, laid by the blood, allowed him to perceive how great the slaughter, did not endure to prolong his life amid his stricken fortunes, or to hope for flight; and he fell amid the slaughter of his men[2], eager for death, and valiant with a bravery to which he was forced.

What now avail thee the turmoil of the Rostra and the Forum, from which, with the arts of harangue[3], the standard-

---

[1] *New funeral sacrifices*) ver. 789. "Inferiæ" were propitiatory sacrifices offered to the shades of the dead. He says that this slaughter of Romans by the hand of Romans will be as good as a propitiatory sacrifice to the shades of Hannibal and the Carthaginians who had suffered so much at the hands of their ancestors.

[2] *Amid the slaughter of his men*) ver. 797. The death of Curio is thus related by Cæsar in the Civil War, B. ii. c. 42:—" Cneius Domitius, commander of the cavalry, standing round Curio, with a small party of horse, urged him to endeavour to escape by flight, and to hasten to his camp, and assured him that he would not forsake him. But Curio declared that he would never more appear in Cæsar's sight, after losing the army which had been committed by him to his charge, and accordingly fought till he was slain."

[3] *The arts of harangue*) ver. 799. The "tribunitia ars," or "tribunitial art," of Curio was his eloquence, for which he was famous, and which, as Tribune of the people, when speaking from the Rostra, he knew how to use

bearer of the plebeians, thou didst deal arms to the people?
What, the betrayed rights[1] of the Senate, and the son-in-law
and the father-in-law enjoined to meet in battle? Thou liest
prostrate before dire Pharsalia has brought the chieftains
together, and the civil warfare has been denied thee to behold. Is it thus, forsooth, that to the wretched City you
pay the penalty with your blood? Thus, ye powerful ones,
do you atone with your throats for your warfare! Happy
Rome, indeed, and destined to possess fortunate citizens, if
the care of its liberty had pleased the Gods above as much
as to avenge it pleases them!

Lo, Curio, a noble corpse, covered by no tomb, is feeding
the Libyan birds. But to thee (since it will be to no purpose to be silent upon those things from which their own
fame repels all the lengthened age of time) we grant, O
youth, the due praises of a life that deserved them. Not
another citizen of capacity so great did Rome produce, or
to whom the laws owed more, when pursuing what was
right. Then did the corrupt age injure the City, after
ambition and luxury, and the possession of wealth, so
much to be dreaded, had carried along with a torrent that
crossed *his path* his unsettled mind; and the altered Curio
became the controller of events, charmed by the spoils of
the Gauls and the gold of Cæsar.

Although powerful Sulla acquired rule over our lives by the
sword, and the fierce Marius, and the blood-stained Cinna,
and the long line of Cæsar's house[2]; to whom was power so
great *ever* granted? They all bought the City, he sold it[3].

to dangerous purpose. See B. i. l. 275, where Curio, in his speech, alludes
to the Rostra at Rome.

[1] *The betrayed rights*) ver. 801. In allusion to the charge made against
him of having been bribed by Cæsar.

[2] *The long line of Cæsar's house*) ver. 823. Lucan must clearly have
been on bad terms with Nero when he penned this line, as he would not
otherwise have joined the "series" of the house of Cæsar, of which Nero
was a member (through adoption), with Sulla, Marius, and Cinna, whom he
repeatedly mentions as monsters of cruelty.

[3] *He sold it*) ver. 824. Virgil is supposed to refer to him in a somewhat
similar manner in the Sixth Book of the Æneid, l. 621. "He sold his
country for gold, and imposed upon it a powerful tyrant."

BOOK THE FIFTH.

CONTENTS.

Thus did Fortune reserve the two[1] generals who had suffered the alternate wounds of warfare for the land of the Macedonians, mingling adversity with prosperity. Now had the winter sprinkled the snows on Hæmus, and the daughter

---

[1] *Reserve the two*) ver. 3. "Pares." This term, used in the athletic sports, to signify the two athletes or gladiators that were "comparati," "pitted" against each other, is often used by the Poet.

of Atlas[1] who sets in the cold Olympus; the day, too, was at hand which gives a new name to the Calendar[2], and which is the first to worship Janus[3], who introduces the seasons. But while the latter part still remained of their expiring sway, each Consul invited the Senators dispersed amid the duties of the warfare to Epirus. A foreign and a lowly retreat received the Roman nobles, and a foreign senate under a distant roof heard the secrets of the state. For who could call so many axes wielded by the laws, so many fasces[4], a camp? The venerable order taught the people that it was not the party of Magnus, but that Magnus was their partisan.

When first silence pervaded the sorrowing assembly. Lentulus[5] from a lofty seat *thus* spoke :—" If strength exists in your minds worthy of the Latian spirit, if of your ancient blood, consider not in what land you are banished, and how far we are located from the abodes of the captured City; but think of the aspect of your own assembly; and, able to command everything, first, Senators, decree this, which to realms and to nations is manifest, that we are the Senate. For whether Fortune shall lead us beneath the icy Wain of the Hyperborean Bear, or where the burning region and the clime shut up in vapours permits not the nights nor yet the days, unequal, to increase, the dominion of the world will attend us, and empire as our attendant. When the Tarpeian seat was consumed by the torches of the Gauls, and when Camillus was dwelling at Veii[6].

---

[1] *The daughter of Atlas*) ver. 4. "Atlantis;" "the Atlantis," or "daughter of Atlas," is here used for the "Atlantides" or "Pleiades," who were fabled to have been originally the seven daughters of Atlas. He alludes to the middle of November, when the Pleiades set cosmically.

[2] *Gives a new name to the Calendar*) ver. 5. The Calends or first day of January, on which the new Consuls came into office and gave their name to the commencing year in the "Fasti" or Calendar. See the Fasti of Ovid, B. i. l. 53, *et seq.*

[3] *To worship Janus*) ver. 6. The month of January was sacred to the God Janus. See the Fasti of Ovid, B. i. l. 63, *et seq.*

[4] *So many fasces*) ver. 12. He alludes to the presence at the camp of the Consuls with the fasces and axes, the emblems of state.

[5] *Lentulus*) ver. 16. This was L. Cornelius Lentulus, one of the Consuls for that year. He raised two legions for Pompey in Asia. He was finally put to death by Ptolemy, the tyrant of Egypt.

[6] *Dwelling at Veii*) ver. 28. Veii, now called Isola Farnese, was one

there was Rome. Never by change of place has *our* order lost its rights.

" Sorrowing abodes does Cæsar possess, and deserted houses, and silenced laws, and judgment seats shut up in sad cessation from the law. That Senate-house beholds those Senators alone[1], whom from the full City it banished. Whoever was not expelled *by us* from an order so mighty, is here. Unacquainted with crimes, and at rest during a lengthened peace, the first fury of warfare dispersed us ; once again do all the members *of the state* return to their place. Behold ! with all the might of the world do the Gods above recompense us for Hesperia *lost;* the enemy lies overwhelmed in the Illyrian waves[2] ; in the loathsome fields of Libya, Curio, a large portion of Cæsar's Senate[3], has fallen. Generals, raise your standards ; urge on the course of fate ; entrust to the Gods your hopes, and let fortune give us courage as great, as the cause gave when you fled from the foe. Our rule is closing with the finished year ; you, whose power is destined to experience no limit, Senators, consult for the common welfare, and bid Magnus be your leader."

With joyous applause the Senate received the name, and entrusted to Magnus his own and his country's fate. Then honors *were* distributed among kings and nations that deserved *them;* both Rhodes sacred to Phœbus[4] and powerful by sea, *was* decorated with gifts, and the unpolished youth

of the most ancient cities of Etruria, situate on the river Cremera, about twelve miles from Rome. It was here that the Senate were convened when the Gauls had destroyed Rome, on which they appointed Camillus Dictator. The Romans at this time were anxious to make Veii their capital, and were only dissuaded by the eloquence of Camillus.

[1] *Those Senators alone*) ver. 32-4. The meaning is that "the Senate-house at Rome now only beholds those Senators whom the senate has expelled as enemies to the state at the time when the City was full, and not deserted as it now is."

[2] *In the Illyrian waves*) ver. 39. He alludes to the fate of Vulteius and his Opitergians, related in the last Book.

[3] *A large portion of Cæsar's Senate*) ver. 40. By reason of his eloquence and activity in Cæsar's cause.

[4] *Rhodes sacred to Phœbus*) ver. 51. The isle of Rhodes, off the coast of Caria in Asia Minor, was said to be especially beloved by Phœbus, who raised it from beneath the waves. There was a splendid temple of Apollo there, and the Colossus erected there was a statue of that God.

of cold Taygetus[1]. In fame is ancient Athens praised, and for her own Massilia[2] is Phocis presented with freedom *from tribute.* Then do they extol Sadales[3], and brave Cotys, and Deiotarus[4] faithful in arms, and Rhasipolis[5], the ruler of a frozen region; and, the Senate decreeing it, they bid Libya pay obedience to the sceptre-bearing Juba. Alas, sad destinies! behold! Ptolemy, to thee[6], most worthy of the sway of a faithless race, the shame of Fortune and the disgrace of the Gods[7], it is permitted to bind thy pressed locks with the Pellæan diadem. A remorseless sword, O boy, dost thou receive over thy people; and would it were over thy people *alone!* The palace of Lagus has been given; *to this* the life of Magnus is added; and *by*

---

[1] *Youth of cold Taygetus*) ver. 52. The Lacedæmonians are here meant, whose country was separated from Messenia by the mountain range of Taygetus.

[2] *For her own Massilia*) ver. 53. This could not in reality be the ground for the honours paid to Phocis in Greece, inasmuch, as has been already remarked, Massilia was a colony from Phocæa in Asia Minor. See B. iii. 1. 340.

[3] *Extol Sadales*) ver. 54. Sadales was the son of Cotys, king of Thrace, and was sent with his father at the head of some cavalry, to assist Pompey. He was forgiven by Cæsar after the battle of Pharsalia, and left his kingdom to the Roman people. Of his father, Cotys, nothing further is known.

[4] *And Deiotarus*) ver. 55. Deiotarus was Tetrarch and king of Galatia, who, though extremely advanced in years, came to the aid of Pompey with six hundred horsemen. He was afterwards pardoned by Cæsar, but, according to Cicero, Cæsar deprived him of his Tetrarchy and kingdom, though he suffered him to retain his title.

[5] *And Rhasipolis*) ver. 55. This person, whose name is also spelt "Rhascuporis," was chieftain of a Thracian tribe, lying between Mount Rhodope and the sea. He joined Pompey with two hundred horse at Dyrrhachium. Cæsar, in the Civil War, B. iii. c. iv., speaks of his troops as coming from Macedonia, and as being of extraordinary valour.

[6] *Ptolemy, to thee*) ver. 59. This was Ptolemy XII., king of Egypt, by some said to have been surnamed Dionysus. Lucan justly expresses his disgust that this unprincipled youth should succeed to a throne founded by "him of Pella," Alexander the Great. More particulars relative to this king will be found in the Ninth Book. He was accidentally drowned in the Alexandrian war against Cæsar.

[7] *Disgrace of the Gods*) ver. 60. By his father's will, the throne was given to Ptolemy and his sister Cleopatra jointly; but he succeeded in expelling her after she had reigned jointly with him for three years. By his murder of Pompey, he saved Cæsar, doubtless to our Poet's sorrow, the criminality of having murdered his son-in-law Pompey.

this a realm has been snatched away from a sister, and crime from a father-in-law.

Now, the assembly broken up, the multitude takes up arms. When the people and the chieftains were resorting to these with uncertain chances, and with indiscriminate allotment, alone did Appius[1] fear to embark upon the doubtful events of the warfare ; and he entreated the Gods of heaven to unfold the destiny of events, and opened again the Delphic shrine of fate-foretelling Phœbus, that had been closed for many a year.

Just as far removed[2] from the western as from the eastern clime, Parnassus with its twofold summit[3] reaches to the skies, a mountain sacred to Phœbus and to Bromius[4]; on which, the Deities united, the Theban Bacchanals celebrate the triennial Delphic festival[5]. This peak alone, when the deluge covered the earth[6], rose aloft, and was the mid division of the sea and the stars. Thou even, Parnassus, raised above the sea, didst

---

[1] *Alone did Appius*) ver. 68. This was Appius Claudius Pulcher, noted for his avarice and rapacity. He sided with Pompey, and died in the isle of Eubœa, before the battle of Pharsalia. He was distinguished for his legal and antiquarian knowledge, and was a firm believer in augury and divination, in which he was deeply skilled.

[2] *Just as far removed*) ver. 71. Delphi was said to be in the very centre of the earth, and for that reason was called the "navel of the earth."

[3] *With its twofold summit*) ver. 72. These two peaks or heights were called Hyampeum and Tithoreum.

[4] *And to Bromius*) ver. 73. Bacchus was said to be called "Bromius," from the Greek verb βρεμεῖν, " to make a noise," in allusion to the shouts of his devotees. Macrobius, in the Saturnalia, B. i. c. 18, tries to prove that Apollo, or the Sun, and Bacchus were the same deity.

[5] *Triennial Delphic festival*) ver. 74. The "Trieterica" was a festival celebrated in honor of Bacchus every three years, probably to commemorate his conquest of India. Ovid, in the Metamorphoses, B. vi. l. 587, *et seq.,* thus speaks of these rites :—" It was now the time when the Sithonian matrons are wont to celebrate the triennial festival of Bacchus. Night is conscious of their rites ; by night Rhodope resounds with the tinkling of the shrill cymbal." See the Translation of the Metamorphoses in Bohn's Classical Library, pp. 116 and 216.

[6] *Deluge covered the earth*) ver. 75. He alludes to the tradition that in the flood of Deucalion the peaks of Parnassus alone arose above the waters. See the Metamorphoses of Ovid, B. i. l. 315, *et seq.* The height called Tithoreum was afterwards said to be sacred to Bacchus, while Hyampeum was devoted to Apollo and the Muses.

scarcely lift the top of thy rocks, and as to one ridge
thou didst lie concealed. There, when her offspring extended her womb, did Pæan, the avenger of his persecuted
mother, lay Python prostrate [1], with his darts till then unused, when Themis [2] was occupying the sway and the
tripods. When Pæan beheld that the vast chasms of the
earth breathed forth divine truths, and that the ground
exhaled prophetic winds [3], he enshrined himself in the
sacred caves, and there, become prophetic, did Apollo
abide in the inmost shrines.

Which of the Gods of heaven lies here concealed?
What Deity, descended from the skies, deigns, enclosed, to
inhabit the darkened caverns? What God of heaven puts
up with the earth, preserving all the secrets of the eternal
course *of fate,* and conscious of the future events of the
world, and ready, himself, to disclose them to nations, and
enduring the contact of mortals [4], both mighty and powerful, whether it is that he prophesies destiny, or whether it
is that that becomes destiny which by prophesying he
commands? Perhaps a large portion [5] of the entire Jove,
pervading the earth *by him* to be swayed, which sustains the

---

[1] *Lay Python prostrate*) ver. 79.   He alludes to the slaughter by
Apollo with his arrows of the serpent Python, which had been sent by
the malignant Juno to persecute Latona when pregnant with Apollo and
Diana.

[2] *When Themis*) ver. 81.   Themis was said to have preceded Apollo in
giving oracular responses at Delphi.   She was the daughter of Cœlus and
Terra, and was the first to instruct men to ask of the Gods that which was
lawful and right, whence she received the name of Themis, signifying in
Greek "that which is just and right."

[3] *Prophetic winds*) ver. 83.   "Ventos loquaces."   These were cold exhalations which were said to arise from a hollow cleft in the mountain
rock, and, when received into the body of the priestess, to inspire her with
prophetic frenzy.

[4] *Contact of mortals*) ver. 91.   In allusion to the divine spirit animating
a mortal, the Pythia, or priestess of the God.

[5] *Perhaps a large portion*) ver. 93.   He suggests that possibly that
divine spirit which pervades all things and keeps the earth poised in air,
finds a vent in the Cirrhæan caverns or shrines of Parnassus.   So Virgil, in
the Æneid, B. vi. l. 726, speaks of a spirit "pervading all things," "spiritus
intus alit."   See also B. i. l. 89.   Lemaire somewhat fancifully suggests that
this passage refers to a supposed axis of the earth, which the Poet imagined
to run through it at Delphi, its so-called navel, and to be connected with the
heavens.

globe poised in the empty air, passes forth through the
Cirrhæan caves, and is attracted, in unison with the ætherea.
Thunderer[1]. When this divine inspiration has been conceived in the virgin's breast, coming in contact with the
human spirit, it re-echoes, and opens the mouth of the
prophetess[2], just as the Sicilian peaks undulate when the
flames press upon Ætna; or as Typhœus, buried beneath
the everlasting mass of Inarime[3], roaring aloud, heats the
Campanian rocks.

This Deity, however, made manifest to all and denied
to none, alone denies himself to the pollution of human
criminality. Not there in silent whispers do they conceive
impious wishes. For, prophesying what is destined and
to be altered for no one, he forbids mortals to wish, and,
benignant to the just, full oft has he assigned an abode
to those quitting entire cities, as to the Tyrians[4]; he has
granted to drive back the threats of war, as the sea of Salamis[5] remembers; he has removed the wrath of the earth[6]

[1] *With the æthereal Thunderer*) ver. 96. The meaning probably is that
an inspiration is derived thence, which, being an emanation from Jupiter, is
still connected with him, and derives its vigour from him.

[2] *The mouth of the prophetess*) ver. 99. It has been suggested that in
this passage there is a hiatus after "solvit," and that probably some lines
are lost, as the likening of the Pythia to Mount Ætna seems forced and
unnatural.

[3] *Of Inarime*) ver. 101. Inarime, now called Ischia, and formerly called
Ænaria as well, was an island not far from the coast of Campania. The name
is supposed by some to have been coined by Virgil from the expression of
Homer, ἐν Ἀρίμοις, as that writer is the first found to use it, and is followed
by Ovid and our Poet in the present instance. Strabo tells us that
"aremus" was the Etrurian name for an ape; if so, the name of the island
may have been derived from, or have given name to, certain adjoining
islands which were called "Pithecusæ," or the "Ape islands."

[4] *As to the Tyrians*) ver. 108. He alludes to the Tyrians, who were
said to have built Sidon and Tyre and Gades by the command of the
Delphic oracle.

[5] *As the sea of Salamis*) ver. 109. In the war of Xerxes against Greece,
the Athenians were advised by the oracle to put their trust in wooden walls;
on which they forthwith took to their ships, and soon afterwards, under the
command of Themistocles, conquered the fleet of Xerxes at Salamis.

[6] *Removed the wrath of the earth*) ver. 110. Egypt was said to have
been relieved from famine by following the directions of the oracle, on
Thrasius being killed by Busiris. Phrygia was, according to Diodorus
Siculus, similarly relieved on burying Atys. So was Attica after it had, by
direction of the oracle, given satisfaction to Minos, whose son Androgeus
had been slain by the Athenians.

when barren, the end of it being shown; he has cleared the air when generating pestilence[1]. Our age is deprived of no greater blessing of the Deities, than that the Delphic seat has become silent, since monarchs have dreaded[2] events to come, and have forbidden the Gods of heaven to speak. Nor yet, a voice denied them, do the Cirrhæan prophetesses mourn; and they have the benefit of the cessation of the Temple's rites. For if the God enters any breast, a premature death is either the punishment[3] of the Deity being received, or the reward; inasmuch as under the vehemence and the fitfulness of the frenzy the human frame sinks, and the impulses of the Gods shake the frail spirit.

Thus does Appius, an enquirer into the remotest *secrets* of the Hesperian destiny, make application to the tripods for a length of time unmoved, and the silence of the vast rocks. The priest, requested to open the dreaded seats, and to admit to the Gods a trembling prophetess, seizes Phemonoë[4], roving amid her wanderings around the streams of Castalia and the recesses of the groves, and compels her to burst open the doors of the Temple. The maid inspired by Phœbus, dreading to stand within the awful threshold, by a vain stratagem attempts to wean the chieftain from his ardent longing to know the future.

[1] *When generating pestilence*) ver. 111. The Thebans were delivered from a plague on banishing, by advice of the oracle of Delphi, the murderer of Laius. The Lucanians experienced a similar relief on appeasing the shade of Palinurus. Livy, B. ix., and Ovid in the Metamorphoses, B. xv. l. 622, *et seq.*, speak of the delivery of the Romans from pestilence on sending to Epidaurus for the God Æsculapius.

[2] *Monarchs have dreaded*) ver. 113. One of the Scholiasts suggests that Lucan alludes to Pyrrhus, king of Epirus; while another says that the Emperor Nero is here alluded to, and that on his making enquiries of the oracle, the answer was that a matricide ought not to be let into the knowledge of the future, on which Nero, fearing the oracle might be harder still upon his crimes, sacrificed an ass to the God, and forbade any sacrifices to be offered to him in future, on which the oracle ceased. According to another account, the oracle gave answer that Nero would be slain by the populace, which caused him to order the temple to be closed.

[3] *Either the punishment*) ver. 117. Death being deemed a punishment or reward, according as the priestess was attached to or weary of life.

[4] *Seizes Phemonoë*) ver. 126. This is probably intended as a general appellation for the Pythia or priestess of Apollo, as it was the name given to his first priestess at Delphi before the times of Homer.

"Why, Roman," says she, "does an unbecoming hope *of hearing* the truth attract thee? Its chasms dumb, Parnassus holds its peace, and has silenced the God; whether it is that the spirit has forsaken these yawning clefts, and has turned its changed course towards the far regions of the world; or whether, when Python was consumed by the barbarian torch[1], the ashes entered the immense caverns, and obstructed the passage for Phœbus; or whether, by the will of the Gods, Cirrha is silent, and it is sufficient that the secrets of future fate have been entrusted to yourselves in the lines of the aged Sibyl; or whether Pæan, wont to drive the guilty from his temples, finds not in our age mouths by which to disclose *the Fates.*"

The deceit of the maiden is manifest, and, the Deities being denied, her very fear imparts confidence. Then does the wreathed fillet[2] bind her locks in front, and, her hair streaming down her back a white head-dress encircles with Phocæan laurel. She, dreading the fate-foretelling recess of the deep-seated shrine, in the first part of the Temple comes to a stop, and, feigning *the inspiration of* the God, utters from her breast, undisturbed beneath, fictitious words, testifying a spirit moved by no divine frenzy with no murmurs of a hurried voice, *and* not so much about to injure the chieftain to whom she is prophesying falsely, as the tripods and the credit of Phœbus.

Her words broken with no trembling sound, her voice not sufficing to fill the space of the capacious cavern, the laurels shaken off, with no standing of her hair on end, and the summits of the Temple without vibration, the grove, too, unshaken, *all these* betrayed that she dreaded to yield herself to Phœbus. Appius beheld the tripods unoccupied, and raging, exclaimed:—

"Impious woman, thou shalt both pay the deserved penalty

[1] *By the barbarian torch*) ver. 134. This has been generally said to refer to the plunder and burning of the Temple at Delphi by Brennus and his Gauls, who invaded Greece from Pannonia, B.C. 279; but on examination it would appear that Brennus was utterly thwarted in his attempts by the bravery of the Delphians, 4000 in number. The passage may possibly refer to the attack made by Pyrrhus, king of Epirus, upon the Temple.

[2] *The wreathed fillet*) ver. 143. The "vittæ," "fillets," and "infulæ," "bands," formed an especial part of the costume of the priestesses who were devoted to the worship of the Gods. The Vestal virgins at Rome wore them.

to me and to the Gods of heaven, whom thou art feigning *as inspiring thee*, unless thou art hidden in the caverns, and, consulted upon the tumults so vast of the trembling world, dost cease, thyself, to speak."

At length, the affrighted maiden flies for refuge to the tripods, and, led away within the vast caverns, *there* remains, and receives the Deity in her unaccustomed breast; who pours forth the spirit of the rock, now for so many ages unexhausted, into the prophetess; and at length having gained the Cirrhæan breast[1], never more fully did Pæan enter into the limbs of female inspired by him; and he banishes her former mind, and throughout her whole breast bids the mortal[2] give way to himself. Frantic, she rages throughout the cave, bearing her neck possessed, and, shaking from her upright hair both the fillets of the God and the garlands of Phœbus, through the empty space of the Temple she whirls round with her neck shaking to and fro, and throws prostrate the tripods that stand in her way as she roams along, and boils with mighty flames, enduring thee, Phœbus, raging with wrath.

Nor dost thou employ the lash alone and goads[3], flames, too, dost thou bury in her entrails; and the bridle she submits to; nor is it permitted[4] the prophetess to disclose as much as to know. All time comes in a single mass; and ages so many press upon *her* afflicted breast. Such a vast chain of events is disclosed, and all the future struggles for the light of day; and fates are striving that demand utterance: not the first day, not the last of the world; not the laws of ocean, not the number of the sands, is wanting. Such did the Cumæan prophetess[5], in the Eubœan

[1] *Gained the Cirrhæan breast*) ver. 165. The God now fully inspiring the priestess.

[2] *Bids the mortal*) ver. 168. The mortal part, or human mind.

[3] *The lash alone and goads*) ver. 175. The meaning is, that in her frenzy the priestess seems to be driven along with whips and goads.

[4] *Nor is it permitted*) ver. 177. You hinder her from disclosing more than you wish the enquirer to be informed of.

[5] *The Cumæan prophetess*) ver. 183. According to some accounts, Cumæ in Italy, which was the abode of one of the Sibyls, was founded by a colony from Chalcis in the isle of Eubœa. He alludes to the occasion on which the Sibyl offered the books which revealed the destinies of Rome for sale to Tarquinius Superbus, and says that she favoured the Roman people done by putting the prophecies in writing, which bore reference to them.

retreat, indignant that her frenzy should be at the service
of many nations, cull with proud hand the Roman from
the heap of destinies so vast.

Thus does Phemonoë, filled with Phœbus, struggle,
while thee, O Appius, consulter of the Deity hidden in
the Castalian land, with difficulty she discovers, long amid
fates so mighty seeking thee concealed. Then, first the
foaming frenzy flows forth about her maddened lips, and
groans and loud murmurs from her gasping mouth ; then
are there mournful yells in the vast caverns, and at last
voices resound, the maiden now overcome :—

" O Roman, thou dost escape from the vast threatenings
of war, free from dangers so great; and alone shalt thou
take thy rest in the wide valley of the Eubœan quarter."[1]
The rest Apollo suppresses, and stops her speech.

Ye tripods, guardians of the Fates, and *ye* secrets of the
world, and thou, Pæan, powerful in the truth, uninformed
by the Gods of heaven of no day of the future, why dost
thou hesitate to reveal the latest moments of the falling
state, and the slaughtered chieftains, and the deaths of potentates, and nations so numerous falling amid Hesperian
bloodshed ? Is it that the Deities have not yet decreed
mischief so great, and are destinies so numerous withheld,
while the stars yet hesitate to doom the head of Pompey ?
Or art thou silent upon the crimes of the avenging sword[2],
and the penalties of *civic* frenzy and tyrannies falling
to the avenging Bruti[3] once again, that Fortune may fulfil
her aim ?

Then, smitten by the breast of the prophetess the doors
open, and, hurried on, she leaps forth from the Temple.
Her frantic fit *still* lasts ; and the God whom *as yet* she has

---

[1] *Of the Eubœan quarter*) ver. 196. " Lateris ;" literally, " side," in
allusion to the situation of the long narrow island of Eubœa, which skirts
the eastern side of Greece. According to Lucan and some other authors,
Appius thought that this prophecy, which was really significant of where he
should die, bore reference to a kingdom reserved for him by destiny.

[2] *Of the avenging sword*) ver. 206. He alludes to the swords of Brutus
and his fellow conspirators.

[3] *Falling to the avenging Bruti*) ver. 207. By alluding to the Bruti, he
means that Junius Brutus is to take the same part in ridding his country of
Cæsar's tyranny that Junius Brutus, of the same family, did in the expulsion
of the tyrant Tarquins.

not expelled still remains in her not having said the whole. She still rolls her fierce eyes, and her looks wandering over the whole sky, now with timid, now stern with threatening, features; a fiery blush tints her face and her livid cheeks, and a paleness exists, not that which is wont to be in one who fears, but inspiring fear. Nor does her wearied heart find rest; but, as the swelling sea after the hoarse blasts of Boreas moans, so do silent sighs relieve the prophetess. And while from the sacred light by which she has beheld the Fates she is being brought back to the sunbeams of ordinary day, shades, intervening, come on. Pæan sends Stygian Lethe into her entrails, to snatch *from her* the secrets of the Gods. Then from her breast flies the truth, and the future returns to the tripods of Phœbus, and, hardly come to herself, she falls *to the ground.*

Nor yet, Appius, does the nearness of death alarm thee, deceived by ambiguous responses; but, the sway of the world being matter of uncertainty, hurried on by vain hopes thou dost prepare to found the kingdom of Eubœan Chalcis. Alas, madman! what one of the Gods, Death excepted, can possibly grant for thee to be sensible of no crash of warfare, to be exempt from the woes so numerous of the world? The secret recesses of the Eubœan shore thou shalt possess, buried in a memorable tomb, where rocky Ca-rystos[1] straitens the outlets of the sea, and where Rhamnus

---

[1] *Rocky Carystos)* ver. 232. Carystos was a town on the south-eastern coast of Eubœa, looking towards the Cyclades; consequently Lucan is wrong in representing it as situate on the straits of Eubœa. It was situate at the foot of Mount Oche, and was said to have been founded by Dryopes; and, according to tradition, it was named after Carystus, son of Chiron. The mineral called "asbestus" was found in the neighbourhood. The spot is now called Karysto or Castel Rosso.

[2] *Where Rhamnus)* ver. 233. Rhamnus was a demus or borough of Attica, situate on a rocky peninsula on the eastern coast, about seven miles from Marathon. The Poet refers to the worship in this place of Nemesis, the Goddess of Retribution, the avenger of crime and the punisher of presumption. She had a famous temple here, in which was her statue carved by Phidias out of a block of marble which the Persians brought to Greece for the purpose of making a statue of Victory, and which was thus appropriately devoted to the Goddess of Retribution. It wore a crown and had wings, and, holding a spear of ash in the right hand, was seated on a stag. According to another account the statue was the work of Agoracritus, the disciple of Phidias.

worships the Deity hostile to the proud   where the sea
boils, enclosed in its rapid tide, and the Euripus[1] hurries
along, with waves that change their course, the ships of
Chalcis to Aulis, hostile to fleets[2].

In the meantime, the Iberians subdued, Cæsar returned,
about to carry his eagles into another region; when almost
did the Gods turn aside the course so mighty of fate
amid *his* prosperity. For, in no warfare subdued, within
the tents of his camp did the chieftain fear to lose the
profit[3] of his excesses; when almost, the bands, faithful
throughout so many wars, satiated with blood, at last forsook
their leader: whether it was that the trumpet-call ceasing for a time from its melancholy sound, and the sword
sheathed and cold, had expelled the mania for war; or
whether, while the soldier looked for greater rewards, he
condemned both the cause and the leader, and even then
held on sale his sword stained with crime. Not in any
danger[4] was Cæsar more tried, as now, not from a firm
height, but from a trembling one, he looked down on
everything, and stood propped up upon *a* stumbling *spot;*
deprived of hands so many, and left almost to his own
sword, he who dragged so many nations to war, was sensible
that it is the sword not of the general, but of the soldier,
that is unsheathed.

There was now no timid murmuring, nor yet anger concealed in the secret breast; for the cause which is wont to
check doubting minds, while each is afraid of those to whom

---

[1] *And the Euripus*) ver. 235.   He is alluding to that part of the Euripus,
or straits of Eubœa, which was the " Cœle," or " Hollows of Eubœa,"
between the promontories Caphareus and Chersonesus, which were very
dangerous to ships; here a part of the Persian fleet was wrecked,
B.C. 480.

[2] *Aulis, hostile to fleets*) ver. 236.   He alludes to the violence of the tide,
which, flowing and ebbing seven times each day and night, was in the
habit of carrying ships, in spite of the wind, away from Chalcis, in
Eubœa, towards Aulis, on the opposite coast of Bœotia.

[3] *To lose the profit*) ver. 242.   Through the mutinous spirit of his
soldiers.

[4] *Not in any danger*) ver. 249.   Suetonius tells us that during his ten
years' campaigns against the Gauls, Cæsar had not experienced any mutiny
or sedition among his troops, but that he had several times to encounter it
during the Civil Wars.   The mutiny here described took place at Placentia,
in the north of Italy.

he is a cause of fear, and thinks that the injustice of tyranny
oppresses himself alone, does not withhold them : inasmuch
as the daring multitude itself has laid *all* its fears aside.
Whatever offence is committed by many goes unpunished.
Thus they pour forth their threats :—

"Let it be permitted us, Cæsar, to depart from the
frantic career of crime. By land and by sea thou dost seek
a sword for these throats, and our lives, held so cheap, thou
art ready to throw away upon any foe. Gaul has snatched
from thee a part of us ; Spain, with her severe wars, a part ;
a part lies in Hesperia ; and the whole world over, thee
being the conqueror, does the army perish. What profits it
to have poured forth our blood in the northern regions, the
Rhone and the Rhine subdued? In return for so many
woes to me thou hast given civil war When, the Senate
expelled, we captured the abodes of our country, which of
mortals or which of the Gods was it allowed us to spoil?
Guilty with hands and weapons we incur every crime,
pious, *however*, in our poverty. What limit is sought for
our arms?

"What is enough, if Rome *is* too little? Now look upon
our hoary locks and our weak hands, and behold our feeble
arms. The prime of our life is past, our years we have
consumed in wars ; dismiss *us*, aged men, to die. Behold
our unreasonable request! to allow us not to lay our dying
limbs upon the hard turf; not with our breath as it flies
to beat against the clod[1], and to seek in death the right
hand that shall close *our* eyes[2]; to sink amid the tears of
our wives, and to know that a pile is prepared for each.
May it be allowed us by disease to end our old age Besides the sword let there be under Cæsar's rule some *other*
death. Why by hopes dost *thou* draw us on, as though
ignorant for what monstrous crimes we are being trained?
As though, indeed, we alone are not aware, amid civil war,
of which treason the reward is the greatest? Nothing has
been effected by the wars, if he has not yet discovered that
these hands are capable of doing everything.

[1] *To beat against the clod*) ver. 279. With the violent pulsation or
palpitation consequent on the struggles of death.
[2] *Shall close our eyes*) ver. 280. He alludes to the custom of the nearest
relative closing the eyes of the dying person.

N

"Nor do right or the bonds of law forbid *us* to attempt
this. Amid the waves of the Rhine Cæsar was my chieftain,
here *he is* my comrade. Those whom criminality defiles, it
renders equal. Add that, under a thankless estimator of our
deserts, our valour is lost; whatever we do is entitled 'fortune.' Let him be aware that we are his destiny. Though
thou shouldst hope for every favour of the Gods, the soldiers
enraged, Cæsar, there will be peace." Thus having said,
they began to rush to and fro throughout all the camp, and
with hostile looks to demand the chief.

Thus may it be, O Gods of heaven! when duty and
fidelity forsake us, and it is left to place our hopes in evil
ways, let discord make an end in civil war. What chieftain
could not that tumult alarm? But Cæsar comes, accustomed headlong to meet the Fates, and rejoicing to exercise
his fortunes amid extreme dangers; nor does he wait until
their rage may abate: he hastens to tempt their fury in full
career. Not to them would he have denied cities and temples
to be spoiled, and the Tarpeian abode of Jove, and the matrons of the Senate[1], and brides doomed to suffer disgraceful
indignities. He wishes indeed for everything to be asked of
him; he wishes the rewards of warfare to be courted; only
the recovered senses of the disobedient soldiery are feared.

Alas! Cæsar, art thou not ashamed for wars now to prove
pleasing to thyself alone that have been condemned by thy
own bands? Shall these be weary first of bloodshed? Shall
the law of the sword prove burdensome to them? Wilt thou
thyself rush through all right and wrong? Be tired *at last*,
and learn to be able to endure *existence* without arms; let it
be possible for thee to put an end to criminality. Barbarous
man, why dost thou press on? Why now dost thou urge on
the unwilling? Civil war is flying from thee. On a mound[2]
of turf built up he stood, intrepid in countenance, and not
alarmed, deserved to be feared; and, anger dictating, thus
he spoke:—

[1] *And the matrons of the Senate)* ver. 305. For his own purposes, the
Poet does not scruple to libel the memory of Cæsar, and in no instance
more so than in the present passage.
[2] *On a mound)* ver. 316. It was the usual custom in the Roman
camp to erect a tribunal formed of turf, from which the commander
harangued his soldiers.

" Him, against whom, when absent, soldiers, just now with countenance and right hands you were raging, you have. with breast bared and exposed to wounds. Fly, if an end of the warfare pleases you, your swords left here[1]. Sedition, that dares nothing bravely, proves faint hearts, and youths that meditate flight alone, and wearied with the prospering successes of their unconquered general. Go, and leave me, with my own destinies, to the warfare ; these weapons will find hands, and, yourselves rejected, Fortune will give in return heroes as many as the weapons that shall be unemployed. Do the nations of Hesperia attend the flight of Magnus with a fleet so great, *and* shall victory give us no *attending* multitude, to bear off the rewards of the shortened warfare, only receiving the concluding stroke, and, the price of your labours snatched away, to attend with no wound the laurel-bearing chariot? You, aged men, a crowd neglected and destitute of blood, then the commonalty of Rome, shall behold my triumphs.

" Do you suppose that the career of Cæsar can possibly feel ill results from your flight? Just as, though all the rivers should threaten to withdraw the streams which they mingle with the deep, the sea would never decrease the more, its waters diminished, than now it swells. Do you suppose that you have imparted any weight to me? Never does the care of the Gods thus lower itself, that the Fates should have leisure to attend to your death and your safety. On the movements of the great do all these things attend. Through a few does the human race exist. Soldiers, beneath my fame the terror of the Iberian and of the native of the north, certainly, Pompey your leader, you would have fled. Amid the arms of Cæsar Labienus was brave[2] ; now, a worthless

---

[1] *Your swords left here*) ver. 321. "Run away, your swords being left here," pointing to his breast.
[2] *Labienus was brave*) ver. 345. T. Labienus had been an able and active officer under Cæsar in his campaigns against the Gauls, by whom he was amply rewarded for his services. Notwithstanding the favours he had received from Cæsar, he took the earliest opportunity of deserting him, and became a zealous adherent of Pompey, who appointed him one of his legates during the campaign in Greece. Cæsar relates that he obtained from Pompey all the soldiers of Cæsar who had been taken prisoners at Dyrrhachium, and after parading them before the army of Pompey, and taunting them as his "fellow soldiers," and upbraiding them with asking if it was the cus-

runaway, with the chief whom he has preferred he wanders over land and sea.

"Nor more pleasing to me *will be* your fidelity, if, myself neither your foe nor your leader, you *do not* carry on the war. Whoever deserts my standards, and does not deliver up his arms to Pompey's party, he never wishes to be on my side. Undoubtedly this camp is a care' to the Gods, who have been desirous only to intrust me to wars so mighty upon a change of my soldiers. Alas! how vast a weight does Fortune now remove from my shoulders, wearied with the burden! It is granted me to disarm right hands that hope for everything, for which this earth does not suffice. Now at least, for myself will I wage the war; depart from the camp, base Quirites, deliver up my standards to men. But the few, in whom as the prompters this madness has raged, not Cæsar, but retribution, detains *here*. Fall down upon the earth, and extend your faithless heads and your necks to suffer the stroke; and you, raw recruits, by whose strength alone my camp shall henceforth stand, be witnesses of the punishment, and learn how to strike, learn how to die."

The motionless throng trembled beneath his stern voice as he threatened; and of one person did a force so great, able to make him a private man, stand in awe; as though he could command the swords themselves, able to wield the weapons in spite of soldiers. Cæsar himself is apprehensive lest weapons and right hands may be denied him for this dreadful deed; their endurance surpasses the hopes of their stern leader, and affords throats[1], not swords

torn for veterans to run away, put them to death in the presence of the assembled troops. By his overweening confidence he contributed to the disastrous issue of the battle of Pharsalia. After that battle, flying from place to place, he at last arrived in Africa, and joined Scipio and Cato, after whose defeat at Thapsus he fled into Spain and joined Cneius, the son of Pompey. He fell at the battle of Munda, which, very probably, was lost through his carelessness.

[1] *And affords throats*) ver. 370. Suetonius thus mentions this circumstance:—"He disbanded the entire ninth legion at Placentia, with ignominy; and only with difficulty after many prayers and entreaties, and not without punishing the guilty, did he reinstate it." Appian, in his Second Book on the Civil War, says,—"A decimation being ordered of the ninth legion, which had been the first mover in the sedition, amid the lamentations of all, the Prætors on their knees suppliantly asked pardon of him. Cæsar,

alone. Nothing does he fear more than to lose spirits
inured to crime, and that they should be lost; with ratification so dire[1] of the treaty is peace obtained, and, appeased
by punishment, the youths return *to their duty.*

This *force,* after ten encampments[2], he orders to reach
Brundisium, and to call in all the shipping, which the
winding Hydrus[3], and the ancient Taras[4], and the secret
shores of Leuca[5], which the Salapian fens[6] receive, and
the Sipus[7], situate below the mountains; where the fruitful
Garganus[8] from Apulia, winding through the Ausonian

with difficulty getting the better of his feelings of irritation, granted that
only one hundred and seventy of the seditious should be selected from the
principal ones, out of whom twelve were selected by the rest for punishment."

[1] *Ratification so dire*) ver. 372.   This is said sarcastically, and, not improbably, there is a play intended upon the use of the word "ictus," in
allusion to the resemblance between "ictus jugulorum," the "blows on the
necks" of those punished, and the "ictus fœderis," the "conclusion" or "ratification" of the treaty.

[2] *After ten encampments*) ver. 374.   "Decimis castris," literally, "in ten
encampments," meaning ten days' march.

[3] *Winding Hydrus*) ver. 375.   Hydrus was a winding river of Calabria,
which flowed past Hydrus, or Hydruntum, an ancient town of that district,
with a good harbour, and near a mountain called Hydrus. It was frequently
a place of transit.   The town is now called Otranto.

[4] *The ancient Taras*) ver. 376.   Taras was the Greek name of the city of
Tarentum, situate on the western coast of the Peninsula of Calabria.   Near
its walls flowed a river named Taras.   It was said to have been founded by
the Iapygians and Cretans, and to have derived its name from Taras, a son
of Neptune, or Poseidon.   Its present name is Taranto.

[5] *Shores of Leuca*) ver. 376.   Leuca was a town at the extremity of the
Iapygian Promontory, in Calabria, with a fetid spring, under the bed of
which the Giants who were vanquished by Hercules were said to have been
buried.

[6] *The Salapian fens*) ver. 377.   Salapia was an ancient town of Apulia,
in the Daunian district, situate on a lake which was named after it. According to the common tradition, it was founded by Diomedes.   In the second
Punic war it revolted to Hannibal after the battle of Cannæ, who is said
here to have indulged in the debaucheries of Campania. It afterwards surrendered to the Romans, and delivered up to them its Carthaginian garrison.
The original site was at some distance from the sea, but in consequence of its
unhealthy situation it was removed to a new town on the sea-coast, which
was built by M. Hostilius, about B.C. 200.

[7] *And the Sipus*) ver. 377.   Sipus was the Grecian name of Sipuntum,
town of Apulia, between Mount Garganus and the sea-shore.   It was
Roman colony, and a place of considerable commercial importance.

[8] *The fruitful Garganus*) ver. 380.   Garganus was the name of a mountain and promontory of Apulia, famous for its forests of oak.

.land, enters into the Adriatic waves, opposed to the Dalmatian Boreas and the southern breeze of Calabria.

In safety, without his soldiers, he himself repairs to trembling Rome, now taught to obey the requirements of peace[1]; and, indulgent to the entreating people, forsooth, as Dictator[2] he attains the highest honor, and, himself Consul, renders joyous the annals. For all the expressions[3] by means of which now for long we have lied to our rulers this age was the first to invent. That in no way any legality in wielding weapons might be wanting to him, Cæsar was desirous to unite the Ausonian axes with his swords. He added the fasces, too, to the eagles; and, seizing the empty name of authority, stamped the sad times with a worthy mark. For by what Consul will the Pharsalian year be better known? The Field *of Mars* feigns[4] the solemnity, and divides the suffrages[5] of the commonalty not admitted, and cites the tribes, and to no purpose *turns* the votes into the urn.

[1] *Obey the requirements of peace*) ver. 382. "Servire togæ." This is said ironically, meaning, "now ready to be enslaved by him while pretending to exercise the arts of peace."

[2] *As Dictator*) ver. 383. Cæsar had himself appointed Dictator, and Consul with P. Servilius Vatia Isauricus; but thinking that his continuing to hold the Dictatorship was likely to alienate the affections of many of his own party, he resigned it in eleven days after. See the Civil War, B. iii. c. 2.

[3] *All the expressions*) ver. 385. This line must have been penned in a bitter spirit against Nero: his meaning is, that this year was the first one of the despotism of the Cæsars, from which all those titles of honour which fear and adulation heaped upon the tyrant took their rise. Some of these titles were "Divus," "the divine;" "Semper augustus," "the ever venerable;" "Pater patriæ," "the father of his country;" "Dominus," "the lord;" 'Fundator quietis," "author of repose."

[4] *The Field of Mars feigns*) ver. 392. By the use of the word "fingit," he means to say that the proceedings were spurious and illegal, and that Cæsar and Servilius were not Consuls, but only Pseudo-Consuls. The votes for the Consulship were given by the tribes assembled on the Campus Martius.

[5] *Divides the suffrages*) ver. 393. He means that Cæsar, in which example was followed by the succeeding emperors, cited the tribes of the people to the election of the Consuls on the Campus Martius, but that he did not admit them to give their votes, although, "dirimebat," he distributed the pebbles or ballots among them as though for the purpose, although, too, the herald cited (decantabat) the tribes by name, and although he drew lots (versabat) from the urn, as to the order in which the tribes were to give their votes.

Nor is it allowed to prognosticate from the heavens ; the augur *remaining* deaf, it thunders, and the birds are sworn to be propitious, the ill-omened owl *presenting itself.* From that time first fell a power once venerated, stripped of its rights ; only, lest time should be wanting an appellation, the Consul of the month[1] distinguishes the ages in the annals. Besides, the Divinity who presides at Ilian Alba[2], not deservedly[3], Latium subdued, *still* beholds the solemn rites, the Latin sacrifices[4] performed in the flaming night.

Then he hurries on his course, and speeds across the fields which the inactive Apulian has deserted with his harrows, and has yielded up to slothful grass, quicker than both the flames of heaven and the pregnant tigress ; and, arriving at the Minoïan abodes of the winding Brundisium[5], he finds the waves pent up by the winds of winter, and the fleets alarmed by the wintry Constellation[6]. Base does it seem to the chieftain for the moments for hurrying on the war to pass in slow delay, and to be kept in harbour while the sea is open in safety, even to those who are unsuc cessful. Spirits unacquainted with the sea thus does he fill with courage :—

[1] *Consul of the month*) ver. 399. He laments that from this time the office of Consul was entirely stripped of its authority, and that only for the purpose of giving a name to the periods in the " Fasti Consulares," or annals, from their Consulships, were the Consuls elected ; and in many instances only for a month, according to the whim of the emperor. Suetonius speaks of Caligula, Claudius, and Nero as acting thus, and Tacitus mentions the same practice with regard to the Emperor Otho.

[2] *At Ilian Alba*) ver. 400. Alba was said to have been founded by Ascanius, or Iulus, the son of Æneas, the Trojan.

[3] *Not deservedly*) ver. 401. He means that Jupiter Latialis was not worthy of this sacrifice being performed in his honor, in consequence of his neglect in having allowed Latium to be subjected to the tyranny of Cæsar.

[4] *The Latin sacrifices*) ver. 402. As to the Latinæ, or rites of Jupiter Latialis, see the First Book, l. 550, and the Note to the passage.

[5] *Winding Brundisium*) ver. 406. See a description of the shores of Brundisium in the Second Book, l. 613 : Lucan calls them " Minoïa" from the tradition which represented the Cretans, over whom Minos reigned, as being the founders of the colony.

[6] *Wintry Constellation*) ver. 408. " Hiberno sidere." It is not precisely known to which of the heavenly bodies he refers as the "Hibernum sidus." The Constellations of the Dolphin and the Pleiades have been suggested ; but it is not unlikely that he alludes to the wintry aspect of the sun, which, by reason of his absence during the prolonged nights of winter, causes cold.

" More constantly do the wintry blasts possess the heavens and the main, when they have *once* begun, than those which the perfidious inconstancy of the cloudy spring forbids to prevail with certainty. No windings are there of the sea, and *no* shores are there to be surveyed by us, but straight onward are the waves to be cleaved, and by *the aid of* the north wind alone. O that he would bend the head of our topmost mast, and press on in his fury, and waft us to the Grecian walls, lest the partisans of Pompey should come with impelled oars from all the shore of the Phæacians[1] upon our languid sails; sever the cables which retain *our* conquering prows; already are we losing[2] .he clouds and the raging waves."

. The first stars of the sky[3], Phœbus concealing himself beneath the waves, had come forth, and the moon had now spread her shadows, when they both unmoored the ships, and the ropes unfurled the full sails; and the sailor, the end of the yard being bent by the rope towards the left, slants the canvass *to catch the wind*, and expanding the loftiest top-sail, catches the gales that might die away. When first a slight breeze has begun to move the sails. and they swell a little, soon, returning to the mast, they

---

[1] *Of the Phæacians*) ver. 420. The Phæacians were the ancient inhabitants of the island of Corcyra, now Corfu. His fear is ·lest the ships of war of Pompey should be enabled to overtake his heavy transports. Cæsar says, in his Civil War, B. iii. c. 5,—" Pompey had resolved to fix his winter quarters at Dyrrhachium, Apollonia, and the other seaports, to hinder Cæsar from passing the sea, and for this purpose had stationed his fleet along the sea-coast."

[2] *Already are we losing*) ver. 423. He means that they are losing the opportunity afforded them by the stormy weather, which will hinder the enemy from obstructing their passage over.

[3] *First stars of the sky*) ver. 424. This important period is thus referred to by Cæsar in his Civil War, B. iii. c. 6 :—" When Cæsar came to Brundisium, he made a speech to the soldiers :—' That since they were now almost arrived at the termination of their toils and dangers, they should patiently submit to leave their slaves and baggage in Italy, and to embark without luggage, that a greater number of men might be put on board: that they might expect everything from victory and his liberality.' They cried out with one voice, that he might give what orders he pleased, that they would cheerfully fulfil them. He accordingly set sail the fourth day of January, with seven legions on board, as already remarked. The next day he reached land, between the Ceraunian rocks and other dangerous spots."

fall into the midst of the ship; and, the land left behind, the wind itself is not able to accompany the vessels which has brought them out. The sea lies becalmed, bound by a heavy torpor. More sluggish do the waves stand than unmoved swamps.

So stands the motionless Bosporus[1] that binds the Scythian waves, when, the ice preventing, the Danube does not impel the deep, and the boundless sea is covered with ice; whatever ships they have overtaken the waves keep fast; and the horseman breaks through the waters not pervious to sails, and the wheel of the migrating Bessan[2] cleaves the Mæotis, resounding with its waves lying concealed. Fearful *is* the calm of the sea, and sluggish *are* the stagnant pools of becalmed water on the dismal deep; as though deserted by[3] stiffened nature the seas are still, and the ocean, forgetful to observe its ancient laws, moves not with its tides, nor shudders with a ripple, nor dances beneath the reflection of the sun.

Detained, to dangers innumerable were the barks exposed. On the one side *were* fleets hostile and ready to move the sluggish waves with *their* oars; on the other was famine threatening to come on them blockaded by the calm on the deep. Unwonted vows were found for unwonted fears, both to pray for the billows and the exceeding might of the winds,

---

[1] *The motionless Bosporus*) ver. 436. Under this name it is probable that he refers to the Black Sea, or Pontus Euxinus in general. The name was given by the ancients to two places:—1. The Thracian Bosporus, now the "Straits of Constantinople," uniting the Propontis, or sea of Marmora, with the Euxine or Black Sea; which received its name, according to the tradition, from Io, when changed by Jupiter into an heifer. 2. The Cimmerian Bosporus, now the Straits of Caffa, which unites the Palus Mæotis, or sea of Azof, with the Black Sea. It derived its name from the Cimmerii, a nation supposed to live in the neighbourhood.

[2] *The migrating Bessan*) ver. 441. The Bessi were a fierce people of Thrace, who dwelt in the districts extending from Mount Hæmus to the Euxine. Ovid mentions them in his Tristia, or Lament, B. iii. El. 10, l. 5:—" The Sauromatæ, a savage race, the Bessi, and the Getæ surround me, names how unworthy of my genius to mention!" The Poet here alludes to the custom of the migratory nations passing over the Palus Mæotis when frozen, with their waggons.

[3] *As though deserted by*) ver. 443-4. " Veluti deserta rigente æquora naturâ, cessant." Lemaire suggests that this is the proper translation of this passage :—" Just like places rendered uninhabited by frozen nature the sea is still."

so long as the waves should release themselves from their
torpid stagnation, and there should be a sea. Clouds and
indications of waves are there nowhere; the sky and the
sea languid, all hope of shipwreck departs[1]. But, the night
dispersed, the day sends forth its beams obscured by clouds,
and by degrees arouses the depths of the ocean, and for the
mariners sets Ceraunia in motion[2]. Then do the ships
begin to be borne along, and the furrowed waves to follow
the fleet, which now moving on with fair wind and tide,
pierces with its anchors the sands of Palæste[3]

The region was the first to see the generals pitch their
adjoining camps, which the swift Genusus[4] and which the
more gentle Apsus[5], surround with their banks. The cause
for the Apsus being able to carry ships is a fen, which,
deceiving by its water slowly flowing, it empties. But the
Genusus, snows, now dissolved by the sun, and now
dissolved by showers, render of headlong course; neither
wearies itself by a long course, but, the sea-shore being
near, is acquainted with but very little land. In this spot
did Fortune bring together two names of a fame so great,
and the hopes of the wretched world were deceived, that

[1] *All hope of shipwreck departs*) ver. 455. Amid the calm they despair
of a storm which may cause them the risk of shipwreck.

[2] *Sets Ceraunia in motion*) ver. 457. Probably this expression is used in
reference to the optical illusion which appears to represent the ship as sta-
tionary to those on board, and the shore as though in motion.

[3] *Sands of Palæste*) ver. 460. Palæste was a town of Epirus, on the
coast of Chaonia, to the south of the Acroceraunian Mountains. From a line
in the Fasti of Ovid, it would seem that the Furies had a temple at this
place, B. iv. l. 236. The town on its site at the present day is called
Palasa.

[4] *The swift Genusus*) ver. 462. The Genusus is a river of Illyria, which
separated Dyrrhachium from Apollonia. It is now called the Iskumi.

[5] *More gentle Apsus*) ver. 462. The Apsus, a river of Illyria, now
called the Crevasta, flows into the Ionian Sea. This period of the War,
when the rivals first met each other, is thus referred to in the Civil
War, B. iii. c. 15:—"Cæsar, finding the road to Dyrrhachium already in
the possession of Pompey, was in no great haste, but encamped by the river
Apsus, in the territory of Apollonia, that the states which had deserved his
support might be certain of protection from his outposts and forts; and there
he resolved to await the arrival of his other legions from Italy, and to winter
in tents. Pompey did the same, and pitching his camp on the other side of
the river Apsus, collected there all his troops and auxiliaries." The trans-
actions in Illyria, from the time of Cæsar's landing up to this period, are
related in the Civil War, B. iii. c. 7-13.

the chieftains might possibly, when separated by the trifling distance of a plain, condemn the criminality *now* brought home. For they have the opportunity to see their countenances and to hear their voices; and for many a year, Magnus, not personally did thy father-in-law, beloved by thee, after pledges so great[1] of blood, the birth and the death of a luckless grandson, behold thee, except upon the sands of the Nile.

A part of *his forces*[2] left behind compelled the mind of Cæsar, aroused for mingling in the conflict, to submit to delay in crime. Antony was the leader, daring in all warfare, even then, in civil war, training for Leucas[3]. Him delaying full oft by threats and by entreaties[4] does Cæsar summon forth :—

" O cause of woes so mighty to the world, why dost thou retard the Gods of heaven and the Fates ? The rest has been effected by my speed; Fortune demands thee as the finishing hand to the successes of the hastened warfare. Does Libya, sundered with her shoaly quicksands,

---

[1] *After pledges so great*) ver. 473-4. " Pignora tanta " refers to the marriage of Julia, the daughter of Cæsar, with Pompey, and in the word " soboles " he refers to the child of which she was delivered, but which lived only for a very short period.

[2] *A part of his forces*) ver. 477. He alludes to the several legions which he had left behind him at Brundisium, under the command of Marc Antony.

[3] *Training for Leucas*) ver. 479. " Jam tunc civili meditatus Leucada bello." This is said ironically, and the Poet means to say that even then Antony was practising, by engaging in civil warfare, for the part he was to take at the battle of Actium, which he fought against Augustus off the Leucadian Promontory.

[4] *By threats and by entreaties*) ver. 480. This is thus expressed by Cæsar himself in his account of the Civil War, B. iii. c. 25 :—" Those who commanded Pompey's fleet received frequent reproofs from him by letter, that as they had not prevented Cæsar's arrival at the first, they should at least stop the remainder of his army ; and they were expecting that the season for transporting troops would every day become more unfavorable, as the winds grew calmer. Cæsar, feeling some trouble on this account, wrote in severe terms to his officers at Brundisium, and gave them orders that as soon as they found the wind to answer, they should not let the opportunity of setting sail pass by, if they were even to steer their course to the shore of Apollonia, because there they might run their ships aground. That these parts principally were left unguarded by the enemy's fleet, because they dared not venture too far from the harbour."

divide us with uncertain tides? Have I in any way entrusted thy arms to an untried deep, and art thou dragged
into dangers unknown? Sluggard, Cæsar commands thee
to come, not to go. I myself, the first, amid the foe touched
upon sands in the midst of them, *and* under the sway of
others. Dost thou fear my camp? I lament that the hours
of fate are wasting; upon the winds and the waves do I
expend my prayers. Keep not those back who desire to go
on the shifting deep; if I judge aright, the youths would
be willing by shipwreck *even* to repair to the arms of Cæsar.
Now must I employ the language of grief; not on equal
terms have we divided the world. Cæsar and the whole
Senate occupy Epirus; thou alone dost possess Ausonia."

After he sees that he, summoned three or four times
in this language, is *still* delaying, as he believes that it is
he himself who is wanting to the Gods, and not the Deities
to him, of his accord amid the unsafe shades *of night* he
dares to try the sea, which they, commanded, stand in fear
of, having experienced that venturous deeds have prospered
under a favoring Divinity; and waves, worthy to be feared
by fleets, he hopes to pass over in a little bark.

Night with its languor had *now* relaxed the wearied care
of arms; rest *was* obtained for the wretched, into whose
breasts by sleep a more humble lot inspires strength. Now
was the camp silent; now had *its* third hour[1] brought
on the second watch; Cæsar with anxious step amid the
vasty silence attempted things hardly by his servants[2] to be
dared; and, all left behind, Fortune alone pleased him as his
companion. After he had gone through the tents, he passed
over the bodies of the sentinels which had yielded to sleep,
silently complaining that he was able[3] to elude them. He

---

[1] *Now had its third hour*) ver. 507.   This would be from 11 to 12 o'clock
at night, as the " vigiliæ," or watches, of the Roman armies were divided
into four, of three hours each, the first beginning at six o'clock in the evening.

[2] *Hardly by his servants*) ver. 509.   Plutarch says that Cæsar disguised
himself in the dress of a servant.   Appian states that he sent three servants
before to get ready the vessel, as though for the use of a messenger from
Cæsar.

[3] *Complaining that he was able*) ver. 512.   That they were tasting of
tranquil slumbers to which he himself was a stranger; or perhaps it may
mean that he was sorry to find the watch so badly kept.

passed along the winding shore, and at the brink of the waves found a bark attached by a cable to the rocks eaten away.

Not far from thence a house, free from all cares, propped up with no stout timbers, but woven with barren rushes and the reeds of the marsh, and covered on its exposed side with a boat[1] turned bottom upwards, sheltered the pilot and the owner of the bark. Cæsar twice or thrice knocked with his hand at this threshold, that shook the roof. Amyclas arose from the soft couch, which the sea-weed afforded. "What shipwrecked person, I wonder," said he, "repairs to my abode? Or whom has Fortune compelled to hope for the aid of our cottage?" Thus having said, the tow now raised[2] from the dense heap of warm ashes, he nourished the small spark into kindled flames; free from care of the warfare, he knew that in civil strife cottages are no prey. O safe the lot of a poor man's life, and his humble home! O gifts of the Deities not yet understood! What temples or *what* cities could this befall, to be alarmed with no tumult, the hand of Cæsar knocking?

Then, the door being opened, the chieftain says:— "Look for what is greater than thy moderate wishes, and give scope to thy hopes, O youth. If, obeying my commands, thou dost carry me to Hesperia, no more wilt thou be owing everything to thy bark, and by thy hands dragging on a needy old age. Hesitate not to entrust thy fate to the God who wishes to fill thy humble abode with sudden wealth."

---

[1] *With a boat*) ver. 518. "Phaselo." The vessel which was called "phaselus" was long and narrow, and probably received its name from its resemblance to the shape of a kidney-bean, which was called "phaselus." They were especially used by the Egyptians, and were of various sizes, from that of a mere boat to a vessel suited for a long voyage. Appian mentions them as being a medium between ships of war and merchant vessels. Being built for speed, they were more noted for their swiftness than their strength. Juvenal, Sat. xv. l. 127, speaks of them as being made of clay; but of course that can only refer to "phaseli" of the smallest kind. The one here mentioned was perhaps of this description.

[2] *The tow now raised*) ver. 524. Among the poor it was the custom to keep a log of wood smouldering beneath a heap of embers on the hearth from day to day, to be in readiness for cooking or giving a light when wanted. In the present instance we find an old rope or piece of tow used for a similar purpose.

Thus he says, unable to be taught to speak as a private man, though clad in a plebeian garb. Then *says* the poor Amyclas, " Many things indeed forbid me to trust the deep to-night. For the sun did not take down into the seas ruddy clouds, and rays of one hue[1]; one portion of Phœbus invited the southern gales, another, with divided light, the northern. Dimmed, too, and languid in the middle of his orb, he set, not dazzling the eyes that looked on him, with his weakly light. The moon, also, did not rise, shining with slender horn, or hollowed with clear cavities in her mid orb ; nor did she describe tapering points on her straitened horn, and with the signs of wind she was red ; besides, pallid, she bears a livid aspect, sad with her face about to sink beneath the clouds.

" But neither does the waving of the woods, nor the lashings of the sea-shore, nor the fitful dolphin, that challenges the waves[2], please me ; nor yet that the sea-gull loves the dry land ; the fact, too, that the heron ventures to fly aloft, trusting to its hovering wing ; and that, sprinkling its head with the waves, as though it would forestall the rain, the crow paces the sea-shore with infirm step. But if the weight of great events demands, I would not hesitate to lend my aid. Either I will touch the commanded shore, or, on the other hand, the seas and the winds shall deny it."

Thus having said and unmooring his craft, he spreads the canvass to the winds ; at the motion of which, not only meteors gliding along the lofty air, as they fall, describe tracks in all quarters *of the heavens ;* but even the stars which are held fixed in the loftiest skies, appear to shake. A dusky swell pervades the surface of the sea; with many a heaving along their lengthened track the threatening waves boil up, uncertain as to the impending blasts ; the swelling seas betoken the winds conceived. Then says the master of the quivering bark :—

" Behold, how vast dangers the raging sea is preparing. Whether it presages the Zephyrs, or whether the east

[1] *Rays of one hue*) ver. 542. " Concordes radii " may mean either " rays of like colour," or " rays pointing in the same direction," which latter meaning is amplified in the succeeding words.

[2] *Challenges the waves*) ver. 552. Burmann remarks that the dolphins seem by their gambols to challenge the ocean to rise in waves.

winds, it is uncertain. On every side the fitful waves are beating against the bark. In the clouds and in the heavens are the southern blasts ; if we go by the murmurs of the sea, Corus is skimming along the deep. In a storm thus mighty neither will bark nor shipwrecked person reach the Hesperian shores. To despair of making our way, and to turn from the forbidden course, is our only safety. Let it be allowed *me* to make for shore with the tossed bark, lest the nearest land should be too distant."

Cæsar, confident that all dangers will give way for him, says, "Despise the threats of the deep, and spread sail to the raging winds. If, heaven prompting thee, thou dost decline Italy, myself *thy prompter*, seek it. This alone is thy reasonable cause for fear, not to have known thy freight ; one whom the Deities never forsake; of whom Fortune deserves badly then, when after his wishes *expressed* she comes. Secure in my protection, burst through the midst of the storms. This is the labour of the heavens and of the sea, not of our bark ; that, trod by Cæsar, the freight will protect from the waves. Nor will long duration be granted to the raging fury of the winds ; this same bark will advantage the waves. Turn not thy hands ; avoid, with thy sails, the neighbouring shores; believe that then thou hast gained the Calabrian port, when no other land can be granted to the ship and to our safety. Art thou ignorant what, amid a tempest so great, is preparing? Amid the tumult of the sea and sky, Fortune is enquiring how she shall favour me."

No more having said, a furious whirlwind, the stern being struck, tears away the shrouds rent asunder, and brings the flapping sails upon the frail mast; the joints overstrained, the vessel groans. Then rush on perils gathered together from the whole universe. First, moving the tides, Corus, thou dost raise thy head from the Atlantic Ocean ; now, as thou dost lift it, the sea rages, and uplifts all its billows upon the rocks. The cold Boreas meets it, and beats back the ocean, and doubtful stands the deep, un-decided which wind to obey. But the rage of the Scythian north wind conquers and hurls aloft the waves, and makes shallows of the sands entirely concealed. And Boreas does not carry the waves on to the rocks, and he dashes his own seas against the billows of Corus; and the aroused waves, even with the winds lulled, are able to meet in conflict.

I would surmise that the threats of Eurus were not with-held, and that the winds of the South, black with showers, did not lie beneath the dungeons of the Æolian rocks; that all, rushing from their wonted quarters, with violent whirl-winds defended their own regions, *and* that thus the ocean remained in its place. No small seas do they speak of as having been carried along by the gales; the Tyrrhenian runs into the Ægean waves; the wandering Adriatic echoes in the Ionian sea. O how often did that day overwhelm mountains *before* beaten in vain by the waves! What lofty summits did the subdued earth permit to be overcome! Not on that shore do waves so tremendous rise, and, rolling from another region of the earth, from the vast ocean have they come, and the waves that encircle the world speed on their monstrous billows.

Thus did the ruler of Olympus[1] aid his wearied light-nings against the world with his brother's trident, and the earth was added to the secondary realms *of Neptune,* when Tethys was unwilling to submit to any shores, content to be bounded by the skies *alone.* Now as well would the mass of sea so vast have increased to the stars, if the ruler of the Gods of heaven had not kept down the waves with clouds. That was not a night of the heavens[2]; the air lay concealed infected with the paleness of the infernal abodes, and, op-pressed with storms, was kept down, and the waves received the showers in the clouds. Even the light *so* dreadful is lost, and the lightnings flash not with their brilliance, but the cloudy atmosphere obscurely divides *for their flashes.*

Then do the convex abodes of the Gods of heaven resound, and the lofty skies re-echo, and, the structure strained, the poles re-echo. Nature dreads Chaos, the elements seem to have burst from their concordant repose, and night once more[3]

[1] *Did the ruler of Olympus*) ver. 620. The meaning is, that with storms like this Jupiter determined to punish the world for its wickedness, both by means of his own lightnings and the seas, the realms of his brother Neptune.
[2] *Not a night of the heavens*) ver. 627. It was not a common darkness aloft, overspreading the heavens, but as though brought from the shades of hell.
[3] *And night once more*) ver. 656. "Nox." Night, in the sense of Chaos.

to return about to mingle the shades below with the Gods *of heaven.* The sole hope of safety *is,* that not as yet have they perished amid ruin of the universe so great. As far as from the Leucadian heights the calm deep is beheld below, so far do the trembling mariners look down upon the headlong sea from the summits of the waves; and when the swelling billows gape open once again, hardly does the mast stand above the surface. The clouds are touched by the sails, and the earth by the keel. For the sea, in the part where it is at rest, does not conceal the sands; it arises in mountains, and all the waters are in waves. Fears conquer the resources of art, and the pilot knows not which to break, to which wave to give way.

The discord of the sea comes to their aid in their distress, and billow is not able to throw over the vessel against billows; the resisting wave supports the yielding side, and the bark rises upright amid all the winds. They dread not the lowly Sason [1] with its shallows, nor yet the rocky shores of curving Thessaly, and the dangerous harbours of the Ambracian coast [2]; of the summits of rocky Ceraunia the sailors are in dread. Now does Cæsar believe there to be a danger worthy of his destiny.

" Is it a labour so great," says he, " with the Gods above to overwhelm me, whom, sitting in a little bark, they have assaulted with seas so vast? If the glory of my end has been granted to the deep, and I am denied to the warfare, fearlessly will I receive whatever death, ye Deities, you send me. Although the day hurried on by the Fates should cut short *my* mighty exploits, things great enough have I done. The nations of the north have I conquered; hostile arms have I subdued with fear; Rome has beheld Magnus second to me. The commonalty ordered *by me,* I have obtained by warfare the fasces which were denied unto me. No Roman dignity will be wanting to my titles.

" No one will know this, except thee, Fortune, who alone

<hr />

[1] *The lowly Sason*) ver. 650. See the Note to B. ii. l. 627.

[2] *The Ambracian coast*) ver. 652. Ambracia was a town of Epirus, situate on the left bank of the river Aracthus, to the north of the Ambracian Gulf. It was originally colonized by the Corinthians about B.C. 660. Pyrrhus, king of Epirus, made it the capital of his dominions. The Ceraunia, or Acroceraunia, "the heights of thunder," were precipitous rocks of the coast of Epirus.

art conscious of my wishes, that I, although I go loaded with
honors and Dictator and Consul, to the Stygian shades, die
as a private person. There is need, O Gods of heaven, of
no funereal rites for me ; retain my mangled carcase in the
midst of the waves ; let tomb and funeral pile be wanting
to me, so long as I shall be always dreaded and looked for
by every land."

Him, having thus said, a tenth wave[1], wondrous to be said,
lifts with the frail bark on high ; nor again does it hurl it
down from the lofty heights of the sea, but the wave bears
it along, and casts it on dry land, where the narrow shore
is free from rugged cliffs. At the same moment, the land
being touched, realms so many, cities so many, and his own
fortune does he regain.

But not so easily did Cæsar, now returning[2], on the following day deceive his camp and his adherents, as on the
occasion of his silent flight. Thronging around their general
the multitude wept, and accosted him with their lamenta
tions and not displeasing complaints[3]. " Whither, cruel
Cæsar, has thy rash valour carried thee, or to what fate
abandoning us, valueless lives, didst thou give thy limbs to
be scattered by the reluctant storm? Since the existence and
the safety of so many nations depend upon this life *of thine,*
and the world so great has made thee its head, it is cruelty
to wish to die. Did no one of thy followers deserve, not to
be able to be a survivor of thy fate? When the sea was
hurrying thee along, slothful slumber was in possession of
our bodies. Alas! we are ashamed! This was the cause
of thy seeking Hesperia; it seemed cruel to commit any

[1] *A tenth wave*) ver. 672. It was a notion among the ancients that every
tenth wave (probably reckoning from the beginning of the storm) was more
violent than the others. Thus Ovid says, in his Tristia, or Lament, B. i.
El. 2, ll. 49, 50 :—" The wave that is now coming on o'ertops all the others;
'tis the one that comes after the ninth and before the eleventh." He also
refers to the same belief in the Metamorphoses, B. xi. l. 530.

[2] *Did Cæsar, now returning*) ver. 678. The meaning is, that having
landed at Brundisium he returned forthwith to his army in Epirus, but that,
coming ashore in the broad light of day, his return could not be so easily
concealed from his army as his departure had been.

[3] *Not displeasing complaints*) ver. 681. Inasmuch as they attested their
affection for him. Appian says that on this occasion some expressed their
admiration of Cæsar's boldness, while others complained to him aloud that he
had done what rather befitted a brave soldier than a considerate general.

one to a sea so boisterous. The last lot of events is wont to precipitate *men* into doubtful dangers and the headlong perils of death.

" For one now holding the rule of the world to have entrusted *himself* to the sea ! Why thus greatly dost thou tempt the Deities ? Is this favour and effort of Fortune sufficient for the crisis of the war, which has impelled thee to our sands? Has this service of the Deities pleased thee. not that thou shouldst be ruler of the world, not chief of the state, but fortunate in shipwreck ?" Uttering such things, the night dispersed. the day with its sunshine came upon them, and the wearied deep lulled the swelling waves, the winds permitting.

The captains also [1] in Hesperia, when they beheld the sea weary of waves, and the clearing Boreas [2] rising in the heavens to subdue the deep, unmoored the barks, which the wind and the right hands, plied with equal time, long kept mingled ; and over the wide sea, the ships keeping close together, *the fleet* united. just as a troop on land. But relentless night took away from the sailors the steadiness of the breeze, and the even course of the sails, and threw the barks out of their line.

Thus, Nile, do the cranes, about to drink of thee, the winter driving them away, leave the frozen Strymon, and at their first flight describe various figures [3] as chance directs

---

[1] *The captains also*) ver. 703. Those chiefs of the Cæsarian party who were at Brundisium, namely, Antony, Gabinius. Posthumius, and Calenus.

[2] *The clearing Boreas*) ver. 705. This is contrary to Cæsar's account, who says that they passed over with a southerly wind. He thus relates the circumstance of their setting sail, in the Civil War, B. iii. c. 26 :—" Cæsar's officers exerting boldness and courage, aided by the instructions of Antony and of Fufius Calenus, and animated by the soldiers strongly encouraging them, and declining no danger for Cæsar's safety, having got a southerly wind. weighed anchor, and the next day were carried past Apollonia and Dyrrhachium, and being seen from the main land, Quintus Coponius, who commanded the Rhodian fleet at Dyrrhachium, put out of port with his ships ; and when they had almost come up with us, in consequence of the breeze dying away, the south wind sprang up afresh and rescued us. However, he did not desist from his attempt, but hoped by the labour and perseverance of his seamen to be able to bear up against the violence of the storm ; and although we were carried beyond Dyrrhachium by the violence of the wind, he nevertheless continued to chase us."

[3] *Describe various figures*) ver. 713. He alludes to the straggling flight of cranes in winter from the banks of the Strymon, in Thrace, towards the

them. Afterwards, when the south wind prevailing more on
high has impelled their spread wings, mixed indiscriminately
they are crowded into confused masses, and the letter, disarranged[1], is destroyed by their wings scattered in all directions. When first, the day returning, a stronger breeze
blew upon the ships, aroused at the rising of Phœbus. they
passed by the shores of Lissus[2] attempted in vain, and
made for Nymphæum[3]. Already had the south wind, succeeding Boreas, made into a harbour the waves exposed[4] to
the north.

The arms of Cæsar being collected in strength from every
side, Magnus, beholding the extreme dangers of the dreadful
warfare now drawing near his own camp, determined to

warmer regions of the Nile.   The figures described by them in their flight
are said to have been of the shape of V, A, or L.

[1] *And the letter, disarranged*) ver. 716.   The figures alluded to in the
last Note.

[2] *The shores of Lissus*) ver. 719.   Lissus, now called Elisso, was a town
on the coast of Epirus, at the mouth of the river Drilon.   It was situate on
a hill, and had a strongly-fortified citadel, which was considered impregnable.
Cæsar, in the Civil War, B. iii. c. 26, thus relates the circumstances here
referred to:—"Our men, taking advantage of the favour of fortune, for they
were still afraid of being attacked by the enemy's fleet, if the wind abated,
having come near a port called Nymphæum, about three miles beyond Lissus,
put into it (this port is protected from a south-west wind, but is not secure
against a south wind); and they thought less danger was to be apprehended
from the storm than from the enemy.   But as soon as they were in harbour.
the south wind, which had blown for two days, by extraordinary good luck
veered round to the south-west.   Here one might observe the sudden turn of
Fortune.   We who, a moment before, were alarmed for ourselves, were
safely lodged in a very secure harbour; and they who had threatened ruin to
our fleet were forced to be uneasy on their own account; and thus, by a
change of circumstances, the storm protected our ships, and damaged the
Rhodian fleet to such a degree that all their decked ships, sixteen in number,
foundered without exception, and were wrecked; and of the prodigious number of seamen and soldiers, some lost their lives by being dashed against the
rocks, others were taken by our men; but Cæsar sent them all safe home."

[3] *Made for Nymphæum*) ver. 720.   Nymphæum was the name of several
places.   The one here mentioned was a port and Promontory on the coast of
Illyricum, three Roman miles from Lissus.

[4] *The waves exposed*) ver. 720.   By "undas," literally "waves," the Poet
means the harbour of Nymphæum.   His meaning is that the harbour was
exposed to the north wind, by means of which Cæsar's ships had entered it;
immediately after which the wind veered to the south, by reason of which
the ships were secure.   Cæsar makes the wind to veer from south to south
west, Lucan from north to south.

deposit in safety the charge of wedlock, and to conceal thee, Cornelia, removed to Lesbos[1], afar from the din of cruel warfare. Alas! how greatly does virtuous passion prevail in well-regulated minds! Even thee, Magnus, did love render doubtful and anxious as to the result of battles; thy wife alone thou wast unwilling to be subject to the stroke of Fortune, beneath which was the world and the destiny of Rome.

Now do words forsake his mind, made up, and it pleases him, putting off what is about to come, to indulge a pleasing delay, and to snatch the moment from the Fates. Towards the close of the night, the repose of slumber banished, while Cornelia cherishes in her embrace his breast weighed down with cares, and seeks the delightful kisses of her husband who turns away; wondering at his moistened cheeks, and smitten with a secret wound, she dares not to arraign Magnus with weeping. He, sighing, says:—

" Wife, dearer to me than life, not now when tired of life, but in joyous times; the sad day is come, and one which both too much and too little we have deferred: now is Cæsar at hand for battle with all his might. To war must we give way: during which for thee Lesbos will be a safe retreat. Forbear making trial of entreaty; already have I denied myself[2]. Thou wilt not have to endure a prolonged absence[3] from me. Events will succeed with headlong speed; ruin hastening on, the highest interests are downward speeding. 'Tis enough to have heard of the dangers of Magnus; and thy love has deceived me, if thou canst be witness of the civil war. For I am ashamed now, the line of battle drawn up, to have been enjoying tranquil slumbers together with my wife, and to arise from thy bosom, when the trumpet-call is shaking the distracted world.

---

[1] *Removed to Lesbos*) ver. 725. Lesbos, now called Metelin, was the largest of the islands of the Ægean along the coast of Asia Minor. The inhabitants were greatly favoured by Pompey, and were restored by him to the enjoyment of freedom after the Mithridatic war, in consideration of the sufferings they had undergone.

[2] *Have I denied myself*) ver. 744. He exercises self-denial, as he is anxious to retain her with him in Epirus.

[3] *A prolonged absence*) ver. 745. " Longas" is supposed by some to apply to the distance between Lesbos and Thessaly. It is more probable however, that it relates to the duration of their separation.

" I dread to engage Pompey in civil warfare sorrowing with no loss. More safe meantime than nations, and more safe than every king, far and wide, and removed afar, the fortune of thy husband may not overwhelm thee with all its weight. If the Deities shall overthrow my ranks, let the better part of me survive; and let there be for me, if the Fates and the blood-stained victor shall overwhelm me, whither I may desire to fly."

In her weakness hardly did she sustain grief so great, and her senses fled from her astounded breast. At length, with difficulty was she able to utter her sorrowing complaints :—

" Nothing, Magnus, is left me to say in complaint of the destiny of our union and of the Gods of heaven; death does not divide our love, nor the closing torch of the sad funereal pile : but, sent away, by a common and too vulgar lot[1] am I separated from my husband. At the approach of the foe let us sever the union of our marriage torch; let us appease thy father-in-law. Has, Magnus, my fidelity been thus experienced by thee? And dost thou believe that anything can be more safe to me than to thee? Have we not for long depended on one lot? Dost thou, relentless one, command me, absent, to expose my life to lightnings and to ruin so mighty? Does my lot seem a tranquil one to thee, to be perishing *with apprehension*, when even now thou art entertaining hopes? As I shall be reluctant to be the slave of the wicked, still, by a ready death, I shall follow thee to the shades; until the sad report reaches the regions removed afar, I, forsooth, shall be living, the survivor of thee.

" Add *this*, that thou dost accustom me to my fate, and, in thy cruelty, to endure grief so great. Pardon me confessing it; I fear to be able to endure it. But if my prayers are *realized*, and I am heard by the Gods, last *of all* will thy wife know the result of affairs. The rocks will be detaining me, full of anxiety, thou being already the conqueror; and I shall be dreading the ship which may be bringing destinies

---

[1] *Too vulgar lot*) ver. 765. By the use of the word "plebeia" she probably refers to the divorces or separations which were of every-day occurrence among the Roman people. One of the Scholiasts thinks that Cornelia alludes to the life of rustics who separate themselves from their wives for the purpose of sending them to market or to work in the fields.

so joyous.   Nor will the successes of the war, heard of by
me, end my fears, when, exposed in an undefended place, I
may be taken by Cæsar even in his flight.   The shores will
grow famous through the exile of a famous name, and, the
wife of Magnus abiding there, who will possibly be ignorant
of the retreat of Mitylene[1]?   This, the last thing do I
entreat, if thy conquered arms shall leave thee nothing
more safe than flight, when thou hast entrusted thyself to
the waves, to any quarter in preference turn thy unlucky
bark; on my shores thou wilt be sought for."

Thus saying, distractedly she leaps forth, the couch[2]
abandoned, and wishes to defer her woes by no delay.   In
her sweet embrace she does not endure to clasp the breast of
the sorrowing Magnus, nor yet his neck; and the last enjoyment of love so prolonged passes away; and their own sorrows they hasten on, and neither on withdrawing can endure
to say, "farewell;" and throughout all their lives no day
has there been so sad.   For other griefs with a mind now
strengthened by woes, and resolute, did they submit to.
She falls fainting in her wretchedness, and, received in the
hands of her attendants, is carried down to the sands of
the sea, and *there* prostrates herself, and clings to the very
shore, and at length is borne to the ship.

Not thus unhappy[3] did she leave her country and the
Hesperian harbours, when the arms of ruthless Cæsar were
pressing.   The faithful companion of Magnus *now* goes alone,
the chieftain left behind, and from Pompey does she fly.

The next night that came to her *was* without sleep.   Then
for the first time was her rest chilled and not as usual, alone

[1] *Retreat of Mitylene*) ver. 786.   Mitylene was the chief city of the isle
of Lesbos, situate on a Promontory, and having two excellent harbours.   Its
foundation was ascribed to the Carians and Pelasgians.

[2] *The couch*) ver. 791.   "Stratis:" literally "bed-clothes," which consisted
of blankets or counterpanes called "peristromata," or "peripetasmata."   In
the houses of the wealthy Romans these were of a costly description, and
generally of a purple colour, and embroiqered with beautiful figures in gold.
They were called "peripetasmata Attalica," from having been first used at
the court of King Attalus.

[3] *Not thus unhappy*) ver. 802.   From the beginning of this line to the
end of the Fifth Book is considered by Weise not to have been the composition of Lucan, but an addition by some later hand.   The use of the word
"vadit" in l. 804, of "sibi" in l. 805, "frigida quies" in l. 807, and the
silly remarks in ll. 811, 12, seem to him to justify such a conclusion.

in her widowed bed, and with no husband pressing her unprotected side. How often, overpowered with sleep, with deceived hands [1] did she embrace the empty couch, and, forgetful of her flight, seek her husband in the night! For, although the flame [2] in silence pervaded her marrow, it pleased her not to extend her body over all the bed; the one part of the couch [3] was kept.

She was afraid of losing Pompey; but the Gods above did not ordain things so joyous. The hour was pressing on which was to restore Magnus to her in her wretchedness.

[1] *With deceived hands*) ver. 809. There is a similar passage in the Metamorphoses of Ovid, B. xi. l. 674, where Alcyone, on being separated from Ceyx, her husband, "groans aloud and moves her arms in her sleep, and, catching at his body, grasps the air."

[2] *Although the flame*) ver. 811. The meaning of this passage, which has been censured by Weise as either spurious or corrupt, seems to be, that in her sleep she deceived herself by stretching out her arms to touch her husband, for, although penetrated by grief, from habit and from a sort of impression that her husband was still with her, she kept to her own side of the couch when surrendering herself to sleep.

[3] *The one part of the couch*) ver. 813. She was afraid, when laying herself on her couch, to act as though she were fully certain of the loss of Pompey; and was, unconsciously, reluctant to acknowledge to herself the full extent of her bereavement.

BOOK THE SIXTH.

CONTENTS.

AFTER the chieftains[1], now nearing *each other* with an intention of fighting, had pitched their camps on the hills, *and* arms were brought hand to hand, and the Gods be-

---

[1] *After the chieftains*) ver. 1. The events which happened after they left the camps at the river Apsus (B. v. l. 461), and which are here omitted, are thus related by Cæsar, in the Civil War, B. iii. c. 30 :—" Cæsar and Pompey received intelligence [of the arrival of Antony] almost at the same time·

held their equals, Cæsar scorned to take all the towns of
the Greeks, and now refused to be indebted to the Fates for
any prosperous warfare except against his son-in-law. In
all his prayers he asks for the hour *so* fatal to the world,
that is to bring everything to a crisis. The die of destiny
that is to sink the head of the one or the other *alone* pleases
him. Three times on the hills he draws out all his troops[1]
and his standards that threaten battle, testifying that he is
never wanting to the downfall of Latium.

When he beholds that his son-in-law can be aroused by
no alarms to battle, but confides in his close entrenchments, he moves *his* standards, and, sheltered by a path
through fields o'erspread with woods, with headlong haste
he marches to seize the towers of Dyrrhachium[2]. This
march Magnus forestalls by following the sea-line, and

for they had seen the ships sail past Apollonia and Dyrrhachium. They
directed their march after them by land ; but at first they were ignorant to
what part they had been carried ; but when they were informed of it, they
each adopted a different plan : Cæsar, to form a junction with Antony as
soon as possible ; Pompey, to oppose Antony's forces on their march to
Cæsar, and, if possible, to fall upon them unexpectedly from ambush ; and
the same day they both led out their armies from their winter encampment
along the river Apsus, Pompey secretly by night, Cæsar openly by day.
But Cæsar had to march a longer distance round, along the river, to find a
ford. Pompey's route being clear, because he was not .obliged to cross
the river, he advanced rapidly and by forced marches, against Antony, and
being informed of his approach, chose a convenient situation, where he posted
his forces ; and kept his men close within camp and forbade fires to be
kindled, that his arrival might be the more secret. An account of this was
immediately carried to Antony by the Greeks. He dispatched messengers
to Cæsar and confined himself in his camp, for one day. The next day
Cæsar came up with him. On learning his arrival, Pompey, to prevent his
being hemmed in between two armies, quitted his position, and moved with
all his forces to Asparagium, in the territory of Dyrrhachium, and there encamped in a convenient situation."

[1] *Draws out all his troops*) ver. 8. These circumstances are thus related
by Cæsar in the Civil War, B. iii. c. 41 :—" As soon as Cæsar heard that
Pompey was at Asparagium, he set out for that place with his army, and
having taken the capital of the Parthenians on his march, where there was
a garrison of Pompey's, he reached Pompey in Macedonia on the third day,
and encamped beside him ; and on the day following, having drawn out all
his forces before his camp, he offered Pompey battle. But perceiving that
he kept within his trenches he led his army back to the camp, and thought
about pursuing some other plan."

[2] *Dyrrhachium*) ver. 14. This is the same city which is called Epidamnus
in the Second Book, l. 264. See the Note to that passage.

the hill which the native Taulantian[1] calls Petra he pitches upon with his camp[2], and guards the walls[3] of Ephyre[4], defending a city safe even in its towers alone[5]. No work of the ancients or bulwark erected defends this *city,* or human labour, liable, though it should elevate on high, to yield either to wars or to years that move everything ; but it has fortifications able to be shaken by no iron, the nature and the locality of the spot. For, enclosed on every side by the deep sea and by rocks that discharge the waves, it owes to a small hill that it is not an island. Rocks terrible to ships support the walls; and when the raging Ionian sea is raised by the boisterous south wind, the ocean shakes temples and houses, and sends its foam to their summits.

Hither did lawless hopes attract the mind of Cæsar, greedy of the warfare, that he might surround the

[1] *The native Taulantian*) ver. 16. The Taulantii were a people of Illyria in the vicinity of Epidamnus or Dyrrhachium. Glaucias, one of their most powerful kings, waged war against Alexander the Great.

[2] *He pitches upon with his camp*) ver. 15. From the present passage it would appear that Pompey was the first to arrive at Dyrrhachium. Cæsar, however, says that he himself was the first to arrive, and that Pompey was cut off from the city. " Pompey at first, not knowing Cæsar's design, because he imagined he had taken a route in a different direction from that country, thought that the scarcity of provisions had obliged him to shift his quarters ; but having afterwards got true intelligence from his scouts, he decamped the day following, hoping to prevent him by taking a shorter road by the sea shore ; which Cæsar suspecting might happen, encouraged his troops to submit cheerfully to the fatigue, and having halted a very small part of the night, he arrived early in the morning at Dyrrhachium, when the van of Pompey's army was visible at a distance, and there he encamped."—Civil War, B. iii. c. 41.

[3] *And guards the walls*) ver. 16. Cæsar says, in the Civil War, B. iii. c. 42 :—" Pompey, being cut off from Dyrrhachium, as he was unable to effect his purpose, took a new resolution, and entrenched himself strongly on a rising ground which is called Petra, where ships of a small size can come in, and be sheltered from some winds. Here he ordered a part of his gallies to attend him, and corn and provisions to be brought from Asia, and from all the countries of which he kept possession."

[4] *Of Ephyre*) ver. 17. The walls of Dyrrhachium are called " Ephyrean " because it was supposed to have been colonized from Corcyra, which was originally a Corinthian colony ; and the city of Corinth was called Ephyre, from the nymph Ephyra, the daughter of Oceanus and Tethys.

[5] *Safe even in its towers alone*) ver. 18. He means to say that it was sufficiently strong in its natural position and fortifications to resist an enemy without the aid of troops.

enemy unawares dispersed on the vast hills, with bulwarks of intrenchments described afar.   The ground he
surveys with his eyes; and not content with frail turf alone
to construct the walls so suddenly raised, he carries across
vast rocks, and stones dug up from quarries, and the houses
of the Greeks, and the walls torn asunder. *A wall* is built
up, which not the ruthless battering-ram, *nor* any engine
of destructive warfare, is able to throw down. Mountains
are broken down, and Cæsar draws the work on a level
right through lofty hills, and he opens fosses, and disposes
towered castles on the highest ridges, and with a great
circuit enclosing boundaries, thickets, and woody lonesome
spots, and forests and wild beasts, with a vast net he shuts
them in.

Fields are not wanting, pastures are not wanting to Magnus, and, surrounded by the bulwarks of Cæsar, he shifts
his camp *at pleasure*[2]. Rivers so many rising there, *and*
ceasing there, exhaust their course; and that he may revisit
the most distant of the works, Cæsar, wearied, abides in
the midst of the fields. Now let ancient story raise the
Ilian walls[3], and ascribe them to the Gods; let the flying

---

[1] *That he might surround the enemy*) ver. 30.   Cæsar thus relates these
operations in the Civil War, B. iii. c. 43 :—"Cæsar, on being informed of
these matters, pursued measures suggested by the nature of the country.
For around Pompey's camp there were several high and rugged hills.
These he first of all occupied with guards, and raised strong forts on them.
Then drawing a fortification from one fort to the other, as the nature of
each position allowed, he began to draw a line of circumvallation around
Pompey ; and with these views, as he had but a small quantity of corn,
and Pompey was strong in cavalry, that he might furnish his army with
corn and other necessaries from all sides with less danger; secondly, to
prevent Pompey from foraging, and thereby render his horse ineffectual in
the operations of the war; and thirdly, to lessen his reputation, on which
he saw he depended greatly among foreign nations, when the report should
have spread throughout the world, that he was blockaded by Cæsar and
dared not hazard a battle."

[2] *He shifts his camp at pleasure*) ver. 44. "Mutat;" literally "changes;"
meaning that he has the power or opportunity to change his camp, although
surrounded by Cæsar's lines ; in allusion to the vast extent of space enclosed
thereby.

[3] *Ancient story raise the Ilian walls*) ver. 48.   He alludes to the alleged
extent of the walls of Ilium or Troy, which were said to be forty miles in
circumference, and to have been built by the hands of Apollo and Neptune
for King Laomedon.

Parthians admire the walls of Babylon, surrounded with frail pottery[1]. Lo, as much as Tigris, as much as swift Orontes surrounds[2], as much as suffices for their realms to the Assyrian nations in the eastern world, does a work, suddenly formed and hurried on amid the tumult of warfare. enclose. *There* perish labours as mighty[3].

Hands thus many had been able to unite Sestos to Abydos[4], and, by heaping earth into it to exclude the sea of Phryxus[5], or to sever Ephyre from the wide realms of Pelops, and to cut short for shipping[6] the circumnavigation of the lengthy Malea[7], or to change any spot of the world,

---

[1] *Walls of Babylon, surrounded with frail pottery*) ver. 50. He alludes to the brick-built walls of Babylon; which city, though in a ruinous state, was, in the Poet's day, in the hands of the Parthians. In the time of Nebuchadnezzar these walls surrounding the city, which was in form of a square, were forty-eight miles in extent, and two hundred cubits high, and fifty thick. They were built of burnt brick, while some of the buildings in the city were only constructed with bricks sun-dried and cemented with bitumen or mortar. Ovid, in the Metamorphoses, B. iv. l. 68, speaks of the "coctiles muri," or "brick-built walls," of Babylon.

[2] *As much as swift Orontes surrounds*) ver. 51. The meaning is, "as much ground as the Tigris (into which the Euphrates discharges itself) surrounds at Babylon, as much as the Orontes surrounds at Antioch, and as much as is required for the royal city of Nineveh, so much does Cæsar on a sudden emergency surround with lines of circumvallation." These lines were fifteen miles in circumference.

[3] *There perish labours as mighty*) ver. 54. "Periere" may either mean that these lines were thrown away as failing in their object of hemming in Pompey, or that they were soon destroyed in the sallies of Pompey's troops.

[4] *Unite Sestos to Abydos*) ver. 55. He alludes to the bridges which Xerxes constructed across the Hellespont from Sestos to Abydos. See the Second Book, l. 674, and the Note to the passage.

[5] *To exclude the sea of Phryxus*) ver. 56. In allusion to Xerxes building up large mounds of earth in the Hellespont. Phryxus was the brother of Helle, who gave her name to the Hellespont. See the Fourth Book, l. 57, and the Note to the passage.

[6] *To cut short for shipping*) ver. 57. He says that it would have been about an equal labour to cut off Corinth, or Ephyre, from the Peloponnesus, by cutting through the Isthmus.

[7] *Circumnavigation of the lengthy Malea*) ver. 58. Malea was a Promontory on the south of Laconia, extending many miles into the sea, the passage round which was much dreaded by sailors. By the use of the word "donare," meaning "to save the passage of," he probably means by cutting through the promontory where it commences to project, and thus save the necessity of going round it. Farnaby, however, takes the passage to be only an amplification of the last line, and to mean that the result of cutting through the

although Nature should forbid it, for the better. The quarters of the warfare are contracted; here is nourished blood destined to flow in all lands; here both the Thessalian and the Libyan slaughters[1] are kept in store. The civil fury rages on a narrow slip of sand.

First indeed, on rising, the structure of the works escapes Pompey; just as he who, safe in the fields of mid Sicily, knows not that ravening Pelorus is barking[2]; or as, when roaming Tethys and the Rutupian shores[3] are raging, the waves aroused escape the ears of the Caledonian Britons. When first he beholds the earth enclosed with a vast rampart, he himself also leading forth his troops[4] from secure Petra scatters them over the different hills, that he may weaken the arms of Cæsar, and extend his line, as he hems him in, with his soldiers spread far and wide; and as much of the land enclosed in the trenches does he

Isthmus of Corinth would be to save sailors the necessity of going round the Peloponnesus and rounding the Malean promontory.

[1] *Both the Thessalian and the Libyan slaughters*) ver. 62. "Here in this space are enclosed persons who are doomed to fall, some at Thessalian Pharsalia, some at African Munda."

[2] *Knows not that ravening Pelorus is barking*) ver. 66. Just as the person who lives in the interior of Sicily does not hear the howling of the whirlpools of Scylla and Charybdis, which are in the vicinity of Pelorus, a Promontory of that island.

[3] *And the Rutupian shores*) ver. 67. Rutupiæ, or Rutupæ, was a Roman town on the coast of Kent, supposed to have been the present Richborough. It was a place of transit for Gaul, and was famed for the goodness of its oysters, which were much prized by the Roman epicures. The Poet's meaning is, "just as the native of Caledonia (now Scotland) does not hear the roaring of the ocean on the Rutupian shore (the coast of Kent)."

[4] *Leading forth his troops*) ver. 71. These operations on the part of Pompey are thus fully explained in Cæsar's narrative of the Civil War, B. iii. c. 44:—"Nothing was left to Pompey but to adopt the last resource, namely, to possess himself of as many hills as he could, and cover as great an extent of country as possible with his troops, and divide Cæsar's forces as much as possible; and so it happened; for having raised twenty-four forts, and taken in a compass of fifteen miles, he got forage in this space, and within this circuit there were several fields lately sown, in which the cattle might feed in the meantime. And as our men, who had completed their works by drawing lines of communication from one fort to another, were afraid that Pompey's men would sally out from some part and attack us on the rear; so the enemy were making a continued fortification in a circuit within ours, to prevent us from breaking in on any side, or surrounding them in the rear. But they completed their wokrs first; both because they had a greater number of men, and because they had a smaller compass to enclose."

claim for himself, as little Aricia of the grove, consecrated to Diana of Mycene, is distant from lofty Rome[1]; and the distance at which[2] Tiber, gliding by Rome, descends into the sea. if it were not to wind in its course.

No trumpet-call re-echoes[3]. and, contrary to orders, the darts roam; and full oft, while the arm tries the javelin, is a crime committed. Greater anxieties deter the chieftains from engaging in arms. Pompey *care deters* by reason of the land being exhausted for affording fodder, which the horseman in his course has trodden down, and with quickened steps the horny hoof has beaten down the shooting field. The warlike charger wearied in the fields cropped short, while the full racks are holding the sedge that has been brought[4], falls dying, requiring for his mouth fresh grass, and cuts short with faltering knees the exercises of the ring in the midst *of them*.

While consumption wastes their bodies[5] and relaxes their

[1] *Aricia is distant from lofty Rome*) ver. 75. He says that the extent of ground which Pompey enclosed within his lines was the same as the distance from Aricia to Rome; namely, about sixteen miles. In speaking of the Mycenæan Diana, he alludes to the worship of Diana, which was said to have been brought from Tauris to Aricia by Iphigenia and Orestes, the children of Agamemnon, king of Mycenæ. See the Third Book, l. 86, and the Note to that passage.

[2] *And the distance at which*) ver. 76. "Modo" signifies "measure" or "distance" here. His meaning is, that the extent is the same as that of the Tiber would be from Rome to Ostia, where it discharges itself into the sea, if it flowed in a straight line. This can hardly be correct, for Ostia was generally said to be but fourteen miles from Rome.

[3] *No trumpet call re-echoes*) ver. 78. "When Cæsar attempted to gain any place, though Pompey had resolved not to oppose him with his whole force, or to come to a general engagement; yet he detached archers and slingers, with which his army abounded, and several of our men were wounded and were filled with great dread of the arrows."—Civil War, B. iii. l. 46.

[4] *The sedge that has been brought*) ver. 85. "Culmos" here signifies, according to some, "hay," or else "straw," while others take it to mean "sedge." The passage has caused considerable discussion, but its meaning clearly is, that although the racks are full of hay, or straw, or sedge, as the case may be, the horses pine away for want of fresh grass.

[5] *While consumption wastes their bodies*) ver. 88. These circumstances are thus alluded to in Cæsar's narrative of the Civil War, B. iii. c. 49:— "Cæsar's troops were often told by deserters, that they could scarcely maintain their horses, and that their other cattle were dead; that they themselves were not in good health, from their confinement within so narrow a compass, from the noisome smell, the number of carcases, and the constant

limbs, the close atmosphere contracts the contagion of the
floating pestilence in a dense cloud. With such an exhalation does Nesis[1] send forth the Stygian air from its clouded
rocks, and the caves of the deadly Typhon[2] puff forth his
rage. Thence do the multitudes perish, and the water,
more ready than the air to contract all infection, hardens
the entrails with mud *collecting there.* Now the blackened
skin grows hard, and bursts the distended eyes; fiery
throughout the features[3], and glowing with erysipelas, the
disease breaks out, and the weary head refuses to support
itself. Now more and more suddenly does destiny sweep
away everything, nor do intervening diseases separate life
and death, but the weakness comes on with death; and by
the multitude of the perishing *is* the pestilence increased,
while the bodies are lying unburied, mingled with the living.
For to throw the wretched citizens outside of the tents is
their burial. Still, these woes, the sea at their backs, and
the air stirred by the north winds, and the sea-shore and the
ships filled with foreign harvests, relieve[4].

But ranging upon the expansive hills the enemy is not

fatigue to them, being men unaccustomed to work, and labouring under a
great want of water."

[1] *With such an exhalation does Nesis*) ver. 90. Nesis, now called "Nisita."
is a small island on the coast of Campania, not far from Puteoli. It was a
favorite residence of some of the Roman nobles. The elder Pliny speaks of
it as in certain places emitting fetid vapours, probably by reason of its volcanic origin. Cicero, Seneca, and Statius also make mention of it.

[2] *The caves of the deadly Typhon*) ver. 92. He alludes to the sul-
phureous vapours of the isle of Inarime, beneath which the giant Typhœus,
or Typhon, was said to be buried. It is mentioned in the Fifth Book,
l. 101; see the Note to that passage.

[3] *Fiery throughout the features*) ver. 96. They were attacked with
erysipelas, or Saint Anthony's fire, which the Romans called the "Sacer
morbus," or "Sacred disease." Celsus mentions this malady as a forerunner of the plague. Some authorities, however, consider "sacer morbus"
to mean "epilepsy."

[4] *Filled with foreign harvests, relieve*) ver. 105. Probably because, as
one of the Scholiasts says, that which grew on the spot was tainted with
the plague. These supplies are thus referred to in the Civil War, B. iii.
c. 47 :—"The usual design of a siege is to cut off the enemy's supplies.
On the contrary, Cæsar, with an inferior force, was enclosing troops sound
and unhurt, and who had abundance of all things. For there arrived every
day a prodigious number of ships, which brought them provisions. Nor
could the wind blow from any quarter that would not be favourable to some
of them."

distressed by pent-up air or stagnant water ; but he endures
cruel famine, as though surrounded in strict siege. The
blades not as yet rising to a crop, the wretched multitude
he sees falling down [1] to the food of cattle, and gnawing
the shrubs and spoiling the grove of its leaves, and
tearing from unknown roots [2] doubtful herbs that threaten
death. Whatever they are able to soften with flames, whatever to pull asunder by biting, and whatever to put into
their stomachs through their chafed throats, *that they devour*,
and the soldiers tearing asunder many a thing before this
unknown to human tables, still besiege a well-fed foe.

When first, the barriers burst, it pleased Pompey to escape,
and to open to himself all lands, he did not choose for
himself the obscure hours of stealthy night, and he disdained
a march stolen by theft, the arms of his father-in-law delaying ; with ruin brought upon him he sought to come forth,
and, the trenches attacked, to break down the towers, and
amid all *his* swords, and where by slaughter a way must be
made. However, a part of the entrenchment close at hand
seems fit, which they call the tower of Minutius [3], and a
shrubbery rough with trees thick set conceals. Hither, be-

[1] *Sees falling down*) ver. 110. "Cecidisse;" falling flat on the ground,
after the manner of cattle. This passage hardly corresponds with what
we learn from Cæsar, in the Civil War, B. iii. c. 49 :—"But Cæsar's
army enjoyed perfect health and abundance of water, and had plenty
of all sorts of provision, except corn ; and they had a prospect of better
times approaching, and saw greater hopes laid before them by the ripening
of the grain." Cæsar, however, acknowledges, in c. 47, that, "having
consumed all the corn far and near, he was in very great distress, but his
soldiers bore all with uncommon patience."

[2] *And tearing from unknown roots*) ver. 113. He probably refers to
the same root which is mentioned by Cæsar, in the Civil War, B. iii. c. 48 :
"There was a kind of root called ' chara,' discovered by the troops which
served under Valerius. This they mixed up with milk, and it greatly contributed to relieve their want. They made it into a sort of bread.—Having
great plenty of it, loaves made thereof, when Pompey's men upbraided ours
with want, they frequently threw among them, to damp their hopes." It was
on this occasion that Pompey, on seeing the loaves, exclaimed that surely he
must be fighting with wild beasts.

[3] *They call the tower of Minutius*) ver. 126. Appian seems to consider
this Minutius as the same person with the centurion Scæva, whose exploits
are afterwards recounted by the Poet, and whose shield Cæsar speaks of
as being pierced in two hundred and thirty places, while Appian mentions a
hundred and twenty arrows as sticking in it. They hardly, however, seem
to have been the same persons, as Suetonius calls the latter Cassius Scæva.

P

trayed by no dust, he speeds *his* band, and suddenly comes to the walls. At the same moment so many Latian birds shine from the plain[1], so many trumpets sound.

That victory might not be owing anything to the sword, fear had stricken the astounded foe. What valour alone could effect, slain they lay, on the spot where they should be standing; those to endure the wounds were now wanting, and the cloud that bore darts so many was of no avail. Then did the hurled torches roll down pitchy fires; then did the shaken towers nod and threaten their fall; the bulwark groaned at the frequent blows of the oak battered against it. Now over the heights of the lofty entrenchment had Pompey's eagles gone forth; now was the rule of the world open *to him*. That place which not with a thousand troops together, nor with the whole force of Cæsar, Fortune had been able to take away, a single man snatched from the victors and forbade to be captured; and, himself wielding arms, and not yet laid prostrate, he denied that Magnus was the conqueror.

Scæva *was* the name of the hero; he had served in the ranks of the camp before the fierce nations of the Rhone[2]; there, amid much bloodshed, promoted in the lengthened rank, he wielded the Latian vine[3]; ready for all daring[4], and one who knew not in civil warfare how great criminality is valour. He, when, the war now left behind, he beheld his companions seeking the safety of flight, said :—

" Whither does an undutcous fear[5] drive you and one un-

---

[1] *So many Latian birds shine from the plain*) ver. 129. He alludes to the eagles or standards of the legions.

[2] *Before the fierce nations of the Rhone*) ver. 144. He means that Scæva had served as a common soldier in Cæsar's army, in the wars with the Gauls, during which he had been promoted to the rank of centurion.

[3] *He wielded the Latian vine*) ver. 146. A vine sapling was one of the badges of office of the centurion, who carried it for the purpose of punishing negligent or disobedient soldiers. " Longo ordine," the " lengthened rank," probably refers to the troop of a hundred men which was under his command.

[4] *Ready for all daring*) ver. 147. " Pronus ad omne nefas." By the use of the word " nefas " the Poet implies, as he says in the next line, that military valour exerted in civil war is no better than criminality.

[5] *Whither does an undutcous fear*) ver. 150. Cæsar thus refers to the exploits of Scæva on this occasion, in the Civil War, B. iii. c. 53 :—" In the shield of the centurion Scæva, which was brought to Cæsar, were counted

known to all the arms of Cæsar? O base slaves, servile beasts[1], do you, without bloodshed, turn your backs upon death? Are you not ashamed to be wanting in the heap of heroes, and to be sought in vain for the tomb among the carcases? Will you not, youths, through anger at least, duty set aside, come to a stand? Out of all, through whom the enemy might sally forth, have we been chosen. With *cost of* no little blood to Magnus shall this day pass. More happily before the face of Cæsar could I seek the shades. Him as a witness Fortune has denied; Pompey praising me, I shall fall. Break their weapons by opposing your breasts, and with your throats blunt the sword. Now does the dust reach him from afar, and the sound of the ruin, and the crash has broken upon the unsuspecting ears of Cæsar. We conquer, O companions; he will come to avenge *these* towers while we die."

That voice arouses fury as great as the trumpet-call, not at the first signal, inflames; and wondering at the hero, and eager to behold, the youths follow *him* to know whether valour, exceeded in numbers and in position, can give *anything* more than death. On the falling rampart he takes his stand, and first of all rolls down carcases from the tower full *of them*, and overwhelms the foes with *dead* bodies as they come on; the whole of the ruins, too, afford weapons to the hero; both wood, and heavy masses, and himself does he threaten to the foe[2]. Now with stakes, now with a sturdy pole, he thrusts down opposing breasts from the walls, and with the sword he cuts off the hands that cling to the upper parts of the rampart; heads and bones he dashes to pieces with stones, and knocks out brains use-

two hundred and thirty holes. In reward for this man's services, both to himself and the public, Cæsar presented him with a reward in money, and declared him promoted from being eighth to first centurion. For it appeared that the fort had been in a great measure preserved by his exertions; and he afterwards very amply rewarded the cohorts with double pay, corn, clothing, and other military honors." It is to be regretted that the account of the commencement of this attack by the troops of Pompey is lost in the narrative of Cæsar.

[1] *O base slaves, servile beasts*) ver. 152. " O famuli turpes, servum pecus, absque cruore." This line is universally considered to be spurious.

[2] *And himself does he threaten to the foe*) ver. 173. " Seque ipse minatur," meaning that he threatens that he himself will leap down upon them.

lessly defended by a frail construction, of another the flame
sets on fire the hair and the cheeks; their eyes burning, the
fires crackle.

As soon as, the heap increasing, the carcases made the
wall level with the ground, a leap brought him down and
threw him upon their arms in the midst of the troops, not
less nimble than *that which* hurries the swift leopard on the
tops of the hunting spears. Then, compressed amid the
dense masses and hemmed in by all the war, whatever foe
he looks upon he conquers. And now, the point of the
sword of Scæva, blunted and through clotted blood no
longer sharp, bruises the smitten foe, *and* wounds him not[1].
The sword loses its use, *and* breaks limbs without a wound[2].
Him does the entire mass aim at, at him do all the weapons *aim;* no hand is unerring, no javelin not fortunately
aimed, and Fortune beholds a new pair *of combatants*
meeting together, an army and a man. The stout shield
resounds with frequent blows, and the compressed fragments
of the hollow helmet bruise his temples; nor does anything
now protect[3] his exposed vitals, except the darts that pro-
trude on the surface of his bones.

Why now, madmen, with javelins and light arrows do
you waste wounds that will never attach to the vital parts?
Let either the wild-fire[4] hurled from the twisted cords overwhelm him, or masses of vast stone torn from the walls; let
the battering-ram with its iron head, and the balista remove
him from the threshold of the gate. He stands, no frail wall

---

[1] *And wounds him not*) ver. 187. The inelegant repetition of "frangit"
in the next line, which is also found in this, shows that most probably one
of them is spurious.

[2] *Breaks limbs without a wound*) ver. 188. His sword was so blunted
that it would no longer pierce and make wounds, but by the force of the
blow broke the limb it struck.

[3] *Nor does anything now protect*) ver. 194. The meaning of this piece
of bombast seems to be that the weapons of the enemy, sticking in his body
in all directions, supply the place of his armour, which, broken to pieces,
now leaves his body exposed. One of the Scholiasts suggests that the
meaning is that his vitals are now exposed, but are prevented from falling
out by reason of the darts pinning his flesh to his bones.

[4] *Let either the wild-fire*) ver. 198. As to the "phalarica" see the
Third Book, l. 681, and the Note to the passage. The "tortiles nervi" are
the cords used to give impetus to the balista, which was used to discharge
the phalarica.

for Cæsar's cause, and he withstands Pompey. Now he no
longer covers his breast with arms, and, fearing to trust his
shield and to be inactive with the left hand, or to live by
his own remissness, alone he submits to the wounds so
many of the warfare, and, bearing a dense thicket *of darts*
on his breast, with now flagging steps he chooses an enemy
on whom to fall.

Like *was he* to the monsters of the deep[1]. Thus the
beast of the Libyan land, thus the Libyan elephant,
overwhelmed by dense arms, breaks every missile as it
bounds off from his rough back, and moving his skin
shakes forth the darts that stick there; his entrails lie safe
concealed within, and without blood do the darts stand in
the pierced wild beast; wounds made by arrows so many,
by javelins so many, suffice not for a single death. Behold!
afar, a Gortynian shaft is aimed against Scæva by a Dictæan
hand[2], which, more unerring than all expectation, descends
upon his head and into the ball of the left eye. He tears
away the impediment of the weapon and the ligaments of
the nerves, fearlessly plucking forth the arrow fastened in
the eye-ball hanging to it, and tramples upon the weapon
together with his own eye.

Not otherwise does the Pannonian she-bear[3], more infuriate after a wound, when the Libyan has hurled the javelin
retained by the slender thong[4], wheel herself round upon the

---

[1] *Like was he to the monsters of the deep*) ver. 207. This is most probably
a spurious line, from the repetition of part of it in the next. "Par pelagi
monstris" is supposed by Farnaby to mean, that he acts as the whale does in
rushing upon a ship and sinking it with its weight. This, if connected with
what precedes, seems to be the right sense of the passage. The Scholiast Sulpitius, however, thinks that it alludes to the circumstance of trees being supposed to grow on the backs of whales, which cause them to resemble islands
and rocks: a meaning which may have possibly been intended if taken in
connection with what follows.

[2] *A Gortynian shaft is aimed against Scæva by a Dictæan hand*) ver. 214.
Gortyna or Gortyn was one of the most ancient cities of Crete, situate on the
river Lethæus. It was the second city of the island, and inferior only to
Cnossus; and under the dominion of the Romans became the capital. The
Cretans were renowned for their skill in the use of the bow.

[3] *Pannonian she-bear*) ver. 220. Pannonia was one of the Roman
provinces, embracing the eastern part of the present Austria, Styria, Carin-
thia, Carniola, the whole of Hungary between the Danube and the Save,
Slavonia, and a part of Croatia and Bosnia.

[4] *Has hurled the javelin retained by the slender thong*) ver. 221. "Parvâ

wound[1], and infuriate seek the dart she has received, and run round after the weapon as it flies together with herself[2]. His fury has *now* destroyed his features[3], with the bloody stream his face stands disfigured; a joyous shout of the conquerors re-echoes to the sky; a wound beheld on Cæsar would not have caused greater joyousness to the men by reason of a little blood. He, concealing the pangs deeply seated in his mind, with a mild air, and, fury from his features entirely removed, says :—

"Spare *me*, fellow-citizens; far hence avert the war. Wounds now will not contribute to my death; *that* requires not weapons thrust in, but *rather* torn away from my breast. Lift me up, and alive remove me to the camp of Magnus; this do for your own general; let Scæva be rather an instance of Cæsar deserted[4], than of a glorious death."

The unhappy Aulus believed *these* deceitful words, and did not see him holding his sword with the point upright; and, about to bear away both the body of the prisoner and his arms, he received his lightning blade in the middle of his throat. His valour waxed hot, and by one slaughter refreshed, he said :—

amentavit habenâ." The spears of the ancients, both those used in war and in the chase, often had a thong of leather tied to the middle of the shaft, which was called ἀγκύλη by the Greeks, and by the Romans "amentum," and was of assistance in throwing the spear. It is not known how the "amentum" added either to the force or the correctness of the aim in the use of the spear; but it has been suggested that it was through imparting volution to it, and perhaps thereby giving it steadiness in its course. This is rendered more probable from the frequent use of the verb "torquere," "to whirl."

[1] *Wheels herself round upon the wound*) ver. 222. "Se rotat in vulnus;" wheels round and round, endeavouring with her mouth to pull out the arrow that sticks in her flanks.

[2] *As it flies together with herself*) ver. 223. "Fugientem" may either mean that the lance or dart is borne round by her, and eludes her endeavours as she wheels round and round, or else that it flies with her as she flies.

[3] *His fury has now destroyed his features*) ver. 224. His frantic valour had deformed his countenance by reason of his tearing out his eye together with the arrow.

[4] *An instance of Cæsar deserted*) ver. 234. He pretends that he is ready to abandon Cæsar and join Pompey's party. This description is certainly not consistent with probability, and indeed the conduct of Scæva, however valorous, merits the reproof that is always due to treachery, for whatever purpose employed.

"Let him pay the penalty, whoever has hoped that Scæva is subdued; if Magnus seeks for peace from this sword, let him, Cæsar being entreated, lower his standards. Do you think me like yourselves, and afraid of death? Less is the cause of Pompey and of the Senate to you, than is the love of death to me."

At the same moment he thus says, and the dust raised on high attests that Cæsar's cohorts are at hand. He removed from Magnus the shame and the disgrace of the war, that whole troops, Scæva, had fled from thee ; who, the warfare withdrawn, dost sink; for while blood was being shed, the combat gave thee strength. ⌐ The throng of his comrades raise him as he falls, and are delighted to bear him exhausted on their shoulders ; and they adore as it were a Divinity enclosed in his pierced breast, and a living instance of transcendent valour; and they adorn the Gods ¹ and Mars with his naked breast, Scæva, with thy weapons ; happy in the glories of this fame ², if the hardy Iberian, or if the Cantabrian with his small ³, or the Teutonian with his long weapons ⁴, had turned his back on thee. Thou canst not adorn with the spoils of warfare the Temples of the Thunderer, thou *canst*

¹ *And they adorn the Gods*) ver. 256. Probably this means that they hung up his arms in the Temples of the Gods, and placed his coat of mail on the statue of Mars, which before was without one. Sulpitius thinks it means that they erected statues of the Gods decorated with his arms in the tower or fort which he had so bravely defended.

² *Happy in the glories of this fame*) ver. 257. From the account given by Cæsar, who does not mention the loss of his eye, it appears that Scæva recovered from his wounds. He is made mention of by Cicero in his Epistles to Atticus, B. xiii. Ep. 23, and B. xiv. Ep. 10, as one of the partisans of Cæsar, about the period of his death.

³ *The Cantabrian with his small*) ver. 259. The Cantabri were a people in the north of Spain, whose country was bounded on the east by the Astures, and on the west by the Autrigones. The name, however, was commonly given to all the people in the north of Spain. By his reference to their "exigua arma," or "small arms," he perhaps refers to the use of the bow and arrow.

⁴ *The Teutonian with his long weapons*) ver. 259. The Teutones were of large stature, and famed for the length of their spears and bucklers. Virgil, in the Æneid, B. viii. l. 662, makes mention of the latter.

⁵ *The Temples of the Thunderer*) ver. 260. The Poet means that, notwithstanding his valorous deeds, being engaged in civil war, he will never have the opportunity, in conformity with the laws of the state, of accompanying his general in his triumphal procession to the Temple of Jupiter on the Capitoline Hill.

not shout aloud in the joyous triumph[1]. Wretched man, with valour how great didst thou obtain a tyrant[1]

Nor yet, repulsed from this part of the camp[2], did Magnus rest, the war being deferred, within the entrenchments, any more than the sea is wearied, when, the east winds arousing themselves, the billows dash against the rock that breaks them, or the wave eats away the side of the lofty mountain, and prepares a late ruin for itself. On the one side, attacking the fortresses adjacent to the placid deep with the onset of a twofold warfare[3] he seizes them ; and he scatters his arms far and wide, and expands his tents upon the open plain ; and the liberty of changing *their* ground delights them.

Thus does the Padus, swelling with full mouth, run over its shores protected with embankments, and confound whole fields ; if anywhere the land gives way and yields, not resisting the raging volume *of water*, then with all its stream it passes on, and with its flood opens fields to itself unknown. These owners the land forsakes ; on these husbandmen are additional fields bestowed, the Padus bestowing the gift.

Hardly was Cæsar aware of the combat, of which a fire elevated from a look-out gave notice. The dust now laid, he found the walls beaten down ; and when he discovered the *now* cold marks, *as though* of ancient ruin,

---

[1] *Shout aloud in the joyous triumph*) ver. 261. " Ululare." In the use of this word he refers to the cries of " Io triumphe " with which the soldiers saluted the victorious general, as they accompanied him in triumph to the Capitoline Hill.

[2] *Repulsed from this part of the camp*) ver. 263. These operations are thus related by Cæsar, in the Civil War, B. iii. c. 65 :—" And now the Pompeians, after great havoc of our troops, were approaching the camp of Marcellinus, and had struck no small terror into the cohorts, when Antony was observed descending from the rising ground with twelve cohorts. His arrival checked the Pompeians, and encouraged our men to recover from their affright. And shortly after, Cæsar, having got notice by the smoke from all the forts, which was the usual signal on such occasions, drafted off some cohorts from the outposts and proceeded to the scene of action. And having there learned the loss he had sustained, and perceiving that Pompey had forced our works, and had encamped along our coast, so that he was at liberty to forage, and had a communication with his shipping, he altered his plan for conducting the war, as his design had not succeeded, and ordered a strong encampment to be made near Pompey."

[3] *A twofold warfare*) ver. 269. By sea and land.

the very quietude of the spot inflamed him, and the rest of the partisans of Pompey and their slumbers, Cæsar overcome. He hastens to speed on even into slaughter, so long as he may disturb their joyousness. Then does he rush, threatening, upon Torquatus[1]; who not less speedily perceives[2] the arms of Cæsar, than does the sailor, as the mast totters, take in all his sails against the Circeian storm[3]; his troops, too, he withdraws within a more limited wall, that in a small compass he may more densely dispose his arms.

Cæsar had crossed the ramparts of the outer trenches, when Magnus sent down his troops from all the hills[4] above,

[1] *Threatening, upon Torquatus*) ver. 285. This is the same Lucius Torquatus (or rather Lucius Manlius Torquatus) who is mentioned by Cæsar in his narrative of the Civil War, B. iii. c. 11, as the governor of Oricum. He was a friend of Cicero and an ardent partisan of Pompey and the aristocratic faction. On the breaking out of the war he was Prætor, and was stationed at Alba, which he afterwards abandoned ; on which he joined Pompey in Greece. He was obliged to surrender Oricum to Cæsar, who dismissed him uninjured. After the defeat at Pharsalia he went to Africa, and attempting to escape thence to Spain with Scipio, was taken prisoner by P. Sittius, and put to death.

[2] *Who not less speedily perceives*) ver. 286. This passage will be better understood by a reference to Cæsar's account of this attack, in the Civil War, B. iii. c. 66-69, a portion of which narrative is to the following effect :—" This place was half a mile distant from Pompey's new camp. Cæsar, hoping to surprise this legion, and anxious to repair the loss sustained that day, left two cohorts employed in the works to make an appearance of entrenching himself, and by a different route, as privately as he could, with his other cohorts, amounting to thirty-three, he marched in two lines against Pompey's legion and his lesser camp. Nor did this first opinion deceive him. For he reached the place before Pompey could have notice of it ; and though the works were strong, yet having made the attack with the left wing, which he commanded in person, he obliged the Pompeians to quit the rampart in disorder. A barricade had been raised before the gates, at which a short contest was maintained, our men endeavouring to force their way in, and the enemy to defend the camp. But the valour of our men prevailed, and having cut down the barricade, they first forced the greater camp, and after that the fort which was enclosed within it ; and as the legion on its repulse had retired to this, they slew several defending themselves there."

[3] *Against the Circeian storm*) ver. 287. Circeium was a promontory of Latium on which was the ancient town of Circeii. The navigation round this point was considered dangerous, and it was the custom on approaching it to furl the sails and ply the oars with vigour.

[4] *Magnus sent down his troops from all the hills*) ver. 292. The movement of Pompey to the rescue is thus related in the Civil War, B. iii. c 69 :— " In the meantime, Pompey, by the great delay which this occasioned, being informed of what had happened, marched with the fifth legion, which he

and poured forth his ranks upon the blockaded foe.
Not thus does he who dwells in the valleys of Ætna[1]
dread Enceladus[2], the south wind blowing, when Ætna
utterly empties its caverns, and, flowing *with fire*, streams
down upon the plains ; as do the soldiers of Cæsar, conquered by the thickening dust[3] *already* before the battle, *and*
alarmed beneath a cloud of blinded fear, meet the enemy
as they fly, and by their alarm rush on to destruction itself.
Then might all the blood have been shed[4] for the civil warfare, even to the procuring of peace; the chieftain himself
restrained the raging swords.

Happy and free, Rome, under thy laws, mightst thou

called away from their work, to support his troops ; and at the same time
his cavalry was advancing towards ours, and an army in order of battle was
seen at a distance by our men, who had taken possession of the camp, and
the face of affairs was suddenly changed. For Pompey's legion, encouraged
by the hope of speedy support, attempted to make a stand at the Decu-
man gate, and made a bold charge on our men. Cæsar's cavalry, who had
mounted the rampart by a narrow breach, being apprehensive of their retreat,
was the first to flee. The right wing, which had been separated from the
left, observing the terror of the cavalry, to prevent their being overpowered
in the lines, were endeavouring to retreat by the same way as they burst in ;
and most of them, lest they should be engaged in the narrow passes, threw
themselves down a rampart ten feet high into the trenches ; and the first
being trodden to death, the rest procured their safety and escaped over their
bodies. The soldiers of the left wing, perceiving from the rampart that
Pompey was advancing, and their own friends flying, being afraid that they
should be enclosed between the two ramparts, as they had an enemy both
within and without, strove to secure their retreat the same way they came."

[1] *Dwells in the valleys of Ætna*) ver. 293. He alludes to the inhabitants of the town of Catana, or Catina, which was situate at the foot of
Mount Ætna, and who were exposed to danger from its eruptions.

[2] *Enceladus*) ver. 294. Enceladus the giant, son of Tartarus and Terra,
having been struck by the thunderbolts of Jupiter, was said to have been
buried under Mount Ætna, the eruptions of which were occasioned by his
turning his sides. They were also sometimes attributed to the winds raging
within its caverns.

[3] *Conquered by the thickening dust*) ver. 296. On seeing the clouds of
dust raised by the troops of Pompey on their approach.

[4] *Then might all the blood have been shed*) ver. 300. Cæsar, in the Civil
War, thus described this engagement so disastrous to his forces, B. iii. c. 69 :—
"All was disorder, consternation, and flight ; insomuch that, when Cæsar
laid hold of the standards of those who were running away, and desired
them to stop, some left their horses behind, and continued to run in the
same manner ; others, through fear, even threw away their standards, nor
did a single man face about."

be, and thy own mistress, if on that occasion a Sulla
had conquered for thee¹. We lament, alas! and ever
shall lament, that the greatest of thy crimes is successful
for thee, to have fought with a duteous son-in-law.   O sad
fate !   *Then* Libya would not have bewailed the slaughter
of Utica, *and* Spain of Munda, nor would the Nile, polluted
with shameful blood², have borne along a carcase more noble
than the Pharian king ; nor would the naked Juba³ have
pressed the Marmaric sands, and Scipio appeased the
ghosts⁴ of the Carthaginians by pouring forth his blood;
nor would life⁵ have been deprived of the hallowed Cato.
This might, Rome, have been the last day of woe to thee ;
Pharsalia might have been wrested from the midst of the
Fates.

The spot occupied against the will of the Divinities Cæsar
forsakes, and with his mangled troops seeks the Emathian
lands.   His followers, by their exhortations, attempt to
dissuade Magnus, about to pursue⁶ the arms of his

¹ *A Sulla had conquered for thee*) ver. 303. He attributes the forbear-
ance of Pompey to pursue to his leniency and humane disposition, and says,
that if he had been as fond of bloodshed as Sulla was, he might, on that
occasion, by following up the victory, have put an end to the war. Cæsar,
however, in the Civil War, B. iii. c. 70, assigns a different reason for the
moderation of Pompey :—" In this calamity the following favourable circumstance occurred to prevent the ruin of our whole army, namely, that Pompey,
suspecting an ambuscade (because, as I suppose, his success had far exceeded
his hopes, as he had seen his men, a moment before, flying from the camp),
did not dare for some time to approach the fortification, and that his horse
were retarded from pursuing, because the passes and gates were in possession
of Cæsar's soldiers. Thus a trifling circumstance proved of equal importance
to each party; for the rampart drawn from the camp to the river interrupted
the progress and certainty of Cæsar's victory, after he had forced Pompey's
camp. The same thing, by retarding the rapidity of the enemy's pursuit,
preserved our army."
² *The Nile, polluted with shameful blood*) ver. 307. The Nile would not
then have borne on its waves the corpse of Pompey, more noble than the
body of the Egyptian king himself.
³ *Nor would the naked Juba*) ver. 309. See the Note to B. iii. l. 293.
⁴ *And Scipio appeased the ghosts*) ver. 311. He alludes to the death of
Metellus Scipio, who fell at the same time as Juba. See the Note to B. ii.
l. 472.
⁵ *Nor would life*) ver. 311. Burmann thinks that " vita " here means
" mankind;" who, according to the Poet, suffered a loss in the death of
Cato.
⁶ *Magnus, about to pursue*) ver. 316. Cæsar tells us that after this battle
Pompey was saluted " Imperator," which title he retained, and thenceforth

father-in-law, wherever he may fly; that he may repair
to his native land and Ausonia *now* free from the enemy.

"Never," said he, "will I, after the example of Cæsar,
betake myself again to my country, and never shall Rome
behold me, except returning, *my* forces dismissed. Hesperia I was able, the war commencing, to hold, if I had
been willing to entrust *my* troops in the temples of my
country, and to fight in the midst of the Forum. So
long as I could withdraw the war, I would march on to the
extreme regions of the Scythian frosts, and the burning
tracks. Victorious, shall I, Rome, deprive thee of repose,
who, that battles might not exhaust thee, took to flight?
Oh! rather, that thou mayst suffer nothing in this warfare,
may Cæsar deem thee to be his own."

Thus having said, he turns his course towards the rising
of Phœbus, and, passing over trackless regions of the earth,
where Candavia[1] opens her vast forest ranges, he reaches
Emathia, which the Fates destined for the warfare.

The mountain rock of Ossa[2] bounds Thessaly, on the
side on which Titan in the hours of winter brings in the
day. When the summer with its higher rising brings
Phœbus to the zenith of the sky, Pelion opposes his
shadow to the rising rays[3]. But the midday fires of heaven
and the solstitial head of the raging Lion the woody
Othrys averts. Pindus receives the opposing Zephyrs and
Iapyx[4], and, evening hastening on, cuts short the light.
The dweller, too, on Olympus, not dreading Boreas, is

allowed himself to be addressed by it. The movements of Cæsar immediately after this defeat are described in the Civil War, B. iii. c. 73-75.

[1] *Where Candavia*) ver. 331. Candavia was a mountain range commencing in Epirus, which separated Illyricum from Macedonia.

[2] *Mountain rock of Ossa*) ver. 334. He means that Ossa bounds Thessaly on the north-east. The present description is supposed to have been borrowed from Herodotus.

[3] *Opposes his shadow to the rising rays*) ver. 335, 36. There is considerable doubt among the Commentators as to the meaning of this passage. Rowe has the following Note:—"According to Cellarius, Lucan must be out in his geography, as well as astronomy; for, as the days lengthen, the sun rises to the northward of the east; whereas Cellarius places Pelion to the southward. For the rest, Othrys lies to the south, Pindus to the west-south-west, and Olympus to the north."

[4] *And Iapyx*) ver. 339. Iapyx was the wind which blew from the west-north-west, off the coast of Apulia, in the south of Italy, the ancient name of which was Iapygia.

unacquainted throughout all his nights with shining
Arctos.

Between these mountains, which slope downwards with
a valley between, formerly the fields lay concealed amid
marshes extending far and wide, while the plains retained
the rivers, and Tempe, affording a passage[1] through, gave
no outlet to the sea; and their course was as they filled a
single standing water to increase it. After that, by the hand
of Hercules, the vast Ossa was divided from Olympus, and
Nereus was sensible of[2] the onward rush of the water *thus*
sudden; better destined to remain beneath[3] the waves, Emathian Pharsalus, the kingdom of the sea-descended Achilles[4]
rose forth, and Phylace[5] that touched with the first ship
the Rhœtean shores[6], and Pteleus[7], and Dorion lamenting[8]

[1] *Tempe, affording a passage*) ver. 345. This was a valley in the north
of Thessaly, lying between Mounts Olympus and Ossa, through which the
Peneus ran into the sea. It was famed among the ancients for its romantic
beauty. It is the only channel through which the waters of the Thessalian plains run to the sea; and the Poet here alludes to the common
opinion of the ancients, that these waters had once covered the country with
a vast lake, till an outlet was formed for them by a great convulsion of
nature, which rent asunder the rocks of Tempe.

[2] *And Nereus was sensible of*) ver. 349. The name of the sea-god
Nereus is here used to signify the sea, which, the Poet says, was sensible of
the vast influx of waters.

[3] *Better destined to remain beneath*) ver. 349. More fortunate for posterity if the plains of Pharsalia had remained under the waves.

[4] *Of the sea-descended Achilles*) ver. 350. Thessaly, once the realm of
Achilles, the son of the sea-goddess Thetis.

[5] *And Phylace*) ver. 352. Phylace was a town of Phthiotis in Thessaly,
east of the Enipeus, on the northern side of Mount Othrys. Protesilaüs was
its king, and was the first Greek who landed on the shores of Troy, at the
commencement of the Trojan war, notwithstanding the prediction that certain death awaited him that should do so. See the Epistle of Laodamia to
Protesilaüs in the Heroides of Ovid, p. 124, *et seq.*, in the Translation in
Bohn's Classical Library.

[6] *The Rhœtean shores*) ver. 351. Meaning thereby the shores of Troy,
near which was the Promontory Rhœteum.

[7] *And Pteleus*) ver. 352. Pteleos, or Pteleum, was an ancient seaport
town in the Phthiotian district in Thessaly.

[8] *And Dorion lamenting*) ver. 352. Dorion, or, as it was more generally
called, Dotion or Dotium, was an ancient town and plain of Thessaly, near
Lake Bœbe. It was here that, according to tradition, Thamyris challenged
the Muses to a contest in song, in consequence of which he was deprived of
his sight and his musical powers. Pierides was a surname of the Muses,
which they derived either from Pieria, near Mount Olympus, where they
were first worshipped, or else from Pierus, an ancient king of Thrace, who
first established their worship.

the wrath of the Pierides; Trachyn[1], and Melibœa[2], brave
with the quiver of Hercules, the reward of the direful
torch[3]; and once-powerful Larissa[4]; where they now
plough over Argos once renowned[5]; where story speaks of
ancient Thebes of Echion[6]; where once the exiled Agave
bearing the head and neck of Pentheus committed them to
the closing fire, complaining that this alone of her son she
had recovered[7].

The marsh then, burst asunder, divided into numerous
streams. On the west Æas thence flows[8] clear into the
Ionian sea, but with a small stream; nor stronger with his
waves does the father of ravished Isis[9] flow, and, Œneus,

[1] *Trachyn*) ver. 353. See B. iii. l. 178.

[2] *Melibœa*) ver. 354. This was a town on the coast of Magnesia in
Thessaly, between Mounts Ossa and Pelion. Horace mentions it as belong-
ing to the dominions of Philoctetes, who is here alluded to, to whom also
Trachyn belonged.

[3] *The reward of the direful torch*) ver. 354. Philoctetes, at the request
of Hercules, lighted the funereal pile on which that hero was burnt on Mount
Œta; in return for which, he bestowed on Philoctetes his bow and arrows,
without the presence of which at the siege, it was fated that Troy could
not be taken.

[4] *Once-powerful Larissa*) ver. 355. There were several Pelasgian places
of this name, and it is uncertain which of the two in Thessaly is here referred
to; one was an important town of Pelasgiotis in Thessaly, situate on the
Peneus, in an extensive plain; the other, famed as the birthplace of Achilles,
and surnamed Cremaste, was in Phthiotis.

[5] *Argos once renowned*) ver. 356. This was a town of Pelasgian Thessaly, which had long been in ruins. By the epithet " nobile " he probably
alludes to the breed of high-spirited horses which were reared there for the
contests at the Olympic games.

[6] *Thebes of Echion*) ver. 357. Echion was one of the five surviving
Sparti who remained of those who had sprung up from the dragon's teeth
which Cadmus had sown. He was the husband of Agave, and the father of
Pentheus. Thebes, in the district of Phthiotis, was an important city of
Thessaly; the Poet probably calls it " Echionia," for the reason stated by
him that Agave, after she had murdered her son, fled thither in exile. See
B. i. l. 574, and the Note to the passage.

[7] *She had recovered*) ver. 359. He seems to mean, that on recovering her
senses, Agave complained that so small a portion of the limbs had been
left for her to place on the funeral pile, the rest having been torn to
pieces by the frantic Bacchanals, who had aided her in the murder.

[8] *Æas thence flows*) ver. 361. This river is called by Pliny the Elder,
Aous. It was a small limpid stream, running through Epirus and Thessaly,
and discharging itself into the Ionian Sea.

[9] *The father of ravished Isis*) ver. 362. There were two rivers of the
name of Inachus; the one here alluded to, now called the Banitza, was a
river of Acarnania, which rises in Mount Lacmon, in the range of Pindus,

he, almost thy son-in-law[1] covers the Echinades[2] with mud
from his turbid waves[3]; and Evenus[4], stained with the blood
of Nessus[5], cuts through Calydon, *the city* of Meleager.
Spercheus, with hastening course[6], cleaves the Malian
waters; and with pure stream Amphrysus waters the
pastures[7] where Phœbus served as shepherd; Anauros,

and falls into the Acheloüs. He was fabled to be the father of Io, who was
carried away by Jupiter, and transformed by him into the shape of a cow,
by some considered to be the same as the Egyptian Goddess Isis. Ovid,
however, seems to imply that the Inachus of Argolis was the sire of Io.
See the story related at length in the Metamorphoses of Ovid, B. i., and
the explanation in the Translation in Bohn's Classical Library, p. 36.

[1] *Almost thy son-in-law*) ver. 363. The river Acheloüs had been promised the hand of Deianira, the daughter of Œneus, king of Calydon, in
Ætolia; but being conquered in single combat by Hercules, he was forced to
resign her to the hero. The story of this contest is related at the commencement of the Ninth Book of the Metamorphoses.

[2] *Covers the Echinades*) ver. 364. The Echinades were said to have been
five Naiad nymphs, whom, in a fit of jealousy, the river Acheloüs hurled into
the sea, on which they were transformed into islands. See their story related
in the Metamorphoses of Ovid, B. viii. l. 570, *et seq.* They are now called
Curzolari, and the largest, which was called Dulichium, is now united to the
mainland.

[3] *With mud from his turbid waves*) ver. 364. The Acheloüs, more anciently called Thoas, Axenus, and Thestius, is the largest river in Greece.
It rises in Mount Pindus and falls into the Ionian Sea, opposite the Echinades, which, as the Poet here hints, were amplified by the earth discharged
by its waters.

[4] *And Evenus*) ver. 366. This river, now called Fidhari, was more anciently called the Lycormas. It rises in Mount Œta, and flows with a rapid
stream through Ætolia into the sea.

[5] *Stained with the blood of Nessus*) ver. 365. The river Evenus, on the
banks of which the Centaur Nessus was slain by the arrow of Hercules,
passes by Calydon, a city of Ætolia, which was formerly reigned over by
Meleager, the lover of Atalanta, and who was slain through the jealousy of
his own mother, Althea. See the story of the death of Nessus related at
length in Ovid's Metamorphoses, B. viii. l. 261, *et seq.*

[6] *Spercheus, with hastening course*) ver. 367. The Spercheus, now called
the Elladha, rises in Mount Tymphrestus, in the north of Thessaly, and
runs easterly, through the Malian districts, falling into the Sinus Maliacus,
or Malian Gulf, now called the Bay of Zeitun, off the coast of the south of
Thessaly, north-west of the Isle of Eubœa, and north of the present Straits
of Negropont.

[7] *Amphrysus waters the pastures*) ver. 368. Amphrysus was a small
river of Thessaly, which flows into the Pagasæan Gulf; on the banks of
which Apollo, in the guise of a shepherd, kept the flocks of King Admetus,
when he had been banished from heaven by Jupiter, for slaying the Cyclops

too [1], who neither breathes forth damp fogs, nor air moistened with dew, nor light breezes; and whatever stream of
itself not known presents its waves in the Peneus [2] to the
ocean: with violent flood flows the Apidanus [3]; and the
Enipeus [4] never swift unless mingled.

Asopus takes his course [5], and Phœnix, and Melas [6].
Alone does Titaresos [7], where he comes into a stream of another name, keep distinct his waters, and, gliding from above,
uses the stream of Peneus as though dry fields. The re-

who had made the bolts with which his son Æsculapius was slain by Jupiter
for daring to raise Hippolytus to life by his medical skill.

[1] *Anauros, too*) ver. 370. The Anauros was a river of Thessaly which
flows into the Pagasæan Gulf. The story that it sent forth no mists or
exhalations probably originated from the resemblance of its name to the
Greek words ἄνευ, "without," and αὔρα, "an exhalation."

[2] *In the Peneus*) ver. 372. The Peneus here mentioned was the chief
river of Thessaly, and is now called the Salambria. It rises in Mount
Lacmon, a branch of the Pindus chain, and after receiving many streams,
the chief of which are the Enipeus, the Lethæus, and the Titaresius, flows
through the vale of Tempe into the sea.

[3] *Flows the Apidanus*) ver. 373. This was a river of Thessaly, joining
the Enipeus near Pharsalus. Ovid, in the Metamorphoses, B. i. l. 580, calls
it "senex Apidanus," "the aged;" which some take to mean "slow,"
whereas here the force of its current is spoken of. Ovid likewise speaks of
the "irrequietus," "restless" Enipeus, which Lucan, on the contrary,
pronounces to be sluggish until its confluence with the Apidanus.

[4] *And the Enipeus*) ver. 373. The Enipeus rises in Mount Othrys in
Thessaly, receives the Apidanus near Pharsalus, and flows into the Peneus.
There were rivers in Elis and Macedonia of the same name.

[5] *Asopus takes his course*) ver. 374. There were several rivers of this
name. The one here alluded to rises in Mount Œta, in Phthiotis, and
flows into the Sinus Maliacus, after its conjunction with the Phœnix, a
small stream of the south of Thessaly, which joins it near Thermopylæ.

[6] *And Melas*) ver. 374. Melas was the name of several rivers whose
waters were of a dark colour. There were two of this name in Thessaly,
one of which rising in the Malian district, and, flowing past Trachyn, fell
into the Sinus Maliacus, while the other, rising in Phthiotis, fell into the
Apidanus.

[7] *Alone does Titaresos*) ver. 376. The Titaresos, or Titaresius, was a
river of Thessaly, called also Europus, rising on Mount Titarus and falling
into the Peneus. Lucan here alludes to the words of Homer in the Iliad,
B. ii. l. 752, who states that the Titaresius "does not mingle with the
Peneus, but flows on the surface of it, just like oil, for it flows from the
waters from Styx in Orcus." Its waters are supposed by physiologists to
have been impregnated with an oily substance, whence it was said to be a
branch of the Styx, and that it disdained to mingle with the rivers of
mortals.

port is that this river flows from the Stygian marshes, and that, mindful of his rise, he is unwilling to endure the contact of an ignoble stream, and preserves the veneration of the Gods for himself [1].

As soon as the fields were open to the rivers sent forth, the rich furrow divided beneath the Bœbycian ploughshare [2]; then, pressed by the right hand of the Lelegians,[3] the plough sank deep. The Æolian [4] and Dolopian husbandmen [5] cleared the ground, both the Magnetes [6], a nation known by their horses, and the Minyæ [7], by their oars. There did the pregnant cloud pour forth in the Pelethronian caverns [8], the Centaurs sprung from Ixion [9], half beasts;

---

[1] *The veneration of the Gods for himself*) ver. 380. As the Gods fear to swear by the river Styx and break their oath, this river, as a branch of it, wishes still to insure the same respect for the Deities.

[2] *Beneath the Bœbycian ploughshare*) ver. 382. He means that the land which was cultivated by the people of the town of Bœbe was then, for the first time, left dry. Bœbe was a town of Pelasgiotis, in Thessaly, on the western shore of Lake Bœbeis.

[3] *Of the Lelegians*) ver. 383. The Leleges were an ancient people, supposed to have inhabited Greece before the Hellenes. They were a warlike and a migratory race, but their origin is enveloped in the greatest obscurity. Pliny mentions them as inhabitants of the country of the Locrians, adjacent to Thessaly; Strabo says that they were the same people that Pindar calls Centaurs.

[4] *The Æolian*) ver. 384. The Æolians were an ancient people of Thessaly, said to have been descended from Æolus, the son of Hellen. It was, however, a name long given to all the inhabitants of Greece beyond the Peloponnesus, except the people of Athens and Megara.

[5] *And Dolopian husbandmen*) ver. 384. The Dolopians were a people of Thessaly, who dwelt on the banks of the Enipeus, but, in later times, at the foot of Mount Pindus.

[6] *Both the Magnetes*) ver. 385. These were the inhabitants of the country of Magnesia, the most easterly part of Thessaly, extending from the Peneus on the north to the Pagasæan Gulf on the south, and including Mounts Ossa and Pelion; like their neighbours, the Centaurs, the Magnetes were famed for their skill in horsemanship.

[7] *The Minyæ*) ver. 385. The Minyæ were an ancient people, who dwelt in Thessaly, in the vicinity of Iolcos. The greater part of the Argonauts, who probably were among the earliest to give attention to naval affairs, were of the Minyan race.

[8] *In the Pelethronian caverns*) ver. 387. Pelethronium was a mountainous district of Thessaly, part of Mount Pelion, where the Lapithæ dwelt, and from whose king, Pelethronium, it was said to have derived its name.

Sprung from Ixion) ver. 386. Ixion was king of the Lapithæ, or Phlegyans, and the story was, that being introduced to the table of Jupiter,

Q

thee, Monychus ', breaking the rugged rocks of Pholoë², and
thee, fierce Rhœtus³, hurling beneath the heights of Œta
the mountain ashes, which hardly Boreas could tear up;
Pholus, too, the host⁴ of great Alcides; and thee, treacherous
ferryman⁵ over the river, destined to feel the arrows tipped
with Lernæan venom, and thee, aged Chiron⁶, who,
shining with thy cold Constellation, dost drive away the
greater Scorpion⁷ with the Hæmonian bow.

In this land *first* shone the seeds of fierce warfare. From

he fell in love with Juno, and offered violence to her, on which Jupiter substituted a cloud in her form, by which Ixion became the father of Centaurus,
from whom descended the Centaurs, a people of Thessaly.

¹ *Monychus*) ver. 388.　He was one of the Centaurs, and is mentioned
by Ovid in the Metamorphoses, B. xii. l. 499, as taking part in the battle
against the Lapithæ, where he is represented as exclaiming,—"'Heap upon
Cæneus stones and beams and entire mountains, and dash out his long-lived
breath by throwing whole woods upon him. Let a wood press on his jaws;
and weight shall be in place of wounds.' Thus he said; and by chance
having got a tree thrown down by the power of the boisterous south wind,
he hurled it against the powerful foe; and he was an example to the rest;
and in a short time, Othrys, thou wast bare of trees, and Pelion had no
shades." Monychus is also mentioned by Juvenal and Valerius Flaccus.

² *The rugged rocks of Pholoë*) ver. 388. Pholoë, now called Olono, was
a mountain forming the boundary between Arcadia and Elis, being a southern continuation of the Erymanthian chain.

³ *Thee, fierce Rhœtus*) ver. 390.　Rhœtus was one of the Centaurs mentioned by Ovid as present at the battle with the Lapithæ, in the Metamorphoses, B. xii. l. 296, where being wounded he takes to flight. He is also
mentioned by Virgil.

⁴ *Pholus, too, the host*) ver. 391. Pholus was a Centaur who hospitably entertained Hercules in his travels. Having taken up one of the arrows tipped
with the poison of the Hydra in order to examine it, it fell upon his foot,
and he died of the wound, on which Hercules buried him on Mount Pholoë,
which from that circumstance received its name. He is mentioned by Ovid
as being present at the battle with the Lapithæ, in the Metamorphoses,
B. xii. l. 306.

⁵ *Thee, treacherous ferryman*) ver. 392.　He alludes to the fate of the Centaur Nessus, who on carrying Deianira across the river Evenus attempted to
offer violence to her, on which he was slain by Hercules with an arrow
tipped with the venom of the Lernæan Hydra.

⁶ *And thee, aged Chiron*) ver. 393.　The Centaur Chiron was famed for his
skill in physic and music, and was the tutor of Achilles. After his death
he was transferred to heaven, and made one of the Zodiacal Constellations,
under the name of Sagittarius, "the archer," which follows the sign of the
Scorpion.

⁷ *The greater Scorpion*) ver. 394. The Constellation Scorpio occupies
more space than any other one of the Zodiacal Constellations.

the rocks, struck with the trident, first did the Thessalian charger [1], an omen of direful wars, spring forth; first did he champ the steel and the bit [2], and foam at the unwonted reins of the Lapithan subduer from the Pagasæan shore [3]. The first ship cleaving the ocean, exposed earth-born man upon the unknown waves. [Itonus, the ruler [4] of the Thessalian land, was the first to hammer masses of heated metal into form, and to melt silver with the flames and stamp gold into coin, and liquefy copper in immense furnaces. There was it *first* granted to number riches, *a thing* which has urged on nations to accursed arms.

Hence did Python [5], *that* most huge serpent, descend, and glide along the fields of Cyrrha; whence, too, the Thessalian laurels come to the Pythian games [6]. Hence the impious Aloeus [7] sent forth his progeny against the Gods of heaven, when Pelion raised itself almost to the lofty stars, and Ossa, meeting the constellations, impeded their course.

When upon this land the chieftains have pitched the

---

[1] *First did the Thessalian charger*) ver. 397. He alludes to the horse, which, in his contest with Minerva who should give name to the capital of Attica, Neptune caused at a blow of his trident to spring from out of the earth. According to most accounts he created the horse in Attica; but Lucan here says (in which statement he is supported by Homer and Apollodorus) that it took place in Thessaly; where also he made a present of the famous horse to Peleus.

[2] *First did he champ the steel and the bit*) ver. 398. Pelethronius, king of the Lapithæ, was said to have been the inventor of the bridle and the bit.

[3] *From the Pagasæan shore*) ver. 400. He alludes to the sailing of the Argonautic expedition from Pagasæ in Thessaly, where the Argo was built.

[4] *Itonus, the ruler*) ver. 408. Itonus was an ancient king of Thessaly, said to have been a son of Deucalion, or, according to some, of Apollo.

[5] *Hence did Python*) ver. 408. The serpent Python was said to have been generated in Thessaly from the slime and putrescence left after the deluge of Deucalion had subsided. It was slain by the shafts of Apollo, who covered the sacred tripod at Delphi with its skin, and instituted the Pythian games as a memorial of his victory.

[6] *Come to the Pythian games*) ver. 409. At the celebration of the Pythian games at Delphi, the Temple of Apollo was adorned with laurel brought for the purpose from Thessaly.

[7] *The impious Aloeus*) ver. 410. Aloeus was the son of Neptune and Canace. He married Iphimedia, the daughter of Triops, who was beloved by Neptune, and had by him the twin sons Otus and Ephialtes, giants who, at the age of nine years, threatened the Gods with war, and attempted to pile Ossa on Olympus and Pelion on Ossa.

camps destined by the Fates, their minds, presaging the
future warfare, engage all, and it is clear that the momentous
hour of the great crisis is drawing nigh. Because their fates
are now close approaching, degenerate minds tremble, and
ponder on the worst. A few, courage preferred, feel both
hopes and fears as to the event. But mingled with the
timid multitude is Sextus [1], an offspring unworthy of
Magnus for a parent, who afterwards, roving, an exile, on
the Scyllæan waves, a Sicilian pirate, polluted his triumphs
on the deep, who, fear spurring him on to know beforehand the events of fate, both impatient of delay and faint-
hearted about all things to come, consults not the tripods of
Delos, not the Pythian caves, nor does he choose to enquire
what sounds Dodona, the nourisher on the first fruits [2],
sends forth from the brass of Jove [3], who from the entrails
can reveal the fates [4], who can explain the birds, who can ob

---

[1] *Is Sextus*) ver. 420. Sextus was the younger son of Pompey, by his
wife Mucia. During the greater part, if not the whole, of his father's campaign in Greece, he was in the island of Lesbos, so that most probably there
is not any foundation for the story here told by Lucan. After the defeat of
his brother Cneius at the battle of Munda, he for some time supported himself
by rapine and plunder in Spain, and many years afterwards, having gained
possession of Sicily, Sardinia, and Corsica, his fleets plundered all the supplies of corn which came from Egypt and the eastern provinces, so that
famine seemed for a time inevitable at Rome. He was taken prisoner by
the troops of Antony in the neighbourhood of Miletus, and was there put to
death.

[2] *The nourisher on the first fruits*) ver. 426. "Frugibus." The fruits of
the woods of Dodona were acorns (or as May, in his Translation, quaintly
calls them, "akehornes"), upon which the primitive races of mankind were
said to have fed.

[3] *Sends forth from the brass of Jove*) ver. 427. It was said by some that
in the oracles of Jupiter at Dodona the will of heaven was divulged by the
ringing of certain cauldrons there suspended. Stephanus Byzantinus informs
us that in that part of the forest of Dodona where the oracle stood, there
were two pillars erected at a small distance from each other; on one there
was placed a brazen vessel about the size of an ordinary cauldron, and on
the other a little boy, probably a piece of mechanism, who held a brazen
whip with several thongs, which hung loose and were easily moved. When
the wind blew, the lashes struck against the vessel, and occasioned a noise
while the wind continued. He says that it was from these that the forest
took the name of Dodona; "dodo," in the ancient language of the vicinity,
signifying "a cauldron."

[4] *From the entrails can reveal the fates*) ver. 427. The meaning is, that
he is not willing in a righteous manner to learn the decrees of fate by consulting the entrails of animals, auspices derived from birds, auguries derived

serve the lightnings of heaven and search the stars with Assyrian care, or if there is any *method*, secret, but lawful[1].

He had gained a knowledge of[2] the secrets of the ruthless magicians detested by the Gods above, and the altars sad with dreadful sacrifices, and the aid of the shades below and of Pluto; and to him, wretched man, it seemed clear that the Gods of heaven knew too little[3].

The vain and direful frenzy the very locality promotes, and, adjoining to the camp, the cities of the Hæmonian women, whom no power over any prodigy that has been invented can surpass, whose art is each thing that is not believed. Moreover, the Thessalian land produces on its crags both noxious herbs, and rocks that are sensible to the magicians as they chaunt their deadly secrets. There spring up many things destined to offer violence to the Deities[4]; and the Colchian stranger gathers[5] in the Hæmonian lands those herbs which she has not brought.

from thunder and lightning, nor yet the astrological art derived from the Chaldæans of Assyria.

[1] *Any method, secret, but lawful*) ver. 430. He means those secret arts of divination which it was not unrighteous to use, such as geomancy and astrology; but instead of resorting to these, Sextus employs the forbidden practices of the art of necromancy.

[2] *He had gained a knowledge of*) ver. 432. "Noverat" does not necessarily mean that Sextus was skilled himself in the necromantic art, but that he was aware of its existence and of the cultivation of it by the sorceresses of Thessaly. Weise, however, thinks that it implies that Sextus had studied the art.

[3] *That the Gods of heaven knew too little*) ver. 433-4. He believed that the Gods of heaven 'were not so likely to be acquainted with the future as the Infernal Deities and the shades of the dead.

[4] *To offer violence to the Deities*) ver. 441. To be able to gain power over the reluctant Gods was one of the pretensions of the sorceresses of antiquity. Thus, in the Heroides of Ovid, in the Epistle of Hypsipyle to Jason, she says, speaking of the enchantress Medea, l. 83, *et seq.* :—" By her incantations has she influenced thee; and with her enchanted sickle does she reap the dreadful plants. She endeavours to draw down the struggling moon from her chariot, and to envelop the horses of the sun in darkness. She bridles the waves and stops the winding rivers; she moves the woods and the firm rocks from their spot." For an account of the magic rites and spells of the sorceresses of antiquity the reader is referred to the Third Volume of the Translation of Ovid in Bohn's Classical Library, pages 56-7, and 278-9.

[5] *The Colchian stranger gathers*) ver. 442. He alludes to the magical incantations of the Colchian Medea when she had arrived with Jason in Thessaly, and says that she found no lack of plants there suited to aid her in her

The impious charms of the accursed nation turn the ears of the inhabitants of heaven that are deaf to peoples so numerous, to nations so many. That voice alone goes forth amid the recesses of the heavens, and bears the stringent words to the unwilling Deities, from which the care of the skies and of the floating heavens never calls them away. When the accursed murmur has reached the stars, then, although Babylon of Perseus and mysterious Memphis[1] should open all the shrines of the ancient Magi, the Thessalian *witch* to foreign altars draws away the Gods of heaven.

Through the charms of the Thessalian *witches* a love not induced by the Fates has entered into hardened hearts; and stern old men have burned with illicit flames. And not only do noxious potions avail; or when they withdraw the pledges swelling with its juices from the forehead of the mother about to show her affection[2]. The mind, polluted by no corruption of imbibed poison, perishes by force of spells[3]. Those whom no unison of the bed jointly occu-

enchantments. It was there that by her magical arts she restored the aged Æson to youth, and likewise contrived the death of his brother Pelias. See the Metamorphoses of Ovid, B. vii. l. 223, *et seq.*, where her culling of the Thessalian herbs is thus described:—"She looked down upon Thessalian Tempe below her, and guided her dragons towards the chalky regions; and observed the herbs which Ossa and which the lofty Pelion bore, Othrys too, and Pindus, and Olympus still greater than Pindus; and part she tore up by the root gently worked, part she cut down with the bend of a brazen sickle. Many a herb, too, that grew on the banks of Apidanus pleased her; many, too, on the banks of Amphrysus; nor, Enipeus, didst thou escape. The Peneian waters, and the Spercheian as well, contributed something, and the rushy shores of Bœbe. She plucks, too, enlivening herbs by the Eubœan Anthedon."

[1] *And mysterious Memphis*) ver. 449. Memphis is here used to signify Egypt in general, which at all times, from the time of the magicians who endeavoured by their enchantments to compete with the miracles of Moses down to the present day, has especially cultivated the magic art.

[2] *The mother about to show her affection*) ver. 456. He alludes to the use in philtres, or love potions, of the substance called "hippomanes," which was by some said to flow from mares when in a prurient state, but more generally, as Pliny the Elder tells us, was thought to be a poisonous excrescence of the size of a fig, and of a black colour, which grows on the head of the mare, and which the foal at its birth is in the habit of biting off, which if it neglects to do, it is not allowed by its mother to suck. Hesiod, however, says, that hippomanes was a herb that produced madness in the horses that ate of it.

[3] *Perishes by force of spells*) ver. 457. They are able by muttering charms alone to deprive men of their senses.

pied binds together, and influence of alluring beauty, they attract by the magic whirling of the twisted threads [1] The courses of things are stayed, and, retarded by lengthened night, the day stops short. The sky obeys not the laws *of nature;* and on hearing the spells the headlong world is benumbed; Jupiter, too, urging them on, is astounded that the poles *of heaven* do not go on, impelled by the rapid axles.

At another time, they fill all *places* with showers, and, while the sun is hot, bring down the clouds; the heavens thunder, too, Jupiter not knowing it. By those same words, with hair hanging loose, have they scattered abroad far and wide soaking clouds and showers. The winds ceasing, the sea has swelled; again, forbidden to be sensible of the storms, the south wind provoking it, it has held its peace; and bearing along the ship the sails have swelled against the wind. From the steep rock has the torrent hung suspended; and the river has run not in the direction in which it was descending. The summer has not raised the Nile; in a straight line the Mæander has urged on his waters; and the Arar has impelled headlong [2] the delaying Rhone; their tops lowered, mountains have levelled their ridges.

Olympus has looked upwards [3] to the clouds, and with no sun the Scythian snows have thawed, while the winter was freezing. Impelled by the stars, the shores protected, the charms of the Hæmonian *witches* have driven Tethys

---

[1] *By the magic whirling of the twisted threads*) ver. 460. He alludes to the use of the "rhombus," or spinning-wheel, in magical incantations, the object of which was to regain the affections when lost. The spinning-wheel was much used in magical incantations, not only among the people of Thessaly and Italy, but those of northern and western Europe. The practice was probably founded on the supposition of the existence of the so-called threads of destiny, and it was the province of the wizard or sorceress, by his or her charms, to lengthen or shorten those threads as required. Some think that the use of the threads implied that the minds of individuals were to be influenced at the will of the enchanter or the person consulting him. See the use of the spinning wheel in magical incantations described in the Fasti of Ovid, B. ii. l. 572, *et seq.*, and the Eighth Eclogue of Virgil.

[2] *The Arar has impelled headlong*) ver. 476. See the First Book, l. 434. The Arar was noted for its slowness, the Rhone for its rapidity.

[3] *Olympus has looked upwards*) ver. 477. Olympus, which towers above the clouds, by magical arts is brought beneath them.

back [1]. The earth, too, has shaken the axle of her unmoved weigh:. and, inclining with the effort, has oscillated
in her mid regions [2]. The weight of a mass so vast smitten
by their voice, has gaped open, and has afforded a prospect through it of the surrounding heavens. Every animal
powerful for death, and produced to do injury, both fears the
Hæmonian arts and supplies them with its deadly qualities. Them do the ravening tigers and the magnanimous wrath of the lions fawn upon with gentle mouth; for
them does the serpent unfold his cold coils, and is extended in the frosty field. The knots of the vipers unite,
their bodies cut asunder; and the snake dies, breathed
upon by human poison.

What failing *is* this of the Gods of heaven in following
after enchantments and herbs, and *what* this fear of disre-
garding them? Of what compact do the bonds keep the
Deities *thus* bound? Is it obligatory, or does it please them
to obey? For an unknown piety only do the *witches* deserve
this, or by secret threats do they prevail? Have they this
power against all the Gods of heaven, or do these imperious
charms sway but a certain Deity [3], who, whatever he himself
is compelled, can compel the world, *to do?* There, too, for
the first time *were* the stars brought down from the headlong sky; and serene Phœbe, beset by the dire influences
of their words, grew pale and burned with dusky and earthy
fires, not otherwise than if the earth hindered her from the
reflection of her brother, and interposed its shade between
the celestial flames; and, arrested by spells, she endures

---

[1] *Have driven Tethys back*) ver. 479-80. The sea, accustomed to be
aroused by the influence of the Moon and certain Constellations, such as
Arcturus, Orion, and the Hyades, is no more influenced by them when the
Thessalian sorceresses will otherwise.

[2] *Has oscillated in her mid regions*) ver. 480-1. This passage is
either in a corrupt state, or one to which it is not improbable that the Poet
himself would have been unable to attach any very definite meaning.

[3] *Sway but a certain Deity*) ver. 497. Rowe has the following Note here:
—"The Poet seems to allude here to that God whom they called Demogorgon,
who was the father and creator of all the other Gods; who, though he himself
was bound in chains in the lowest hell, was yet so terrible to all the others
that they could not bear the very mention of his name; as appears towards
the end of this Book. Him Lucan supposes to be subject to the power of
magic, as all the other Deities of what kind soever were to him."

labours so great, until, more nigh, she sends her foam[1] upon the herbs situate beneath.

These rites of criminality, these spells of the direful race, the wild Erictho[2] has condemned as being of piety too extreme, and has applied the polluted art to new ceremonies. For to her it is not permitted to place her deadly head within a roof or a home in the city; and she haunts the deserted piles, and, the ghosts expelled, takes possession of the tombs, pleasing to the Gods of Erebus. To hear the counsels of the dead, to know the Stygian abodes and the secrets of the concealed Pluto, not the Gods above, not a life *on earth*, forbids.

Leanness has possession of the features of the hag, foul with filthiness, and, unknown to a clear sky, her dreadful visage, laden with uncombed locks, is beset with Stygian paleness. If showers and black clouds obscure the stars, then does the Thessalian *witch* stalk forth from the spoiled piles, and try to arrest the lightnings of the night. The seeds she treads on of the fruitful corn she burns up, and by her breathing makes air noxious that was not deadly *before*. She neither prays to the Gods of heaven, nor with suppliant prayer calls the Deity to her aid, nor does she know of the propitiating entrails; upon the altars she delights to place funereal flames, and frankincense which she has carried off from the lighted pile[3].

Her voice now first *heard* as she demands, the Gods of heaven accede to all the wickedness, and dread to hear a second address. Souls that live, and still rule their respective limbs, she buries in the tomb; and death reluctantly creeps on upon those who owe *lengthened* years to the Fates; the funeral procession turning back, the dead bodies

---

[1] *She sends her foam*) ver. 506. It was a belief among the ancients that the moon was arrested in her course and brought down upon the earth by means of the Thessalian incantations, and that at those times she shed a kind of venomous foam upon certain plants, which were consequently much sought for, to be applied to magical purposes.

[2] *The wild Erictho*) ver. 508. Erictho is mentioned as a famous enchantress in the Epistle from Sappho to Phaon, in Ovid's Heroides, l. 139. She is also spoken of by Apuleius as skilled in sepulchral magic. The name was probably used to signify an enchantress in general.

[3] *Carried off from the lighted pile*) ver. 526. In ordinary life it was deemed the height of disgrace to be guilty of taking away anything that had been placed on the funeral pile.

she rescues from the tomb; corpses fly from death. The smoking ashes of the young and the burning bones she snatches from the midst of the piles, and the very torch which the parents have held[1]; the fragments, too, of the funereal bier[2] that fly about in the black smoke, and the flowing robes does she collect amid the ashes, and the embers that smell of the limbs.

But when corpses are kept within stone[3], from which the moisture within is taken away, and, the corruption withdrawn, the marrow has grown hard; then does she greedily raven upon all the limbs, and bury her hands in the eyes, and delight to scoop out the dried-up balls[4], and gnaw the pallid nails[5] of the shrunken hand; with her mouth she tears asunder the halter[6] and the murderous knots; the bodies as they hang she gnaws, and scrapes the crosses[7]; the entrails, too, smitten by the showers she rends asunder, and the parched marrow, the sun's heat admitted *thereto*. Iron fastened into the hands[8], and the black corruption of the filthy matter that distils upon the limbs, and the slime

[1] *Parents have held*) ver. 534. It was the duty of the parent to set fire to the funeral pile of his children.

[2] *Of the funereal bier*) ver. 536. The corpse was carried to the funeral pile on a couch which was called "feretrum" or "capulus;" but the bodies of the poorer classes, or of slaves, were borne on a common kind of bier called "sandapila." The couches on which the bodies of the rich were carried were sometimes made of ivory and covered with gold and purple. On the top of the pile the corpse was laid upon the couch on which it had been carried, and burnt with it. The "vestes" here mentioned were probably the coverings of the funeral couch.

[3] *Corpses are kept within stone*) ver. 538. He alludes to bodies which, after the eastern fashion, are preserved as mummies, by drawing the moisture out and then preserving them in tombs of stone.

[4] *Scoop out the dried-up balls*) ver. 542. The practices here imputed to the Thessalian enchantress are similar to those of the Ghouls of the East, who were said to feast on the bodies of the dead, a practice frequently alluded to in the Arabian Nights.

[5] *And gnaw the pallid nails*) ver. 543. The nails of the human hand continue to grow after death, and turn of a white hue.

[6] *Tears asunder the halter*) ver. 543. She gnaws the knot of the noose to obtain the body that is hanging, for the purposes of her incantations.

[7] *And scrapes the crosses*) ver. 545. She scrapes off the clotted gore that adheres to the crosses on which malefactors hang, and tears out their entrails which have been long exposed to the drenching showers.

[8] *Iron fastened into the hands*) ver. 547. The iron nails driven through the hands and feet of those fastened to the cross.

that has collected, she bears off, and hangs *to the bodies*, as the sinews hold fast her bite.

⌠Whatever carcase, too, is lying upon the bare ground, before the beasts and the birds of the air does she sit; nor does she wish to separate the joints with iron and with her hands, and about to tear the limbs from their parched jaws, she awaits the bites of the wolves. Nor do her hands refrain from murder, if she requires the life-blood, which is the first to spring[1] from the divided throat. Nor does she shun slaughter, if her rites *demand* living gore, and her funereal tables demand the quivering entrails. So, through the wounds of the womb, not the way in which nature invites, is the embryo torn out, about to be placed upon the glowing altars. And as often as she has need of grim and stalwart shades, she herself makes the ghosts; every kind of death among mankind is in her employ.

She from the youthful body tears the down of the cheek; she with her left hand[2] from the dying stripling cuts off the hair. Full often, too, at her kinsman's pile has the dire Thessalian *witch* brooded over the dear limbs, and imprinting kisses, has both cut off the head, and torn away the cheeks pressed with her teeth, and biting off the end of the tongue as it cleaves to the dried throat, has poured forth murmurs into the cold lips, and has dispatched accursed secrets to the Stygian shades.

When the rumours of the spot brought her to the notice of Pompey[3], amid the depths of the night of the sky, at the time when Titan is bringing the midday beneath *our* earth, along the deserted fields he takes his way. The faithful and wonted attendants upon his crimes, wandering amid the ruined tombs and graves, beheld *her* afar, sitting upon a lofty crag, where Hæmus, sloping down, extends the Pharsalian ridges. She was conning over spells unknown to the magicians and the Gods of magic, and was trying charms for unwonted purposes. For, fearing lest the shifting warfare

[1] *Which is the first to spring*) ver. 555. The blood just drawn being deemed efficacious in enchantments, she will not scruple to commit murder for the sake of obtaining it.
[2] *With her left hand*) ver. 563. The left hand was especially employed in magical operations, as also by thieves in the pursuit of their vocation.
[3] *To the notice of Pompey*) ver. 570. To Sextus, the son of Pompey.

might remove to another region, and the Emathian land be deprived of slaughter so vast, the sorceress has forbidden Philippi[1], polluted with spells and sprinkled with dreadful potions, to transfer the combats, about to claim so many deaths as her own, and to enjoy the blood of the world ; she hopes to maim the corpses of slaughtered monarchs[2], and to turn *to herself* the ashes of the Hesperian race, and the bones of nobles, and to obtain ghosts so mighty.   This *is* her pursuit, and her sole study, what she is to tear away from the corpse of Magnus when exposed, what limbs of Cæsar she is to brood over.   Her does the degenerate offspring of Pompey first address :—

" O *thou* honor to the Hæmonian females, who art able to reveal their fates to nations, and who *art able* to turn them away from their course when about to come to pass, I pray thee that it may be permitted me to know the assured end which the fortune of war provides.   Not the lowest portion am I of the Roman multitude; the most renowned offspring of Magnus, either ruler of the world, or heir to a fall so great[3].   Smitten with doubts, my mind is in alarm, and again is prepared to endure the fears that spring from certainty.   This power do thou withdraw from events, that they may not rush on sudden and unseen ; either extort it from the Deities, or do thou spare the Gods, and force the truth from the shades below.   Unlock the Elysian abodes, and Death herself, called forth[4], compel to confess to thee whom of us it is that she demands.   Not mean is the task ; *it is* worthy for even thee to have a care to seek which way inclines the hazard of destinies so mighty."

The impious Thessalian *witch* rejoices at the mention of

---

[1] *The sorceress has forbidden Philippi*) ver. 582.   The Poet again commits the same mistake as in B. i. l. 675, and other places, in confounding Philippi, a town of Thrace, with Pharsalia in Thessaly.

[2] *Corpses of slaughtered monarchs*) ver. 584.   Who had come to the assistance of Pompey ; see B. vii. l. 227.

[3] *Heir to a fall so great*) ver. 595.   It must be remembered that Sextus was only a younger son ; but if he was a person of the character here depicted by Lucan, he would not improbably be guilty of misrepresentation.

[4] *Death herself, called forth*) ver. 601.   He speaks of Death here as a Divinity.   She was worshipped by the Greeks under the name of Thanatos. Sacrifice was probably offered to this Divinity, but no Temples of Death are mentioned by the ancient writers.

her fame *thus* spread abroad, and *answers* on the other hand :—

" O youth, if thou wouldst have influenced more humble destinies, it had been easy to force the reluctant Gods to any action thou mightst wish. To *my* skill it is granted, when with their beams the constellations have urged on death, to interpose delays[1]; and although every star would make a man aged, by drugs do we cut short his years in the midst. But together does the chain of causes work downward from the first origin of the world, and all the fates are struggling, if thou shouldst wish to change anything, and the human race stands subject to a single blow; then do we, the Thessalian throng, confess, Fortune has the greater might. But if *thou art* content to learn the events beforehand, paths easy and manifold will lie open to truth; earth, and sky, and Chaos[2], and seas, and plains, and the rocks of Rhodope, will converse with us. But *it is* easy, since there is a supply so vast of recent deaths, to raise a single body from the Emathian plains, that, with a clear voice, the lips of a corpse just dead and warm may utter their sounds, and no dismal ghost, the limbs scorched by the sun, may send forth indistinct screechings."

Thus she says ; and, the shades of night redoubled by her art, wrapped as to her direful head in a turbid cloud, she wanders amid the bodies of the slain, exposed, sepulchres being denied. Forthwith the wolves take to flight, their talons loosened, the birds fly unfed, while the Thessalian *witch* selects *her* prophet, and, examining the marrow cold in death, finds the fibres of the stiffened lungs standing without a wound[3], and in the dead body seeks a voice. Now stand in doubt destinies full many of men who have been slain, which one she is to choose to recall to the world above. If she had attempted to raise

---

[1] *To interpose delays*) ver. 608-9. She can cut short or lengthen the lives of individual men at her pleasure, despite the Fates; but over the destinies of states she can exercise no influence.

[2] *And sky, and Chaos*) ver. 617. " Chaos" here means Tartarus, or the place of departed spirits. She enumerates the different classes of magic arts : geomancy, aeromancy, necromancy, hydromancy, and soothsaying derived from inspection of the entrails of animals.

[3] *Standing without a wound*) ver. 630. She seeks the body of a person recently slain, in which the lungs are uninjured.

whole armies from the plains. and to restore *them* to the war, the laws of Erebus would have yielded, and a people dragged forth by the powerful miscreant from Stygian Avernus, would have mingled in fight.

A body selected at length with pierced throat she takes, and, a hook being inserted with funereal ropes, the wretched carcase is dragged over rocks, over stones, destined to live *once again*[1]; and beneath the lofty crags of the hollowed mountain, which the dire Erictho has destined for her rites, it is placed.

Downward sloping, not far from the black caverns of Pluto, the ground precipitately descends, which a wood covers, pale with its drooping foliage, and with no *lofty* tops looking upwards to the heavens, *and* a yew-tree shades, not pervious to the sun. Within is squalid darkness, and mouldiness pallid within the caves amid the lengthened gloom; never, unless produced by charms, does it receive the light. Not within the jaws of Tænarus[2], the baleful limit of the hidden world, and of our own, does the air settle thus stagnant; whither the sovereigns of Tartarus would not fear[3] to send forth the shades. For although the Thessalian *witch* uses violence against destiny, it is matter of doubt whether she beholds the Stygian ghosts because she has dragged them thither[4], or whether because she has descended *to Tartarus*.

A dress, of various colours and fury-like with varied garb, is put on *by her;* and her locks removed, her features are revealed, and, bristling. with wreaths of vipers her hair is fastened round. When she perceives the

---

[1] *Destined to live once again)* ver. 640. Destined to live for the purpose of answering her questions as to the future.

[2] *The jaws of Tænarus)* ver. 648. Tænarus was the name of a cavern at the foot of the Malean promontory in Laconia ; it emitted powerful mephitic vapours, and through it Hercules was said to have dragged Cerberus from the Infernal Regions.

[3] *The sovereigns of Tartarus would not fear)* ver. 650. Her cave is so gloomy, fetid, and dismal, that the rulers of Tartarus would not object to the ghosts, their subjects, taking up their abode there, it being no way preferable to their own realms.

[4] *Because she has dragged them thither)* ver. 652. If she evokes a ghost by her magic rites, it is matter of doubt whether she has really brought the spirit from hell, or whether in inhabiting her cave she has not really descended to hell herself.

youth's attendants alarmed, and himself trembling, *and*, casting down his eyes with looks struck with horror, she says:—

" Banish the fears conceived in your timid mind; now anew, now in its genuine form shall life be restored, that even tremblers may endure to hear him speak. But if I can show the Stygian lakes[1], and the shores that resound with flames; if, I being present, the Eumenides[2] can be beheld, and Cerberus shaking his necks shaggy with serpents, and the Giants chained *with their hands* to their backs, what dread is there, cowards, to behold the frightened ghosts?"

Then in the first place does she fill his breast, opened by fresh wounds, with reeking blood, and she bathes his marrow with gore, and plentifully supplies venom from the moon[3]. Here is mingled whatever, by a monstrous generation, nature has produced. Not the foam of dogs to which water is an object of dread, not the entrails of the lynx[4], not the excrescence[5] of the direful hyæna is wanting, and the marrow of the stag that has fed upon serpents[6];

[1] *The Stygian lakes*) ver. 662. He alludes to Pyriphlegethon, the burning Lake of hell.

[2] *The Eumenides*) ver. 664. The name "Eumenides," in the Greek, literally signifies " the well-meaning" or "propitiated Goddesses." This was a euphemism given to the Furies, because the superstitious were afraid to mention them by their real names, and was said to have been first given them after the acquittal of Orestes by the court of the Areopagus, when their anger had become soothed.

[3] *Venom from the moon*) ver. 669. See the Note to l. 506.

[4] *Not the entrails of the lynx*) ver. 672. It is not improbable that the Scholiast rightly suggests that the popular superstition is here alluded to which believed that the urine of the lynx hardens into a precious stone. Ovid says, in the Metamorphoses, B. xv. l. 413, *et seq.* :—" Conquered India presented her lynxes to Bacchus crowned with clusters; and, as they tell, whatever the bladder of these discharges is changed into stone and hardens by contact with the air." Pliny says, that this becomes hard and turns into gems like the carbuncle, being of a fiery tint, and that the stone has the name of "lyncurium." Beckmann, in his History of Inventions, thinks that this was probably the jacinth or hyacinth, while others suppose it to have been tourmaline or transparent amber.

[5] *The excrescence*) ver. 672. "Nodus." This word probably means the spine, or the upper part of it which joins the neck. Pliny the Elder tells us that the neck is fastened to, or, rather, forms part of, the back-bone of the hyæna.

[6] *Fed upon serpents*) ver. 673. It was a superstition among the an-

not the sucking fish, that holds back the ship[1] in the
midst of the waves, while the eastern breeze stretches the
rigging; the eyes of dragons, too[2], and the stones that resound[3], warmed beneath the brooding bird; not the winged
serpent[4] of the Arabians, and the viper produced in the
Red Sea, the guardian of the precious shell[5]; or the
slough of the horned serpent[6] of Libya that still survives
or the ashes of the Phœnix[7], laid upon an eastern altar.

With this, after she has mingled abominations, vile,

cients that deer when grown old have the power of drawing serpents from
their holes with their breath, which they destroy with their horns, and then
eat, on which they become young again.

[1] *That holds back the ship*) ver. 674. The "echeneis remora," or sucking
fish, was supposed, by sticking to the keel or rudder of a vessel in sail, to he
able to stop its course. Ovid says, in his Halieuticon, l. 99, "There is, too,
the little sucking-fish, wondrous to tell! a vast obstruction to ships."

[2] *The eyes of dragons, too*) ver. 675. It was a notion that those who had
their eyes anointed with a mixture made from serpents' eyes beaten up with
honey were proof against the sight of nocturnal spectres.

[3] *The stones that resound*) ver. 676. He alludes to the aëtites or eagle-
stone, which was said to be found in the nest of the eagle; by whose incu-
bation when warmed it exploded with a loud noise. See Pliny's Natural
History, B. ix. c. 3, and B. xxxvi. c. 21.

[4] *Not the winged serpent*) ver. 677. He may either mean a winged serpent, the existence of which was currently believed in the East, or may
allude to the "jaculus," which he again mentions in the Ninth Book, and
which Pliny, in his Eighth Book, c. 23, speaks of as darting upon passers-by
from the branches of trees.

[5] *Guardian of the precious shell*) ver. 678. It was supposed that there
were serpents upon the shores of the Red Sea that watched the shells of the
oysters in which the pearls are inclosed.

[6] *Slough of the horned serpent*) ver. 679. The cerastes or horned serpent
of Africa is again mentioned in the Ninth Book.

[7] *Or the ashes of the Phœnix*) ver. 680. This allusion to the fabulous bird,
called the Phœnix, will be best explained by the account of Ovid, in the Metamorphoses, B. xv. l. 303, *et seq.*: "The Assyrians call it the Phœnix. It
lives not on corn or grass, but on drops of frankincense and the juices of the
amomum. This bird, when it has completed the five ages of its life, with its
talons and its crooked beak constructs for itself a nest in the branches of a
holm-oak, or on the top of a quivering palm. As soon as it has strewed on this
cassia and ears of sweet spikenard, and bruised cinnamon, with yellow myrrh,
it lays itself down on it, and finishes its life in the midst of odours. They
say that thence, from the body of its parent, is reproduced a little Phœnix,
which is destined to live as many years. When time has given it strength,
and it is able to bear the weight, it lightens the branches of the lofty tree of the
burden of the nest, and dutifully carries both its own cradle and the sepulchre
of its parent; and having reached the city of Hyperion through the yielding
air, it lays it down before the sacred doors in the Temple of Hyperion."

and possessing no names [1], she added leaves steeped in
accursed spells, and herbs upon which, when shooting up,
her direful mouth had spat, and whatever poisons she herself gave unto the world; then, a voice, more potent than
all drugs to charm the Gods of Lethe, first poured forth its
murmurs, discordant, and differing much from the human
tongue. The bark of dogs has she, and the howling of
wolves; she sends forth the voice in which the scared owl,
in which the screech of the night, complain, in which wild
beasts shriek and yell, in which the serpent hisses, and the
wailing of the waves dashed upon the rocks; the sounds,
too, of the woods, and the thunders of the bursting cloud.
Of objects so many there is the voice in one. Then afterwards in a Hæmonian chaunt she unfolds the rest, and
her voice penetrates to Tartarus :—

" Eumenides, and Stygian fiends, and penalties of the
guilty, and Chaos, eager to confound innumerable worlds ;
and *thou*, Ruler of the earth [2], whom the wrath of the Gods,
deferred for lengthened ages, does vex ; Styx, and the
Elysian *fields*, which no Thessalian *sorceress* is deserving of:
Persephone, who dost detest heaven and thy mother [3], *and*

---

[1] *And possessing no names*) ver. 681. There is a similar passage in the
Metamorphoses of Ovid, where he is describing the incantations of Medea,
B. vii. 1. 270 :—" She adds, too, hoar-frost gathered at night by the light of
the moon, and the ill-boding wings of a screech-owl together with its flesh,
and the entrails of a two-formed wolf that was wont to change its appearance
of a wild beast into that of a man. Nor is there wanting there the thin
scaly slough of the Cinyphian water-snake and the liver of the long-lived
stag ; to which, besides, she adds the bill and head of a crow that had sustained an existence of nine ages. When with these and a hundred other
things without a name, the barbarian princess has completed the medicine
prepared for the mortal body, with a branch of the peaceful olive, long since
dried up, she stirs them all up, and blends the lowest ingredients with the
highest."

[2] *Thou, Ruler of the earth*) ver. 697. Dis, or Pluto; to whom was allotted
the government of the Earth, and the regions beneath, when his brother
Jupiter received that of Heaven and Neptune that of the Sea. The passage
may either mean that Pluto repines at the lengthened existence of the Deities
who do not through death descend to his realms, or that he is tired of the
prolonged existence which lie in common with the other Gods enjoys.

[3] *Detest heaven and thy mother*) ver. 699. She preferred to remain with
her husband Pluto in the Infernal Regions to returning to heaven and rejoin-
ing her mother Ceres ; on which it was agreed that she should spend six
months in the year with Pluto and six months with Ceres. The story of the

R

who art the lowest form of our Hecate[1], through whom the
ghosts and I[2] have the intercourse of silent tongues ; *thou*
porter, too[3], of the spacious abodes, who dost scatter our
entrails before the savage dog; and *you*, Sisters, about to
handle the threads[4] renewed, and thou, O ferryman of the
burning stream, now, aged man, tired with the ghosts returning to me ; listen to my prayers, if you sufficiently I
invoke with mouth accursed and defiled, if, never fasting
from human entrails, I repeat these charms, if full oft I
have given you the teeming breasts, and have smothered
your offerings[5] with warm brains ; if any infant, when I
have placed its head and entrails on your dishes, had been
destined to live[6]; listen to my entreaty.   A soul we ask
for, that has not lain hid in the caves of Tartarus, and
accustomed long to darkness, *but* one *just* descending, the

rape of Proserpine is related in the Fasti of Ovid, B. iv. l. 389-620, and in
the Metamorphoses, B. v. l. 537, *et seq.*

[1] *Lowest form of our Hecate*) ver. 700. "Pars ultima." The meaning of
this passage has caused much discussion, but it seems to imply that Proserpine is the third form or aspect of the Goddess called Hecate on earth, and
probably Diana in heaven. By the use of the word "nostræ" the sorceress
seems to imply that she worships the infernal Goddess Proserpine under
the name of Hecate. Ovid, in the Metamorphoses, B. vii., represents her as
the daughter of Perses, who, according to Diodorus Siculus, was the son of
Phœbus and the brother of Æetes ; and as, on marrying her uncle, the
mother of Circe, Medea, and Absyrtus. This person, however, can hardly
be considered identical with the Goddess who, under the form of Hecate,
was considered the patroness of magic.

[2] *Through whom the ghosts and I*) ver. 701. Who aids her in receiving
the secret communications from the ghosts of the dead.

[3] *Thou porter, too*) ver. 702. This passage has caused much discussion ;
but it seems most probable that the "janitor" or "porter" of hell here alluded to is Mercury, whose office it was to deliver over the bodies of the
dead to Cerberus, the three-headed dog, stationed at the entrance of hell,
whose name, according to some, was derived from χριῶν βορὰ, "feeding upon
flesh."

[4] *About to handle the threads*) ver. 703. She addresses the Fates, who are
about to spin the threads of existence over again for the person whose body
is going to be restored to life.

[5] *Have smothered your offerings*) ver. 709. Those parts of the animals
which were burnt on the altars of the Gods were called "prosiciæ," "pro-
secta," or "ablegmina."

[6] *Had been destined to live*) ver. 710. She means, if she has torn away
any infant from the womb for sacrifice to her, which otherwise might have
lived.

light but lately withdrawn; *and which* still delays at the
very chasm of pallid Orcus. Although it may listen to
these spells, it shall come to the shades once again[1]. Let
the ghost of one but lately our soldier repeat the destinies
of Pompey to the son of the chieftain, if the civil warfare
deserves well at your hands."

When, having said these things, she lifted up her head
and her foaming lips, she beheld the ghost of the extended
corpse standing by, dreading the lifeless limbs and the hated
place of its former confinement. It was dreading to go into
the gaping breasts, and the entrails torn with a deadly wound.
Ah wretch! from whom unrighteously the last privilege of
death is snatched, to be able to die [2]! Erictho is surprised
that this delay has been permitted by the Fates, and, enraged
with death, with living serpents she beats the unmoved
body; and through the hollow clefts of the earth, which
with her charms she opens, she barks forth to the shades
below, and breaks the silence of the realms :—

"Tisiphone, and Megæra[3], heedless of my voice, are ye
not driving the wretched soul with your ruthless whips
through the void space of Erebus? This moment under
your real name[4] will I summon you forth, and, Stygian
bitches, will leave you in the light of the upper world;
amid graves will I follow you, amid funereal rites, your
watcher; from the tombs will I expel you, from all the urns
will I drive you away. And thee, Hecate, squalid with thy
pallid form, will I expose to the Gods, before whom in false
shape with other features thou art wont to come, and I will
forbid thee to conceal the visage of Erebus. I will disclose,
damsel of Enna[5], under the boundless bulk of the earth,

---

[1] *Shall come to the shades once again*) ver. 716.   She promises that
when the reanimated corpse shall have done what she wishes, the spirit shall
return to the shades once for all.

[2] *To be able to die*) ver. 725.   " Non posse mori;" the "non" is redundant
here.

[3] *Tisiphone, and Megæra*) ver. 730.   Tisiphone, Alecto, and Megæra were
the names of the three Eumenides or Furies.

[4] *Under your real name*) ver. 732.   She will not call them Eumenides or
Erinnys, by which names they were usually called among mortals, but will
call them by the titles used in incantations, " Stygian bitches."

[5] *Damsel of Enna*) ver. 740.   He calls Proserpine " Ennæa," because she
was carried off by Pluto on the plains of Enna in Sicily.   The story was

what feasts are detaining thee, upon what compact thou dost love the gloomy sovereign. to what corruption having submitted, thy parent was unwilling to call thee back[1].

"Against thee, most evil ruler of the world[2], into thy burst caverns will I send the sun[3], and with sudden daylight thou shalt be smitten. Are you going to obey? Or will he have to be addressed, by whom never, when named[4], the shaken earth fails to tremble[5], who beholds the Gorgon exposed to view[6], and with his stripes chastises the quailing Erinnys, who occupies *depths of* Tartarus by you unseen; in whose power you are[7], ye Gods above; who by the Stygian waves forswears."[8]

Forthwith the clotted blood grows warm, and nourishes the blackened wounds, and runs into the veins and the extremities of the limbs. Smitten beneath the cold breast, the lungs palpitate: and a new life creeping on is mingled with the marrow *so lately* disused. Then does every joint throb; the sinews are stretched: and not by degrees throughout the limbs does the dead body lift itself from the earth, and it is spurned by the ground, and raised erect at the same

that on arriving in the Infernal regions she ate the grains of a pomegranate, on which Jupiter forbade her return from hell without the sanction of Pluto. See the Note to l. 699 and the passage of Ovid there referred to.

[1] *Was unwilling to call thee back*) ver. 742. "Why thy parent Ceres was unwilling (or, rather, unable) to procure thy return to the world above."

[2] *Most evil ruler of the world*) ver. 743. She calls Pluto the "pessimus arbiter mundi;" the most evil sharer in the world, in allusion to the dismal regions of hell falling to his share.

[3] *Will I send the sun*) ver. 743. Titana. Literally "Titan," one of the epithets of the Sun.

[4] *By whom never, when named*) ver. 745. He probably alludes to the terrible God Demogorgon, who is mentioned in the Note to l. 497. One of the Scholiasts says that he was the first and most powerful of the Gods, and was the father of Omago, Omago of Coelus, and Coelus of Saturn. Demiurgus was another name of this mysterious Divinity.

[5] *The shaken earth fails to tremble*) ver. 746. On the very mention of whose name earthquakes ensue.

[6] *Who beholds the Gorgon exposed to view*) ver. 746. It was the fate of all who looked upon the head of the Gorgon Medusa to be changed into stone: from this the God here alluded to alone was exempt.

[7] *In whose power you are*) ver. 748. "Cujus vos estis." Literally "whose" or "of whom you are."

[8] *By the Stygian waves forswears*) ver. 749. Who is not afraid to swear falsely by the river Styx, a thing which the other Gods dread to do.

instant. The eyes with their apertures distended wide are opened. In it not as yet is there the face of one living, *but* of one now dying. His paleness and his stiffness remain, and, brought back to the world, he is astounded. But his sealed lips resound with no murmur. A voice and a tongue to answer alone are granted unto him.

"Tell me," says the Thessalian *witch*, "for a great reward, what I command *thee*; for, having spoken the truth, by the Hæmonian arts I will set thee free in all ages of the world; with such a sepulchre *will I grace* thy limbs, with such wood will I burn them with Stygian spells, that thy charmed ghost shall hearken to no magicians. Of such great value be it to have lived once again; neither charms nor drugs shall presume to take away from thee the sleep of Lethe prolonged [1], death being bestowed by me. Obscure responses befit the tripods and the prophets of the Gods; well assured he may depart whoever asks the truth of the shades, and boldly approaches the oracles of relentless death. Spare not, I pray. Give things their names, give the places, give the words by which the Fates may converse with me."

She added a charm as well, by which she gave the ghost the power to know whatever she consulted him upon. Sad, the tears running down, the corpse *thus* said :—

"Called back from the heights of the silent shores I surely have not seen the sad threads of the Destinies ; but, what from all the shades it has been allowed me to learn, fierce discord agitates the Roman ghosts [2], and impious arms disturb the rest of hell. Coming from different spots, some chieftains have left the Elysian abodes, and some the gloomy Tartarus; what fate is preparing these have disclosed. Sad was the countenance of the spirits of the blessed. The Decii [3] I beheld, both son and father, the souls that expiated the warfare, and Camillus weeping [4], and the Curii [5];

---

[1] *Sleep of Lethe prolonged*) ver. 769. Lethe was one of the rivers of hell ; the waters of which being drunk induced forgetfulness.

[2] *Discord agitates the Roman ghosts*) ver. 780. Even the shades of the Romans are at discord among themselves, belonging to the different factions.

[3] *The Decii*) ver. 785. See B. ii. l. 308, and the Note to the passage.

[4] *And Camillus weeping*) ver. 786. See B. xi. l. 545, and the Note to the passage.

And the Curii) ver. 787. See B. i. l. 169.

Sulla, too, Fortune, complaining of thee[1]. Scipio is deploring his hapless descendant[2], doomed to perish in the Libyan lands. The elder Cato, the foe of Carthage[3], bemoans the destiny of his nephew who will not be a slave.

" Thee, Brutus, first Consul, the tyrants expelled[4], alone rejoicing did I behold among the pious shades. Threatening Catiline, his chains burst asunder and broken, exults, the fierce Marii, too, and the Cethegi with their bared arms[5]. I beheld the Drusi exulting, names beloved by the populace[6]; the Gracchi, exorbitant with their laws, and who dared such mighty exploits. Hands, bound with the eternal knots of iron, and in the dungeon of Dis, clap in applause, and the guilty multitude demands the fields of the blessed. The possessor of the empty realms is opening the pallid abodes, and is sharpening rocks torn off, and adamant hard with its chains, and is preparing punishment for the conqueror. Take back with thee, O youth, this comfort, that in their placid retreat the shades await thy father and thy house, and in the serene quarter of the realms are preparing room for Pompey.

[1] *Fortune, complaining of thee*) ver. 787. He alludes to the successful career of Sulla, who attributed his prosperity to the Goddess Fortuna, and took the name of Felix after the death of the younger Marius, and called his son Faustus and his daughter Fausta. He complains of Fortune because the Patrician faction which he had headed is being worsted by the arms of Cæsar.

[2] *Deploring his hapless descendant*) ver. 788. "Scipio Africanus the elder deplores the fate of his descendant Metellus Scipio, who is doomed to fall by the sword in Africa." See the Note to l. 311.

[3] *Elder Cato, the foe of Carthage*) ver. 789. Cato, the Censor, or the Elder, the implacable enemy of Carthage, is grieved for the destiny of his great grandson Porcius Cato, who is doomed to fall by his own sword at Utica. See l. 311 and B. ii. l. 238.

[4] *First Consul, the tyrants expelled*) ver. 791. L. Junius Brutus, the first Consul, on the expulsion of the Tarquins, is alone glad, inasmuch as the tyrant Cæsar is destined to fall, and in part by means of his descendants Marcus and Decius Brutus.

[5] *The Cethegi with their bared arms*) ver. 794. See B. ii. l. 543, and the Note to the passage.

[6] *The Drusi exulting, names beloved by the populace*) ver. 795. He probably alludes to M. Livius Drusus, who, to conciliate the Roman populace, renewed several of the propositions and imitated the measures of the Gracchi. He proposed and carried laws for the distribution of corn, or for its sale at a low price, and for the assignment of the public lands.

"And let not the glory of a short life cause thee anxiety; the hour will come that is to mingle all chieftains *alike*. Make ye haste to die, and proud with *your* high spirit go down though from humble graves, and tread under foot the ghosts of Romans deified[1]. It is sought to know which tomb the wave of the Nile, *and* which *that* of the Tiber is to wash, and only is the combat among the chieftains as to[2] their place of burial. Seek not thou to know thy own destiny; the Fates, while I am silent, will declare; a prophet more sure, Pompey himself, thy sire, will declare all things to thee[3] in the Sicilian fields; he, too, uncertain whither he shall invite thee, whence warn thee away, what regions to bid thee avoid, what Constellations of the world. Wretched *men*, dread Europe, and Libya, and Asia[4]; according to your triumphs[5] does Fortune distribute *your* sepulchres. O wretched house, nothing throughout the whole earth wilt thou behold more safe than Emathia."[6]

After he has thus revealed the Fates, gloomy with speechless features he stands, and demands death once again. Magic incantations are needed, and drugs, that the carcase may fall, and the Fates are unable to restore the soul to themselves, the law *of hell* now once broken. Then, with plenteous wood she builds up a pile; the dead man comes to the fires; the youth placed upon the lighted heap

---

[1] *The ghosts of Romans deified*) ver. 809. He alludes to the deification of Julius Cæsar, the victorious opponent of Pompey, and that of the Roman Emperors his successors. This line must certainly have been penned in a hostile spirit towards the Emperor Nero.

[2] *Is the combat among the chieftains as to*) ver. 811. This is somewhat similar to the line in Gray's Elegy:—
"The paths of glory lead but to the grave."

[3] *Will declare all things to thee*) ver. 814. He probably alludes to a future scene which was to have been depicted in his Poem, in which Pompey was to appear to his son Sextus in his Sicilian campaign, and warn him of his approaching destruction: the Poem being unfinished comes to an end long antecedent to that period.

[4] *Dread Europe, and Libya, and Asia*) ver. 817. The meaning is, "Your father shall die in Egypt in Africa, your brother at Munda in Spain, and you yourself at Miletus in Asia Minor."

[5] *According to your triumphs*) ver. 818. Pompey the elder enjoyed triumphs for his campaign against Sertorius in Spain, against Mithridates in Asia Minor, and for his successes in Egypt.

[6] *More safe than Emathia*) ver. 819. "From Thessaly you will escape alive, from other regions you will not."

Erictho leaves, permitting him at length to die; and she
goes attending Sextus to his father's camp.

The heavens wearing the aspect of light, until they
brought their footsteps safe within the tents, the night,
commanded to withhold the day[1], afforded its dense shades.

---

[1] *Commanded to withhold the day*) ver. 830.   The meaning is, that the
night was prolonged by Erictho, that Sextus might have time to return to his
father's camp unobserved.

BOOK THE SEVENTH.

CONTENTS.

NEVER more tardy from the ocean than the eternal laws demand, did mournful Titan speed on his steeds along the heavens; and he checked his chariot, as the skies whirled him along. He was both ready to endure eclipse, and the grievance of light withdrawn; and he attracted clouds, not as food for his flames[1], but lest he might shine serenely upon the regions of Thessaly.

But the night, the last portion of fortunate existence for Magnus, deceived his anxious slumbers with vain prospects For he seemed to himself, in the seat of the Pom-

---

[1] *Not as food for his flames*) ver. 5. It was the notion of some of the ancient philosophers, and particularly of Heraclitus and the Stoics, that the heat of the sun was nourished by the moisture of the clouds.

peian Theatre[1], to behold forms innumerable of the commonalty of Rome, and his own name raised with joyous
voices to the stars, and the resounding tiers[2] contending
in applause. Such were the looks and the shouts of the
applauding populace, when formerly, a young man, and at
the period of his first triumph, after the nations which
the rushing Iberus surrounds were subdued, and the arms
which the flying Sertorius[3] urged on, the West having been
reduced to peace, revered as much in his white toga[4] as in
that which adorned the chariot, the Senate giving applause,
he sat, as yet but a Roman knight.

Whether, at the end of successes, anxious for the future,
sleep flew back to joyous times, or whether, prophesying
by its wonted perversions, things contrary to what is seen,
it bore the omens of great woe; or whether to thee, forbidden any more to behold thy paternal abodes, Fortune in
this fashion presented Rome. Break not his slumbers, *ye*
sentinels of the camp; let no trumpet resound in his ears.
The rest of the morrow, direful, and saddened with the
image of the day, will from every quarter bring the blood-

---

[1] *In the seat of the Pompeian Theatre*) ver. 9. Pompey erected the first
stone Theatre at Rome, near the Campus Martius. It was of great magnificence and was built after the model of that of Mitylene in the isle of Lesbos,
but on a much larger scale, as it was able to contain 40,000 persons.

[2] *And the resounding tiers*) ver. 11. " Cuneos," literally " wedges." The
tiers or sets of seats in the theatres of Greece and Rome were divided into
a number of compartments, which converging, resembled cones from which
the tops are cut off; hence they were termed κερκίδες, and in Latin " cunei,"
or " wedges." It was the custom for the populace to applaud such of the
great as were their favourites on their entrance into the theatre. Plutarch
relates that the night before the battle of Pharsalia Pompey dreamed that as
he went into the theatre the people received him with great applause, and
that he himself was adorning the Temple of Venus Victrix, or " the Victorious," with spoils. He was partly encouraged and partly disheartened
by this dream; but the latter feeling was predominant, inasmuch as he feared
lest the adorning a place consecrated to Venus should be performed by Cæsar
with the spoils taken from himself, who boasted of being descended from that
Goddess through the line of Iulus or Ascanius.

[3] *The arms which the flying Sertorius*) ver. 16. In allusion to his triumph
over Sertorius, the leader of the Marian party in Spain. See B. ii. l. 549,
and the Note to the passage, and the Note to B. vii. l. 25.

[4] *In his white toga*) ver. 17. The white toga, or the " toga pura," was
worn by the Senators in the time of peace, while a robe of purple covered with
embroidery was worn by the victorious general in the triumphal chariot.
The family of Pompey was of the Equestrian order.

stained ranks, from every side the war. Whence canst thou *then* obtain the slumbers of the populace[1] and a happy night? O blessed, if even thus thy Rome could behold thee!

Would that, Magnus, the Gods of heaven had granted a single day to thy country and to thee, on which either, assured of destiny, might have enjoyed the last blessing of affection so great[2]. Thou goest as though destined to die[3] in the Ausonian city. She, conscious to herself of her assured wishes in behalf of thee, has not believed that this evil ever existed in destiny; that thus she is to lose the tomb even of Magnus. Thee, with mingling griefs, would both old men and youths have bewailed, and the child untaught. The female throng, their locks dishevelled, would, as at the funeral of Brutus[4], have torn their breasts. Now even, although they may fear the darts of the unscrupulous victor, although Cæsar himself may bring word of thy death, they will weep; but, while they are bringing frankincense, while laurel wreaths to the Thunderer[5]. O wretched *people*, whose groans devour their griefs! who equally lament thee in the Theatre no longer full!

The sunbeams had conquered the stars, when, with the

---

[1] *Obtain the slumbers of the populace*) ver. 28. "Unde pares somnos populi, noctemque beatam?" The Commentators are at variance as to what is the meaning of this line, and it is undecided whether "pares" is a verb or an adjective, and whether the sentence should be read with or without a note of interrogation. It seems, however, most likely that "pares" is a verb; in which case the sentence may either mean "How, Pompey, are you to enjoy in future the placid slumbers common to the lower classes?" or, "How, Pompey, are you to provide placid slumbers for your harassed country?"

[2] *The last blessing of affection so great*) ver. 32. "Would that, aware of your approaching end, the Fates had granted one day on which you and the Roman populace might have bid each other an eternal farewell."

[3] *As though destined to die*) ver. 33. That is, "in your present dream."

[4] *As at the funeral of Brutus*) ver. 39. The matrons of Rome mourned a whole year for Lucius Junius Brutus, the avenger of Lucretia, who expelled the Tarquins from the city.

[5] *Laurel wreaths to the Thunderer*) ver. 42. "They will now weep for you though forced to carry frankincense and garlands to the Capitol in honor of the triumph of the victorious Cæsar." The Poet covertly implies the lawlessness of which Cæsar will be guilty in insisting upon a triumph for a victory gained in civil war, contrary to the laws of his country, which expressly forbade it.

mingled murmur of the camps the multitude resounded, and, the Fates dragging on the world *to ruin*, demanded the signal for combat. The greatest part of the wretched throng, not destined to behold the day throughout, murmurs around the very tent of the general, and, inflamed, with vast tumult, urges on the speeding hours of approaching death. Direful frenzy arises; each one desires to precipitate his own destinies and those of the state. Pompey is called slothful and timorous, and too sparing of his father-in-law, and attached to his sway of the world[1], in desiring to have at the same moment so many nations from every part under his own control, and being in dread of peace. Still more, both the kings and the eastern nations, too, complain that the war is prolonged, and that they are detained at a distance from their native land.

Is it your pleasure, O Gods of heaven, when it is your purpose to overthrow all things, to add to our errors *this* crime[2]? We rush on upon slaughter, and arms that are to injure *ourselves* we demand. In the camp of Pompey, Pharsalia is an object of desire! Tullius, the greatest author of Roman eloquence, beneath whose rule and *Consular* toga the fierce Catiline trembled at the axes[3], producers of peace, enraged with the warfare, while he longed for the Rostra and the Forum, having, as a soldier, submitted to a silence

---

[1] *And attached to his sway of the world*) ver. 54. Pompey was accused of being too fond of his sway over monarchs gathered from all regions of the world, and unwilling to bring the contest to a conclusion. We learn from Plutarch and Appian that on this occasion he was styled "Agamemnon," and the "King of kings." Cæsar, in his account of the Civil War, B. iii. c. 82, confirms the present statement of Lucan. "The forces of Pompey, being thus augmented by the troops of Scipio, their former expectations were confirmed, and their hopes of victory so much increased, that whatever time intervened was considered as so much delay to their return to Italy; and whenever Pompey was acting with slowness and caution, they used to exclaim that it was the business only of a single day, but that he had a passion for power, and was delighted in having persons of Consular and Prætorian rank in the number of his slaves."

[2] *To add to our errors this crime*) ver. 59. "Is it your determination that, in addition to the fatality which decrees our downfall, we shall be guilty of perverseness amounting to criminality?"

[3] *Catiline trembled at the axes*) ver. 64. He alludes to the part which Cicero, then Consul, took in quelling Catiline's conspiracy. It was in a great measure by his prudence that it was suppressed.

so prolonged, reported the language of all.   Eloquence
added its powers[1] to the feeble cause :—

    " Fortune requests this only of thee, Magnus, in return
for favours so numerous, that thou wilt be ready to make
use of her; both we, the nobles in thy camp, and thy kings,
with the suppliant world pressing around thee, entreat that
thou wilt permit thy father-in-law to be overcome.   Shall
Cæsar for so long a time be cause of war[2] to mankind?
With reason is it distasteful to nations subdued *by thee* when
speeding past them, that Pompey should be slow in victory.
Whither has thy spirit fled, or where *is* thy confidence in
destiny?   Dost thou have apprehensions, ungrateful man,
as to the Gods of heaven?   And dost thou hesitate to trust
the cause of the Senate to the Deities?

    " The troops themselves will tear up thy standards, and
will spring forward *to the combat.*   Let it shame thee to
have conquered by compulsion.   If by thee *as* our appointed
leader, if by us wars are waged, be it their right to meet
upon whatever field they please.   Why dost thou avert the
swords of the *whole* world from the blood of Cæsar?   Hands
are brandishing weapons; with difficulty does each await the
delaying standards; make haste that thy own trumpet-call
may not forsake thee.   Magnus, the Senate long to know[3]

---

[1] *Eloquence added its powers*) ver. 67.   It has been generally supposed
by the learned that during Cicero's residence in the camp of Pompey he was
in declining health, affected with low spirits, and in the habit of inveighing
against everything that was going on there, and giving way to the deepest
despondency.   A knowledge that this was the case may possibly have caused
Lucan to represent him as one of those who urged Pompey, against his own
inclination, to fight the battle of Pharsalia; but it is the fact that he really
was not present at that battle.

[2] *De cause of war*) ver. 72.   " Bellum" has here the meaning of "a cause
of warfare."

[3] *The Senate long to know*) ver. 84–5.   " Scire Senatus avet, miles te,
Magne, sequatur. An comes."   This passage admits of two modes of interpretation :—" The Senate wishes to know whether you think that you have
despotic sway over them, and that they are only your obedient soldiers, or
whether you look upon them as your equals and sharers in the command."
This is the old interpretation, but Lemaire suggests another, which seems
much more consistent with probability: " Do you look upon the Senators as
soldiers who have placed themselves under your command, ready to fight, or
merely as fellow travellers, forsooth, in your journey and flight from the
arms of Cæsar ?"

whether they are to follow thee as soldiers or whether as companions."

The leader groaned, and perceived that *this* was a subterfuge of the Gods, and that the Destinies were opposed to his own feelings.

" If this is the pleasure of all," he said ; " if the occasion requires Magnus as a soldier, not a general, no further will I delay the Fates. In one ruin let Fortune involve the nations, and let this day be to a large portion of mankind the very last. Still, Rome, I call thee to witness, that Magnus has received[1], the day on which all things came to ruin. The labour of the war might have cost thee no wound[2]; it might have delivered up the leader, subdued without slaughter and a captive, to violated peace[3]. What frenzy is this in crimes, O ye, blind *to fate?* Do they dread to wage a civil war, so as not to conquer with blood ? The earth we have wrested *from him*[4], from the whole ocean we have excluded *him;* his famishing troops we have compelled to premature rapine of the crops[5]; and in the enemy have we wrought the wish to prefer to be slaughtered with swords, and to mingle the deaths of his partisans with my own.

" A great part of the warfare has been accomplished in those *measures*, by which it has been brought about that the raw recruit is in no dread of the combat, if only under the excitement of valour and in the heat of resentment they demand the standards *to be raised.* The very fear of an evil about to come has committed many a one to extreme dangers. He is the bravest man, who, ready to endure what is deserving of fear, if it impends close at hand, can also defer it. Is it your pleasure to abandon this so pros-

[1] *That Magnus has received*) ver. 92. Has had this fatal day forced upon him by necessity, and has not sought it.

[2] *Might have cost thee no wound*) ver. 93. He means that the war might have been prolonged so as to weary out the enemy without any bloodshed.

[3] *Delivered up the leader to violated peace*) ver. 94. " Tradere paci," according to some of the Commentators, simply means " to reduce to peace " by subduing him; but Burmann thinks that it signifies " to immolate Cæsar as a victim to that peace which he has so wantonly violated."

[4] *The earth we have wrested from him*) ver. 97. He means the regions of the East, the richest part of the Roman provinces, which were favouring the cause of Pompey against Cæsar.

[5] *To premature rapine of the crops*) ver. 99. During the war in Epirus.

perous state of things to Fortune, to leave the hazard of
the world to the sword? They wish rather for their leader
to fight than to conquer. Fortune, thou hadst granted me
the Roman state to rule; receive it *still* greater, and protect
it amid the blindness of warfare.

" War will be neither the crime nor the glory of Pompey.
Before the Gods of heaven, thou dost conquer me, Cæsar, by
thy hostile prayers. The battle is *now* fought. What an
amount of crimes, and of evils an extent how vast will this day
bring upon nations! how many kingdoms will lie *in ruin!*
How turbid will Enipeus run[1] with Roman blood! I could
wish that the first dart of this lamentable warfare would strike
this head, if without the ruin of the state and the downfall
of the party, it were about to fall; for not more joyous to
Magnus *will* victory *prove.* To nations, this slaughter perpetrated, Pompey will be this day either a hated or a pitied
name[2]. Every woe that the allotted destiny of things shall
bring will belong to the conquered, to the conqueror every
crime."

Thus he speaks, and allows the combat to the nations,
and gives loose rein to them as they rage with anger; and
just as the mariner, overpowered by the boisterous Corus,
leaves the rudder to the winds, and, skill abandoned, a
sluggish burden, the ship is borne along. Confused, with
an anxious murmuring the camp resounds, and bold hearts
throb against their breasts with uncertain palpitations. On
the countenances of many is the paleness of approaching
death, and an aspect strongly indicating their destiny.
It is clear that the day is come, which is to bestow a fate
for everlasting upon human affairs, and it is manifest, that
in that combat it is sought what Rome is to be[3]. His
own dangers each man knows not, distracted with greater
fears.

Who, beholding the shores overwhelmed by sea, who,

---

[1] *How turbid will Enipeus run*) ver. 116. See B. vi. l. 373.

[2] *A hated or a pitied name*) ver. 120-1. "If I gain this victory it will
only be through the slaughter of my fellow citizens, and the nations who entrust their fortunes to me; if I am conquered, I myself am irretrievably
ruined."

[3] *Is sought what Rome is to be*) ver. 132. Whether it is destined to
remain a free republic, or is to become a monarchy under the sway of a
tyrant.

seeing the ocean on the summits of mountains, and the sky, the sun hurled down, falling upon the earth, the downfall of things so numerous, could feel fear for himself? There is no leisure to have apprehensions for one's self; for the City and for Magnus is the alarm.

Nor have they confidence in their swords, unless the points shine sharpened with the whetstone. Then is every javelin pointed against the rock; with better strings they tighten the bows; it is a care to fill the quivers with chosen arrows [1]. The horseman increases the spurs, and fits on the thongs of the reins. If it is lawful to compare the labours of men with the Gods of heaven, not otherwise, Phlegra supporting the furious Giants [2], did the sword of Mars grow warm upon the Sicilian anvils [3]; and a second time the trident of Neptune grew red with flames, and, Python lying prostrate, Pæan renewed his darts. Pallas scattered the locks of the Gorgon upon her Ægis, and the Cyclops moulded anew the Pallenæan thunderbolts of Jove [4].

Fortune, however, did not forbear by various marks to disclose the woes about to ensue. For while they were repairing to the Thessalian fields, the whole sky opposed them

[1] *To fill the quivers with chosen arrows*) ver. 142. The "pharetra," or quiver filled with arrows, was used by most of the ancient nations that excelled in archery, among whom were the Scythians, Persians, Lycians, Thracians, and Cretans. It was made of leather, and was sometimes adorned with gold and colours. It had a lid, and was suspended by a belt from the right shoulder. Its usual position was on the left hip, and it was thus worn by the Scythians and Egyptians. The Cretans, however, wore it behind the back, and Diana in her statue is represented as so doing.

[2] *Phlegra supporting the furious Giants*) ver. 145. See B. iv. l. 597, and the Note to the passage.

[3] *Grow warm upon the Sicilian anvils*) ver. 146. He alludes to the preparations which, previous to the battle of the Gods with the Giants, Vulcan and the Cyclops made at the forge which they had at Mount Ætna in Sicily. There they furbished the lance or sword ("ensis" may mean either) of Mars, the trident of Neptune, the arrows with which Pæan, or Apollo, had slain the serpent Python, the Ægis or shield of Minerva, on which was the head of the Gorgon Medusa, and the thunderbolts of Jupiter.

[4] *The Pallenæan thunderbolts of Jove*) ver. 150. So called because about to be employed at Pallene, which was more anciently called Phlegra, where this battle was said to have taken place. It was a Peninsula jutting out into the sea from Chalcidice in Macedonia. On the Isthmus which connected it with the main land stood the town of Potidæa.

as they come, and in the eyes of the men the lightnings
rent asunder the clouds; and torches meeting them, and
columns of immense flames, and *the sky* presented serpentine forms, greedy of the waves[1], with fiery meteors,
intermingled, and with hurled lightnings dimmed their
eyes. The crests it struck off from their helmets[2], and
dissolved the hilts of their melted swords, and liquefied
the darts torn away[3], and made the hurtful weapon to
smoke with sulphur from the skies.

Moreover, the standards, covered with swarms innumerable[4], and with difficulty torn up from the ground[5],
bowed the head of the standard-bearer, weighed down with
an unusual burden, soaking with tears, even as far as
Thessaly the standards of Rome and of the republic[6].
The bull, urged onward for the Gods above, flies from the
spurned altar, and throws himself headlong along the
Emathian fields; and for the sad rites no victim is found.

But thou, Cæsar, what heavenly Gods of criminality,
what Eumenides, didst thou with due ceremonials invoke[7]?

[1] *Serpentine forms, greedy of the waves*) ver. 156. "Pythoras aquarum"
probably means "water-spouts" assuming a serpentine shape.

[2] *The crests it struck off from their helmets*) ver. 158. The helmets of the
ancients were very commonly surmounted by crests of horse-hair. In the
Roman army the crest was not only used for ornament, but to distinguish
the different centuries, each of which wore one of a different colour.

[3] *And liquefied the darts torn away*) ver. 160. Most of these portentous
occurrences are related by Valerius Maximus as having happened to Pompey
in his march from Dyrrhachium to Thessaly; and, according to him, they
were so many warnings for him to avoid a battle with Cæsar.

[4] *Covered with swarms innumerable*) ver. 161. Weise takes "examen"
here to mean "flocks of birds;" but it is more probable that swarms of bees
are meant, which Valerius Maximus mentions on the same occasion as clinging
to the standards of Pompey's troops, B. i. c. 6.

[5] *With difficulty torn up from the ground*) ver. 162. The standards stuck
so fast in the ground that it was only with the utmost difficulty that they
were withdrawn from it, and then they were so weighty that the standard-
bearers were forced to incline their heads forwards in supporting them; they
were dripping, too, with water, as though weeping for the public calamities.

[6] *The standards of Rome and of the republic*) ver. 164. The word
"signa" is repeated in this line by the figura anaphora. They grieved because
hitherto they had been the standards of the whole Roman republic, whereas
in future they were doomed to serve in the cause of but one individual,
namely, Cæsar, and his successors.

[7] *What Eumenides didst thou invoke*) ver. 169. Lucan, with his usual hos-

What Deities of the Stygian realms, and *what* infernal
fiends, and monsters steeped in night, didst thou propitiate, so ruthlessly about to wage the impious warfare?
Now (*it is* matter of doubt whether they believed the portents of the Gods, or their own excessive fears), Pindus
seemed to many to meet with Olympus, and Hæmus to
sink in the deep valleys, Pharsalia to send forth by night
the din of warfare, flowing blood to run along Ossæan
Bœbeis[1]; and in turn they wondered at their features
being concealed amid gloom[2], and at the day growing
pale, and at night hovering over their helmets, and their
departed parents and all the ghosts of their kindred flitting
before their eyes. But to their minds this was one consolation, in that the throng, conscious of their wicked intentions,
who hoped for the throats of their fathers, who *longed for*
the breasts of their brothers, exulted in *these* portents and
the tumultuous feelings of their minds, and deemed the
sudden portents to be omens of their impious deeds.

What wonder, that nations, whom[3] the last day *of liberty*
was awaiting, trembled with frantic fear, if a mind fore
knowing woes is granted to mankind? The Roman, who, a

tility to Cæsar, implies that on the night before the battle he sacrificed to the
Infernal Deities; he is censured by Burmann for implying that the Gods
of heaven might sanction criminality, and for not knowing that victory was
never supposed to lie in the hands of the Infernal Deities. Appian, B. ii.
c. 116, informs us that in the middle of the night before the battle Cæsar
performed sacrifice, and invoked Mars, and Venus his ancestress, and vowed
a temple to Victory if he should gain the battle.

[1] *To run along Ossæan Bœbeis*) ver. 176. See B. vi. l. 382, and the Note
to the passage.

[2] *Being concealed amid gloom*) ver. 177. Florus, B. iv. c. 2, mentions the
deep gloom that came over in the middle of the day. Badius Ascensius
thinks that the following remarks of Lucan here apply to the partisans of
Cæsar; it is, however, pretty clear that he is censuring the Pompeian party
for their readiness to enter upon the civil strife.

[3] *What wonder, that nations, whom*) ver. 185-7. "Quid mirum, populos,
quos lux extrema manebat, Lymphato trepidàsse metu? præsaga malorum Si
data mens homini est." This passage admits of three modes of interpretation: "What wonder is it that people were alarmed who had now arrived
at the last day of their lives?" or, "What wonder if they were alarmed when
the waning light of liberty was forsaking them?" or, "What wonder if nations who saw the light at the extremities of the world had apprehensions at
that time of the scene of horror then acting in Thessaly?"

stranger, lies adjacent to Tyrian Gades[1], and he who drinks of Armenian Araxes[2], beneath whatever clime, beneath whatever Constellation of the universe *he is*, is sad, and is ignorant of the cause, and chides his flagging spirits; he knows not what he is losing on the Emathian plains. An augur, if *there is* implicit credit[3] *to be given* to those who relate it, sitting on the Euganean hill[4], where the steaming Aponus[5] arises from the earth, and the waters of Timavus of Antenor[6] are dispersed in various channels, exclaimed:— " The critical day is come, a combat most momentous is being waged, the impious arms of Pompey and of Cæsar are meeting." Whether *it was that* he marked the thunders and the presaging weapons of Jove, or beheld the whole sky and the poles standing still in the discordant heavens; or whether the saddening light in the sky pointed out the fight by the gloomy paleness of the sun.

The day of Thessaly undoubtedly did nature introduce unlike to all the days which she displays; if, universally, with the experienced augur, the mind of man had marked[7]

[1] *Adjacent to Tyrian Gades*) ver. 187. Gades, now Cadiz, in Spain, was said to have been a Phrygian or Tyrian colony.

[2] *Of Armenian Araxes*) ver. 188. See B. i. l. 19, and the Note to the passage.

[3] *If there is implicit credit*) ver. 192. He alludes to the story which is related by Plutarch and Aulus Gellius, B. xvi. c. 18, that on the day when the battle of Pharsalia was fought C. Cornelius, a celebrated soothsayer, was then at Patavium, and that, observing the portentous signs given by his science, he told those who were then standing by him that that very instant the battle was beginning; and then, turning again to the signs, he suddenly sprang forward as though inspired, and exclaimed, " Cæsar, thou hast conquered."

[4] *Sitting on the Euganean hill*) ver. 192. The Euganean Hills were near the city of Patavium, now Padua, in the north of Italy, which was said so have been founded by a people called the Euganei.

[5] *Where the steaming Aponus*) ver. 193. The Aponus or " Aponi Fons," "Aponian Springs," was a medicinal spring in the neighbourhood of Patavium, much valued for its healing qualities.

[6] *Timavus of Antenor*) ver. 194. Timavus is a stream now called Timavo or Friuli, forming the boundary between Istria and Venetia, and falling into the Sinus Tergestinus in the Adriatic or Gulf of Venice. Antenor, who fled from Troy with some Trojans, was said to have been the founder of Patavium.

[7] *The mind of man had marked*) ver. 203. " If mankind had been endowed with the augur's skill, they might have known by the signs prevalent throughout the world the contest that was then going on at Pharsalia."

the unusual phenomena of the heavens, Pharsalia might have been beheld by the whole world. O mightiest of men, the indications of whom Fortune afforded throughout the earth, to whose destinies all heaven had leisure to attend! These *deeds*, both among future nations and the races of your descendants, whether by their own fame alone they shall come down to remote ages, or whether the care of my labours is in any degree able as well to profit mighty names, when the wars shall be read of, will excite both hopes and fears, and wishes destined to be of no avail; and all, moved, shall read of thy fate as though approaching *and* not concluded, and still, Magnus, shall wish thee success.

The soldiers, when, gleamed upon by the opposite rays of Phœbus, descending, they have covered all the hills with *glittering* brightness, *are* not promiscuously sent forth upon the plains; in firm array stand the doomed ranks. To thee, Lentulus, is entrusted the care of the left wing[1], together with the first legion, which then was the best in war, and the fourth; to thee, Domitius[2], valiant, with the Deity adverse, is given the front of the army on the right. But the bravest troops redouble the strength of the centre of the battle, which, drawn forth from the lands of the Cilicians, Scipio commands[3], the chief commander in the

---

[1] *To thee, Lentulus, is entrusted the care of the left wing*) ver. 218. On the other hand, Appian assigns the right wing to Lentulus Spinther, and Plutarch to Pompey, while he gives the left to Domitius. Cæsar says, in the Civil War, B. iii. c. 88 :—" On the left wing were the two legions delivered over by Cæsar at the beginning of the disputes in compliance with the Senate's decree, one of which was called the first, the other the third. Here Pompey commanded in person." This is the more likely, as, from the strength of these legions, they would probably be placed opposite to Cæsar's strongest legion, the tenth, which was on his right.

[2] *To thee, Domitius*) ver. 220. This was L. Domitius Ahenobarbus, who had been taken and released by Cæsar at Corfinium, and had opposed his arms at Massilia; on both of which occasions, as here remarked, he had been singularly unfortunate.

[3] *Scipio commands*) ver. 223. This was Metellus Scipio, the father-in-law of Pompey, who had arrived a few days before with eight legions from Syria. Cæsar says, in the Civil War, B. iii. c. 88 :—" Scipio, with the Syrian legions, commanded the centre. The Cilician legion, in conjunction with the Spanish cohorts, which we said were brought over by Afranius, were disposed on the right wing. These Pompey considered his steadiest troops."

Libyan land[1], a soldier in this.   But near the streams and
the waters[2] of the flowing Enipeus, the mountain cohorts
of the Cappadocians[3], and the Pontic cavalry with their
loose reins[4], take their stand.

But most of the positions on the dry plain[5] Tetrarchs
and Kings[6] and mighty potentates held, and all the purple
which is obedient to the Latian sword.   Thither, too, did
Libya send her Numidians[7], and Crete her Cydonians[8];
thence was there a flight for the arrows of Ituræa[9]; thence,

[1] *In the Libyan land*) ver. 223.   After the death of Pompey, Scipio took
the command of the war in Africa.

[2] *But near the streams and the waters*) ver. 224.   The rest of the disposition
of Pompey's forces is thus stated by Cæsar, in the Civil War, B. iii. c. 88 :—
" The rest he had interspersed between the centre and the wing, and he had
a hundred and ten complete cohorts ; these amounted to forty-five thousand
men.   He had, besides, two cohorts of volunteers, who, having received favours from him in former wars, flocked to his standard ; these were dispersed
through his whole army.   The seven remaining cohorts he had disposed to
protect his camp and the neighbouring forts.   His right wing was secured by
a river with steep banks; for which reason he placed all his cavalry, archers,
and slingers on his left wing."

[3] *Mountain cohorts of the Cappadocians*) ver. 225.   The Cappadocians
from Asia Minor were commanded by their king, Ariobarzanes.   See B. ii.
l. 344, and the Note to the passage.   It is not known whether the epithet
"montana" is given to them from living in mountainous districts in their
native country, or from their being encamped on the hills near Pharsalia ;
most probably the former is the fact.

[4] *Pontic cavalry with their loose reins*) ver. 225.   "Largus habenæ."
These were the ancestors of the Cossacks of the present day, and seem to
have similarly excelled in horsemanship.

[5] *Positions on the dry plain*) ver. 226.   "Sicci ;" meaning that part of
the plain which was at a distance from the river.

[6] *Tetrarchs and Kings*) ver. 227.   A Tetrarch was originally one who had
the fourth part of a kingdom to govern; hence the word came to be applied
to small potentates, who, though enjoying regal dignity and power, were not
considered worthy of the name of " Rex," or " King."

[7] *Libya send her Numidians*) ver. 229.   The subjects of Juba, the ally
of Pompey.

[8] *And Crete her Cydonians*) ver. 229.   Cydonis, or Cydon, was one of
the principal cities of the isle of Crete, on the north-west coast of which it
was situate.   The inhabitants were among the most skilful archers of Crete ;
and it was the first place from which quinces were brought to Rome, which
were thence called "mala Cydonia," afterwards corrupted into " Melicotone,"
the old English name of the fruit.

[9] *For the arrows of Ituræa*) ver. 230.   The country of Ituræa was situate
on the north-eastern border of Palestine.   Its people were of the Arab race,
and of warlike and predatory habits.   Pompey had recently reduced them,

fierce Gauls, did you[1] sally forth against your wonted foe;
there did Iberia wield her contending bucklers[2] Tear
from the victor the nations[3], Magnus, and, the blood of the
world spilt at one moment, cut short *for him* all triumphs.

On that day, by chance, his position being left, Cæsar,
about to move his standards for foraging in the standing
corn[4], suddenly beholds the enemy descending into the level
plains, and sees the opportunity presented to him, a thousand
times asked for in his prayers, upon which he is to submit
everything to the last chance. For, sick of delay, and
burning with desire for rule, he had begun, in *this* short space
of time, to condemn the civil war as slow-paced wickedness.

in a great degree, under the Roman rule, and many of their warriors entered
the Roman army, in which they distinguished themselves by their skill in
archery and horsemanship. They were not, however, reduced to complete
subjection to Rome till after the Civil Wars.

[1] *Thence, fierce Gauls, did you*) ver. 231. Burmann thinks that the Galatians of Asia Minor are here referred to, who were said to be descendants of
the people of Gaul, and were aiding Pompey under their aged king Deiotarus.
It is, however, more probable, from the allusion to their "wonted foe,"
that the Allobroges are alluded to, the desertion of two of whom to Pompey,
Roscillus and Ægus, is mentioned by Cæsar in the Civil War, B. iii. c. 59-
61. He says that they went over " with a great retinue."

[2] *Wield her contending bucklers*) ver. 232. The "cetra" was a target or
small round shield, made of the hide of a quadruped. It was worn by the
people of Spain (as here mentioned) and of Mauritania. By the latter
people it was sometimes made from the skin of the elephant. As Tacitus
mentions the " cetra " as being used by the Britons, it is probably the same
with the " target " used by the Highlanders of Scotland.

[3] *Tear from the victor the nations*) ver. 233. By causing the blood to be
shed of so many nations, leave none for Cæsar to triumph over.

[4] *For foraging in the standing corn*) ver. 236. Cæsar thus relates the
circumstances here alluded to, in the Civil War, B. iii. c. 75 :—" Cæsar,
seeing no likelihood of being able to bring Pompey to an action, judged it
the most expedient method of conducting the war, to decamp from that post,
and to be always in motion : with this hope, that by shifting his camp and
removing from place to place, he might be more conveniently supplied with
corn, and also, that by being in motion he might get some opportunity of
forcing them to battle, and, by constant marches, harass Pompey's army,
which was not accustomed to fatigue. These matters being settled, when
the signal for marching was given, and the tents struck, it was observed that
shortly before, contrary to his daily practice, Pompey's army had advanced
further than usual from his entrenchments, so that it appeared possible to
come to an action on even ground." According to another account, Cæsar
had sent out three legions the night before, to forage, which, on perceiving
Pompey's advance, he forthwith recalled.

After he saw the fates of the chieftains drawing nigh,
and the closing combat *at hand*, and perceived the falling
ruins of destiny tottering, this frenzy even, most eager for
the sword, flagged in a slight degree, and his mind, which
his own fortunes did not permit to fear, nor *those* of Magnus
to hope, bold to engage for a prosperous result, hesitated
in suspense[1]. Fear thrown aside, confidence sprang up,
better suited for encouraging the ranks :—

"O soldiers, subduers of the world[2], the stay of my fortunes[3], the opportunity for the fight so oft desired is come.
No need is there for prayers ; now hasten your destinies by
the sword. You have in your own power how mighty Cæsar
is to prove. This is that day which I remember being promised me[4] at the waves of Rubicon, in hope of which
we took up arms, to which we deferred the return of our
forbidden triumphs[5]. This is that same which is this day[6]
to restore *our* pledges, and which *is to give us back our*
household Gods, and, your period of service completed, is to

[1] *Hesitated in suspense*) ver. 247-8. His own previous successes will
not allow him to despair, while those of Pompey will not allow him to hope
for the victory.

[2] *O soldiers, subduers of the world*) ver. 250. Cæsar, in the Civil War,
B. iii. c. 85, gives the following account of the first of his two brief speeches
on this occasion :—" Cæsar addressed himself to his soldiers, when they were
at the gates of the camp, ready to march out. ' We must defer,' said he,
' our march at present, and set our thoughts on battle, which has been our
constant wish : let us, then, meet the foe with resolute minds. We shall
not hereafter easily find such an opportunity.'" This betokens none of the
hesitation which the Poet ascribes to Cæsar on the present occasion.

[3] *The stay of my fortunes*) ver. 250. Conquerors of those regions comprehended under the names of Gaul, Hispania, and part of Britain and of
Germany. Appian, in the speech which he attributes to Cæsar on the
present occasion, makes him refer to the four hundred nations which he, by
his victories, had added to the Roman sway.

[4] *Which I remember being promised me*) ver. 255. Promised by Lælius,
the Tribune, and assented to by the shouts of the whole army. See B. i.
l. 359, *et seq.*, and l. 388, *et seq.*

[5] *The return of our forbidden triumphs*) ver. 256. "The triumph over
the conquered Gauls, which the jealousy of Pompey and the Senate has not
hitherto allowed us to enjoy."

[6] *That same which is this day*) ver. 257-8. "This is the day which will
restore us who have been banished and declared the enemies of our country
to our homes and our wives and children, to which we have been forbidden
to return, and will be the means of procuring for you allotments of land, on
which, as cultivators, discharged from war (emeriti), you will be enabled to
settle."

make you tillers of the land. This *the day*, which, fate being
the witness, is to prove who the most righteously has taken
up arms ; this battle is destined to make the conquered the
guilty one.

"If for me with sword and with flames you have attacked
your country, now fight valiantly, and absolve your swords
from blame. No hand, the judge of the warfare being
changed[1], is guiltless. Not my fortunes are at stake, but
that you yourselves may be a free people do I pray, that
you may hold sway over all nations. I, myself, anxious to
surrender myself to a private station, and to settle myself *as
an humble citizen in a plebeian toga*[2], refuse to be nothing[3]
until all *this* is granted to you. With the blame my own do
you obtain the sway. And with no great bloodshed do you
aspire to the hope of the world : a band of youths selected
from the Grecian wrestling schools, and *rendered* effeminate
by the pursuits of the places of exercise[4], will be before you,
and wielding their arms with difficulty; the discordant barbarism, too, of a mingled multitude, that will not be able
to endure the trumpets, nor, the army moving on, their
own shouts. But few hands *with them*[5] will be waging a

[1] *The judge of the warfare being changed*) ver. 263. Meaning that neither
side is guiltless, if it has its adversary as the judge of its conduct.

[2] *An humble citizen in a plebeian toga*) ver. 267. He is ready to resign
the Consulship, and with it the "toga prætexta," which was the garment worn
by the magistrates, and assume the "toga plebeia," or garment worn by
private persons in time of peace.

[3] *Refuse to be nothing*) ver. 268. "Nihil esse recuso." There have been
two meanings suggested for these words. That adopted by Marmontel and
some of the Commentators is, "So long as I obtain for you your rights,
there is nothing that I would refuse to be." The other, which seems the
more probable, is, "In order that I may gain your liberty for you, I do
refuse to be as nothing," *i. e.*, to be trodden under foot by the Senate, or to
be treated like a private person.

[4] *By the pursuits of the places of exercise*) ver. 271. "Palæstræ." He
means that, compared with the real hardships which his own veterans have
undergone, the exercises of the Grecian "palæstræ" and "gymnasia" have but
tended to render the partisans of Pompey less hardy. The "palæstræ" were
places of exercise, probably intended for such as were about to contend in the
public games, while the "gymnasia" were for the use of the public in general.
It has, however, been suggested that the "palæstræ" were for the use of the
boys and youths, while the "gymnasia" were intended for the men.

[5] *But few hands with them*) ver. 274. Notwithstanding this remark, it is
most probable that by far the greater part of Pompey's army consisted of
Roman citizens, as it is solely by poetic licence that Lucan represents

civil war; a great part of the combat will rid the earth of
these nations, and will break down the Roman foe. Go
onward amid dastard nations and realms known by report,
and with the first movement of the sword lay prostrate the
world; and let it be known that the nations which, so
numerous, Pompey at his chariot led into the City, are not
worth a single triumph [1].

"Does it concern the Armenians to what chieftain the
Roman sway belongs? Or does any barbarian wish to place
Magnus over the Hesperian state, purchased with the least
bloodshed? All Romans they detest, and most do they hate
the rulers whom they have known. But me Fortune has
entrusted to bands of whom Gaul has made me witness in
so many campaigns. Of which soldier shall I not recognize
the sword? And when a quivering javelin passes through
the air, I shall not be deceived in pronouncing by what arm
it has been poised. And if I behold the indications that
never deceived your leader, both stern faces and threatening
eyes, *then* have you proved the victors. Rivers of blood do
I seem to behold, and both Kings trodden under foot, and
the corpses of Senators scattered, and nations swimming
in boundless carnage.

"But I am delaying my own destinies in withholding you
by these words from rushing upon the weapons. Grant *me*
pardon for procrastinating the combat. I exult in hopes;
never have I beheld the Gods of heaven about to present
gifts so great, so close at hand for me; at the slight distance
of *this* plain are we removed from our wishes. I am he
who shall be empowered, the battle finished, to make dona-
tions of what nations and monarchs possess. By what
commotion in the skies, by what star of heaven turned
back, ye Gods above, do ye grant thus much to the Thessalian land?

"This day, either the reward of the warfare or the

Pompey's army as such a vast multitude. We find Cæsar, who had no
interest in underrating his numbers, representing them as forty-five thousand
men, and Plutarch, in the Life of Pompey, says that Cæsar's army consisted
of twenty-two thousand, and Pompey's, double that number.

[1] *Are not worth a single triumph*) ver. 280. "Show, by conquering them
all united with ease, that these nations, for the conquest of whom Pompey
has enjoyed so many triumphs, were not worthy of being the cause for a
single triumph even."

punishment is awarded. Behold the crosses for Cæsar's partisans[1]; behold the chains! this head, too, exposed on the Rostra[2], and *my* torn limbs, and the criminal doings at the voting-places[3], and the battles in the enclosed Plain *of Mars*. With a chieftain of Sulla's party are we waging civil war. It is care for you that moves me. For a lot, free from care, sought by my own hand, shall await myself; he who, the foe not yet subdued, shall look back, shall behold me piercing my own vitals. Ye Gods, whose care the earth and the woes of Rome have drawn down from the skies, let him conquer, who does not deem it necessary to unsheathe against the conquered the ruthless sword, and who does not think that his own fellow-citizens, because they have raised hostile standards, have committed a crime. When he enclosed your troops in a blockaded place, your valour forbidden to be employed, with how much blood[4] did Pompey glut the sword!

" Still, youths, this do I ask of you, that no one will be ready to smite the back of the foe; he who flies, let him be a fellow-citizen[5]. But while the darts are glittering, let not any fiction of affection, nor *even* parents beheld with adverse front, affect you ; mangle with the sword[6] the venerated fea-

[1] *The crosses for Cæsar's partisans*) ver. 305. "Cæsareas cruces ;" meaning the crosses erected with which to punish the adherents of Cæsar.

[2] *Exposed on the Rostra*) ver. 305. In the civil war between Marius and Sulla, the heads of those who were slain were exposed by the dominant party at the Rostra. Cicero's head and hands were placed there subsequently to this by his revengeful enemy, Antony.

[3] *The criminal doings at the voting-places*) ver. 306. "Septorumque nefas." See this allusion explained in the Note to B. ii. l. 197.

[4] *With how much blood*) ver. 317. We have already seen Lucan representing Pompey as leaving Dyrrhachium, and not pushing on his successes there, in consequence of his extreme unwillingness to shed the blood of his fellow-citizens. It is probably the fact that Pompey acted with neither any remarkable relentlessness nor humanity, but with more prudence than either, on that occasion. Of course, Lucan would not miss the opportunity of putting an untruth in the mouth of Cæsar.

[5] *Let him be a fellow-citizen*) ver. 319. Cæsar, long before this, had stated at Rome that he should treat those as his friends who should adopt neither party ; whereas Pompey, on leaving Rome, had declared that he should consider all such persons his enemies.

[6] *Mangle with the sword*) ver. 322. It is generally related by the historians that, on this occasion, Cæsar especially requested his soldiers to aim at the faces of Pompey's cavalry, who, being in a great measure composed of

tures. Whether one shall rush with hostile weapon against
a kinsman's breast, or whether with his wound he shall
violate no ties *of relationship*, let him attack the throat of an
unknown foe, just the same as *incurring* the criminality *of
slaughtering a relative*. Forthwith lay the ramparts low, and
fill up the trenches with the ruins, that in full maniples,
not straggling, the army may move on. Spare not the
camp; within those lines[1] shall you pitch your tents, from
which the army is coming doomed to perish."

Cæsar having hardly said all this[2], his duties attract each
one, and instantly *their* arms *are* taken up by the men.
Swiftly they forestall the presage of the war[3], and, *their* camp
trodden under foot, they rush on; in no order[4] do they

the young Patricians of Rome, would dread a scar on the face even more
than death itself.

[1] *Within those lines*) ver. 328. "You shall pitch your next tents within
the lines of the enemy." Appian represents Cæsar as saying on this occasion, "As you go forth to battle, pull down the ramparts and level the outworks, that we may be in possession of nothing but as conquerors. Let the
enemy themselves behold us destitute of a camp, and know that it is imposed on us, as a matter of necessity, either to gain their camp, or to die
in battle."

[2] *Cæsar having hardly said all this*) ver. 329. Cæsar, in his Civil War,
B. iii. c. 90, mentions that he addressed his soldiers in the following terms,
just before the onset:—"He could call his soldiers to witness the earnest-
ness with which he had sought peace, the efforts that he had made, through
Vatinius, to gain a conference [with Labienus], and likewise, through Claudius, to treat with Scipio; and in what manner he had exerted himself at
Oricum to gain permission from Libo to send ambassadors; that he had
been always reluctant to shed the blood of his soldiers, and did not wish to
deprive the republic of either of her armies."

[3] *Forestall the presage of the war*) ver. 331. They swiftly obey Cæsar's
command, and, destroying their lines and ramparts, adopt it as an omen of
victory.

[4] *In no order*) ver. 332. This is not the truth, and purely an invention
of the Poet, to show the determination with which the troops of Cæsar
began the engagement. Cæsar, in his Civil War, B. iii. c. 89, gives the
following account of his line of battle:—"Cæsar, observing his former
custom, had placed the tenth legion on the right, the ninth on the left,
although it was very much weakened by the battles at Dyrrhachium.
He placed the eighth legion so close to the ninth as to almost make one of
the two, and ordered them to support one another. He drew up on the field
eighty cohorts, making a total of twenty-two thousand men. He left two
cohorts to guard the camp; he gave the command of the left wing to Antony,
of the right to P. Sulla, and of the centre to Cn. Domitius; he himself took
his post opposite Pompey. At the same time, fearing, from the disposition

stand, with no disposition made by their general; everything
they leave to destiny. If in the direful combat you had
placed so many fathers-in-law of Magnus, and so many
aspiring to the sway of their own city, not with course so
precipitate would they have rushed to the combat.

When Pompey beheld the hostile troops coming forth
straight on, and allowing no respite for the war, but that
the day was pleasing to the Gods of heaven, with frozen
heart he stood astounded; and for a chieftain so great thus
to dread arms was ominous. Then he repressed his fears,
and, borne on a stately steed along all the ranks, he said:—

" The day which your valour demands, the end of the
civil warfare which you have looked for, is at hand. Show
forth all your might; the last work of the sword is at hand,
and one hour drags on nations *to their fate.* Whoever looks
for his country and his dear household Gods; who *looks for
his* offspring, and conjugal endearments, and *his* deserted
pledges *of affection,* let him seek them with the sword;
everything has the Deity set at stake in the midst of the
plain. *Our* cause the better one bids us hope for the Gods
of heaven as favouring; they themselves will direct the
darts through the vitals of Cæsar; they themselves will be
desirous with this blood to ratify the Roman laws. If they
had been ready to grant to my father-in-law kingly sway and
the world, they were able, by fatality, to hurry on my old age.
It is not the part of the Gods, angered at nations and the
City, to preserve Pompey as *their* leader.

" Everything that could possibly conquer have we contributed. Illustrious men have of their own accord submitted to dangers, and the veteran soldier, with his holy
resemblance *to the heroes of old.* If the Fates at these *troublous*
times would permit the Curii and the Camilli to come back,
and the Decii, who devoted their lives to death, on this side
would they take their stand. Nations collected from the

of the enemy which we have previously mentioned, lest his right wing might
be surrounded by their numerous cavalry, he rapidly drafted a single cohort
from each of the legions of the third line, formed of them a fourth line, and
set them opposite to Pompey's cavalry, and, acquainting them with his wishes,
admonished them that the success of that day depended on their courage.
At the same time he ordered the third line, and the entire army, not to
charge without his command; that he would give them the signal whenever
he wished them to do so."

remote East. and cities innumerable, have aroused bands to battle so mighty as *they* never *sent forth before.* At the same moment the whole world do we employ. Whatever men there are included within the limits of the heavens[1] that bear the Constellations, beneath Notus and Boreas, *here* are we, arms do we wield. Shall we not with our wings extended around place the collected foe in the midst *of us?* Few right hands does victory require; and many troops will only wage the warfare with their shouts. Cæsar suffices not for our arms[2].

"Think that your mothers, hanging over the summits of the walls of the City, with their dishevelled hair, are encouraging you to battle. Think that a Senate, aged, and forbidden by years to follow arms, are prostrating at your feet their hallowed hoary locks; and that Rome herself, dreading a tyrant, comes to meet you. Think that that which now is the people, and that which shall be the people, are offering their mingled prayers. Free does this multitude wish to be born; *free does* that *wish* to die. If, after pledges so great, there is any room for Pompey, suppliant with my offspring and my wife, if with the majesty of command preserved it were possible, I would throw myself before your feet. *I,* Magnus, unless you conquer, an exile, the scorn of my father-in-law, your own disgrace, do earnestly deprecate my closing destinies, and the disastrous years of the latest period of my life, that I may not, an aged man, learn to be a slave."

At the voice of their general uttering *words* so sad their spirits are inflamed, and the Roman valour is aroused, and it pleases them to die if he is in fear of the truth.

Therefore on either side do the armies meet with a like impulse of anger; the fear of rule arouses the one, the hope *of it* the other. These right hands shall do what no age can supply, nor the human race throughout all ages repair, even though it should be free from the sword. This warfare shall overwhelm future nations, and shall cut short

---

[1] *Within the limits of the heavens*) ver. 363. "Limite cœli" probably means the circle of the Zodiac.

[2] *Cæsar suffices not for our arms*) ver. 368. "Cæsar's numbers are too few for us to slay each one his man."

to the world the people of ages to come, the day of their
birth being torn away *from them*.   Then shall all the Latin
name be a fable; the ruins concealed in dust shall hardly
be able to point out Gabii[1], Veii[2], and Cora[3], and the
deserted fields *shall hardly show* the homes of Alba and the
household Gods of Laurentum[4], which the Senator would
not inhabit, except upon the night ordained[5], with reluctance, and complaining that Numa has *so* ordained.
These monuments of things devouring time has not
consumed, and has left *still* crumbling away; the crime
of civil war we behold, cities so many deserted[6].   To what
has the multitude of the human race been reduced?   We
nations who are born throughout the whole world are
able to fill neither the fortified places nor the fields with
men ; one City receives us *all*.   By the chained delver[7] are

---

[1] *To point out Gabii*) ver. 392.   Gabii, near the present town of Casti-
glione, was a city of Latium, near the Gabinian Lake, between Rome and
Præneste, said to have been founded by a colony from Alba Longa ; and,
according to tradition, Romulus was brought up there.   It was taken by
stratagem by Tarquinius Superbus (see the Fasti of Ovid, B. ii. l. 690,
et seq.), and was in ruins, as we learn from Horace, in the time of Augustus.

[2] *Veii*) ver. 392.   See B. v. l. 29, and the Note to the passage.

[3] *And Cora*) ver. 392.   This was an ancient town of Latium, in the
mountains of the Volsci, said to have been founded by an Argive named
Corax.   It is mentioned by Virgil in the Æneid, B. vi. l. 776. ·

[4] *Household Gods of Laurentum*) ver. 394.   Laurentum was one of the
most ancient towns of Latium, situate on a high ground between Ostia and
Ardea, not far from the sea, and said to have been surrounded by a grove of
laurels, whence it was supposed to have derived its name.   According to
Virgil, it was the residence of King Latinus, and the capital of Latium, and,
historically speaking, it appears to have been a place of some importance in
the time of the Roman kings.

[5] *Except upon the night ordained*) ver. 395.   He is supposed obscurely
to allude here to the " Latinæ feriæ," or Latin festival, which was celebrated
at Alba Longa by night, and has been alluded to in a preceding Note.
Burmann thinks that he alludes to some other rites now unknown, inasmuch
as Tarquinius Superbus, and not Numa, instituted that festival in honor of
the confederate towns of Latium.

[6] *Cities so many deserted*) ver. 399.   See B. ii. l. 24, *et seq.*

[7] *By the chained delver*) ver. 402.   He means that, in consequence of the
scarcity of freemen, slaves in chains will have to till the lands of Italy.
Tibullus mentions the chained slave singing at his work, B. ii. El. vi. l. 26:—
" His legs rattle with the iron, but he sings at his work."   Ovid also, in his
Tristia, or Lament, B. iv. El. i. l. 5, mentions the chained " fossor " (though
there the word may possibly mean "a miner"): " This, too, is the reason

the corn-fields of Hesperia tilled; mouldering with its ancestorial roofs stands the house, about to fall upon none; and Rome, thronged with no citizens of her own, but filled with the dregs of the world, did we surrender to that extent of slaughter that thenceforth for a period so long no civil war could possibly be waged. Of woes so great *was* Pharsalia the cause. Let Cannæ yield, a fatal name[1], and Allia, long condemned in the Roman annals[2]. Rome has marked *these as* occasions of lighter woes, this day she longs to ignore[3].

Oh shocking destinies! The air pestilential in its course, and shifting diseases, and maddening famine, and cities abandoned to flames, and earthquakes about to hurl populous cities[4] headlong, those men might have repaired, whom from every side Fortune has dragged to a wretched death, while, tearing away the gifts[5] of lengthened ages, she displays them, and ranges both nations and chieftains upon the plains; through whom she may, Rome, disclose to thee, as thou dost come to ruin, how mighty thou dost fall. The more widely she has possessed the world, the more swiftly through her prospering destinies has she run. Throughout all ages, has every war given *subdued* nations unto thee;

why the miner sings chained with the fetter, when he lightens his heavy labour with his untaught numbers."

[1] *Cannæ yield, a fatal name*) ver. 408. See B. ii. l. 46, and the Note to the passage.

[2] *Long condemned in the Roman annals*) ver. 408. Allia was a river about fifteen miles from Rome, near which the Roman army was cut to pieces by the Gauls under Brennus. The 17th day of the Calends of July, or the 16th of that month, on which this defeat happened, was ever after set down as "ater," or "unlucky," in the Roman Fasti.

[3] *This day she longs to ignore*) ver. 411. While the Calendar records the defeats of the Allia and Cannæ, it will not endure to take any notice of the disaster of Pharsalia. One of the Scholiasts remarks that Cæsar ordered that no notice should be taken of this battle, probably, in the Fasti Consulares.

[4] *Populous cities*) ver. 414. "Mœnia plena." "Fortified cities, full of inhabitants."

[5] *Tearing away the gifts*) ver. 416–17. "Dum munera longi explicat eripiens ævi." "While Fortune is now ranging in battle array, for the purpose of withdrawing them, the gifts which she has in such a lapse of years bestowed on all-powerful Rome." Burmann understands this as meaning that Fortune is cutting short what, to many, had been destined as the gift of a prolonged life.

thee has Titan beheld advancing towards the two poles[1]. Not much space was there remaining of the eastern earth, but what for thee the night, for thee the entire day, for thee the *whole* heavens should speed on, and the wandering stars behold all things belonging to Rome. But the fatal day of Emathia bore back thy destinies, equal to all *these* years[2].

On this blood-stained morn *was it* caused that India does not shudder[3] at the Latian fasces, and that she does not lead the Dahæ[4] into walled cities forbidden to wander, and that *no* tightly-girt Consul presses on[5] a Sarmatian plough. *This is the cause* that Parthia is ever owing to thee a cruel retribution ; that flying from civil strife, and never to return, Liberty has withdrawn beyond the Tigris and the Rhine, and, so oft sought by us at hazard of our throats[6], *still* wanders abroad, a blessing to Germany and Scythia, and no further looks back upon Ausonia. Would that she had been unknown to our people, *and that* thou, Rome, from the time when first Romulus filled the walls founded at the left-hand flight of the vultures from the guilty grove, even unto the Thessalian downfall, hadst remained enslaved.

Fortune, of the Bruti do I complain[7]. Why have we framed the periods of our laws, or *why made* the years to

[1] *Advancing towards the two poles*) ver. 422. In her victories approached to both the northern and southern poles.

[2] *Equal to all these years*) ver. 426. " Par omnibus annis." " Able in its results to overthrow the work of so many ages."

[3] *Caused that India does not shudder*) ver. 428. This disaster has cut short the victorious progress of Rome, and India needs not fear being subjugated.

[4] *She does not lead the Dahæ*) ver. 429. See the Second Book, 1. 296, and the Note to the passage.

[5] *No tightly-girt Consul presses on*) ver. 430. He probably refers to the custom of the Roman Consul, in the Gabinian habit, marking out with a plough drawn by a cow and a bull the trenches for the foundations of the walls of a new city in the subjugated country. Burmann thinks that the passage bears reference to the custom of ploughing over the surface of conquered cities which had been razed to the ground, but the expression in the previous line, " in mœnia ducat," seems to forbid such a construction being put upon the passage.

[6] *At hazard of our throats*) ver. 434. " Jugulo." " With the throat presented to the sword ;" or, " at the hazard of our lives."

[7] *Of the Bruti do I complain*) ver. 440. He complains of Lucius Junius Brutus, who, by the expulsion of the Tarquins, had introduced liberty into Rome.

take their name from the Consul? Happy the Arabians, and the Medes, and the Eastern lands, which the Fates have kept under continued tyrants. Of the nations which endure rule our lot is the last, who are ashamed to be slaves. Assuredly we have no Divinities; whereas ages are hurried along by blind chance, we falsely allege that Jupiter reigns. Will he look down from the lofty skies upon the Thessalian carnage, while he is wielding the lightnings[1]? Will he, forsooth, hurl at Pholoë, hurl at Œta with his flames, the groves, too, of the guiltless Rhodope, and the pine-woods of Mimas[2], shall Cassius, in[3] preference, smite this head? The stars against Thyestes did he urge on, and condemn Argos to sudden night[4]; shall he afford the light of day to Thessaly that wields the kindred swords so numerous of brothers and of parents?

Mortal affairs are cared for by no God. Still for this slaughter do we obtain satisfaction, as much as it is proper for the Deities to give to the earth. The civil wars will create Divinities[5] equal to the Gods of heaven. The shades will Rome adorn[6] with lightnings and with rays and stars:

[1] *While he is wielding the lightnings*) ver. 447-8. "Is it credible that Jupiter will rather hurl his thunders against these mountains than against the Pharsalian plains or the guilty head of Cæsar?"

[2] *The pine-woods of Mimas*) ver. 450. Mimas was a mountain of Ionia, near Colophon, and opposite to the Isle of Chios. It was sacred to Bacchus.

[3] *Shall Cassius, in*) ver. 451. He alludes to Caius Cassius Longinus, one of the murderers of Cæsar, who was a violent partisan of the Pompeian faction, and was forgiven by Cæsar, the man whom he afterwards murdered: he must not be confounded with his cousin Quintus Cassius Longinus, the tribune of the people, who is mentioned, in B. ii. l. 266, as leaving Rome to join Cæsar.

[4] *Condemn Argos to sudden night*) ver. 451-2. Did Jupiter hurry on the night at Argos on beholding the crime committed by Atreus against Thyestes? See B. i. l. 544, and the Note to the passage.

[5] *The civil wars will create Divinities*) ver. 457. This is probably said in a spirit of sarcasm against Nero. He says that one result of the Civil War, and indeed a just punishment of the Gods, is the deification of mortals, in allusion to the practice of deifying the Roman emperors, which began with Julius Cæsar.

[6] *The shades will Rome adorn*) ver. 458. One of the Scholiasts says that Cæsar was represented in his Temple arrayed in the habit of Jove, and as wearing rays in resemblance of the sun. It is, however, more probable that Lucan refers to the lightnings and the comet which appeared at the time of the death of Cæsar, and which were supposed to signify his deification.

T

and in the temples of the Gods will she swear by the shades *of men.*

When with a rapid step they have *now* passed over the space that delays the closing moments of destiny, separated by a small strip of ground, thence do they look upon the bands and seek to recognise their features, where their javelins are to fall, or what fate is threatening themselves, what monstrous deeds they are to perpetrate. Parents they behold with faces fronting them, and the arms of brothers in hostile array, nor do they choose to change their positions[1]. Still, a numbness binds all their breasts; and the cold blood, their feelings of affection smitten, congeals in their vitals; and whole cohorts for a long time hold the javelins in readiness with outstretched arms.

May the Gods send thee, Crastinus[2], not the death which is prepared as a punishment for all, but after thy end sensation in thy death, hurled by whose hand the

Indeed, the comet, which appeared for seven days, was supposed to be the spirit of Cæsar received into the heavens. See the History of Suetonius, Cæsar, c. 88; the Eclogues of Virgil, ix. l. 47; the Epistles of Horace, B. ii. Ep. 1. l. 16; and the Metamorphoses of Ovid, B. xv. l. 841, *et seq.*

[1] *Nor do they choose to change their positions*) ver. 466. So bent on each other's destruction are they that no one is desirous to change his place, and thereby avoid collision with a parent or a brother. May seems to be wrong in his translation of this passage, as he renders " nec libuit mutare locum," " yet would not change their side."

[2] *May the Gods send thee, Crastinus*) ver. 470-1. This Crastinus was an old soldier of Cæsar, who had been " emeritus," or discharged from service, but was now serving as a volunteer in his army. Cæsar, in the Civil War, B. iii. c. 91, thus relates the circumstance here alluded to:—" There was in Cæsar's army a volunteer of the name of Crastinus, who the year before had been first centurion of the tenth legion, a man of distinguished bravery. He, when the signal was given, said, ' Follow me, my old comrades, and display such exertions in behalf of your general as you have resolved to display ; this is our last battle, and when it shall have been won, he will recover his dignity, and we our liberty.' At the same time he looked back towards Cæsar, and said, ' General, I will act in such a manner to-day, that you will feel grateful to me, living or dead.' After uttering these words he was the first to charge on the right wing, and about one hundred and twenty chosen volunteers of the same century followed." In c. 94, Cæsar says, " In this battle, Crastinus, of whom mention was made before, fighting most courageously, lost his life by the wound of a sword in the mouth; nor was that false which he declared when marching to battle ; for Cæsar entertained the highest opinion of his behaviour in that battle, and thought him most deserving of his approbation."

javelin commenced the battle, and first stained Thessaly with Roman blood. O headlong frenzy, when Cæsar withheld the darts, was there found any hand more forward! Then *was* the resounding air rent by clarions[1], and the battle call given by the cornet; then did the trumpets presume to give the signal; then did a crash reach the skies, and burst upon the arched top of loftiest Olympus, from which the clouds are far removed *and* whither no lightnings last *to penetrate.* With its re echoing valleys Hæmus received the noise, and gave it to the caves of Pelion again to redouble; Pindus sent forth the uproar, and the rocks of Pangæum resounded, and the crags of Œta groaned, and the sounds of their own fury did they dread re-echoed throughout all the land.

Darts innumerable are scattered abroad with various intents. Some wish for wounds, some to fix the javelins in the earth, and to keep their hands in purity. Chance hurries everything on, and uncertain Fortune makes those guilty, whom she chooses. But how small a part[2] of the slaughter is perpetrated with javelins and flying weapons! For civil hatred the sword alone suffices, and guides right

---

[1] *The resounding air rent by clarions*) ver. 476–7. In these two lines he makes mention of the "lituus" or "clarion," the "cornu," "cornet" or "horn," and the "tuha" or "trumpet." "Cornu" seems to have been a general name for the horn or trumpet, but here it probably means the same as the "buccina" mentioned in B. ii. l. 689, which see, with the Note to the passage. The "tuba" was a straight trumpet, while the "lituus" assumed a spiral shape. Lydus says that the "lituus" was the sacerdotal trumpet, and that it was employed by Romulus when he proclaimed the title of his newly-founded city. Acro says that it was peculiar to the cavalry, while the "tuba" belonged to the infantry. The notes of the "lituus" are usually described as being harsh and shrill.

[2] *But how small a part*) ver. 489. Cæsar says, in the Civil War, B. iii. c. 93 :—" Our men, when the signal was given, rushed forward with their javelins ready to be launched, but perceiving that Pompey's men did not run to meet their charge, having acquired experience by custom, and being practised in former battles, they of their own accord repressed their speed, and halted almost midway, that they might not come up with the enemy when their strength was exhausted, and after a short respite, they again renewed their course, and threw their javelins, and instantly drew their swords, as Cæsar had ordered them. Nor did Pompey's men fail at this critical moment, for they received our javelins, stood our charge, and maintained their ranks; and, having launched their javelins, had recourse to their swords."

hands to Roman vitals. The ranks of Pompey, densely
disposed in deep bodies, joined their arms, their shields
closed together in a line[1]; and, hardly able to find room
for moving their right hands and their darts, they stood
close, and, wedged together, kept their swords sheathed.

With headlong course the furious troops of Cæsar are
impelled against the dense masses, and, through arms,
through the foe do they seek a passage. Where the twisted
coat of mail[2] presents its links, and the breast, beneath
a safe covering, lies concealed, even here do they reach
the entrails, and amid so many arms it is the vitals
which each one pierces. Civil war does the one army
suffer, the other wage; on the one hand the sword stands
chilled, on Cæsar's side every guilty weapon waxes hot.
Nor is Fortune long, overthrowing the weight of destinies so vast, in sweeping away the mighty ruins, fate
rushing on.

When first the cavalry of Pompey[3] extended his wings
over the whole plain, and poured them forth along the extremities of the battle, the light-armed soldiers, scattered
along the exterior of the maniples, followed, and sent forth
their ruthless bands against the foe. There, each nation
is mingling in the combat with weapons its own; Roman
blood is sought by all. On the one side arrows, on the
other torches and stones are flying, and plummets, melting
in the tract of air and liquefied with their heated masses[4].
Then do both Ituræans, and Medians, and Arabians, a

[1] *Their shields closed together in a line*) ver. 493. "Nexis umbonibus"
probably does not mean that their shields were fastened together, but that
they stood in close and serried ranks in one continued line.
[2] *Where the twisted coat of mail*) ver. 498. He alludes to the flexible
cuirasses or hauberks of chain mail which were worn by the Roman
"hastati" or spearmen; probably such as are mentioned by Virgil as made
of rings, linked or hooked into one another.
[3] *Where first the cavalry of Pompey*) ver. 506. This part of the battle
is thus described by Cæsar, B. iii. c. 93 :—"At the same time Pompey's
horse, according to their orders, rushed forth at once from his left wing, and
his whole host of archers poured after them. Our cavalry did not withstand
their charge, but gave a little, upon which Pompey's horse pressed
them more vigorously, and began to file off in troops and flank our army."
[4] *Liquefied with their heated masses*) ver. 513. It was a notion of the ancients
that the stones or metal plummets discharged from their slings became red-
hot in their course, from the swiftness of their motion, and they occasionally

multitude threatening with loosened bow, never aim their arrows, but the air alone is sought which impends over the plain; thence fall *various* deaths. But with no criminality of guilt[1] do they stain the foreign steel; around the javelins stands collected all the guiltiness[2]. With weapons the heaven is concealed, and a night, wrought by the darts, hovers over the fields.

Then did Cæsar, fearing lest his front rank might be shaken by the onset, keep in reserve some cohorts in an oblique position behind the standards[3], and on the sides of his line, whither the enemy, scattered about, was betaking himself, he suddenly sent forth a column, his *own* wings unmoved. Unmindful of the fight, and to be feared by reason of no sense of shame, they openly took to flight; not well *was* civil warfare ever entrusted to barbarian troops. As soon

went so far as to assert that they melted and disappeared entirely. Thus, Ovid says in the Metamorphoses, B. ii. l. 727, *et seq.*:—" As when the Balearic sling throws forth the plummet of lead; it flies and becomes red-hot in its course, and finds beneath the clouds the fires which it had not before;" and B. xiv. l. 826:—"Just as the leaden plummet, discharged from the broad sling, is wont to dissolve itself in mid-air." The "glandes," or "plummets" mentioned by Lucan, were called in Greek, μολύβδιδες, and were of a form between acorns and almonds, cast in moulds. They have been frequently dug up in various parts of Greece, and particularly on the plains of Marathon. Some have the device of a thunderbolt, while others are inscribed with δίξαι, "take this."

[1] *But with no criminality of guilt*) ver. 517. The weapons used by the foreign nations are exempt from the criminality of destroying fellow-citizens.

[2] *Stands collected all the guiltiness*) ver. 519. All the wickedness of the warfare is confined to the "pilum," or the javelin used especially by the Roman soldiers. See the Note to B. i. l. 7.

[3] *In an oblique position behind the standards*) ver. 522. It appears from the expression "obliqua," that Cæsar had placed these reserved cohorts at right angles to his other three lines; probably keeping them in the background, and not in extended line, that they might take the cavalry of Pompey by surprise, wheeling round and flanking them. The account given by Lucan is not easy to be understood, and the same may be said of that of Cæsar, in the Civil War, B. iii. c. 93:—" When Cæsar perceived this, he gave the signal to his fourth line, which he had formed of the six cohorts. They instantly rushed forward and charged Pompey's horse with such fury, that not a man of them stood his ground; but all, wheeling about, not only quitted their post, but galloped forward to seek a refuge in the highest grounds. By their retreat, the archers and slingers, being left destitute and defenceless, were all cut to pieces. The cohorts, pursuing their success, wheeled about upon Pompey's left wing, whilst his infantry still continued to make battle, and attacked them in the rear."

as the charger, his breast pierced with the weapon, trod
upon the limbs of the rider hurled upon his head, each
horseman fled from the field, and, crowded together, turning
bridle, the youths rushed on upon their own ranks. Then
did the carnage lose *all* bounds, and it was no battle that
ensued, but on the one hand with their throats[1], on the other
with the sword, the war was waged ; nor was the one army
able to lay low as many as were able to perish on the other
side.

Would that, Pharsalia, for thy plains that blood which
barbarian breasts pour forth would suffice : that the streams
might be changed by no other gore; that this throng might
for thee cover whole fields with bones; or if thou dost prefer
to be glutted with Roman blood, spare the others, I entreat ; let the Galatians and Syrians live, the Cappadocians
and the Gauls, and the Iberians from the extremity of the
world, the Armenians and the Cilicians ; for after the civil
wars these will form the Roman people. Once commenced,
the panic reaches all, and to the Fates is an impulse given
in favour of Cæsar.

They had *now* come to the strength of Magnus and the
mid ranks. The war, which, in its wandering course, had
strayed over whole fields, here paused, and the fortune of
Cæsar delayed. On this spot no youths collected by the
aid of kings are waging the war, and no alien hands[2] wield
the sword ; this spot contains their brothers, this spot their
fathers. Here *is* frenzy, here frantic rage ; here, Cæsar, are
thy crimes. My soul, fly from this portion of the warfare[3],
and leave it to the shades of night, and, myself the Poet of

---

[1] *On the one hand with their throats*) ver. 533. The Pompeians stand only
to be killed, the people of Cæsar fight only to slay.

[2] *No alien hands*) ver. 549. "Rogatæ ;" meaning mercenary or foreign
troops enlisted.

[3] *Fly from this portion of the warfare*) ver. 552. It is singular that in a
similar manner Cæsar omits to give any further particulars of the battle after
the charge made on the cavalry by his fourth line, except the following few
words, c. 94 :—"At the same time Cæsar ordered his third line to advance,
which till then had not been engaged, but had kept their post. Thus, new
and fresh troops having come to the assistance of the fatigued, and others
having made an attack on their rear, Pompey's men were not able to maintain their ground, but all fled : nor was Cæsar deceived in his opinion that
the victory, as he had declared in his speech to his soldiers, must have its
beginning with those six cohorts, which he had placed as a fourth line to

woes so great, let no age learn how great is the licence in civil warfare.   Perish rather these tears, and perish *these* complaints.   Whatever, Rome, in this battle thou hast done, upon it I will be silent.

Here Cæsar, the *prompting* fury of his people, and the exciter of their rage, lest upon any side his guilt may prove unavailing, goes to and fro around the troops and adds flames to their fired hearts; he examines the swords, too[1], which ones are dripping all over with gore, which ones are shining stained with blood *just* at the point only, which hand falters in pressing home the sword, who it is that bears his weapons *but* languidly, who tightly grasped, who with alacrity wages the war at command, who takes a pleasure in fighting, who changes countenance on a fellow-citizen being slain; he surveys the carcases strewed over the wide plains. The wounds of many, about to pour forth all their blood, he himself stanches[2], by placing his hand against them. Wherever he roves, just as Bellona[3], shaking her blood-stained whip, or Mars inciting[4] the Bistonians, if with severe lashes he urges on his chariot steeds frightened by the Ægis of Pallas, a vast night of crimes and slaughters ensues, and groans like *one* immense cry, and arms resound with the weight of the falling breast, and swords shivered against swords.

He himself with *his own* hand supplies falchions, and provides darts, and bids them mangle the opposing faces[5]

oppose the horse.   For by them the cavalry was routed; by them the archers and slingers were cut to pieces; by them the left wing of Pompey's army was surrounded, and obliged to be the first to fly."

[1] *He examines the swords, too*) ver. 560-65.   All this is only an invidious way of informing us that Cæsar was everywhere, a witness to the martial prowess of his soldiers.

[2] *He himself stanches*) ver. 567.   He stanches the blood of his men, by pressing down the severed vein with his fingers.

[3] *Just as Bellona*) ver. 568.   Bellona, the wife or sister of Mars, is represented also by Horace and Virgil, as brandishing a blood-stained scourge.   See B. i. l. 565, and the Note to the passage.

[4] *Or Mars inciting*) ver. 569.   " Mavors."   Mavers, or Mavors, was the original form of the name " Mars."   Varro says that Mamers was the Sabine name of the God; but the word is more generally thought to have belonged to the Oscan dialect.   Mars was especially an object of worship with the Bistonian or Thracian nations.

[5] *The opposing faces*) ver. 575.   It is probable that he here obscurely refers to the order given by Cæsar to his men to aim at the faces of the Ro-

with their weapons. He himself urges on the ranks; *and*
onward drives the backs of his own men; those slackening
he forces on with blows of his lance reversed. He forbids
their hands to be directed against the common people, and
points out the Senators[1]. He knows well which is the blood
of the state, which *are* the vitals of the republic; in which
direction he is to speed on to Rome[2], in which spot stands
to be smitten the final liberty of the world. Mingled with
the second rank[3], the nobles and the venerated bodies are
pressed upon by the sword; Lepidi they slay, Metelli, too,
they slay, Corvini as well, and *those with* the names of Torquatus[4], often the rulers of kings, and the chiefs of men,
thee, Magnus, excepted.

There, concealing thy features[5] in a plebeian helmet, and
unknown to the foe, what a weapon, Brutus[6], thou didst
wield! O honor to the state, O final hope of the Senate,
last name of a race for ages so renowned, rush not too
rashly through the midst of the foe, and hasten not for

man patricians. One of the Commentators, Janus Rutgersius, thinks that
the meaning is, that Cæsar, being afraid that the spirits of his men might
be damped on beholding the countenances of their relatives and friends,
had given an order that aim should be taken at the faces of all indiscriminately, so that they might not be able to recognize individuals; and that
this conjecture is supported by what is said in ll. 320 and 627.

[1] *Points out the Senators*) ver. 578. He points out the patricians as the
especial objects of attack.

[2] *He is to speed on to Rome*) ver. 580. Through the shedding of whose
blood he will arrive at the sovereignty of Rome.

[3] *Mingled with the second rank*) ver. 581. Patricians are slaughtered
indiscriminately with those of the Equestrian order.

[4] *And those with the names of Torquatus*) ver. 584. It does not appear
that the names have come down to us of any of the Lepidi, Metelli, Corvini,
or Torquati, who fell at the battle of Pharsalia.

[5] *There, concealing thy features*) ver. 586. He means that Brutus was disguised as a common soldier, for the purpose of slaying Cæsar if he could find
the opportunity. If this story is true, it certainly contrasts unfavourably with
the fact that at this battle Cæsar had given orders to his men not to slay
Brutus, probably for the sake of his mother Servilia, who had implored Cæsar
to spare him. After the battle Brutus escaped to Larissa, but did not accompany Pompey any further. Here he wrote a letter to Cæsar entreating his
pardon, which was generously granted by the conqueror without hesitation;
on which, according to Plutarch, Brutus informed Cæsar of Pompey's flight
to Egypt.

[6] *What a weapon, Brutus*) ver. 587. "Quod ferrum," meaning, "a sword
intended for what a purpose."

thyself too soon the fatal Philippi, doomed to perish in a Thessaly of thy own [1]. Nothing there dost thou avail by aiming at Cæsar's throat; not yet has he arrived at the summit of power, and having surpassed *that* human elevation, by which all things are swayed, has by the Fates been made deserving of so noble a death. Let him live, and that he may fall the victim of Brutus, let him reign.

Here perished all the glory of *thy* native land; in large heaps patrician corpses lay on the plain [2], the vulgar not intermingled. Still, however, amid the slaughter of illustrious men the death of the valiant Domitius [3] was distinguished, whom the Destinies led through every reverse [4]. Never did the fortunes of Magnus fail without him; conquered by Cæsar so oft, his liberty saved, he dies. Then joyously did he fall amid a thousand wounds, and he rejoiced to have been spared a second pardon [5]. Cæsar beheld him rolling his limbs amid the clotted blood, and, upbraiding him, *exclaimed*, "Now, *my* successor, Domitius", thou dost abandon the arms of Magnus; without thee now is the warfare waged."

[1] *In a Thessaly of thy own*) ver. 592. The Poet here falls into his usual error of confounding Thessaly with Thrace.

[2] *Patrician corpses lay on the plain*) ver. 598. Because in especial Cæsar had ordered those of patrician rank to be slain. Cæsar thus recounts the losses of both sides in this battle; Civil War, B. iii. c. 99:—"In that battle, no more than two hundred privates were missing, but Cæsar lost about thirty centurions, valiant officers; of Pompey's army there fell about fifteen thousand; but upwards of twenty-four thousand were made prisoners; for even the cohorts which were stationed in the forts, surrendered to Sulla. Several others took shelter in the neighbouring states."

[3] *Death of the valiant Domitius*) ver. 600. Cæsar says, in the Civil War, B. iii. c. 99:—"Lucius Domitius fleeing from the camp to the mountains, his strength being exhausted by fatigue, was slain by the cavalry." .

[4] *Through every reverse*) ver. 600. He alludes to the ill success which always attended Domitius in his campaigns against Cæsar. See l. 479, and the Note to the passage.

[5] *To have been spared a second pardon*) ver. 604. In allusion to the pardon which he received from Cæsar at Corfinium. See B. ii. l. 512-522.

[6] *My successor, Domitius*) ver. 607. Domitius was designed by Pompey and the Senate to be Cæsar's successor in the province of Gaul. There is no doubt that this passage is the pure result of Lucan's malevolent feelings against the memory of Cæsar, as it is pretty clear that Cæsar was not even present at his death.

He spoke, but the breath *of Domitius* struggling in his breast sufficed him for a voice, and he *thus* opened his dying lips : " Beholding thee, Cæsar, not *yet* in possession of the direful reward of thy crimes, but doubtful of thy fate, and less mighty than thy son-in-law, I go to the shades free and void of care, Magnus being my leader : for thee *to be* subdued in the ruthless warfare, and to be about to pay a heavy penalty to Pompey and to us, while I die, it is allowed me to hope." Life fled from him having said no more, and dense shades pressed upon his eyes.

I scruple to expend tears at the downfall of the world upon deaths innumerable, and, tracing them out, to enquire into individual fates ; through whose vitals the deadly wound made its way ; who it was that trod upon entrails scattered on the ground ; who, the hostile sword being thrust into his jaws, dying, breathed forth his soul ; who fell down at the blow ; who, while his limbs dropped down, *lopped off*, stood upright ; who received the darts right through the breast, or whom the lance pinned to the plain ; whose blood, the veins being severed, gushed through the air, and fell upon the arms of his foe ; who pierced the breast of his brother, and that he might be able to spoil the well-known carcase, threw afar the head cut off ; who mangled the features of a parent, and by his extreme fury would prove to lookers-on that he whom he stabbed was not his father.

No death is deserving of a lament its own, and no individuals have we the leisure to mourn. Pharsalia had not those features of combat which other slaughters *had*[1] ; there did Rome perish by the fates of individuals, here by multitudes ; that which was there the death of a soldier, was here *that* of a nation ; there flowed Achæan blood, Pontic *and* Assyrian ; the gore of all did the Roman torrent forbid to remain and stagnate upon the plain. Greater wounds do nations receive from this battle-field than their own times can endure ; that which perishes is more than life and safety ; to all ages of the world are we laid prostrate ; by these swords is every generation conquered which shall be

---

[1] *Which other slaughters had*) ver. 633. Such as the Roman defeats at Allia, Trebia, Thrasymenus, Ticinum, and Cannæ.

a slave. How have the succeeding race, or how the grand-children, deserved to be born to thraldom? Did we wield arms with fear? Or did we cover up *our* throats? The punishment of others' fears sits *heavy* upon our necks. If, Fortune, to those born after the battle thou dost give a tyrant, thou shouldst have given warfare as well.

Now had the wretched Magnus perceived that the Gods and the destinies of Rome had forsaken him; hardly pre-vailed upon by the whole slaughter to rebuke his own for-tune. He stood upon a rising ground of the plain, on high, whence he could behold all the carnage scattered over the Thessalian fields, which, while the battle hindered, lay concealed. With weapons so many he beheld his destinies attacked, so many bodies lying prostrate, and himself pe-rishing with bloodshed so great. Nor yet, as is the way of the unfortunate, does he take pleasure in dragging, together with himself, everything to sink, by involving nations in his own ruin; that after himself the greatest part of the Latian multitude may survive, he endures even yet to deem the inhabitants of heaven worthy of his prayers, and reflects upon *this* solace of his misfortune[1].

"Forbear, ye Gods of heaven," he says, "to lay all na-tions prostrate; the world *still* existing and Rome surviving, Magnus can possibly be wretched. If still more wounds of mine please you, I have a wife, I have sons; so many pledges have I given to the Fates. Is it too little for a civil war if myself and mine thou dost overwhelm? Is our down-fall a trifle, the world being exempted? Why dost thou rend everything; why dost thou strive to destroy all things? Now, Fortune, nothing is my own."

Thus he speaks, and he rides around the arms and the standards and the smitten troops on every side, and he calls them back as they rush upon a speedy death, and denies that he is of value so great. Nor to the chieftain is courage wanting to rush upon the swords, and to submit to death with throat or with breast; but he fears lest, the body of Magnus laid low, the soldiers may not fly, and over the chieftain the earth may fall; or else from Cæsar's eyes he

[1] *Reflects upon this solace of his misfortune*) ver. 653. Revolves in his mind appeals to the clemency of the Gods, by way of some consolation for the magnitude of his calamities.

wishes to remove his death. In vain. Unhappy man, to thy father-in-law, willing to behold it[1], must the head be shown in some place. But thou, too, *his* wife, *art* the cause of his flight, and thy features, *so well remembered;* and by the Fates has it been decided that he shall die in thy presence.

Then, spurred on, the charger bears Magnus away[2] from the combat, not fearing the darts at his back, and showing magnanimity amid *this* extremity of fate. No sighing, no weeping, is there, and his grief is deserving of respect, its dignity preserved, such as, Magnus, it becomes thee to show for the woes of Rome. With countenance not changed thou dost look upon Emathia; neither shall the successes of war behold thee proud, nor *its* losses *see thee* dejected; and as much as faithless Fortune has proved below thee when exulting in three triumphs, so much has she when unfortunate. Now, the weight of fate laid aside, free from care thou dost depart; now thou hast leisure to look back upon joyous times; hopes never to be fulfilled have gone; what thou wast thou now hast the opportunity to know.

Fly from direful battles, and call the Gods to witness, that not one who continues in arms[3] now, Magnus, dies

---

[1] *Willing to behold it*) ver. 675. "It is fated that Cæsar must be the witness of thy death, which he will willingly be."

[2] *The charger bears Magnus away*) ver. 677. Cæsar, in the Civil War, B. iii. c. 96, thus records the flight of Pompey after the battle :—" Pompey, as soon as our men had forced the trenches, mounting his horse, and stripping off his general's habit, went hastily out of the back gate of the camp and galloped with all speed to Larissa—nor did he stop there, but, with the same dispatch, collecting a few of his flying troops, and halting neither day nor night, he arrived at the sea-side, attended by only thirty horse, and went on board a victualling ship, often complaining, as we have been told, that he had been so deceived in his expectation, that he was almost persuaded that he had been betrayed by those from whom he expected victory, as they began the flight."

[3] *Not one who continues in arms*) ver. 690. He alludes to the battle which continued at the camp of Pompey after he himself had fled; we find it thus mentioned in the Civil War, B. iii. c. 97 :—" The camp of Pompey was bravely defended by the cohorts which had been left to guard it, but with much more spirit by the Thracians and foreign auxiliaries. For the soldiers who had fled for refuge to it from the field of battle affrighted and exhausted by fatigue, having thrown away their arms and military standards, had their thoughts more engaged on their further escape than on the defence of the camp. Nor could the troops who were posted on the battlements long withstand the immense number of our darts, but, fainting under their wounds,

for thee; just as Africa to be lamented with her reverses, and just as fatal Munda, and the carnage on the Pharian stream [1], so too, after thy *departure is* the greatest portion of the Thessalian fight. No longer now *shall* Pompey's name *be* revered by nations throughout the world, nor *be* the prompter of the war; but the pair *of rivals* which we always have, will be Liberty and Cæsar; and thyself expelled thence, the dying Senate shows that it was for itself it fought. Driven *afar*, does it not give thee pleasure to have left the warfare, and not to have beheld those horrors, the troops drenched in gore?

Look back upon the rivers clouded by the influx of blood, and have pity upon thy father-in-law. With what breast shall he enter Rome, made more happy by these fields? Whatever, an exile alone in unknown regions, whatever placed in the power of the Pharian tyrant, thou shalt endure, believe the Gods, believe the lasting favour of the Fates, to conquer was still worse. Forbid lamentations to resound, prevent the people from weeping; forego tears and mourning. As much shall the world venerate the woes of Pompey as his successes. Free from care, with no suppliant features behold potentates; behold cities won *by thee*, and kingdoms bestowed, Ægypt and Libya, and select a region for thy death.

Larissa, as the first witness [2] of thy downfall, beholds thy head, noble and unconquered by the Fates. With all her citizens [3] does she pour forth her entire strength through

quitted the place, and under the conduct of their centurions and tribunes fled, without stopping, to the high mountains which joined the camp." In c. 98 we learn that these capitulated to Cæsar.

[1] *The carnage on the Pharian stream*) ver. 692. He probably means the Alexandrian war, a sequel to the Civil War. The meaning is, " Neither the battle commenced at Pharsalia after the flight of Pompey, nor yet the war waged in Africa by Scipio, Cato, and Juba, nor yet the battle of Munda fought by Cneius and Sextus, the sons of Pompey, nor yet the Alexandrian war, fought by the Egyptians against Cæsar, can be said to have been engaged in for the cause of Pompey, but rather in a struggle where Cæsar and Liberty were the antagonists."

[2] *Larissa, as the first witness*) ver. 712. There were several places of this name, and two in Thessaly, one in Pelasgiotis, the other in Phthiotis, near the Malian Gulf; the latter is probably the one to which Pompey fled.

[3] *With all her citizens*) ver. 714. This does not agree with the account given by Cæsar of the flight of Pompey through Larissa without staying there. See the Note to l. 677.

the walls ; weeping they send before to thee, as though suc cessful, gifts to meet thee on thy way; *their* temples, *their* houses they open ; themselves they wish to be partners in *thy* reverses.   It is clear that much of thy illustrious name is left; and less than thy *former* self alone, thou canst again urge all nations to arms, and again resort to the fatality *of war*.   But, "What need has a conquered man of nations or of cities ?" he says; "put faith in the conqueror."   Thou Cæsar, still on the high heap of carnage art wading amid the entrails of thy country; but now does thy son-in-law present the nations unto thee [1].

The charger bears Pompey away from there; sighs and tears follow *him;* and many a rebuke of the multitude against the relentless Gods.   Now, Magnus, to thee is granted real experience of the love which thou didst seek, and its reward.   While prosperous one knows not that he is beloved [2].

Cæsar, when he beheld that the fields had sufficiently overflowed with Hesperian blood, now thinking that he ought to spare the swords and the hands of his men, left the troops to live as though worthless lives, and about to perish for no purpose.   But, that the camp may not invite them back when routed, and rest by night dispel their fears, forth-with he resolves to attack the entrenchments of the enemy, while Fortune waxes hot, while terror effects everything, not fearing lest this command may prove harsh to *soldiers* wearied and overpowered with the battle.   Through no great exhortation are the soldiers to be led to the plunder :—

"Men, we have an abundant victory," says he ; "for *our* blood the reward is *now* remaining [3], which it is my office to point out ; for I will not call it bestowing that which each one will give unto himself.   Behold, the camp, filled with all kinds of metal, is open ; here lies the gold torn from the Hesperian nations, and the tents are covering the treasures

[1] *Present the nations unto thee*) ver. 723.   Pompey, in his hatred of blood-shed, surrenders unto thee the mastery of nations.

[2] *Knows not that he is beloved*) ver. 727.   Because he might suppose that regard was had rather to his elevated position than to himself.

[3] *The reward is now remaining*) ver. 738.   Cæsar says the contrary in his Civil War, B. iii. c. 97 :—"Cæsar having possessed himself of Pompey's camp, urged his soldiers not to be too intent on plunder, and lose the oppor-tunity of completing their conquest."

of the East. The collected wealth of so many kings and of Magnus together, waits for possessors; make haste, soldiers, to get before those whom you pursue; and let the wealth be torn from the conquered which Pharsalia has made your own."

And no more having said, he urged them on frantic and blinded with greed for gold, to rush over swords, and upon the carcases of parents, and to tread under foot the slaughtered chieftains. What trench, what rampart could withstand them seeking the reward of war and of crimes? Onward they flew to know for how great wages they had been guilty. They found indeed, the world having been spoiled, full many a mass of bullion heaped up [1] for the expenses of the wars; but it did not satisfy minds craving for everything. Though they should seize whatever gold the Iberian digs up [2], whatever the Tagus yields, whatever the enriched Arimaspian [3] gathers from the surface of the sands, they will think that this criminality has been sold at a trifling price. When the victor has bespoken for himself the Tarpeian towers [4], when he has promised *himself* everything in hopes of the spoil of Rome, he is deceived in plundering a camp *alone*.

The unscrupulous commonalty take their slumbers upon the Patrician sods [5]; the worthless private soldier presses the couches left empty by kings; and on the beds of fathers,

---

[1] *Full many a mass of bullion heaped up*) ver. 753. Cæsar gives the following short account of what was found in Pompey's camp, B. iii. c. 96 :— "In Pompey's camp you might see arbours in which tents were laid, a large quantity of plate set out, the floors of the tents covered with fresh sods, the tents of Lucius Lentulus and others shaded with ivy, and many other things which were proofs of excessive luxury, and a confidence of victory; so that it might readily be inferred that they had no apprehensions of the issue of the day, as they indulged themselves in unnecessary pleasures, and yet upbraided with luxury Cæsar's army, distressed and suffering troops, who had always been in want of common necessaries."

[2] *Whatever gold the Iberian digs up*) ver. 755. See the Note to B. iv. l. 298. The Tagus, in Portugal, was noted in the times of the Romans for its golden sands.

[3] *The enriched Arimaspian*) ver. 756. See B. iii. l. 281, and the Note to the passage.

[4] *Bespoken for himself the Tarpeian towers*) ver. 758. Not content with the spoil, their hopes were fixed upon sacking the Capitol (in which was the public treasury) of Rome.

[5] *Take their slumbers upon the Patrician sods*) ter. 761. See the Note to l. 753.

and on *those* of brothers the guilty men lay their limbs;
whom a frenzied rest, and frantic slumbers agitate; wretched,
they revolve the Thessalian combat in their breasts. The
ruthless bloodshed stands before them all in their sleep,
and in all their thoughts they brandish arms, and, the hilt
away, their hands are in motion. You would suppose that
the plains were groaning, and that the guilty earth had exhaled spirits, and that the whole air was teeming with
ghosts, and the night above with Stygian horrors. Of them,
wretched *men*, does victory demand a sad retribution, and
sleep presents hissings and flames [1]; the shade of the slaughtered fellow-citizen is there; his own image of terror weighs
heavy upon each. This one sees the features of aged men,
that one the figures of youths; another one do the carcases
of brothers affright throughout all his slumbers; in this
breast is a father; with Cæsar *are* the ghosts of all [2].

No otherwise, not purified as yet at the Scythian altar [3],
did Orestes, descendant of Pelops, behold the features of
the Eumenides; nor, when Pentheus raved, or when Agave
had ceased *to rave* [4], were they more sensible of astounding
tumults in their minds. Him do all the swords, which
either Pharsalia has beheld or the day of vengeance is destined to behold, the Senate unsheathing them, upon that
night oppress; him do the monsters of hell scourge. Alas!
how vast a punishment does his conscience-stricken mind

---

[1] *Presents hissings and flames*) ver. 772. The hissings of the Furies as
they shake their burning brands and viperous locks.

[2] *With Cæsar are the ghosts of all*) ver. 776. "Each one sees the spirit
of some slain relative, but Cæsar is haunted by the ghosts of all."

[3] *Not purified at the Scythian altar*) ver. 777. When Orestes, the son of
Agamemnon and descendant of Pelops, had killed his mother Clytemnestra,
he was haunted by the Furies, until his sister Iphigenia, at the altar of the
Tauric Diana in Scythia, of whom she was the priestess, had purified him;
from which circumstance the Furies were said to have received, as a Euphemism, their name of Eumenides.

[4] *When Pentheus raved, or when Agave had ceased to rave*) ver. 780.
"Quum fureret, Pentheus, aut quum desisset, Agave." This line, differently
punctuated, may be translated two different ways. "When Pentheus raged,
or when Agave ceased to rage," or "Than Pentheus did, when Agave raged
or when she ceased to rage." The former, though not adopted by Grotius, is
probably the correct translation. Probably the contempt with which Pentheus regarded the rites of Bacchus (for which he was torn to pieces by his
mother and the Bacchanalian women) is the madness or frenzy here alluded
to by the Poet.

inflict upon him [1] in his wretchedness, in that. Pompey surviving, he beholds Styx, in that *he beholds* the shades below,
and Tartarus heaped upon him in his slumbers!

Still, having suffered all *these things,* after the bright day
has unveiled *to him* the losses of Pharsalia, not at all does
the aspect of the place call away his eyes riveted upon the
fatal fields. He beholds rivers swollen with gore, and
he looks upon bodies equalling in heaps the lofty hills, and
piles flattened down in corrupted gore, and he counts the
people of Magnus [2]; and that spot is made ready for a
banquet, from which he may recognize *their* features and
faces as they lie. He is delighted not to see the Emathian
ground, and to survey with his eyes the plains lying hid
beneath the carnage; in the blood does he behold Fortune and the Gods of heaven his own.

And that in his fury he may not lose the joyous spectacle
of his crimes, he denies the fires of the pile to the
wretched *slain,* and exposes Emathia to a noisome atmosphere. Not him do the Carthaginian burier of the Consul [3],
and Cannæ, lighted up with the Libyan torch, instruct how
to observe the customs of men with regard to his foes ; but
he remembers, his wrath not yet satiated with slaughter, that
they were his own fellow-citizens. Not individual graves,
and separate funeral piles do we ask ; grant but one fire to
whole nations ; and in no distinct flames let the bodies be
burned. Or if vengeance on thy son-in-law pleases thee,
heap up the groves of Pindus ; pile up the woods raised
aloft with the oaks of Œta ; let Pompey from the main behold the Thessalian flames.

Nought by this wrath dost thou avail ; whether putrefac-
tion, or whether the pile destroys the carcases, it matters

[1] *Inflict upon him*) ver. 784. "Donat;" this word may admit of two
interpretations : "How much punishment does his conscience remit to him,
by seeing the horrors of hell, Pompey being yet alive, whereas on his death
they will be increased?" or, "How great pangs does his conscience cause him
while seeing," &c.

[2] *He counts the people of Magnus*) ver. 792. No doubt this is an untruth, having its origin in the Poet's imagination. Cæsar was more humane
than most of the conquerors of ancient times.

[3] *Carthaginian burier of the Consul*) ver. 799. Hannibal had the body
of Paulus Æmilius, the Roman Consul, who was slain at the battle of Cannæ,
burned, with all the funeral honours due to his rank.

not ; nature receives back everything into her placid bosom, and an end of themselves to themselves do the bodies owe. These nations, Cæsar, if now the fire does not consume *them*, with the earth it will consume [1], with the waters of the deep it will consume. *One* pile in common is left for the world [2], destined to mingle the stars with its bones. Whithersoever Fortune shall summon thine own, *thither* these souls as well are wending. Not higher *than they* shalt thou ascend into the air, not in a more favoured spot shalt thou lie beneath Stygian night. Death is secure from Fortune ; the earth receives everything which she has produced ; he who has no urn is covered by the heavens. Thou, to whom nations are paying the penalty by a death ungraced with burial, why dost thou fly from this slaughter ? Why dost thou desert the *carnage*-smelling fields ? Quaff these waters, Cæsar ; inhale, if thou canst, this air [3]. But from thee do the putrefying nations snatch the Pharsalian fields, and, the victor put to flight, possess the plains.

Not only the Hæmonian, *but* the Bistonian wolves [4] came to the direful banquet of the war, and the lions left Pholoë, scenting the carnage of the bloody combat. Then did bears desert their dens. obscene dogs their abodes and homes, and whatever *besides* with acute scent was sensible of the air impure and tainted by carrion. And now the

[1] *With the earth it will consume*) ver. 813. At the time when the world shall burn in the universal conflagration.

[2] *One pile in common is left for the world*) ver. 814. Plato, in the Timæus, expresses a belief that the world will be destroyed by a universal conflagration. Cicero, in his Treatise on the Nature of the Gods, speaks of the world being subjected in cycles to the action of fire and water. Ovid says, in the Metamorphoses, B. i. l. 256-7:—" He remembers, too, that it was in the decrees of Fate, that a time should come, at which the sea, the earth, and the palace of heaven, seized by the flames, should be burned, and the laboriously-wrought fabric of the universe should be in danger of perishing." Lactantius also mentions that the Sibyls predicted that the world should perish by fire. Seneca, in his Consolation to Marcia and his Quæstiones Naturales, mentions the same destined termination of the present state of the universe. It was a doctrine of the Stoic philosophers that the stars were nurtured with moisture, and that on the cessation of this nourishment the conflagration of the universe would ensue.

[3] *Inhale, if thou canst, this air*) ver. 822. " Hoc utere cœlo." Literally, "use this heaven ;" alluding to the air being tainted by the bodies of the dead.

[4] *Bistonian wolves*) ver. 826. The wolves scented the dead even from distant Thrace.

fowls of the air, that long had followed the civic warfare, flocked together. You, birds, who are wont to change [1] the Thracian winters for the Nile, departed later *than usual* [2] for the balmy south. Never with vultures so numerous did the heavens cover themselves, or did wings more numerous beat the air. Every grove sent forth its fowls, and every tree dripped with gouts of gore from the blood-stained birds.

Full oft upon the features of the victor and the impious standards did either blood or corrupt matter flow down from the lofty sky, and from its now weary talons the bird threw down the limbs. And thus, not all the people were reduced to bones, and, torn to pieces, disappeared in the beasts of prey; the entrails within they cared not for, nor were they greedy to suck out all the marrow; they lightly tasted of the limbs. Loathed, the greatest part of the Latian multitude lay; which the sun, and the showers, and lapse of time, mingled, when decomposed, with the Emathian earth.

Thessaly, unhappy land, with what guilt so great hast thou offended the Gods of heaven, that thee alone with deaths so numerous, with the fatal results of crimes so numerous, they should afflict? What length of time is sufficient for forgetful antiquity to pardon thee the calamities of the warfare? What crop of corn will not rise discoloured with its tinted blade? With what ploughshare wilt thou not wound a Roman ghost? First shall fresh combats ensue [3], and for a second crime shalt thou afford the fields not yet dry from this bloodshed. Should it be allowed us to overthrow all the tombs of our ancestors, both the sepulchres that stand, and those which beneath the ancient roots [4]

[1] *You, birds, who are wont to change*) ver. 832. He uses the licence of the Poet in making the Thracian cranes scent the dead and hasten to feed upon them. Buffon admits that they are carnivorous as well as granivorous, but only to the extent of feeding upon worms, insects, and small reptiles. See B. iii. l. 199, and B. v. l. 512.

[2] *Departed later than usual*) ver. 833. Inasmuch as they stopped short in Thessaly, on their way to the banks of the Nile.

[3] *Shall fresh combats ensue*) ver. 853. The Poet commits his usual error of taking Philippi to be identical with Pharsalia; a mistake, as already mentioned, common to him with others of the Latin poets.

[4] *Beneath the ancient roots*) ver. 856. "Radice vetustâ." One of the Scholiasts takes "radice" here to mean the roots of the trees which had taken fast hold of the foundation of the tombs, and thinks that fig-trees

have emptied *their* urns, *their* structures burst asunder; ashes more numerous are ploughed up in the furrows of the Hæmonian earth, and more bones are struck against by the harrows that cultivate the fields.

No mariner would have loosened the cable from the Emathian shore, nor any ploughman have moved the earth, the grave of the Roman race; the husbandmen, too, would have fled from the fields of the ghosts; the thickets would have been without flocks; and no shepherd would have dared to allow to the cattle the grass springing up from our bones; and, as though uninhabitable by men either by reason of the tract of unendurable heat, or of freezing, bare and unknown thou wouldst have lain, if thou hadst not *only* first, but alone, been guilty of the criminality of the warfare.

O Gods of heaven, be it allowed us to hate *this* hurtful land! Why do ye render guilty [1] the whole, why absolve the whole world? The carnage of Hesperia [2], and the tearful wave of Pachynus, and Mutina, and Leucas, have rendered Philippi free from guilt.

are alluded to, which were planted near the graves, at least of the more humble classes. Juvenal and Martial mention a superstition that these trees grow from the liver of the dead, and are able to penetrate even through rocks. Lemaire thinks that "radice vetustâ" merely means the lowest foundations of the tombs themselves worn out with old age.

[1] *Why do ye render guilty*) ver. 870. "By setting the example of bloodshed you lead the world to be guilty; by the readiness with which it follows your example, it shows itself equally guilty."

[2] *The carnage of Hesperia*) ver. 871-2. He alludes to the battle of Munda in Spain, where the forces of Pompey were defeated; of Mutina, where the Consuls Hirtius and Pansa were defeated; (see B. i. l. 41, and the Note to the passage;) of Actium, which was fought by Augustus and Antony, near the Leucadian Promontory; and of Naulochus and Mylæ off the coast of Sicily (of which Pachynus was a Promontory), where M. Vipsanius Agrippa, the lieutenant of Augustus, defeated Sextus, the younger son of Pompey, and destroyed his naval supremacy.

BOOK THE EIGHTH.

CONTENTS.

Now, beyond the vales of Hercules[1] and the woody
Tempe, seeking the desert by-paths of the Hæmonian
wood[2], Magnus, urging on the steed exhausted with the
flight and refusing the spur, in his wanderings confuses
the uncertain traces of his flight and the intricate paths. He

[1] *Beyond the vales of Hercules*) ver. 1. This was the valley that lay
between Mounts Ossa and Olympus, through which the Peneus running,
discharges itself into the Thermaic Gulf, not far from Thermopylæ. See
B. vi. l. 345-8, and the Note to the passage.
[2] *Of the Hæmonian wood*) ver. 2. These were the woods that lay at the
foot of Mount Ossa, in the vicinity of Lake Nassonis.

(r.

starts with fear at the sound of the groves moved by the
winds; and that of his own attendants, which reaches
him from behind, startles him, fearful and afraid *that the
enemy is* at his side.) Although fallen from his lofty summit,
he knows that not yet is the price of his blood valueless,
and, mindful of his destiny, he believes that [1] he himself
still possesses a life of value as great as that which he
himself would give for the torn-off head [2] of Cæsar.

As he followed the desert tracks the noble features of the
hero did not allow him to conceal his station in a safe
retreat. Many, as they were repairing to the Pharsalian
camp, rumour not as yet having disclosed his downfall, were
astounded on meeting the chieftain [3], at the mutations of
events [4]; and hardly was he himself a trustworthy inform-
ant on his own ruin. Grievous is it to Magnus, whoever is
the witness of *his* woes. He would prefer to be unknown
to all nations, and in safety to pass through the world with
an obscure name; but Fortune demands from him in his
affliction the punishment of her prolonged favours, who
presses hard upon his adversity with the weight of a fame
so great, and burdens him with his former lot.

Now is he sensible that honors were too much hastened
for him, and he condemns the exploits in Sulla's day [5] of his

[1] *He believes that*) ver. 11. "Credit." He *believes* so only, and the Poet
seems to imply, from his abject condition, that he is mistaken, and only flat-
ters himself in thinking so.

[2] *For the torn-off head*) ver. 12. "Avulsâ cervice." Literally, " the
neck wrenched asunder."

[3] *Astounded on meeting the chieftain*) ver. 16. Rowe has the following
Note relative to this description of the flight of Pompey:—" This is one of
the passages which, if Lucan had lived to give the last hand to this work, I
cannot but think he would have altered. The fear that he gives to Pompey
on occasion of his flight, is very unlike the character he himself, or indeed
any writer, has given him. It is something the more remarkable, from a
passage in the latter end of the foregoing Book, where he is said to leave the
battle with great bravery and constancy of mind. Though it is very judi-
ciously observed, on comparing the passage and this together, by Martin
Lasso de Oropesa, the Spanish Translator, that the desire of seeing his wife,
which was the occasion of his resolution to leave the field, and survive such
a loss as that battle was, in the Seventh Book, might in this place likewise
be the reason for the fear and anxiety which he showed in his flight."

[4] *At the mutations of events*) ver. 16. "Vertigine rerum;" a strong expression, signifying "the sudden revolution" of his fortunes.

[5] *Condemns the exploits in Sulla's day*) ver. 25. He probably alludes

laurel-crowned youth. Now hurled down it grieves him to recollect both the Corycian fleets[1] and the Pontic standards[2]. Thus does an age too lengthened destroy great spirits, and a life that survives empire. Unless the last day comes with the end of *our* blessings, and anticipates sorrows by a speedy death, fortune is the prelude to disgrace. Does any one dare to surrender himself to a prosperous lot, except on having prepared for death[3]?

He had reached the shore[4], through which the river Peneus, now red with the Emathian carnage, discharged itself into the sea. From there a bark, unsuited for the wind and waves, hardly safe on the shallows of a river, bore him in trepidation, upon the deep. He, with whose oars even yet Corcyra shakes[5], and the Leucadian bays, the master of the Cilicians and of the Liburnian land, stole away, a timid passenger, in a little boat. Partner of his cares, thou didst bid him turn his sails towards the secret shores of Lesbos! in which land at that time thou didst lie concealed, Cornelia, more sad than if thou wast standing in the midst of the plains of Emathia. Pre-

to the triumph of Pompey over Hiarbas, king of Numidia, which, contrary to the wishes of Sulla, he gained when only in his twenty-fifth year. The Poet is guilty of an error in the Seventh Book, l. 14, where he mentions the triumph over Sertorius as the first of Pompey's triumphs.

[1] *Both the Corycian fleets*) ver. 26. He alludes to Pompey's victories over the Cilician pirates. The Corycus here named was a city of Cilicia Aspera, with a capacious harbour, between the mouths of the Lamus and the Calycadnus. Near it was the Corycian cave mentioned B. iii. l. 226.

[2] *And the Pontic standards*) ver. 26. The victories which he gained over Mithridates, king of Pontus, are those here alluded to.

[3] *Except on having prepared for death*) ver. 32. " Who can presume to look for prosperity, unless he is ready to meet death in case of failure?" Weise, however, thinks that by " secundis fatis," a second destiny, or " adversity," is meant. The passage is obscure, and the Commentators are by no means agreed upon its meaning.

[4] *He had reached the shore*) ver. 33. We learn from Appian that on reaching the sea-shore Pompey lodged that night in the cottage of a fisherman; in the morning he embarked in a little boat, in which he coasted along till he met with a ship of greater burden, of which an officer named Petilius was captain, who, recognizing Pompey, took him on board, and conveyed him to Lesbos. Plutarch gives a similar account.

[5] *Even yet Corcyra shakes*) ver. 37. He whose fleet was then master of Corcyra, the Leucadian coast, the Cilicians, and the Liburnians, some of the most skilful among the naval powers, was at that moment obliged to take refuge in a little boat.

sages arouse sad anxieties; thy slumber is convulsed by
trembling fears; Thessaly does each night present; and,
the shades departed, thou dost run along the crags of steep
rocks and the verge of the shore, looking out upon the
waves; fluttering afar thou art always the first to behold
the sails of the approaching ship, nor dost thou venture to
make any enquiries about thy husband's fate.

Lo! a bark, which spreads its canvas [1] towards your
harbours! what it is bringing thou knowest not; and now,
the sum of thy fears, a sad messenger of arms *is come*, and
ill-boding report. Thy vanquished husband is come. Why
dost thou lose the moments for grief? When now thou
couldst be weeping, thou art stricken with fear. Then, the
ship drawing nigh, she leaps forward, and marks the cruel
judgment of the Gods, the chieftain disfigured with paleness, and having his countenance overhung with white
hairs, and his garments squalid with black dust. Darkness
coming over her, afflicted, with its shades, takes away the
heavens and the light, and grief besets her soul; all *her*
limbs, forsaken by *their* sinews, totter; her heart grows
contracted, and long does she lie deceived with the hope
of death.

Now, the cable fastened to the shore, Pompey surveys the
vacant sands. After the faithful handmaids behold him close
at hand, no further than silent sighs do they allow them

---

[1] *Which spreads its canvas*) ver. 50. Pompey's movements, after he had
left the field of Pharsalia, are thus described by Cæsar, in the Civil War,
B. iii. c. 102:—"A proclamation was issued by Pompey at Amphipolis, that
all the young men of that province, Grecians and Roman citizens, should
take the military oath; but whether he issued it with an intention of preventing suspicion, and to conceal as long as possible his design of fleeing
thither, or to endeavour to keep possession of Macedonia by new levies, if
nobody pursued him, it is impossible to judge. He lay at anchor one night,
and calling together his friends at Amphipolis, and collecting a sum of money
for his necessary expenses, upon advice of Cæsar's approach, set sail from
that place, and in a few days arrived at Mitylene. Here he was detained
two days, and having added a few galleys to his fleet, he went to Cilicia,
and thence to Cyprus. There he was informed, that by consent of all the
inhabitants of Antioch and the Roman citizens who traded there, the castle had
been seized in order to shut him out of the town; and that messengers had
been dispatched to all those who were reported to have taken refuge in
the neighbouring states, that they should not come to Antioch; that if
they did, it would be attended with imminent danger to their lives."

selves *with which* to rebuke the Fates, and in vain do they attempt to raise their lifeless mistress from the ground; whom Magnus, clasps to his breast, and with his embraces warms her enervated limbs. The blood *now* recalled to the surface of her body, she had begun to feel the hands of Pompey, and to be able to meet the sad looks of her husband; Magnus forbids her to yield to fate, and with his voice reproves her immoderate grief :—

"Why, at the first wound of Fortune, dost thou fail in thy high-born courage, woman, rendered illustrious by the titles of ancestors so great[1]? Thou hast a road to a fame destined to endure for ages. In this sex *of thine* the sole ground for praise is not the enactment of laws, nor yet arms, *but* an unfortunate husband. Elevate thy mind, and let thy duty struggle with destiny, and love myself because I have been conquered. Now am I a still greater glory to thee, because the emblems of state[2], and because the virtuous throng of Senators, and troops so vast of Kings, have departed from me. Begin to be the only one to follow Magnus. Misplaced the grief, *which*, while thy husband survives, *is* extreme, and forbidden *is it* to increase. It ought to be thy last token of fidelity to mourn for thy husband. In my warfare thou hast borne ho losses. After the battles Magnus *still* lives, but his fortunes have perished ; that which thou dost bewail, that *alone* hast thou loved."

Rebuked by these words of her husband, with difficulty she raised her weak limbs from the ground, with lamentations breaking forth into such complaints :—

"O would that I had entered the marriage bed of hated Cæsar, an unhappy wife, and joyous in no husband[3]! Twice have I proved injurious to the world ; Erinnys has conducted me as my bridal attendant[4], and the shades of the Crassi ;

---

[1] *By the titles of ancestors so great*) ver. 73. He alludes to her descent from the family of the Scipios.

[2] *The emblems of state*) ver. 79. " Fasces ;" literally, " the fasces," the emblems of the Consular dignity.

[3] *Joyous in no husband*) ver. 89. Neither in her first husband, P. Crassus, the son of M. Crassus the Triumvir, both of whom were slain in the Parthian war, nor yet in the unfortunate Pompey, her second husband.

[4] *Erinnys has conducted me as my bridal attendant*) ver. 90. Erinnys, or one of the Furies, being " Pronuba," would be inauspiciously occupying the place of Juno " Pronuba." The "pronubæ" were also the women who directed

and devoted to those ghosts I have borne the disasters of
Assyria [1] to the civil warfare, and have hurled nations headlong, and have scared all the Gods from the better cause.
O most famous husband, O *thou,* unworthy of my marriage
bed, had Fortune this control over a head so mighty? Why
impiously did I marry *thee,* if I was doomed to make thee
wretched? Now take revenge, but *such as* I shall willingly
submit to. In order that the ocean may be more propitious
to thee, the fidelity of kings assured, and the whole world
more hospitable, hurl *me,* thy partner, into the sea. More
do I wish that I had laid down *this* life for the fortune of
arms; now at last, Magnus, expiate thy overthrow. Wherever
ruthless Julia, thou dost lie, having by civil strife taken
vengeance upon my nuptials, do thou come hither and
exact the penalty, and appeased, thy rival slain [2], spare thy
Magnus." Thus having said, and again sinking into the
bosom of her husband, she melts the eyes of all to tears.
The heart of stern Magnus relents, and eyes that were dry
in Thessaly does Lesbos fill.

Then does the multitude of Mitylene [3] upon the thronged
shore *thus* address Magnus:—

" If it shall always prove to us the greatest glory to have
preserved the *precious* pledge of a husband so mighty, do
thou, as well, we entreat, deign to grace for even one night
the walls devoted to thee by a sacred treaty, and *our* household Gods thy allies; make *this,* Magnus, a place which all
ages shall revisit, which the Roman stranger on coming shall
venerate. By thee vanquished, no walls ought in preference
to be entered. All *places* are able to hope for the favour of
the conqueror; this has already committed a crime. And

the marriage ceremony on the part of the bride, or "the bridewomen." Ovid
has a similar passage to this in the Epistle of Phyllis to Demophoon, in the
Heroides, Ep. ii. ver. 117-120 :—"Over that match did presiding Tisiphone
howl, and the solitary bird uttered its mournful notes. Alecto was there,
her hair wreathed with short serpents, and the light was waved with the
sepulchral torch."

[1] *Borne the disasters of Assyria*) ver. 92. Disasters such as the Romans
had suffered in their campaigns against the Parthians, the inhabitants of
ancient Assyria.

[2] *Appeased, thy rival slain*) ver. 104. "Pellice." "Pellex" is here
used in the same sense as in B. iii. l. 23. See the Note to the passage.

[3] *The multitude of Mitylene*) ver. 109. See B. v. l. 786, and the Note
to the passage.

what if this lies, an island, on the sea? Cæsar is in want of ships. A great part of thy nobles will collect *here*, assured of thy locality. Upon a known shore must the war be renewed. Take the wealth of the Temples and the gold of the Gods; if these youths are better suited for the land, if for ships, take them; make use of all Lesbos, so far as it is of service. Take them; lest Cæsar should seize them, do thou, vanquished, accept them. This charge alone do thou remove from a land that deserves well *of thee*, that thou mayst not appear both to have obtained our alliance when fortunate, and to have repudiated it when unsuccessful."

Glad in his adversity at such affection in *these* men, and rejoicing for the sake of the world that fidelity *still* exists, he says :—

"That there is no land[1] in all the world more dear to me, I have shown to you by no slight pledge. By this hostage did Lesbos retain my affection; here was my hallowed home and my dear household Gods, here was Rome to me. To no shores in my flight have I before this turned my ship, as I knew that Lesbos had already earned the wrath of Cæsar, my wife being sheltered *there*, not having feared to entrust to you so great a ground for pardon[2]. But now, sufficient is it to have rendered you guilty; over the whole world my destinies must be pursued by me. Alas! too happy Lesbos, with everlasting fame, whether thou dost teach nations and kings to receive Magnus, or whether thou alone dost show fidelity to me. For I am resolved to seek in what lands there is righteousness, *and* where is guilt. Receive, O Deity, if still thou art in any degree favourable to me, the extreme of my prayers: grant *me* nations like to Lesbos who will not forbid me, subdued in war, Cæsar my foe, to enter their harbours, nor yet to leave them."

He spoke, and he placed his sorrowing partner on board the ship. You would have supposed that all were changing

---

[1] *There is no land*) ver. 129. Plutarch informs us that when the people of Mitylene entreated Pompey to enter their city, he declined to do so, and entreated them to be of good heart, and submit to Cæsar, who was full of goodness and clemency; a very different account from that here given.

[2] *So great a ground for pardon*) ver. 136. He means to say that he did not hesitate to put himself in their power, although, by his betrayal, they had the opportunity of easily making their peace with Cæsar.

their land and their paternal soil; in such a manner did
they lament throughout all the shore, *and* reproaching right
hands were extended to the skies; and less for Pompey, whose
fortunes had aroused their grief, but *rather* for her, whom,
throughout the whole period of the war, they had looked on
as their own fellow-citizen, did the people lament on beholding her depart; whom hardly, if she had been repairing
to the camp of a victorious husband, could the matrons
have now supposed to depart with dry eyes; with so great
love had her virtue attached to her some, some her inte-
grity and the modesty of her chaste features, inasmuch as,
humble in the extreme, a sojourner, cause of offence to not
one of the multitude, she lived, her fortunes still erect, just
as though her husband had been conquered.

Now Titan, sinking to his mid fires[1] in the sea, was
not entire to those from whom he conceals, nor to those to
whom, if any, he discloses his orb; the watchful anxieties in
Pompey's breast now revert to the allied cities of the Roman
confederacy and the varying dispositions of kings, now
to the remote regions of the world beyond oppressive suns
extending, and the south. Full oft the sad struggle of
cares and a distrust in the future cast aside the wearying
fluctuations of his undecided breast, and he consults the
pilot of the ship about all the stars[2]; in which quarter he
marks the land[3]; what is his method of dividing the sea by
the heavens; by means of what Constellation he makes for
Syria, or which fire in the Wain[4] rightly points to Libya. To

[1] *To his mid fires*) ver. 159. He means that half of the orb of the
sun was above the horizon, and half below it, so as to be seen in its en-
tirety neither by those to whom it was setting, nor to their antipodes (if
any), to whom it was rising. He expresses some doubt as to the antipodes,
because it was a matter of discussion among the ancients whether they
existed. It is clear that the Poet here alludes to the setting sun; but Rowe
translates the passage as though describing the break of day.

[2] *About all the stars*) ver. 167. All this astronomical parade of the Poet
has been generally deemed frigid, and misplaced in the extreme.

[3] *In which quarter he marks the land*) ver. 168-9. He enquires how, by
means of observing the stars, he traverses the sea, and what stars he watches
in steering for Syria.

[4] *Which fire in the Wain*) ver. 170. "Which star in the Constellation of
the Greater Bear is observed in steering for the coast of Africa." This Constellation was called "plaustrum," from its fancied resemblance to a waggon
and a team of horses. By us it is sometimes called Charles's Wain.

these *words* the skilled observer of the silent heavens makes answer :—

" The Constellations which fleet on in the star-bearing sky, deceiving wretched mariners, the heavens never standing still, we do not follow; but that pole which never sets, most bright with the twofold Arcti², guides the ships.　Here, always when the Lesser Bear rises vertically ³ before me and stands over the summit of the ropes of the mainmast yards ⁴ *then* do we look towards the Bosporus and the sea that winds along the shores of Scythia.　Is Arctophylax descending ⁵ at all from the summit of the mast, and is the Cynosure brought nearer to the sea, *then* is the bark making towards the harbours of Syria.　Then does Canopus receive us⁶, a star content to wander in the southern sky, dreading Boreas: speed onward with it also to the left, beyond Pharos, the bark in the mid sea will touch the Syrtes.　But in what direction dost thou command the sails to be set, in what the canvas to be now spread with the sheet?"

To him, on the other hand, with doubting breast Magnus answered:—" Observe this alone throughout the whole ocean, that thy bark is always afar from the Emathian shores, and leave Hesperia to the sea and sky; leave the rest to the winds.　My partner and deposited pledge have I regained; then was I assured what shores I desired; now Fortune will provide a harbour."

¹ *Observer of the silent heavens*) ver. 171.　"Servator Olympi."　Literally, " the watcher," or " keeper of Olympus "—a rather periphrastic description of a pilot.

² *Most bright with the twofold Arcti*) ver. 175.　The Greater and Lesser Bears, or Helice and Cynosura.

³ *The Lesser Bear rises vertically*) ver. 176-7.　He means that when he steers towards the Bosporus and the North, the Lesser Bear rises towards the zenith, but when he steers southwards, towards Syria, it declines.

⁴ *Summit of the ropes of the mainmast yards*) ver. 177.　" Ceruchi."　It is not well ascertained what is the meaning of the word " ceruchus."　Some Commentators take it to have been the extremity of the sailyard, while others consider it to have been the name of the rope which ran from the end of the sailyard to the top of the mast.

⁵ *Is Arctophylax descending*) ver. 180.　As to Arctophylax, or Bootes, and Cynosura, or the Lesser Bear, see B. ii. L 722; B. iii. l. 218, and l. 252; and B. ix. l. 540.

⁶ *Then does Canopus receive us*) ver. 181.　" After passing Syria southward, we observe Canopus, a star of the south, unknown to northern climes."　This star was also called " Coma Berenices," or " Berenice's Hair."

Thus he speaks; but he turns the sails hanging in equal degree from the level ends of the sailyards, and guides the ship to the left, and that he may cleave the waves which the Samian rocks and which Chios renders rugged, these ropes he loosens at the prow, those he tightens [1] at the stern. The seas are sensible of the change, and now, the beak in another direction cleaving the deep, and the bark not looking the same way, they change their sound. Not so *dexterously* does the guide of the horses, when he sweeps round the left end of the axle [2] with the right-hand wheel, force the chariot to keep close to the turning-place untouched [3].

Titan has *now* disclosed the earth and concealed the stars. Each one dispersed by the Emathian storms, follows after Magnus [4], and first from the shores of Lesbos his son comes to meet him [5], and then a faithful band of nobles. For not from Magnus when hurled down by the Fates and worsted in fight, has Fortune taken kings as his attend-

---

[1] *Loosens at the prow, those he tightens*) ver. 196. Weise seems to understand "dedit" and "tenet" as meaning the same thing; that he draws tight the sailyards both at stem and stern; which, however, seems not to be the case. The meaning apparently is, that he loosens or lets out the ropes at the prow, and tightens them at the stern, for the purpose of running in a south-easterly course, his object being to open out one angle of the sail (these being generally three-cornered), and to draw in the others." See the description in B. v. l. 428, *et seq.*

[2] *Sweeps round the left end of the axle*) ver. 200. "Dexteriore rotâ lævum quum circuit axem." When turning sharply round the turning-place the outer or right-hand wheel takes a circuit round the other end of the axle-tree, the inner or left-hand wheel standing almost still.

[3] *Close to the turning-place untouched*) ver. 201. Among the Romans, the chariot-race consisted of seven circuits of the "spina," or wall in the midst of the Circus, at each end of which was the "meta" or "goal," or rather, "turning-place." Of course it was the object of the charioteers to save as much space as possible, by getting the inside place and turning close to the "meta," without touching it.

[4] *Follows after Magnus*) ver. 204. Those who have escaped the Thessalian catastrophe, on learning the direction in which Pompey has sailed, hasten to follow him.

[5] *His son comes to meet him*) ver. 204. This was Sextus, his younger son, who had been in Lesbos during the Pharsalian campaign, at the time when, in his fervent imagination, the Poet represents him as consulting the Thessalian enchantress. He was probably in another part of the island during his father's short stay there. This is the more probable as his mother Mucia having been Pompey's divorced wife, he may not have felt any regard or sympathy for Cornelia, who was then at Mitylene.

ants; an exile, he has the rulers of the earth and those who wield the sceptres of the East as his companions. He bids Deiotarus [1], who follows the flying track of his leader, go to the remote regions of the world.

"Since," says he, "most faithful of kings, the earth, wherever it is Roman, has been lost by the Emathian defeat, it remains *for us* to try the fidelity of the East, and the nations that drink of Euphrates, and Tigris still safe from Cæsar. Object not, seeking the destinies of Magnus, to penetrate to the remote abodes of the Medians and the Scythian retreats, and to change the entire clime, and to carry my words to the proud descendant of Arsaces [2].

" If *your* ancient treaties with me are *still* in force, sworn unto me by the Thunderer of Latium, ratified by your magicians [3], fill your quivers, and stretch the Armenian bows with Getan strings; if, you, O Parthians, when I sought the Caspian strongholds, and pursued the hardy Alani [4] with their eternal wars, permitting *you* to range at large in the Achæmenian plains [5], I never drove trembling *in flight* to well-defended Babylon. Beyond the realms of Cyrus, and the confines of the Chaldæan sway, where the rapid Ganges and where the Nysæan Hydaspes [6] approach the sea, nearer was I then to the fires of rising Phœbus than

[1] *He bids Deiotarus*) ver. 210. See B. v. l. 55, and the Note to the passage. Deiotarus had made his escape from the coast of Thessaly in the same ship with Pompey.

[2] *Proud descendant of Arsaces*) ver. 218. The royal family of Parthia were descended from Arsaces; see B. i. l. 108.

[3] *Ratified by your magicians*) ver. 220. He means " confirmed and ratified by the Chaldæan priesthood," who also aspired to the credit of being deemed magicians.

[4] *Pursued the hardy Alani*) ver. 223. The Alani were a warlike people of Asia, included under the general name of Scythians, but probably a branch of the Massagetæ. They excelled in horsemanship, and at the time when Lucan wrote were probably dwelling on the east of the Caucasus. They finally became absorbed with the Huns and the Vandals.

[5] *In the Achæmenian plains*) ver. 224. See B. ii. l. 49, and the Note to the passage.

[6] *The Nysæan Hydaspes*) ver. 227. The name Nysa was given to several places which, for various reasons, were held sacred to Bacchus. The Indian Nysa, which is here alluded to, was in the country of Goryæa, the Punjaub of the present day. It was situate at the confluence of the rivers Cophen and Choaspes, and was probably the same place as Dionysopolis, or Nagara, the Naggar of the present day.

Persia *was;* still, subduing all places, I endured that
yourselves alone [1] should be wanting to my triumphs;
and alone in the number of kings of Eastern lands does
the Parthian approach me on equal terms. Nor once
do the descendants of Arsaces stand *saved* by the favour
of Magnus. For who was it that, after the wounds of the
Assyrian slaughter, restrained the just wrath of Latium [2]?
Bound by so many obligations to me, now let Parthia,
the limits burst open [3], pass beyond the banks forbidden
for ages, and the Zeugma of him of Pella [4]. Conquer
for Pompey, ye Parthians; Rome will be ready to be conquered.'"

The King does not hesitate to obey him commanding
an enterprise so difficult; and, the insignia of the palace
laid aside [5], he goes forth, clad in the assumed garb of a
menial. In doubtful *enterprises* it is safe for the monarch
to counterfeit the needy man. How much more securely,
then, does the man who is truly poor pass his life than the
rulers of the world! The king having been dismissed upon

[1] *I endured that yourselves alone)* ver. 230. If we may judge from the
circumstances of the utter overthrow of the army of the Crassi, Pompey, in
not following up the war with the Parthians and finally triumphing over
them, made a virtue of necessity.

[2] *Restrained the just wrath of Latium)* ver. 234. See B. i. l. 104. After
the defeat of the Crassi, Pompey dissuaded the Senate from continuing the
Parthian warfare while they were engaged in the Gallic war.

[3] *The limits burst open)* ver. 236. This passage has been generally thought
to refer to the boundaries of the Parthian Empire (which were considered to
be the line of the Euphrates), agreed upon between Pompey and King
Phraates. But, unless we agree with Burmann that " per sæcula" here
means " for future ages," having a prospective signification, that cannot be
the meaning of the passage, as the treaty had been only recently made,
and we must adopt the suggestion of one of the Scholiasts, that the
Euphrates is alluded to as the boundary assigned, together with the city of
Zeugma, by Alexander the Great, to the Parthian Empire.

[4] *The Zeugma of him of Pella)* ver. 237. Zeugma was a city built,
according to some, by Alexander the Great, which opinion Lucan seems to
adopt, from his using the epithet " Pellæus." Its foundation is, however,
more generally attributed to Seleucus Nicator ; it was situate on the western
bank of the Euphrates, where a bridge of boats had been constructed by
Alexander, from which it received its name, a Greek word signifying " the
junction." Pella in Macedon, as already remarked, was the birthplace of
Alexander the Great.

[5] *The insignia of the palace laid aside)* ver. 239. He lays aside the
robes of a monarch, and, disguising himself, assumes the dress of a servant.

the shore, he himself amid the rocks of Icaria[1], leaving behind both Ephesus, and Colophon[2] with its tranquil seas, skims past the foaming rocks of little Samos[3]; the floating breeze blows off from the shores of Cos[4]; next does he fly past Cnidos[5] and leave Rhodes behind, made illustrious by the sun[6], and by the mid-sea[7] he cuts short the great bays of the Telmessian waves[8].

The Pamphylian land presents itself to the ship; and not as yet venturing to entrust himself to any walls, to thee, little Phaselis[9], does Magnus first repair. For thee

[1] *Amid the rocks of Icaria*) ver. 244. Icaria, now called Nicaria, is an island of the Ægean Sea, one of the Sporades, and west of Samos. It was also called Doliche, " the Long Island." It was famed for its rich pastures, and received its name from the adjacent Icarian Sea, which was so called from the fabled fall there of Icarus, the son of Dædalus, when flying with his father from Crete.

[2] *Both Ephesus, and Colophon*) ver. 245. Colophon, like Ephesus, was one of the twelve Ionian cities of Asia Minor, and stood on the sea-coast, at the mouth of the river Halesus. It claimed to be the birth-place of Homer. A small village now stands on its site.

[3] *The foaming rocks of little Samos*) ver. 246. Samos, now called Samo by the Greeks, was one of the principal islands in the Ægean Sea. It lies off the coast of Ancient Ionia, from which it is only separated by a narrow strait. It was famed for its architecture, painting, and pottery. Pythagoras was a native of this island.

[4] *From the shores of Cos*) ver. 246. Cos, now called Stanco, was one of the Sporades, lying off the coast of Caria, in Asia Minor. It was the birth-place of the famous painter Apelles.

[5] *Fly past Cnidos*) ver. 247. Cnidos, or Gnidus, was a celebrated city of Asia Minor, on the coast of Caria. It was much resorted to by travellers, led thither by curiosity to behold the statue of Venus by Praxiteles, which stood in her Temple there.

[6] *Rhodes behind, made illustrious by the sun*) ver. 247-8. See B. v. l. 50, and the Note to the passage.

[7] *By the mid-sea*) ver. 249. " Compensat medio pelago." He probably means by this expression that Pompey did not coast along the Telmessian Gulf, but stood out to sea straight in his course from point to point, at the extremities of the bay.

[8] *Of the Telmessian waves*) ver. 248. There were two cities of the name of Telmessus. The one here referred to was a city of Lycia, near the borders of Caria, on a gulf called Telmessicus Sinus, and close to the Promontory Telmessis.

[9] *Little Phaselis*) ver. 251. Phaselis was a seaport of Lycia, near the borders of Pamphylia, on the Pamphylian Gulf. It was at one period a place of considerable importance, and, having the command of three harbours, enjoyed an extensive commerce. Becoming the head-quarters of the pirates

X

thy scanty inhabitants forbid to be distrusted, and thy
homes exhausted of *their* people; and greater is the multitude in the ship than thine. Hence, again spreading the
canvas, now he beholds Taurus, and Dipsus, that flows
down from Taurus[1].

Could Magnus have believed this[2], that when he gave
peace to the waves provision was made for himself as well?
Safe, in his little bark he flies along the shores of the Cilicians. A great part of the Senate, collected, overtakes the
flying chieftain; and at little Celendræ[3], at which port Selinus both sends forth and receives its ships, in an assembly
of the nobles, at length does Magnus open his sorrowing
lips, in these words:—

"Companions in the war and in *my* flight, and dear as
my native land, although on a naked shore, in the region
of the Cilicians, *and* surrounded by no arms, I take counsel,
and consider of a commencement for a new career, *still*, do
you bring courageous spirits. Not utterly have I fallen on
the fields of Emathia, nor so far are my destinies depressed
that I am not able to raise my head again, and shake off
the reverse I have sustained. Were the ruins of Libya able

who infested the coasts of Asia Minor, it was destroyed by P. Servilius Isauricus. It was rebuilt, but never recovered its former importance, or, perhaps,
magnitude; and this is probably the reason which prompts the Poet to
style it " parva," "little." It is not improbable that the inhabitants were
forbidden by the Romans to surround it with walls. It is said by some that
the light vessels, called " phaseli," were first built here. According to Plutarch, Attalia was the first place in Asia Minor at which Pompey touched.
The Poet, perhaps, means in l. 253, that the inhabitants of this place had all
deserted it for the standards of Pompey.

[1] *Dipsus, that flows down from Taurus*) ver. 255. Under the name
" Dipsus," or " Dipsas," Burmann thinks that the river Catarrhactes is
alluded to. This is a river of ancient Pamphylia, which descends from the
mountain chain of Taurus, in a vast broken waterfall, whence it received its
name. After flowing beneath the earth in a portion of its course, it falls
into the sea to the east of Attalia.

[2] *Could Magnus have believed this*) ver. 256. " Could Pompey have fore-
seen, at the time when he defeated the Cilician pirates, and made the southern
coasts of Asia Minor secure from piracy, that he should one day as a fugitive
have to seek a refuge there?"

[3] *And at little Celendræ*) ver. 259. Celendræ was a town founded by
the Samians in Cilicia. It had a harbour of the same name at the mouth of
the river Selinus, and was probably the same place as Syedra, or Syedræ,
which indeed, in some of the Editions, is the reading here.

to elevate Marius[1] to the Consular dignity[2] and restore him
to the filled annals[3], *and* me shall Fortune keep depressed
by a lighter hand? A thousand ships of mine[4] are tossed
upon the Grecian seas, a thousand captains ; rather does
Pharsalia disperse our resources, than subvert them.

"But me even the fame alone of my exploits is able to
protect, which throughout the whole earth I have achieved,
and a name which the world loves. Do you weigh *these*
realms[5], both as to their strength and their fidelity—Libya,
and the Parthians, and Pharos—which of them ought to
succour the Roman state. But I, nobles, will disclose the
secrets of my cares, and in which direction the prepon-
derance of my thoughts inclines. The age of the monarch
of the Nile[6] is suspected by me, because strict fidelity demands ripened years. On the other hand the two-faced
subtlety of the doubtful Moor alarms me ; for, mindful
of his race, the ruthless descendant of Carthage[7] longs for
Hesperia, and much of Hannibal is in *his* fickle breast.
He who defiles his kingdom with collateral blood[8], and

---

[1] *Able to elevate Marius*) ver. 269. See B. ii. l. 89, and the Note. He
alludes to the downfall of Marius, and his being found sitting amid the ruins
of Carthage, after which, with the aid of Cinna, he regained his lost position,
and entered Rome once more as a conqueror.

[2] *To the Consular dignity*) ver. 270. "In fasces ;" literally, " to the
fasces."

[3] *To the filled annals*) ver. 270. In allusion to the " Fasti Consulares," in which Marius appeared as Consul seven times, a number never
before equalled by any person.

[4] *A thousand ships of mine*) ver. 272. His large fleet was at this time
in the Adriatic Sea, and the neighbourhood of Corcyra.

[5] *Do you weigh these realms*) ver. 276. " Take into consideration the
comparative resources and fidelity of Juba, king of Numidia, Phraates, king
of Parthia, and Ptolemy, king of Egypt, who are all allies of the Roman
people, of which you are the representatives."

[6] *The age of the monarch of the Nile*) ver. 281. This was Ptolemy XII.,
king of Egypt, who was but thirteen years of age at this period ; on account
of which Pompey doubts whether he will have sufficient strength of mind
to adhere with fidelity to his allies. The result proved how well founded
were these doubts.

[7] *The ruthless descendant of Carthage*) ver. 284. One of the Scholiasts
asserts that Juba was descended from a sister of Hannibal.

[8] *Defiles his kingdom with collateral blood*) ver. 286. It has been suggested
that by the words " obliquo sanguine" he hints that Juba is of illegitimate
birth. But it is much more probable that by it he intends to denote the kind
of relationship which existed between Hannibal and Juba ; probably mean-

reaches up to Numidian forefathers, has now become puffed
up with pride, on Varus being a suppliant[1], and has looked
upon *the destinies* of Rome in a secondary rank.

" Come, then, *my* companions, let us hasten to the
Eastern climes. Euphrates with his tide divides the vast
earth, and the Caspian strongholds set apart boundless retreats, and another pole measures the Assyrian nights and
days, and a sea of different colour[2] in its waves is severed
from ours, and an ocean their own. Their sole desire *is*
rule[3]. More lofty *is* the war-horse in the plains, and
more strong *their* bow; neither boy nor aged man is slow
to stretch the deadly string, and from no arrow is death
matter of uncertainty. They were the first with the bow
to repulse the lances of Pella[4]; and Bactria, the abode[5] of
the Medians, and Babylon, proud of its walls[6], the home
of the Assyrians.

" Nor yet are our javelins much feared by the Parthians;
and they dare to engage in war, having made trial of the
Scythian arrows, when Crassus died. Nor do they scatter

ing, that though not lineally they were collaterally related. Oudendorp
thinks that Hannibal may have descended from a daughter or sister of one
of the former kings of Numidia, and thus through his maternal ancestors
have been related to the forefathers of Juba.

[1] *Varus being a suppliant*) ver. 287. He thinks that he may have become overweening and arrogant, on seeing Varus appealing to him for assistance, and then having conquered Curio and his troops. See B. iv. l. 668–
715, et seq.

[2] *A sea of different colour*) ver. 293. No doubt he here alludes to the
Red Sea.

[3] *Their sole desire is rule*) ver. 294. " They are not greedy for wealth,
and therefore will not be traitors to us; while their love of conquest will aid
our cause."

[4] *The lances of Pella*) ver. 298. " Sarissas." The " sarissa" is supposed
to have been a kind of pike with which the soldiers of the Macedonian phalanx were armed. Their ordinary length was twenty-one feet, but those used
by the phalanx were twenty-four feet in length. As to the Eastern expedition of Alexander the Great, here alluded to, see B. iii. l. 233.

[5] *And Bactria, the abode*) ver. 299. Bactria was a province occupying
pretty nearly that part of Asia now called Bokhara. It was inhabited by
a rude and warlike race, who were subjugated by either Cyrus or one of the
later Medo-Persian kings, who are here spoken of as " Medi." It afterwards
formed the Greek kingdom of Bactria, which was ultimately subdued by the
Parthians.

[6] *Proud of its walls*) ver. 299. See B. vi. l. 50, and the Note to the
passage.

darts that trust in iron alone, but the whizzing shafts are steeped in plenteous venom. Small wounds are fatal, and there is death in the blood on the surface *of the skin.* Oh! would that I had not dependence so great upon the ruthless descendants of Arsaces! Destinies too strongly rivalling our own destinies influence the Medians, and greatly do the Gods favour the race[1].

" Nations will I pour forth summoned from other lands ; and the East will I send against him, awakened from its retreats. But if Eastern faith and barbarian confederacies betray us, let Fortune bear our wreck beyond the intercourse of the ordinary world. I will not go suing to realms which I have created; but I shall enjoy a great solace in my death, as I lie in another clime, that nothing to these limbs my father-in-law has done with bloody, nothing with pious intent. But revolving all the destinies of my life, always was I venerated in that part of the world. Beyond Mæotis how mighty[2]! How mighty at Tanais, in the sight of the whole East! Into what lands did my name make its way with deeds more glorious, or whence with greater triumphs did it return?

" Rome, favour my purpose ; for what could the Gods of heaven ever grant to thee more welcome than for thee to wage the civil war with Parthian troops, *and* to overthrow a nation so mighty, and to confound it with our woes? When the arms of Cæsar shall engage with the Medians, it follows that Fortune must avenge either me or the Crassi."

Thus having said, he perceives by the murmurs that the men disapprove of his plans ; all of whom Lentulus exceeded in his incentives to valour and in the dignity of his grief, and uttered words worthy of one so late a Consul :—

" Have the Thessalian reverses so far impaired thy mind ?

---

[1] *Greatly do the Gods favour the race*) ver. 308. " Multumque in gente Deorum est;" literally, "and much of the Gods is in the race ;" meaning that they were clearly highly favoured by the Gods. One of the Scholiasts thinks that it means that " the Chaldæans worship many Gods," which, however, would be a very frigid translation of the passage.

[2] *Beyond Mæotis how mighty*) ver. 319. Alluding to his victories over Tigranes and Mithridates, he supposes the fame of them to have extended beyond the " palus Mæotis " or " sea of Azof," and the river " Tanais " or " Don." " Lis datur."

Has a single day sealed the destinies of the world? Is
a contest so mighty decided[1] by Emathia? Does all aid
lie prostrate for *this* blood-stained wound? Has Fortune
left to thee, Magnus, the feet of the Parthians alone[2]?
Why, flying through the world, abhorring the entire regions
of *our* earth[3] and *our* sky, dost thou seek the opposite
poles and remote stars, about to venerate Chaldæan Gods,
and barbarian rites[4], a servant of the Parthians? Why
is the love of liberty[5] the pretext alleged for our arms?
Why dost thou deceive the wretched world, if thou canst
be a slave? Thee, whom he dreaded to hear of when
ruling the Roman state, whom he beheld leading captured
kings from the Hyrcanian woods[6], and from the Indian
shores, shall he behold cast down by the Fates, humble
and abject, and madly raise his aspirations for the Latian
world, Pompey his suppliant, measuring himself and Rome
together?

" Thou wilt be able to say nothing worthy of thy spirit
and thy destiny. Ignorant of converse in the Latin
tongue, he will demand, Magnus, that thou shouldst ask
him by tears. Are we to endure this wound on our shame,

[1] *Is a contest so mighty decided*) ver. 333. "Litem dare" signified "to
pronounce sentence," and was especially applied to the Roman Prætor
giving judgment. The meaning is, "Is the Thessalian disaster so entirely to
pronounce judgment upon and influence our future destinies?"

[2] *Left to thee, Magnus, the feet of the Parthians alone*) ver. 334–5.
"Solos tibi, Magne, reliquit Parthorum Fortuna pedes?" This has been
generally taken to mean, "Has Fortune left it as your only resource to go and
kiss the feet of the Parthians while imploring their aid?" and in that sense
the Scholiasts have understood the passage. It is much more probable that
the meaning is, "Has Fortune left it as your only resource to trust in the
swiftness of foot of the Parthian troops?" a quality for which they were
especially famed.

[3] *The entire regions of our earth*) ver. 336. "Terrarum;" meaning "our
regions of the earth," in contradistinction to the distant climes of the Parthians and Assyrians. See l. 292.

[4] *And barbarian rites*) ver. 338. He probably alludes to the fire worship
of the Chaldæans and Magi; which has descended to the Parsees of the present day.

[5] *Why is the love of liberty*) ver. 339. "Why pretend that love of liberty
influences us, if it is only a desire to serve the Parthians that prompts us to
continue the warfare?"

[6] *From the Hyrcanian woods*) ver. 343. He says this with the licence of
the poet, in allusion to the Parthian and Syrian campaigns of Pompey.

that Parthia shall avenge the woes of Hesperia, before Rome *does* her own? Thyself it was she chose as *her* chieftain in the civil strife. Why dost thou spread our wounds among the Scythian tribes, and our slaughters that *at present* lie concealed? Why dost thou teach the Parthians to come beyond[1]? Rome loses *thereby* the solace of woes so great in bringing in no kings, but becoming the slave of her own citizen.

"Does it give thee delight to go throughout the world leading savage nations against the walls of Rome, and following standards from the Euphrates, captured with the Crassi[2]? He who alone among the kings, who, while Fortune concealed her preference, was wanting to Emathia[3], will he now challenge the resources so mighty of him heard of as the conqueror, or be ready, Magnus, to unite his fortunes with thee? Not this trustworthiness is there in the race.

---

[1] *Teach the Parthians to come beyond*) ver. 354. "Why give the Parthians an excuse for passing the Euphrates, which, by the treaty made with yourself, is their limit?"

[2] *Standards captured with the Crassi*) ver. 358. See B. i. l. 10, and the Note to the passage. The standards here alluded to were eventually restored by Phraates to Augustus, on hearing that the Romans were preparing an expedition to obtain their restitution, which had been previously promised, by force of arms. Ovid, in the Fasti, B. v. l. 578, *et seq.*, has the following interesting passage relative to these circumstances :—"Nor is it enough for Mars to have but once merited this epithet of avenger; he pursues the standards detained in the hands of the Parthians. This was a nation protected both by their plains, their horses, and their arrows, and inaccessible from the rivers that surrounded them. The slaughter of the Crassi imparted daring to the nation, when soldiers, general, and standards were lost together. The Parthian was in possession of the Roman standards, the token of honor in warfare ; and an enemy was the bearer of the Roman eagle. And still would that disgrace have been remaining, had not the empire of Ausonia been protected by the valiant arms of Cæsar. 'T was he that removed the ancient stains and the disgrace of such long duration; the standards when recovered recognized their friends. What then, thou Parthian, availed thee the arrows wont to be discharged behind thy back ? What thy inaccessible places ? What the management of thy fleet steed ? Parthian, thou dost restore the eagles. Thy conquered bows, too, thou dost extend! Now no pledges of our disgrace hast thou."

[3] *Was wanting to Emathia*) ver. 360–61. He reminds Pompey that Phraates was the only monarch, in alliance with the Roman people, who did not send forces to Thessaly to the aid of Pompey, and suggests that his object was to see who would prove the victor, and side with the strongest.

" Every nation which is born amid the Arctoan frosts *is* unsubdued in war and a lover of death. Whatever glides towards the Eastern lands and the warm regions of the world, the mildness of the climate makes the nations effeminate. There do you behold both the flowing vestments[1] and the loose coverings of the men. The Parthian amid the Median fields, upon the Sarmatian plains and the lands of Tigris extending with level track, is conquerable by no enemy in his powers of flight; but where the earth swells he will not ascend the rugged mountain ridges; nor will he wage the warfare in darkening shades, weak with his uncertain bow, nor by swimming cleave the current with its strong eddies; nor, besprinkled in battle over all his limbs with blood, will he endure the summer's sun beneath the heated dust. No battering-rams have they, no engines of war; they are not able to fill up trenches; and, the Parthian pursuing, whatever shall be able to resist the arrow, *that same* shall prove a wall[2].

" Skirmishing *are* their battles, and flying their fights, and straggling their squadrons, and more skilled are the troops at giving way than at repulsing. Steeped *are their* weapons with treachery, nor have they valour ever to endure the combat hand to hand, but *rather* to stretch the strings *of their bows* from afar, and to leave their wounds to the winds, wherever they choose to carry them. The sword requires strength, and every nation that exists of men wages the warfare with the sword; but the Medians the first onset disarms, and *their* emptied quivers bid them retreat. No confidence have they in their hands, in poison is it all.

" Dost thou, Magnus, deem *those to be* men for whom it is too little to come to the hazard of the battle with the sword? Is it so greatly worth thy while to try a disgraceful aid, that, separated from thy country by the whole world, thou mayst die? Is barbarian earth to press upon thee? Is a little and a homely tomb to cover thee, matter of envy still,

[1] *Both the flowing vestments*) ver. 367–8. He regards the flowing vestments, and probably the loose trowsers of the Eastern nations, as so many symptoms of luxury and effeminacy. In the later times of the Empire the use of this kind of dress was much affected by the more fashionable Romans.
[2] *That same shall prove a wall*) ver. 379. Meaning that by their arrows alone they are formidable.

while Crassus wants a sepulchre[1]. But lighter is thy lot, since death is the extreme punishment, and one not to be feared by men

" But Cornelia dreads not death[2] alone under a wicked king. Is the barbarian lust unknown to us, which blindly, after the manner of wild beasts, pollutes the laws and the compacts of the marriage tie with wives innumerable? The secrets, too, of the unrighteous bed lie there exposed. Amid a thousand wives, royalty, maddened with revelry and with wine, abhors not any intercourse[3] interdicted by the laws; amid the embraces of women so many one night wearies not one man. Sisters lie in the beds of brothers, the sacred ties of mothers, as well. The woful story among nations condemns Thebes, stained by Œdipus[4], for a crime not voluntarily committed; how often is the Parthian ruler, descended from Arsaces, born of blood thus mixed! To him to whom it is lawful to unite with a parent, what can I deem to be unlawful? The progeny so illustrious of Metellus[5] will be standing, the thousandth wife, at a barbarian couch, although, Magnus, to no woman will royal lust more readily devote itself than to her when cruelty stimulates it, and the titles of her husbands[6].

" For, in order that still more portents may delight the Parthian, he will know that she was the wife of Crassus

[1] *Crassus wants a sepulchre*) ver. 394. Plutarch informs us that the body of Crassus was thrown into the Euphrates. Ovid calls the Crassi " sepulti," or " entombed," in his Art of Love, B. i. l. 180, when speaking of the expedition of Caius Cæsar, the grandson of Augustus, against the Parthians. Seneca, however, and Valerius Maximus confirm the account given by Plutarch.

[2] *But Cornelia dreads not death*) ver. 397. He now speaks of the numerous wives and concubines of the Eastern kings, and suggests that if Pompey places himself in the power of the Parthians, Cornelia may be torn away from him to grace the harem of the tyrant.

[3] *Abhors not any intercourse*) ver. 402. "Concubinage with no female relations whatever is forbidden by the laws of the Parthians "

[4] *Thebes, stained by Œdipus*) ver. 407. He says that Thebes was disgraced by the incest of Œdipus, who married his mother Jocasta; though that was comparatively pardonable, as it happened unknowingly.

[5] *The progeny so illustrious of Metellus*) ver. 410. Cornelia, the wife of Pompey, the daughter of Metellus Scipio.

[6] *And the titles of her husbands*) ver. 413. He will be inflamed the more by remembering who her husbands were—P. Crassus and Pompey, both of whom had fought against Parthia.

too; as though owed already to the Assyrian destinies, she is dragged along, the captive of the former overthrow[1]. Let the woful wound to our eastern destinies be impressed *upon thee;* not only to have asked aid from the ruthless king, but to have waged civil war before that thou wilt be ashamed. For what crime among nations of thy father-in-law and of thyself will be greater, than that, you engaging in arms, vengeance for the Crassi has been lost? All the chieftains ought to have rushed to attack Bactria; and no arms should have been spared, even to laying bare the northern sides of *our* empire to the Dacians[2] and the bands of the Rhine, until perfidious Susa[3], falling upon the tombs of the heroes[4], and Babylon, had lain prostrate.

"An end, Fortune, do we pray for, to the Assyrian peace; and if the civil war of Thessaly has terminated, against the Parthians let him, who has proved the victor, go. It is the only nation of the world at a triumph over whom by Cæsar I could rejoice. Will not, when first thou shalt pass over the cold Araxes, the shade of the sorrowing old man[5], transfixed with the Scythian arrows, utter these words to thee: 'Dost thou, whom we hoped for as the avenger of the ashes of *our* unburied ghosts[6], come for treaties and for peace?'

[1] *Captive of the former overthrow*) ver. 416. "As though owing to the fortune of war, she will be considered as a part of the spoil which fell to the Parthians on their victory gained at Carrhæ."

[2] *To the Dacians*) ver. 424. He means that it is the duty of all even to leave the extremities of the Empire exposed to the attacks of the Dacians and Germans of the Rhine, in order to employ the troops in dealing vengeance against the perfidious Parthians.

[3] *Until perfidious Susa*) ver. 425. See B. ii. l. 49, and the Note to the passage.

[4] *Upon the tombs of the heroes*) ver. 426. "Virûm;" meaning those of the soldiers of Crassus.

[5] *The shade of the sorrowing old man*) ver. 432. Of Crassus; who at the time of his death had passed his sixtieth year. Orodes, or Arsaces XIV., king of Parthia, caused melted gold to be poured in his head, which had been cut off, exclaiming, "Sate thyself now with that metal of which in life thou wast so greedy."

[6] *Ashes of our unburied ghosts*) ver. 434. "Cinerum nudæ umbræ;" literally "to the naked" or "unburied shade of my ashes," which is almost tantamount to a blunder; inasmuch as on the body being reduced to ashes, that was considered tantamount to a burial. The word "cinerum," therefore, must here have the more extended meaning of "bones" or "dead body." It was the belief that the souls of those who remained unburied were doomed to wander for a hundred years on the banks of the Styx.

Then will many a memorial of the slaughter meet thee ;
the walls which the decapitated chieftains surveyed[1], where
Euphrates overwhelmed names so mighty, and Tigris
threw our carcases on shore, and *hen* took them back *to
himself*[2].

" If, Magnus, thou art able to submit to these things,
thou art able also to appease thy father-in-law, paramount in
the midst of Thessaly. Why dost thou not look upon the
Roman world? If thou dost dread the realms situate beneath
the south, and the faithless Juba, we repair to Pharos[3] and
the fields of Lagus. On the one side Egypt is safe in the
Libyan Syrtes ; then, on the other, the rapid stream disturbs the sea by its seven mouths. *It is* a land contented
with its own blessings, not standing in need of merchandize or of showers[4]; in the Nile alone is its trust. The boy
Ptolemy wields a sceptre, Magnus, owed to thee[5], entrusted
to thy guardianship. Who should dread the *mere* shadow of
a name? His age is free from guile[6]; hope for neither jus-

[1] *Decapitated chieftains surveyed*) ver. 436. The word "lustrarunt" is
capable of two significations here : " the walls which the heads of the chieftains
purified" with their blood; or, " the walls which the heads surveyed" or
" looked upon;" which latter is most likely the real signification. Not improbably the report was that the heads of the Crassi were exposed on the walls of
Parthian cities; we are informed by Plutarch that the head of the elder
Crassus was sent by Surenas to Orodes at Seleucia, and the head of the
younger one, who had slain himself on being unable to escape, was exultingly
shown to his father on the end of a spear.

[2] *Took them back to himself*) ver. 439. He alludes to the violence of the
Tigris in sometimes throwing the bodies ashore, and then again sweeping
them away in its tide. The more placid nature of the tide of the Euphrates
is well expressed by the use of the verb " obruit." The bodies, when thrown
there, were not carried away by the tide, but sank at once.

[3] *We repair to Pharos*) ver. 443. Pharos, the island at the mouth of the
Nile, here signifies Egypt in general ; the founder of the then royal house of
which was Ptolemy, the son of Lagus.

[4] *Or of showers*) ver. 447. " Jovis;" literally " of Jupiter;" signifying
"rain," or portraying the vivifying principle.

[5] *A sceptre, Magnus, owed to thee*) ver. 448. He alludes to the fact that
Ptolemy XI., or Auletes, after having been expelled from the Egyptian throne
by his subjects, was reseated on his throne by A. Gabinius the Proconsul of
Syria, who was influenced by the request of Pompey, and a bribe of ten
thousand talents from Ptolemy.

[6] *His age is free from guile*) ver. 449. He alludes to the youthful age of
the present monarch of Egypt, and considers him as holding only " the
shadow of the title of king."

tice and honor, nor reverence for the Gods in an aged court. Those used to the sceptre are ashamed of nothing; mildest is the lot of realms under a youthful king." No more having said, he inclined their minds in that direction. How much freedom does the last hope of success obtain! The opinion of Magnus was overruled.

Then did they leave the territory of the Cilicians, and urge on their hastening barks to Cyprus, to which no altars has the Goddess preferred, remembering the Paphian waves[1], if we are to believe that the Deities have birth, or it is right *to suppose* that any one of the Gods has had a beginning. When Pompey has departed from these shores, coasting along all the rocks of Cyprus, in which it projects towards the south, thence is he turned aside[2] by the obliquely-flowing tides of the vast ocean; nor does he make for the mountain cheering at night with its light[3]; and, with struggling sails, with difficulty he reaches the lower shores of Egypt, where the largest portion of the divided Nile, the seventh channel, flows into the Pelusian fords[4].

[1] *Remembering the Paphian waves*) ver. 458. According to some accounts Venus rose from the sea in the vicinity of Paphos.

[2] *Thence is he turned aside*) ver. 462. He coasts along the rocky shores of Cyprus to the south of the island, whence he is carried along transversely by the tide.

[3] *The mountain cheering at night with its light*) ver. 463. "Nec tenuit gratum nocturno lumine montem." This is one of the few instances in which May gives a wrong translation. He renders it—

"Nor by the night's weak light could he attain
    Mount Casius."

Whereas the Poet alludes to the high rocks of the isle of Pharos, off the coast of Egypt, pleasing (gratum) to sailors, as giving them timely warning against danger. Here was the most celebrated of the light-houses of antiquity, which was situate at the entrance to the port of Alexandria. It was erected by Sostratus of Cnidos, at the expense of Ptolemy II., or Philadelphus. It was of vast dimensions, square, and constructed of white stone, consisting of several stories, diminishing in width from below upwards. Torches or fires, probably in cressets or fire-pans, were kept burning during the night.

[4] *Into the Pelusian fords*) ver. 466. Pelusium, on the site of which is the modern Tineh, and which was also more anciently called Abaris, stood on the eastern side of the most easterly mouth of the Nile, about two miles from the sea, in the midst of marshes, from the mud (πηλὸς) of which it received its name. It was the frontier city of Egypt towards Syria and Arabia, and was strongly fortified. In later times it was the capital of the district of Augustamnica.

It was the time at which the Balance poises[1] the level hours, but equal on not more than a single day, and then the decreasing light pays back to the winter nights a consolation for their losses in the spring.

When he understood that the King was staying at Mount Casius[2] he changed his course; as yet neither was Phœbus gone down, nor did the sails flag[3]. Now with rapid speed along the shore the horsemen scouts[4] had filled the trembling court with the arrival of the stranger. Hardly was there time for counsel; still, all the miscreants of the Pellæan household[5] met together; among whom, Achoreus[6], now calmed by old age and more moderate through bending years (to him Memphis gave birth, frivolous in her rites[7], the observer of the Nile[8] increasing upon the fields; he the worshipper of the Gods, not one Apis only had lived[9]

[1] At which the Balance poises) ver. 467. The time of the Autumnal Equinox.

[2] Was staying at Mount Casius) ver. 470. Casius, or Casium, was a mountain on the coast of Egypt, east of Pelusium, with a temple of Jupiter on the summit. At its foot stood the town of Casium.

[3] Neither was Phœbus gone down, nor did the sails flag) ver. 471. "Nec Phœbus adhuc, nec carbasa languent." Literally, "neither does Phœbus as yet, nor the sails grow weak ;" meaning, that the sun was not setting, nor the wind going down.

[4] Along the shore the horsemen scouts) ver. 472. All the historians agree that the king was informed by a deputation of Pompey's arrival, and not by scouts or spies, as here mentioned.

[5] All the miscreants of the Pellæan household) ver. 474. "Monstra." All the iniquitous counsellors of the court of Alexandria, founded by Alexander of Pella; the principal of whom were Pothinus the eunuch, Theodotus of Chios, the rhetorician, and Achillas an Egyptian.

[6] Among whom, Achoreus) ver. 475. Most probably this Achoreus is entirely a fictitious character. See B. x. l. 175.

[7] Frivolous in her rites) ver. 478. He alludes to the superstitious worship by the Egyptians of bulls, cats, dogs, and other objects, which was especially cultivated at Memphis. See the story of Iphis and Ianthe related in the Metamorphoses of Ovid, B. ix. l. 666, et seq., and the Notes in Bohn's Translation, pp. 335-6.

[8] The observer of the Nile) ver. 477. He alludes to the well which existed at Memphis, connected with the river Nile, by the rise or fall of the waters of which the height of the waters in the river was denoted.

[9] Not one Apis only had lived) ver. 479. "Lustra suæ Phœbes non unus vexerat Apis." He means hereby to denote the extreme old age of Achoreus, during whose priesthood   than one Apis had died. "Lustra suæ Phœbes" mean the periods allotted for the existence of the sacred bull, which were measured by the course of the moon. "Suæ," "his own," is used in reference to the worship of Apis, who was supposed to be the same

through the changes of his moon), was the first speaker in
the council; and he alleged the merits and the fidelity *of
Pompey*, and the sacred ties of the deceased parent[1] *of
Ptolemy*. But more skilled in persuading the ill disposed,
and in understanding tyrants, Pothinus, presuming to condemn Pompey to death, *thus* said :—

" Justice and right, Ptolemy, have rendered many a one
guilty[2]. Fidelity, bepraised *as it is*, pays the penalty when
it upholds those whom Fortune depresses. Concur with
the Fates and the Gods, and pay court to the fortunate; fly
from the wretched. As different as are the stars from the
earth, as the flames from the sea, so *is* the profitable from
the right. The entire power of sceptres perishes if it begins
to weigh what is just; and regard for what is honorable overthrows citadels. It is the liberty to commit crimes which
protects a hated sway, and *all* restraint removed from the
sword. Everything may you do in cruelty with no impunity,
except when you *dare to* do it. Let him who wishes to be
virtuous remove from a court. Goodness and supreme
power do not agree together; he will be always afraid whom
cruelty shall shame. Not with impunity let Magnus have
despised thy years, who thinks that thou art not able to
drive away even the vanquished from our shores.

" Nor let a stranger deprive thee of thy sceptre; nearer
pledges hast thou; if thou art tired of reigning, yield up
Nile and Pharos to thy condemned sister[3]. Let us at least
protect Egypt from Latian arms. Whatever has not be-

Deity with Phœbe or the moon, and of whom probably the sacred bull called
" Apis " was the symbol. It was the rule with the priesthood not to allow the
" Apis " to live beyond a certain time. When his allotted period had ex-
pired they drowned him in the sacred well, and then amid tears and lamentations sought another to substitute in his place ; which was recognized by
certain marks on the forehead.

[1] *And the sacred ties of the deceased parent*) ver. 481. He alleged the
obligations which the father of Ptolemy lay under to Pompey.

[2] *Have rendered many a one guilty*) ver. 484. " Scrupulous attention to
the laws, human and divine, often makes persons appear guilty in the eyes
of those who are thwarted thereby."

[3] *To thy condemned sister*) ver. 500. He alludes to Cleopatra, the sister of
Ptolemy, who, by the will of Ptolemy Auletes, was to share the throne with
her younger brother Ptolemy, whom she was to marry; she had been
expelled from the throne about a year before this period, through the arti-
fices of Achillas and Pothinus, and had retreated into Syria, and there collected an army with which to compel her brother to reinstate her.

longed to Magnus, while the war was being waged[1], will not belong to the conqueror. Now from the whole world expelled after there is no confidence remaining in his fortunes, he seeks a nation with which to fall; he is distracted by the ghosts of fellow-citizens. And not only from the arms of his father-in-law does he fly; from the faces of the Senate he is flying, of whom a great part is gorging the Thessalian birds[2]; he dreads the nations, too, whom, mingled in one carnage, he has abandoned; kings, also, does he fear, all of whose *fortunes* he has ruined; guilty, too, of Thessaly, in no land received, he appeals to our land, which not as yet he has betrayed.

"A more just cause of complaint, Ptolemy, has been given to us against Magnus. Why dost thou stain[3] with the crimes of war Pharos distant and ever at repose, and *why* make our lands suspected by the conqueror? Why has this region alone pleased *thee*, on thy fall, upon which to bring the fortunes of Pharsalia and thy own punishment? Already do we incur a blame[4], to be wiped away with the sword, in that on us, at thy persuasion, the Senate conferred the sceptre. By our wishes we have encouraged thy arms. This sword, which the Fates bid us únsheathe, I have provided, not for thee, but for the conquered one. Magnus, thy vitals I will pierce; *those* of thy father-in-law I could have preferred. Whither everything is being borne[5], we are hurried on.

"Dost thou have a doubt whether it is necessary for me to destroy thee while yet I may? What confidence in our kingdom brings thee hither, unhappy man? Dost thou not behold our people unarmed, and, the Nile receding, hardly able to dig the softened fields[6]? It is right to take measure of one's kingdom, and to confess one's strength.

[1] *While the war was being waged*) ver. 502. He alludes to the circumstance of Egypt having given no assistance to Pompey during his campaign in Thessaly.

[2] *Is gorging the Thessalian birds*) ver. 507. See B. vii. l. 831, and the Note to the passage.

[3] *Why dost thou stain*) ver. 513. He here apostrophizes Pompey.

[4] *Already do we incur a blame*) ver. 517. "Already we are guilty of a crime only to be expiated by the sword of Cæsar, in having been indebted for the kingdom to the Roman senate influenced by Pompey."

[5] *Whither everything is being borne*) ver. 522. To the side of Cæsar.

[6] *The softened fields*) ver. 526. "Mollia," "pliant for the purposes of hus-bandry."

Art thou, Ptolemy, able to support the downfall of Magnus,
beneath which Rome lies prostrate? Dost thou presume
to stir the graves and the ashes of Thessaly, and to summon
war against thy realms? Before the Emathian combat with
no arms did we side; is the camp of Pompey now to please
thee, which the *whole* earth forsakes? Dost thou now provoke
the resources of the victor and destinies that have been
ascertained? It befits not to desert in adversity, but *it so
befits those* who have attended upon the prosperity. No
fidelity ever made choice of unfortunate friends."

All assent to the villany. The boy king rejoices at the
unusual honor, that now his servants allow matters of such
importance to be entrusted to him. For the crime Achillas *is*
chosen. Where the perfidious land[1] projects in the Casian
sands, and the Egyptian shallows attest the adjoining
Syrtes, he provides a little bark, with companions for the
monstrous crime[2], and with swords. O Gods of heaven!
have Nile and barbarian Memphis and the multitude so
effeminate of Pelusian Canopus[3] such a disposition as this?
Does civil strife thus depress the world? Do the Roman
fortunes thus lie prostrate? Is there any room left for Egypt
in these disasters, and is the Pharian sword introduced?
At least, *ye* civil wars, preserve this fidelity; afford kindred
hands[4], and drive afar misdeeds committed by foreign hands,
if, with a name so illustrious Magnus has deserved to be
the ground for Caesar's crimes.

[1] *Where the perfidious land*) ver. 539. "Perfida;" either on account of
the unsteady footing of the sands for passengers, or, as Burmann thinks, by
reason of the shoals and quicksands, or by reason of the treachery of its inhabitants. The part of the shore here mentioned lay at the foot of Mount
Casius.

[2] *For the monstrous crime*) ver. 541. "Monstri" may either mean "the
dreadful crime," or "the monster of wickedness," in allusion to himself.

[3] *Of Pelusian Canopus*) ver. 543. Weise justly observes that the expression "Pelusian Canopus" is incongruous, inasmuch as Pelusium lay on the
extreme eastern and Canopus near the most westerly mouth of the Nile.
Its inhabitants are justly spoken of as "mollis turba," "an effeminate multitude," for Canopus was proverbially famed for its voluptuousness. Strabo
informs us that there was a temple there dedicated to Serapis, to which multitudes resorted by the canal from Alexandria. He says that the canal was
filled, night and day, with men and women dancing to music on board the
vessels, with the greatest licentiousness.

[4] *Afford kindred hands*) ver. 548. He means that at least Pompey merits to
fall by the hands of his own countrymen, and not by those of foreign miscreants.

Dost thou not dread, Ptolemy, the downfall of a name so great? The heavens, too, thundering[1], dost thou, impure one and but half a man[2], presume to interpose thy profane hands?. Not *that he was* the subduer of the world, and not that he was thrice borne in his chariot[3] to the Capitol, the ruler, too, of kings, the avenger of the Senate, and the son-in-law of the conqueror; what might have been for a Pharian tyrant enough, he was a Roman. Why dost thou lay open our entrails with the sword? Thou knowest not, dishonorable boy, thou knowest not, in what position thy fortunes are[4]; now without any right dost thou wield the sceptre of the Nile; in civil fight has he fallen who gave to thee thy realms.

Now had Magnus denied his sails to the wind, and by the aid of oars[5] was making for the accursed shores; to meet whom, borne in a two-oared boat, not long the wicked band pushed on; and pretending that the realms of Pharos lie

[1] *The heavens, too, thundering*) ver. 551. "Cœlo tonante" admits of two significations: "While the heavens are pursuing Pompey with their thunders, dost thou interpose?" or, "While the heaven is rent with the thunders of the Civil War, dost thou interpose?"

[2] *And but half a man*) ver. 552. "Semivir." By this epithet he may either allude to the effeminate boy Ptolemy, or to his eunuch minister Pothinus.

[3] *Thrice borne in his chariot*) ver. 553. He alludes to the three triumphs of Pompey, namely, over Hiarbas, king of Numidia, over Sertorius, the Marian leader in Spain, and over Mithridates, the king of Pontus. See B. vii. l. 685.

[4] *In what position thy fortunes are*) ver. 558. Being no longer under the protection of Pompey.

[5] *And by the aid of oars*) ver. 561. The application of Pompey to Ptolemy for his aid is thus related by Cæsar in the Civil War, B. iii. c. 103 :—" Pompey having sailed for Pelusium, it happened that king Ptolemy, a minor, was there with a considerable army, engaged in war with his sister Cleopatra, whom, a few months before, by the assistance of his relations and friends, he had expelled from the kingdom ; and her camp lay at a small distance from his. To him Pompey applied to be permitted to take refuge in Alexandria, and to be protected in his calamity by his powerful assistance, in consideration of the friendship and good feeling which had subsisted between his father and him. But Pompey's deputies having executed their commission, began to converse with less restraint with the king's troops, and to advise them to act with friendship to Pompey, and not to think meanly of his bad fortune. In Ptolemy's army were several of Pompey's soldiers, of whom Gabinius had received the command in Syria, and had brought them over to Alexandria, and, at the conclusion of the war, had left with Ptolemy, the father of the young king."

Y

open to Magnus, bade him come from the prow of the lofty ship into the little bark, and censured the unfavourable shore, and the tides from the two seas[1] upon the shoals that break them, which forbid foreign fleets to approach the land. And had not the laws of the Fates, and the approach of a wretched death destined by the command of an eternal ordination, forced Magnus, condemned to destruction, unto the shore, to no one of his attendants were wanting omens of the crime; for, if their fidelity had been unstained, if the palace had been with true good feeling open to Magnus, the giver of the sceptre, *it was clear that* the Pharian monarch would have come, together with all his fleet.

But he yields to his destiny[2]; and, bidden to leave his fleet, he obeys, and delights to prefer death to fear. Cornelia was going straightway into the enemy's ship, through this more impatient at being absent from her departing husband because she apprehended calamity. " Stay behind, daring wife," said he, "and thou, son, I pray, and afar from the shore await my fate; and upon this neck make trial of the fidelity of the tyrant."

But towards him, *thus* harshly refusing, frantic Cornelia extended her two hands[3]. " Whither, cruel one," *she said,*

---

[1] *And the tides from the two seas*) ver. 566. He probably alludes to the two tides coming from the opposite sides of the Casian promontory, and meeting on the shoals.

[2] *But he yields to his destiny*) ver. 575. The circumstances of Pompey's death are thus related by Cæsar in the Civil War, B. iii. c. 104 :—" The king's friends, who were regents of the kingdom during the minority, being informed of these things, either induced by fear, as they afterwards declared, lest Pompey should corrupt the king's army, and seize on Alexandria and Egypt, or despising his bad fortune, as, in adversity, friends commonly change to enemies, in public gave a favourable answer to his deputies, and desired him to come to the king; but secretly laid a plot against him, and dispatched Achillas, captain of the king's guards, a man of singular boldness, and Lucius Septimius, a military tribune, to assassinate him. Being kindly addressed by them, and deluded by his acquaintance with Septimius, because in the war with the pirates the latter had commanded a company under him, he embarked in a small boat with a few attendants, and was there murdered by Achillas and Septimius. In like manner, Lucius Lentulus was seized by the king's order, and put to death in prison."

[3] *Extended her two hands*) ver. 583. Plutarch relates that, embracing her, he left Cornelia in tears, and ordered two centurions, a freedman named Philippus, and a servant, to go on board the boat. When the attendants of Achillas held out their hands to help him on board, he turned

"dost thou depart without me? Am I left again, removed
afar from the Thessalian woes'? Never with joyous omens
are we wretched _persons_ severed asunder. Couldst thou not
have guided thy ship elsewhere when thou didst fly, and
have left me in the retreats of Lesbos, if thou didst intend
to drive me away from all lands? Or do I only please thee
as thy companion upon the waves?" When in vain, she
had poured forth these _words_, still in her anxiety did she
hang over the end of the stern; and with astounded fear
neither was she able in any direction to turn her eyes away,
nor yet to look on Magnus.

The fleet stands anxious upon the fate of the chieftain,
fearing not arms and crime, but lest with submissive prayers
Pompey should venerate the sceptre presented by his own
hands. As he is preparing to pass on board, Septimius, a
Roman soldier², salutes him from the Pharian ship; who
(oh shame to the Gods of heaven!), the javelin laid aside³,
as a body-guard was bearing the disgraceful weapons of
royalty; fierce, violent, unrelenting, and less inclined to
carnage than no one of the wild beasts. Who, Fortune,
may not suppose that thou didst spare the nations, in that
this right hand was wanting in the war, and that thou didst
drive afar from Thessaly weapons so baneful? Thou dost _so_
dispose the swords, alas! that in no quarter of the world a
civil crime may not be perpetrated for thee.

To the victors themselves a disgrace, and a tale never to
be free from shame to the Gods of heaven: thus did a
Roman sword obey a king; and the Pellæan boy, Magnus,
cut thy throat with a sword thy own. With what character
shall posterity hand down Septimius to _future_ ages? By

to his wife and younger son, and exclaimed in the words of Sophocles,—
"Whoever goes to a tyrant, becomes a slave, even though he goes thither a
free man."

¹ _Removed afar from the Thessalian woes_) ver. 585. "Thessalicis submota
malis." "Separated from you on the eve of woes as great as those which
you suffered in Thessaly."

² _Septimius, a Roman soldier_) ver. 597. Appian, evidently by mistake,
calls this miscreant, Sempronius.

³ _The javelin laid aside_) ver. 598. "Pilo." See B. i. l. 7, and the Note to
the passage. The meaning is, that he was no longer serving in the Roman
army.

what name shall they speak of this crime who have pronounced that of Brutus a wickedness[1]?

Now had arrived the period of *his* closing hour, and borne
off in the Pharian boat he had now lost the disposal of himself. Then did the royal miscreants prepare to unsheathe
their swords[2]. When he beheld their weapons closing upon
him, he covered up his features, and, disdaining to expose
to Fortune his bared head, then did he close his eyes, and
hold his breath, that he might be able to utter no words
and spoil his eternal fame by lamentations. But after the
murderous Achillas had pierced his side with his pointed
weapon, with not a groan he submitted to the stroke[3], and
despised the villany, and kept his body unmoved, and
proved himself when dying *to be Pompey*, and revolved these
things in his breast :—

"Ages, never to be silent, wait upon the woes of Rome,
and generations to follow look from the whole earth upon
this bark and the Pharian faith. Now think upon thy fame.
The prospering fortunes of a lengthened life have flowed
on for thee. Nations know not, if at thy death thou dost not
prove it, whether thou dost know how to endure adversity.
Give way to no shame, nor grieve at the author of thy fate.
By whatever one thou art smitten, think it the hand of
thy father-in-law. Though they should rend and tear me,
still, O Gods of heaven, I am happy, and no God has the
power to deprive me of that. The prosperity of my life is
changed; through death a person does not become wretched.

[1] *That of Brutus a wickedness*) ver. 609-10. "If Brutus who slew Cæsar
was a murderer, what was this Septimius?"
[2] *Prepare to unsheathe their swords*) ver. 612. According to Plutarch,
when Pompey had got to a considerable distance from the ship, and near the
shore, and perceived that he was not very courteously treated, he turned to
Septimius, and addressing him, asked him if he did not remember him as
having formerly fought under him, on which Septimius, not deigning to give
him an answer, only nodded his head. When Pompey was rising to get out
of the boat, Septimius was the first to run him through the back with his
sword, after which Salvius and Achillas drew their swords, and dispatched
him.
[3] *With not a groan he submitted to the stroke*) ver. 619. "Nullo gemitu
consensit ad ictum." This may either mean that, by uttering no sigh, he, as
it were, resigned himself to death; or that he did not, by any sigh, indicate
that he had been pierced by the sword.

Cornelia beholds this murder and my Pompey. So much more patiently, grief, restrain thy sighs. I entreat; my son and my wife *truly* love me, if they admire me in my death."[1]

Such was the self-possession of the mind of Magnus; this power had he over his dying spirit.

But Cornelia, not so well able to behold the ruthless crime as to endure it with courage, fills the air with lamentable words : "O husband. I, wicked that I am, have murdered thee ; the cause of the fatal delay to thee was Lesbos *so* remote thy course, and Cæsar has arrived the first[2] at the shores of the Nile. For who else had the right to commit the crime? But thou, whoever thou art, sent down, by the Gods of heaven against that life, having a view either to Cæsar's wrath, or to thyself. knowest not, cruel one, where are the vitals themselves of Magnus : thou dost hasten and redouble thy blows, where *such* is the wish of the vanquished. Let him pay a penalty not less than death, and first let him behold my head *cut off*. Not free *am* I from the fault of the warfare, who alone of the matrons. an attendant on the waves and in the camp, scared away by no fatalities, sheltered him conquered, which even monarchs feared *to do*. Have I, husband, deserved this, to be left in safety in the ship? Perfidious one, didst thou spare me? Thou coming to thy latest hour, have I been deserving of life? I will die, and *that* not by the favour of the king. Either. sailors, allow me a headlong leap, or to place the halter and the twisted ropes around my neck; or let some companion worthy of Magnus provide a sword. For Pompey he may do that which he may lay to the charge of the arms of Cæsar. O cruel men, do ye restrain me hurrying on to my fate? Still, husband, thou dost survive, and now. Magnus, Cornelia has not the disposal of herself. They hinder me from hastening on my death ; for the conqueror I am reserved."

---

[1] *If they admire me in my death*) ver. 634-5. "If they show more admiration of my fortitude than grief at my death, they will be showing greater affection for me."

[2] *And Cæsar has arrived the first*) ver. 641. In her ignorance of the circumstances, she accuses herself of being the cause of his death. She thinks that, by his coming out of his way to meet her at Lesbos, Cæsar has gained time to reach Egypt before him, and give orders for him to be put to death.

Thus having said, and having fallen into the arms of
her friends, she was carried off, the alarmed ship hastening
away.

But when the back and the breast of Magnus resounded
with the sword, those who beheld the lacerated head confess that the majestic gracefulness of his hallowed form still
remained, and that his _features_ were angered at the Gods,
and that the last moments of death changed nothing of the
mien and features of the hero. But ruthless Septimius
in this act of villany invents a villany still greater; and,
the covering cut asunder[1], he uncovers the sacred features
of the half-dead Magnus, and lays hold of the breathing
head, and places the languid neck crosswise upon a bench.
Then he cuts the nerves and veins, and is long in breaking
the knotty bones; not as yet was it an art[2] to whip off a
head with the sword.

But after the neck, divided, shrunk back from the trunk,
the Pharian courtier[3] claimed to carry this in his right hand.
Roman soldier, degenerate and playing a second part[4], dost
thou with the ruthless sword cut off the sacred head of
Pompey, not to bear it away thyself? O fate, treated with
extreme indignity! That the impious boy may recognize
Magnus, that flowing hair revered by kings, and the long
locks graceful with his noble forehead are seized by the
hand, and while the features are alive, and the sobs of the
breath are moving the mouth to murmurs, and while the
unclosed eyes are stiffening, the head is fixed on a Pharian
spear[5], which when ordering war never was there peace; this

---

[1] *The covering cut asunder*) ver. 669. He alludes to the "toga," which
Pompey had wrapped about his head when he was first struck. See l. 614.

[2] *Not as yet was it an art*) ver. 673. The meaning is, that decapitation
had not as yet come to be an art. Suetonius tells us that Caligula trained an
executioner to the art of cutting off a head at a single blow.

[3] *The Pharian courtier*) ver. 675. Achillas claims it as his right to carry
the head to his sovereign.

[4] *Playing a second part*) ver. 676. "Operæ secundæ." This is a thea-
trical simile. He expresses his surprise that a Roman soldier could consent
to play a second part, in cutting off the head of Pompey for another to carry
it as his trophy.

[5] *On a Pharian spear*) ver. 681. "Veruto." The "verutum" was the
spear of the light infantry of the Roman army, the use of which was derived
from the Samnites and the Volsci. The shaft was three and a half feet long,
and the point five inches.

it was that swayed the laws, and the Plain[1], and the Rostra with this face, Fortune of Rome, didst thou gratify thyself.

Nor enough was it for the disgraceful tyrant to have beheld this; he wished a memorial to survive the crime. Then, by an accursed art[2], the moisture was extracted from the head, and, the brains removed, the skin *was* dried, and the putrid juices flowed forth from within, and the head was hardened by drugs poured into it.

Last offspring of the race of Lagus[3], and about to perish degenerate, *and* destined to yield to the rule of thy unchaste sister[4]; whilst by thee the Macedonian is preserved[5] in the sacred vaults, and with mountains piled over them, the ashes of kings are at rest, while the Pyramids[6] and Mausolean graves[7], unworthy of them, enclose the shades of the Ptolemies and their abandoned line, are the shores to be beating against Pompey, and is the trunk to be tossed to and fro by the waves on the shoals? Was it so burdensome a care to save the corpse entire for the father-in-law? Fortune with this fidelity ended the fates of Magnus so prosperous; with this death did she hurl him down from

---

[1] *The Plain*) ver. 685. "Campum." The "Campus Martius," where the magisterial elections of Rome took place.

[2] *Then, by an accursed art*) ver. 688. He alludes to the process of embalming, which, as to the head, was performed by drawing out the moisture through the nostrils; although in the present case, probably, there was no necessity to adopt that course. It was embalmed for the purpose of showing it to Cæsar, and proving that Pompey was really slain.

[3] *Last offspring of the race of Lagus*) ver. 692. He perished shortly after, in the Alexandrian war against Cæsar, being drowned in the Nile.

[4] *The rule of thy unchaste sister*) ver. 693. He alludes to Cleopatra, who was notorious for her unchaste conduct, and who was restored to the Egyptian throne by Cæsar.

[5] *The Macedonian is preserved*) ver. 694. Alexander the Great was buried at Alexandria (which city he had founded, B.C. 332) by Ptolemy Lagus. He was buried in a sarcophagus of gold, under a tomb of stupendous size and gorgeous magnificence. His name is here expressed by "Macedon," as with the glory of Macedonia he was identified.

[6] *While the Pyramids*) ver. 697. It is probable that at least some of the Pyramids were devoted to funereal purposes.

[7] *Mausolean graves*) ver. 697. "Mausolea" was a general term for tombs erected to the great, in imitation of that which Artimesia caused to be built at Halicarnassus, in honor of her husband Mausolus, king of Caria. The Roman Mausolea were in general formed of a succession of terraces, in imitation of the "rogus," or "funeral pile."

the highest summit of power, and cruelly centred all the
calamities in one day, from which she granted him years
so many of freedom; and Pompey was one who never saw
joys mingled with sorrows; happy in no one of the Gods
molesting him, and wretched in no one sparing him.
Once for all with delaying hand did Fortune hurl him down.
He is beaten to and fro on the sands, he is mangled on the
rocks, the waves received into his wounds, the sport of the
ocean; and, no figure remaining, the only mark of Magnus
is the loss of the head torn off.

Still, before the conqueror touched upon the Pharian
sands, Fortune suddenly provided for Pompey a tomb, lest
he might lie in none, or lest in a better sepulchre. From
his hiding-place Cordus, trembling[1], runs down to the sea-
shore. The seeker had been the unhappy attendant[2] of
Magnus from the Idalian shores[3] of Cyprus, the abode of
Cinyras. He amid the shades daring to move his steps,
repressed his fear, overcome by affection, that he might
bring the body, sought in the midst of the waves, to land,
and draw Magnus to the shore. But little light does sorrowing Cynthia afford amid the thickening clouds; but the
trunk, of different colour from the hoary sea, is perceived.
He seizes the chieftain in his strict embrace, as the sea
drags him away; now overpowered by a burden so vast
he awaits the waves, and, the sea aiding him, moves on the

[1] *Cordus, trembling*) ver. 715. This story of Cordus is probably an invention of the Poet. Plutarch distinctly says that the body was burnt by
Philippus, Pompey's freedman, who had accompanied him from the ship. He
made the funeral pile with pieces of wreck which he found on the sea-shore,
and while he was so employed an aged Roman came up by accident, and
assisted him, having served under Pompey in his youth. It is just possible
that his name may have been Cordus, which was not an uncommon cognomen
among the Romans. The word "quæstor" has been thought to mean that
Cordus held some office known by that name. It is much more likely that
it means "a seeker," in allusion to his search for the body, mentioned in
l. 719.

[2] *The unhappy attendant*) ver. 717. Philippus probably escaped unharmed,
during the confusion attendant on the murder of Pompey at his landing.

[3] *From the Idalian shores*) ver. 716. Idalus was a mountain in the Isle
of Cyprus, of which Cinyras had been king, who unknowingly committed
incest with his daughter Myrrha, who became the mother of Adonis. See
the story related in the Tenth Book of Ovid's Metamorphoses, l. 299, *et seq.*
Some ancient writers say that Cyprus was so called from Cyprus, the son, or,
according to others, the daughter of Cinyras, king of Assyria.

corpse. After he has now seated himself upon the dry shore, he leans over Magnus, and pours forth his tears into every wound, and to the Gods of heaven and the darkened stars he says:—

" Thy Pompey, Fortune, asks not a sepulchre precious with heaped-up frankincense[1]; not that the unctuous smoke may bear eastern odours from his limbs unto the stars; that duteous necks of Romans may bear[2] their parent, that the funereal procession should carry before it his ancient triumphs, that with the song of sorrow the market-places may re-echo[3]; that the whole army, grieving, may go round the flames with arms reversed[4]. Grant to Magnus the lowly coffin[5] of the plebeian funeral, which may lower his torn corpse into the dry flames[6]. Let not

[1] *With heaped-up frankincense*) ver. 729. It was the custom to throw frankincense and other costly aromatics on the funeral piles of the wealthy, although this practice was forbidden by the Twelve Tables.

[2] *Romans may bear*) ver. 732. The "lecticæ," or "feretra," the biers on which the more wealthy were carried to the funeral pile, were often carried on the shoulders of the nearest relations of the deceased. Metellus was carried by his sons, Julius Cæsar by the officers of state, and Augustus by the Senators.

[3] *The market-places may re-echo*) ver. 734. It is difficult to say whether "fora" here means the judicial "fora," or the market-places at Rome, through which the funeral procession would have to pass, attended by musicians called "cornicienes," or "siticines," who played mournful strains. It is, however, ascertained that if the deceased was of illustrious rank, it was the custom for the funeral procession to go through the Forum, and to stop before the "Rostra," where a funeral oration in praise of the deceased was delivered. This practice was said to have been first introduced by Valerius Publicola, who pronounced a funeral oration in honor of his colleague L. Junius Brutus. Probably this practice is obscurely referred to in the present passage.

[4] *With arms reversed*) ver. 735. By the word "projectis," some have suggested that the Poet means "throwing" their arms upon the funeral pile, which, however, is probably not the sense of the passage. It means "reversing," or "lowering their arms;" at the funeral of a general it was the custom for the troops to march three times round the funeral pile.

[5] *Grant to Magnus the lowly coffin*) ver. 736. "Vilem arcam" has been taken by some of the Scholiasts to mean the "sandapila," or "bier," on which the bodies of the lower classes were carried to the funeral pile. The word, however, thus used, properly signifies a coffin made of stone, in which bodies were buried which were not burnt. In later times, however, the word came to be applied to any kind of coffin or tomb.

[6] *Into the dry flames*) ver. 737. On which there was no one present to pour oil and aromatics.

wood be wanting for him ill-fated, nor yet a humble burner.
Be it enough, O Gods of heaven, that Cornelia does not lie
prostrate, with flowing locks, and, embracing her husband,
command the torch to be applied, but, unhappy wife, is
absent from the last rites of the tomb, and still is not far
distant from the shore."

Thus having said, afar the youth beholds a little fire,
with no watcher, burning a body[1], unregarded by its friends.
Thence he bears off the flames, and taking the half-burnt
wood from beneath the limbs, he says: "Whoever thou art,
neglected ghost, and dear to no friend of thine, but more
happy than Pompey, grant pardon that now a stranger's
hand despoils thy constructed pyre. If there is any sense
left after death, thou thyself dost yield up thy funeral pile,
and dost submit to this spoiling of thy tomb, and dost feel
ashamed for thee to burn the shades of Pompey, scattered
abroad."

Thus does he speak, and with his bosom filled with the
burning embers he flies away to the trunk, which, almost
carried back by the waves, is hovering on *the edge of* the
shore. He moves away the surface of the sands, and, trembling, places in the little trench the fragments collected
from afar of a vessel broken up. No oaken beams press
upon the noble corpse, upon no built-up wood do the limbs
recline ; applied, not placed beneath, the fire receives Magnus. Sitting near the flames, he said: "O greatest chieftain,
and sole glory of the Hesperian name, if more sad to thee
this pile than the tossing on the deep, if *more sad* than
no funereal rites, withdraw thy shade and thy mighty spirit
from my *duteous* offices. The injustice of Fate declares this
to be right; lest a monster of the sea, lest a wild beast,
lest the birds, lest the wrath of cruel Cæsar should venture
aught, accept, so far as thou canst, *these* flames, *thus* burnt
by a Roman hand.

"If Fortune should grant *me* a return to Hesperia, not
in this spot shall ashes so sacred repose ; but, Magnus,
Cornelia shall receive thee, and by my hand transfer thee

---

[1] *Beholds a little fire, with no watcher, burning a body*) ver. 743. The
improbability of this part of the story is very striking, and it is somewhat
surprising that the Poet did not, in preference, adopt the historical account
alone.

to the urn. In the meantime let me mark the shore with a little stone, that there may be a memorial of thy grave; if any one, perchance, should wish to appease thee *thus* cut off, and to render the full rites due to death, he may find the ashes of thy trunk, and may know the sands to which, Magnus, he is to bring back thy head."

Thus having said, with fuel heaped on he arouses the sluggish flames. Magnus is consumed, and disappears in the fire slowly burning, with his moisture feeding the pile. But now the day had dimmed the stars, the harbingers of dawn; he, the ceremonial of the funeral interrupted, alarmed, seeks his hiding-place upon the shore. What punishment, simple man, dost thou dread for this crime, for which loud-mouthed fame has taken charge of thee for all years *to come?* The unnatural father-in-law, *even,* will commend the burial of the bones of Magnus; only go, secure of pardon, and disclosing the sepulchre, demand the head.

Affection compels him to place the finishing stroke to his duteous offices. He takes up the bones half-burnt and not yet quite decomposed, full of ligaments and of marrow unconsumed he quenches them with sea-water, and, collected together, encloses them in a little spot of earth. Then, that the light breeze may not bear away the ashes uncovered, he presses down the sand with a stone; and that the sailor may not disturb the grave for fastening the cable, he inscribes the sacred name with a half-burnt stake, HERE MAGNUS LIES. Fortune, it pleases thee to call this the tomb of Pompey, in which his father-in-law would rather that he were interred[1], than deprived of the earth.

Rash right hand, why dost thou block up the tomb of Magnus, and shut in the wandering ghost? Wherever the

---

[1] *Would rather that he were interred*) ver. 795. As Lucan would not readily attribute humanity to Cæsar, it is suggested that Cæsar may have wished this for two reasons: lest, if the body of Pompey should remain unburied, he should be haunted by his ghost; and because he might deem it a greater disgrace to Pompey's remains to be entombed in this homely manner than to be deprived of burial altogether. Another reason would be that, in consequence of the burial, Cæsar would feel more sure of his death, than if he was merely told of it, and that the body was lost. Appian mentions another inscription as being placed upon the tomb of Pompey:—" Hardly could a Temple have contained him who is covered with a little sand."

extremity of the earth hangs steep over the ocean flowing back does he lie. The Roman name and all its empire is the limit of the tomb of Magnus. Overwhelm the stone replete with the disgrace of the Gods. If to Hercules belongs the whole of Œta¹, and the whole mountain ridges of Nysa make room for Bromius, why for Magnus in Egypt *is* there a single stone? All the fields of Lagus he might possess, if upon no clod his name was inscribed. Let us nations *still* be ignorant, and, Magnus, through respect for thy ashes, let us tread upon no sands of Nile.

But if thou dost deign to grace a stone with name so holy, add thy deeds so mighty, and the most glorious memorials of thy exploits; add the fierce rebellion of Lepidus², and the Alpine wars; the conquered arms, too, of Sertorius³, the Consul recalled; the triumphs, too, which, *still* a knight⁴, he enjoyed; commerce, *too*, rendered safe to nations, and the Cilicians, fearful of the sea. Add barbarism subdued⁵, and the wandering nations⁶, and whatever realms lie beneath the eastern breeze and Boreas. Say how that after arms he always sought again the toga of the citizen; how that, thrice his chariot speeding on *in triumph*, he was content to make present to his country of full many a triumph. What tomb can contain these things? *Here* rises a wretched sepulchre, filled with no titles, with no recital so vast of his annals; and after being wont to be read above⁷

¹ *Belongs the whole of Œta*) ver. 801. See l. 227, and the Note to the passage.

² *Rebellion of Lepidus*) ver. 808. See B. ii. l. 547.

³ *The conquered arms, too, of Sertorius*) ver. 809. He alludes to the doubtful victories which Pompey gained over Sertorius in Spain, who had, during eight years, withstood the arms of the Proconsul, Q. Cæcilius Metellus Pius. Lucan is incorrect *in* hinting that Metellus was " Consul revocatus," as he was neither Consul during the war with Sertorius, nor was he recalled, but was obliged to summon to his aid the armies of Gaul and Nearer Spain, and to send to Rome for the assistance of Pompey as Proconsul. See B. ii. l. 549.

⁴ *Which, still a knight*) ver. 810. He alludes to the triumphs which Pompey enjoyed, contrary to usage, while of Equestrian rank.

⁵ *Barbarism subdued*) ver. 812. His victories gained over Mithridates, and the people of Pontus, Armenia, Paphlagonia, Cappadocia, and the nomad or wandering Scythians.

⁶ *And the wandering nations*) ver. 812. His conquests of the Iberi, the Basternæ, the Syrians, and the Jews.

⁷ *Wont to be read above*) ver. 818. He here alludes to the inscriptions

the lofty heights of the Gods and the arches built up[1] with the spoils of the foe, not far is the name of Pompey from the lowest sand, crouching low on his tomb, which the sojourner cannot read standing upright, which, unless pointed out, the Roman stranger would be passing by.

Egyptian land, rendered guilty by civil fate, not undeservedly indeed was warning given[2] by the lines of the prophetess of Cumæ, that the soldier of Hesperia was not to touch the Pelusian shores of the Nile, and the banks swelling in summer-time. What, ruthless land, ought I to pray for thee for a crime so great? May Nile, detained in the region from which he springs, change the course of his streams, and may the barren fields miss the wintry waters[3], and mayst thou be entirely lost in the loose sands of the Æthiopians. We in Roman Temples have received thy Isis[4], and the half-dog Deities[5], and the sistra command-

on the Temples of the Gods, which, when votive, in conspicuous characters bore the names of the founders.

[1] *And the arches built up*) ver. 819. "Arcus" has been supposed to refer to the Theatre of Pompey; but it is much more probable that the triumphal arches which were erected in honor of victorious generals are here alluded to; as they were covered with spoils and trophies taken from the enemy.

[2] *Was warning given*) ver. 824. The Sibylline books are said to have stated that harm would come to the soldiers of the west who should land in Egypt. We learn from Cicero, in one of his Epistles, that the Quindecimviri, or fifteen guardians of the sacred Books, interpreted this prophecy in reference to the orders given by Pompey and the Senate to the Proconsul Gabinius, to restore Ptolemy Auletes to his kingdom.

[3] *Miss the wintry waters*) ver. 829. "Imbribus" cannot here mean "showers," inasmuch as there are no showers in Egypt, a fact to which the Poet has already alluded in the present Book, l. 447. The word must therefore signify high inundations of the Nile, fertilizing the lands. May, however, translates the line,—

"May thy unfruitful fields want winter rain."

[4] *Have received thy Isis*) ver. 831. Isis was said to be the same Deity as Io, the daughter of Inachus. See the Metamorphoses of Ovid, B. i. l. 747. Apuleius tells us that the worship of Isis was introduced at Rome in the time of Sulla. Many enactments were passed to check the licentiousness of her worship, but were resisted by the populace. It was, in a great measure, kept without the City walls. The most important Temple was in the Campus Martius, whence she obtained the epithet of Isis Campensis. Those initiated in her mysteries wore, in the public processions, masks resembling the heads of dogs.

[5] *And the half-dog Deities*) ver. 832. He probably alludes to Anubis, an

ing grief [1], and Osiris, whom [2] thou by mourning dost attest
to have been a man; thou, Egypt, art keeping our shades [3]
in the dust.

Thou, also, although thou hast now granted Temples to
the ruthless tyrant [4], hast not yet sought, O Rome, the ashes
of Pompey; still lies in exile the ghost of the chieftain.
If former ages dreaded the threats of the conqueror, now,
at least, receive the bones of thy Magnus, if, not yet rooted
up by the waves, they remain in the hated land. Who will
respect the tomb [5]? Who will be afraid to disturb a ghost
deserving of sacred rites? I wish that Rome would enjoin
this wickedness on me, and be ready to employ my bosom [6];
enough, and O too greatly blessed, if me it should befall to

Egyptian Deity, which had the body of a man and the head of a dog.
Some writers say that it was Mercury who was thus represented, and that
this form was given him in remembrance of the fact of Isis having employed dogs in her search for Osiris, when he was slain by his brother
Typhon. Other authors say that Anubis was the son of Osiris, and that he
distinguished himself with a helmet wearing the figure of a dog, when he
followed his father to battle. Herodotus mentions the worship of dogs by
the Egyptians.

[1] *The sistra commanding grief*) ver. 832. The "sistrum" was a mystical
musical instrument, used by the ancient Egyptians in the worship of Isis,
and other ceremonials. It was shaken with the hand, and emitted a tinkling sound. Plutarch tells us that the shaking of its four cross-bars was
supposed to represent the agitation of the four elements, earth, air, fire, and
water; and that the cat which was usually sculptured on the end of it,
represented the moon. Apuleius says that these instruments were sometimes
made of silver, and even of gold. It was introduced at Rome with the worship of Isis, and it is said to be used in Nubia and Abyssinia at the present
day.

[2] *And Osiris, whom*) ver. 833. Osiris was the chief male Divinity of the
Egyptians, and the husband of Isis. Heliodorus says that he was God of
the Nile, while Isis was Goddess of the earth. Lucan here suggests that the
lamentations of Isis for the death of Osiris at the hands of his brother Typhon proves that he was a mortal and not a Divinity.

[3] *Art keeping our shades*) ver. 834. " Nostros Manes." Literally, " our
shades;" meaning, " the shade of Pompey worthy of our worship and veneration."

[4] *Granted Temples to the ruthless tyrant*) ver. 835. He alludes to the
deification of Julius Cæsar by public decree of the Roman Senate, and the
erection of Temples in his honor. On this subject see the Translation of
Ovid's Metamorphoses, in Bohn's Classical Library, pp. 553-4.

[5] *Who will respect the tomb*) ver. 840. " Who, in such a case, would have
any superstitious fear of violating his tomb?"

[6] *Be ready to employ my bosom*) ver. 843. " Sinu." In the folds of the

transfer to Ausonia the ghost removed, if of a chieftain to violate such a tomb.

Perhaps, when Rome shall be desirous to ask of the Gods of heaven either an end for the barren furrows, or for the fatal south winds[1], or for heat too great, or for the earth moving the houses, by the counsel and command, Magnus, of the Gods, thou wilt remove to thy City, and the highest Priest[2] will carry thy ashes. Now, who will go to Syene[3], scorched by the burning Crab, and Thebes, parched beneath[4] the showery Pleiad, a spectator of the Nile? who, Magnus, will repair to the waters of the deep Red Sea, or the ports of the Arabians, a barterer of the merchandize of the East, whom the venerable stone upon the tomb, and the ashes scattered perchance upon the surface of the sands will not attract, and who will not delight in propitiating thy shade, and in preferring thee to Casian Jove[5]?

In no degree will that grave prove injurious to thy fame. Buried in a Temple and in gold, shade of higher worth thou wouldst be; now is Fortune in place of the greatest Divinity, lying buried in this tomb[6]. More august than[7]

bosom of the dress. The same expression is used in l. 752. So in the Metamorphoses of Ovid, B. xiii. l. 425-6,—" Dulichian hands have dragged her away, while clinging to their tombs and giving kisses to their bones : yet the ashes of one has she taken out, and, so taken out, has carried with her in her bosom, the ashes of Hector."

[1] *For the fatal south winds*) ver. 847. " Feralibus." Blowing from Africa, and causing pestilence.

[2] *The highest Priest*) ver. 850. " Summus sacerdos." The " Pontifex Maximus," who was the chief in influence of the Roman priesthood, but second in rank to the " Flamen Dialis," or high priest of Jupiter.

[3] *Who will go to Syene*) ver. 851. See B. ii. l. 587, and the Note to the passage.

[4] *And Thebes, parched beneath*) ver. 852. He speaks of Thebes in Egypt as situate in a climate a stranger to rain. This city, which is called in Scripture No, or No-Ammon, was the capital of Thebais, or Upper Egypt. It stood on both banks of the Nile, and was said to have been founded by the Æthiopians. Its later name was Diospolis Magna, or the Great City of Jove. The ruins of Thebes are the most magnificent in modern Egypt.

[5] *Preferring thee to Casian Jove*) ver. 858. There was a Temple of Jupiter on Mount Casius.

[6] *Lying buried in this tomb*) ver. 861. " Fortune seems to be buried here with Pompey, so long her favourite."

[7] *More august than*) ver. 861-2. More august than the Temple and altars erected to Cæsar in the Capitol at Rome, by Augustus and the Senate.

the altars of the conqueror is the stone beaten against upon the Libyan shore. Those who have full oft denied their frankincense to the Tarpeian Gods[1] would venerate the Deity enclosed beneath the dusky clod.

This in future time will advantage thee, that the lofty mass of thy sepulchre, destined to endure, has not soared aloft with its ponderous marble. No great length of time will scatter the heap of scanty dust, and the tomb will fall, and the proofs of thy death will perish. An age more blest will come, in which there will be no credit *given* to those who point out that stone; and to the generations of posterity Egypt will be as lying in the tomb of Magnus, as Crete *in that*[2] of the Thunderer.

---

[1] *To the Tarpeian Gods*) ver. 863. He seems to refer here to a reluctance on the part of the Egyptians to worship the Gods of Rome.

[2] *As Crete in that*) ver. 872. Universal testimony seems to have been given by the ancient writers to the untruthfulness of the Cretans. St. Paul, in his Epistle to Titus, c. i. v. 12, says, quoting from the Cretan poet Epimenides, "One of themselves, even a prophet of their own, said, 'The Cretans are alway liars, evil beasts, slow bellies.' This witness is true." Callimachus says, "The Cretans are always liars; for, O Jove, they have thy tomb! But thou didst not die; for thou art for everlasting." Ovid also says, in his Art of Love, B. i. l. 298, "Crete, which contains its hundred cities, cannot gainsay them, untruthful as it is."

BOOK THE NINTH

CONTENTS.

z

Troy, 950-965. Which is described, 966-999. He arrives in Egypt,
where a soldier, sent by the king, meets him with the head of Pompey,
1000-1033. Cæsar, though really overjoyed, sheds tears, and reproaches
Pompey's murderers, and then commands them to appease the shade of
Pompey, 1034-1108.

But not in the Pharian embers lay the shade, nor did a few
ashes contain a ghost so mighty; forth from the tomb did
he issue, and, leaving the limbs half burnt and the unworthy
pile, he reached the concave of the Thunderer[1], where the
swarthy air[2] meets with the starry poles, and where it
extends between the earth and the courses of the moon
(half-deified shades[3] inhabit it, whom, guiltless in their
lives, an ardent virtue[4] has made able to endure the lower
tracts of heaven), and he withdrew his spirit to the eternal
spheres. Not thither do those come entombed in gold, or
buried amid frankincense.

There, after he had filled himself with genuine light,
and admired[5] the wandering planets, and the stars fixed in
the skies, he beheld beneath how vast a night our day lies
concealed, and he laughed at the mockery of his headless
body. Hence did he hover over the plains of Emathia,
and the standards of the blood-stained Cæsar, and the fleets
scattered upon the waves; and, the avenger of crimes, he

[1] *The concave of the Thunderer*) ver. 4.   "Convexa Tonantis;" literally, " the convex places of the Thunderer," meaning the heavens.
According to some of the ancients the Elysian fields or abodes of the Blessed
were situate in the western world, either in Spain or in the Fortunate
Islands, beyond the pillars of Hercules.   These were probably only imaginary islands, though on the discovery by the Romans of the Canary Islands
the name of " Fortunatæ insulæ" was applied to them.   The Platonics considered the abode of the Blessed to be in the heavens, while others placed
them in an imaginary region near the moon.

[2] *Where the swarthy air*) ver. 5.   He probably calls the atmosphere
" black " or " swarthy" in comparison with the brightness of the heavens
and the stars.

[3] *Half-deified shades*) ver. 7.   He speaks of "æther," or the upper regions
of the air, as inhabited by the Heroes or Demigods.

[4] *An ardent virtue*) ver. 7.   "Their ardent or fire-born (ignea) virtue is
able to make them endure the æther, which is the source of fire, amid which
they have taken their place among the stars."

[5] *And admired*) ver. 12-13.   It has been suggested that Lucan had here
in view a passage in the Eclogues of Virgil, E. v. l. 56-7 :—" Candidus
insuetum miratur limen Olympi, Sub pedibusque videt nubes et sidera
Daphnis."   " The beauteous Daphnis admires, unusual sight, the threshold
of Olympus, and sees beneath his feet the clouds and stars."

seated himself in the hallowed bosom of Brutus[1], and implanted himself in the breast of the unconquered Cato. He, while the chances were undecided, and it remained in doubt, which one the civil wars were to make ruler of the world, had hated Magnus too, although he had gone as his follower in arms, hurried on by the auspices of his country and by the guidance of the Senate; but after the disasters of Thessaly, then with all his heart he was a partisan of Pompey.

His country, wanting a protector, he took *into his own protection*, the trembling limbs of the people he cherished once more, the swords thrown away he placed again in timid hands, and neither desiring rule, nor yet fearing to serve *under another*[2], he waged the civil war. Nothing in arms did he do for the sake of self; after the death of Magnus it was entirely the party of liberty; and, lest victory should sweep this away scattered along the shores, with the rapid speed of Cæsar, he sought the secret retreats of Corcyra[3], and in a thousand ships[4] carried off with him the fragments of the Emathian downfall. Who could have supposed that flying troops were speeding on in barks so numerous? Who, that conquered ships were crowding the seas?

[1] *In the hallowed bosom of Brutus*) ver. 17. Meaning that the soul of Pompey inspires Brutus to avenge his cause, by slaying Cæsar. It is more than probable that Brutus was a weak and restless man, and merely joined the conspiracy against Cæsar, because he was completely under the influence of Cassius. Gratitude alone should have prevented him from thus requiting the favours he had received from his benefactor; but Lucan would probably have deemed gratitude too mean a virtue for a patriot and a hero.

[2] *To serve under another*) ver. 28. He did not hesitate to obey the commands of another, when the good of his country required it. It has been suggested that "nec servire timens" means that he had no fear of becoming a slave, as he was determined to kill himself to avoid that necessity, a thing which it was always in his power to do.

[3] *Secret retreats of Corcyra*) ver. 32. When Pompey followed Cæsar into the interior of Thessaly, he left Cato with some troops in the vicinity of Dyrrhachium. With these troops and the remnant of those who fled from Pharsalia, he passed over from the continent to the Island of Corcyra (now Corfu), near which Pompey's navy then lay, in order, if possible, to join Pompey.

[4] *And in a thousand ships*) ver. 32. This is probably a hyperbolical mode of expression. Three hundred is more generally said to have been the number of the ships.

Then does he repair to Dorian Malea[1], and Tænarus open to the shades[2], and next Cythera[3]; and Crete vanishes, Boreas speeding on the barks; the waves moderating, he coasts along the Dictæan shores[4]. Then, Phycus, that dared[5] to shut its ports against the fleet, and that well deserved ruthless rapine, he burst into and sacked; and thence, Palinurus, was he borne by the calm breezes along the deep to thy shores[6]; (for not only in the Ausonian seas[7] dost thou possess memorials; Libya, also, testifies that her quiet ports were pleasing to the Phrygian pilot;) when, spreading their sails afar upon the deep, some ships kept their minds in suspense[8], whether they were conveying partners in their misfortunes, or whether foes. The con-

[1] *To Dorian Malea*) ver. 36. Malea, the promontory of Laconia, is called "Dorian," from the Dorians being supposed to have colonized Laconia.

[2] *Tænarus open to the shades*) ver. 36. He alludes to the cavern of Tænarus in Laconia, which was supposed to communicate with the Infernal Regions. See B. vi. l. 648, and the Note to the passage.

[3] *And next Cythera*) ver. 37. Cythera was a mountainous island off the south-eastern coast of Laconia. It was colonized by the Phœnicians, who, at a very early period, introduced there the worship of Aphrodite or Venus, whence her epithet Cytheræa. According to some traditions she rose from the sea in the neighbourhood of this island. At the present day it is called Cerigo.

[4] *The Dictæan shores*) ver. 38. See B. ii. l. 610, and the Note to the passage.

[5] *Phycus, that dared*) ver. 40. Phycus was a town on the coast of Cyrenaica, west of Apollonia, and north-west of Cyrene. It was the most northerly headland of eastern Libya, and the nearest point of land in Africa to the coast of Europe, the distance from Phycus to the Tænarian promontory being 208 miles. The inhabitants having refused to receive Cato and his troops, he took and sacked the town.

[6] *Palinurus, to thy shores*) ver. 42. There was a Promontory on the coast of Cyrenaica, which, according to Ptolemy the Geographer, was called "Paliurus." It is not improbable that the Poet has mistaken the name and incorrectly represented it as being called Palinurus, after the pilot of Æneas of that name.

[7] *In the Ausonian seas*) ver. 42-3. On the coast of Italy in the Velian Gulf, near Naples, there was a Promontory called Palinurus; according to tradition it was so called, because Palinurus, the pilot of Æneas, was murdered there by the natives, or, according to Virgil, Æn. B. vi. l. 366, he was drowned off that spot.

[8] *Kept their minds in suspense*) ver. 46. They were at a loss to say whether the ships of Cornelia and Sextus, now on their way from Egypt, were those of friends or foes.

queror, *so* swiftly moving, made everything to be dreaded, and in no ship was he not believed to be. But these barks were bearing grief and lamentation, and woes to move the tears of even the stern Cato.

For after by entreaties Cornelia had in vain tried to detain the sailors and the flight of her step-son[1], lest by chance, beaten back from the Pharian shores, the trunk might return to sea, and *when* the flames disclosed the pile with funeral rites unworthy of him, she exclaimed :—

" Have I, then, Fortune, proved unworthy to light the pile for my husband, and, stretched upon his cold limbs, to throw myself upon my spouse? To burn my hair torn out[2]? And to gather up the limbs of Magnus dispersed upon the sea? To pour abundant tears into all his wounds? To cover my garments with the bones and the heated embers[3], about to scatter in the Temples of the Gods whatever I might be allowed to take from the extinguished pyre? Without any honor of funereal rites is the pile to burn ; perhaps an Egyptian hand has performed this office repulsive to his shade[4]. O well *did* the ashes of the Crassi *lie* exposed! By greater enmity of the Gods has the fire fallen to Pompey's lot. Shall there always be to me a like fatality in my woes? Shall I never be allowed to provide a grave for my husband? Shall I never lament over a filled urn? What further need, sorrow, hast thou of tombs, or *why* require any instruments *of grief?* Dost thou not, unnatural one, retain Pompey throughout all thy breast? Does not his image dwell in thy inmost vitals? Let one look for the ashes, who is destined long to survive.

" Still, however, now does the fire that from afar shines with scanty light[5], as it rises from the Pharian shore, pre-

[1] *Of her step-son*) ver. 52. Sextus, the younger son of Pompey, by his wife Mucia.

[2] *To burn my hair torn out*) ver. 57. It was the custom for the female relatives of the deceased to lay locks of their hair upon the funeral pile.

[3] *With the heated embers*) ver. 60. See B. viii. l. 843, and the Note to the passage.

[4] *Office repulsive to his shade*) ver. 64. See B. viii. l. 671-3.

[5] *With scanty light*) ver. 73. " Luce maligna." Literally, " With malignant light." The question may be asked, how she could know that this was the funeral pile of Pompey ?—unless, indeed, we suppose the ship to have stood in very close to the shore.

sent to me something, Magnus, of thee. Now has the flame subsided, and the smoke that bears Pompey away vanishes at the rising of the sun, and, hateful to me, the winds spread the sails. Not now if any land conquered by Pompey were affording a triumph, *would it be* more dear to me, nor yet the chariot as it wears away the lofty Capitol; Magnus *as* prosperous has vanished from my breast. Him do I wish for whom the Nile retains, and at remaining on the guilty land I do not complain; the crime makes welcome the sands. If I am believed at all, I wish not to leave the Pelusian shores.

" Do thou, Sextus, *try* throughout the world the chances of war, and bear thy father's standards; for Pompey left this charge to you *his sons*, entrusted to my care:

"' When the fated hour shall have doomed me to death, take up, O my sons, the civil war, and never, while on earth any one of my race shall remain, let opportunity be given to the Cæsars to reign. Urge on even monarchies, even cities powerful in their own liberty, by the fame of my name. This party, these arms, to you do I leave. He will find fleets whichever Pompey[1] shall launch upon the waves; and to no nations shall my heir not cause war; only do you have feelings unsubdued and mindful of your father's rights. Cato alone will it be right to obey, if he shall espouse the cause of liberty.'

" Magnus, I have performed my trust to thee; thy injunctions I have complied with. Thy stratagem has taken effect[2], and, deceived, I have survived, that I might not, breaking my faith, carry away the words entrusted to me. Now then, husband, through empty Chaos will I follow thee, through Tartarus, if any *such* there is: how long respited from death it is uncertain; upon itself will I first wreak vengeance for my long-enduring life. It endured, Magnus, beholding thy wounds, not to take refuge in death; smitten with blows in wailing it shall end, it shall flow forth in tears; never shall I have to resort to the sword or

---

[1] *Whichever Pompey*) ver. 93. Whether Cneius or Sextus.

[2] *Thy stratagem has taken effect*) ver. 99. She means that Pompey's entrusting her with this commission was a plan to deceive her, and to make her live on, contrary to her own inclination.

the halter, or the headlong leap[1] through the empty *realms of air*. It is disgraceful, after thee not to be able to die of grief alone."

When thus she had spoken, she covered her head with a mourning veil, and resolved to endure darkness, and lay hid in the recesses of the ship; and, strictly embracing cruel grief, she enjoyed her tears, and cherished mourning for her husband. Not the billows moved her, and the eastern gales howling through the rigging, and the cries that rose in extreme peril; and conceiving wishes opposed to the anxious sailors, composed for death she lay, and wished success to the storms.

Cyprus with its foaming waves first receives the ship; thence, the eastern gales, retaining possession of the deep, but now more moderate, impel them towards the Libyan settlements[2], and the camp of Cato. Sad, as is his presaging mind amid much fear, Magnus from the shore[3] beholds the companions of his father, his brother, too; headlong is he then borne through the midst of the waves. "Say, brother, where is our father; does the summit and head of the earth exist, or are we undone? Has Magnus borne away *the destinies* of Rome to the shades?"

Thus he says; him, on the other hand, his brother *addresses in* such words as these:—" O happy *thou*, whom fate has separated in other regions, and who dost *only* hear of *this* wickedness: brother, I have eyes guilty of looking on my father *when dying*. Not by the arms of Cæsar did he fall, and *so* perish by a worthy author of his downfall; under the impure king who owns the fields of Nile, relying on the Gods of hospitality, and his services so great to his progenitors[4], he fell, the victim of the realm he had presented

[1] *Or the headlong leap*) ver. 107. "She will not have occasion to resort to a violent death by hanging herself, or by the sword, or by throwing herself from a precipice."

[2] *Towards the Libyan settlements*) ver. 119. Having touched at Cyprus she proceeds towards Africa, and meets Cato off the coast of Cyrenaica.

[3] *Magnus from the shore*) ver. 121. Lucan now calls Cneius, the eldest son of Pompey, by the epithet "Magnus," "Great," which had been given by the Roman people to his father, and descended to his children. Sextus did not remain long in Africa, but repaired to Spain to levy troops there.

[4] *To his progenitors*) ver. 132. Meaning the father of Ptolemy, whom he had been instrumental in restoring to his kingdom.

I myself beheld them wounding the breast of our noble
sire, and not believing that the Pharian tyrant could pos
sibly *commit* so great *a crime*, I imagined that[1] already his
father-in-law was standing on the shores of the Nile.

" But me neither did the blood nor the wounds of our
aged *sire* so much affect, as the head of the chieftain carried
through the city, which we saw borne aloft on a javelin
thrust through it; the report is that this is saved for the
eyes of the ruthless conqueror, and that the tyrant wishes
to ensure belief in his guilt. But, whether Pharian dogs
and greedy birds have torn the body in pieces, or whether
a stealthy fire[2] which we saw consumed it, I am ignorant.
Whatever injustice of fate has carried away these limbs, for
these crimes do I forgive the Gods of heaven; as to the
portion preserved do I lament."

When Magnus heard such *words* as these, he did not
pour forth his sorrow in groans and tears; and inflamed
with righteous affection he thus spoke :—"Launch forth, *ye*
sailors, the ships from the dry shore; with its oars let the
fleet cleave onward against the opposing gales; come on. *ye*
chieftains, with me; never for civil war was there a reward
so great, to inter the unburied ghost, to satiate Magnus with
the blood of the effeminate tyrant. Shall I not sink the
Pellæan towers, and the corpse of Alexander, torn from its
shrine, in the sluggish Mareotis[3]? Dragged forth from the
sepulchres of the pyramids, shall not Amasis[4] and the

[1] *I imagined that*) ver. 135. So Cornelia thought, B. viii. l. 641.

[2] *Or whether a stealthy fire*) ver. 142. He does not speak so positively as
Cornelia did in her lamentations, as to the fire being that of the funeral pile
of Pompey.

[3] *In the sluggish Mareotis*) ver. 154. Mareotis was a large lake in the
north-west of Lower Egypt, separated from the Mediterranean by the narrow
neck of land on which Alexandria stood, and supplied with water from the
Nile by canals. It was probably of a sluggish and stagnant nature, and
served as the port for the vessels that repaired to Alexandria. Its present
name is Birket-Mariouth, or El-Kreit.

[4] *Shall not Amasis*) ver. 155. See B. viii. l. 697. He probably refers
to Amasis, a very ancient king of Egypt, whom Pliny mentions as having
been buried in a pyramid which received its name from a figure of the
Sphynx. There was a more modern king of the same name, who was buried
at Sais, in the tomb which he himself had constructed in the temple of
Athene or Minerva. His body was dragged from his tomb by order of
Cambyses, and subjected to shameful indignities.

other kings float for me upon the stream of the Nile? For thee unburied, Magnus, let all the sepulchres pay the penalty; I will hurl forth Isis from her tomb, now a Divinity among the nations, and over the ashes of Magnus shall sacred Apis be slain. Osiris, too [1], clad in linen, I will scatter among the crowd; and, the Gods placed beneath, I will burn *Pompey's* head. This penalty shall the land pay to me; the fields I will leave deprived of cultivation, and no one shall there be for whom Nile shall increase; and thou, my sire, shalt possess Egypt alone, the people and the Deities banished."

He said, and was hurrying the fleet into the ruthless waves. But Cato restrained the praiseworthy resentment of the youth.

In the meantime, the death of Magnus being heard of, the sky resounded, smitten by lamentations; there was grief, too, wanting a parallel and known to no age, the people bewailing the death of a great man. But, still more, when, exhausted by tears, having her dishevelled locks streaming over her features, Cornelia was seen coming forth from the ship, did they again lament with redoubled blows [2] As soon as she reached the shores of a friendly land, she collected the garments and the memorials of the ill-fated Magnus, and the spoils embossed with gold, which he had formerly worn, and the embroidered robes [3], vestments thrice beheld [4] by supreme Jove, and she threw them into a funereal fire. To her *thus* sorrowing these were the ashes of Magnus. All feelings of affection followed her example, and throughout all the shore funeral piles arose, giving their

[1] *Osiris, too*) ver. 160. When Osiris had been torn to pieces by his brother Typhon, the story was that the fragments of the body were picked up by Isis and placed in a linen cloth, from which circumstance his statues were clothed in linen. The priests and devotees of both Isis and Osiris were also clothed in the same material.

[2] *With redoubled blows*) ver. 173. "Geminato verbere plangunt." This refers to the blows upon the breast by which the ancients (and especially females) were wont to denote violent paroxysms of grief.

[3] *The embroidered robes*) ver. 177. "Togæ" embroidered with palms, the emblems of conquest, and worn by victorious generals when celebrating their triumphs.

[4] *Vestments thrice beheld*) ver. 178. In allusion to his three triumphs. See B. vii. l. 635, and the Note to the passage. The triumphant procession proceeded to the Temple of Jupiter Capitolinus.

fires to the Thessalian shades [1]. Thus, when the Apulian [2] is preparing to reproduce the grass on the plains eaten bare, and to renew the wintry herbage, does he warm the earth with fires, and together do both Garganus [3] and the fields of Vultur [4] and the pastures for oxen on warm Matinus [5] shine.

Still, not more pleasing did all that the common people dared *to utter* in censure of the Gods of heaven, and in which it rebuked the Deities as to Pompey, reach the ghost of Magnus, than *did* the words of Cato, few, but coming from a breast replete with truth.

" A citizen has perished," he said, " much inferior to our forefathers [6] in knowing moderation in his sway, but still, useful in this age, which has had no respect [7] for justice, powerful, liberty still safe, and the only one who was a private man when the people were ready to be his slaves, and the ruler of the Senate, but of that *still* reigning. Nothing in right of war did he demand; whatever he wished to be granted him he wished it to be possible for it to be refused him. Wealth unbounded did he possess, but more did he

[1] *To the Thessalian shades*) ver. 181. In imitation of the honorary pile which Cornelia erects and sets fire to in honor of Pompey, they erect funeral piles in honor of their friends who have fallen at Pharsalia.

[2] *When the Apulian*) ver. 182-5. He refers to the custom among the husbandmen of Apulia of lighting fires throughout the fields, in order to renew the exhausted earth, and to destroy the old roots, thus leaving room for the young blade to spring up.

[3] *Together do both Garganus*) ver. 184. Garganus was a mountain and Promontory on the coast of Apulia, famous, according to Horace, for its forests of oak. It is still called Monte Gargano.

[4] *Fields of Vultur*) ver. 185. Vultur was a mountain near Venusia, dividing Apulia from Lucania. Horace mentions it as one of the haunts of his youthful days. From it the south-east wind was called Vulturnus by the Romans.

[5] *On warm Matinus*) ver. 185. Matinus was a mountain of Apulia, near Mount Garganus. As here mentioned, it was famous for the excellence of its pastures.

[6] *Inferior to our forefathers*) ver. 190. " A good citizen, though far inferior to the Bruti, the Camilli, the Curii, the Decii, the Fabii, the Fabricii, the Cincinnati, the Catos, and the Scipios of former times." Cato was especially a " laudator temporis acti."

[7] *Which has had no respect*) ver. 192. " Cui " here, though considered by some to refer to Pompey, clearly relates to " ævum," " the age," of which Cato is complaining.

present *to the public* than what was retained ; the sword he took up, but he knew how to lay it down. Arms he preferred to civil life [1]; but. amid arms, he loved peace.

" Authority assumed pleased the chieftain ; laid down, it pleased him. Chaste *was* his household, and void of luxury, and never corrupted by the *good* fortune of its lord. A name illustrious and revered by nations, and one that has advantaged our City much. Long since, on Sulla and Marius being received [2] *into the City*, real confidence in liberty disappeared ; now, Pompey taken away from the State, even a feigned one perishes. No longer now will there be shame at holding kingly sway ; neither the colour of authority, nor yet any front of the Senate, will there be. O happy man, whom, when conquered, his last day came to meet, and to whom the Pharian villany presented a sword deserving to be sought! Perhaps under the sway of his father-in-law he might have been able to live. To know how to die *is* the first blessing to man, but the next, to be compelled. To me, too, if by the Fates we fall into the power of another, Fortune, grant Juba *to be* such ; I do not beg not to be reserved for an enemy, so long as [3] he reserves me, my head cut off."

By these words more honor in his death accrued to the noble shade, than if the Roman Rostra had resounded with praises of the chieftain.

In the meantime, the discord of the people in the camp creates murmurs, and after the death of Magnus they are weary of the war, when Tarchondimotus [4] raises the standard

[1] *Preferred to civil life*) ver. 199. "Togæ ;" literally, " to the toga," the garb of peace.

[2] *Sulla and Marius being received*) ver. 204. "Receptis." He alludes to the returns of Sulla and Marius, at different periods after having recovered from their defeats, which they celebrated with almost indiscriminate slaughter of their fellow-citizens.

[3] *So long as*) ver. 214. He does not refuse to suffer the same treatment from Juba as Pompey did from the hands of Ptolemy.

[4] *When Tarchondimotus*) ver. 219. Tarchondimotus was the king of Cilicia, or perhaps more properly a chieftain of some portion of its piratical population. He fought on the side of Pompey, but was afterwards pardoned by Cæsar, and allowed to retain his dominions. After the death of Cæsar he joined Cassius, and subsequently espoused the cause of Antony against Augustus. He was slain in a sea-fight in the year B.C. 31, while fighting under Sosius against M. Agrippa.

for leaving Cato. Following him to the edge of the shore, as he flies with his fleet hurrying off, Cato censures him in such words: "O Cilician, never reduced to peace, dost thou again go to thy rapine on the main? Fortune has removed Magnus; now as a pirate thou art returning to the seas." Then he gazes upon all the men in groups and in commotion; one of whom, disclosing his mind as to the flight, in such words addresses the chief:—

"Cato, grant us pardon, it was the love of Pompey, not of civil war, that moved us to arms, and through affection did we espouse a faction. He lies prostrate, whom the earth preferred to peace, and fallen is our cause; allow us to revisit our country's household Gods, and our deserted homes and dear children. For what end of the contest will there be, if neither Pharsalia nor Pompey shall be *so?* The moments of our lives have been wasted; let death come upon us in our retreat; let our old age look forward to the flames its due. Civil warfare can hardly afford sepulchres to chieftains. No barbarian sway awaits the conquered; no cruel Fortune threatens me with an Armenian or a Scythian yoke; I come beneath the rule of a citizen who wears the toga.

"Whoever, while Magnus was living, *was* the second, the same to me shall be the first; the highest honor shall be paid to the hallowed shade; the ruler whom disaster forces *me to have*, I will have; general, Magnus, none. Thee alone having followed to the war, next after thee will I follow destiny[1], for it is neither right nor lawful for me to hope for success. All things are embraced by the fortune of Cæsar; victory has destroyed the Emathian sword. *All* confiding is closed against us in our wretchedness, and in the whole earth there is one alone, who is willing and is able to give safety to the conquered. Pompey slain, civil war is a crime, who living it was fidelity. If, Cato, thou wilt always obey the public laws, if *always* thy country, let us follow the standards which *Cæsar*, the Roman Consul, raises."

Thus having said, he leaped on board ship, the cheers of the youths accompanying him. There was an end of the state of Rome, and in want of servitude all the multitude

Will I follow destiny) ver. 243. "Fata;" meaning "the fortune of war."

thronged upon the shore. *These* words burst forth from
the hallowed breast of their leader: — "Did you then,
youths, wage the war with like hopes[1], were you too for
tyrants, and were you a Pompeian, not a Roman, army?
Because for no one's sway you toil, because for yourselves,
not for your leaders, you live and die, because for no one
you win the world, because now it is safe for you to conquer, do you fly from war, and do you seek a yoke, your
necks *yet* free, and know you not how to endure to be without a king?

"Now *is* the cause of danger worthy of men. Pompey
might have made bad use of your blood; now to your
country do your refuse your throats and swords, when
liberty *is* nigh? Of three lords Fortune has now left but
one[2]. Be ashamed *of yourselves;* more has the court of the
Nile conferred upon the laws, the bows, too, of the Parthian
soldiers. Away, O degenerate men, despise the gift and the
arms of Ptolemy[3]. Who could suppose that your hands were
guilty of any slaughter? He will believe that you readily
turned your backs, he will believe that you were the first to
fly from Emathian Philippi[4].

"Go in security; in Cæsar's judgment you have deserved
life, subdued by no arms, in no siege. O base slaves, after
the death of your first master you descend to his heir. Why
do you not choose to merit more than life and pardon?
Let the unhappy wife of Magnus, and the offspring of
Metellus[5] be hurried off upon the waves; carry off the
Pompeys, surpass the gift of Ptolemy. My own head as
well. whoever shall present to the hated tyrant, will give it
for no small reward. This force will know that at the price

[1] *With like hopes)* ver. 250. "Pari voto." "With just the same party
spirit as the followers of Cæsar, and not influenced by any feelings of pa-
triotism."

[2] *Now left but one)* ver. 266. "Cæsar is the only tyrant now left you out
of the Triumvirate, Crassus and Pompey being dead."

[3] *Of Ptolemy)* ver. 268. He means to say that the death of Pompey
has at least procured them a greater share of liberty, and ironically calls it
"munus," the "gift" of Ptolemy.

[4] *From Emathian Philippi)* ver. 271. As usual, he confounds the field
of Pharsalia with that of Philippi.

[5] *Offspring of Metellus)* ver. 277. Cornelia, the daughter of Metellus Scipio.

of my life it has well followed my standards. Come on, then, and in *one* vast slaughter earn your deserts ; cowardly treason only is flight."

He *thus* said, and all the ships did he recall from the midst of the sea, no otherwise than *as when* the swarms together leave the teeming wax, and, forgetful of the combs, mingle not their wings[1] in clusters, but each one takes flight for itself, nor now slothfully tastes the bitter thyme ; the sound of the Phrygian brass[2] censures *them;* astounded, they cease their flight, and seek again the pursuits of their flower-gathering labours, and their fondness for the scattered honey ; freed from care, glad is the shepherd on the grass of Hybla[3], that he has preserved the wealth of his cottage: thus by the words of Cato was patience recommended to the men in a righteous warfare.

. And now by the movements of war, and by a continuance of labours he determines to exercise their minds, not taught to endure repose. First, the soldiers are wearied on the sands of the sea-shore ; at the walls and fortifications[4] of Cyrene[5] is their next labour; excluded, by no wrath does he avenge himself; and the sole vengeance of Cato upon

---

[1] *Mingle not their wings*) ver. 286. It is more generally supposed that he alludes here to the bees flying in thick swarms together, and not to their hanging in clusters, the one fastened to the other, as described in Virgil's Georgics, B. iv. l. 558, although at first sight the passage seems to have that meaning.

[2] *Sound of the Phrygian brass*) ver. 288. Cymbals were originally used by the Phrygians in the worship of the Goddess Cybele. He alludes to the calling the bees together by the noise of the cymbals. Virgil has a similar passage in the Georgics, B. iv. l. 64, where, speaking of bees, he says,— " Tinnitusque cie, et Matris quate cymbala circum." " And make a tinkling noise, and shake the cymbals of the Mother round about."

[3] *On the grass of Hybla*) ver. 291. Hybla was a mountain of Sicily famed for its honey. There were three places in that island thus named, Hybla Major, Minor, and Heræa.

[4] *And fortifications*) ver. 297. Cato really did not take the city of Cyrene, as the inhabitants voluntarily opened their gates to him, when they had refused to do so for Labienus, an adherent of Pompey.

[5] *Of Cyrene*) ver. 297. Cyrene was the chief city of Cyrenaica. It stood about eight miles from the sea, on an eminence 1800 feet above the sea, in the midst of most picturesque scenery. Its harbour was Apollonia, and its ruins are still very extensive. Cyrene is the scene of the Rudens, perhaps the most interesting of all the plays of Plautus.

the conquered is the having conquered them. Thence does it please him to repair to the realms of Juba [1], adjoining to the Moors; but nature forbids a passage by the Syrtes [2] lying between; a dauntless valour trusts that these even will give way to it. Either nature, when she gave its first figure to the world, left the Syrtes in a doubtful position between sea and land (for neither did the land subside entirely in order that it might receive the waters of the deep, nor did it protect itself from the sea; but a tract lay impassable, by reason of the ambiguous nature of the place; the seas *are* broken by shoals, and the land *is* torn away by the deep, and the waves intervening, resound behind many a shallow. Thus did nature heedlessly forsake it, and she wrought for no use this portion of herself); or else the Syrtis once was more full of the deep ocean, and was entirely deluged *with waters;* but the scorching sun [3], feeding his light with the sea, drew up the adjacent waters of the burnt-up zone; and now, the sea still contends with Phœbus as he dries it up. At a future day, when destroying time shall have *enough* applied the rays, the Syrtis will be *dry* land; for now shallow water floats above, and the waves are failing, destined far and wide to come to an end.

When first all the force of the fleet impelled the sea urged by its oars, the south wind, black with showers, roared, raging throughout his realms [4]; with a whirlwind he defends the deep invaded by the fleets, and far from the Syrtes he drives the billows, and dashes the sea upon the extending shores. Then, the sails of some which he finds *extended* on

[1] *Realms of Juba*) ver. 301. He heard that Scipio and Atius Varus had repaired to the court of Juba, king of Numidia, and was anxious to join them.

[2] *By the Syrtes*) ver. 302. The Syrtis Major, or Greater Syrtis, is the one here alluded to, lying between Cyrenaica and the river Cinyps. Its situation is exactly opposite to the mouth of the Adriatic Sea, between Sicily and Peloponnesus. Its depth is about 110 miles, and its width between the Promontories, anciently called Cephalæ and Boreum, about 230 miles. The great desert through which Cato marched comes down close to its shores, forming a sandy and desolate coast.

[3] *But the scorching sun*) ver. 313. Literally, "Titan," an epithet of the sun, as, according to some accounts, being the offspring of the Titans Hyperion and Thia, or Euryphaessa.

[4] *Throughout his realms*) ver. 321. The regions particularly exposed to its influence, and whence it was supposed to take its rise.

the upright masts, he tears away from the mariners; and the ropes having vainly attempted to deny the canvas to the southern gales, they surpass the length of the ship, and beyond the prow swells the bellying sail. If any one with foresight has fastened beneath all the cloth to the topmost yard, he, too, with bared rigging is driven out of his course.

Better *was* the lot of the fleet which happened upon deep waves, and *was* tossed by a steady sea. Whatever *ships* lightened by their masts cut down avoided the raging blast, the tide at liberty bore these on, rolling *them* in a contrary direction to the winds, and victorious drove them against the struggling south wind. Some barks do the shallows forsake, and the earth broken in upon by the deep strikes them; and exposed to a doubtful fate, one part of the ship rests *on land*, the other part is poised in the waves. Then still more *is* the sea dashed upon the quicksands, and the earth rages rising to meet it in its path; although repelled by the south wind, still full oft the wave masters not the hills of sand. There stands aloft upon the surface of the main afar from all the fields, untouched by the water, a heap of now dry sand; the wretched sailors stand *confounded*, and the ship run on land they behold no shore.

Thus does the sea intercept a part; a greater portion of the ships obey the rudder and the helm; safe in flight, and having obtained pilots well acquainted with the spot, unhurt it arrives at the stagnant swamps of Triton [1]. This, as the report *is*, the God loves, whom throughout all the shore the ocean hears, as he raises his murmurs on his windy shell [2]; this does Pallas [3] love as well, who, springing

---

[1] *Stagnant swamps of Triton*) ver. 347. This was probably a place at the mouth of the river Triton, or Tritonis, which was supposed to flow from Lake Tritonis, in the interior of the country, which is thought to have been the great Salt Lake in the south of Tunis, now called El Sibkah. As it has now no opening to the sea, the river, if ever it existed, must have been long since choked up by the sands.

[2] *On his windy shell*) ver. 349. The sea-God Triton, the son of Neptune and Amphritite, or Celæno. It was his office to blow his trumpet, made ot a conch shell, at the command of his father, in order to soothe the restlessness of the sea.

[3] *This does Pallas*) ver. 350. Pallas, or Minerva, was said to have received her surname Trito, or Tritogeneia, from this spot, where she was also said to have been born. According to other versions, she had that name from the river Triton, in the vicinity of Alalcomenæ, in Bœotia, where she

from her father's head touched Libya first of *all* lands (for
nearest is it to heaven, as the heat itself proves[1]), and beheld her features[2] in the quiet water of the pool, and on
the margin set her feet, and named herself Tritonis from
the beloved waves.

Near to which does Lethon[3], silent river, flow along;
bringing obliviousness, as *is* the report, from the streams of
hell; and, once the care of the sleepless dragon, the poor
garden of the Hesperides[4], spoiled of its boughs. Spiteful
the man, who robs old times of their credit, *and* who summons poets to the truth. There was a golden wood, and
branches weighed down with riches and with yellow fruit;
a virgin troop[5], too, *were* the guardians of the shining
grove, and a serpent with its eyes never condemned to
sleep, entwining around the boughs bending with shining

was worshipped, and by some was said to have been born. Grammarians
derive the name from an ancient word, *ρεισω*, signifying " the head," in allusion to the story of her having sprung from the head of her father Jupiter.

[1] *As the heat itself proves*) ver. 352. This is a very good instance of what
we may call a *non sequitur.*

[2] *Beheld her features*) ver. 353. The modest Minerva was especially
represented by the ancients as repudiating the use of the mirror, and as
viewing herself solely in the stream. So in the Fasti of Ovid, where she is
describing the invention of the pipe, she is represented as saying (B. vi.
l. 700),—" The melody pleased me; but in the clear waters that reflected
my face, I saw the swelling out of my cheeks."

[3] *Near to which does Lethon*) ver. 355. Lucan is probably mistaken here
in his geography, as Lethe was generally said to be a river in Spain, called
also Limæa, which flowed into the Atlantic Ocean. Some, however, assert
that Lethe was a different river from the one, which the Poet here calls
"Lethos," and which is said to have flowed past a town called Berenice,
near the Syrtis.

[4] *Garden of the Hesperides*) ver. 358. In the earliest versions of the
story of the Hesperides, or guardians of the Golden apples, these nymphs
are described as living on the river Oceanus, in the extreme west; but the
later poets and geographers mention other parts of Libya as their locality,
such as the vicinity of Cyrene (as in the present instance), Mount Atlas, or
the islands on the western coast of Africa. It was one of the labours of
Hercules to obtain possession for Eurystheus of these golden apples, which
were said to be guarded by a sleepless dragon.

[5] *A virgin troop*) ver. 362. Some accounts mention three as the number
of the Hesperides, Ægle, Arethusa, and Hesperia; others four, Ægle, Cytheia,
Hestia, and Arethusa; while other accounts make seven to have been their
number. They are called in poetic story the daughters of Night, or of Erebus, or of Phorcys and Ceto, or of Atlas and Hesperia, or of Hesperus, or
of Zeus and Themis.

A A

metal. Alcides took away the prize from the trees; and, allowing the branches *to be* valueless without their load, brought back the shining apples to the tyrant of Argos[1].

Pushing off from these spots[2], therefore, and driven away from the Syrtes, the fleet did not proceed beyond the waves of the Garamantes[3], but under the command of Pompey remained on the coasts of more wealthy Libya. But the valour of Cato, impatient at delaying, ventured to lead his band among unknown nations, and to skirt the Syrtes by land, trusting in his arms. This did the same wintry season prompt, which had shut up the deep; and showers were objects of their hopes, as they feared the excessive heats; that the year would temper their march, severe with neither the sun's heat nor with extreme cold, on the one hand with the clime of Libya, on the other with the winter season. And, about to enter upon the barren sands, he thus spoke :—

" O ye, to whom, following my camp, one safety alone has proved pleasing, to die with necks unenslaved, make up your minds to the great work of constancy and labours extreme. We are going unto sterile plains and scorched regions of the world, where are excessive heat of the sun and scanty water in the springs, and the parched fields are horrid with deadly serpents, a toilsome march. For the sake of the laws and for the love of their falling country, through the midst of Libya let them come, and let them attempt *these places so* remote, if any have centered their wishes in no escape, if to any to march onward is enough. Nor indeed is it my intention to deceive any one, and by concealing my fears to draw on the multitude.

[1] *To the tyrant of Argos*) ver. 367. Eurystheus, the king of Argos, who, by the command of Jupiter, imposed his tasks upon Hercules in the hope of destroying him.

[2] *Pushing off from these spots*) ver. 368-70. The meaning of this passage is obscure, but it seems to be that, fearful of the dangers of the Lesser Syrtis, with its quicksands and shoals, Cneius, the elder son of Pompey, who had taken command of the fleet, put in at some seaport on the coast, and remained there, declining to coast along Africa, a delay which the restless spirit of Cato could not brook, on which he determined to make his way by land across the Great Desert.

[3] *Waves of the Garamantes*) ver. 369. The Poet is here guilty of a great mistake, as the Garamantes were a nation far in the interior of Africa, adjoining Æthiopia.

" Let those be my companions, whom the dangers them selves would lead, who, myself the witness, would deem it glorious and befitting a Roman to endure even the most shocking *fate*. But the soldier who wants a surety for his safety, and is influenced by the sweetness of life, let him go to a tyrant by an easier way. So long as I am the first to set foot upon the sands, and the first to imprint my steps in the dust, upon me let the heat of the sky strike [1]. me let the serpent, filled with venom, meet ; and try beforehand your perils in my fate; whoever shall behold me drinking, let him thirst; or whoever *shall see me* seeking the shade of the groves, let him swelter with heat, or on horseback going before troops of foot, let him flag ; if *in fact* it shall by any difference be known whether as general or as soldier I am marching. Serpents, thirst, heat, sand, *are* sweet to valour; in adversity patience delights. More pleasing is that which is honorable, as often as it costs itself a heavy price. Libya alone can present a multitude of woes that it would beseem men to fly from."

Thus did he with valour and with the love of difficulties inflame their wavering minds, and commence upon a path not to be retraced with its desert track : and, destined in a little tomb to enclose a hallowed name, Libya secured the death of Cato, free from care.

Libya *is* the third part of the earth, if you are ready to trust report in everything ; but if you trace the winds and climate, it will be a portion of Europe. For, not more distant are the shores of Nile, than *is* the Scythian Tanais from the nearest Gades, in which quarter Europe separates from Libya, and by their retreat the shores make room for the ocean : but a larger portion of the world composes Asia singly [2]. For whereas [3], these in common send forth Zephyrus, the other touching upon the left-hand side of Boreas, and

---

[1] *Heat of the sky strike*) ver. 396. By the use of the word " feriat," he probably refers to the effects of sun-stroke, or coup-de-soleil.

[2] *Composes Asia singly*) ver. 416-17. He means that Asia is larger than Europe and Africa joined together.

[3] *For whereas*) ver. 417-420. His meaning is that Asia is as large as Europe and Africa, inasmuch as it includes all the eastern part of the earth, besides part of the north and of the south ; while Europe and Africa together occupy the whole of the west, with part of the north and of the south.

the right-hand side of the South, slopes away to the East, alone possessing Eurus. That which is the fertile *part* of the Libyan land lies to the Westward ; but even this is not relaxed with any springs ; with few Northern breezes does it receive the Arctoan showers, and refresh its fields with our serene weather.

It is corrupted by no riches[1]; neither for copper nor for gold is it melted, with no faultiness of the soil, *it is* pure, and is mould throughout. The Maurusian wood[2] is the only wealth of the race, the use of which it knows not, but it lives content with the foliage of the cedar, and its shade. To unknown groves have our axes come, and in the extremities of the earth have we sought our banquets and our tables[3]. But whatever region skirts around the shifting Syrtis, extended beneath heat too intense, adjacent to a parching sky, it scorches the corn and chokes up the grape[4] with dust, and, crumbling, is held by no root. A temperature suited to life is wanting, and under no care of Jove[5] is that land ; nature lying slothful, the region is torpid, and with its unmoved sands is not sensible of the *changing* year.

Still, this soil so dull puts forth a few herbs, which the Nasamonian[6], a hardy race, collects, who, bare of *all comforts*, possesses the country adjacent to the sea ; *and* whom the barbarian Syrtis feeds[7] with the losses of the world. For the wrecker hovers over the sands of the shore, and, no

[1] *It is corrupted by no riches*) ver. 424. "Africa has no mines of metal, the sources of vice."

[2] *The Maurusian wood*) ver. 426. "The only wealth of the people of Mauritania is their woods, which they do not value for their material, like the Romans, but for their shade from the sun."

[3] *Our banquets and our tables*) ver. 430. The wood of the African "citrus," which is generally supposed to have been a kind of cedar, was much prized by the Romans for the purpose of making tables, and "triclinia," or couches, used for reclining on at meals, and other articles of furniture.

[4] *Chokes up the grape*) ver. 433. Literally, "Bacchus," the guardian Divinity of the grape.

[5] *Under no care of Jove*) ver. 436. Jupiter, in his character of "pluvius," or the God of showers, is here alluded to. "Nulla sub illâ" is here put by Hypallage for "Illa sub nullâ."

[6] *The Nasamonian*) ver. 439. See B. iv. l. 679, and the Note to the passage.

[7] *The barbarian Syrtis feeds*) ver. 441. "To whom the whole world is a common prey, when falling into their power through shipwreck."

keel touching at his harbours, he knows of wealth. Thus in shipwrecks do the Nasamonians have traffic with the whole world. This way does resolute valour bid Cato march. There *is* the youthful band regardless of the winds, and, dreading no storms by land, suffers the terrors of the deep[1]. For upon the dry shore does the Syrtis with greater violence receive the south winds than on the sea, and more injurious is it to the land

With no mountains opposing does Libya break its *force*, and scatter it repelled by rocks, and change it from a hurricane into serene air: nor does it rush into woods, and weary itself with hurling down aged oaks ; all the land lies open, and in its passage it works out the rage of Æolus, free from all rein ; and the sand whirled *aloft*, sweeping along it drives in wreaths a cloud teeming with no rain. The greater portion of the land is raised *on high*, and, in a whirlwind[2] never dissolved, hangs aloft. The poor Nasamonian sees *his* possessions[3] floating in the wind, and his home rent asunder ; and, the Garamantian laid bare, the cottages, torn away, fly from the roofs. Not higher does fire bear aloft what it consumes ; and as far as it is possible for smoke to arise and to obscure the day, so high does the sand possess the air.

Then, too, more violently than usual does it attack the Roman troops, and not a soldier is able to keep his footing, infirm of hold, even the sands being borne away on which he treads. It would shake the earth, and would move the region away from the spot, if Libya, of solid texture and of hard substance, all covered with crags, were to enclose the southern blasts in *its* caverns eaten away; but because it is easily moved with its shifting sands, by never struggling it remains firm, and the lower part of the land stands fast, because the upper gives way.

With its violent impulse the blast hurls away helmets

[1] *Suffers the terrors of the deep*) ver. 447. They suffered disasters there from the winds equal to those which they might have experienced at sea.

[2] *And, in a whirlwind*) ver. 457. He describes a whirlwind, or Typhoon, and its dreadful effects.

[3] *Sees his possessions*) ver. 458. " Regna " means the humble cottages of the unfortunate Nasamonians. Lucan has probably taken the idea from the first Eclogue of Virgil, l. 70, where Tityrus styles his humble cottage " mea regna," " my realms," or " kingdoms."

and shields and the javelins of the men, and, without ceasing, bears them through the void realms of the wide heavens. Perhaps on some foreign and far remote land that is
a prodigy; and nations are alarmed at weapons falling from
the skies, and, torn away from the arms of men, they think
them sent down[1] by the Gods of heaven. Thus undoubtedly did those fall for sacrificing Numa, which the chosen
youths[2] wore on their Patrician necks; the South wind or
Boreas had spoiled nations bearing our ancilia[3].

Notus thus attacking the region, the Roman troops lay
down, and, dreading to be borne away, girded fast their
clothes, and thrust their hands into the earth; nor by their
weight alone did they lie, but by their efforts *to hold fast*,
hardly thus unmoved by the southern blasts; which rolled
upon them vast heaps of sand, and covered the men with
earth.

Hardly is the soldier able to raise *his* limbs, sticking fast
in a large pile of dust. Some even standing the vast mass
of drifted sand overpowers; and, unable to move, they
are held fast in the rising ground. Stones does it bear
afar, torn away from the walls shaken down, and scatter them
at a distance, with a wondrous kind of disaster; they
who beheld no houses, behold the ruins. And now all the
path lies hid; nor is there *now* any difference in *the sky
and* earth, except the lights of heaven, as though in the
midst of the sea. By the Constellations they know the way,

[1] *Think them sent down*) ver. 476. He suggests an explanation for those
prodigies which, according to the accounts of his time, were occasionally
creating alarm among nations; he thinks that such objects as arms, which
occasionally fell, and were supposed to be sent down from heaven, may have
been borne away by whirlwinds from people in distant regions, and suggests
that this was the origin of the "ancile," or sacred shield of Numa, which
was supposed to have fallen from heaven.

[2] *Which the chosen youths*) ver. 478. "Lecta juventus." He alludes to
the Salii, or guardians of the "ancilia," who were chosen from the noble
families of Rome. See B. i. l. 603, and the Note to the passage. The Salii
hung the "ancilia" round their necks, or in their left hands, beating them
with rods, and keeping time with their voices and the movements of the
dance. This took place on the festival of Mars, or the 1st of March.

[3] *Bearing our ancilia*) ver. 480. Though he speaks of "ancilia" in the
plural, we read of but one that was said to have descended from heaven.
The other eleven were made by Mamurius exactly to resemble it, in order
that it might not be distinguished by those inclined to steal it.

nor does the horizon, the limit of the Libyan region, show the well-known Constellations, and it conceals many *of them* by the margin of the earth downward sloping.

And when the heat released the air which the wind had borne to and fro, and the day *was* inflamed, their limbs flowed with perspiration, their mouths were parched with thirst. A little water was beheld afar in a scanty streamlet : which a soldier, with difficulty scooping it up from the dust, poured forth into the wide concavity of a helmet and offered to the general. The jaws of all were clogged with dust; and, receiving the tiny *draught* of water, the general himself was an object of envy

" What," said he, " degenerate soldier, didst thou suppose that I alone in this multitude was devoid of manliness ? Did I seem so very tender and unequal to the morning's heat? How much more worthy of this punishment art thou, to be drinking while the people thirsts !" Thus, aroused with anger, he dashed down the helmet, and the water sufficed for all [1].

They had *now* come to the Temple, the only one which among the Libyan nations the uncivilized Garamantes possess. There stands Jupiter, the foreteller of destiny, as they relate; but not either brandishing the lightnings or like to ours, but Ammon with crooked horns [2]. Not there

---

[1] *Water sufficed for all*) ver. 510. Rowe remarks here that this action was not much unlike that of David, when he refused to drink of the water of the well of Bethlehem, which three men had ventured their lives to fetch. 1 Chron. xi. 15.

[2] *Ammon with crooked horns*) ver. 514. This was the Libyan or Æthiopian Deity, Amun or Ammun, whose worship extended throughout Egypt, the northern coast of Africa, and various parts of Greece, and who was by some believed to be the same Deity as Zeus, or Jupiter, under another form. Rowe has the following note on this passage :—" Lucan has made no scruple of committing here another great fault in geography, for the sake of bringing Cato to the Temple of Jupiter Ammon. This famous oracle was certainly situate between the less and the greater Catabathmus, to the west of Egypt, in what is now called the desert of Barca, a great way distant from the march Cato was then taking in the kingdom of Tunis. The description of the place itself, except that (as I understand him) he places it under the Æquator, is agreeable to most other ancient authors. It is pretty well known that Jupiter was worshipped in this place under the shape of a Ram (at least the upper part), and there are still to be found among the Egyptian idols, in the cabinets of the curious, some with the body of a man and a ram's head."

have Libyan nations erected costly Temples, nor do shrines
glitter with eastern gems. Although among the tribes of the
Æthiopians¹ and the rich nations of the Arabians and the
Indians, Jupiter Ammon is the only *God*, still he is a poor
God, possessing sanctuaries polluted in no age with wealth,
and a Divinity of primitive habits, he protects the Temple
from Roman gold. That there are Deities in the spot a
wood attests, the only one verdant² throughout all Libya.

For whatever *country* with its parching sand separates
burning Berenice from hot Leptis, is destitute of shrubs;
Ammon alone produces a grove. A fountain on the spot is
the cause of the woods, which knits together the crumbling
particles of earth, and unites the sand subdued by *its* waters.
Here, as well, nothing resists Phœbus, when in the highest
zenith the day stands poised; hardly does the tree over-
shadow its trunk, so small a shadow is thrown down
perpendicularly by the rays. It has been ascertained that
this is the spot where the circle³ of the elevated solstice
cuts through the mid sphere of the Constellations. Not obliquely do they proceed, nor does the Scorpion go more
vertically than the Bull, nor does the Ram give his hours⁴
to the Balance, nor does Astræa bid the lagging Fishes to go
down. Chiron is equally⁵ matched with the Twins, and just
as the burning Carcinus *is* the watery Ægoceros⁶, nor is the
Lion raised higher than the Urn.

---

¹ *Of the Æthiopians*) ver. 517.   This epithet is used here with reference
to the Æthiopians, who, with the confused notions of geography of the
ancients, were considered to be the same race with the inhabitants of eastern
India.

² *The only one verdant*) ver. 523.   Sallust mentions the fact that all the
district which lies between Leptis and Berenice, one of the five cities which
constituted Pentapolis, was entirely devoid of trees and shrubs; consequently
the Temple here described was situate in what we call an Oasis.

³ *Where the circle*) ver. 531.   This passage has given rise to much discussion; but there can be little doubt but that the Poet means to say that the
region of Ammonitis lies under the Equator, in which, however, he is mistaken, as it does not lie even within the Tropic of Cancer.

⁴ *The Ram give his hours*) ver. 534.   He means the counterpoise, as it
were, of Aries to Libra, they being opposite Constellations; as many hours as
there are of day when the sun is in Aries, so many hours of night are there
the sun being in Libra, and vice versâ.

⁵ *Chiron is equally*) ver. 536.   Chiron is the Constellation which we call
Sagittarius, or the Archer. Carcinos is the Greek name for Cancer, the Crab.

⁶ *Watery Ægoceros*) ver. 537.   By Ægoceros he means the Constellation

But whatever race thou art, cut off by the Libyan fires, for thee the shadows fall to the south, which with us go towards the north ; and the Cynosure, slowly moving, sets [1] ; thou dost think that *its* dry Wain is immersed in the deep, and dost deem no star in the loftiest heights *of the northern sky* exempt from the sea [2]. Afar is either pole, and the course of the Constellations hurries on all of them in the intermediate heavens.

Before the doors stood the nations whom the East had sent, and by the warning of horned Jupiter they sought the approaching destinies ; but for the Latian chieftain they gave way ; and his attendants entreated Cato that he would enquire of the Deity famed throughout the Libyan world, and form a judgment as to the report of such lengthened ages. Labienus was [3] the principal adviser to enquire into events by the voice of the Gods.

" Chance," said he, " and the fortune of the way has presented the lips of a Deity so great and the counsel of a God : a guide so mighty amid the Syrtes we may employ, and learn the destined events of the warfare. For to whom could I suppose that the Gods of heaven would rather reveal and disclose their secrets than the truth to the hallowed Cato ? Assuredly thy life has ever been regulated according to the laws of heaven, and thou art a follower of the God. Lo ! the opportunity is granted thee of communing with Jove ; make enquiry into the fates of wicked Cæsar, and search into the future manners of *thy* country ; whether it will be possible for nations to enjoy their own rights and *those of* the laws, or whether civil war is hopeless. Fill thy heart with the sacred words ; ever a lover of strict virtue, seek what is virtue, and request an example of right."

He, filled with the God, whom in his silent mind he bore, poured forth from his breast words worthy of the shrines :—

" What, Labienus, dost thou request to be asked ? Whe-

Capricorn, that being its Greek name. Urna is the urn or pitcher of the sign Aquarius, the Water-bearer.

[1] *And the Cynosure, slowly moving, sets*) ver. 540. The Constellation " Ursa Minor," or the Lesser Bear. See B. iii. l. 219.

[2] *Exempt from the sea*) ver. 542. So Ovid, in the Metamorphoses, B. xiii. l. 293, speaking of the same Constellation, says, " Immunemque æquoris Arcton," " and the Bear that is exempt from the sea."

[3] *Labienus was*) ver. 550. See B. v. l. 340, and the Note to the passage.

ther, a free man, I would rather die in arms than behold a
tyranny? Whether life is nothing at all, even *though it be*
a long one? Whether age makes any difference? Whether
any violence can injure the good man? Whether Fortune
wastes her threats on virtue being opposed *to her?* And
whether it is enough to wish for what is to be commended,
and *whether* rectitude is never crowned by a successful result?

" *These things* we know, and Ammon will not engraft
them more deeply. We all of us depend upon the Gods
of heaven, and, *his* Temple silent, nothing do we effect but
by the will of the God. Nor does the Divinity stand in
need of any voice ; and, once for all, *our* author has told *us*
at our birth[1] whatever we may be allowed to know : nor
has he chosen barren sands that he may prophesy to a few,
and in this dust concealed the truth. The abode of God,
too, is, wherever *is* earth, and sea, and air, and sky, and
virtue. Why further do we seek the Gods of heaven?
Whatever thou dost behold and whatever thou dost
touch, that is Jupiter. Let the apprehensive need di-
viners, and those that are ever doubtful on future events ;
it is not oracles, but a certain death that makes me certain.
Both the coward and the brave must fall ; this is enough for
Jove to have pronounced."

Thus does he speak ; and, the credit of the Temple preserved, he departs from the altars, leaving Ammon untried
· by the people.

He himself, in his hand wielding a javelin, on foot, goes
before the faces of the panting soldiers. He shows them
how to endure labours, he does not command ; and, with
face uplifted[2] on no necks is he borne, or sitting in a
chariot. Most sparing is he himself of sleep, the last
drinker of the water. When, at last, a spring discovered,
the youthful band longing for the stream endeavour to
drink, he stands until the camp follower[3] has drunk. If

---

[1] *Told us at our birth*) ver. 575. "That all must die." Some, however,
seem to think that he alludes to conscience, or the perception of right and
wrong.

[2] *With face uplifted*) ver. 589. He does not travel in a " lectica," or
litter, carried upon men's shoulders.

[3] *Until the camp follower*) ver. 593. The " lixæ " had much the same
duties in the Roman campaigns as the " calones," with this difference—that
the " calones " were generally slaves, while the " lixæ " were freemen. They
followed the camp for the purposes of gain and merchandize ; and it is not

by real merits great fame is acquired, and if, success disregarded, unadorned virtue is looked at, whatever in any one of our forefathers we praise was *merely* Fortune.

Who by prosperous warfare, who by the blood of nations, has deserved a name so great? This triumph I would rather conduct through the Syrtes and the extremities of Libya than thrice with the chariot of Pompey ascend the Capitol, than break the neck of Jugurtha[1]. Behold a true parent of his country, most worthy, Rome, of thy altars; by whom it will never shame *thee* to swear; and whom, if ever thou shalt stand with neck released, then at last *thou art* destined to make a God.

Now *was* the heat more intense, and a region, beyond which none[2] in the southern climes have the Gods created, was traversed, and the water *was* more scarce. *There was* found in the middle of the sands a single spring abounding in water, but which a multitude of serpents possessed, the spot hardly containing *them.* Parched asps[3] were standing at the brink, in the midst of the waves the Dipsas[4] thirsted. The chieftain, when he saw them likely to perish, the spring left behind, addressed *them:* "Alarmed with the false show of death, fear not, soldiers, in safety to quaff the stream. Noxious is the poison of serpents when mixed with the blood; they have venom in their sting, and they threaten destruction with their teeth; the draughts are devoid of deadliness."

improbable that they originally received their name from the fact of their supplying ready-cooked provisions, "elixos cibos," to the Roman armies.

[1] *Break the neck of Jugurtha*) ver. 600. He probably alludes to the belief that, immediately after the triumph of Marius over him, Jugurtha was thrown into prison and there strangled. Other accounts say that he was starved to death.

[2] *Beyond which none*) ver. 605. Rowe remarks upon this passage, "The hyperbole is very strong here; and one would think Cato had penetrated into the very depth and middle of Africa, whereas, in all appearance, his march could never be very far from the Mediterranean."

[3] *Parched asps*) ver. 610. Galen mentions three destructive kinds of asps, the Chersæan, the Ptyades, and the Chelidonian, which frequented the banks of rivers, and especially of the Nile. Those bitten by them were said to die in a state of torpor. Cleopatra put an end to her life by the bite of an asp, which she caused to be introduced to her in a basket of fruit.

[4] *The Dipsas*) ver. 610. The Dipsas was said to be so called from the Greek verb διψάω, "to be thirsty," as it was said that those bitten by it died of thirst.

He spoke, and quaffed the supposed poison; and throughout the whole sands of Libya that was the only stream of
which he was the first to demand the water for himself.

Why the Libyan climate, fruitful in deadliness, should
abound in plagues so great, or what nature has secretly
mixed in the noxious soil, our care and labour are not able
to ascertain; except that a story, spread throughout *all* the
world, has deceived ages, in place of the real cause. In
the extreme parts of Libya, where the glowing earth receives the ocean warmed by the setting sun, far and wide
lay parched the fields of Medusa, the daughter of Phorcys[1];
not overshadowed by the foliage of the groves, not softened
by ridges, but rugged with rocks[2] looked upon by the countenance of its mistress. In this body first did noxious
nature produce deadly plagues; from those jaws snakes
poured forth whizzing hisses with vibrating tongues, which,
after the manner of a woman's hair flowing along the back,
flapped about the very neck of the delighted Medusa.
Upon her forehead turned towards you erect did serpents
rise, and viper's venom flowed from her combed locks.

This *alone* does unhappy Medusa possess, which with impunity[3] it is permitted all to look upon; for who has dreaded
the mouth and the head of the monster? Whom, that with
glance direct[4] has seen her, has Medusa suffered to die?
She arrested doubting destiny, and prevented fear; the life

---

[1] *Daughter of Phorcys*) ver. 626. Medusa, and her two Gorgon sisters,
Stheno and Euryale, were said to be the daughters of Phorcys and Ceto,
and were represented by Hesiod as living in the Western Ocean, in the
neighbourhood of Night and the Hesperides. Later traditions, which the
Poet here follows, place them in Libya. See the subject of the Gorgons
considered at length in the Translation of the Metamorphoses of Ovid, in
Bohn's Classical Library, pp. 149-50.

[2] *Rugged with rocks*) ver. 628. The sight of Medusa was said to turn
everything into stone.

[3] *Which with impunity*) ver. 635-9. The meaning of this passage is
somewhat obscure, but it seems to be this: "the serpents on Medusa's head
are the only part that can be looked on with impunity, for what person is
there that ever beheld her head, face to face, and survived to express his
alarm? having been instantly changed into stone."

[4] *With glance direct*) ver. 638. He uses the expression, "qui recto se
lumine vidit," probably in allusion to the story that it was possible to behold
the reflection of her in a mirror, with impunity, which was the method used
by Perseus when he slew her.

retained, the limbs died, and spirits not sent forth grew rigid beneath the bones. The locks of the Eumenides produced madness alone; Cerberus moderated his hissing at the song of Orpheus; the son of Amphitryon[1] beheld the Hydra when he had conquered it. This monster did Phorcus dread, her father, and the second Deity in the waves, her mother Ceto, also, and her Gorgon sisters themselves. This was able to threaten to the heavens and to the sea an unwonted numbness, and from the universe to withdraw the world.

From the skies the birds fell with sudden weight; in rocks wild beasts stood fast; whole nations of Æthiopians, inhabiting the vicinity, grew hard in marble. No animal *was there that* could brook the sight; and the serpents themselves, streaming in a backward direction, shunned *her* countenance. She turned Atlas[2] the Titan into rock, as he stood beneath the Hesperian pillars; and, formerly, the heavens dreading the Giants standing on Phlegræan serpents[3] *for feet*, the Gorgon raised mountains aloft, and in the midst of the breast of Pallas ended the mighty warfare of the Gods. Hither, after the Parrhasian wings[4] of the Arcadian inventor of the lyre and of the oily palæstra[5] had carried Perseus born of the womb of Danaë[6] and the enriched shower, and the winged steed,

---

[1] *Son of Amphitryon*) ver. 644. He calls Hercules " Amphitryoniades," from Amphitryon, his putative father, the husband of his mother Alcmena.

[2] *She turned Atlas*) ver. 655. He alludes to the transformation of Atlas, the son of Iapetus the Titan, into a mountain, in the vicinity of the columns of Hercules (now Gibraltar). This was effected by Perseus, who showed to him the head of the Gorgon Medusa. See the Metamorphoses of Ovid, B. iv. l. 656.

[3] *Standing on serpents*) ver. 656. " Stantes serpente." This is an Hypallage for " pedibus angues habentes," having serpents for their feet. He alludes to the war of the Giants with the Gods on the Phlegræan plains.

[4] *The Parrhasian wings*) ver. 660. The " Parrhasiæ pennæ" of Perseus were the " talaria," or winged shoes, said to have been given him by Mercury, who was born on Mount Cyllene in Arcadia, of which Parrhasia was one of the most famous towns.

[5] *The oily palæstra*) ver. 661. By the use of the word " liquidæ," he refers to the " ceroma," or " wrestler's oil," which was used by those engaged in athletic exercises.

[6] *Born of the womb of Danaë*) ver. 659. Perseus was the son of Jupiter and Danaë, the daughter of Acrisius, king of Argos, whom Jupiter debauched, by means of descending into her prison in a shower of gold.

that suddenly sprung up, had borne aloft the Cyllenian
falchion[1], the falchion reddened already by the slaughter
of another monster (the watcher of the heifer beloved by
Jove, *by it* destroyed), unwedded Pallas gave aid to her swift
brother[2], having stipulated for[3] the head of the monster;
and she bade Perseus turn towards the rising of Phœbus
on the margin of the Libyan land, cleaving the realms of
Gorgon in *his* flight with averted face; she gave him, too,
a shield for his left hand, shining with yellow gold, in
which she bade[4] him look at the stone-transforming Medusa, whom sleep, destined to bring on eternal slumber in
death, did not entirely overpower.

A great part of her locks are awake, and the snakes, extending along the hair, protect her head; on the midst of
her features some lie, and upon the lid of her eye[5].
Pallas herself guides him palpitating, and in his shaking
right hand directs the Cyllenian falchion of the averted
Perseus, cutting asunder the broad extremities of the ser-
pent-bearing neck. What a countenance had the Gorgon,
the head cut off by the wound of the hooked sword! With
how much poison I could conceive her mouth breathing
forth! What death, too, her eyes shooting forth! Not
even Pallas was able to look upon her; and they would
have congealed the features of the averted Perseus, if
Tritonia had not spread her dense hair, and covered her
face with the serpents.

[1] *The Cyllenian falchion*) ver. 663. The "harpe," or "falchion," of
Perseus had been given him by Mercury. With it he slew Argus, the
hundred-eyed guardian set by Juno to watch Io when transformed into a
cow. See the Metamorphoses of Ovid, B. i. l. 611, *et seq.*

[2] *To her swift brother*) ver. 665. They being both of them the children of Jupiter.

[3] *Having stipulated for*) ver. 666. On condition that she should have
the head to place in her Ægis.

[4] *In which she bade*) ver. 670. In order to slay her, he beheld the reflection of her head in the bright shield which Pallas had given him, and
instructed him how to use.

[5] *Upon the lid of her eye*) ver. 674. "Oculique tenebras." This expression probably means the eyelid of her one eye. Some of the Commentators think that it means the eye itself "closed in sleep," while Weise suggests that it may mean the other eye devoid of sight; or, more properly, its
socket: but it is more generally represented that the Gorgons had their
single eye in the middle of the head.

Thus, the Gorgon spoiled, the winged *hero* flew towards heaven. He, indeed, was shortening his path, and by a nearer course was cleaving the air; if he should cut through the midst of the cities of Europe, Pallas enjoined him not to hurt the fruitful lands, and to spare the nations. For who, an object so great flying aloft, would not look up at the sky?

Towards the west he, winged, turns, and over Libya he goes, which, sowed by no agriculture, is exposed to the stars and to Phœbus; the course of the sun oppresses *it* and parches up the soil; nor in any part of the earth does a shadow fall from a loftier height upon the heavens, and impede the course of the moon, if at any time forgetful of her oblique route she runs straight onward through the signs *of the Zodiac*, and escapes not the shade *by swerving* to the north or to the south. Still, that sterile land, and the fields prolific in nothing good, conceive the venom from the gore of the bleeding Medusa, and dreadful moisture from the fell blood, which the heat promotes and anneals in the loose sand.

Here, the gore which first from the sand lifted a head raised the drowsy asp with puffed-out neck[1]. More thick did the blood and the drops of the clogged venom fall on this; in no serpent is it more dense. Itself wanting heat, it passes not to a cold clime of its own will, and near the Nile it inhabits the sands. But what shame shall we have in profit? Thence are brought hither the deadly plagues of Libya, and the asp we have made an object of traffic[2]. But the huge Hæmorrhois[3] unfolds its scaly wreaths, that will not allow their blood to remain in the wretched *sufferers;* the Chersydros, too, *is* produced to haunt the plains of the doubtful Syrtis, and the Chelydri, trailing along with

[1] *Puffed-out neck*) ver. 701. The head of the asp is depressed, and the neck puffed out on each side.

[2] *Made an object of traffic*) ver. 707. He laments that asps are imported into Italy as a commodity of merchandize; probably this was for the purposes of secret poisoning.

[3] *The huge Hæmorrhois*) ver. 709. Nicander, in his Theriaca, informs us that those bitten by the Hæmorrhois died with the blood flowing from the nose and ears, whence its name.

smoking track[1]; the Cenchris, also[2], ever to move in a straight path; this is painted with more marks on its speckled belly than the Theban Ophites[3], tinted with little spots. The Ammodytes[4], of the same colour with the parched sands, and not to be distinguished *therefrom*, and the Cerastæ, moving with twisting back-bone[5]; the Scytale, too, alone, even now, the hoar-frost lying scattered *on the ground*, about to cast its slough; and the scorching Dipsas; the dangerous Amphisbæna[6], also, that moves on at both of its heads; the water-serpent, also, the tainter of the water; and the swift Jaculi, and the Pareas[7], content with its tail to cleave its track; the greedy Prester[8], too, distending its foaming jaws; and the deadly Seps[9], dissolving the body together with the bones.

The Basilisk[10], too, sending forth hisses that terrify all the plagues, hurtful before its venom, removes from itself far and wide all the race, and rules upon the deserted

[1] *Along with smoking track*) ver. 711. Nicander informs us that the Chelydri live altogether in the water; in such case "fumante" will apply to the foam which they raise in their course. Some interpreters, who have not attended to this fact, have considered it to mean "strong-smelling," while others have thought it signifies "raising a dust."

[2] *The Cenchris, also*) ver. 712. Nicander calls this serpent Cenchrena.

[3] *The Theban Ophites*) ver. 714. One of the Scholiasts explains this epithet by stating that at Thebes in Egypt there was found a kind of spotted marble, which was called Ophites.

[4] *The Ammodytes*) ver. 716. So called from ἄμμος, "sand," and δῦμι, "to go."

[5] *With twisting back-bone*) ver. 716. One of the Scholiasts relates the story that when Helen was eloping with Paris, she trod on the back of a Cerastes, and broke it, from which time the whole race moved with a crooked course.

[6] *The dangerous Amphisbæna*) ver. 719. It was a superstition that the Amphisbæna had two heads, and could move either way, being so called from ἀμφίς, "both ways," and βαίνω, "to go."

[7] *And the Pareas*) ver. 721. Those darting from trees on the passers by were called "jaculi," from "jaculum," a javelin. See l. 822. They are also mentioned by Pliny and Solinus. The Pareas was said to have feet near its tail.

[8] *The greedy Prester*) ver. 722. See l. 791.

[9] *The deadly Seps*) ver. 723. Said to be so called from σηπομαι, "to putrefy." See l. 776.

[10] *The Basilisk*) ver. 726. The Basiliscus, or kingly serpent, was said to have a white spot on the head resembling a diadem.

sands. You also, the Dragons [1], shining with golden brightness, who crawl in all *other* lands *as* innoxious Divinities, scorching Africa renders deadly. With wings you move the air on high, and, following whole herds, you burst asunder vast bulls, embracing them with your folds. Nor is the elephant safe through his size ; everything you devote to death, and no need have you of venom for a deadly fate.

Amid these pests, Cato, with his hardy soldiers, moved on upon his scorching march, seeing the sad fates of so many of his men and extraordinary deaths through a little wound. A Dipsas trodden on, turning back its head, bit Aulus, a young standard-bearer of Etrurian blood. Hardly was there pain or *any* feeling of the sting, and his face itself was free from the anguish of death, nor did the wound threaten anything. Behold! the venom creeps silently on, and a devouring flame consumes his marrow, and burns his entrails with the heating poison. The virus sucks up the moisture flowing around the vitals, and begins to scorch the tongue with the dried palate ; no perspiration is there to run down his wearied limbs, and the fountain of tears flies from his eyes. Not the ensign of the state [2], not the orders of the sorrowing Cato, restrained the parched man from daring to hurl down the standard, and, infuriate, seeking over all the fields the water which the venom, thirsting in his heart, demanded.

He, sent even to Tanais and Rhone and Padus, would be parched, and *even if* drinking of Nile as it wanders through the fields. Libya promoted his death [3], and the Dipsas has a fame unequal to its deadliness, when aided by the scorching regions. Deep down he seeks for rain in the glowing sands; now to the Syrtes he returns, and takes sea-water

[1] *You also, the Dragons*) ver. 727-8. The serpent called the Dragon was worshipped by the nations of the East, and even by the people of Greece and Rome. Æsculapius was worshipped at Rome in the form of a serpent. The dragons, from their alleged harmlessness, were called ἀγαθοὶ δαίμονες, or Good Genii. Solinus tells us that the mouth of the dragon was so small that it was impossible for it to bite.

[2] *Not the ensign of the state*) ver. 747. The eagle or standard that he was carrying.

[3] *Libya promoted his death*) ver. 753. The climate of Libya added to the fatality of the venom of the Dipsas.

in his mouth, and the moisture of the deep is grateful, but suffices not for him. Nor is he sensible of the nature of the death and the fatality of the venom, but he thinks that it is thirst *alone*, and brooks to open the swelling veins, and to fill his mouth with blood. Instantly does Cato order the standard to be taken up; to no one is it allowed to learn that thirst can have this effect.

But a more sad death than that was before their eyes; and upon the thigh of the wretched Sabellius there stood a little Seps, which, hanging with its barbed tooth, he both tore off with his hand, and pinned with his javelin to the sand; a little serpent only, but than which not one is so sure a source of a bloody death. For the skin nearest the wound, torn off, disappears, and discloses the pallid bones. And now with open surface, without a body *left*, the wound is bare; the limbs swim in corrupt matter; the calves fall off; without any covering are the hams; of the thighs, too, every muscle is dissolved, and the groin distils black matter. The membrane that binds the stomach snaps asunder, and the bowels flow away; nor does just so much of the entire body as may be expected flow upon the earth, but the raging venom melts the limbs; soon does the poison convert all the ligaments of the nerves, and the textures of the sides, and the hollow breast, and what is concealed in the vital lungs, everything that composes man, into a diminutive corrupt mass. By a foul death does nature lie exposed; the shoulders and strong arms melt; the neck and head flow away.

Not more quickly does the snow fall away, dissolved by the warm south wind, nor is wax influenced by the sun. Trifling things I mention, how that the body flowed away scorched up by corruption; this flame can *do* as well. But what pile has *ever* dissolved the bones? These, too, disappear, and, following the crumbling marrow, suffer no vestiges of their rapid destruction to remain. Among the Cinyphian plagues[1] thine is the palm in destroying; all take away the life, thou alone the carcase.

---

[1] *The Cinyphian plagues*) ver. 787. The Cinyps, or Cinyphus, was a small river on the northern coast of Africa, between the Syrtes, forming the eastern boundary of the African Tripolis. The district around it was called by the same name.

Behold! a form occurs quite different from *this* wasting death. A scorching Prester stung Nasidius, a cultivator of the Marsian fields. A fiery redness lighted up his face, and, his shape destroyed, a swelling, confounding all *features*, now larger than the whole body, stretched out his skin; and, exceeding the human growth, the corrupt matter puffed up throughout all the limbs; the poison prevailing far and wide, he himself lay concealed, completely hidden within his swollen body: nor did the coat of mail withhold the increase of the distended body. Not thus does the foaming mass of water boil over on the cauldron being heated, nor do the sails under the effects of Corus swell out into a bellying form so vast. Now he wielded not his limbs a deformed bloated mass, and a trunk in a confused heap. Not daring to commit *it* to the tomb, they fled from the increasing carcase, untouched, *and* destined to afford a feast to the beaks of the birds and to the wild beasts, not with impunity, the swelling not even ceasing *after death*.

But sights more monstrous do the Libyan pests provide. A fierce Hæmorrhois thrust its fangs into Tullus, a noble youth, and an admirer of Cato. And just as the pressure[1] of the Corycian saffron[2] is wont to discharge itself from all the statues *of the Theatre*, in such manner do all the members at the same moment send forth a red virus instead of blood. His tears are blood; whatever outlets the moisture finds, from them the gore distils in streams; his mouth is running over, the distended nostrils too; his sweat is red; all his members flow from the gorged veins; his whole body is as though *one* wound.

[1] *Just as the pressure*) ver. 808-10. There has been much discussion on the meaning of this passage; but though probably the reading is in some measure corrupt, there is little doubt that it alludes to the custom of discharging saffron-water over the Theatres with pipes, which the Greeks called κρόκου ῥαγισμός. Sometimes the saffron was even mixed with wine for this purpose. The Poet uses the term "pressura," in allusion to the force that was used to discharge it through pipes of very minute bore, so that it fell upon the spectators in the form of the finest dust. If "signis" is a correct reading, it would imply that these "nimbi," or showers of saffron-water, were made to start forth from orifices in the statues with which the Theatres were decorated.

[2] *The Corycian saffron*) ver. 809. The finest saffron grew on Mount Corycus in Cilicia. One of the Scholiasts says that a giant was buried beneath this mountain, and his blood, squeezed out, distilled in the form of saffron.

But thy heart, wretched Levus, has the gore, congealed by the serpent of the Nile, benumbed; and, attesting the sting by no pain, in sudden darkness thou dost receive thy death, and in sleep descend to the Stygian shades. Not with a fate so swift[1] do the slips of the yew, which, resembling the shoots of the Sabine tree, when ripe, the death-gathering Sabæans cut from the deadly trunk, corrupt the draughts.

Behold! afar, around the trunk of a barren oak a fierce serpent (Africa calls it the Jaculus) wreathes itself, and *then* darts forth; and through the head and pierced temples of Paulus it takes its flight; nothing does venom there effect, death seizes him through the wound. It was *then* understood how slowly fly *the stones* which the sling hurls, how sluggishly whizzes the air of the Scythian arrow.

What avails a Basilisk being pierced by the spear of the wretched Murrus? Swift flies the poison along the weapon, and fastens upon the hand; which, instantly, with sword unsheathed, he smites, and at the same moment severs it entirely from the arm; and, looking upon the dreadful warning of a death his own, he stands in safety, his hand perishing. And who could suppose that the Scorpion has the power to cause a rapid death? He, threatening with knotted tail[2], and furious with stroke direct, heaven being the witness, bore off the honors of Orion's death[3]. Who, Solpuga[4], would be afraid to tread upon thy abodes? And yet to thee do the Stygian sisters give power over[5] their threads.

---

[1] *Not with a fate so swift*) ver. 819-21. Probably the whole of this passage is corrupt. If, however, we read " taxica " instead of " toxica," it may possibly mean that the people of Saba in Arabia extracted a poison hardly so fatal from the yew, that resembled the " brathy," " savin-tree," or " tree of the Sabines." However, the words " virgas mentita Sabæas Toxica fatilegi " are more generally rejected as spurious.

[2] *With knotted tail*) ver. 835. " Nodis," " with the joints of his tail." " Recto verbere," " the stroke of his tail raised upright."

[3] *Honors of Orion's death*) ver. 836. According to some accounts, Orion, who was of gigantic size, was, for his arrogance and for his attempt on the chastity of Diana, stung to death by a scorpion, which for its services was made a Constellation.

[4] *Who, Solpuga*) ver. 837. The " solipuga," or " solpuga," was a kind of venomous ant.

[5] *Give power over*) ver. 838. " The Fates sometimes permit you to cut short the threads of human life by the virulence of your sting."

Thus does neither bright day nor dark night bring rest:
it is matter for suspicion for them in their wretchedness
upon what ground they are lying. For neither do leaves,
heaped up, form their beds, nor are their couches made
larger with reeds; but, exposing their bodies to death, they
roll upon the ground, and by the warm vapour attract the
pests, chilled by the rigor of the night; and among their
limbs they warm the jaws for a time innocuous from the
poison having grown torpid.

Nor, the heavens their guide, do they know what is the
length of their wanderings, or what the limit. Full oft
complaining, they cry aloud: " Restore, ye Gods, to us distressed, the warfare from which we have fled; restore *us*
Thessaly. Why do we suffer a coward's death, a band
sworn to the sword? The Dipsas fights for Cæsar, and
the Cerastes wages the civil war. It would please me to
go where the *torrid* zone *is* red, and the sky scorched by
the steeds of the sun; it would delight me to ascribe to
causes of climate that I perish, and to die by reason of the
temperature. Not at all, Africa, of thee, nor, nature, of
thee do I complain; thou hadst devoted to the serpents a
region bearing monsters so numerous, *and* removed from
nations; and, a soil unable to produce corn, cultivators being
denied, thou hast condemned, and hast willed that men
should be afar from *their* venom. To the regions of the
serpents have we come; demand retribution, thou, whoever
thou art, of the Gods above, who, vexed at our trespass,
bounding the region by the burning districts on the one
side, by the dubious Syrtes on the other, hast placed destruction in the middle space. Through the secret spots
of thy retreat does the warfare proceed; and, with thee
sharing the knowledge of the secrets of the earth, the soldier
repairs to the confines of the world.

" Perhaps greater *misfortunes* remain for us, having made
the entrance. The fires meet in the hissing waves[1], and
the fabric of the sky is convulsed. But, in that direction[2],

---

[1] *In the hissing waves*) ver. 866. It was the opinion of some of the
ancients, following the doctrines of Posidonius the philosopher, that the sun
when setting plunged into the ocean, emitting the same hissing noise as red-
hot iron, when thrown into water.

[2] *In that direction*) ver. 867. " Isthinc " seems a preferable reading here
to " ista."

there lies no land further than *lie* the sad realms of Juba, known to us by fame. Perhaps we shall *then* be longing for these regions of the serpents; the heavens, too, are productive of some comfort; still, something does live. I seek not the fields of my native land, and Europe, beholding other suns, and Asia; under what part of the sky, in what region, Africa, did I leave thee? At Cyrene, even still was the winter freezing. In *so* small a distance do we change the course of the year? We are proceeding towards the opposite pole; our world we leave behind; our backs we present to be smitten by the southern blasts[1]. Now, perhaps, is Rome herself beneath our feet[2]. This solace in death do we ask; let the enemy come, and let Cæsar follow whither we fly."

Thus does enduring patience disburden itself of its complaints; the extreme valour of their leader compels them to endure hardships so great, who lies extended on the bare sand, and at every hour challenges Fortune. In all vicissitudes he alone is at hand; and, wherever he is called, thither he flies, and a great boon, and one larger than health, does he confer—strength to undergo death; and they are ashamed, he the witness, to die uttering groans. What power over him could any misery have? Sorrows in the breast of another does he subdue, and, a looker on, he shows that mighty pains are powerless.

Hardly did Fortune, wearied with dangers so great, grant them a tardy aid in their wretchedness. A single nation inhabits the land, unhurt by the cruel sting of the serpents, the Marmarian Psylli[3]; their tongues are equal to powerful drugs; their very blood *is* safe, and can admit no venom, even their charms unemployed. The nature of the place has commanded, that, mingled with the serpents, they should be unharmed. It has profited them to have placed

---

[1] *Smitten by the southern blasts*) ver. 877. It being their notion that the south wind blew northward from the Equator, on passing which they would have their backs to it.

[2] *Rome herself beneath our feet*) ver. 877-8. "Perhaps the people at Rome are now our antipodes."

[3] *The Marmarian Psylli*) ver. 893. These were probably a race of people, skilled in the practice of serpent charming. Pliny states that serpents fled even at the smell of them. Being a nation of Marmarica, which Cato had now left, the Poet probably means that some of them had purposely accompanied Cato on his march.

their abodes in the midst of venom. Peace has been made between them and death. So great is their confidence in their blood; when a little babe, *newly born*, falls upon the earth, fearing lest there may be any contamination by foreign intercourse, they test the doubtful offspring by the deadly asp; and as the bird of Jove, when from the heated egg it has brought forth its unfledged young ones, turns them to the rising of the sun; those which can endure the rays, and with direct glance can sustain the light of heaven, are preserved for rearing; those which flinch from Phœbus, it leaves exposed; so does the Psyllian consider it a pledge of its origin, if any infant does not shudder at the snakes when touched, if any one plays with the presented serpents.

Nor is that race only contented with its own safety; the Psyllian is on the watch for strangers, and assists people against the hurtful monsters. And these, then following the Roman standards, as soon as the general ordered the tents to be pitched, in the first place, purged the sands which the compass of the trenches enclosed, with charms and words that put the snakes to flight. A fire made with drugs surrounds the extremity of the camp. Here does wall-wort crackle, and foreign galbanum[1] steam, and tamarisk[2] rejoicing in no foliage, and eastern costus, and pungent all-heal, and Thessalian centaury[3]; and sulphur-wort resounds in the flames, and the thapsus of Eryx[4]. Larch-trees, too, they burn, and southern-wood, with its smoke stifling to serpents, and the horns of stags bred afar.

Thus *is* the night made safe for the men. But if any one in the day receives the fatal sting from the pest

[1] *Foreign galbanum*) ver. 916. Coming from Mount Amanus in Syria The smell of it burnt, when pure, was said to drive away serpents.

[2] *And tamarisk*) ver. 917. The tamarisk was a tree that grew to a small height. One of the Scholiasts says that it was much used for planting over the graves of the poor.

[3] *Thessalian centaury*) ver. 918. The virtues of the herb centaury were discovered by the Centaur Chiron, from whom it was said to have taken its name. His abode was in Thessaly.

[4] *Thapsus of Eryx*) ver. 919. Thapsos, or Thapsia, was the name of a shrub resembling the "ferula." It was said to have been so called from Thapsus in Sicily, where it grew, and of which island Eryx was a Promontory.

then are the miracles of the magic nation *seen*, and the mighty struggle of the Psylli and of the imbibed venom. For, in the first place, he marks the limbs by the contact of spittle, which restrains the virulence, and retains the poison in the wound. Then, with foaming tongue, he hurries over many a charm in a continuous murmur, nor does the rapid spread of the wound give time for breathing, or death allow him for an instant to be silent. Full oft, indeed, the venom, received into the blackening marrow, charmed forth, takes to flight; but if any poison obeys too tardily, and, summoned forth and commanded, refuses to depart, then, lying down upon the pallid wounds, he licks them, sucking the poison with his mouth, and squeezes the limbs with his teeth, and, holding the deadly matter drawn forth from the cold body, spits it out; and even from the taste of the poison it is quite easy for the Psylli to tell what serpent's bite it is that has taken effect. Relieved, then, at last, by this aid, the Roman youth wandered far and wide in the glowing fields. Phœbe, her flames twice laid aside[1], her light twice recovered, rising and departing, beheld Cato wandering on the sands.

And now for them, more and more did the sands begin to harden, and Libya, growing more compact, to return to glebe. And now afar a few branches of woods *began* to raise themselves; *and* rude cottages of piled-up reeds to appear. How great joy in their wretchedness did it afford them by reason of an improved land, when first they beheld, facing them, the savage lions[2]! Leptis was nearest[3] at hand,

---

[1] *Her flames twice laid aside*) ver. 940. Rowe has the following Note here :—" That is, during the space of two months. The express time of Cato's march is diversely related by Plutarch, Strabo, and Lucan ; the first allowing but seven days for it, the second thirty, and the last, as we see here, two months. This is of no great consequence, since they might fix the beginning of his journey, and reckon his departure from several places."

[2] *Facing them, the savage lions*) ver. 947. Rowe has the following Note here :—" Some of the Commentators upon this verse fancy that it refers to a custom which the natives of this country had to hang up the lions, which they had caught or killed, upon crosses, and they were these crucified lions which Cato's soldiers were so glad to meet with. But I can see no reason for such a far-fetched interpretation ; the meaning seems to me to be that, by meeting with those beasts, who usually prey upon tame cattle, they found that they were come into or near an inhabited country."

[3] *Leptis was nearest*) ver. 948. This was the " Leptis Parva," or

in whose harbour they passed a quiet winter, devoid of clouds and heat.

When Cæsar, satiated with the Emathian slaughter, withdrew, the other weights of care he threw aside, thinking of his son-in-law alone; vainly tracking whose footsteps scattered throughout the dry land, rumour his guide, he resorted to the waves, and coasted along the Thracian straits, and the sea famed for love[1], and the tower of Hero on the tearful shore, where Helle, daughter of Nephele[2], took away its name from the deep.

Not anywhere do the waves of a more limited tract of water divide Asia from Europe, although Pontus, by a narrow channel, divides Byzantium[3] and Chalcedon[4], that produces the purple, and Propontis, carrying along the Euxine, rushes from a small mouth. An admirer, too, of glory, he seeks the Sigæan sands, and the waters of Simois, and Rhœteum, ennobled[5] with the Grecian tomb, and the ghosts that owe[6] so much to the Poets. He goes around the name of burnt Troy, and seeks for the vast traces of the Phœbean wall. Now have barren woods and crumbling trunks of oak overwhelmed the abodes of Assaracus, and they take hold upon the Temples of the Gods with roots now wearied; and the whole of Pergamus is covered with brambles; even the ruins are gone.

"Minor," the "Lesser Leptis," a Phœnician estuary on the coast of Byzacium in Africa, between Adrumetum and Thapsus; it was an important place under both the Carthaginians and the Romans.

[1] *The sea famed for love*) ver. 954. The Hellespont, famed for the loves of Hero and Leander, and the tower from which she gave the signal with her torch when he was swimming across.

[2] *Daughter of Nephele*) ver. 955. Helle, the daughter of Nephele, who was carried across the Hellespont by the Golden Ram, where, falling off, she was drowned, and gave it the new name of Hellespont.

[3] *Divides Byzantium*) ver. 958. Byzantium, on the site of the present Constantinople, was situate on the Thracian Bosporus. It was subject successively to the Athenians, Lacedæmonians, Macedonians, and Romans.

[4] *And Chalcedon*) ver. 959. Chalcedon was in Bithynia, nearly opposite to Byzantium. It was fortified by the Romans, who made it the chief city of Bithynia.

[5] *And Rhœteum, ennobled*) ver. 262. Ajax Telamon, one of the bravest of the Grecian chiefs at Troy, was buried on the Promontory of Rhœteum.

[6] *And the ghosts that owe*) ver. 963. The shades of many of the dead there buried, who owe their praises to Homer and other Poets, such as Priam, Achilles, Hector, and Ajax Telamon.

He beholds the rocks of Hesione[1], and the concealed groves, the nuptial retreat of Anchises[2]; in what cave[3] the umpire took his seat; from what spot[4] the boy was carried to the heavens; upon what mountain height the Naiad Œnone disported[5]; no rock is there without a name[6]. Unknowingly he passed over a rivulet creeping along the dry sand, which *once* was Xanthus. Unthinkingly he was placing his step in the thick grass, a Phrygian native forbade him to tread upon the ghost of Hector. Torn asunder lay the stones, and showing no appearance of aught that was sacred. "Dost thou not behold," said the guide, "the Hercæan altars?"[7]

O sacred and mighty labours of the Poets, all things do ye rescue from fate, and immortality do ye bestow on mortal men! Cæsar, be not touched with envy at their hallowed fame; for if it is allowable to promise aught to the Latian Muses, so long as the honors of the Smyrnæan Poet shall last, those to come will read both me and thee[8]; my

---

[1] *The rocks of Hesione*) ver. 970. On which she was exposed to a sea-monster, when she was rescued by Hercules.

[2] *Nuptial retreat of Anchises*) ver. 971. The woods of Ida, where Anchises was courted by Venus.

[3] *In what cave*) ver. 971. Where Paris gave his decision, which of the three Goddesses was entitled to the Golden Apple.

[4] *From what spot*) ver. 972. Ganymede, the son of Tros, who was carried away by the eagle of Jupiter, to become cupbearer to the Deities, in place of Hebe.

[5] *Œnone disported*) ver. 972. The Naiad, or wood-nymph, Œnone, the mistress of Paris. See her Epistle to Paris in the Heroides of Ovid.

[6] *Without a name*) ver. 973. This idea is probably derived from the words of Ovid in the Epistle of Œnone to Paris, l. 21-6:—" The beech-trees cut by thee, still preserve my name; and marked by thy pruning-knife, I, Œnone, am read of as thine; and as the trunks increase, so does my name grow on; grow on then, and rise upward in my praise. There is a poplar (I remember it), planted on the banks of the river, on which there is an inscription carved, a memorial of ourselves. Flourish, thou poplar, I pray, which, planted on the margin of the banks, hast these lines inscribed on thy rough bark; ' When Paris shall be able to exist, his Œnone deserted, the waters of Xanthus, turning back, shall flow towards their source.'"

[7] *Hercæan altars*) ver. 979. The altar of Hercæan Jove was consecrated to him as the keeper of the house and family. He was so named from the Greek word ἑρκος, which signified "an enclosure;" as his altar was placed close to the wall.

[8] *Read me and thee*) ver. 985. "Thy fame, and my lines." It is just

Pharsalia will survive, and by no age shall we be condemned to obscurity.

When venerable antiquity had satisfied the view of the chieftain, he erected momentary altars with piles of turf heaped-up, and poured forth *these* prayers over flames that burned frankincense, to no purpose :—

"Ye Gods who guard[1] *these* ashes, whoever haunt the Phrygian ruins; and *ye* Lares[2] of my Æneas[3], whom now the Lavinian abodes and Alba preserve, and upon whose altars still does the Phrygian fire glow, and Pallas, by no male beheld[4], the memorable pledge *of empire* in the hidden shrine, the most illustrious descendant of the Julian race offers on your altars the pious frankincense, and solemnly invokes you in your former abodes : grant *me* for the future a fortunate career. I will restore the people[5]; in grateful return the Ausonians shall return to the Phrygians their walls, and a Roman Pergamus shall arise."

Thus having said, he seeks the fleet once more, and gives full sail to the prospering Cori; and desirous, the gale speeding him on, to compensate for the delays of Ilium, he is both carried past powerful Asia *Minor*, and leaves Rhodes behind with the foaming main. The seventh night, Zephyrus never allowing the ropes to flag, shows by the Pharian flames the Egyptian shores. But rising day obscures the torch of the night, before he enters the still waters.

There he hears the shores filled with tumult, and confused voices with uncertain murmurs ; and, hesitating to

possible that Lucan may here allude to Cæsar's labours as an historian, namely, his Commentaries.

[1] *Ye Gods who guard*) ver. 990. The " Di Manes," or " shades of the dead."

[2] *And ye Lares*) ver. 992. The household Gods which Æneas rescued from the flames of Troy.

[3] *Of my Æneas*) ver. 991. The Julian family was said to be descended from Æneas, through his son Iulus or Ascanius.

[4] *Pallas, by no male beheld*) ver. 994. The Palladium, or image of Pallas, brought by Æneas from Troy, which was kept by the Vestal virgins, and on which no male was permitted to look.

[5] *I will restore the people*) ver. 998. Ilium, or Troy, had been long rebuilt in part, but the Poet alludes to the privileges which Cæsar granted to it. The inhabitants of Ilium having sided with the party of Sulla, C. Flavius Fimbria, a violent partisan of Marius, took it by stratagem, and wantonly destroyed it.

entrust himself to a doubtful power, he keeps the ships off
from the shore.   But a courtier[1], bearing the dreadful gift
of the monarch, launching forth into the mid sea, carries
the head of Magnus, concealed in a Pharian mantle, and
first with impious words justifies the crime :—

"Subduer of the earth, greatest of the Roman race, and,
what as yet thou dost not know, secure, thy son-in-law
slain; the Pellæan monarch spares thee thy labours by land
and by sea, and bestows on thee what alone has been wanting to the Emathian arms : for thee in thy absence has the
civil war been finished.   Magnus, seeking to repair the
Thessalian ruin, lies prostrate by my sword: with a pledge
so mighty, Cæsar, do we purchase thee; by this blood has
a treaty been concluded with thee.   Accept the realms of
Pharos, obtained with no bloodshed.   Accept the rule of
the streams of Nile, accept whatever thou wouldst give for
the head of Magnus; and deem him a dependant worthy of
thy camp, to whom the Fates have willed that there should
be power so great over thy son-in-law.   And think not this
merit worthless, in that it has been acquired by an easy
slaughter.   He was the friend of his grandsire; to his
banished parent he had restored the sceptre.   Why mention
more?   Thou shalt find a name for an exploit so great;
or at least consult the fame of the world.   If it is a crime,
confess that thou dost owe the more to us, in that thou
thyself dost not commit this crime."

Thus having said, he uncovered the concealed head and
held it up.   The features, now languid in death, had
changed the expression of the well-known face.   Not at the
first sight did Cæsar condemn the gift, and turn his eyes
away; his looks were fixed *upon it* until he recognized it.
And when he saw that there was truth in *the assertion of* the
crime, and thought it safe now to be an affectionate father-
in-law, he poured forth tears that fell not of their own ac-

---

[1] *But a courtier*) ver. 1010.   This was Theodotus, a rhetorician of Samos,
or of Chios, and preceptor to king Ptolemy.   When Cæsar arrived in Egypt,
he hastened to meet him, bearing the head and signet-ring of Pompey.
Cæsar turned from him in disgust, and would have put him to death, had he
not made his escape.   Five years after he was apprehended and executed in
Asia, by order of M. Brutus.   Appian says that he was crucified by order
of Cassius.   "Satelles" may perhaps more strictly mean "an officer of the
body-guard," than a courtier.

cord, and uttered groans from a joyous heart[1], not thinking otherwise to conceal the transparent joyousness of his
mind than by tears; and he cancelled the vast merit of the
tyrant, and chose rather to mourn the severed head of his
son-in-law, than to be under an obligation *for it.*

He, who with features unmoved had trodden upon the
limbs of Senators[2], who with dry eyes had beheld the
Emathian plains, to thee, Magnus, alone. dares not refuse a
sigh.   O most unhappy turn of fate!   Didst thou, Cæsar,
pursue him with accursed warfare who was worthy to be
bewailed by thee?   Do not the ties of the united families
influence thee, nor thy daughter and grandchild[3] bid thee
mourn?   Dost thou suppose that among the people who
love the name of Magnus this can avail thy cause?
Perhaps thou art moved with envy of the tyrant, and art
grieved that others have had this power over the vitals of
the ensnared Magnus, and dost complain that the revenge
of war has been lost, and that thy son-in-law has been
snatched from the power of the haughty victor.   Whatever,
impulse compels thee to weep, far from true affection does
it differ.   With these feelings, forsooth, art thou hunting over
land and sea, that nowhere thy son-in-law, cut off, may
perish?   O how fortunately has this death been rescued from
thy award!   How much criminality has sad Fortune spared
the Roman shame, in that, perfidious man. she did not suffer
thee to have compassion on Magnus when *still* alive!   Still
further, in these words does he presume to dissemble, and he
gains credit for the grief pretended by his countenance :—

"Remove, courtier, from my sight, the melancholy gift of
thy king; worse has your wickedness deserved from Cæsar
than from Pompey.   The sole reward of civil war, to give
safety to the vanquished[4], have I lost.   Were not his sister

hated[1] by the Pharian tyrant, I might have given to the king
in return what he has deserved, and have sent, Cleopatra, thy
head in return for such a present. Why has he wielded[2] secret
arms, and intruded his own weapons into my task? Did we
create a sway for the Pellœan sword in the Thessalian fields?
Was licence sought for in your realms? I would not endure Magnus ruling the Roman destinies together with me;
Ptolemy, am I to put up with thee? In vain have we involved nations in civil war, if in this earth there is any other
power than Cæsar; if any land belongs to two. I would
have turned the Latian prows from your shore; but regard
for my fame forbids it, lest I should seem not to have condemned, but to have dreaded the blood-stained Pharos.

"And do not suppose that you can deceive me, the conqueror. For us as well *was* provided the like hospitality
on your shores. That my own head is not borne in like
fashion, the fortune of Thessaly causes. With greater
danger, in truth, than could be dreaded, did we wield
arms in the conflict; of exile and of the threats of my
son-in-law and of Rome did I stand in dread; Ptolemy
was the punisher of defeat. But I spare his years, and
forgive him the crime. Let the tyrant know that for this
murder nothing more than pardon can be granted. Do you
bury in the tomb the head of a chieftain so mighty; but
not alone that the earth may hide your guilt; give frankincense to the sepulchre, his due, and appease the head, and
collect the ashes scattered on the shore, and give but one
urn to the dispersed shades. Let the ghost be sensible of
the arrival of his father-in-law, and hear his affectionate
voice as he complains.

" Since he preferred everything to me, since his life he
had rather owe to his Pharian dependant, a joyous day has
been snatched away from nations; our reconcilement has
been lost to the world. My prayers have been denied favouring Gods, that, embracing thee, Magnus, my victorious
arms laid aside, I might beg of thee thy former affection
and thy life[3]; and, content with a sufficient reward of my

---

[1] *Were not his sister hated*) ver. 1068. Cleopatra was then engaged in
warfare with her brother.

[2] *Why has he wielded*) ver. 1071. " What business had he to wield arms
in a cause not his own, and to meddle in the civil wars of Rome?"

[3] *And thy life*) ver. 1100. " Vitam;" " willingness still to survive, although conquered by me."

labours, to be thy equal, then, by an enduring peace, I would have caused that, though conquered, thou mightst have been able to forgive the Gods, thou wouldst have caused that Rome *would have been able to forgive* me."

Having thus said, he neither found a sharer in his grief, nor did the multitude believe him *thus* complaining; they suppressed their sighs, and concealed their feelings by joyous features, and dared with delight to behold the blood-stained deed, (O happy freedom!) while Cæsar mourned[1].

---

[1] *While Cæsar mourned*) ver. 1108. Rowe has the following remark here :—" This is a very satirical irony. He means that those standing by durst not show any sign but that of joy, since Cæsar, though outwardly he seemed to grieve, was in his heart pleased with that execrable action. But this is an instance of Lucan's prejudice against Cæsar, a fault of which I am sorry an author, who seems to have been a lover of his country, should be so often guilty."

BOOK THE TENTH.

WHEN Cæsar, following the head of Pompey[1], first reached the shore, and trod upon the direful sands, the fortune of the chieftain and the fate of guilty Egypt struggled, as to whether the realms of Lagus should come under the Roman sway, or whether the Memphitic sword should snatch from the world the head of both conqueror and conquered. Magnus, thy shade prevailed[2], thy ghost rescued thy father-in-law from bloodshed, that after thee the Roman people might not esteem the Nile.

Thence is he borne into the Parætonian city[3], secure in the pledge of a crime so ruthless, following his own

[1] *Following the head of Pompey*) ver. 1. Following Theodotus on shore, who had presented to him the head of Pompey.
[2] *Thy shade prevailed*) ver. 6. Meaning that Cæsar took warning against the treachery of the Egyptians, from the fate of Pompey.
[3] *The Parætonian city*) ver. 9. See B. iii. l. 295, and the Note to the passage.

insignia[1]. But, in the shouts of the mob complaining that the fasces and the Roman authority are encroaching upon their own, he perceives discordant breasts and doubtful feelings, and that Magnus has perished not for him. Then, his looks always concealing his fears[2], without hesitation he goes about the abodes of the Gods of heaven and the Temples of the ancient Divinity[3], that attest the former strength of the Macedonians; and, touched by no beauty of the objects, not by the gold and the rites of the Gods, not by the walls of the city, he eagerly descends into a cavern dug out among the tombs. There, the mad offspring of Pellæan Philip, the fortunate robber, lies interred, snatched away by Fate[4], the avenger of the earth. The members of the man that should have been scattered over the whole globe they placed in a shrine. Fortune spared his shade, and the fortunes of his kingdom lasted until recent times[5].

For, if Liberty had ever taken unto herself the earth, as a laughing-stock he would have been kept, shown as no useful precedent to the world, that countries so numerous could be under a single man. The limits of the Macedonians and the lurking-holes of his own people he forsook, and Athens, subdued by his father, he despised; and driven onward

[1] *Following his own insignia*) ver. 10. Cæsar mentions the same circumstance in the Civil War, B. iii. c. 106 :—" At Alexandria Cæsar was informed of the death of Pompey: and, on his landing there, heard a cry among the soldiers whom the king had left to garrison the town, and saw a crowd gathering towards him, because the fasces were carried before him ; for this the whole multitude thought an infringement of the king's dignity. Though this tumult was appeased, frequent disturbances were raised for several days successively, by crowds of the populace, and a great many of his soldiers were killed in all parts of the city."

[2] *Always concealing his fears*) ver. 14. Frontinus, in his book on Stratagems, remarks, that if Cæsar had shown the slightest alarm on this occasion his destruction would have been certain.

[3] *Of the ancient Divinity*) ver. 16. He alludes to the Temple of Isis built there by the Macedonians under Alexander the Great.

[4] *Snatched away by Fate*) ver. 21. The Poet alludes to the suddenness of Alexander's death, which rescued the earth from his conquering hand.

[5] *Lasted until recent times*) ver. 24. It is not clear whether "regni duravit ad ultima fatum" means that the reign of Alexander still lasted, as it were, in his being worshipped, when entombed, or that the kingdom of Egypt, which he had founded, was lasting at the time of Cæsar, a period of about 280 years.

through the nations of Asia by the impelling fates, amid
human slaughter he rushed on, and thrust his sword
through all nations; unknown streams he stained, the
Euphrates with the blood of the Persians, the Ganges *with
that* of the Indians; a deadly mischief to the earth, and a
thunderbolt that shook all peoples alike, and a star malevolent to nations. Fleets he was preparing to launch on
the ocean in the Outer Sea [1]. No heat withstood him, nor
waves, nor sterile Libya, nor Ammon [2] on the Syrtis. To
the west he would have gone, following the incline of the
world, and he would have compassed the poles, and have
drunk of Nile at its source; his last day met him, and
nature alone was able to put this period to the frantic
King; who, with the *same* greed with which he had taken
the whole earth, bore off with himself the empire, and, no
heir to all his fortune being left, gave the cities to be rent
asunder [3]. But he died, feared in Babylon, his own, and by
the Parthian. O shame! the Eastern nations dreaded the
lances more close at hand, than now they dread the
javelins [4]. Though we reign even beneath Arctus, and
frequent the abodes of Zephyrus and lands behind the
back of scorching Notus, we shall yield in the East to the
lord of the descendants of Arsaces. Parthia, not fortunate
to the Crassi, was a secure province to little Pella.

Now, coming from the Pelusian [5] mouth of the Nile, the
effeminate boy king had appeased the wrath of the unwarlike
multitude; who being the security for peace, Cæsar was
safe in the Pellæan court; when, in a little two-oared boat,

[1] *In the Outer Sea*) ver. 36-7. Burmann seems to think that this passage
means that Alexander the Great was thinking of bringing round his ships to
the Eastern or Indian Ocean by the exterior ocean, or that beyond the Pillars
of Hercules or straits of Gibraltar, and that this interpretation is confirmed
by l. 39.

[2] *Nor Ammon*) ver. 38. The Poet alludes to the visit of Alexander the
Great to the Temple of Jupiter Ammon. He falls into a geographical error
in calling it " Syrticus," as it was at a very great distance from either of the
Syrtes.

[3] *The cities to be rent asunder*) ver. 45. He alludes to the division of the
kingdom and conquests of Alexander among his generals.

[4] *The lances—the javelins*) ver. 47–8. The " sarissa," or " long spear,"
and " pilum," or " javelin," are here mentioned antithetically, as being the
national weapons of the Macedonians and Romans.

[5] *From the Pelusian*) ver. 53. From Mount Casius near Pelusium.

Cleopatra, the guard having been bribed to loosen the chains [1] of Pharos, betook herself, unknown to Cæsar [2], to the Emathian abodes [3]; the disgrace of Egypt, the fatal Erinnys of Latium, unchaste, to the undoing of Rome. As much as did the Spartan *female* by her fatal beauty bring ruin on Argos and the homes of Ilium, so much did Cleopatra increase the frenzy of Hesperia [4].

She, if *so* it is allowable *to say*, alarmed the Capitol by her sistrum, and with unwarlike Canopus attacked the Roman standards [5], about to conduct the Pharian triumph, Cæsar *her* captive [6]; and doubtful was the event on the Leucadian main [7], whether in fact a woman should not hold our sway. This pride did that night create which first united in the couch with our chieftains the unchaste daughter of Ptolemy. Who will not, Antony, grant thee pardon for thy frantic passion, when the hardy breast of Cæsar caught the flame, and in the midst of frenzy and the midst of fury, and in a palace haunted by the shade of Pompey, the paramour, sprinkled with the blood of the Thessalian carnage, admitted Venus amid his cares, and mingled with his arms both illicit connexion and issue not by a wife?

[1] *To loosen the chains*) ver. 57. There is no doubt that Lucan is guilty of an historical error here, for Cæsar, in the Civil War, B. iii. c. 107, and other historians, mention that Cleopatra was at this time at the head of an army, with which she had marched against Alexandria for the purpose of enforcing her rights.

[2] *Unknown to Cæsar*) ver. 58. According to some accounts, Cleopatra introduced herself into the palace at the request of Cæsar; while others state that she clandestinely effected an entrance into the palace where Cæsar was residing, by being packed in a bale of cloth, which was brought by Apollodorus, her attendant, as a present for Cæsar.

[3] *To the Emathian abodes*) ver. 58. The palace founded by Alexander the Great, the king of Emathia or Macedonia. Some Commentators suggest that it means the palace now occupied by Cæsar the recent conqueror in Emathia or Thessaly.

[4] *Increase the frenzy of Hesperia*) ver. 62. The Civil Wars of Rome, first between Cæsar and the adherents of Pompey, and then between Augustus and Antony, the lover of Cleopatra.

[5] *Attacked the Roman standards*) ver. 64. He alludes to the aid which she gave to Antony in his wars against Augustus.

[6] *Cæsar her captive*) ver. 65. Meaning Augustus Cæsar. One of the Scholiasts suggests that there is purposely an ambiguity here, as "captivo" may either mean that she intended to lead Augustus away the captive of warfare or of love.

[7] *On the Leucadian main*) ver. 66. At Actium, near Leucas or Leucadia.

O shame! forgetful of Magnus, to thee, Julia, did he give brothers[1] by an obscene mother; and, suffering the routed faction to unite in the distant realms of Libya, he disgracefully prolonged his stay for an amour of the Nile, while he was preferring to present her with Pharos, while not to conquer[2] for himself. Confiding in her beauty, Cleopatra approaches him, sad without any tears, arrayed for simulated grief, so far as is consistent with beauty, as though tearing her dishevelled hair, and thus she begins to speak :—

" If there is, O most mighty Cæsar, any nobleness, I, the most illustrious offspring of Pharian Lagus, an exile for everlasting, expelled from the sceptre of my father, a queen, embrace thy feet, if thy right hand may restore me to my former destiny. A gracious Constellation to our race thou dost appear. I shall not be the first woman to rule the cities of the Nile; making no distinction of sex, Pharos knows how to endure a queen. Read the last words of my deceased father, who gave me common rights to the sway, and a union with my brother. That boy, if only he were free, loves his sister; but he holds his inclination and his sword under the control of Pothinus. · Nothing of my paternal rights do I myself ask to gain; from a censure and a stain so great do thou free our house; remove the ruthless arms of the courtier, and command the king to rule. What swelling pride does the menial feel in his mind, the head of Magnus struck off! Now (but may the Fates avert that afar!) he *even* threatens thee. Cæsar, disgrace enough has it proved to the world and to thee that Pompey has been the guilt and the merit of Pothinus."

In vain would she have appealed to the obdurate ears of Cæsar, *but* her features aid her entreaties, and her unchaste face pleads *for her*. A night of infamy she passes, the arbitrator being *thus* corrupted. When peace was obtained by the chieftain[3] and purchased with vast presents, feast-

---

[1] *Did he give brothers*) ver. 77. Cleopatra had but one child by Cæsar, who was called Cæsarion, and was afterwards put to death by Augustus.

[2] *While not to conquer*) ver. 81. He devotes his time to reinstating Cleopatra on the Egyptian throne, instead of marching against Cato, Scipio, and Juba, the partisans of Pompey.

[3] *Obtained by the chieftain*) ver. 107. A seeming reconciliation having been made between Cleopatra and Ptolemy through Cæsar's intervention. See the account of this intervention, in the Civil War, B. iii. c. 107–1..

ing crowned the joyousness of events so momentous, and Cleopatra amid great tumult displayed her luxuries, not as yet transferred to the Roman race. The place itself was equal to a Temple, which hardly a more corrupt age [1] could build; and the roofs adorned with fretted ceilings displayed riches, and solid gold concealed the rafters. Nor did the palace shine resplendent, encrusted with marble on the surface and in sections; the agate and the purple stone [2] stood of themselves in no infirm way [3]'; and, laid down throughout the whole palace, onyx was trodden upon. Ebony from Meroë [4] did not cover the massive posts, but it stood as though common oak, the support, *and* not the ornament of the palace.

Ivory covers the halls, and backs of Indian tortoises, fastened by the hand, are placed upon the doors, dotted in their spots with plenteous emeralds. Gems shine upon the couches, and the furniture *is* yellow with jasper; the coverlets glisten [5], of which the greater part, steeped long in the Tyrian dye, have imbibed the drug not in one cauldron only [6]. A part shines, embroidered with gold; a part, fiery with cochineal [7], as is the method of mingling the threads in the Pharian webs. And then, the number of the servant train and the attendant crowd! Some, the blood differing in colour, others, their ages had distinguished; this *part has* Libyan *hair, another* part has hair so light, that Cæsar

---

[1] *A more corrupt age*) ver. 111. One of the Scholiasts suggests that this is aimed at Nero, who was noted for his extravagant passion for building.

[2] *And the purple stone*) ver. 116. Probably "porphyry;" though Weise suggests that carnelian is meant.

[3] *In no infirm way*) ver. 115. "Non segnis;" meaning, "not in layers resting on other stones, but in solid columns for the purpose of supporting the roof."

[4] *Ebony from Meroë*) ver. 117. See B. iv. l. 333, and the Note to the passage. Ebony is the production of Æthiopia and other southern climes. The meaning is, that it was not used for the purposes of veneering, but in a solid state.

[5] *The coverlets glisten*) ver. 123. "Strata" here means the coverlets or tapestry used on the "triclinia" or couches, on which they reclined at meals.

[6] *Not in one cauldron only*) ver. 124. He alludes to the "dibapha" or cloths twice steeped in the Tyrian purple, which were of extreme value.

[7] *Fiery with cochineal*) ver. 125. "Cocco." The "coccum" was thought by the ancients to be a berry; but it is now known to be an insect, which we call cochineal, or kermes, and which is found on the scarlet oak, or Quercus coccifera. The "coccum," or "granum Cnidium," was used in medicine, and was produced from the plant "thymelæa."

declares that in no regions of the Rhine has he seen locks so bright; some *are* of scorched complexion, with curly hair, wearing their locks thrown back from their foreheads. Unhappy youths, as well, rendered effeminate by the iron, and deprived of virility. Opposite stands an age more robust, still with hardly any down[1] darkening the cheeks.

There do kings recline, and Cæsar a *still* higher power; and having immoderately painted up her fatal beauty, neither content with a sceptre her own, nor with her brother her husband[2], covered with the spoils of the Red Sea[3], upon her neck and hair Cleopatra wears treasures, and pants beneath her ornaments. Her white breasts shine through the Sidonian fabric, which, wrought in close texture by the sley of the Seres[4], the needle of the workman of the Nile has separated, and has loosened the warp by stretching out the web. Here do they place circles[5], cut from the snow-white teeth in the forests of Atlas, such as not even when Juba was captured, came before the eyes of Cæsar.

O frenzy, blind and maddened by ambition, to him who is waging a civil war to disclose one's own riches, to inflame the mind of an armed stranger! Although he were not prepared in accursed warfare to seek riches in the downfall of the world; set *there* the ancient chieftains and the names of poorer days, the Fabricii and the grave Curii; here let that humble Consul[6] recline, taken away from the Etrurian

---

[1] *With hardly any down*) ver. 135. This has been supposed to mean that those individuals had purposely plucked out their beards; but Weise takes it to signify that the Africans are naturally beardless.

[2] *With her brother her husband*) ver. 138. She was probably only nominally married to this brother, according to the wish of her father signified in his will: she was also afterwards nominally married to her younger brother, who was also named Ptolemy.

[3] *Spoils of the Red Sea*) ver. 139. He alludes to pearls.

[4] *The sley of the Seres*) ver. 142. He probably alludes to the textures made by the Seres or Chinese, which we call Chinese crapes. The Egyptians had probably the art of making a peculiar kind of open work on them. It is curious to find here the names of the Seres and the Egyptians in juxtaposition. Sir Gardiner Wilkinson states that vases and bottles with Chinese inscriptions have been found in the tombs of ancient Egypt.

[5] *Do they place circles*) ver. 145. He means round tables supported on pillars made of ivory tusks, taken from elephants in the woods of Mauritania near Mount Atlas.

[6] *That humble Consul*) ver. 153. Quintius Cincinnatus, who, while ploughing, was saluted Dictator.

ploughs, he would long to gain for his country a triumph so great.

They poured forth the viands into gold, whatever the earth, whatever the air, whatever the sea and the Nile afforded, whatever luxury, raging with vain ambition, had sought in the whole earth, hunger not demanding it. Both many birds and *many* wild beasts did they set before them, the Gods of Egypt; and crystal supplied the water of the Nile for their hands; and capacious bowls, studded with gems, received the wine, but not of the grape of Mareotis, but noble Falernian [1], to which in a few years Meroë had imparted maturity, compelling it, *otherwise* full of roughness, to ferment. They received chaplets wreathed with the flowering nard [2], and the never-fading rose; and upon their dripping locks they poured forth plenteous cinnamon, that had not yet faded in the air nor lost its scent in a foreign land. The fresh amomum, too, of the adjacent harvests *was* brought. Cæsar learnt how to waste the wealth of the despoiled world, and was ashamed to have waged war with a poor son-in-law, and longed for a cause of strife with the Pharian race.

After pleasure wearied with feasting and with wine had put an end *to the revelry*, Cæsar began with long discourse to prolong the night, and in gentle words addressed the linen-clad Achoreus [3], who reclined at the highest seat :—

"O aged man, devoted to sacred rites, and, what *thy* age proves, not neglected by the Gods, disclose the origin of the Pharian race, and the situation of the country, and the manners of the people, and the rites and the forms of the Gods; and relate whatever is engraved [4] *in characters* in

---

[1] *Noble Falernian*) ver. 163. The Falernian wine, produced on the Massic hills of Italy, was naturally harsh, and was not considered fit for drinking unless it was ten years old; from the present passage it seems to have been thought to be improved by being sent to Meroë, near the borders of Æthiopia, in order to be mellowed by the heat, probably in much the same way that, at the present day, Madeira wine is sent for a voyage to the East or West Indies.

[2] *The flowering nard*) ver. 164. The nard was an odoriferous shrub bearing leaves and a kind of ear called spikenard, from which was extracted a perfume of costly price.

[3] *Linen-clad Achoreus*) ver. 175. As being a priest of Isis or Osiris.

[4] *Whatever is engraved*) ver. 180. He enquires into the meaning of the inscriptions in hieroglyphics.

the shrines of ancient days, and reveal the Gods that are
willing to be known.   If thy forefathers taught Cecropian
Plato · their rites, what stranger was there ever more worthy
to be heard than this one, or more able to scan the world?
Rumour, indeed, about my son-in-law brought me to the
Pharian cities, but still about yourselves as well.   Always in
the midst of battles have I spared time for the courses of
the stars and of the heavens and for the Gods above, nor
shall my year² be surpassed by the Calendar of Eudoxus .
But although aspirations thus great exist beneath my breast,
thus great is my love of truth, there is nothing that I would
rather wish to know than the causes of the stream¹ that
have lain hid through so many centuries, and its unknown
head.   Let me have an assured hope of seeing the sources
of the Nile, I will forego civil war."

He had finished, and on the other hand thus began
the sacred Achoreus :—

"Let it be allowable for me, Cæsar, to disclose the
secrets of my mighty forefathers, hitherto unknown to the
profane multitude.   Let it be piety to others to be silent on
miracles so great; but I deem it pleasing to the inhabitants
of heaven for these works to be disclosed to all, and for the

---

¹ *Taught Cecropian Plato*) ver. 181.   It is generally believed that Plato,
the Athenian philosopher, travelled into Egypt, among other foreign countries,
where he probably acquainted himself with the learning of the Egyptians ;
but no evident traces of this knowledge are to be found in his works.

² *Nor shall my year*) ver. 187.   Cæsar alludes to his own reformation of
the Calendar which he had made when Pontifex Maximus at Rome.   Finding
that the first of January had retrograded nearly to the Autumnal Equinox, in
order to bring that day to its proper place he made the current year to con-
sist of 445 days, by adding two intercalary months of 67 days to the usual
intercalary month Mercedonius.   This year in consequence was styled " the
year of confusion."   Finding also that the year would be too short by a
quarter of a day, he provided for the deficiency, by the insertion, every fourth
year, of an extra day immediately after the 23rd of February, which was to
be esteemed as a duplicate of the 24th of February, or, as the Romans called
it, the sixth of the Calends of March.   It is this double day which gave the
name of Bissextile to the leap year.

³ *The Calendar of Eudoxus*) ver. 187.   Eudoxus of Cnidus studied for
some time under Plato, and afterwards travelled in Egypt, where he remained
for sixteen months.   He is said to have been the first to regulate the year
according to the revolutions of the moon in Greece.   Strabo also attributes to
him the introduction of the odd quarter of a day into the value of the year.

⁴ *Causes of the stream*) ver. 190.   The sources of the river Nile.

sacred laws to be revealed to nations. To the planets, which alone modify the course of the heavens and run counter to the sky, a different power was given by the original laws of the world. The sun divides the seasons of the year, he changes the day for the night, and with his powerful rays forbids the stars[1] to move onward, and modifies their wandering courses in their track. The moon, by her changes, mingles Tethys and the regions of the earth. To Saturn has fallen[2] the cold ice and the snowy zone. The winds and the uncertain thunderbolts has Mars. Under Jove is a moderate temperature, and an atmosphere never rendered dense. But fruitful Venus holds sway over the seeds of all things; the Cyllenian God[3] is the ruler of the boundless waves. When the part of the sky has received him where the stars of the Lion are mingled with the Crab, where Sirius puts forth his glowing fires, and where the Circle, the changer of the varying year[4], possesses Ægoceros and the Crab, placed beneath which the mouths of the Nile lie concealed; when the ruler of the waters has smitten these with his fires hovering above, then does the Nile, its fountains opened, spring forth, just as the ocean, bidden at the increase of the moon, moves on, and it does not check its own increase before the night has recovered the hours of summer from the sun.

"Vain *was* the opinion of the ancients that the snows of the Æthiopians aid the Nile for it to swell upon the fields. No Arctos *is there*[5] in those mountains, or *any*

[1] *Forbids the stars*) ver. 203. Rowe has the following Note here:— "That is, drives them back, and makes them become retrograde, when they come to their nearest distance to the sun. The other offices, which he gives to the rest of the planets, were according to their astronomy at that time."

[2] *To Saturn has fallen*) ver. 205. Saturn was supposed especially to hold influence in the northern climates : whence the extreme Northern Ocean was styled the "Chronian sea." "Zona nivalis" probably means the "Arctic circle."

[3] *The Cyllenian God*) ver. 209. The planet of Mercury, who was said to have been born on Mount Cyllene in Arcadia.

[4] *Circle, the changer of the varying year*) ver. 212. Some suppose this to mean the Zodiac, others the Solstitial Colure ; it is very doubtful which is meant, as the whole of the Poet's astronomical system is involved in the greatest obscurity.

[5] *No Arctos is there*) ver. 220. ●The Poet was not aware that to those who travel southward from the Equator, the cold increases. It was the opinion of Anaxagoras, Euripides, and others of the ancient philosophers, that the Nile took its rise in the snows of Æthiopia.

Boreas. Your witness *is* the colour itself of the scorched people, and the south winds warm with vapours. Besides, every head of a river, which thawed ice hurries onward, on the approach of spring, swells with the first washing away of the snow; *but* the Nile neither raises its waves before the rays of the Dog-star, nor confines its stream to the banks before Phœbus is equalled with the night, under Libra for arbitrator. From this, likewise, it knows not the laws of other streams: nor does it swell in the winter, when, the sun far removed, the wave performs not its duties[1]; ordered to give a moderate temperature to the oppressive weather, in the midst of summer it comes forth. Under the torrid tracts, lest fire should impair the earth, the Nile comes to the aid of the world, and swells in opposition to the inflamed face of the Lion; and, the Crab scorching its own Syene, implored it comes: nor does it liberate the fields from the waves until Phœbus declines in the autumn and Meroë extends the shades. Who can explain the causes? Thus has the parent Nature commanded the Nile to run; thus has the world need *of it*.

"The Zephyrs, also, does antiquity vainly allege *as the cause of* these waters, the times of whose blasts *are* fixed and the days continuous, and of long duration *is* their sway over the air; either because from the western sky they drive so many clouds beyond the south, and compel the showers to hover over the river; or because so often they beat back with constancy the waters of the Nile when bursting forth at the sea-shore[2], and compel the waves to flow back. Through the impeding of its course, and the resistance of the opposing sea[3], it overflows upon the plains.

[1] *Performs not its duties*) ver. 230. Of irrigating and refreshing the earth.

[2] *Bursting forth at the sea-shore*) ver. 244. Where it enters the ocean at its seven mouths.

[3] *Resistance of the opposing sea*) ver. 246. The Libyan Sea, roused by the winds, beats back the waters of the Nile as they flow from the mouths of the river. The opinion which the Poet here mentions attributes the cause of the inundations of the Nile to the western winds in two ways: either by reason of their blowing constantly against the stream for many days together, and keeping it from running into the sea as usual; or else by their conveying a large quantity of rain from other parts of the world towards the sources of the Nile, and so causing it to overflow.

"Some there are who think that there are channels in the earth, and vast inlets in the hollow structure. This way through secret courses does the water glide from the interior, attracted to the mid region *of the earth* from the arctic colds, when Phœbus presses upon Meroë, and the scorched earth thither draws the waters. Both Ganges and Padus are drawn through the secret *regions* of the world. Then is Nile, discharging all the rivers from one source, unable to give them vent at a single mouth.

"*There is* a report that from the Ocean which bounds all lands, overflowing, the impetuous Nile breaks out afar, and that the salt of the sea becomes tasteless from the length of the course.

"Besides, we believe that both Phœbus and the sky are fed by the Ocean ; it, when he has touched the claws of the heated Crab, the sun draws up, and more waters are raised than the air can digest. This do the nights draw back, and discharge again into the Nile.

"But I, Cæsar, if it is permitted me to dispose of a question so great, imagine that certain waters, since the last ages of the completion of the world, burst forth from the ruptured veins of the earth, God not willing it, *and* that certain *waters* at the very creation took their origin with the universe, which *last* the Creator himself and the Maker of things restrains by certain laws.

"The desire that thou hast of knowing the Nile, O Roman, existed both in the Pharians and in the Persians and in the tyrants of the Macedonians; and no age is there that has not wished to bestow the knowledge on posterity; but still does its propensity for concealment prevail. Alexander, the greatest of the kings whom Memphis adores, envied the Nile *its concealment*, and sent chosen persons through the remotest *regions* of the land of the Æthiopians; them the red zone[1] of the scorched sky kept back, they beheld the Nile warm. Sesostris came[2] to the west and to the extremities of the world, and drove the Pharian chariots over the necks of

---

[1] *The red Zone*) ver. 275. Meaning the torrid zone.

[2] *Sesostris came*) ver. 276. It is probable that the great Egyptian conqueror Rameses Sesostris turned his attention to the sources of the Nile, as his conquest of Æthiopia is attested by numerous monuments found in that country, and memorials of him still exist as far as the south of Nubia.

kings; still, Rhone and Padus[1]. of your streams did he
drink at their sources before the Nile. The mad Cambyses
came to the long-lived people[2] in the East, and, falling
short of food and fed by the slaughter of his men, he returned, Nile, thee undiscovered.

" No lying fable has dared to speak about thy source.
Wherever thou art seen, thou art enquired into; and the
glory falls to no nation's lot for it to be joyous over the
Nile its own. Thy streams will I disclose so far as, Nile,
the God, the concealer of thy waves, has granted me to
know of thee. From the southern pole dost thou rise, ven
turing to raise thy banks towards the scorching Crab ; towards Boreas and the midst of Bootes dost thou go straight
onward with thy waters; *then* with windings is thy course
turned towards the west and the east, now favoring the
tribes of the Arabians, now the Libyan sands; and thee do
the Seres[3] first see, yet even these, as well, seek *to trace thy
source;* and with a foreign stream thou dost beat upon the
plains of the Æthiopians, and the earth knows not to what
region it is indebted for thee. *Thy* hidden source nature
has not disclosed to any one, nor has it been allowed
peoples to behold thee, Nile, but small; and thy springs
has she removed, and has willed rather that nations should
wonder at than know thy sources.

" At the very solstice it is thy privilege to rise, *and,*
winter removed, to increase, and to bring on wintry floods of
thy own ; and to thee alone is it permitted to wander between each pole. At the one is sought the rising, at the
other the end of thy waters. Far and wide with thy divided
stream is Meroë surrounded, fruitful for black husbandmen,

---

[1] *Rhone and Padus*) ver. 278. " He was no more able to discover the
mouths of the Nile than he was those of the Rhone and the Padus :" implying
that Sesostris in his European conquests penetrated as far as Gaul and Italy,
whereas he is more generally said to have conquered Thrace only.

[2] *To the long-lived people*) ver. 280. He alludes to the invasion by Cambyses, after having conquered Egypt, of Æthiopia, and his conflicts with the
" Macrobii," or " long-lived" Æthiopians. The miseries which his army there
suffered by famine are described in the pages of Herodotus.

[3] *Do the Seres*) ver. 292. He probably means a nation called Seres, in
the south of Africa ; who are mentioned by Heliodorus, B. ix. If so, he will
not be amenable to the censure of Scaliger, who blames him for supposing
that the Nile rises in the country of the Chinese.

joyous with the foliage of the ebony tree; which, although it is green with many a tree, moderates its summer with no shade [1], so straight through the Lion does that line of the world [2] cut. Thence art thou conveyed past the tracks of Phœbus, suffering no loss of thy waters [3], and long dost thou wander along the desert sands, at one time collecting all thy might into a single stream, at another wandering and undermining the banks that readily yield to thee.

"Again does thy sluggish channel recall the waves, divided into many parts, where Philæ, the key [4] of the kingdom, divides the fields of Egypt from the tribes of the Arabians. Next, a gentle course speeds thee on, cutting through the deserted regions, where the track of commerce divides our sea from the Red. Who, Nile, could suppose that thou, so gently flowing, couldst arouse such mighty anger of a stream so impetuous? But when the abruptness of the path and the precipitate cataracts have intercepted thy passage, and thou art indignant that any rocks should resist thy waters nowhere forbidden, then with foam dost thou challenge the stars; all sides roar with thy waters; and with a vast murmur of the mountains does the foaming river grow white with unconquered waves.

"After this, a powerful land, which our revered antiquity styles Abatos [6], assaulted by it, feels the first attacks, and the rocks which they have thought fit to call the springs of the river, because they first give the manifest signs of its

[1] *With no shade*) ver. 305. He alludes to the impossibility of trees, under a vertical sun, throwing a shade obliquely.

[2] *That line of the world*) ver. 306. Meaning the equator.

[3] *No loss of thy waters*) ver. 307. From the vast body of its waters the diminution of them by evaporation is not perceptible.

[4] *Philæ, the key*) ver. 313. Rowe has the following Note here :—" I have translated this literally ; though Philæ, which is an island on the Nile, and at a good distance from the Red Sea or Gulf of Arabia, is much rather to be looked upon as a boundary between Egypt and Æthiopia than between Egypt and Arabia. It lies a little above the lesser Cataracts."

[5] *Track of commerce*) ver. 314. He alludes to the Isthmus now called the Isthmus of Suez, which divides the Red Sea from the Mediterranean or Libyan Sea, and over which there was an intercourse by land with Asia.

[6] *Styles Abatos*) ver. 323. Abatos, or "the Inaccessible," was a rock or inaccessible island in the Nile, overgrown with shrubs, lying between Philæ and Elephantina. Seneca, in his Quæstiones Naturales, mentions it as only able to be trodden by the priests. One of the Scholiasts says that Isis buried Osiris in this neighbourhood.

recent swelling. After this, nature has placed mountains around the wandering waves, which, Nile, deny thee to Libya; among which, in a deep valley, the waves now speed on, lying within dams *thus* regained. First does Memphis allow to thee the fields and the open country, and forbid banks to place an obstacle to thy increase."

Thus without care, as though in the safety of peace, do they prolong the course of midnight; but the frenzied mind of Pothinus[1], once stained with blood so sacred, does not rest from the contemplation of crimes. Magnus slain, nothing does he now deem to be wickedness; his ghost dwells in his breast, and the avenging Goddesses direct his frenzy to new misdeeds. He is for gracing vile right hands with that blood[2] as well, with which Fortune is preparing to drench the vanquished Senators; and punishment for the civil war, vengeance for the Senate, is almost granted to a slave.

Avert afar, ye Fates, this crime, that, Brutus absent, this neck should be smitten! The punishment of the Roman tyrant is going to be counted a Pharian crime, and the example is being lost. Audaciously did he plan things not purposed by the Fates; nor did he prepare to entrust the murder to secret fraud, and in open warfare he challenged the unconquered chieftain. Courage so great did his crimes afford that he gave orders to strike off the head of Cæsar, and thy father-in-law, Magnus, to be joined unto thee; and he bade faithful slaves to carry these commands to Achillas, his partner in the murder of Pompey, whom the

[1] *Mind of Pothinus*) ver. 333.   These circumstances are thus related by Cæsar, in the Civil War, B. iii. c. 108 :—" A eunuch named Pothinus, the tutor of the young king, was regent of the kingdom on account of his youthfulness.   He at first began to complain among his friends, and to express his indignation, that the king should be summoned to plead his cause; but afterwards, having prevailed on some of those whom he had made acquainted with his views to join him, he secretly called the army away from Pelusium to Alexandria, and appointed Achillas, already spoken of, commander-in-chief of the forces.   Him he encouraged and animated by promises both in his own and the king's name, and instructed by letters and messages how he should act."

[2] *With that blood*) ver. 338.   " Fortune almost deigns to stain the base hands of Pothinus and Achillas with that blood which is doomed to be shed among the nobles in the Senate of Rome, who have been conquered by him at Pharsalia."

weak boy had appointed over all arms, and had given *to him* the sword, against all and against himself as well, no authority being retained for himself:—

"Now lie down on thy bed," said he, "and enjoy sound slumbers; Cleopatra has surprised the palace. Nor has Pharos been betrayed[1] only, but given away. Dost thou delay, alone, to run to the couch of thy mistress? The guilty sister is married to her brother, *guilty, I say*, for already is she married to the Latian chieftain; and running to and fro between her husbands she sways Egypt and has won Rome. Cleopatra has been able to subdue an old man[2] by sorceries; trust, wretched one, a child; whom if one night shall unite *with her*, and he shall once, submitting to her embrace with incestuous breast, satisfy an obscene passion under the name of affection, probably between each kiss he will be granting to her myself, and thy own head. By crosses and by flames shall we atone for it, if his sister shall prove beauteous[3]. No aid remains on any side; on the one hand there is the king the husband, on the other, Cæsar the paramour.

"And we are, though I confess it, convicted before so vengeful a judge; which one of us will Cleopatra not deem guilty, with regard to whom she has been chaste? By the deed which we jointly committed, and did in vain[4], and by the treaty ratified by the blood of Magnus, do thou come; with a sudden outburst arouse the warfare; rush on by night; let us quench the marriage torches in death; and the cruel mistress let us slaughter in the very bed with either husband. Nor let the fortune of the Hesperian chieftain deter us from the enterprise. The glory which has elevated him and set him over the earth *is* common to ourselves; us, too, does Magnus render illustrious. Look

[1] *Nor has Pharos been betrayed*) ver. 355-6. "Egypt has not only been betrayed to Cæsar, but has been given by him as a spoil to Cleopatra."

[2] *To subdue an old man*) ver. 360. "Senem." Cæsar, who was at this time fifty-two years of age, is thus styled in comparison with the boy Ptolemy. He suggests that Cleopatra has gained her influence over Cæsar by means of philtres and magic potions.

[3] *Shall prove beauteous*) ver. 366. "If the brother and sister are reconciled, our death will be the certain consequence."

[4] *Did in vain*) ver. 371. "Perdidimus." Literally, "we have lost," or "have gained nothing by."

upon the shore, the hope of our guilt; consult the stained waves what we may attempt; and behold a tomb with *its* little sand covering not *even* all the limbs of Pompey. He whom thou dost dread was *but* his peer.

"*We are* not illustrious in blood; what matters? Nor do we wield the resources of nations and the sway *of kings:* we have mighty powers for criminality. Fortune betrays them into our hands. Behold, another more noble victim comes! Let us by a second murder propitiate the Hesperian nations. The divided throat of Cæsar can afford this for me, that the Roman people will love us, though guilty in the death of Pompey. Why do we shudder at names so great, and the forces of the chieftain, which, left behind, he will be *but* a common soldier? This night will put an end to the civil wars, and will offer an appeasing sacrifice to the people, and will send to the shades the head which is still due to the world. Rush fiercely upon the throat of Cæsar: let the Lagæan band do this for their king, the Roman[1] for themselves. Do thou forbear delaying; filled with the banquet and drenched with wine, and prepared for lust, thou wilt find him; dare *the deed;* the Gods of heaven will bestow on thee ·the fulfilment of so many aspirations of the Catos and of the Bruti."

Achillas *is* not slow to obey one persuading to villany. To his camp, about to be moved, he does not give, as is the wont, a loud signal, nor does he betray his arms by the sound of any trumpet; in his temerity he employs all the appurtenances of savage warfare. The greatest part of the multitude are of the Latian commonalty, but so great obliviousness has taken possession of their minds, the soldiers being corrupted by foreign manners, that they can serve under a slave for their general, and under the command of a dependant of the court, whom to obey the Pharian tyrant it would have disgraced. No faith and piety *is there* in men

---

[1] *The Roman*) ver. 395. He alludes to those Romans who were then in the Egyptian army. They are thus mentioned by Cæsar in the Civil War, B. iii. c. 110:—"The forces of Achillas consisted partly of the soldiers of Gabinius, who were now become habituated to the licentious mode of living at Alexandria, and had forgotten the name and discipline of the Roman people, and had married wives there, by whom the greatest part of them had children." Septimius, who slew Pompey, was one of these mercenaries.

who follow camps, and let out for a little money their venal
hands, there the right *is* where *are* the highest wages[1];
and they engage to attack the life of Cæsar not for them
selves.

O right! where has not the wretched fate of our empire
met with civil war? Troops far removed from Thessaly
rage after the manner of their country on the banks of the
Nile. What more, Magnus, thyself received with hospitality,
could the house of Lagus have dared? Every right hand
performs, forsooth, that which is due to the Gods of heaven;
and to no Roman is it permitted to be unemployed. Thus
has it pleased the Gods to rend the Latian body; the people
do not separate in partisanship for the father-in-law and the
son-in-law: a dependant on a court arouses the civil war,
and Achillas sides with a faction of the Romans. And unless the Fates avert their hands from the blood of Cæsar,
this faction will prove the conqueror.

Ready prepared did each[2] come, and, engaged in feasting,
the palace was exposed to all treachery, and the blood of
Cæsar might have been poured forth amid the royal cups,
and his head have fallen on the table. But they feared
the startling alarms of war in the night, lest the slaughter,
promiscuous and sanctioned by the Fates, might, Ptolemy,
destroy thee. So great was their confidence in the sword.
They did not hasten on their guilt; the opportunity for a
deed so momentous was despised; it seemed to the slaves
a loss that might be made good to let that hour pass for
slaying Cæsar. To pay the penalty in open light was he
reserved. One night was granted to the chieftain, and Cæsar,
reprieved till the rising of Phœbus, lived by the favour of
Pothinus.

Lucifer looked down from the Casian rock, and sent the
day over Egypt, warmed even by the rising sun, when, afar
from the walls, troops were beheld, not scattered in maniples,

[1] *Where are the highest wages*) ver. 408. Weise thinks that this means
that where, as Romans, they could with the greatest justice and highest glory
have warred against Cæsar in the character of partisans of the Senate and
of Pompey, they preferred to act as the mercenaries of Ptolemy. That,
however, does not seem to be the sense of the passage.

[2] *Prepared did each*) ver. 421. Pothinus within, and Achillas without,
the palace.

nor yet unmarshalled, but just as they march with straight front against an equal foe. Ready to stand the attack hand to hand and to make it, they rushed on. But Cæsar, distrusting[1] the walls of the city, protected himself within the gates of the closed palace, submitting to an unworthy retreat. Nor for him, pent up, was the whole palace available; in the smaller portion of the house he had collected his forces; both anger and fear affected their minds; he both dreaded the onset and he disdained to dread.

Thus rages the noble brute confined within the narrow cage, and, the prison gnawed, breaks his frantic teeth; not otherwise would thy flames grow furious, Mulciber, in the caverns of Sicily, if any one were to block up the summits of Ætna[2] for thee. He who, in his boldness, so lately beneath the heights of Thessalian Hæmus, feared not all the nobles of Hesperia and the ranks of the Senate and Pompey their leader. the cause forbidding[3] him to look at them, and promised for himself an unmerited success, dreaded the guilty attempts of slaves, and within a house[4] was assailed with darts; he, whom not the Alanian would have provoked, not the Scythian, not the Moor, who sports with the stranger fastened up[5]; he, for whom the space of the Roman world does not suffice, and who deems the Indians with the Tyrian Gades a trifling realm, just like an unwarlike boy, just like a woman in a captured city, seeks the safe retreats of a house; his hope of life he places in a closed threshold, and, wandering about with uncertain steps, surveys the halls; not without the king, however, whom he takes in every quarter with him, to exact vengeance and

[1] *Cæsar, distrusting*) ver. 440. Cæsar says, in the Civil War, B. iii. c. 111:—"Full of confidence in his troops, and despising the small numbers of Cæsar's soldiers, Achillas seized Alexandria, except that part of the town which Cæsar occupied with his troops. At first he attempted to force the palace; but Cæsar had disposed his cohorts through the streets, and repelled his attack."

[2] *Summits of Ætna*) ver. 448. See B. i. l. 545.

[3] *The cause forbidding*) ver. 451. "When the badness of the cause ought to have forbidden him even to face Pompey and the Senate."

[4] *Within a house*) ver. 453. "Intraque Penates." Literally, "And within the Penates."

[5] *The stranger fastened up*) ver. 455. Alluding to those savage nations who amuse and exercise themselves with making strangers marks for their arrows.

a grateful expiation for his death, and determined to hurl, Ptolemy, thy head against the slaves, if there be not darts or flames. Thus is the barbarian fair one of Colchis[1] believed, fearing the avenger both of *his* kingdom and of *her* flight, with her sword and with the head of her brother as well, ready prepared, to have awaited her father.

However, the emergency of affairs forces the chieftain to have recourse to hopes of peace; and a royal attendant[2] is sent to corrupt the slaves in the name of their absent monarch, *to tell* by whose advice they commenced the attack. But neither does the law of the world[3] avail, nor the ties that are ratified by nations. The ambassador of the king and the pleader for peace, guilty of so many misdeeds, gives proof of what is to be placed in the number of thy crimes. Not the Thessalian land, and the vast realms of Juba, not Pontus, and the impious standards of Pharnaces, and the region flowed around by the cold Iberus, not the barbarian Syrtis, have perpetrated crimes so great as thy effeminacy.

The warfare presses him on every side, and now within the house the darts are falling, and the household Gods are trembling. No battering-ram *is there* to move the threshold at a single shock, and to break down the house; no engine of war is there; nor is the work entrusted to flames; but the troops, devoid of counsel, straggling, surround the vast

---

[1] *Fair one of Colchis*) ver. 464. Medea the Colchian tore her brother Absyrtus to pieces, and strewed his limbs in the way, when pursued by her father Æetes.

[2] *And a royal attendant*) ver. 468. Cæsar, in the Civil War, B. iii. c. 109, thus mentions the circumstance here referred to:—"Cæsar's only resource was to keep within the town in the most convenient places, and to get information of the designs of Achillas. However, he ordered his soldiers to repair to their arms, and advised the king to send some of his friends, who had the greatest influence, as deputies to Achillas, and to signify his royal pleasure. Dioscorides and Serapio, the persons sent by him, who had both been ambassadors at Rome, and had been in great esteem with Ptolemy, the father, went to Achillas. But as soon as they appeared in his presence, without hearing them, or learning the occasion of their coming, he ordered them to be seized and put to death. One of them, after receiving a wound, was taken up and carried off by the attendants as dead; the other was killed on the spot."

[3] *The law of the world*) ver. 471. "Jus mundi." Meaning the law universally observed by civilized nations, of holding inviolate the person of an ambassador.

abode, and nowhere does a body attack with its entire force.
The Fates forbid, and Fortune, in place of a wall, defends
Cæsar. With ships likewise[1] is the palace attempted, where
the luxurious abode extends itself with proud extremities
into the midst of the waves.

But Cæsar is present everywhere defending, and these
does he keep from entering with the sword, those with
flames; and, blockaded (so great is his presence of mind),
he does the work of the besieger. He orders torches dipped
in pitch and fat to be hurled against the sails in the joined
barks. Nor is the fire slow amid shrouds of tow and amid
planks dripping with wax; and at the same moment do
both the benches of the sailors and the topmost ropes of
the sailyards catch fire. Now almost are the half-burnt
ships sunk in the deep, and now both enemies and weapons
are floating. Nor on the ships alone do the flames take
hold; but the roofs which are near to the sea, with extending
smoke, catch fire. The south winds, too, feed the destruction, and the flame, smitten by a whirlwind, runs along the
roofs with no other motion than a meteor is wont to run
along the æthereal track, both lacking fuel, and burning in
the desert air.

This disaster for a short time called away the people
from the besieged palace to the aid of the city. Nor did
Cæsar lose the moments for destruction in sleep, but in the
darkness of the night he leapt aboard ship, always successfully employing the sudden turns of war and the opportunity
seized. Then he took Pharos, the key to the main. Once
did it stand as an island[2] in the mid sea, at the time of the
prophet Proteus; but now it is adjoining to the Pellæan

---

[1] *With ships likewise*) ver. 486. These naval contests are described at
length by Cæsar in the Civil War, B. iii. c. 111-112. In the latter chapter
he says:—"In this quarter of the town was a wing of the king's palace, in
which Cæsar was lodged on his first arrival, and a theatre adjoining the
house, which served for a citadel, and commanded an avenue to the port and
other docks."

[2] *Stand as an island*) ver. 510. Homer describes the Isle of Pharos as
a whole day's sail from Egypt. In the Odyssey, B. iv. l. 355-385, he describes Proteus, the prophetic old man of the sea, as dwelling in the Isle of
Pharos. Virgil mentions the Isle of Carpathos, between Crete and Rhodes,
as his abode. By some, Proteus is supposed to have been an ancient king
of Egypt.

walls. A double aid in war did that afford to the chieftain:
it cut off the power of making incursions and the outlets of
the main from the foe; and to the aid of Cæsar, it left an
inlet and free access to the sea.

Nor then did he any further delay the punishment of
Pothinus; but not with the wrath his due, not with the
cross, not with the flames, not with the ravenous teeth of
wild beasts. Oh shame! his head unbecomingly struck off
with the sword[1] atoned; he died by the death of Magnus!

Moreover, escaping by a stratagem[2] prepared by the slave
Ganymedes, Arsinoë goes over to the foes of Cæsar; and
she holds the camp deprived of its monarch, as the offspring
of Lagus, and pierces the grim Achillas[3], the slave of the
king, with a righteous sword. Now, Magnus, another victim
is dispatched to thy shade; nor does Fortune deem this
enough. Afar be it, that this should be the sum of thy
vengeance. Not the tyrant himself suffices for retribution,
not the whole palace of Lagus. Until the swords of his
country reach the vitals of Cæsar, Magnus will be unre-
venged.

But, the author of the commotion removed, the frenzy did
not cease; for again did they have recourse to arms, under
the guidance of Ganymedes[4]; and many battles did they

[1] *Struck off with the sword*) ver. 518. Cæsar says, in the Civil War, B. iii.
c. 112:—"While the enemy was thus employed, Pothinus, tutor to the
young king, and regent of the kingdom, who was in Cæsar's part of the
town, sent messengers to Achillas, and encouraged him not to desist from
his enterprise, or to despair of success; but his messengers being discovered
and apprehended, he was put to death by Cæsar."

[2] *Escaping by a stratagem*) ver. 520. Cæsar thus speaks of the escape
of Arsinoë, the younger sister of Cleopatra, in the Civil War, B. iii. c. 112:—
"In the meantime, Ptolemy's younger daughter, hoping the throne would
become vacant, made her escape from the palace to Achillas, and assisted
him in prosecuting the war. But they soon quarrelled about the command,
which circumstance enlarged the presents to the soldiers, for each endeavoured,
by great sacrifices, to secure their affection."

[3] *Pierces the grim Achillas*) ver. 523. We are told in the Alexandrian
War of Aulus Hirtius, c. v., that "after having mutually endeavoured to
supplant one another, each striving to engross the supreme authority, Arsinoë,
by the assistance of the eunuch Ganymedes, her governor, at length prevailed,
and slew Achillas."

[4] *Guidance of Ganymedes*) ver. 531. We learn from Hirtius, c. 5, that
"after the death of Achillas, Arsinoë possessed the whole power without a
rival, and raised Ganymedes to the command of the army, who, on his

fight with successful warfare. That day might, with fatal results to Cæsar, have been handed down to fame and to future ages.

His arms being crowded within the compass of a slight rampart, while the Latian chieftain is preparing to disembark his forces in empty ships, he is surrounded with all the dangers of a sudden attack; on the one side, numerous ships line the shores; on the other, foot soldiers are attacking in the rear; no way *is there* for safety, no flight, no *room for* valour; hardly, even, *is there* the hope of an honorable death. With no army routed, and with no heaps of vast carnage, was Cæsar then about to be conquered, but with no bloodshed, captured through the fatality of the spot.

He hesitates whether, in his doubt, to fear, or whether to wish to die. He recollects Scæva[1] amid the dense mass, who had already earned the glory of everlasting fame, Epidamnus, on thy plains, when, alone, the ramparts thrown open, he besieged Magnus treading upon the walls[2] ——

entrance upon that high office, augmented the largesses of the troops, and with equal diligence discharged all other parts of his duty."

[1] *Recollects Scæva*) ver. 544. The fate of Scæva now recurs to him, who on a similar occasion opposed the whole force of the enemy. See B. vi. l. 141, *et seq.*

[2] *Treading upon the walls*) ver. 546. It is rather singular that the work of Lucan breaks off at the same point as Cæsar's narrative of the Civil War. The death of Achillas, and the revolt under the command of Ganymedes, are the only events here stated which appear to have taken place after the close of the period comprised in Cæsar's work.

INDEX.

No citation.

commits an error as to the first of
Pompey's triumphs, 295 ; an astronomical description in his poem
deemed frigid and misplaced, 300 ;
commits errors in geography, 320.
340. 353, 354. 359, 360. 366 ;
probably had passages of Virgil in
view, 338. 357 : guilty of an historical error, 357 ; the obscurity of
his astronomical system, 393 ; his
poem finishes at the same period as
Cæsar's Commentaries, 406.
Lucian quoted, 334.
" Lustrare," the double meaning of,
315.
" Lustrum," the meaning of, 17.
Lycidas, the death of, 121.
Lycurgus, king of Thrace, punished
with insanity, 36.
Lydus quoted, 275.
Lygdamus, the death of, 123.
Lynx, the entrails of the, used for
magical purposes, 239.

Macedonia called Emathia, 1.
Macra, the river, 69.
Macrobii, or long-lived Æthiopians,
the, 168.
Macrobius quoted, 168.
Mænalus, the mountain of, 98.
Magnetes, the nation of the, 225.
Magnus, the surname, when first given
to Pompey, 9 ; the name by which
he is usually called by Lucan, 8 ;
the name given to Cneius, the son
of Pompey, by Lucan, after his fa-
ther's death, 343.
Malea, the promontory of, 205. 340.
Mallus, the city of, 103.
Maniple, the meaning of the word, 18.
" Manus," meaning grappling-irons, 87.
Mapalia, Numidian huts or cottages,
51.
Marbodus Andinus, his supposed in-
terpolation in Lucan's Pharsalia,
28.
Marcellus, C. Claudius, the Consul, 19.
Marcia, her visit to Cato after the
death of Hortensius. 63 ; the nature
of her second marriage to Cato dis-

cussed, ib. ;
in presence
Mareotis, the
Marica, the N
Marius, Caius,
marshes of
50 ; his def
of Jugurtha
death, ib.,
to the slav
Cinna, ib. ;
who do no
enjoys sevel
the bloodsh
Rome, 347.
Marius, the yo
Marmaridæ, t
157.
Marmontel, hi
sage in the
Marsi, the nat
Marsyas, his
the river so
Massagetæ, tl
sucked the
107.
Massilia, the
Phocæans,
Cæsar, 111
inhabitants
can, 116.
Massilians, the
109 ; their
Cæsar, 125.
Matinus, the
Mausolea, 327
May, probabl
316. 333.
Mazagians, th
Medea, her
Jason, the
syrtus, the
Medians, the,
Meduana, the
Medusa and P
Megæra, the
cules, 37.
Melas, the riv
Melibœa, the
Memphis, the

Samos, the island of, 305.

Sand, used by wrestlers, 154.

Santones, or Santoni, the, 26.

Sapis, the river, 68.

Sarissa, the land of the Macedonians, 308.

Sarnus, the river, 69.

Sarmatians, the, mentioned as wearing trowsers, 27.

Sason, or Saso, the island of, 82.

Saturn, the treasury in the Temple of, plundered by Cæsar, 95.

Scæva, his exploits, 214, 215 ; his address to his comrades, 210 ; his perfidy, 214 ; is mentioned by Cicero as a partizan of Cæsar, 215.

Scævola, Mutius, the murder of, 54.

Scaliger, his censure of Lucan, 396.

Scamnum, or bedsteps, made of ivory, 65.

Scholiasts on the Pharsalia, quoted, 3. 5. 27. 35, 36. 38. 53. 60. 171. 208. 273. 291. 307. 309. 371. 375. 387. 389. 397.

Scorpio, the Constellation, occupies more space than any other, 226.

Scorpion, the, 372.

Scylla, the whirlpool of, 70.

Scytale, 368.

Sea-fight off Massilia, described, 122.

Sellæ, the people of, 98 ; the extinction of the oracle, ib.

Sena, the river, 68.

Senate, the Roman, expels the Tribunes from Rome, 16; commands the Consuls to march against Cæsar, 32; is convoked by Cæsar in the Temple of Apollo, 94.

Seneca quoted, 7. 290. 313. 397.

Senones, or Senonian Gauls, the, 15.

Seps, the serpent, described, 368, 370.

Septemviri Epulones, alluded to, 39.

Septimius, prepares to murder Pompey, 323 ; murders him, 324.

Seres or Chinese, the, 2 ; their probable intercourse with Egypt, 390.

Serpents, winged, 240 ; a mixture made from their eyes proof against spectres, 240.

Sertorius, Q., opposed by Pompey in Spain, 78.

Servius quoted, 38. 69.

Sesostris, the extent of his conquests, 395.

Sestos and Abydos, the towns of, 85.

Sextus, the younger son of Pompey, his defeat in Sicily alluded to, 4 ; has recourse to necromantic arts, 229 ; addresses the sorceress Erictho, 236 ; a corpse restored to life prophesies to him, 245 ; meets his father when flying from Cæsar, 302 ; probably in another part of Lesbos during Cornelia's stay there, 302 ; meets his brother Cneius, 343, and addresses him on the fall of his father, 343.

Showers, not known in Egypt, 315. 333.

Sibyl, the prophecies of the, 35. 173. 333.

Sicily, said to have been once connected with Italy, 70. 91.

Sicoris, the river, 127.

Sidon, the city of, 102.

Siler, the river, 69.

Silius Italicus quoted, 140.

Sinus, the folds of the bosom of the dress, 334.

Sipus, the town of, 181.

Sistrum, the use and origin of the, 334.

Solipuga, or Solpuga, the, 372.

"Sonipes," the war-horse so called ? Lucan, 13.

Sophene in Armenia, 80.

Spartacus the Thracian, 78.

Standards of the Romans, captured by the Parthians, 311.

Stags, supposed to feed on serpents, 239.

Stephanus Byzantinus quoted, 228.

Stœchades, the islands, 117.

Stoic philosophers, their doctrine as to the destruction of the universe, 290.

Storm, description of a, 192.

Strabo quoted, 317.

Strata or coverlets 389.

Strongyle, or Stromboli, probably alluded to, 71.

Strymon, the river, frequented by cranes, 100.

Suessones, or Suessiones, the nation of the, 26; famous for the length of their weapons, *ib.*

Suetonius quoted, 120. 180. 183. 274.

Suevi, the nation of the, 49.

Suez, the isthmus of, 397.

Sugar, probably alluded to by the Poet, 103.

Sulla, L. Cornelius, his retirement from public life, 20; his funeral in the Campus Martius, 37; where his ghost appears, *ib.*; his victories at Sacriportus and the Collinian Gate, 55; calls himself Felix, or Fortunate, 59; Fortuna his patron Divinity, 246; the bloodshed on his return to Rome, 347.

Sulla, Faustus Cornelius, flies from Italy, 72.

Sulpitius, the Scholiast on the Pharsalia, quoted, 44. 60. 213. 215.

Sun, a notion that its heat was supplied from the clouds, 249; an opinion as to its setting, 373.

Sunstroke, probably alluded to, 355.

Superstitions, the Roman, introduced from Etruria, 37.

Supparus, or supparum, what garment it was, 65.

Susa, or Shushan, the city of, 48. 314.

Syene, a city of Upper Egypt, 80.

Syrtes of Africa, what, 22; the march of Cato over the, 45; description of the, 351.

Tacitus quoted, 27. 183.

Tæda, or marriage torch, 8.

Tænarus, the cavern of, 340.

Tages, the diviner, 37. 42.

Tagus, the death of, 119, 120.

Talaria, worn by Perseus, 365.

Tamarisk, planted near the graves of the poor, 375.

Tanais, the river, forms the boundary between Europe and Asia, 107.

Taprobana, a story told of the natives of, 104.

Taranis, a Gallic Divinity, 29.

Taras, the city of, 181.

Tarbela, the city of, 25.

Tarchondimotus, the Cilician, attempts to revolt, 347; is censured by Cato, 348; one of his men addresses Cato, *ib.*

Tarsus, the city of, 103.

Taulantii, the nation of the, 203.

Taurians, the nation of the, 80.

Tauromenus, or Tauromenium, the town of, 148.

Taygetus, the river, 167.

Telmessus, two cities so called, 305.

Telon, the death of, 120.

Tempe, the valley of, 221.

Terence, the comic Poet, said to have betrayed M. Bæbius, 53.

"Testudo," or tortoise, its meanings in a military sense, 115.

Tethys, the Goddess, 25.

Tetrarch, the dignity of, 261.

Teutas, or Teutates, a Gallic Divinity, 29.

Teutones, the nation of the, 215; conquered by C. Marius, 50.

Thapsus, the shrub, 375; grew in Sicily, *ib.*

Theatre of stone, the first at Rome built by Pompey, 9. 250.

Theatres, saffron water discharged in them, 371.

Thebes, the city of, in Egypt, 335.

Themis, her oracles at Delphi, 169.

Theodotus, meets Cæsar with the head of Pompey, 380; his address to Cæsar, *ib.*; is answered by Cæsar, 381.

Thermus, Q. Minutius, flies from Umbria, 72.

Thesproti, the nation of the, 98.

Thessaly, called Emathia, 1; described, 221.

Threshold, the bride lifted over the, 65.

Thucydides quoted, 70.

Thyestes and Atreus, the story of, alluded to, 34.

LONDON :

PRINTED BY WILLIAM CLOWES AND SONS, LIMITED,
STAMFORD STREET AND CHARING CROSS.

A

CLASSIFIED CATALOGUE

OF

SELECTED WORKS .

INCLUDING AN ALPHABETICAL LIST

OF BOHN'S LIBRARIES

PUBLISHED BY

GEORGE BELL & SONS

LONDON : YORK ST., COVENT GARDEN

NEW YORK : 66 FIFTH AVENUE; & BOMBAY

CAMBRIDGE : DEIGHTON, BELL & CO.

1896

CONTENTS.

London, December 1896.

MESSRS. BELL'S
CLASSIFIED CATALOGUE
OF
SELECTED WORKS.

** *Messrs. Bell will be glad to send their Complete Catalogue, Catalogue of Bohn's Libraries, or Educational Catalogue, to any address, post free.*

POETRY.

Aidé (Hamilton). Songs without Music. 3rd edition. With additional Pieces. Fcap. 8vo. 5s.

Aldine Edition of the Poets. *See List, page 7.*

Barry Cornwall. English Songs and Lyrics. 2nd edition. Fcap. 8vo. 6s.

Bridges (R.) Shorter Poems. 4th edition. Fcap. 8vo. 5s. net.

—— **Eros and Psyche: A Poem in Twelve Measures.** The Story done into English from the Latin of Apuleius. 2nd edition revised. Fcap. 8vo. 5s. net.

—— **Prometheus the Firegiver.** [*Out of print.*

—— **A Series of Plays.** Fcap. 4to. printed on hand-made paper, double columns, paper wrappers, each 2s. 6d. net (except No. 8). The eight Plays are paged consecutively, and are intended to form a Volume:—

1. NERO. The First Part. History of the first five years of Nero's reign, with the Murder of Britannicus to the Death of Agrippina.
[*Out of print at present.*

2. PALICIO. A Romantic Drama in Five Acts, in the Elizabethan manner.

3. THE RETURN OF ULYSSES. A Drama in Five Acts, in a mixed manner.

4. THE CHRISTIAN CAPTIVES. A Tragedy in Five Acts, in a mixed manner, without change of scene.

5. ACHILLES IN SCYROS. A Drama in Five Acts, in a mixed manner, without change of scene.

6. THE HUMOURS OF THE COURT. A Comedy in Three Acts, in the Spanish manner.

7. THE FEAST OF BACCHUS. A Comedy in Five Acts, in the Latin manner, without change of scene.

8. NERO. The Second Part. In Five Acts: comprising the Conspiracy of Piso to the Death of Seneca, in the Elizabethan manner. 3s. net, with general title-page, &c., for the volume.

—— **Achilles in Scyros.** New Edition. Fcp. 8vo. 2s. 6d. net.

—— **Eden.** A Cantata in Three Acts, set to music by C. Villiers Stanford. Words only, by Robert Bridges. 2s. net.

Browning's Strafford. With Notes by E. H. Hickey, and an Introduction by S. R. Gardiner, LL.D. 2nd edition. Crown 8vo. 2s. 6d.

Handbook to Robert Browning's Works. By Mrs. Sutherland Orr. 6th edition, with additions and full bibliography. Fcap. 8vo. 6s.

Stories from Robert Browning. By Frederic M. Holland. With an Introduction by Mrs. Sutherland Orr. Wide fcap. 4s. 6d.

Calverley (C. S.) Works by the late C. S. Calverley, M.A,, late Fellow of Christ's College, Cambridge.

New and Cheaper uniform Edition in 4 vols. Crown 8vo. 5s. each.

Vol. I. LITERARY REMAINS, with Portrait and Memoir. Edited by Sir Walter J. Sendall, K.C.M.G.

Vol. II. VERSES AND FLY LEAVES.

Vol. III. TRANSLATIONS into English and Latin.

Vol. IV. THEOCRITUS, in English Verse.

Original Editions.

FLY LEAVES. 17th edition. Fcap. 8vo. 3s. 6d.

VERSES AND TRANSLATIONS. 15th edition. Fcap. 8vo. 5s.

De Vere (Sir Aubrey). Mary Tudor : an Historical Drama, in Two Parts. By the late Sir Aubrey De Vere. New edition. Fcap. 8vo. 5s.

De Vere (Sir Stephen). Translations from Horace. By Sir Stephen E. De Vere, Bart. 3rd edition enlarged. Imperial 16mo. 7s. 6d. net.

Fanshawe (R.) Two Lives. A Poem. By Reginald Fanshawe, M.A. 4s. 6d. net.

Ferguson (Sir S.) Congal: A Poem in Five Books. By the late Sir Samuel Ferguson, Knt., Q.C., LL.D., P.R.I.A. Fcap. 8vo. 2s.

—— Poems. Demy 8vo. 7s. 6d.

Field (Michael). Underneath the Bough. A Book of Verses. 2nd edition. Royal 16mo. 4s. 6d. net.

—— Callirrhoë, Fair Rosamund. 2nd edition. Crown 8vo. parchment cover, 6s.

—— Canute the Great; a Cup of Water. Two Plays. Crown 8vo. 7s. 6d.

—— The Father's Tragedy ; William Rufus; Loyalty or Love ? Crown 8vo. parchment cover, 7s. 6d.

—— The Tragic Mary. On hand-made paper, bound in brown boards, with Design by Selwyn Image, imperial 16mo. 7s. 6d. net.

Large-paper Edition, on Whatman's paper, bound in vellum, with design in gold, 60 copies only (numbered), fcap. 4to. 21s. net.

Lang (Andrew). Helen of Troy. A Poem. 5th edition. Wide fcap. 8vo. cloth, 2s. 6d. net.

Patmore (Coventry). Poems. Collective Edition in 2 vols. 5th edition. Fcap. 8vo. 9s.

—— The Unknown Eros, and other Poems. 3rd edition. Fcap. 8vo. 2s. 6d.

—— The Angel in the House. 7th edition. Fcap. 8vo. 3s. 6d.

Procter (A. A.) Legends and Lyrics. By Adelaide Anne Procter. With Introduction by Charles Dickens. New edition, printed on hand-made paper. 2 vols. pott 8vo., extra binding, 10s.

ORIGINAL EDITION. First Series. 69th thousand. 2s. 6d. Second Series. 61st thousand. 2s. 6d.

CROWN 8VO EDITION. New Issue, with additional Poems, and 10 Illustrations by Ida Lovering. 19th thousand. Post 8vo. cloth, gilt edges, 5s.

CHEAP EDITION, with 18 Illustrations, double columns. 2 Series. 30th thousand. Fcap. 4to. paper cover, 1s. each; or in 1 vol. cloth, 3s.

The Procter Birthday Book. Demy 16mo. 1s. 6d.

Rickards (M. S. C.) Lyrics and Elegiacs. By Marcus S. C. Rickards. Crown 8vo. 4s. net.

—— **Poems of Life and Death.** Crown 8vo. 4s. 6d. net.

—— **The Exiles: A Romance of Life.** Crown 8vo. 4s. 6d. net.

Sweetman (E.) The Footsteps of the Gods, and other Poems. Crown 8vo. 6s. net.

Tennyson (Lord). A Key to Tennyson's 'In Memoriam.' By Alfred Gatty, D.D., Vicar of Ecclesfield and Sub-Dean of York. Fourth edition, with Portrait of Arthur Hallam, 3s. 6d.

Handbook to Lord Tennyson's Works. By Morton Luce. With Bibliography. Fcap. 8vo. 6s.

Trevelyan (Sir G. O.) The Ladies in Parliament, and other Pieces. Republished, with Additions and Annotations. By Sir George Otto Trevelyan. Crown 8vo. 1s. 6d.

Waddington (S.) A Century of Sonnets. Fcap. 4to. 4s. 6d.

—— **Poems.** Fcap. 8vo. 4s.

Beaumont and Fletcher, their finest Scenes, Lyrics, and other Beauties (selected), with Notes and Introduction by Leigh Hunt. Small post 8vo. 3s. 6d.

Butler's Hudibras, with Variorum Notes, a Biography, and a General Index, a Portrait of Butler, and 28 Illustrations. Small post 8vo. 5s.

Chaucer's Poetical Works. With Poems formerly printed with his or attributed to him. Edited, with a Memoir, Introduction, Notes, and a Glossary, by Robert Bell. Revised, with a Preliminary Essay by Rev. Prof. Skeat, M.A. With Portrait. 4 vols. small post 8vo. 3s. 6d. each.

Greene, Marlowe, and Ben Jonson, Poems of. Edited, with Critical and Historical Notes and Memoirs, by Robert Bell. Small post 8vo. 3s. 6d.

Milton's Poetical Works. With a Memoir and Critical Remarks by James Montgomery, an Index to Paradise Lost, Todd's Verbal Index to all the Poems, and a Selection of Explanatory Notes by Henry G. Bohn. Illustrated with 120 Wood Engravings by Thompson, Williams, O. Smith, and Linton, from Drawings by W. Harvey. 2 vols. small post 8vo. 3s. 6d. each.

Pope's Poetical Works. Edited, with copious Notes, by Robert Carruthers. 2 vols. with numerous Illustrations, small post 8vo. 10s.

—— **Homer's Iliad and Odyssey.** With Introduction and Notes by the Rev. J. S. Watson, M.A. Illustrated by the entire Series of Flaxman's Designs. 2 vols. small post 8vo. 5s. each.

Sheridan's Dramatic Works. Complete. With Life by G. G. S., and Portrait, after Reynolds. Small post 8vo. 3s. 6d.

Shakespeare. Dramatic Works. Edited by S. W. Singer. With a Life of Shakespeare by W. W. Lloyd. Uniform with the Aldine Edition of the Poets. In 10 vols. fcap. 8vo. cloth, 2s. 6d. each.

——— **Plays and Poems.** With Notes and Life by Charles Knight. Royal 8vo. 10s. 6d.

——— **Pocket Volume Edition.** Comprising all his Plays and Poems. Edited from the First Folio Edition by T. Keightley. 13 vols. royal 32mo. in a cloth box, price 21s.

Critical Essays on the Plays. By W. W. Lloyd. Uniform with Singer's Edition of Shakespeare, 2s. 6d.

Lectures on Shakespeare. By Bernhard ten Brink. Translated by Julia Franklin. Small post 8vo. 3s. 6d.

Shakespeare's Dramatic Art. The History and Character of Shakespeare's Plays. By Dr. Hermann Ulrici. Translated by L. Dora Schmitz. 2 vols. sm. post 8vo. 3s. 6d. each.

Shakespeare : A Literary Biography by Karl Elze, Ph.D., LL.D. Translated by L. Dora Schmitz. Sm. post 8vo. 5s.

Coleridge's Lectures on Shakespeare, &c. Edited by T. Ashe. Sm. post 8vo. 3s. 6d.

Hazlitt's Lectures on the Characters of Shakespeare's Plays. Sm. post 8vo. 1s.

Jameson's Shakespeare's Heroines. Sm. post 8vo. 3s. 6d.

Lamb's Specimens of English Dramatic Poets of the Time of Elizabeth. With Notes, together with the Extracts from the Garrick Plays. Sm. post 8vo. 3s. 6d.

Ballads and Songs of the Peasantry of England, taken down from oral recitation, and transcribed from private manuscripts, rare broadsides, and scarce publications. Edited by Robert Bell. Sm. post 8vo. 3s. 6d.

Percy's Reliques of Ancient English Poetry. Collected by Thomas Percy, Lord Bishop of Dromore. With an Essay on Ancient Minstrels, and a Glossary. A new edition by J. V. Prichard, A.M. 2 vols. Sm. post 8vo. 7s.

English Sonnets by Living Writers. Selected and arranged, with a Note on the History of the Sonnet, by S. Waddington. 2nd edition, enlarged. Fcap. 8vo. 2s. 6d.

English Sonnets by Poets of the Past. Selected and arranged by S. Waddington. Fcap. 8vo. 2s. 6d.

Who Wrote It? A Dictionary of Common Poetical Quotations in the English Language. 4th edition. Fcap. 8vo. 2s. 6d.

Bohn's Dictionary of Quotations from the English Poets, arranged according to subjects. 4th edition. Post 8vo. 6s.

New Editions, fcap. 8vo. 2s. 6d. each net.

THE ALDINE EDITION
OF THE
BRITISH POETS.

'This excellent edition of the English classics, with their complete texts and scholarly introductions, are something very different from the cheap volumes of extracts which are just now so much too common.'—*St. James's Gazette.*
'An excellent series. Small, handy, and complete.'—*Saturday Review.*

Akenside. Edited by Rev. A. Dyce.

Beattie. Edited by Rev. A. Dyce.

*Blake. Edited by W. M. Rossetti.

*Burns. Edited by G. A. Aitken. 3 vols.

Butler. Edited by R. B. Johnson. 2 vols.

Campbell. Edited by his son-in-law, the Rev. A. W. Hill. With Memoir by W. Allingham.

Chatterton. Edited by the Rev. W. W. Skeat, M.A. 2 vols.

Chaucer. Edited by Dr. R. Morris, with Memoir by Sir H. Nicolas. 6 vols.

Churchill. Edited by Jas. Hannay. 2 vols.

*Coleridge. Edited by T. Ashe, B.A. 2 vols.

Collins. Edited by W. Moy Thomas.

Cowper. Edited by John Bruce, F.S.A. 3 vols.

Dryden. Edited by the Rev. R. Hooper, M.A. 5 vols.

Falconer. Edited by the Rev. J. Mitford.

Goldsmith. Edited by Austin Dobson.

*Gray. Edited by J. Bradshaw, LL.D.

Herbert. Edited by the Rev. A. B. Grosart.

*Herrick. Edited by George Saintsbury. 2 vols.

*Keats. Edited by the late Lord Houghton.

Kirke White. Edited by J. Potter Briscoe. [*Preparing.*

Milton. Edited by Dr. Bradshaw. 3 vols.

Parnell. Edited by G. A. Aitken.

Pope. Edited by G. R. Dennis. With Memoir by John Dennis. 3 vols.

Prior. Edited by R. B. Johnson. 2 vols.

Raleigh and Wotton. With Selections from the Writings of other COURTLY POETS from 1540 to 1650. Edited by Ven. Archdeacon Hannah, D.C.L.

Rogers. Edited by Edward Bell, M.A.

Scott. Edited by John Dennis. 5 vols.

Shakespeare's Poems. Edited by Rev. A. Dyce.

Shelley. Edited by H. Buxton Forman. 5 vols.

Spenser. Edited by J. Payne Collier, 5 vols.

Surrey. Edited by J. Yeowell.

Swift. Edited by the Rev. J. Mitford. 3 vols.

Thomson. Edited by the Rev. D. C. Tovey. 2 vols. [*Preparing.*

Vaughan. Sacred Poems and Pious Ejaculations. Edited by the Rev. H. Lyte.

Wordsworth. Edited by Prof. Dowden. 7 vols.

Wyatt. Edited by J. Yeowell.

Young. Edited by the Rev. J. Mitford. 2 vols.

* These volumes may also be had bound in Irish linen, with design in gold on side and back by Gleeson White, and gilt top, 3s. 6d. each net.

BIOGRAPHY AND HISTORY.

Memoir of Edward Craven Hawtrey, D.D., Headmaster, and afterwards Provost, of Eton. By F. St. John Thackeray, M.A. With Portrait and 3 Coloured Illustrations. Small crown 8vo. 7s. 6d.

Memorials of the Hon. Ion Keith-Falconer, late Lord Almoner's Professor of Arabic in the University of Cambridge, and Missionary to the Mohammedans of Southern Arabia. By the Rev. Robert Sinker, D.D. With new Portrait. 6th edition. Crown 8vo. 2s. 6d.

A Memoir of Edward Steere, Third Missionary Bishop in Central Africa. By the Rev. R. M. Heanley, M.A. With Portrait, Four Illustrations, and Map. 2nd edition, revised. Crown 8vo. 5s.

François Severin Marceau. A Biography. By Captain T. G. Johnson. With Portraits and Maps. Crown 8vo. 5s.

Robert Schumann. His Life and Works. By August Reissmann. Translated by A. L. Alger. Sm. post 8vo. 3s. 6d.

Schumann's Early Letters. Translated by May Herbert. With a Preface by Sir George Grove, D.C.L. Sm. post 8vo. 3s. 6d.

William Shakespeare. A Literary Biography by Karl Elze, Ph.D., LL.D. Translated by L. Dora Schmitz. Sm. post 8vo. 5s.

Boswell's Life of Johnson, with the Tour in the Hebrides, and Johnsoniana. New edition, with Notes and Appendices by the late Rev. Alexander Napier, M.A., Trinity College, Cambridge, Vicar of Holkham, Editor of the Cambridge Edition of the 'Theological Works of Barrow.' With Steel Engravings. 5 vols. Demy 8vo. 3l.; or in 6 vols. sm. post 8vo. 3s. 6d. each.

Johnson's Lives of the Poets. Edited, with Notes, by Mrs. Alexander Napier, and an Introduction by Professor J. W. Hales, M.A. 3 vols. Sm. post 8vo. 3s. 6d. each.

North's Lives of the Norths: Right Hon. Francis North, Baron Guildford, the Hon. Sir Dudley North, and the Hon. and Rev. Dr. John North. Edited by A. Jessopp, D.D. With 3 Portraits. 3 vols. Sm. post 8vo. 3s. 6d. each.

Vasari's Lives of the most Eminent Painters, Sculptors, and Architects. Translated by Mrs. J. Foster, with Notes. 6 vols. Sm. post 8vo. 3s. 6d. each.

Walton's Lives of Donne, Hooker, &c. New edition, revised by A H. Bullen. With numerous illustrations. Sm. post 8vo. 5s.

Helps (Sir Arthur). The Life and Labours of the late Thomas Brassey. 7th edition. Sm. post 8vo. 1s. 6d.

———— The Life of Hernando Cortes, and the Conquest of Mexico. Dedicated to Thomas Carlyle. 2 vols. Small post 8vo. 3s. 6d. each.

———— The Life of Christopher Columbus, the Discoverer of America. 10th edition. Small post 8vo. 3s. 6d.

———— The Life of Pizarro. With some Account of his Associates in the Conquest of Peru. 3rd edition. Small post 8vo. 3s. 6d.

———— The Life of Las Casas, the Apostle of the Indies. 5th edition. Small post 8vo. 3s. 6d.

Irving (Washington). Life of Oliver Goldsmith. 1s.

——— Life and Voyages of Columbus and his Companions. 2 vols. With Portraits. 3s. 6d. each.

——— Life of Mahomet and His Successors. With Pertrait. 3s. 6d.

——— Life of George Washington. With Portrait. 4 vols. 3s. 6d. each.

Life and Letters of Washington Irving. By his nephew, Pierre E. Irving. With Portrait. 2 vols. 3s. 6d. each.

Lockhart's Life of Burns. Revised and corrected with Notes and Appendices, by William Scott Douglas. With Portrait. Sm. post 8vo. 3s. 6d.

Southey's Life of Nelson. With Additional Notes, Index, Portraits, Plans, and upwards of 50 Engravings. Sm. post 8vo. 5s.

——— Life of Wesley, and the Rise and Progress of Methodism. With Portrait. Sm. post 8vo. 5s.

Life of Wellington. By 'An Old Soldier.' From the materials of Maxwell. With 18 Steel Engravings. Sm. post. 8vo. 5s.

Life of Burke. By Sir James Prior. With Portrait. Sm. post 8vo. 3s. 6d.

Life and Letters of Locke. By Lord King. Sm. post 8vo. 3s. 6d.

Life of Pope. By Robert Carruthers. Illustrated. Sm. post. 8vo. 5s.

Cellini's Memoirs. Translated by T. Roscoe. With Portrait. Sm. post 8vo. 3s. 6d.

Memoirs of the Life of Colonel Hutchinson. By his Widow. With Portrait. Sm. post 8vo. 3s. 6d.

Memorials and Letters of Charles Lamb. Talfourd's edition, revised. By W. Carew Hazlitt. 2 vols. Sm. post 8vo. 3s. 6d. each.

Robert Southey: The Story of his Life Written in his Letters. With an Introduction. Edited by John Dennis. Small post 8vo. 3s. 6d.

Letters and Works of Lady Mary Wortley Montagu. Edited, with Memoir, by W. Moy Thomas. Revised edition, with 5 Portraits. 2 vols. small post 8vo. 5s. each.

Memoirs of Philip de Commines. Translated by A. R. Scoble. With Portraits. 2 vols. small post 8vo. 3s. 6d. each.

The Diary of Samuel Pepys. Transcribed from the Shorthand MS. by the Rev. Mynors Bright, M.A. With Lord Braybrooke's Notes. Edited, with Additions, by Henry B. Wheatley, F.S.A. 9 vols. demy 8vo. with Portraits and other Illustrations, 10s. 6d. each.
.˙. The only complete edition.

Evelyn's Diary and Correspondence, with the Private Correspondence of Charles I. and Sir Edward Nicholas, and between Sir Edward Hyde (Earl of Clarendon) and Sir Richard Browne. Edited from the Original MSS. by W. Bray, F.A.S. With 45 Engravings. 4 vols. small post 8vo. 20s.

Pepys' Diary and Correspondence. With Life and Notes by Lord
Braybrooke, and 31 Engravings. 4 vols. small post 8vo. 20s.

The Early Diary of Frances Burney, 1768-1778. With a Selection from her Correspondence and from the Journals of her Sisters, Susan
and Charlotte Burney. Edited by Annie Raine Ellis. 2 vols. demy 8vo. 32s.

The Diary and Letters of Madame D'Arblay. As edited by her
Niece, Charlotte Barrett. With Portraits. 4 vols. demy 8vo. 30s.

Handbooks of English Literature. Edited by J. W. Hales, M.A.,
Fellow of Christ's College, Cambridge, Professor of English Literature at
King's College, London. Crown 8vo. 3s. 6d. each.

> The Age of Pope. By John Dennis.
>
> The Age of Dryden. By R. Garnett, LL.D.
>
> The Age of Milton. By J. Bass Mullinger, M.A., and the
> Rev. J. H. B. Masterman.
>
> The Age of Wordsworth. By Prof. C. H. Herford, Litt.D.
>
> PREPARING.
>
> The Age of Chaucer. By Professor Hales.
>
> The Age of Shakespeare. By Professor Hales.
>
> The Age of Johnson. By Thomas Seccombe.
>
> The Age of Tennyson. By Professor Hugh Walker.

Ten Brink's History of English Literature. Vol. I.—Early
English Literature (to Wiclif). Translated into English by Horace M.
Kennedy, Professor of German Literature in the Brooklyn Collegiate Institute. 3s. 6d. Vol. II.—(Wiclif, Chaucer, Earliest Drama, Renaissance).
Translated by W. Clarke Robinson, Ph.D. 3s. 6d. Vol III.—(To the Death
of Surrey). Edited by Professor Alois Brandl. Translated by L. Dora
Schmitz. Small post 8vo. 3s. 6d.

The British Fleet : the Growth, Achievements, and Duties of the
Navy of the Empire. By Commander Charles N. Robinson, R.N. With 150
Illustrations. Cheaper edition. Crown 8vo. 6s.

Achievements of Cavalry. By General Sir Evelyn Wood, V.C.,
G.C.B., G.C.M.G. Crown 8vo. with Maps and Plans.   [*In the press.*

The Campaign of Sedan: The Downfall of the Second Empire,
August–September 1870. By George Hooper. With General Map and Six
Plans of Battles. Demy 8vo. 14s.

Waterloo: The Downfall of the First Napoleon. A History of the
Campaign of 1815. By George Hooper. With Maps and Plans. New edition,
revised. Small post 8vo. 3s. 6d.

History of the Irish Rebellion in 1798. By W. H. Maxwell.
Illustrated by George Cruikshank. 13th edition. 7s. 6d.

**The War of the Succession in Spain during the Reign of Queen
Anne,** 1702-1711. Based on Original Manuscripts and Contemporary Records.
By Col. the Hon. Arthur Parnell, R.E. Demy 8vo. 14s. With Map, &c.

The Revolutionary Movements of 1848-9 in Italy, Austria, Hungary, and Germany. With some Examination of the previous Thirty-three
Years. By C. Edmund Maurice. With Illustrations. Demy 8vo. 16s.

History of Germany in the Middle Ages. By E. F. Henderson, Ph.D. Crown 8vo. 7s. 6d. net.

England in the Fifteenth Century. By the late Rev. W. Denton, M.A., Worcester College, Oxford. Demy 8vo. 12s.

History of Modern Europe, from the Taking of Constantinople to the Establishment of the German Empire, A.D. 1453-1871. By the late Dr. T. H. Dyer. A new edition. 5 vols. 2l. 12s. 6d.

Lives of the Queens of England. From the Norman Conquest to the reign of Queen Anne. By Agnes Strickland. Library edition. With Portraits, Autographs, and Vignettes. 8 vols. demy 8vo. 7s. 6d. each. Also a Cheaper Edition in 6 vols. with 6 Portraits, small post 8vo. 30s.

Life of Mary Queen of Scots. By Agnes Strickland. With Index and 2 Portraits of Mary. 2 vols. small post 8vo. 10s.

Lives of the Tudor and Stuart Princesses. By Agnes Strickland. With Portraits. Small post 8vo. 5s.

The Works of Flavius Josephus. Whiston's Translation. Thoroughly revised by Rev. A. R. Shilleto, M.A. With Topographical and Geographical Notes by Sir C. W. Wilson, K.C.B. 5 vols. small post 8vo. 17s. 6d.

Coxe's Memoirs of the Duke of Marlborough. 3 vols. With Portraits. Small post 8vo. 3s. 6d. each.

　　*** ATLAS OF THE PLANS OF MARLBOROUGH'S CAMPAIGNS. 4to. 10s. 6d.

────── **History of the House of Austria.** 4 vols. With Portraits. Small post 8vo. 3s. 6d. each.

Draper's History of the Intellectual Development of Europe. 2 vols. Small post 8vo. 3s. 6d. each.

Falckenberg's History of Modern Philosophy. Translated by Professor A. C. Armstrong. Demy 8vo. 16s.

Gibbon's Decline and Fall of the Roman Empire. Complete and Unabridged, with Variorum Notes. With Index, Maps, and Portrait. 7 vols. Small post 8vo. 3s. 6d. each.

Gregorovius's History of the City of Rome in the Middle Ages. Translated by Annie Hamilton. Crown 8vo. Vols. I., II., and III., each 6s. net. Vol. IV., in 2 parts, each 4s. 6d. net.

Guizot's History of Civilisation. Translated by W. Hazlitt. 3 vols. With Portraits. Small post 8vo. 3s. 6d. each.

Lamartine's History of the Girondists. 3 vols. With Portraits. Small post 8vo. 3s. 6d. each.

Machiavelli's History of Florence, the Prince, and other Works. With Portrait. Small post 8vo. 3s. 6d.

Martineau's (Harriet) History of England, from 1800-1815. Sm. post 8vo. 3s. 6d.

────── **History of the Thirty Years' Peace,** A.D. 1815-46. 4 vols. Small post 8vo. 3s. 6d. each.

Menzel's History of Germany. With Portraits. 3 vols. Small post 8vo. 3s. 6d. each.

Michelet's Luther's Autobiography. Translated by William Hazlitt. Small post 8vo. 3s. 6d.

—— **History of the French Revolution** from its earliest indications to the flight of the King in 1791. Small post 8vo. 3s. 6d.

Mignet's History of the French Revolution, from 1789 to 1814. With Portrait of Napoleon as First Consul. Small post 8vo. 3s. 6d.

Motley's Rise of the Dutch Republic. A new Edition, with Introduction by Moncure D. Conway. 3 vols. Small post 8vo. 3s. 6d. each.

Ranke's History of the Popes. Translated by E. Foster. 3 vols. With Portraits. Small post 8vo. 3s. 6d. each.

STANDARD BOOKS.

(See also ' Biography and History,' ' Poetry,' ' Fiction,' &c.)

Addison's Works. With the Notes of Bishop Hurd. Edited by H. G. Bohn. 6 vols. With Portrait and Plates. Small post 8vo. 3s. 6d. each.

Bacon's Essays, and Moral and Historical Works. Edited by J. Devey. With Portrait. Small post 8vo. 3s. 6d.

Bede's Ecclesiastical History, and the Anglo-Saxon Chronicle. Edited by Rev. Dr. Giles. With Map. Small post 8vo. 5s.

Browne's (Sir Thomas) Works. 3 vols. With Portrait. Small post 8vo. 3s. 6d. each.

Burke's Works and Speeches. 8 vols. Sm. post 8vo. 3s. 6d. each.

Burton's Anatomy of Melancholy. Edited, with Notes, by the Rev. A. R. Shilleto, M.A., and an Introduction by A. H. Bullen. 3 vols. Demy 8vo. with binding designed by Gleeson White, 31s. 6d. net. Also a Cheap Edition, in 3 vols. Small post 8vo. 3s. 6d. each.

Coleridge's Prose Works. Edited by T. Ashe. 6 vols. With Portrait. Small post 8vo. 3s. 6d. each.

Defoe's Novels and Miscellaneous Works. 7 vols. With Portrait. Small post 8vo. 3s. 6d. each.

Dunlop's History of Prose Fiction. Revised by Henry Wilson. 2 vols. Small post 8vo. 5s. each.

Emerson's Works. 3 vols. Small post 8vo. 3s. 6d. each.

Goldsmith's (O.) Works. Edited by J. W. M. Gibbs. 5 vols. With Portrait. Small post 8vo. 3s. 6d. each.

Gray's Letters. New Edition, by the Rev. D. C. Tovey, M.A.
[In the press.

Hazlitt (William). Lectures and Essays. 7 vols. Small post 8vo. 3s. 6d. each.

Irving (Washington). Complete Works. 15 vols. With Portraits, &c. Small post 8vo. 3s. 6d. each.

Lamb's Essays of Elia and Eliana. With Portrait. Small post
8vo. 3s. 6d.

Locke (John). Philosophical Works. Edited by J. A. St. John.
2 vols. With Portrait. Small post 8vo. 3s. 6d. each.

Mill (John Stuart). Essays. Collected from various sources by
J. W. M. Gibbs. Small post 8vo. 3s. 6d.

Milton's Prose Works. Edited by J. A. St. John. 5 vols. With
Portraits. Small post 8vo. 3s. 6d. each.

Prout's (Father) Reliques. By Rev. F. Mahony. Copyright edition.
With Etchings by Maclise. Small post 8vo. 5s.

Swift (Jonathan). Prose Works. With Introduction by W. E. H.
Lecky, M.P. In about 8 volumes. Small post 8vo. 3s. 6d. each.
[*Vols. I. and II. shortly.*

Walton's (Izaak) Angler. Edited by Edward Jesse. With 229
Engravings on Wood and Steel. Small post 8vo. 5s.

White's Natural History of Selborne. Edited by Edward Jesse.
With 40 Portraits and Coloured Plates. Small post 8vo. 5s.

Young (Arthur). Travels in France during the Years 1787-89.
Edited by M. Betham-Edwards. With Portrait. Small post 8vo. 3s. 6d.

—— Tour in Ireland during the years 1776-9. Edited by A.
W. Hutton, Librarian, National Liberal Club. With Bibliography by J. P.
Anderson. Index and Map. 2 vols. Small post 8vo., 3s. 6d. each.

———

Comte's Positive Philosophy. Translated and Condensed by
Harriet Martineau. New edition, with Introduction by Frederic Harrison.
3 vols. Small post 8vo. 5s. each.

—— Philosophy of the Sciences, being an Exposition of the
Principles of the 'Cours de Philosophie Positive.' By G. H. Lewes. With
Index. Small post 8vo. 5s.

Hegel's Philosophy of Right (Grundlinien der Philosophie des
Rechts). Translated by Samuel W. Dyde, M.A., D.Sc., Professor of Mental
Philosophy in Queen's University, Kingston, Canada. Crown 8vo. 7s. 6d.

Hugo (Victor). Dramatic Works. Hernani—Ruy Blas—The King's
Diversion. Translated by Mrs. Newton Crosland and F. L. Slons. Small
post 8vo. 3s. 6d.

—— Poems, chiefly Lyrical. Translated by various Writers, collected by J. H. L. Williams. With Portrait. Small post 8vo. 3s. 6d.

Molière's Dramatic Works. Translated by C. H. Wall. 3 vols.
With Portrait. Small post 8vo. 3s. 6d. each.

Montaigne's Essays. Cotton's Translation. Edited by W. C.
Hazlitt. 3 vols. Small post 8vo. 3s. 6d. each.

Montesquieu's Spirit of Laws. Translated by Dr. Nugent. Revised by J. V. Prichard. 2 vols. With Portrait. Small post 8vo. 3s. 6d. each.

Pascal's Thoughts. Translated by C. Kegan Paul. Small post
8vo. 3s. 6d.

Racine's Tragedies. Translated by R. Bruce Boswell. 2 vols. With
Portrait. Small post 8vo. 3s. 6d. each.

Goethe's Works. Including his Autobiography and Annals, Dramatic Works, Poems and Ballads, Novels and Tales, Wilhelm Meister's Apprenticeship and Travels, Tour in Italy, Miscellaneous Travels, Early and Miscellaneous Letters, Correspondence with Schiller and Zelter, and Conversations with Eckermann and Soret. Translated by J. Oxenford, Anna Swanwick, R, D. Boylan, E. A. Bowring, Sir Walter Scott, Edward Bell, L. Dora Schmitz, A. D. Coleridge, and A. Rogers. 16 vols. With Portraits. Small post 8vo. 3s. 6d. each.

———— **Faust.** German Text with Hayward's Prose Translation and Notes. Revised with Introduction by Dr. C. A. Buchheim. Sm. post 8vo. 5s.

Heine's Poems. Translated by E, A. Bowring. Sm. post 8vo. 3s. 6d.

———— **Travel-Pictures.** Translated by Francis Storr. With Map. Small post 8vo. 3s. 6d.

Lessing's Dramatic Works. Edited by Ernest Bell. 2 vols. With Portrait. Small post 8vo. 3s. 6d. each.

———— **Laokoon, Dramatic Notes, &c.** Translated by E. C. Beesley and Helen Zimmern. Edited by Edward Bell. With Frontispiece. Small post 8vo. 3s. 6d.

Richter (Jean Paul). Levana. Translated. Sm. post 8vo. 3s. 6d.

———— **Flower, Fruit, and Thorn Pieces (Siebenkäs).** Translated by Lieut.-Col. A. Ewing. Small post 8vo. 3s. 6d.

Schiller's Works. Including the History of the Seven Years' War, Revolt in the Netherlands, &c., Dramatic and Poetical Works, and Aesthetical and Philosophical Essays. Translated by Rev. A. J. W. Morrison, A. Lodge, E. A. Bowring, J. Churchill, S. T. Coleridge, Sir Theodore Martin, and others. 7 vols. With Portraits. Small post 8vo. 3s. 6d. each.

F. Schlegel's Lectures, and other Works. 5 vols. Small post 8vo. 3s. 6d. each.

A. W. Schlegel's Lectures on Dramatic Art and Literature. Translated by the Rev. A. J. W. Morrison. Small post 8vo. 3s. 6d.

Schopenhauer. On the Fourfold Root of the Principle of Sufficient Reason, and on the Will in Nature. Small post 8vo. 5s.

———— **Essays.** Selected and Translated by E. Belfort Bax. Small post 8vo. 5s.

Alfieri's Tragedies. Translated by E. A. Bowring. 2 vols. Small post 8vo. 3s. 6d. each.

Ariosto's Orlando Furioso, &c. Translated by W. S. Rose. 2 vols. With Portrait and 24 Steel Engravings. Small post 8vo. 5s. each.

Dante. Translated by Rev. H. F. Cary. With Portrait. Small post 8vo. 3s. 6d.

———— Translated by I. C. Wright. With Flaxman's Illustrations. Small post 8vo. 5s.

———— The Italian Text, with English Translation. The Inferno. By Dr. Carlyle. The Purgatorio. By W. S. Dugdale. Sm. post 8vo. 5s. each.

Petrarch's Sonnets, and other Poems. Translated by various hands. With Life by Thomas Campbell, and Portrait and 15 Steel Engravings. Small post 8vo. 5s.

Tasso's Jerusalem Delivered. Translated into English Spenserian
Verse by J. H. Wiffen. With Woodcuts and 8 Steel Engravings. Small
post 8vo. 5s.

Camoëns' Lusiad. Mickle's Translation revised by E. R. Hodges.
Small post 8vo. 3s. 6d.

Antoninus (Marcus Aurelius). The Thoughts of. Translated
literally, with Notes. Biographical Sketch, Introductory Essay on the
Philosophy, and Index. By George Long, M.A. New edition. Printed at
the Chiswick Press, on hand-made paper, and bound in buckram. Pott
8vo. 6s. (Or in *Bohn's Classical Library*, 3s. 6d.)

**Epictetus. The Discourses of, with the Encheiridion and Frag-
ments.** Translated, with Notes and Introduction, by George Long, M.A.
New edition, printed at the Chiswick Press, on hand-made paper, and bound
in buckram. 2 vols. Pott 8vo. 10s. 6d. (Or in *Bohn's Classical Library*,
1 vol., 5s.

Plato's Dialogues, referring to the Trial and Death of Socrates,
Euthyphro, The Apology, Crito and Phædo. Translated by the late William
Whewell, D.D. Printed at the Chiswick Press on hand-made paper, and
bound in buckram. Pott 8vo., 4s. 6d.

Plotinus, Select Works of. Translated by Thomas Taylor. Edited
by G. R. S. Mead, B.A., M.R.A.S. Small post 8vo. 5s.

Horace. The Odes and Carmen Saeculare. Translated into English
Verse by the late John Conington, M.A. 11th edition. Fcap. 8vo. 3s. 6d.

—— **The Satires and Epistles.** Translated into English Verse
by John Conington, M.A. 8th edition. 3s. 6d.

Dictionaries and Books of Reference.

Webster's International Dictionary of the English Language,
being the authentic edition of Webster's Unabridged Dictionary, comprising
the issues of 1847, 1864, and 1880, now thoroughly revised and enlarged under
the supervision of Noah Porter, D.D., LL.D., of Yale University, with
Valuable Literary Appendices. Medium 4to. 2118 pages, 3500 Woodcuts.
Cloth, 1l. 11s. 6d.; half calf, 2l. 2s.; half russia, 2l. 5s.; full calf, 2l. 8s.
Also in 2 vols. cloth, 1l. 14s.
> The Standard in the Postal Telegraph Department of the British Isles.
> The Standard in the United States Government Printing Office.
> Prospectuses with specimen pages sent free on application.

Webster's Brief International Dictionary. A Pronouncing Dictionary of the English Language. Abridged from Webster's International
Dictionary. With 800 Illustrations. Demy 8vo. 3s.

A Dictionary of Slang, Jargon, and Cant. By A. Barrère and
C. G. Leland. 2 vols. Medium 8vo. 7s. 6d. each.

A Biographical and Critical Dictionary of Painters and Engravers.
With a List of Ciphers, Monograms, and Marks. By Michael Bryan. Imperial 8vo. New edition, thoroughly revised and enlarged by R. E. Graves
(of the British Museum) and Walter Armstrong. 2 vols. Imperial 8vo.
buckram, 3l. 3s.

A Biographical Dictionary. Containing Concise Notices (upwards
of 15,000) of Eminent Persons of all Ages and Countries, and more particularly of Distinguished Natives of Great Britain and Ireland. By Thompson
Cooper, F.S.A. With a new Supplement, bringing the work down to 1883.
2 vols. Crown 8vo. 5s. each.

Kluge's Etymological Dictionary of the German Language.
Translated by J. F. Davis, D.Lit., M.A. Cheap Edition. Crown 4to. 7s. 6d.

Grimm's Teutonic Mythology. Translated from the 4th edition, with Notes and Appendix, by James Stephen Stallybrass. Demy 8vo. 4 Vols 8l. 8s.; Vols. I. to III. 15s. each; Vol. IV. (containing Additional Notes and References, and completing the Work), 18s.

French and English Dictionary. By F. E. A. Gasc. 6th edition. 8vo. cloth, 10s. 6d.

    A Pocket Dictionary. 16mo. 52nd Thousand. 2s. 6d.

Synonyms and Antonyms of the English Language. Collected and Contrasted. By the late Ven. C. J. Smith, M.A. Small post 8vo. 5s.

Synonyms Discriminated. A Dictionary of Synonymous Words in the English Language, showing the accurate signification of words of similar meaning. Illustrated with Quotations from Standard Writers. By Ven. C. J. Smith, M.A. Edited by the Rev. H. Percy Smith, M.A., of Balliol College, Oxford. Demy 8vo. 14s.

A History of Roman Literature. By Professor W. S. Teuffel. 5th edition, revised, with considerable Additions, by Professor L. Schwabe. Translated by G. C. W. Warr, M.A., Professor of Classical Literature at King's College, London. 2 vols. Medium 8vo. 15s. each.

Corpus Poetarum Latinorum, a se aliisque denuo recognitorum et brevi lectionum varietate instructorum, edidit Johannes Percival Postgate. Vol. I. Large post 4to. 21s. net. Or in 2 parts, paper wrappers, 9s. each net.
                                                      [Vol. II. preparing.

Lowndes' Bibliographer's Manual of English Literature. Enlarged edition, by H. G. Bohn. 6 vols. Small post 8vo. 5s. each; or 4 vols., half morocco, 2l. 2s.

A Dictionary of Roman Coins, Republican and Imperial. Commenced by the late Seth W. Stevenson, F.S.A., revised in part by C. Roach Smith, F.S.A., and completed by F. W. Madden, M.R.A.S. With upwards of 700 engravings on wood, chiefly executed by the late F. W. Fairholt, F.S.A. 8vo. 2l. 2s.

Henfrey's Guide to English Coins, from the Conquest to the present time. New and revised edition. By C. F. Keary, M.A., F.S.A. With an Historical Introduction by the Editor. Small post 8vo. 6s.

Humphreys' Coin Collector's Manual, or Guide to the Numismatic Student in the Formation of a Cabinet of Coins. By H. N. Humphreys. With Index and upwards of 140 Illustrations on Wood and Steel. 2 vols. Small post 8vo. 5s. each.

Clark's Introduction to Heraldry. 18th edition. Revised and Enlarged by J. R. Planché, Rouge Croix. With nearly 1000 Illustrations. Small post 8vo. 5s.; or with the Illustrations Coloured, half-morocco, roxburgh, 15s.

ART AND ARCHÆOLOGY.

Sir Edward Burne-Jones, Bart. A Record and Review. By Malcolm Bell. Illustrated with over 100 Reproductions of the most popular pictures by the Artist; including many paintings and drawings hitherto unpublished, and a representative selection of his designs for stained glass, tapestry, &c. With full and complete lists of his finished works and of his cartoons. 3rd edition, with binding designed by Gleeson White. Small Colombier 8vo. 21s. net.

Albert Moore: his Life and Works. By A. Lys Baldry. Illustrated with 10 Photogravures and about 70 other Reproductions. Small Colombier 8vo. with binding by Gleeson White, 21s. net.

Sir Frederic Leighton, Bart., P.R.A. An Illustrated Chronicle. Py Ernest Rhys. With Introduction by F. G. Stephens. Illustrated with 15 Photogravures and 100 other Reproductions. Super royal 4to. 3*l*. 3*s*.

The Art of Velasquez. A Critical Study. By R. A. M. Stevenson. With 20 Photogravures and 50 other Illustrations. Small royal 4to. 2*l*. 5*s*. net.

Raphael's Madonnas, and other Great Pictures. Reproduced from the Original Paintings. With a Life of Raphael, and an Account of his Chief Works. By Karl Károly. With 54 Illustrations, including 9 Photogravures. Small Colombier 8vo. 21*s*. net.

Masterpieces of the Great Artists A.D. 1400-1700. By Mrs. Arthur Bell (N. D'Anvers). With 43 full-page Illustrations, including 8 Photogravures. Small Colombier 8vo. 21*s*. net.

Men and Women of the Century. Being a Collection of Portraits and Sketches by Mr. Rudolf Lehmann. Edited, with Introduction and Biographical Notices, by H. C. Marillier, B.A. With 12 Photogravures and 70 facsimile reproductions in Half-tone, some printed in Colour, and all executed and printed by the Swan Electric Engraving Co. Medium 4to. 3*l*. 3*s*.

Richard Cosway, R.A., and his Companions. With numerous Illustrations. By George C. Williamson, Lit.D. Small Colombier 8vo.

Bell (Sir C.) The Anatomy and Philosophy of Expression as Connected with the Fine Arts. By Sir Charles Bell, K.H. 7th edition, revised. Small post 8vo. 5*s*.

Bell's Cathedral Series. A new Series of Handbooks on the great Cathedrals. Edited by Gleeson White and E. F. Strange. Well illustrated. Cloth, 1*s*. 6*d*. each.
*** *Illustrated list on application.*

Bloxam (M. H.) The Principles of Gothic Ecclesiastical Architecture. By M. H. Bloxam. With numerous Woodcuts by Jewitt. 11th edition. Crown 8vo. 2 vols. 15*s*. Companion Volume on CHURCH VESTMENTS. 7*s*. 6*d*.

Bryan's Biographical and Critical Dictionary of Painters and Engravers. With a List of Cyphers, Monograms, and Marks. By Michael Bryan. New edition, thoroughly revised and enlarged by R. E. Graves, of the British Museum, and Walter Armstrong, R.A. 2 vols. imperial 8vo. buckram, 3*l*. 3*s*.

Burn (R.) Ancient Rome and its Neighbourhood. An Illustrated Handbook to the Ruins in the City and the Campagna. By Robert Burn, M.A., Fellow of Trinity College, Cambridge, Author of 'Rome and the Campagna,' &c. With numerous Illustrations. 7*s*. 6*d*.
*** *This volume is also issued in limp red cloth, with Map Pocket, for the convenience of Travellers.*

Connoisseur Series. Edited by Gleeson White.

 Hiatt (C. T. J.) Picture Posters. A Handbook on the History of the Illustrated Placard. With numerous Reproductions of the most artistic examples of all countries. By C. T. J. Hiatt. 8vo. 12*s*. 6*d*. net.

 Strange (E. F.) Japanese Illustration. A History of the Arts of Woodcutting and Colour Printing in Japan. By Edward F. Strange, M.J.S. With 8 Coloured Plates and 88 other Illustrations. Demy 8vo. 12*s*. 6*d*. net.

 Watson (R. M.) The Art of the House. By Rosamund Wheatley, F.S.A. With numerous Reproductions. Deny 8vo. 6*s*. net. Marriott Watson. Illustrated. Demy 8vo. 6*s*. net.

 Wheatley (H. B.) English Historical Portraits. By H. B.

A 2

Cunningham s Lives of the Most Eminent British Painters. A new edition, with Notes and Sixteen fresh Lives. By Mrs. Heaton. 3 vols. small post 8vo. 3s. 6d. each.

Delamotte (P. H.) The Art of Sketching from Nature. By P. H. Delamotte. Illustrated by 24 Woodcuts and 20 Coloured Plates, arranged progressively, from Water-colour Drawings by Prout, E. W. Cooke, R.A., Girtin, Varley, De Wint, and the Author. New edition. Royal 4to. 21s.

Demmin's Illustrated History of Arms and Armour, from the Earliest Period. By Auguste Demmin. Translated by C. C. Black, M.A., Assistant Keeper, South Kensington Museum. With nearly 000 Illustrations. Small post 8vo. 7s. 6d.

Didron's Christian Iconography. A History of Christian Art in the Middle Ages. Translated from the French, with additions, &c., by Margaret Stokes. 2 vols. small post 8vo. 5s. each.

Ex-Libris Series. Edited by Gleeson White.

   English Book-Plates (Ancient and Modern). By Egerton Castle, M.A., F.S.A. With more than 200 Illustrations. 3rd edition. 10s. 6d. net.

   French Book-Plates. By Walter Hamilton. With nearly 200 Illustrations. 2nd edition, revised and enlarged. 8s. 6d. net.

   German Book-Plates. By Dr. Heinrich Pallmann and G. Ravenscroft Dennis. With numerous Illustrations. [*Preparing.*

   American Book-Plates. By Charles Dexter Allen. With Bibliography by Eben Newell Hewins, and numerous Illustrations. 12s. 6d. net.

   Ladies' Book-Plates. By Norna Labouchere. With numerous Illustrations. 8s. 6d. net.

   Printers' Marks. By W. Roberts, Editor of the 'Bookworm,' &c. With about 250 Examples. 7s. 6d. net.

   The Decorative Illustration of Books. By Walter Crane. With more than 150 Illustrations. 10s. 6d. net.

   Modern Book Illustration. By Joseph Pennell. With 172 Illustrations. 10s. 6d. net.

   Bookbindings, Old and New. By Brander Matthews. With numerous Illustrations. 7s. 6d. net.

   Decorative Heraldry. By G. W. Eve. [*Preparing.*

   Durer's Little Passion. Printed from stereotypes taken from the original wood-blocks. With Introduction by Austin Dobson, and Photogravure Portrait of Dürer, by himself. 5s. net.

Fairholt's Costume in England. A History of Dress to the end of the Eighteenth Century. 3rd edition. Revised by the Hon. H. A. Dillon, F.S.A. Illustrated with above 700 Engravings. 2 vols. sm. post 8vo. 5s. each.

Flaxman's Classical Compositions, reprinted in a cheap form for the use of Art Students. Oblong demy, paper cover, 2s. 6d. each.

   THE ILIAD OF HOMER, 39 Designs. THE ODYSSEY OF HOMER, 34 Designs. THE TRAGEDIES OF AESCHYLUS, 36 Designs. THE WORKS AND DAYS AND THEOGONY OF HESIOD, 37 Designs. SELECT COMPOSITIONS FROM DANTE'S DIVINE DRAMA. 37 Designs. Oblong, paper cover, 2s. 6d.

Flaxman. Lectures on Sculpture. as delivered before the President and Members of the Royal Academy. By J. Flaxman, R.A. With 53 Plates. New edition. Small post 8vo. 6s.

Gatty (Mrs.) The Book of Sun-dials. Collected by Mrs. Alfred Gatty, Author of 'Parables from Nature,' &c. Edited by Horatio K. F. Eden and Eleanor Lloyd. With numerous Illustrations. 3rd edition. Fcap. 4to. 15s.

Heaton (Mrs.) A Concise History of Painting. By Mrs. Charles Heaton. New edition, revised, by Cosmo Monkhouse. Small post 8vo. 5s.

Lanzi's History of Painting in Italy, from the Period of the Revival of the Fine Arts to the End of the Eighteenth Century. With a Biographical Notice of the Author, Indexes, and Portraits. Translated by Thomas Roscoe. 3 vols. small post 8vo. 3s. 6d. each.

Law (E.) The History of Hampton Court Palace. Profusely Illustrated with Copper-plates, Autotypes, Etchings, Engravings, Maps, and Plans. By Ernest Law, B.A. In 3 vols. fcap. 4to. Vol. I.—IN TUDOR TIMES, 21s.; Vol. II.—IN STUART TIMES, 21s.; Vol. III.—IN ORANGE AND GUELPH TIMES, 21s.
** Vol. II. will be sold in sets only. Vols. I. and III. may be obtained separately.

Leonardo da Vinci's Treatise on Painting. With a Life of Leonardo. New edition, revised, with numerous Plates. Small post 8vo. 5s.

Moody (F. W.) Lectures and Lessons on Art. By the late F. W. Moody, Instructor in Decorative Art at South Kensington Museum. With Diagrams to illustrate Composition and other matters. 5th edition. Demy 8vo. sewed, 4s. 6d.

Patmore (C.) Principle in Art. By Coventry Patmore. 2nd edition. Fcap. 8vo. 5s.

Petit (J. T.) Architectural Studies in France. By the late Rev. J. T. Petit, F.S.A. New edition, revised by Edward Bell, M.A., F.S.A. Fcap. 4to. with 260 Illustrations, 15s. net.

Planché's History of British Costume, from the Earliest Time to the close of the Eighteenth Century. By J. R. Planché, Somerset Herald. With Index and upwards of 400 Illustrations. Small post 8vo. 5s.

Renton (E.) Intaglio Engraving, Past and Present. By Edward Renton. With numerous Illustrations from Gems and Seals. Fcap. 8vo. 3s. 6d.

Roberts (W.) Memorials of Christie's. By W. Roberts. With 64 Collotype Reproductions and Coloured Frontispiece. 2 vols. 8vo. 25s. net.

Stokes (Margaret). Three Months in the Forests of France. A Pilgrimage in Search of Vestiges of the Irish Saints in France. With numerous Illustrations. By Margaret Stokes, Hon. M.R.I.A. Fcap. 4to. 12s. net.

Strange (E. F.) Alphabets. A Handbook of Lettering for the use of Artists, Architects, and Students. With 200 Illustrations. Crown 8vo. 5s.

Vasari's Lives of the Most Eminent Painters, Sculptors, and Architects. Translated by Mrs. J. Foster, with Notes, Index, and Portrait. 6 vols. small post 8vo. 3s. 6d. each.

Way (T. R.) Reliques of Old London. Drawn in lithography by T. R. Way. With Introduction and Explanatory Letterpress by H. B. Wheatley, F.S.A. Small 4to. 21s. net.

Wedmore (F.) Etching in England. By Frederick Wedmore. With numerous Illustrations. Small 4to. 8s. 6d. net.

White (Gleeson). Practical Designing. A Handbook on the Preparation of Working Drawings, showing the Technical Methods employed in preparing them for the Manufacture, and the Limits imposed on the Design by the Mechanism of Reproduction and the materials employed. Freely Illustrated. Edited by Gleeson White. 2nd edition. 6s. net.

THEOLOGY.

À Kempis. On the Imitation of Christ. A New Translation.
By the Rt. Rev. R. Goodwin, D.D. 3rd edition. With fine Steel Engraving after Guido, 3s. 6d.; without the Engraving, 2s. 6d. Cheap edition, 1s. cloth; 6d. sewed.

Alford (Dean). The Greek Testament. With a critically revised
Text; a Digest of various Readings; Marginal References to Verbal and Idiomatic Usage; Prolegomena; and a Critical and Exegetical Commentary. For the Use of Theological Students and Ministers. By the late Henry Alford, D.D., Dean of Canterbury. 4 vols. 8vo. 5l. 2s. Sold separately.

———— **The New Testament for English Readers. Containing the**
Authorised Version, with additional Corrections of Readings and Renderings, Marginal References, and a Critical and Explanatory Commentary. In 4 Parts, 2l. 14s. 6d. Sold separately.

Augustine (St.): De Civitate Dei. Books XI. and XII. By the
Rev. Henry Gee, B.D., F.S.A. I. Text only, 2s. II. Introduction, Literal Translation, and Notes, 3s.

———— **In Joannis Evangelium Tractatus. XXIV.-XXVII. Edited**
by the Rev. Henry Gee, B.D., F.S.A., 1s. 6d. Also the Translation by the late Rev. Canon H. Brown, 1s. 6d.

Barrett (A. C.) Companion to the Greek Testament. For the
Use of Theological Students and the Upper Forms in schools. By A. C. Barrett, M.A., Caius College. 5th edition, revised. Fcap. 8vo. 5s.

Barry (Dr.) Notes on the Catechism. For the Use of Schools.
By the Rev. Canon Barry, D.D., Principal of King's College, London. 10th edition. Fcap. 2s.

Birks (T. R.) Horæ Evangelicæ, or the Internal Evidence of the
Gospel History. By the Rev. T. R. Birks, M.A., late Hon. Canon of Ely. Edited by the Rev. H. A. Birks, M.A., late Scholar of Trin. Coll., Camb. Demy 8vo. 10s. 6d.

Bleek (F.) An Introduction to the Old Testament. By Friedrich
Bleek. Edited by Johann Bleek and Adolf Kamphausen. Translated from the Second Edition of the German by G. H. Venables, under the supervision of the Rev. E. Venables, Residentiary Canon of Lincoln. 2nd edition, with Corrections. With Index. 2 vols. 10s.

Burbidge (Rev. E.) Liturgies and Offices of the Church for the use
of English Readers, in illustration of the Growth and Devotional value of the Book of Common Prayer, with a Catalogue of the remains of the Library of Archbishop Cranmer. By Edward Burbidge, M.A., Prebendary of Wells. Cr. 8vo. 9s.

———— **The Parish Priest's Book of Offices and Instructions for**
the Sick: with Appendix of Readings and Occasional Offices. 4th edition, thoroughly revised, with much additional matter. Small post 8vo. 3s. 6d.

Burgon (Dean). The Traditional Text of the Holy Gospels
Vindicated and Established. By the late John William Burgon, B.D., Dean of Chichester. Arranged, Completed, and Edited by Edward Miller, M.A., Wykehamical Prebendary of Chichester. Demy 8vo. 10s. 6d. net.

———— **The Causes of the Corruption of the Traditional Text of**
the Holy Gospels. Edited by the Rev. Edward Miller, M.A. Demy 8vo. 10s. 6d. net.

Denton (W.) A Commentary on the Gospels and Epistles for the Sundays and other Holy Days of the Christian Year, and on the Acts of the Apostles. By the Rev. W. Denton, M.A., Worcester College, Oxford, and Incumbent of St. Bartholomew's, Cripplegate. In 7 vols. each 9s.

Eusebius. Ecclesiastical History. Translated by Rev. C. F. Cruse, 5s.

Garnier (T. P.) Church or Dissent? An Appeal to Holy Scripture, addressed to Dissenters. By T. P. Garnier, late Fellow of All Souls' College, Oxford. 2nd edition. Crown 8vo. 2s. ; in stiff paper cover for distribution, 1s.

Hardwick (C.) History of the Articles of Religion. By Charles Hardwick. 3rd edition revised. 5s.

Hawkins (Canon). Family Prayers:—Containing Psalms, Lessons, and Prayers, for every Morning and Evening in the Week. By the late Rev. Ernest Hawkins, B.D., Prebendary of St. Paul's. 20th edition. Fcap. 8vo. 1s.

Hook (W. F.) Short Meditations for Every Day in the Year. Edited by the late Very Rev W. F. Hook, D.D., Dean of Chichester. Revised edition. 2 vols. Fcap. 8vo. Large type. 11s. Also 2 vols. 32mo. Cloth, 5s.; calf, gilt edges, 9s.

—— The Christian Taught by the Church's Services. Revised edition. Fcap. 8vo. Large type, 6s. 6d. Royal 32mo. Cloth, 2s. 6d. calf, gilt edges, 4s. 6d.

—— Holy Thoughts and Prayers, arranged for Daily Use on each Day of the Week, according to the stated Hours of Prayer. 8th edition. 16mo. Cloth, red edges, 2s; calf, gilt edges, 3s. Cheap edition, 3d.

Humphry (W. G.) An Historical and Explanatory Treatise on the Book of Common Prayer. By W. G. Humphry, B.D., late Fellow of Trinity College, Cambridge, Prebendary of St. Paul's, and Vicar of St. Martin's-in-the-Fields. 6th edition. Fcap. 8vo. 1s,

Latham (H.) Pastor Pastorum; or, the Schooling of the Apostles by our Lord. By the Rev. Henry Latham, M.A., Master of Trinity Hall, Cambridge. 3rd edition. Crown 8vo. 6s. 6d.

—— A Service of Angels. Crown 8vo. 3s. 6d.

Lewin (T.) The Life and Epistles of St. Paul. By Thomas Lewin, M.A., F.S.A., Trinity College, Oxford, Barrister-at-Law. 5th edition. Illustrated with numerous fine Engravings on Wood, Maps, and Plans. 2 vols. Demy 4to. 2l. 2s.

Miller (E.) Guide to the Textual Criticism of the New Testament. By Rev. E. Millar, M.A. Oxon, Rector of Bucknell, Bicester. Crown 8vo. 4s.

Monsell (Dr.) Watches by the Cross. Short Meditations, Hymns, and Litanies on the Last Seven Words of our Lord. 4th edition. Cloth, red edges, 1s.

—— Near Home at Last. A Poem. 10th thousand. Cloth, red edges. Imp. 32mo. 2s. 6d.

—— Our New Vicar; or, Plain Words about Ritual and Parish Work. Fcap. 8vo. 11th edition, 2s. 6d.

—— The Winton Church Catechism. Questions and Answers on the Teaching of the Church Catechism. 4th edition. 32mo. cloth, 3s.

Neander (Angustus.) History of the Christian Religion and Church. Translated by J. Torrey. 10 vols. small post 8vo. 3s. 6d. each.

—— Life of Jesus Christ, in its Historical Connexion and Development. Translated by J. M'Clintock and C. Blumenthal. Sm. post 8vo.[3s.;6d.

—— History of the Planting and Training of the Christian Church by the Apostles. Together with the Antignostikus, or Spirit of Tertullian. Translated by J. E. Ryland. 2 vols. small post 8vo. 3s. 6d.;each.

—— Lectures on the History of Christian Dogmas. Edited by Dr. Jacobi. Translated by J. E. Ryland. 2 vols. small post 8vo. 3s. 6d. each.

—— Memorials of Christian Life in the Early and Middle Ages. Translated by J. E. Ryland. Small post 8vo, 3s. 6d.

Pascal. The Thoughts of Blaise Pascal. Translated from the Text of M. Auguste Molinier by C. Kegan Paul. 3s. 6d.

Perowne (Bp.) The Book of Psalms: a New Translation, with Introductions and Notes, Critical and Explanatory. By the Right Rev. J. J. Stewart Perowne, D.D., Bishop of Worcester. 8vo. Vol. I. 8th edition, revised, 18s. Vol. II. 8th edition, revised, 16s.

—— The Book of Psalms. An abridged Edition for Schools and Private Students. Crown 8vo. 8th edition, 10s. 6d.

Pearson (Bp.) Exposition of the Creed. Edited by E. Walford, M.A. 5s.

Prudentius. Selected Passages, with Verse Translations on the opposite pages. By the Rev. F. St. John Thackeray, late Assistant Master, Eton College. Crown 8vo. 7s. 6d.

Sadler (M. F.) The Gospel of St. Matthew. By the Rev. M. F. Sadler, Rector of Honiton and Prebendary of Wells. With Notes, Critical and Practical, and Two Maps. 6th edition. Crown 8vo. 7s. 6d.

—— The Gospel of St. Mark. 4th edition. Crown 8vo. 7s. 6d.

—— The Gospel of St. Luke. 4th edition. Crown 8vo. 9s.

—— The Gospel of St. John. 6th edition. Crown 8vo. 7s. 6d.

—— The Acts of the Apostles. 4th edition. Crown 8vo. 7s. 6d.

—— St. Paul's Epistle to the Romans. 3rd edition. Crown 8vo. 7s. 6d.

—— St. Paul's Epistles to the Corinthians. 2nd edition. Crown 8vo. 7s. 6d.

—— St. Paul's Epistles to the Galatians, Ephesians, and Philippians. 3rd edition. Crown 8vo. 6s.

—— St. Paul's Epistles to the Colossians, Thessalonians, and Timothy. 2nd edition. Crown 8vo. 6s.

—— St. Paul's Epistles to Titus, Philemon, and the Hebrews. 2nd edition. Crown 8vo. 6s.

—— The Epistles of SS. James, Peter, John, and Jude. 2nd edition. Crown 8vo. 6s.

—— The Revelation of St. John the Divine. With Notes Critical and Practical, and Introduction. 2nd edition. 6s.

—— Sermon Outlines for the Clergy and Lay Preachers, arranged to accord with the Church's Year. 2nd edition. Crown 8vo. 5s.

Sadler (M. F.) Church Divine—Bible Truth. 49th thousand. Fcap. 8vo. 3s. 6d.

'The objective nature of the faith, the Athanasian Creed, the Baptismal Services, the Holy Eucharist, Absolution and the Priesthood, Church Government and Confirmation, are some of the more prominent subjects treated. And Mr. Sadler handles each with a marked degree of sound sense, and with a thorough mastery of his subject.'—*Guardian.*

—— **The Church Teacher's Manual of Christian Instruction.** Being the Church Catechism expanded and explained in Question and Answer, for the use of Clergymen, Parents, and Teachers. 46th thousand. Fcap. 8vo. 2s. 6d.

—— **Confirmation.** An Extract from the Church Teacher's Manual. 70th thousand. 1d.

—— **The One Offering.** A Treatise on the Sacrificial Nature of the Eucharist. Fcap. 8vo. 11th thousand, 2s. 6d.

—— **The Second Adam and the New Birth;** or, the Doctrine of Baptism as contained in Holy Scripture. 12th edition. Fcap. 8vo. 4s. 6d.

—— **Justification of Life:** its Nature, Antecedents, and Results. 2nd edition, revised. Crown 8vo. 4s. 6d.

—— **The] Sacrament of Responsibility;** or, Testimony of the Scripture to the Teaching of the Church on Holy Baptism, with especial reference to the Cases of Infants; and Answers to Objections. 9th thousand, 6d. With an Introduction and an Appendix. On fine paper, bound in cloth, 7th edition, 2s. 6d.

—— **Scripture Truths.** A Series of Ten Tracts on Holy Baptism, The Holy Communion, Ordination, &c. 9d. per set. Sold separately.

—— **The Communicant's Manual;** being a Book of Self-examination, Prayer, Praise, and Thanksgiving. Royal 32mo. 114th thousand. Cloth, 1s. 6d.; roan, gilt edges, 2s. 6d.; padded calf, 5s. A Cheap edition in limp cloth, 8d.

—— —— **A Larger Edition** on fine paper, red rubics. Fcap. 8vo. 2s. 6d.

Scrivener (Dr.) Novum Testamentum Græce Textus Stephanici, A.D. 1550. Accedunt variæ lectiones editionum Bezæ, Elzeviri, Lachmanni, Tischendorfii, Tregellesii, curante F. H. Scrivener, A.M., D.C.L., LL.D 16mo. 4s. 6d.—EDITIO MAJOR. Small post 8vo. 2nd edition. 7s. 6d.—An Edition with wide Margin for Notes. 4to. half bound, 12s.

—— **A Plain Introduction to the Criticism of the New Testament.** For the Use of Biblical Students. 4th edition, revised and enlarged by the Rev. E. Miller, M A., formerly Fellow and Tutor of New College, Oxford. With Portrait and numerous Lithographed Facsimiles of MSS. Demy 8vo. 2 vols. 32s.

Socrates' and Sozomen's Ecclesiastical Histories. Translated from the Greek. 2 vols. 5s. each.

Steere (E.) Notes of Sermons, arranged in Accordance with the Church's Year. Edited by Rev. R. M. Heanley, M.A. Oxon. With Introduction by the Bishop of Lincoln. Crown 8vo. 3rd Series, 7s. 6d.

Theodoret and Evagrius. Histories of the Church. Translated from the Greek. 5s.

Young (Rev. P.) Daily Readings for a Year on the Life of Our Lord and Saviour Jesus Christ. By the Rev. Peter Young, M.A. 6th edition. 2 vols. 8vo. 1l. 1s.

ROYAL NAVY HANDBOOKS.

Edited by Commander CHARLES N. ROBINSON, R.N.

'The series of Naval Handbooks edited by Commander Robinson has made a most hopeful beginning, and may be counted upon to supply the growing popular demand for information in regard to the Navy, on which the national existence depends.'—*Times.*

Crown 8vo. Illustrated, 5s. each.

Naval Administration: the Constitution, Character, and Functions of the Board of Admiralty and of the Civil Departments it Directs. By Admiral Sir R. Vesey Hamilton, G.C.B., late First Sea Lord of the Admiralty.

The Mechanism of Men-of-War: being a Description of the Machinery to be found in Modern Fighting Ships. By Fleet Engineer Reginald C. Oldknow, R.N.

Torpedoes and Torpedo-Vessels. With a Chapter on the Effects of Torpedo Warfare, by one who was present at the Yalu and Weihaiwei. By Lieutenant G. E. Armstrong, late R.N.

Naval Ordnance and Small Arms. With the Methods of Mounting Guns on Board Modern Men-of-War. By Captain H. Garbett, R.N.

Other Volumes in Preparation.

BOTANY.

By J. G. BAKER, F.R.S., F.L.S., Keeper of the Herbarium of the Royal Gardens, Kew.

A Flora of the English Lake District. Demy 8vo. 7s. 6d.

Handbook of the Fern Allies. A Synopsis of the Genera and Species of the Natural Orders, Equisetaceae, Lycopodiaceae, Selaginellaceae, Rhizocarpeae. Demy 8vo. 5s.

Handbook of the Amaryllideae, including the Alstroemerieae and Agaveae. Demy 8vo. 5s.

Handbook of the Bromeliaceae. Demy 8vo. 5s.

Handbook of the Irideae. Demy 8vo. 5s.

English Botany. Containing a Description and Life-size Drawing of every British Plant. Edited by T. Boswell (formerly Syme), LL.D., F.L.S., &c. The Figures by J. C. Sowerby, F.L.S., J. De C. Sowerby F.L.S., J. W. Salter, A.L.S., F.G.S., and J. E. Sowerby. 3rd edition, entirely revised, with descriptions of all the species by the Editor, and 1937 full-page Coloured Plates. In 12 vols. 24l. 3s. cloth; 27l. 15s. half morocco; and 31l. 13s. whole morocco. Also in 89 parts, 5s. each, except part 89, containing an Index to the whole work, 7s. 6d. Volumes sold separately.

** A Supplement to the third edition is now in preparation. Vol. I. (Vol. XIII. of the complete work) containing orders I. to XL., by N. E. Brown, of the Royal Herbarium, Kew, now ready, 17s. Or in three parts, 5s. each.

Johnson's Gardener's Dictionary. Describing the Plants, Fruits, and Vegetables desirable for the Garden, and explaining the Terms and Operations employed in their cultivation. New edition (1893-4), revised by C. H. Wright, F.R.M.S., and D. Dewar, Curator of the Botanic Gardens, Glasgow. Demy 8vo. 9s. net.

British Fungus-Flora. A Classified Text-book of Mycology. By George Massee. With numerous Illustrations. 4 vols. Post 8vo. 7s. 6d. each.

Botanist's Pocket-Book. By W. R. Hayward. Containing the botanical name, common name, soil or situation, colour, growth, and time of flowering of all plants, arranged in a tabulated form. 8th edition, revised, with a new Appendix. Fcap. 8vo. 4s. 6d.

Index of British Plants, according to the London Catalogue (8th edition), including the Synonyms used by the principal authors, an alphabetical list of English names; also references to the illustrations of Symc's 'English Botany' and Bentham's 'British Flora.' By Robert Turnbull. Paper, 2s. 6d.; cloth, 3s.

The London Catalogue of British Plants. Part I., containing the British Phaenogamia, Filices, Equisetaceae, Lycopodiaceae, Selaginellaceae, Marsileaceae, and Characeae. 9th edition. Demy 8vo. 6d.; interleaved, in limp cloth, 1s.

ECONOMICS AND FINANCE.

The Case against Bimetallism. By Sir Robert Giffen, C.B., LL.D. 4th edition. Crown 8vo. 7s. 6d.

The Growth of Capital. By the same author. Demy 8vo. 7s. 6d.

Ricardo on the Principles of Political Economy and Taxation. Edited by E. C. K. Gonner, M.A., Lecturer, University College, Liverpool. Sm. post 8vo. 5s.

Smith (Adam). The Wealth of Nations. Edited by E. Belfort Bax. 2 vols. Sm. post 8vo. 7s.

The History, Principles, and Practice of Banking. By the late J. W. Gilbart, F.R.S., formerly Director and General Manager of the London and Westminster Bank. New edition, revised by A. S. Michie, of the Royal Bank of Scotland, Glasgow. 2 vols. small post 8vo. 10s.

SPORTS AND GAMES.

Bohn's Handbooks of Athletic Sports. In 8 vols. Sm. post 8vo. 3s. 6d. each.

Vol. I.—Cricket, by Hon. and Rev. E. Lyttelton. Lawn Tennis, by H. W. W. Wilberforce. Tennis, Rackets, and Fives, by Julian Marshall, Major Spens, and Rev. J. A. Tait. Golf, by W. T. Linskill. Hockey, by F. S. Creswell.

Vol. II.—Rowing and Sculling, by W. B. Woodgate. Sailing, by E. F. Knight. Swimming, by M. and J. R. Cobbett.

Vol. III.—Boxing, by R. G. Allanson-Winn. Broadsword and Single Stick, with chapters on Quarterstaff, Bayonet, Cudgel, Shillalah, Walking-Stick, and Umbrella, by R. G. Allanson-Winn and C. Phillipps-Wolley. Wrestling, by Walter Armstrong. Fencing, by H. A. Colmore Dunn.

Vol. IV.—Rugby Football, by Harry Vassall. Association Football, by C. W. Alcock. Baseball, by Newton Crane. Rounders, Bowls, Quoits, Curling, Skittles, &c., by C. C. Mott and J. M. Walker.

Vol. V.—Cycling and Athletics, by H. H. Griffin. Skating, by Douglas Adams.

Vol. VI.—Practical Horsemanship, including Riding for Ladies, by W. A. Kerr, V.C.

Vol. VII.—Camping Out, by A. A. Macdonald. Canoeing, by Dr. J. D. Hayward.

Vol. VIII.—Gymnastics, by A. F. Jenkin. Clubs, by G. T. B. Cobbett and A. F. Jenkin.

Bohn's Handbooks of Games. New edition. In 2 vols. Small post 8vo. 3s. 6d. each.

Vol. I.—TABLE GAMES : Billiards, with Pool, Pyramids, and Snooker, by Major-General A. W. Drayson, F.R.A.S., with a preface by W. J. Peall. Bagatelle, by 'Berkeley.' Chess, by R. F. Green. Draughts, Backgammon, Dominoes, Solitaire, Reversi, Go-Bang, Rouge et Noir, Roulette, E.O., Hazard, Faro, by 'Berkeley.'

Vol. II.—CARD GAMES : Whist, by Dr. William Pole, F.R.S., Author of 'The Philosophy of Whist,' &c. Solo Whist, by R. F. Green. Piquet, Ecarté, Euchre, Bézique, and Cribbage, by 'Berkeley.' Poker, Loo, Vingt-ot-un, Napoleon, Newmarket, Pope Joan, Speculation, &c. &c., by Baxter-Wray.

Morphy's Games of Chess, being the Matches and best Games played by the American Champion, with explanatory and analytical Notes by J. Löwenthal. With short Memoir and Portrait of Morphy. Sm. post 8vo. 5s.

Staunton's Chess-Player's Handbook. A Popular and Scientific Introduction to the Game. With numerous diagrams. 5s.

——— **Chess Praxis.** A Supplement to the Chess-player's Handbook. Containing the most important modern improvements in the Openings; Code of Chess Laws; and a Selection of Morphy's Games. Small post 8vo. 5s.

——— **Chess-Player's Companion.** Comprising a Treatise on Odds, Collection of Match Games, and a Selection of Original Problems. With coloured Frontispiece. Small post 8vo. 5s.

Chess Studies and End-Games. In Two Parts. Part I. Chess Studies. Part II. Miscellaneous End-Games. By B. Horwitz and J. Kling. 2nd edition, revised by the Rev. W. Wayte, M.A. Demy 8vo. 7s. 6d.

Hints on Billiards. By J. P. Buchanan. Illustrated with 36 Diagrams. Crown 8vo. 3s. 6d.

Sturges's Guide to the Game of Draughts. With Critical Situations. Revised, with Additional Play on the Modern Openings, by J. A. Kear, Editor of 'The International Draught Magazine.' Crown 8vo. 3s. 6d.

Hints on Driving. By Captain C. Morley Knight, R.A. Illustrated by G. H. A. White, Royal Artillery. 2nd edition, revised and enlarged. Crown 8vo. 3s. 6d.

Golf, in Theory and Practice. Hints to beginners. By H. S. C. Everard, St. Andrew's. With 22 Illustrations. Crown 8vo. 3s. 6d.

Half-Hours with an Old Golfer; a Pot-pourri for Golfers. By Calamo Currente. With 40 Illustrations and 4 Coloured Plates by G. A. Laundy. Crown 8vo. gilt extra, 5s.

Schools and Masters of Fence, from the Middle Ages to the Eighteenth Century. With a Sketch of the Development of the Art of Fencing with the Rapier and the Small Sword, and a Bibliography of the Fencing Art during that Period. By Egerton Castle, M.A. With numerous Illustrations. 2nd edition. Small post 8vo. 6s.

Oars and Sculls, and How to Use them. By W. B. Woodgate, M.A., Brasenose College, Oxford. Crown 8vo. 2s. 6d.

Dancing as an Art and Pastime. With 40 full-page illustrations from life. By Edward Scott. Crown 8vo. 6s.

THE ALL-ENGLAND SERIES.

HANDBOOKS OF ATHLETIC GAMES.

The only Series issued at a moderate price, by Writers who are in the first rank in their respective departments.

'The best instruction on games and sports by the best authorities, at the lowest prices.'—*Oxford Magazine.*

Small 8vo. cloth, Illustrated. Price 1s. each.

Cricket. By the Hon. and Rev. E. LYTTELTON.

Lawn Tennis. By H. W. W. WILBERFORCE. With a Chapter for Ladies, by Mrs. HILLYARD.

Tennis and Rackets and Fives. By JULIAN MARSHALL, Major J. SPENS, and Rev. J. A. ARNAN TAIT.

Golf. By W. T. LINSKILL.

Rowing and Sculling. By W. B. WOODGATE.

Sailing. By E. F. KNIGHT, dbl.vol. 2s.

Swimming. By MARTIN and J. RACSTER COBBETT.

Camping out. By A. A. MACDON-ELL. Double vol. 2s.

Canoeing. By Dr. J. D. HAYWARD. Double vol. 2s.

Mountaineering. By Dr. CLAUDE WILSON. Double vol. 2s.

Athletics. By H. H. GRIFFIN. With contributions by E. H. Pelling, H. C. L. Tindall, J. L. Greig, T. Jennings, C. F. Daft, J. Kibblewhite, Tom Ray, Sid Thomas, and the Rev. W. Pollock-Hill.

Riding. By W. A. KERR, V.C. Double vol. 2s.

Ladies' Riding. By W.A.KERR,V.C.

Boxing. By R. G. ALLANSON-WINN. With Prefatory Note by Bat Mullins.

Cycling. By H. H. GRIFFIN, L.A.C., N.C.U., C.T.C. With a Chapter for Ladies, by Miss L. C. DAVIDSON.

Wrestling. By WALTER ARM-STRONG ('Cross-buttocker').

Fencing. By H. A. COLMORE DUNN.

Broadsword and Singlestick. By R. G. ALLANSON-WINN and C. PHIL-LIPPS-WOLLEY.

Gymnastics. By A. F. JENKIN. Double vol. 2s.

Indian Clubs. By G. T. B. COR-BETT and A. F. JENKIN.

Football — Rugby Game. By HARRY VASSALL.

Football—Association Game. By C. W. ALCOCK.

Hockey. By F. S. CRESWELL. (In Paper Cover, 6d.)

Skating. By DOUGLAS ADAMS. With a Chapter for Ladies, by Miss L. CHEETHAM, and a Chapter on Speed Skating, by a Fen Skater. Dbl. vol. 2s.

Baseball. By NEWTON CRANE.

Rounders, Fieldball, Bowls, Quoits, Curling, Skittles, &c. By J. M. WALKER and C. C. MOTT.

Dancing. By EDWARD SCOTT. Double vol. 2s.

THE CLUB SERIES OF CARD AND TABLE GAMES.

'No well-regulated club or country house should be without this useful series of books.' *Globe.*

Small 8vo. cloth, Illustrated. Price 1s. each.

Whist. By Dr. WM. POLE, F.R.S.

Solo Whist. By ROBERT F. GREEN.

Billiards. The Art of Practical Billiards for Amateurs, with chapters on Pool, Pyramids, and Snooker. By Major-Gen. A. W. DRAYSON, F.R.A.S. With a Preface by W. J. Peall.

Chess. By ROBERT F. GREEN, Editor of the 'British Chess Magazine.'

The Two-Move Chess Problem. By B. G. LAWS.

Chess Openings. By I. GUNSBERG.

Draughts and Backgammon. By 'BERKELEY.'

Reversi and Go Bang. By 'BERKELEY.'

Dominoes and Solitaire. By 'BERKELEY.'

Bézique and Cribbage. By 'BERKELEY.'

Écarté and Euchre. By 'BERKELEY.'

Piquet and Rubicon Piquet. By 'BERKELEY.'

Skat. By LOUIS DIEHL. *.* A Skat Scoring-book. 1s.

Round Games, including Poker, Napoleon, Loo, Vingt-et-un, New-market, Commerce, Pope Joan, Specu-lation, Spin, Snip-Snap-Snorum, Jig, Cassino, My Bird Sings, Spoil-Five, and Loto. By BAXTER-WRAY.

FICTION.

(See also ' Standard Books.')

Björnson's Arne and the Fisher Lassie. Translated from the Norse with an Introduction by W. H. Low, M.A. Small post 8vo. 3s. 6d.

Burney's Evelina: or, The History of a Young Lady's Entrance into the World. By Frances Burney (Mme. D'Arblay). With an Introduction and Notes by A. R. Ellis. Small post 8vo. 3s. 6d.

——— **Cecilia.** 2 vols. small post 8vo. 3s. 6d. each.

Cervantes' Galatea. A Pastoral Romance. Translated from the Spanish by G. W. J. Gyll. Small post 8vo. 3s. 6d.

——— **Exemplary Novels.** Translated from the Spanish by Walter K. Kelly. Small post 8vo. 3s. 6d.

——— **Don Quixote de la Mancha.** Motteux's Translation, revised. With Lockhart's Life and Notes. 2 vols. small post 8vo. 3s. 6d. each.

Classic Tales, containing Rasselas, Vicar of Wakefield, Gulliver's Travels, and The Sentimental Journey. Small post 8vo. 3s. 6d.

De Staël's Corinne or Italy. By Madame de Staël. Translated by Emily Baldwin and Paulina Driver. Small post 8vo. 3s. 6d.

Ebers' Egyptian Princess. An Historical Novel. By George Ebers. Translated by E. S. Buchheim. Small post 8vo. 3s. 6d.

Edmonds (Mrs.) Amygdala. A Story of the French Revolution. 2s. 6d. net.

Fielding's Adventures of Joseph Andrews and His Friend Mr. Abraham Adams. With Cruikshank's Illustrations. 3s. 6d.

——— **History of Tom Jones, a Foundling.** Roscoe's Edition, with George Cruikshank's Illustrations. 2 vols. small post 8vo. 3s. 6d. each.

——— **Amelia.** Illustrated by George Cruikshank. 5s.

Gift (Theo.) Dishonoured. 6s.

Gil Blas, the Adventures of. Translated by Smollett. Illustrated by Smirke and Cruikshank. Small post 8vo. 6s.

Hauff's Tales. The Caravan—The Sheik of Alexandria—The Inn in the Spessart. Translated by S. Mendel. Small post 8vo. 3s. 6d.

Hawthorne's Tales. 4 vols. Small post 8vo. 3s. 6d. each.

Hoffmann's Tales. The Serapion Brethren. Translated by Lieut.-Col. Ewing. 2 vols. Small post 8vo. 3s. 6d. each.

Holnut (W. S.) Olympia's Journal. Crown 8vo. 3s. 6d.

Manzoni. The Betrothed. By Alessandro Manzoni. With numerous Woodcut Illustrations Small post 8vo. 5s.

Poushkin's Prose Tales. Translated from the Russian by T. Keane. Small post 8vo. 3s. 6d.

Smollett's Roderick Random. With Cruikshank's Illustrations and Bibliography. Small post 8vo. 3s. 6d.

——— **Peregrine Pickle.** With Cruikshank's Illustrations. 2 vols. Small post 8vo. 3s. 6d. each.

——— **Humphry Clinker.** With Cruikshank's Illustrations. Small post 8vo. 3s. 6d.

Steele (Mrs. A. C.) Lesbia. A Study in one volume. 6s.

Stinde (J.) The Buchholz Family. Sketches of Berlin Life. By Julius Stinde. Translated from the 49th edition of the German by L. Dora Schmitz. Popular edition, picture boards, 2s.

Stinde (J.) The Buchholz Family. Second Part. Popular edition. Picture boards, 2s.

——— The Buchholzes in Italy. Translated from the 37th edition of the original by Harriet F. Powell. Crown 8vo. cloth, 3s.

——— Frau Wilhelmine. Being the Conclusion of 'The Buchholz Family.' Translated by Harriet F. Powell. Crown 8vo. cloth, 3s.

BOOKS FOR THE YOUNG.

Andersen (Hans Christian). Fairy Tales and Sketches. Translated by C. C. Peachey, H. Ward, A. Plesner, &c. With numerous Illustrations by Otto Speckter and others. 7th thousand. Crown 8vo. 3s. 6d.

——— Tales for Children. With 48 full-page Illustrations by Wehnert, and 57 small Engravings on Wood by W. Thomas. 13th thousand. Crown 8vo. 3s. 6d.

——— Danish Legends and Fairy Tales. Translated from the Original by Caroline Peachey. With a Short Life of the Author, and 120 Wood Engravings, chiefly by Foreign Artists. Small post 8vo. 5s.

Edgeworth's Stories for Children. With 8 Illustrations by L. Speed. Small post 8vo. 3s. 6d.

Ford (Mrs. Gerard). Master Rex. By Mrs. Gerard Ford. Illustrated by James Cadenhead, Florence M. Cooper, and Louise S. Sweet. 2nd edition. Crown 8vo. 3s.

——— Pixie ; and the Hill-House Farm. Illustrated by James Cadenhead and Florence M. Cooper. 2nd edition. Crown 8vo. 3s.

Gatty's Parables from Nature. With Notes on the Natural History, and numerous full-page Illustrations by W. Holman Hunt, E. Burne Jones, J. Tenniel, J. Wolf, and other eminent artists. Complete edition with short Memoir by J. H. Ewing. Crown 8vo. 5s.
POCKET VOLUME EDITION. 2 vols. Imp. 32mo. 5s.
CHEAP EDITION. Illustrated. 2 vols. Fcap. 4to. paper covers, 1s. each ; or bound in 1 vol. cloth, 3s.

Grimm's Gammer Grethel; or, German Fairy Tales and Popular Stories, containing 42 Fairy Tales. Translated by Edgar Taylor. With numerous Woodcuts after George Crnikshank and Ludwig Grimm. 3s. 6d.

——— Tales. With the Notes of the Original. Translated by Mrs. A. Hunt. With Introduction by Andrew Lang, M.A. 2 vols. 3s. 6d. each.

Harald the Viking. A Book for Boys. By Capt. Charles Young. With Illustrations by J. Williamson. Crown 8vo. 5s.

Stowe's Uncle Tom's Cabin; or, Life among the Lowly. With Introductory Remarks by Rev. J. Sherman. With 8 full-page Illustrations. Small post 8vo. 3s. 6d.

The Wide, Wide World. A Story. By Elizabeth Wetherell. Sm. post 8vo. 3s. 6d.

Uncle Peter's Riddle. By Ella K. Sanders. Illustrated by Florence M. Cooper. 3s. 6d.

CAPT. MARRYAT'S BOOKS FOR BOYS.

Uniform Illustrated Edition. Small post 8vo. 3s. 6d. each.

Poor Jack.
The Mission ; or, Scenes in Africa.
The Pirate, and Three Cutters.
Peter Simple.

The Settlers in Canada.
The Privateersman.
Masterman Ready.
Midshipman Easy.

MRS. EWING'S BOOKS.

Uniform Edition, in 9 vols.

We and The World. A Story for Boys. By the late Juliana
Horatio Ewing. With 7 Illustrations by W. L. Jones. 4th edition. 3s.

A Flat Iron for a Farthing; or, Some Passages in the Life of an
Only Son. With 12 Illustrations by H. Allingham. 16th edition. 3s.

Mrs. Overtheway's Remembrances. Illustrated with 9 fine full-
page Engravings by Pasquier, and Frontispiece by Wolf. 5th edition. 3s.

Six to Sixteen: A Story for Girls. With 10 Illustrations by Mrs.
Allingham. 8th edition. 3s.

Jan of the Windmill: a Story of the Plains. With 11 Illustrations
by Mrs. Allingham. 5th edition. 3s.

A Great Emergency. A very Ill-tempered Family—Our Field—
Madame Liberality. With 4 Illustrations. 3rd edition. 3s.

Melchior's Dream. The Blackbird's Nest—Friedrich's Ballad—A
Bit of Green—Monsieur the Viscount's Friend—The Yew Lane Ghosts—A
Bad Habit—A Happy Family. With 8 Illustrations by Gordon Browne. 7th
edition. 3s.

Lob-Lie-by-the-Fire, or the Luck of Lingborough ; and other Tales.
With 3 Illustrations by George Cruikshank. 4th edition. Imp. 16mo. 3s. 6d.

The Brownies. The Land of Lost Toys—Three Christmas-trees—
An Idyl of the Wood—Christmas Crackers—Amelia and the Dwarfs—Timothy's
Shoes—Benjy in Beastland. Illustrated by George Cruikshank. 7th edition.
Imp. 16mo. 3s. 6d.

THE SHILLING SERIES.

Fcap. 4to. double columns, Illustrated, 1s. each.

Mrs. Ewing's Melchior's Dream, and other Tales.

———— A Flat Iron for a Farthing.

———— Six to Sixteen.

———— We and the World.

———— Mrs. Overtheway's Remembrances.

———— Jan of the Windmill.

———— A Great Emergency, and other Tales.

———— The Brownies, and other Tales.

Mrs. Gatty's Parables from Nature. Two Series, each 1s.

Miss Procter's Legends and Lyrics. Two Series, each 1s

Hector. A Story for Young People. With 12 Illustrations by
W. J. Hennessey. By Flora Shaw, Author of 'Castle Blair.'

Andersen's Tales. Translated by Caroline Peachey.

AN ALPHABETICAL LIST OF BOOKS

CONTAINED IN

BOHN'S LIBRARIES.

769 Vols., Small Post 8vo. cloth.   Price £163 19s.

Complete Detailed Catalogue will be sent on application.

Addison's Works. 6 vols. 3*s.* 6*d.* each.

Aeschylus. Verse Trans. by Anna Swanwick. 5*s.*

—— Prose Trans. by T. A. Buckley. 3*s.* 6*d.*

Agassiz & Gould's Comparative Physiology 5*s.*

Alfieri's Tragedies. Trans. by Bowring. 2 vols. 3*s.* 6*d.* each.

Alford's Queen's English. 1*s.* & 1*s.* 6*d.*

Allen's Battles of the British Navy. 2 vols. 5*s.* each.

Ammianus Marcellinus. Trans. by C. D. Yonge. 7*s.* 6*d.*

Andersen's Danish Tales. Trans. by Caroline Peachey. 5*s.*

Antoninus (Marcus Aurelius). Trans. by George Long. 3*s.* 6*d.*

Apollonius Rhodius. The Argonautica. Trans. by E. P. Coleridge. 5*s.*

Apuleius, The Works of. 5*s.*

Ariosto's Orlando Furioso. Trans. by W. S. Rose. 2 vols. 5*s.* each.

Aristophanes. Trans. by W. J. Hickie. 2 vols. 5*s.* each.

Aristotle's Works. 5 vols, 5*s.* each ; 2 vols, 3*s.* 6*d.* each.

Arrian. Trans. by E. J. Chinnock. 5*s.*

Ascham's Scholemaster. (J. E. B. Mayor.) 1*s.*

Bacon's Essays and Historical Works, 3*s.* 6*d.* ; Essays, 1*s.* and 1*s.* 6*d.* ; Novum Organum, and Advancement of Learning, 5*s.*

Ballads and Songs of the Peasantry. By Robert Bell. 3*s.* 6*d.*

Bass's Lexicon to the Greek Test. 2*s.*

Bax's Manual of the History of Philosophy. 5*s.*

Beaumont & Fletcher. Leigh Hunt's Selections. 3*s.* 6*d.*

Bechstein's Cage and Chamber Birds. 5*s.*

Beckmann's History of Inventions. 2 vols. 3*s.* 6*d.* each.

Bede's Ecclesiastical History and the A. S. Chronicle. 5*s.*

Bell (Sir C.) On the Hand. 5*s.*

—— Anatomy of Expression. 5*s.*

Bentley's Phalaris. 5*s.*

Björnson's Arne and the Fisher Lassie. Trans. by W. H. Low. 3*s.* 6*d.*

Blair's Chronological Tables. 10*s.* Index of Dates. 2 vols. 5*s.* each.

Bleek's Introduction to the Old Testament. 2 vols. 5*s.* each.

Boethius' Consolation of Philosophy, &c. 5*s.*

Bohn's Dictionary of Poetical Quotations. 6*s.*

Bond's Handy-book for Verifying Dates, &c. 5*s.*

Bonomi's Nineveh. 5*s.*

Boswell's Life of Johnson. (Napier). 6 vols. 3*s.* 6*d.* each.

—— (Croker.) 5 vols. 20*s.*

Brand's Popular Antiquities. 3 vols. 5*s.* each.

Bremer's Works. Trans. by Mary Howitt. 4 vols. 3*s.* 6*d.* each.

Bridgewater Treatises. 9 vols. Various prices.

Brink (B. Ten). Early English Literature. 3 vols. 3*s.* 6*d.* each.

—— Five Lectures on Shakespeare 3*s.* 6*d.*

Browne's (Sir Thomas) Works. 3 vols. 3*s.* 6*d.* each.

Buchanan's Dictionary of Scientific Terms. 6*s.*

Buckland's Geology and Mineralogy. 2 vols. 15*s.*

Burke's Works and Speeches. 8 vols. 3*s.* 6*d.* each. The Sublime and Beautiful. 1*s.* & 1*s.* 6*d.* Reflections on the French Revolution. 1*s.*

—— Life, by Sir James Prior. 3*s.* 6*d.*

Burney's Evelina. 3*s.* 6*d.* Cecilia 2 vols. 3*s.* 6*d.* each.

Burns' Life by Lockhart. Revised by W. Scott Douglas. 3*s.* 6*d.*

Burn's Ancient Rome. 7*s.* 6*d.*

Burton's Anatomy of Melancholy. (A. R. Shilleto). 3 vols. 3*s.* 6*d.* each.

Butler's Analogy of Religion, and Sermons. 3*s.* 6*d.*

Butler's Hudibras. 5*s.* ; or 2 vols., 5*s.* each.

Caesar. Trans. by W. A. M'Devitte. 5*s.*

Camoens' Lusiad. Mickle's Translation, revised. 3*s.* 6*d.*

Carafas (The) of Maddaloni. By Alfred de Reumont. 3*s.* 6*d.*

Carpenter's Mechanical Philosophy 5*s.* Vegetable Physiology. 6*s.* Animal Physiology. 6*s.*

Carrel's Counter Revolution under Charles II. and James II. 3*s.* 6*d.*

Cattermole's Evenings at Haddon Hall. 5*s.*

Catullus and Tibullus. Trans. by W. K. Kelly. 5*s.*

Cellini's Memoirs. (Roscoe.) 3*s.* 6*d.*

Cervantes' Exemplary Novels. Trans. by W. K. Kelly. 3*s.* 6*d.*

—— Don Quixote. Motteux's Trans. revised. 2 vols. 3*s.* 6*d.* each.

—— Galatea. Trans. by G. W. J. Gyll. 3*s.* 6*d.*

Chalmers On Man. 5*s.*

Channing's The Perfect Life. 1*s.* and 1*s.* 6*d.*

Chaucer's Works. Bell's Edition, revised by Skeat. 4 vols. 3*s.* 6*d.* ea.

Chess Congress of 1862 By J. Löwenthal. 5*s.*

Chevreul on Colour. 5*s.* and 7*s.* 6*d.*

Chillingworth's The Religion of Protestants. 3*s.* 6*d.*

China : Pictorial, Descriptive, and Historical. 5*s.*

Chronicles of the Crusades. 5*s.*

Cicero's Works. 7 vols. 5*s.* each. 1 vol., 3*s.* 6*d.*

—— Friendship and Old Age. 1*s.* and 1*s.* 6*d.*

Clark's Heraldry. (Planché.) 5*s.* and 15*s.*

Classic Tales. 3*s.* 6*d.*

Coleridge's Prose Works. (Ashe.) 6 vols. 3*s.* 6*d.* each.

Comte's Philosophy of the Sciences. (G. H. Lewes.) 5*s.*

—— Positive Philosophy. (Harriet Martineau.) 3 vols. 5*s.* each.

Condé's History of the Arabs in Spain. 3 vols. 3*s.* 6*d.* each.

Cooper's Biographical Dictionary. 2 vols. 5*s.* each.

Cowper's Works. (Southey.) 8 vols 3*s.* 6*d.* each.

Coxe's House of Austria. 4 vols. 3*s.* 6*d* each. Memoirs of Marlborough. 3 vols. 3*s.* 6*d.* each. Atlas to Marlborough's Campaigns. 10*s.* 6*d.*

Craik's Pursuit of Knowledge. 5*s.*

Craven's Young Sportsman's Manual 5*s.*

Cruikshank's Punch and Judy. 5*s* Three Courses and a Dessert. 5*s.*

Cunningham's Lives of British Painters. 3 vols. 3*s.* 6*d.* each.

Dante. Trans. by Rev. H. F. Cary. 3*s.* 6*d.* Inferno. Separate, 1*s.* and 1*s.* 6*d.* Purgatorio. 1*s.* and 1*s.* 6*d.* Paradiso. 1*s.* and 1*s.* 6*d.*

—— Trans. by I. C. Wright. (Flaxman's Illustrations.) 5*s.*

—— Inferno. Italian Text and Trans by Dr. Carlyle. 5*s.*

—— Purgatorio. Italian Text and Trans. by W. S. Dugdale. 5*s.*

De Commines' Memoirs. Trans. by A. R. Scoble. 2 vols. 3*s.* 6*d.* each.

Defoe's Novels and Miscel. Works 6 vols. 3*s.* 6*d.* each. Robinson Crusoe (Vol. VII). 3*s.* 6*d.* or 5*s* The Plague in London. 1*s.* and 1*s.* 6*d.*

Delolme on the Constitution of England. 3*s.* 6*d.*

Demmins' Arms and Armour. Trans, by C. C. Black. 7*s.* 6*d.*

Demosthenes' Orations. Trans. by C. Rann Kennedy. 4 vols. 5s., and 1 vol. 3s. 6d.

—— Orations On the Crown. 1s. and 1s. 6d.

De Stael's Corinne. Trans. by Emily Baldwin and Paulina Driver. 3s. 6d.

Devey's Logic. 5s.

Dictionary of Greek and Latin Quotations. 5s.

—— of Poetical Quotations (Bohn). 6s.

—— of Scientific Terms. (Buchanan.) 6s.

—— of Biography. (Cooper.) 2 vols. 5s. each.

—— of Noted Names of Fiction. (Wheeler.) 5s.

—— of Obsolete and Provincial English (Wright.) 2 vols. 5s. each.

Didron's Christian Iconography. 2 vols. 5s. each.

Diogenes Laertius. Trans. by C. D. Yonge. 5s.

Dobree's Adversaria. (Wagner). 2 vols. 5s. each.

Dodd's Epigrammatists. 6s.

Donaldson's Theatre of the Greeks. 5s.

Draper's History of the Intellectual Development of Europe. 2 vols. 5s. each.

Dunlop's History of Fiction. 2 vols. 5s. each.

Dyer's History of Pompeii. 7s. 6d.

—— The City of Rome. 5s.

Dyer's British Popular Customs. 5s.

Early Travels in Palestine. (Wright.) 5s.

Eaton's Waterloo Days. 1s. and 1s. 6d.

Eber's Egyptian Princess. Trans. by E. S. Buchheim. 3s. 6d.

Edgeworth's Stories for Children. 3s. 6d.

Ellis' Specimens of Early English Metrical Romances. (Halliwell.) 5s.

Elze's Life of Shakespeare. Trans. by L. Dora Schmitz. 5s.

Emerson's Works. 3 vols. 3s. 6d. each, or 5 vols. 1s. each.

Ennemoser's History of Magic. 2 vols. 5s. each.

Epictetus. Trans. by George Long. 5s.

Euripides. Trans. by E. P. Coleridge. 2 vols. 5s. each.

Eusebius' Eccl. History. Trans. by C. F. Cruse. 5s.

Evelyn's Diary and Correspondence. (Bray.) 4 vols. 5s. each.

Fairholt's Costume in England. (Dillon.) 2 vols. 5s. each.

Fielding's Joseph Andrews. 3s. 6d. Tom Jones. 2 vols. 3s. 6d. each. Amelia. 5s.

Flaxman's Lectures on Sculpture. 6s.

Florence of Worcester's Chronicle. Trans. by T. Forester. 5s.

Foster's Works. 10 vols. 3s. 6d. each.

Franklin's Autobiography. 1s.

Gesta Romanorum. Trans. by Swan & Hooper. 5s.

Gibbon's Decline and Fall. 7 vols. 3s. 6d. each.

Gilbart's Banking. 2 vols. 5s. each.

Gil Blas. Trans. by Smollett. 6s.

Giraldus Cambrensis. 5s.

Goethe's Works and Correspondence, including Autobiography and Annals, Faust, Elective affinities, Werther, Wilhelm Meister, Poems and Ballads, Dramas, Reinecke Fox, Tour in Italy and Miscellaneous Travels, Early and Miscellaneous Letters, Correspondence with Eckermann and Soret, Zelter and Schiller, &c. &c. By various translators. 16 vols. 3s. 6d. each.

—— Faust. Text with Hayward's Translation. (Buchheim.) 5s.

—— Faust. Part I. Trans. by Anna Swanwick. 1s. and 1s. 6d.

—— Boyhood. (Part I. of the Autobiography.) Trans. by J. Oxenford. 1s. and 1s. 6d.

—— Reinecke Fox. Trans. by A. Rogers. 1s. and 1s. 6d.

Goldsmith's Works. (Gibbs.) 5 vols. 3s. 6d. each.

—— Plays. 1s. and 1s. 6d. Vicar of Wakefield. 1s. and 1s. 6d.

Grammont's Memoirs and Boscobel Tracts. 5s.

Gray's Letters. (D. C. Tovey.) [In the press.

Greek Anthology. Trans. by E. Burges. 5s.

Greek Romances. (Theagenes and Chariclea, Daphnis and Chloe, Clitopho and Leucippe.) Trans. by Rev. R. Smith. 5s.

Greek Testament. 5*s.*

Greene, Marlowe, and Ben Jonson's Poems. (Robert Bell.) 3*s.* 6*d.*

Gregory's Evidences of the Christian Religion. 3*s.* 6*d.*

Grimm's Gammer Grethel. Trans. by E. Taylor. 3*s.* 6*d.*

—— German Tales. Trans. by Mrs. Hunt. 2 vols. 3*s.* 6*d.* each.

Grossi's Marco Visconti. 3*s.* 6*d.*

Guizot's Origin of Representative Government in Europe. Trans. by A. R. Scoble. 3*s.* 6*d.*

—— The English Revolution of 1640. Trans. by W. Hazlitt. 3*s.* 6*d.*

—— History of Civilisation. Trans. by W. Hazlitt. 3 vols. 3*s.* 6*d.* each.

Hall (Robert). Miscellaneous Works. 3*s.* 6*d.*

Handbooks of Athletic Sports. 8 vols. 3*s.* 6*d.* each.

Handbook of Card and Table Games. 2 vols. 3*s.* 6*d.* each.

—— of Proverbs. By H. G. Bohn. 5*s.*

—— of Foreign Proverbs. 5*s.*

Hardwick's History of the Thirty-nine Articles. 5*s.*

Harvey's Circulation of the Blood. (Bowie.) 1*s.* and 1*s.* 6*d.*

Hauff's Tales. Trans. by S. Mendel. 3*s.* 6*d.*

—— The Caravan and Sheik of Alexandria. 1*s.* and 1*s.* 6*d.*

Hawthorne's Novels and Tales. 4 vols. 3*s.* 6*d.* each.

Hazlitt's Lectures and Essays. 7 vols. 3*s.* 6*d.* each.

Heaton's History of Painting. (Cosmo Monkhouse.) 5*s.*

Hegel's Philosophy of History. Trans. by J. Sibree. 5*s.*

Heine's Poems. Trans. by E. A. Bowring. 3*s.* 6*d.*

—— Travel Pictures. Trans. by Francis Storr. 3*s.* 6*d.*

Helps (Sir Arthur). Life of Columbus. 3*s.* 6*d.*

—— Life of Pizarro. 3*s.* 6*d.*

—— Life of Cortes. 2 vols. 3*s.* 6*d.* each.

—— Life of Las Casas. 3*s.* 6*d.*

—— Life of Thomas Brassey. 1*s.* and 1*s.* 6*d.*

Henderson's Historical Documents of the Middle Ages. 5*s.*

Henfrey's English Coins. (Keary.) 6*s.*

Henry (Matthew) On the Psalms. 5*s.*

Henry of Huntingdon's History. Trans. by T. Forester. 5*s.*

Herodotus. Trans. by H. F. Cary. 3*s.* 6*d.*

—— Wheeler's Analysis and Summary of. 5*s.* Turner's Notes on. 5*s.*

Hesiod, Callimachus and Theognis. Trans. by Rev. J. Banks. 5*s.*

Hoffmann's Tales. The Serapion Brethren. Trans. by Lieut.-Colonel Ewing. 2 vols. 3*s.* 6*d.*

Hogg's Experimental and Natural Philosophy. 5*s.*

Holbein's Dance of Death and Bible Cuts. 5*s.*

Homer. Trans. by T. A. Buckley. 2 vols. 5*s.* each.

—— Pope's Translation. With Flaxman's Illustrations. 2 vols. 5*s.* each.

—— Cowper's Translation. 2 vols. 3*s.* 6*d.* each.

Hooper's Waterloo. 3*s.* 6*d.*

Horace. Smart's Translation, revised, by Buckley. 3*s.* 6*d.*

—— A New Literal Prose Translation. By A. Hamilton Bryce, LL.D. 3*s.* 6*d.*

Hugo's Dramatic Works. Trans. by Mrs. Crosland and F. L. Slous. 3*s.* 6*d.*

—— Hernani. Trans. by Mrs. Crosland. 1*s.*

—— Poems. Trans. by various writers. Collected by J. H. L. Williams. 3*s.* 6*d.*

Humboldt's Cosmos. Trans. by Otté, Paul, and Dallas. 4 vols. 3*s.* 6*d.* each, and 1 vol. 5*s.*

—— Personal Narrative of his Travels. Trans. by T. Ross. 3 vols. 5*s.* each.

—— Views of Nature. Trans. by Otté and Bohn. 5*s.*

Humphreys' Coin Collector's Manual. 2 vols. 5*s.* each.

Hungary, History of. 3*s.* 6*d.*

Hunt's Poetry of Science. 5*s.*

Hutchinson's Memoirs. 3*s.* 6*d.*

India before the Sepoy Mutiny. 5*s.*

Ingulph's Chronicles. 5*s.*

Irving (Washington). Complete Works. 15 vols. 3*s.* 6*d.* each ; or in 18 vols. 1*s.* each, and 2 vols. 1*s.* 6*d.* each.

—— Life and Letters. By Pierre E. Irving. 2 vols. 3*s.* 6*d.* each.

Isocrates. Trans. by J. H. Freese. Vol. I. 5s.

James' Life of Richard Cœur de Lion. 2 vols. 3s. 6d. each.

—— Life and Times of Louis XIV 2 vols. 3s. 6d. each.

Jameson (Mrs.) Shakespeare's Heroines. 3s. 6d.

Jesse (E.) Anecdotes of Dogs. 5s.

Jesse (J. H.) Memoirs of the Court of England under the Stuarts. 3 vols. 5s. each.

—— Memoirs of the Pretenders. 5s.

Johnson's Lives of the Poets. (Napier). 3 vols. 3s. 6d. each.

Josephus. Whiston's Translation, revised by Rev. A. R. Shilleto. 5 vols. 3s. 6d. each.

Joyce's Scientific Dialogues. 5s.

Jukes-Browne's Handbook of Physical Geology. 7s. 6d. Handbook of Historical Geology. 6s. The Building of the British Isles. 7s. 6d.

Julian the Emperor. Trans by Rev. C. W. King. 5s.

Junius's Letters. Woodfall's Edition, revised. 2 vols. 3s. 6d. each.

Justin, Cornelius Nepos, and Eutropius. Trans. by Rev. J. S. Watson. 5s.

Juvenal, Persius, Sulpicia, and Lucilius. Trans. by L. Evans. 5s.

Kant's Critique of Pure Reason. Trans. by J. M. D. Meiklejohn. 5s.

—— Prolegomena, &c. Trans. by E. Belfort Bax. 5s.

Keightley's Fairy Mythology. 5s. Classical Mythology. Revised by Dr. L. Schmitz. 5s.

Kidd On Man. 3s. 6d.

Kirby On Animals. 2 vols. 5s. each.

Knight's Knowledge is Power. 5s.

La Fontaine's Fables. Trans. by E. Wright. 3s. 6d.

Lamartine's History of the Girondists. Trans. by H. T. Ryde. 3 vols. 3s. 6d. each.

—— Restoration of the Monarchy in France. Trans. by Capt. Rafter. 4 vols. 3s. 6d. each.

—— French Revolution f 1848. 3s. 6d.

Lamb's Essays of Elia and Eliana. 3s. 6d., or in 3 vols. 1s. each.

—— Memorials and Letters. Talfourd's Edition, revised by W. C. Hazlitt. 2 vols. 3s. 6d. each.

—— Specimens of the English Dramatic Poets of the Time of Elizabeth. 3s. 6d.

Lanzi's History of Painting in Italy. Trans. by T. Roscoe. 3 vols. 3s. 6d. each.

Lappenberg's England under the Anglo-Saxon Kings. Trans. by B. Thorpe. 2 vols. 3s. 6d. each.

Lectures on Painting. By Barry, Opie and Fuseli. 5s.

Leonardo da Vinci's Treatise on Painting. Trans. by J. F. Rigaud. 5s.

Lepsius' Letters from Egypt, &c. Trans. by L. and J. B. Horner. 5s.

Lessing's Dramatic Works. Trans. by Ernest Bell. 2 vols. 3s. 6d. each. Nathan the Wise and Minna von Barnhelm. 1s. and 1s. 6d. Laokoon, Dramatic Notes, &c. Trans. by E. C. Beasley and Helen Zimmern. 3s. 6d. Laokoon separate. 1s. or 1s. 6d.

Lilly's Introduction to Astrology. (Zadkiel.) 5s.

Livy. Trans. by Dr. Spillan and others. 4 vols. 5s. each.

Locke's Philosophical Works. (J. A. St. John). 2 vols. 3s. 6d. each.

—— Life. By Lord King. 3s. 6d.

Lodge's Portraits. 8 vols. 5s. each.

Longfellow's Poetical and Prose Works. 2 vols. 5s. each.

Loudon's Natural History. 5s.

Lowndes' Bibliographer's Manual. 6 vols. 5s. each.

Lucan's Pharsalia. Trans. by H. T. Riley. 5s.

Lucian's Dialogues. Trans. by H. Williams. 5s.

Lucretius. Trans. by Rev. . S. Watson. 5s.

Luther's Table Talk. Trans. by W. Hazlitt. 3s. 6d.

—— Autobiography. (Michelet). Trans. by W. Hazlitt. 3s. 6d.

Machiavelli's History of Florence, &c Trans. 3s. 6d.

Mallet's Northern Antiquities. 5s.

Mantell's Geological Excursions through the Isle of Wight, &c. 5s. Petrifactions and their Teachings 6s. Wonders of Geology. 2 vols 7s. 6d. each.

Manzoni's The Betrothed. 5s.

Marco Polo's Travels. Marsden's Edition, revised by T. Wright. 5s.

Martial's Epigrams. Trans. 7*s.* 6*d.*

Martineau's History of England, 1800-15. 3*s.* 6*d.*

—— History of the Peace, 1816-46. 4 vols. 3*s.* 6*d.* each.

Matthew Paris. Trans. by Dr. Giles. 3 vols. 5*s.* cach.

Matthew of Westminster. Trans. by C. D. Yonge. 2 vols. 5*s.* each.

Maxwell's Victories of Wellington. 5*s.*

Menzel's History of Germany. Trans. by Mrs. Horrocks. 3 vols. 3*s.* 6*d.* ca.

Michael Angelo and Raffaelle. By Duppa and Q. de Quincy. 5*s.*

Michelet's French Revolution. Trans. by C. Cocks. 3*s.* 6*d.*

Mignet's French Revolution. 3*s.* 6*d.*

Mill (John Stuart). Early Essays. 3*s.* 6*d.*

Miller's Philosophy of History. 4 vols. 3*s.* 6*d.* each.

Milton's Poetical Works. (J. Montgomery.) 2 vols. 3*s.* 6*d.* each.

—— Prose Works. (J. A. St. John.) 5 vols. 3*s.* 6*d.* each.

Mitford's Our Village. 2 vols. 3*s.* 6*d.* each.

Molière's Dramatic Works. Trans. by C. H. Wall. 3 vols. 3*s.* 6*d.* each.

—— The Miser, Tartufe, The Shopkeeper turned Gentleman. 1*s.* & 1*s.* 6*d.*

Montagu's (Lady M. W.) Letters and Works. (Wharncliffe and Moy Thomas.) 2 vols. 5*s.* each.

Montaigne's Essays. Cotton's Trans. revised by W. C. Hazlitt. 3 vols. 3*s.* 6*d.* each.

Montesquieu's Spirit of Laws. Nugent's Trans. revised by J. V. Prichard. 2 vols. 3*s.* 6*d.* each.

Morphy's Games of Chess. (Löwenthal.) 5*s.*

Motley's Dutch Republic. 3 vols. 3*s.* 6*d.* each.

Mudie's British Birds. (Martin.) 2 vols. 5*s.* each.

Naval and Military Heroes of Great Britain. 6*s.*

Neander's History of the Christian Religion and Church. 10 vols. Life of Christ. 1 vol. Planting and Training of the Church by the Apostles. 2 vols. History of Christian Dogma.

2 vols. Memorials of Christian Life in the Early and Middle Ages. 16 vols. 3*s.* 6*d.* each.

Nicolini's History of the Jesuits. 5*s.*

North's Lives of the Norths. (Jessopp.) 3 vols. 3*s.* 6*d.* each.

Nugent's Memorials of Hampden. 5*s.*

Ockley's History of the Saracens. 3*s.* 6*d.*

Ordericus Vitalis. Trans. by T. Forester. 4 vols. 5*s.* each.

Ovid. Trans. by H. T. Riley. 3 vols. 5*s.* each.

Pascal's Thoughts. Trans. by C. Kegan Paul. 3*s.* 6*d.*

Pauli's Life of Alfred the Great, &c. 5*s.*

—— Life of Cromwell. 1*s.* and 1*s.* 6*d.*

Pausanias' Description of Greece. Trans. by Rev. A. R. Shilleto. 2 vols. 5*s.* each.

Pearson on the Creed. (Walford.) 5*s.*

Pepys' Diary. (Braybrooke.) 4 vols. 5*s.* each.

Percy's Reliques of Ancient English Poetry. (Prichard.) 2 vols. 3*s.* 6*d.* ea.

Petrarch's Sonnets. 5*s.*

Pettigrew's Chronicles of the Tombs. 5*s.*

Philo-Judæus. Trans. by C. D. Yonge. 4 vols. 5*s.* each.

Pickering's Races of Man. 5*s.*

Pindar. Trans. by D. W. Turner. 5*s.*

Planché's History of British Costume. 5*s.*

Plato. Trans. by H. Cary, G. Burges, and H. Davis. 6 vols. 5*s.* each.

—— Apology, Crito, Phædo, Protagoras. 1*s.* and 1*s.* 6*d.*

—— Day's Analysis and Index to the Dialogues. 5*s.*

Plautus. Trans. by H. T. Riley. 2 vols. 5*s.* each.

—— Trinummus, Menæchmi, Aulularia, Captivi. 1*s.* and 1*s.* 6*d.*

Pliny's Natural History. Trans. by Dr. Bostock and H. T. Riley. 6 vols. 5*s.* each.

Pliny the Younger, Letters of. Melmoth's trans. revised by Rev. F. C. T. Bosanquet. 5*s.*

Plotinus: Select Works of. Tom Taylor's Translation. (G. R. S. Mead). 5*s.*

Plutarch's Lives. Trans. by Stewart and Long. 4 vols. 3s. 6d. each.

—— Moralia. Trans. by Rev. C. W. King and Rev. A. R. Shilleto. 2 vols. 5s. each.

Poetry of America. (W. J. Linton.) 3s. 6d.

Political Cyclopædia. 4 vols. 3s. 6d. ea.

Polyglot of Foreign Proverbs. 5s.

Pope's Poetical Works. (Carruthers.) 2 vols. 5s. each.

—— Homer. (J. S. Watson.) 2 vols. 5s. each.

—— Life and Letters. (Carruthers.) 5s.

Pottery and Porcelain. (H. G. Bohn.) 5s. and 10s. 6d.

Poushkin's Prose Tales. Trans. by T. Keane. 3s. 6d.

Propertius. Trans. by Rev. P. J. F. Gantillon. 3s. 6d.

Prout (Father.) Reliques. 5s.

Quintilian's Institutes of Oratory. Trans. by Rev. J. S. Watson. 2 vols. 5s. each.

Racine's Tragedies. Trans. by R. B. Boswell. 2 vols. 3s. 6d. each.

Ranke's History of the Popes. Trans. by E. Foster. 3 vols. 3s. 6d. each.

—— Latin and Teutonic Nations. Trans. by P. A. Ashworth. 3s. 6d.

—— History of Servia. Trans. by Mrs. Kerr. 3s. 6d.

Rennie's Insect Architecture. (J. G. Wood.) 5s.

Reynold's Discourses and Essays. (Beechy.) 2 vols. 3s. 6d. each.

Ricardo's Political Economy. (Gonner.) 5s.

Richter's Levana. 3s. 6d.

—— Flower Fruit and Thorn Pieces. Trans. by Lieut.-Col. Ewing. 3s. 6d.

Roger de Hovenden's Annals. Trans. by Dr. Giles. 2 vols. 5s. each.

Roger of Wendover. Trans. by Dr. Giles. 2 vols. 5s. each.

Roget's Animal and Vegetable Physiology. 2 vols. 6s. each.

Rome in the Nineteenth Century. (C. A. Eaton.) 2 vols. 5s. each.

Roscoe's Leo X. 2 vols. 3s. 6d. each.

—— Lorenzo de Medici. 3s. 6d.

Russia, History of. By W. K. Kelly. 2 vols. 3s. 6d. each.

Sallust, Florus, and Velleius Paterculus. Trans. by Rev. J. S. Watson. 5s.

Schiller's Works. Including History of the Thirty Years' War, Revolt of the Netherlands, Wallenstein, William Tell, Don Carlos, Mary Stuart, Maid of Orleans, Bride of Messina, Robbers, Fiesco, Love and Intrigue, Demetrius, Ghost-Seer, Sport of Divinity, Poems, Aesthetical and Philosophical Essays, &c. By various translators. 7 vols. 3s. 6d. each.

—— Mary Stuart and The Maid of Orleans. Trans. by J. Mellish and Anna Swanwick. 1s. and 1s. 6d.

Schlegel (F.). Lectures and Miscellaneous Works. 5 vols. 3s. 6d. each.

—— (A. W.). Lectures on Dramatic Art and Literature. 3s. 6d.

Schopenhauer's Essays. Selected and Trans. by E. Belfort Bax. 5s.

—— On the Fourfold Root of the Principle of Sufficient Reason and on the Will in Nature. Trans. by Mdme. Hillebrand. 5s.

Schouw's Earth, Plants, and Man. Trans. by A. Henfrey. 5s.

Schumann's Early Letters. Trans. by May Herbert. 3s. 6d.

—— Reissmann's Life of. Trans. by A. L. Alger. 3s. 6d.

Seneca on Benefits. Trans. by Aubrey Stewart. 3s. 6d.

—— Minor Essays and On Clemency. Trans. by Aubrey Stewart. 5s.

Sharpe's History of Egypt. 2 vols. 5s. each.

Sheridan's Dramatic Works. 3s. 6d.

—— Plays. 1s. and 1s. 6d.

Sismondi's Literature of the South of Europe. Trans. by T. Roscoe. 2 vols. 3s. 6d. each.

Six Old English Chronicles. 5s.

Smith (Archdeacon). Synonyms and Antonyms. 5s.

Smith (Adam). Wealth of Nations. (Belfort Bax.) 2 vols. 3s. 6d. each.

—— Theory of Moral Sentiments. 3s. 6d.

Smith (Pye). Geology and Scripture. 5s.

Smollett's Novels. 4 vols. 3s. 6d. each.

Smyth's Lectures on Modern History. 2 vols. 3s. 6d. each.

Socrates' Ecclesiastical History. 5*s.*

Sophocles. Trans. by E. P. Coleridge, B.A. 5*s.*

Southey's Life of Nelson. 5*s.*
—— Life of Wesley. 5*s.*
—— Life, as told in his Letters. By J. Dennis. 3*s.* 6*d.*

Sozomen's Ecclesiastical History. 5*s.*

Spinoza's Chief Works. Trans, by R. H. M. Elwes. 2 vols. 5*s.* each.

Stanley's Dutch and Flemish Painters, 5*s.*

Starling's Noble Deeds of Women. 5*s.*

Staunton's Chess Players' Handbook. 5*s.* Chess Praxis. 5*s.* Chess Players' Companion. 5*s.* Chess Tournament of 1851. 5*s.*

Stöckhardt's Experimental Chemistry. (Heaton.) 5*s.*

Strabo's Geography. Trans. by Falconer and Hamilton. 3 vols. 5*s.* each.

Strickland's Queens of England. 6 vols. 5*s.* each. Mary Queen of Scots. 2 vols. 5*s.* each. Tudor and Stuart Princesses. 5*s.*

Stuart & Revett's Antiquities of Athens. 5*s.*

Suetonius' Lives of the Caesars and of the Grammarians. Thomson's trans. revised by T. Forester. 5*s.*

Sully's Memoirs. Mrs. Lennox's trans. revised. 4 vols. 3*s.* 6*d.* each.

Swift's Prose Works. With Introduction by W. E. H. Lecky. 8 vols. 3*s.* 6*d.* each. [*Vols. 1 & 2 in the Press.*

Tacitus. The Oxford trans. revised. 2 vols. 5*s.* each.

Tales of the Genii. Trans. by Sir. Charles Morell. 5*s.*

Tasso's Jerusalem Delivered. Trans. by J. H. Wiffen. 5*s.*

Taylor's Holy Living and Holy Dying. 3*s.* 6*d.*

Terence and Phædrus. Trans. by H. T. Riley. 5*s.*

Theocritus, Bion, Moschus, and Tyrtæus. Trans. by Rev. J. Banks. 5*s.*

Theodoret and Evagrius. 5*s.*

Thierry's Norman Conquest. Trans. by W. Hazlitt. 2 vols. 3*s.* 6*d.* each.

Thucydides. Trans by Rev. H. Dale. 2 vols. 3*s.* 6*d.* each.
—— Wheeler's Analysis and Summary of. 5*s.*

Thudichum's Treatise on Wines. 5*s.*

Trevelyan's Ladies in Parliament. 1*s.* and 1*s.* 6*d.*

Ulrici's Shakespeare's Dramatic Art. Trans. by L. Dora Schmitz. 2 vols. 3*s.* 6*d.* each.

Uncle Tom's Cabin. 3*s.* 6*d.*

Ure's Cotton Manufacture of Great Britain. 2 vols. 5*s.* each.
—— Philosophy of Manufacture. 7*s.* 6*d.*

Vasari's Lives of the Painters. Trans. by Mrs. Foster. 6 vols. 3*s.* 6*d.* each.

Virgil. Trans. by A. Hamilton Bryce, LL.D. 3*s.* 6*d.*

Voltaire's Tales. Trans. by R. B. Boswell. 3*s.* 6*d.*

Walton's Angler. 5*s.*
—— Lives. (A. H. Bullen.) 5*s.*

Waterloo Days. By C. A. Eaton. 1*s.* and 1*s.* 6*d.*

Wellington, Life of. By 'An Old Soldier.' 5*s.*

Werner's Templars in Cyprus. Trans. by E. A. M. Lewis. 3*s.* 6*d.*

Westropp's Handbook of Archæology. 5*s.*

Wheatley. On the Book of Common Prayer. 3*s.* 6*d.*

Wheeler's Dictionary of Noted Names of Fiction. 5*s.*

White's Natural History of Selborne. 5*s.*

Wieseler's Synopsis of the Gospels. 5*s.*

William of **Malmesbury's** Chronicle 5*s.*

Wright's Dictionary of Obsolete and Provincial English. 2 vols. 5*s.* each.

Xenophon. Trans. by Rev. J. S. Watson and Rev. H. Dale. 3 vols. 5*s.* ea.

Young's Travels in France, 1787-89 (M. Betham-Edwards.) 3*s.* 6*d.*
—— Tour in Ireland, 1776-9. (A. W Hutton.) 2 vols. 3*s.* 6*d.* each.

Yule-Tide Stories. (B. Thorpe.) 5*s.*

'I may say in regard to all manner of books, Bohn's Publication Series is the usefullest thing I know.'—THOMAS CARLYLE.

'The respectable and sometimes excellent translations of Bohn's Library have done for literature what railroads have done for internal intercourse.'—EMERSON.

'An important body of cheap literature, for which every living worker in this country who draws strength from the past has reason to be grateful.'

Professor HENRY MORLEY.

BOHN'S LIBRARIES.

STANDARD LIBRARY	360 VOLUMES.
HISTORICAL LIBRARY	23 VOLUMES.
PHILOSOPHICAL LIBRARY .	21 VOLUMES.
ECCLESIASTICAL LIBRARY . . .	15 VOLUMES.
ANTIQUARIAN LIBRARY . , .	36 VOLUMES.
ILLUSTRATED LIBRARY	76 VOLUMES.
SPORTS AND GAMES	16 VOLUMES.
CLASSICAL LIBRARY . . .	106 VOLUMES.
COLLEGIATE SERIES . .	10 VOLUMES.
SCIENTIFIC LIBRARY . .	44 VOLUMES.
ECONOMICS AND FINANCE . . .	5 VOLUMES.
REFERENCE LIBRARY	30 VOLUMES.
NOVELISTS' LIBRARY .	17 VOLUMES.
ARTISTS' LIBRARY . . .	10 VOLUMES.
CHEAP SERIES	55 VOLUMES.
SELECT LIBRARY OF STANDARD WORKS	31 VOLUMES.

'Messrs. Bell are determined to do more than maintain the reputation of "Bohn's Libraries."'—*Guardian.*

'The imprint of Bohn's Standard Library is a guaranty of good editing.'

Critic (N.Y.)

'This new and attractive form in which the volumes of Bohn's Standard Library are being issued is not meant to hide either indifference in the selection of books included in this well-known series, or carelessness in the editing.'

St. James's Gazette.

'Messrs. Bell & Sons are making constant additions of an eminently acceptable character to "Bohn's Libraries."'—*Athenæum.*

www.ingramcontent.com/pod-product-compliance
Lightning Source LLC
Chambersburg PA
CBHW031813270326
41932CB00008B/413